Islamic Law, Tribal Customary Law and *Waqf*

# Studies in Islamic Law and Society



VOLUME 54

The titles published in this series are listed at *brill.com/sils*

# Islamic Law, Tribal Customary Law and *Waqf*

*Studies in the Legal History of the Modern Middle East and North Africa*

*By*

Aharon Layish

BRILL

LEIDEN | BOSTON

Library of Congress Cataloging-in-Publication Data

Names: Layish, Aharon, 1933–2022 author.
Title: Islamic law, tribal customary law, and Waqf : studies in the legal history of the modern Middle East and North Africa / by Aharon Layish.
Description: Leiden ; Boston : Brill, 2023. | Series: Studies in Islamic law and society, 1384–1130 ; volume 54 | Includes index.
Identifiers: LCCN 2023035646 (print) | LCCN 2023035647 (ebook) | ISBN 9789004314054 (hardback) | ISBN 9789004680920 (ebook)
Subjects: LCSH: Islamic law—Middle East—History. | Islamic law—Africa, North—History. | Customary law (Islamic law) | Waqf. | Islamic law—Sudan. | Islamic law—Israel.
Classification: LCC KBP64 .L39 2023 (print) | LCC KBP64 (ebook) | DDC 340.5/90956—dc23/eng/20230906
LC record available at https://lccn.loc.gov/2023035646
LC ebook record available at https://lccn.loc.gov/2023035647

Typeface for the Latin, Greek, and Cyrillic scripts: "Brill". See and download: brill.com/brill-typeface.

ISSN 1384-1130
ISBN 978-90-04-31405-4 (hardback)
ISBN 978-90-04-68092-0 (e-book)
DOI 10.1163/9789004680920



This book is printed on acid-free paper and produced in a sustainable manner.

*Dedicated to*
*Professor Pessah Shinar*

# Contents

## PART 2
## *Legal Methodologies in Sudan*



## PART 3
## *Modern Trends in Islamic Law*



## PART 4
## Waqf, *Testamentary* Waqf *and Bequests*

## PART 5
## *Islamic Law in a Non-Muslim State*

# In Memoriam: Aharon Layish (1933–2022)

*Ron Shaham and David S. Powers*

It is our sad duty to report the death of Aharon Layish at the age of eighty-eight. Aharon was one of the founders of *Islamic Law and Society*. He served as Associate Editor of the journal from 1994–2011 and as a member of the Advisory Board between 2011 and 2020. In 2021, he became Honorary Associate Editor. Aharon worked tirelessly on behalf of the journal and made important contributions to its scholarly excellence and to the field of Islamic legal history.

Aharon Layish (né Liskovski) was born in Suwalki, a small town in northeastern Poland, on May 25, 1933. He had a difficult childhood. In 1934, in the face of rising anti-Semitism, Aharon's parents took their three boys and immigrated to Palestine, leaving many relatives behind. They settled in Haifa, where, in 1935, Aharon's father succumbed to typhus. Unable to support her children, his widow placed Aharon in an orphanage and sent his two older brothers to a *moshav* agricultural settlement where they lived with foster families. After finishing elementary school, he moved in with his oldest brother, who lived in a mixed Jewish-Arab neighborhood where Aharon was exposed to colloquial Arabic and Arabic culture. In high school Aharon began to study literary Arabic. In 1953, following two and a half years of military service, he enrolled as an undergraduate at the Hebrew University of Jerusalem, where he studied Arabic language and literature and modern Middle Eastern history. As an M.A. student, Aharon developed an interest in the *Tanzimat* reforms, and took his first steps in the study of Islamic law under the supervision of Shlomo Dov Goitein.

Between 1958 and 1966, Aharon served at the office of the Advisor on Arab Affairs in the Bureau of the Prime Minister, where his remit included matters relating to the communal organization and the judicial system of Muslim and Druze communities in Israel. He developed friendly relations with Muslim and Druze religious figures and became familiar with their legal documents. While working in the Bureau, Aharon wrote his M.A. thesis, under the supervision of Gabriel Baer, on Muslim communal organization in Israel, based on qadi court records.

In 1966 Aharon began his doctoral studies at the Hebrew University, where he read classical Islamic law with Eliyahu Ashtor at the Faculty of Law. Between 1966 and 1968, he was Visiting Research Associate at the Shiloah Center for Middle Eastern and African Studies, Tel Aviv University. During the academic year 1971–72, with the support of a British Council fellowship, he was a visiting scholar at the School of Oriental and African Studies at the University of London, where he read Islamic inheritance law with Noel Coulson and Doreen Hinchcliffe, and family law with Norman Anderson. One year later, in 1973, he submitted his Ph.D. thesis, written under Baer's supervision, on the social status of Muslim women in Israel. A revised version of the dissertation was published under the title *Women and Islamic Law in a Non-Muslim State: A Study Based on the Decisions of the* Sharīʿa *Courts in Israel* (1975).

In 1973 Aharon was appointed Lecturer in the Department of the History of the Muslim Countries and the Department of Islamic Civilization at the Institute of Oriental Studies (later, the Institute of Asian and African Studies) at the Hebrew University. He was promoted to Senior Lecturer in 1978, Associate Professor in 1981, and Professor in 1989. Between 1981 and 1993, he served as Chairperson of both departments and – after their unification – as Chair of the Department of Islamic and Middle Eastern Studies. In addition, he taught Islamic law at the Faculties of Law at Tel Aviv University (1978–86) and at the Hebrew University (1981–83, 1987–88); at the Department of Law at the School of Oriental and African Studies, University of London (1979–80); and at the Hagop Kevorkian Center for Near Eastern Studies, New York University (1989).

Aharon was a strict, demanding, and meticulous teacher who was dedicated to the welfare and success of his students. He was widely admired for his integrity, fairness, and reliability. He was a generous colleague who shared with colleagues and students not only his knowledge, wisdom, research materials but also his sharp sense of humor.

Throughout his career, Aharon was fascinated by the relationship between Islamic law (*sharīʿa*) and custom (*ʿāda* or *ʿurf*), the former understood to be a divinely revealed law that is eternal and immutable, the latter an unwritten law shaped by local community practice. For centuries, the two have co-existed in a state of tension and mutual influence. The defining feature of Aharon's scholarship was his focus on original legal documents: qadi court decisions, endowment deeds (*waqfiyya*s), and tribal legal documents. Based on his intimate familiarity with these sources, Aharon argued that in matters of personal status and inheritance, local customary law placed a limit on the rights conferred upon Muslim women by Islamic law.

Aharon was the first Israeli scholar to receive permission to use the records of the Druze courts to conduct research on Druze family law, inheritance, and wills. He was fascinated by the ability of Druze jurists to adapt certain rules relating to e.g., polygamy, remarriage to a divorced wife, and testamentary dispositions, to the needs of the agnatic Druze society; and by the ability of Druze jurists to modify and temper religious restrictions that were no longer consistent with modern ideas and practices.

Aharon was also interested in the methods used to introduce legal reform in contemporary Muslim societies. In his view, codification of the *sharīʿa* has had several consequences, not all of them positive: the transformation of Islamic law from a jurists' law to a statutory law, the decline of classical legal methodology (*uṣūl al-fiqh*), a decline in the influence exercised by expert jurists (*fuqahāʾ*) over the regulation and development of *sharīʿa*; and the weakening of the traditional Muslim patrilineal and patriarchal family.

On occasion, Aharon was asked to issue expert opinions on matters relating to marriage, divorce, inheritance, family endowments, homicide and bodily assault. One of his opinions on a *sharʿī* rule relating to the paternity of a child born out of wedlock was instrumental in the Israeli Supreme Court's creation of a new constitutional norm, namely civil paternity.

Aharon served the Israel Oriental Society as editor of its journal, *Hamizrah Hehadash, The New East* (1976–92), as Deputy Chair of the Executive Committee (1981–98), as Chair of this committee (1998–2004) and, between 2004 and 2006, as President of the Society. In addition, he was a member of the executive committee of *Sikkuy*, the Association for the Advancement of Civic Equality for Arabs in Israel (1991–2004).

Aharon and his wife Bilha traveled frequently in search of knowledge, adventure and new experiences. He was a Visiting Fellow at Clare Hall and Member of the Law Faculty, Cambridge (1979–80); at Eliot College, Kent (1986–87); at New York University (1989); at the Institute of Social Anthropology, Oxford (1993); at the Centre of Middle Eastern and Islamic Studies, Leiden (1995), and at the Centre of Middle Eastern and Islamic Studies, Bergen (1996–97).

In 2002 Aharon retired from the Hebrew University. For the next fifteen years, he continued to pursue his research with enthusiasm and energy. During this period, he published *inter alia Sharīʿa and Custom in Libyan Tribal Society: An Annotated Translation of Decisions from the* sharīʿa *Courts of Ajdābiya and Kufra* (Brill, 2005); "Interplay between Tribal and *Sharʿī* Law: A Case of Tibbāwī Blood Money in the *Sharīʿa* Court of Kufra" (*ILS*, 2006); "Ḥasan al-Turābī" (Brill, 2013); "*Waqf*s of *Awlād al-Nās* in Aleppo in the Late Mamlūk Period as Reflected in a Family Archive" (*JESHO*, 2008), and, most recently, *Sharīʿa and the Islamic State in 19th Century Sudan: The Mahdī's Legal Methodology and Doctrine* (Brill, 2016).[1]

Aharon's remarkable scholarly career came to a sudden end in 2017, when he suffered a fall in his home that caused serious brain injury and left him

1 For a full list of Aharon's publications, see Aharon Layish, "List of Publications," in *Law, Custom, and Statute in the Muslim World: Studies in Honor of Aharon Layish*, ed. Ron Shaham (Brill, 2006), xxiii–xxxi.

partially paralyzed. He died on April 16, 2022 and was buried in Jerusalem, leaving his devoted wife of sixty-three years, Bilha, three children, Galia, Hadara and Dan, and seven grandchildren. He will be sorely missed but remembered with fondness. Verily we belong to God and to Her we return. May the memory of Aharon Layish be for a blessing!

# Acknowledgments

The articles included in this volume are the product of my intellectual activity since the mid-1970s. During this long period many teachers inspired my work, among them Uriel Heyd and Gabriel Baer of the Institute of Asian and African Studies, the Hebrew University of Jerusalem; and Noel Coulson and Norman Anderson of the School of Oriental and African Studies, University of London. Their influence can be traced one way or another in my publications. During my study of the *sijill* of the Sharīʿa Courts of Ajdābiya and Kufra, and the legal documents from the Judean Desert, I was greatly influenced by Pessah Shinar of the Hebrew University of Jerusalem, an outstanding scholar of modern Islam in the Maghrib with special reference to the Salafī and reformist movements. We frequently discussed issues pertaining to the interaction between the *sharīʿa* and tribal customary law and inspiration (*ilhām*) derived from the Prophet and God as a source of law in the revivalist movements that emerged in the course of my research. I am most grateful to him for intellectual inspiration and unfailing friendship over the years. This collected volume is dedicated to his memory.

Thanks are due to the editors and publishers of the journals in which the articles of this volume originally appeared (see below, Copyrights and Permissions) for their willingness to grant permission for this publication. My thanks are due also to Brill, in particular to Ruud Peters and Kevin Reinhart for accepting this volume for publication in their series "Studies in Islamic Law and Society." Thanks are due also to my colleague and friend Amnon Cohen of the Hebrew University, who encouraged me to persevere with the preparation of this volume.

I began my research on modern Islam and its institutions almost fifty years ago. During all this time my wife, Bilha, has stood by me. I would like to take this opportunity to profoundly thank her and my children, Galia, Hadara, and Dan – who grew up with and developed along with my publications – for their patient understanding, moral support, and encouragement throughout this prolonged period of endeavor.

Jerusalem, January 2016

# Note from the Publisher

This volume has been a long time in the making. Professor Layish made the selection of his articles himself, and by the beginning of 2016, he had written an Introduction and the Acknowledgments. All that remained to be done was to go over the articles – all of which had been converted back into Word documents with the use of optical character recognition software – to correct any mistakes as a result of the conversion process. Regrettably, due to a fall and subsequent hospitalization, Professor Layish was unable to do this prior to his death in 2022.

The texts published here have been checked by Maurits van den Boogert, who had already worked with Professor Layish on one of the original articles. The corrections made were so minor (typos, consistency in the transliteration of Arabic, etc.) that they are not indicated in the texts. Where possible, bibliographic references to publications that were forthcoming when the articles were originally published, now include the publication details. In one article the endnotes were converted to footnotes. The first footnote of each article indicates where the text was originally published. The index was made by Laila al-Zwaini.

Leiden, June 2023

# Introduction: The Legal Document as a Source of Legal and Social History

The articles included in this collection are mostly based on legal documents.[1] Each type is an essential source for the legal and social history of the subject matter under review. The articles dealing with the interaction between the *sharīʿa* and tribal customary law are based on the *sijill* (records) of some *sharīʿa* courts in Libya since the early twentieth century as well as private collections of decisions handed down by arbitrators in the Judean Desert since the late nineteenth century. The *sijill* may be the only remaining source of information on matters that are within the jurisdiction of the *sharīʿa* court,[2] especially in cases where the option of reviewing the parties to the dispute is not available. Due to the friendly environment of the *sharīʿa* court, the parties have been ready to reveal even intimate matters to the *qāḍī*. His only concern has been to establish facts and record them in his decisions. He has done so candidly, without taking into account that the *sijill* might someday be used for purposes of research; this candor is of course essential to the credibility of the information. In tribal regions, the *sharʿī qāḍī*, rather than the *muftī*, is confronted on a daily basis with a population nurtured on tribal customary law, and it is he who determines the scheme of relations between the two legal systems. Hence the *sijill* is an indispensable source for obtaining genuine information on the *qāḍīs*' inclination to meet tribal law halfway in an attempt to bring the Bedouin within the orbit of *sharīʿa*.[3] The *fatwā* solicited from a *muftī* by Bedouin to relieve them from occasional distress in matters of personal status is another instrument of the Islamization of tribal society (7). In their written decisions, tribal arbitrators in modern times reveal a consistent tendency to absorb *sharʿī*

1 References to the articles appear in the text in parentheses.

2 On the *sijill* as a source for political and social history, see A. Layish, "The *Sijill* of Jaffa and Nazareth *Sharīʿa* Courts as a Source for the Political and Social History of Ottoman Palestine," in *Studies on Palestine during the Ottoman Period*, ed. M. Maʿoz (Jerusalem: The Magnes Press, 1972), 514–521.

3 A. Layish, *Legal Documents on Libyan Tribal Society in Process of Sedentarizaion. A Selection of Decisions from the* Sijills *of the* Sharīʿa *Courts of Ajdābiya and Kufra. Part 1: The Documents in Arabic*, Mediterranean Language and Culture Monograph 14 (Wiesbaden: Harrassowitz, 1998), 1–6; idem, *Sharīʿa and Custom in Libyan Tribal Society. An Annotated Translation of Decisions from the Sharīʿa Courts of Ajdābiya and Kufra, with a Linguistic Essay by Alexander Borg*, Studies in Islamic Law and Society 24 (Leiden: Brill, 2005), vii–xvii; idem, *Divorce in the Libyan Family. A Study Based on the* Sijill *of the* Sharīʿa *Courts of Ajdābiya and Kufra*, New York University Studies in Near Eastern Civilization xv (New York University Press, 1991), 123–169.

 | DOI:10.1163/9789004680920_002

substantive elements, making it possible for them to survive as a voluntary autonomous judiciary based on tribal customary sureties and capable of competing with a *sharīʿa* court that relies on the executive power of the state.[4]

The articles dealing with *waqf* are based on *waqf* deeds culled from private collections dating from the Mamlūk and Ottoman periods. These documents provide a clear notion of the importance of the *waqf* as a prop for social and political order. Thus a family archive in Aleppo of the late Mamlūk period sheds light on a social stratum in a transition from military to civil elite. It provides vital information on a variety of subjects – such as the religious, social and economic role of the *waqf*, the capacity of women and manumitted slaves to own and dispose of property, and the legal pluralism created by the introduction of *sharīʿa* courts belonging to the four Sunnī schools (13). A copy of a *waqfiyya* in favor of a Ṣūfī *shaykh* related to the Ottoman Sulṭān Selīm I and endorsed by the Qāḍī of Damascus in 1516 was found in the private archive of one of the inhabitants of Dayr al-Asad in western Galilee. The document reveals the importance of the *waqf* as an instrument in carrying out the policy of the Ottoman colonization and Islamization of recently conquered areas (14). *Waqf* deeds collected from the *sijill* of the *sharīʿa* courts in modern times provide important information on the *waqf* property, the founders, the beneficiaries and the administrators (*mutawallīn*) of both family *waqf* and *waqf* for charitable purposes (15, 16). Although the *qāḍī* may have some influence on the content of the *waqf* deed by using standard legal formularies, these documents reflect first and foremost the founder's wish and state of mind. Surprisingly, evidence of complete freedom of testation in Israeli Muslim society, in a glaring departure from the traditional *sharʿī* will, may be found in the *sijill* of some *sharīʿa* courts (17).

The Sudanese Mahdī (d. 1885) led a millenarian, revivalist, reformist movement in Islam in the late nineteenth century, strongly inspired by Salafī and Ṣūfī ideas (8), in an attempt to restore the caliphate of the Prophet Muḥammad and the "Righteous Caliphs" in Medina. He left an enormous number of documents – legal opinions (*fatwā*), decisions in matters of law (*ḥukm*), proclamations (*manshūr*), and "traditions" (*qawl*) attributed to him after his death. He left behind no legal treatise, but this rich material makes it possible to reconstruct his legal methodology and doctrine, and to evaluate their compatibility with Islamic legal theory and *fiqh* (9).[5] Other articles based on statutory

4 A. Layish, *Legal Documents from the Judean Desert: The Impact of the Sharīʿa on Bedouin Customary Law, with the Assistance of Mūsā Shawārbah and including his Linguistic Essay*, Studies in Islamic Law and Society 33 (Leiden: Brill, 2011), 3–15.

5 For a comprehensive study on this subject, see A. Layish, *Sharīʿa and the Islamic State in 19th Century Sudan. The Mahdī's Legal Methodology and Doctrine*, Islam in Africa 19 (Leiden: Brill, 2016).

legislation and decisions of the Supreme Court are indispensable for the analysis of modern trends and transformations in Islamic law as part of the state legal system (11, 12). Application of the *sharīʿa* in Israel is based on the records of the *sharīʿa* courts, judicial decrees (*marsūm qaḍāʾī*) issued by the President of the Sharīʿa Court of Appeals, minutes of conferences of *qāḍīs*, records of the civil family courts and the jurisprudence of the High Court of Justice.[6]

In what follows, short introductions to the topics dealt with in this collection provide the main findings and conclusions of the articles in a historical context with a view to facilitating the reader's orientation.

## 1 Interplay between *sharʿī* and Tribal Law

The study of the interaction between tribal customary law (*ʿāda*, *ʿurf*) and the *sharīʿa* in Libya is based on the *sijill* of the *sharīʿa* courts of Ajdābiya and Kufra. The documents cover a period extending from 1932 (the Italian rule in Cyrenaica, 1932–42) and in the case of Ajdābiya from 1942 down to the abolition of the *sharīʿa* courts in 1973. The study of the interaction in the Judean Desert is based on decisions handed down by tribal arbitrators from the late 19th century to the early 1970s. Ajdābiya is a district center in the cultivable plain near the Mediterranean coast on the road from Tripoli to Benghazi. The people of this area are part of the confederation of *qabīlas* consisting locally of the Maghāriba and the Majābira. Kufra in the south, originally the administrative center for the Sanūsiyya order, consists mainly of the Zuwaya tribe.[7] The Judean Desert is in the Jerusalem-Bethlehem region. The Bedouin in this region comprise al-Taʿāmira (13 tribes), al-Sawāḥira, al-ʿUbaydiyya and al-Rashāʾida; most of the tribes, with the exception of Ḥamūlat al-Radāʾida, are said to have originated from Ḥijāz and Najd. Their sedentarization began in the 1920s and was almost complete by the 1970s. It was furthered by proximity to religious, economic, and administrative centers, and by the consolidation of internal security.[8]

The interaction between tribal customary law and the *sharīʿa* is part of a general process that has been going on since early Islam well into modern

6 A. Layish, "Islamic Law in the Israeli High Court of Justice: The Muslim *Waqf* and the Dignity of the Dead – the Cemetery of Māmillā as a Case Study," in *Muslim Minorities in Modern Times*, ed. Y. Friedmann, Proceedings of the Israel Academy of Sciences and Humanities (Jerusalem 2019).

7 For full details, see John Davis, "A Social Perspective," in Layish, *Legal Documents on Libyan Tribal Society in Process of Sedentarizaion* (*supra*, fn. 3), 7–13.

8 For full details, see Layish, *Legal Documents from the Judean Desert* (*supra*, fn. 4), 16–36 and the references to Avshalom Shmueli's works.

times. A socio-legalistic method is proposed for the distinction between custom and *sharīʿa*: Where the two legal systems share the same technical terms, their connotations should be examined while paying attention to the social substance, which may be quite different in some essential respects in the two laws. The interaction between the two legal systems is most pronounced in the domains of private property, and marriage and divorce (1, 6),[9] but also in inheritance, contracts and obligations, homicide and bodily harm (2), and evidence (3). The main agents of Islamization are the *sharʿī qāḍī* (5, 6),[10] the *sharʿī* marriage solemnizer (*maʾdhūn*) and occasionally also the independent non-institutionalized *muftī*. In the case discussed in this volume a well-known *shaykh* had divorced his wife by an oath of suspended repudiation, intended to emphasize his determination in a matter that had nothing to do with his wife, and repeated his oath several times. When his attention was drawn to the legal consequences of his oath from the *sharʿī* point of view, he resorted to an *ʿālim* – whose legal opinion is binding on no one – to extricate him from the personal predicament into which he had stumbled, i.e., to release his triply divorced wife from intermediate marriage to a third party (*al-muḥallil min al-ṭalāq*) before legally remarrying her. The *muftī*'s remedy was based on three alternative legal solutions: lack of intent to divorce, implying thereby that the marriage remained valid; placing the divorce on a par with a revocable divorce, which enables the husband to reinstate the wife within the waiting period; and admission that the original marriage was based on tribal custom rather than on the *sharʿī* procedure, thus enabling the husband to separate from his wife and remarry her in accordance with the *sharʿī* procedure (7). Tribal customary law is yielding ground to Islamic law on its own territory, i.e., in the domain of the tribal *qāḍī* (*ḥakam, muḥakkam*). The fact that the arbitrators are committed to Islam and tend to identify customary law with the *sharīʿa* facilitates their rapprochement to the *sharʿī* legal system. However, the Islamization of tribal customary law has left its mark on neither Islamic legal methodology nor doctrine; its only result has been the emergence, in the tribal judiciary, of a hybrid

---

9 See also A. Layish and A. Shmueli, "Custom and *Sharīʿa* in the Bedouin Family according to Legal Documents from the Judaean Desert," *Bulletin of the School of Oriental and African Studies* 42 (1979), 29–45; Layish, *Divorce in the Libyan Family* (*supra*, fn. 3), 170–208. For a comprehensive study on this subject, see Layish, *Legal Documents from the Judean Desert* (*supra*, fn. 4); idem, "*Sharīʿa* and Tribal Custom in Libya: Was Tajdīda Married to Two Husbands?" *Archív Orientální* 63 (1995), 488–503; idem, "*Sharīʿa* and Custom in the Muslim Family in Israel," *Hamizrah Hehadash* 23 (1974), 377–409 (Hebrew).

10 A. Layish, "The Islamization of the Bedouin Family in the Judaean Desert as Reflected in the *Sijill*s of the *Sharīʿa* Court," in *The Changing Bedouin*, ed. E. Marx and A. Shmueli (Brunswick, N.J.: Transaction Books, 1984), 39–58.

version of a realistic, pragmatic Islamic customary law, outside the control of the *ʿulamāʾ*. The syncretism in the arbitrators' judicial practice resembles (with due reservations) the eclectic device (*takhayyur*, *talfīq*) in Middle Eastern and North African statutory legislation and judicial practice. This development, in turn, has been instrumental in bringing the Bedouin within the orbit of conventional Islam (4).[11]

## 2 Legal Methodologies in Sudan

Islamic classical legal methodology (*uṣūl al-fiqh*) has survived almost intact into modern times. Since the late nineteenth century, there have been sporadic attempts to create new legal methodologies with a view to adapting Islamic law to contemporary conditions, the most important of which was initiated by the Western-oriented Modernist movement, headed by Muḥammad ʿAbduh (d. 1905).[12] The Mahdī's legal methodology is unique within this category. He, not being a qualified *ʿālim*, rejected the *fiqh* of all the schools as well as their methods of analogical reasoning (*qiyās*) and consensus (*ijmāʿ*). His legal methodology comprised the textual sources of the Qurʾān and the *sunna*, and – in the event of a lacuna – the inspiration (*ilhām*) derived from the Prophet (and occasionally also from God) and such auxiliary sources of law as public interest (*maṣlaḥa*) and necessity (*ḍarūra*). The uniqueness of this methodology derived from its having been molded under the profound impact of both Ṣūfism and Salafism, and in that it was carried out without the cooperation of the *ʿulamāʾ*. In fact, it was meant to deprive the latter of their historic role as the exclusive authoritative interpreters of the will of God. The Mahdī used his legal methodology as an instrument to promote extensive social and political reforms, and to enhance his moralistic agenda. Thus the Mahdī had a consistent policy of denouncing political adversaries as infidels (*takfīr*). Although the institution of slavery was part of his worldview, he was concerned that slaves and concubines be treated kindly and considerately by their masters; moreover, he extended the status of *umm al-walad* to the effect that not only her children by her master but also children she gave birth to afterward who had been fathered by slaves be deemed manumitted even in her master's lifetime.

---

11 Also A. Layish, "Challenges to Customary Law and Arbitration: the Impact of Islamic Law upon Settled Bedouin in the Judaean Desert," *Tel Aviv University Studies in Law* 5 (1980–82), 206–221.

12 See A. Layish, "The Contribution of the Modernists to the Secularization of Islamic Law," *Middle Eastern Studies* 14 (1978), 263–277.

He did not approve of a woman being married against her will. He declared all kinds of repudiation by way of oath – including by implication suspended repudiation – to be null and void (unless God's name has been mentioned in the oath). The Mahdī acknowledged the right of a widow to waiting-period maintenance *out of the estate* with no such preconditions as the consummation of the marriage or pregnancy. The Mahdī underlined the importance of taxes as a state instrument for promoting social justice in terms of the distribution of property. He promoted a land reform according to which everyone was entitled to own a plot of land to be cultivated by himself to satisfy his needs; land beyond this extent should be given to needy people. He condemned leasing land for rent on the grounds that this might weaken the solidarity of the believers. By the same token, the Mahdī did not permit using a pledge as a device for circumventing the prohibition on interest. The Mahdī made a special effort to establish himself as the custodian of public morality in an attempt to maintain a strict, uncompromisingly puritan way of life. He was engaged in intensive reformist and purist legislation. He proved himself to be a pragmatic legislator with no inhibitions about adapting the *sharīʿa* to his political, social, and personal needs – occasionally at a very high price from the point of view of traditional Islamic law. Quite often, the Mahdī's legislation resulted in explicit deviations from the orthodox *sharīʿa*, or at least in what was incompatible with its spirit (8, 9).[13]

Ḥasan al-Turābī, who led the Muslim Brothers in Sudan after 1964, played a decisive role in Jaʿfar al-Numayrī's legal experiment of reinstating the *sharīʿa* in Sudan in 1983. His legal methodology is a combination of traditional Islamic legal theory and Western legal doctrines. In the event of a lacuna in Islamist statutes, the civil judge (the *sharīʿa* courts having been abolished) is to exercise judicial *ijtihād* on the basis of the legal sources and principles in the following order: the Qurʾān and the *sunna*, consensus, analogy, the public interest (*maṣlaḥa*), legal precedent (in the Sudanese national courts), custom and the English principles of natural justice, "justice, equity and good conscience." This methodology, however, can hardly be regarded as a development within the conventional *sharīʿa* or as one legitimized by the *ʿulamāʾ* (10).[14]

13 For a comprehensive study of the Mahdī's legal methodology and doctrine, see Layish, *Sharīʿa and the Islamic State in 19th-Century Sudan* (*supra*, fn. 5).

14 On the application of al-Turābī's legal methodology in Sudan, see A. Layish and Gabriel R. Warburg, *The Reinstatement of Islamic Law in Sudan under Numayrī. An Evaluation of a Legal Experiment in the Light of Its Historical Context, Methodology, and Repercussions* (Leiden: Brill, 2002).

## 3 Modern Trends in Islamic Law

The introduction of legal reforms, especially in the domain of family law, by means of statutory codification caused the *sharīʿa* to lose some of its most salient features. The methods employed by parliaments, such as the eclectic expedient (*takhayyur, talfīq*) from all schools of law and the reinterpretation of the textual sources on the basis of such utilitarian principles as "public interest" and "necessity" (*ḍarūra*), have resulted in the transformation of the *sharīʿa* from a jurists' law to a statutory law (11). The traditional patrilineal and patriarchal Muslim family law that for centuries maintained a balance between the rights and duties of the spouses is now on the verge of complete collapse, without a new balance suited to the conditions of a modern society taking its place.[15] Statutory codification and the jurisprudence of the Supreme Constitutional Court (in Egypt) disrupt the traditional *sharʿī* legal methodology and positive law (*furūʿ*) of the schools on the one hand and contribute to the nationalization of the *sharīʿa* on the other. Consequently, the *ʿulamāʾ* are losing their historic role as the authorized interpreters and exponents of the *sharīʿa* as well as their exclusive monopoly on the formulation of the law. As a reaction to this process, which has been to a great extent inspired by the West, there have been increasing attempts in recent years to reinstate the *sharīʿa* in such countries as Iran, Sudan, and Egypt (12).

## 4 *Waqf*, Testamentary *waqf*, and Bequests

The *waqf* or religious endowment has been one of the most important institutions in Muslim society, from the emergence of Islam until well into modern times. Family (*dhurrī* or *ahlī*) *waqf* has been an important means to prevent the fragmentation of agnatic patrimony through the Qurʾānic prescribed rules of inheritance (14);[16] indeed, family *waqf* is another manifestation of the victory of custom over the *sharīʿa*. The incentive to establish family *waqf* and testamentary *waqf* is especially strong in regions where the Mālikī school is dominant, due to the position of the Public Treasury (*bayt al-māl*) as a residuary heir that completely deprives *dhawū 'l-arḥām* – i.e., relatives that are neither

15 A. Layish, "Reformist Matrimonial Legislation and the Collapse of the Muslim Patrilineal Family," *Awrāq* 21 (2000), 57–80.

16 See also A. Layish, "The Muslim *Waqf* in Jerusalem after 1967: Beneficiaries and Management," in *Le waqf dans le monde musulman contemporain* (*xix*^e^*–xx*^e^ *siècles*), ed. Faruk Bilici, Institut Français d'Etudes Anatoliennes, *Varia Turcica*, xxvi (Istanbul, 1994), 145–166.

Qurʾānic heirs (*dhawū ʾl-farāʾiḍ*) nor male agnates (*ʿaṣaba*) – under all circumstances, of any rights to the estate, as well as depriving Qurʾānic heirs of their rights to the residue of the estate (*radd*) in the absence of male agnates (15). The mechanism of the family *waqf* in regions where the Ḥanafī school is dominant makes it possible to circumvent the inheritance rules and to concentrate entitlement on descendants of the founder as beneficiaries of the first series, which practically means the weakening or even the complete exclusion of the Qurʾānic heirs. The cognates are disadvantaged with regard to entitlement to the income of *waqf*, not only as to the order of beneficiaries but also as to the transmission of entitlement to descendants; cognates get their turn only when no agnates remain. As a rule, females in both the patrilineal and the matrilineal line of descent enjoy the income of the *waqf* but do not transmit their right to their descendants so long as there are sons or agnatic male descendants of the founder. The apportionment of entitlement "in accordance with the *sharʿī* fractional shares" completely ignores the *sharʿī* priorities in and exclusion of inheritance (16).

Statutory freedom of testation – available since 1965 to Israeli Muslims within the *sharīʿa* courts – has replaced the family *waqf* as an instrument for circumventing the Islamic compulsory rules of inheritance. As in the case of family *waqf*, the bequest is being used as a means to prevent the fragmentation of the patrimony and to preserve it in the hands of the testator's sons – or, in their absence, other male agnates – in units as complete and economically sound as possible. While excluding his wife and daughters from the estate, the testator secures their economic well-being by allocating to them subsistence allowances and residential rights – that is, customary maintenance out of the estate. The concern for orphaned children, who are deprived of benefiting from the estate according to the traditional Islamic law of inheritance, is another incentive for making a will. At the same time, the making of bequests demonstrates the capacity of Muslim women to dispose of property (17).[17]

The charitable (*khayrī*) *waqf* has been the main vehicle for providing such public services as social welfare and religious education. Broadly speaking, in the absence of state regulation in this domain beyond care for the poor by means of the alms tax (*zakāt*) system, it was the ruling elite (such as sultans, local governors and well-to-do dignitaries) who established *waqf*s, using their

17 The Druze freedom of testation has made the institution of family *waqf* redundant in that community. See A. Layish, "The Druze Testamentary *Waqf*," *Studia Islamica* 71 (1990), 127–154; idem, *Marriage, Divorce and Succession in the Druze Family. A Study Based on Decisions of Druze Arbitrators and Religious Courts in Israel and the Golan Heights* (Leiden: Brill, 1982), Ch. 12, 287ff.

own private property to this end. The aforementioned family archive in Aleppo of the late Mamlūk period provides a good notion of the religious, social and economic role of the *waqf*. The motives for creating *waqf* include the allocation of cloth, bread and meat to orphans and the poor; the allocation of allowances to readers of the Qur'ān for commemoration of the founder, his parents and the rest of the Muslims; manumission of Muslim female slaves as part of the procedure of *kaffāra*, religious expiation; the allocation of allowances to the mosques in al-Ḥaramayn: Mecca and Medina, as well as the mosques of al-Aqṣā and al-Khalīl; and allocations to the *madrasa* constructed by the founder in Aleppo, etc. (13).[18]

The *waqf* was also instrumental in the Ottoman policy of the colonization and Islamization of recently conquered areas. Thus Selīm I's *waqf* in favor of a miracle-working Ṣūfī shaykh with powerful charisma demonstrates the role played by roving Ṣūfī dervishes and their monasteries in the colonization and Islamization, especially of the border areas, in the Ottoman period. The dervishes provided settlement nuclei combining diligent, sophisticated agricultural manpower with religious zeal (14).

Since the nineteenth century, *waqf* has undergone radical changes in the Middle East and North Africa with a view to introducing reforms in the substance of the institution to the point of its complete abolition. The reform was motivated by economic, social and political considerations: accommodation of *waqf* law to the inheritance rules so as to prevent depriving females and cognates of their inheritance rights; restoration of *waqf* property to the private and national economic cycle; redivision of *waqf* landed property within the framework of agrarian reform; and undermining the traditional leadership closely bound up with the agrarian system. The family *waqf* was abolished in such countries as Egypt, Lebanon, Syria and Libya, and endowed agricultural lands were nationalized within the framework of agrarian reform in Egypt and Algeria.[19]

In Israel, the management of and entitlement to the proceeds of *waqf* became absentees' property to the extent that their administrators or beneficiaries, respectively, left for the Arab states during the 1948 war. The status of absentees' property did not affect the ownership of the *waqf* since according

---

18 It is noteworthy that non-Muslims too resorted to the institution of the Muslim *waqf* for both familial and charitable purposes and preferred to register the *waqf* deeds in the *sharīʿa* courts for reasons of legal certainty. See A. Layish, "A *Sharʿī Waqfiyya* in Favor of the Ashkenazi Community in Jerusalem," in *Jeruslem in the Modern Period*, ed. E. Shaltiel, Yaacov Herzog Memorial Volume (Jerusalem: Yad Ben-Zvi, 1981), 249–254 (Hebrew).

19 See A. Layish, "Waḳf, 5: In the Modern Middle East and North Africa," *Encyclopaedia of Islam*, 2nd ed. XI, 78–81.

to the view dominant in the *sharīʿa* courts in Israel, as part of the Ottoman legal heritage, the ownership is transferred to God and hence is debarred from any transaction. In 1965, the Knesset vested in the Custodian of Absentees' Property, retroactively from 1950, in addition to the right of management and the right to entitlement, the *full ownership* of the property free from any religious legal restriction – implying thereby that the property ceased to be *waqf*. The Custodian may release the full ownership of family *waqf* to beneficiaries residing in Israel in accordance with their proportional shares in the entitlement; the ownership of charitable *waqf* properties has been released to Muslim boards of trustees in towns where Muslim communities exist. The boards may dispose of the property as owners and use its revenues and the price of property sold for such purposes as education, social welfare, health and religious worship – without being bound by the *sharʿī* law pertaining to *waqf* – in favor of the local Muslim communities, with the proviso that they may not sell property on which there is a mosque (18).[20]

## 5 Islamic Law in a Non-Muslim State

Israel is a unique case of the application of the *sharīʿa* in a non-Muslim state. The *sharʿī* judiciary has been integrated into the state judicial system, and its decisions are subject to review by the High Court of Justice. The Knesset (Parliament) consistently endeavors to replace both the Ottoman-Muslim and the English legal heritage with legislation that is inspired by "the principles of freedom, justice, equity and peace of Israel's heritage" (The Foundation of Law, 1980, art. 1). Until 2001, the Ottoman *millet* system remained virtually intact as far as the jurisdiction of the religious courts was concerned (19). In 2001 the civil family courts were vested with jurisdiction concurrent to that of the *sharīʿa* courts, except in matters relating to marriage and divorce, which were left within the latter's exclusive jurisdiction. The Knesset has intervened, through substantive legislation, in various matters pertaining to personal status. However, in matters pertaining to *sharʿī* permission for, or prohibition of, marriage and divorce, the Knesset has resorted to criminal sanctions that do not affect *sharʿī* substantive law.

In the absence of official *muftīs*, *qāḍīs* in Israel adapted the *sharīʿa* to changing conditions by holding (until the early 1970s) periodic conferences to discuss reform in judicial practice by the eclectic device – i.e., by absorbing into their decisions elements from schools other than the Ḥanafī, by handing down

20 For further details, see Layish, "Islamic Law in the Israeli High Court of Justice," *supra*, fn. 6.

liberal decisions based mainly on the doctrine of public interest and legitimized by the ruler's right to issue administrative regulations (*siyāsa sharʿiyya*), and (since 1994) by judicial decrees (*marsūm qaḍāʾī*) issued by the President of the Sharīʿa Court of Appeals. Until the early 1970s *qāḍīs* did not hesitate to apply Knesset legislation, and whenever they came across cases where the husband married another woman or divorced his wife against her will, they would draw the wife's attention of her right to sue her husband in civil court for committing a criminal offense. Since then there has been an increasing tendency among the *qāḍīs* to avoid applying Israeli statutes – even those explicitly addressed to religious courts – and to base the *sharīʿa* courts' decisions on the Qurʾān, *sunna*, and *fiqh*. The Sharīʿa Court of Appeals, however, has been strongly influenced by the Supreme Court's jurisprudence. Thus it has adopted such concepts as "natural justice," "the best interests of the child" and "the right of standing in court," while attempting to Islamize these concepts by enlisting support for them in the *sharīʿa*. The *sharīʿa* is applied in the civil courts in the light of Israeli principles of law and rules of evidence and procedure. As a result, an Israeli version of Islamic law has emerged that resembles in some respects the Anglo-Muhammadan Law in British India. The Supreme Court has created new civil legal norms that are not consistent with Islamic law, such as "civil paternity" based on DNA testing (12, 20).[21]

The articles selected for this collected volume demonstrate that since the late nineteenth century, Islamic law has undergone tremendous transformations, some of which have irrevocably affected the basic features of its nature as jurists' law. Although the West has physically retreated from the Middle East and North Africa, its impact on the process of these transformations, alongside internal developments, is still very strong. Tribal customary law is constantly yielding ground to the *sharīʿa*; custom, however, still plays a central role in regulating property relations within the family. The tension between these two legal norms is most pronounced in the relations between the *sharʿī* inheritance law and the institution of family *waqf*, which though technically anchored in the *sharīʿa*, is greatly inspired by customary considerations

21 A. Layish, *Women and Islamic Law in a Non-Muslim State* (New York: John Wiley, 1975; 2nd ed., New Brunswick, New Jersey: Transactions Publishers, 2006); idem, "Muslim Religious Jurisdiction in Israel," *Asian and African Studies* 1 (1965), 47–79; idem, "*Qāḍīs* and *Sharīʿa* in Israel," *Asian and African Studies* 7 (1971), 237–272; idem, "The Status of the *Sharīʿa* in a Non-Muslim State: The Case of Israel," *Asian and African Studies* 27 (1993), 171–187; idem, "Islamic Law in Israel: A Case Study in Legal Pluralism," *Pluralism, Transnationalism and Culture in Asian Law: A Book in Honor of M.B. Hooker*, Singapore: ISEAS, 2017; idem, "Islamic Law in the Israeli High Court of Justice," *supra*, fn. 6.

aiming at the protection of the agnatic patrimony. In fact, the tension inherent in the *sharʿī* family (and criminal) law is based on the patrilineal and patriarchal system though mitigated by religio-ethical norms. Thus in the domain of inheritance, the power of the male agnates (*ʿaṣaba*), the tribal backbone of the inheritance system, is softened by the precedence of the Qurʾānic heirs consisting of females and cognates closely related to the deceased. Paradoxically, the *sharīʿa* created the devices – one of which is the *waqf* – that make it possible to legitimately circumvent the prescribed inheritance rule sanctioned by the will of God in the Qurʾān. In this sense, the family *waqf* is the authorized agent of tribal customary law. In a way, the combination of inheritance law and family *waqf* – both anchored in the *sharīʿa* – is tantamount to a statement and its contradiction.

The Mahdī's legal methodology in nineteenth-century Sudan is unique due to the Salafī and Ṣūfī environment in which the Mahdī functioned. The methodology was doomed to failure due to a lack of cooperation on the part of the orthodox *ʿulamāʾ* and the political circumstances. The status of the Muslims in Israel is another unique case due to the fact that they are an indigenous population of Palestine, rather than immigrants from abroad. Hence they claim self-determination as a political – religious and national – entity in the State of Israel.[22]

It is hoped that this collected volume will prove a useful contribution to the literature relating to the history of Islamic law and institutions in the modern Middle East and North Africa. It is intended for students and researchers of Islamic law with special reference to legal methodologies, and to the interaction between Islamic law and tribal customary law, *waqf*, and Islamic law in Israel; it will be valuable also to Orientalists, Islamologists, Arabists, legal and social historians, lawyers interested in comparative law, and social scientists.

22 A. Layish, "Social and Political Changes in the Arab Society in Israel," in *The Arabs in Israel: Continuity and Change*," ed. A. Layish (Jerusalem: The Magnes Press, 1981), 241–247.

# PART 1

## *Interplay between* Sharīʿa *and Tribal Law*

CHAPTER 1

# Customary *khulʿ* as Reflected in the *sijill* of the Libyan *Sharīʿa* Courts

## 1 Introduction[1]

*Khulʿ*, according to its *sharʿī* definition, is a wife's 'redemption of herself' from the marriage tie, with the husband's consent, by the use of the word *khulʿ*, or a verb derived from it, in return for consideration. The husband, not the wife, dissolves the marriage tie; he must be legally competent to divorce the wife, and the wife must be legally competent to enter into a contractual divorce agreement for consideration (Anderson, 1970: 367). She is a party to the proceedings for divorce by *sharʿī khulʿ*, just as she is a party to the marriage contract. She generally compensates the husband by returning the dower (which is her property under the *sharīʿa*), wholly or in part, in exchange for her freedom. This is the picture emerging from the *sijill* and confirmed by research elsewhere.

However, the Libyan *sijill* shows far-reaching deviations from the pattern of *sharʿī khulʿ*; they consist mainly in compensating the husband by the dower which the woman is due to receive upon her marriage to another man, or even in making the remarriage conditional on the return of the dower to the first husband. This is attested by dozens of instances, and it seems that we have not to do here with a marginal phenomenon. Although these practices have already been observed in North Africa and other parts of Africa and in the Middle East, the Libyan *sijill* makes it possible to study more exactly the mechanism of this *khulʿ*, hereinafter referred to as 'customary *khulʿ*' since it is mainly inspired by custom. In fact, the *sharīʿa* has deviated from it by adapting its

1 Originally published in the *Bulletin of the School of Oriental and African Studies*, LI/3 (1988), pp. 428–439. This article is based on a paper presented at the BRISMES Annual Conference held at the University of Exeter on 12–15 July, 1987. It is part of a comprehensive study, *Divorce in the Libyan family: a study based on the sijill of the sharīʿa courts of Ajdābiya and Kufra*. My colleague, Professor John Davis, who painstakingly photographed thousands of documents from the *sijill* (see his 'A note on some Libyan archives in Canterbury', *BRISMES* vol. 9, no. 2, 1982, 75–79), invited me to work on them, and I wish to thank him for his generosity and for his advice and guidance throughout my endeavour. I also wish to thank the Eliot College of the University of Kent at Canterbury for the kind hospitality extended to me and the technical assistance provided by its secretarial staff.

 | DOI:10.1163/9789004680920_003

mechanism to the norms required by the transformation of the wife from an object of sale in marriage-by-purchase, under customary law, into a party to a marriage contract under the *sharīʿa* (Layish and Shmueli, 1979: 38).

Scholars agree that *khulʿ* is rooted in pre-Islamic custom, except that according to the latter, the dower was not returned by the wife but by her clan. There is no express reference to *khulʿ* in the Qurʾān though a trace of it may perhaps be found in the wife's right to redeem herself by returning the dower (2:229). Orthodox exegesis too relates that right to the *khulʿ* custom. A hint of *khulʿ* may be found in the *ḥadīth* as well, though the reference here is only to the wife's initiative for dissolution while dissolution itself is reserved to the husband (Stern, 1939: 129 ff.; Linant de Bellefonds, 1965: 422). Bousquet found vestiges of marriage-by-purchase among the Berbers of the Kabyle Mountains, with whom customary *khulʿ* prevails. In his estimation, marriage there is like a sale rather than like a *sharʿī* marriage. Among those Berbers, it is usual to 'sell' the wife to the husband even before she reaches maturity. A woman 'sold' passes to the almost total domination of the husband; she owes him obedience and faithfulness, and he may subject her to corporal punishment. The consideration for the 'sale' or 'delivery' of the woman is the dower. The future husband (or his relatives) must pay it to the wife's father (or to other agnatic relatives). It is a condition of the marriage and essential to its validity. At the same time, such a marriage is not a sale in the full sense of the word, like the sale of a slave, since the woman retains certain succession rights in her father's estate; her share does not become the husband's property and he has no rights in it; in fact, there is complete separation of property between the spouses; the wife cannot be compelled to move into the marital residence. Colucci too notes that the Cyrenaicans treat women like property (*māl*) and that, therefore, he who has a right to them (the agnatic guardian) may sell them. In fact, the only legitimate kind of Cyrenaican marriage is essentially the purchase of a woman. As we shall see, some vestiges of marriage-by-purchase can be detected in Libyan customary *khulʿ* (Bousquet, 1950: 52 f., 59, 64, 68; Bousquet, 1945: 8; Colucci, 1932: 38ff.).

The special feature of the North African *sharīʿa* courts is the encounter of the custom of a tribal society with the *sharīʿa* in its Mālikī version. In fact, the tension between these two poles is the main axis of this article.

## 2 The Features and Application of Customary *khulʿ*

Most customary *khulʿ* divorces involve mutual renunciation of marital rights, such as waiting-period maintenance and dower, arising out of the dissolution of the marriage tie. But the special characteristic of customary *khulʿ* is the undertaking to return the balance of the dower, or to pay compensation in addition to the dower, 'upon her marriage to another man so that he may divorce her for it' (*ʿinda iqtirānihā bi-zawj ākhar* (or: *ghayrihi*) *li-yuṭalliqahā ʿalā dhālika*).[2] Sometimes the wife is a full-fledged, exclusive party to the customary *khulʿ* proceedings. She conducts negotiations with the husband on the exact terms of the *khulʿ*, and each side carries out its part. In one case, e.g., the wife said: 'I redeem myself (*khalaʿtu*) from my husband for my whole dower, the prompt and the deferred, specified in my marriage contract, and I undertake to pay him … when I am able to marry someone else. … I have delivered to him all I have received of the prompt dower and the clothing (*kiswa*), and there is nothing left of my financial liability (*dhimma*) but these … so that he may divorce me in return.' The husband 'consented to this and agreed to wait for the said payment'. Eventually, he divorced her by a single *khulʿī* repudiation. In another case, the wife initiated dissolution after eight months of marriage and undertook to support herself during the waiting period, as well as to pay the husband eight pounds 'upon her marriage to another husband in order that he may divorce her in return'. The husband agreed to these terms and divorced her.[3]

According to the *sharīʿa*, the freedom of marriage of a divorced woman is unlimited provided that there are no *sharʿī* impediments to the marriage, such as non-observance of the waiting period or a forbidden degree of kinship (*maḥram*) to the intended husband; her marriage to another man cannot be made conditional on the payment of a debt to her former husband; non-payment of a debt is merely a ground for a civil claim. Any restrictions on remarriage are apparently imposed by the woman of her own free will. In this respect, we have to do here with a compromise between the *sharīʿa*, according to which the wife is a party to the divorce proceedings, and the custom adopted by the wife of her own choice. However, it is not certain that the *sharʿī* norm appearing from the above examples as to the wife's personal involvement in *khulʿ* proceedings reflects the actual facts. It is possible that the court is trying to couch proceedings conducted according to custom in terms fitting the *sharīʿa* and that the wife is not in fact a party to the proceedings or at any rate not an exclusive party, as we shall see below. In some cases in which the wife is presented in the *sijill* as a full partner in the negotiations for a customary *khulʿ*

2 E.g., KD59–73, K51: p. 20 no. 39, 8.11.59.

3 AP:E4, p. 137, no. 127, 23.5.47 and A:E104, p. 182, no. 314, 28.2.53, respectively. See also ibid., no. 315, 28.2.53; B2:KM38–43: T41–3, K8: p. 62, no. 157, 14.6.42; AP:E2, p. 174, no. 169, 11.10.47; A:E103, p. 150, no. 265, 13.12.52.

divorce, it seems that, owing to difficulties in raising the necessary funds for compensating the husband or because the latter demands it as security for the fulfillment of her financial obligation, she enlists the help of her father in the compensation arrangement. Thus, in one case, the wife redeemed herself by compensating her spouse with the whole of her dower and marital rights. After 'he proved against her that she still owed him seven pounds of her prompt dower, she and her father undertook to pay them to him upon her marriage to another man' – all this in return for (*fī naẓīr*) his divorcing her by *ṭalāq*. Similarly, in another case, it was stated that the wife 'redeemed herself with her deferred dower and she and her father undertook to return the prompt dower to him ... upon her marriage to another man.'[4] Cases of this kind too represent a compromise between custom and *sharīʿa*: the financial arrangement is purely customary, but it is the wife, not her father, who conducts the negotiations, and although the father's support is enlisted he is not a formal party to the transaction; from a technical legal point of view, the obligation to return the dower falls on the wife alone. In this sense, we may see here a transitional stage between customary and *sharʿī khulʿ*, provided that the *qāḍī* does not intervene by smoothing custom so as to adapt it, as far as possible, to the *sharʿī* norm. In one case, the wife appeared in court with her mother (rather than with her father or some other agnatic relative), which demonstrates a wife's competence to conduct negotiations for her freedom.[5]

Still, in most cases of customary *khulʿ*, the wife's agnatic relatives, and especially her father, were directly involved in the proceedings, assuming every financial and other liability for the fulfillment of the conditions agreed upon with the divorcing husband. Thus, in one case, the husband alleged in court, in the absence of the wife, that his father-in-law had undertaken to give him some camels, a sum of money in cash and some jewelry upon his daughter's marriage to another man. The father-in-law confirmed this version and undertook that if his daughter claimed anything from the divorcing husband in contravention of the agreement between them, he, the father-in-law, would indemnify him for any monetary damage incurred through filing the claim in court. In a further case, the wife's father waived all his daughter's marital rights and undertook to pay to the divorcing husband 'what he received of his daughter's dower ... upon her marriage to another man ...'. He added: 'If my daughter demands any marital rights from this her husband, we shall satisfy her out of my own money.' In a similar case, the divorced woman's father undertook to pay a certain amount 'upon my daughter's marriage to another man'. He added:

4 KD59–73, K51: p. 15, no. 29, 27.9.59 and K48: p. 64, no. 125, 18.10.60, respectively.

5 KD59–73, p. 206, no. 496, 10.9.64.

'Furthermore, if, breaking away from my control, she marries without my permission … for less than that amount, I undertake to pay it in full of my own volition without any resistance or delay.'[6] The instances before us reflect the customary norm in its full supremacy with a slight concession to the *sharīʿa* prompted by the character of the authority before which the matter is brought: the wife is not a party to the *khulʿ* proceedings but the object of a transaction between her father (who receives her dower upon her remarriage) and her former husband. But since, in the *Sharīʿa* Court, the wife may, under the *sharīʿa*, claim the fulfillment of her marital rights as a divorced woman, an undertaking by her father to satisfy such claims is required.

Occasionally a male agnatic relative (usually the father) acts as her deputy (*nāʾib*) or agent (*wakīl*) in divorce proceedings. Thus, in one case, the wife's father, by virtue of a power of attorney from her, waived all her marital rights and undertook to pay his son-in-law a certain sum 'when his daughter is able to marry another man'. He also undertook that if his daughter claimed anything contrary to the agreement between them 'he will be liable for it [the claim] to the honourable *Sharīʿa* Court'. In a further case the father, as his daughter's *nāʾib*, undertook to pay a certain sum upon her marriage to another man, adding that if she claimed anything from her former husband 'by virtue of a right due to her under the *sharīʿa*' he will pay it to her out of his own money.[7] According to the Mālikī school, no legal status is required in order to conduct negotiations with the husband concerning *khulʿ*. Even a third party who has no family or legal tie with the wife may stipulate with the husband that he shall divorce her by *khulʿ* – even against her will – provided that he, the third party – and not the wife – pays compensation to the husband (Linant de Bellefonds, 1965: 423, 428 f.). This is a carry-over from the customary concept of marriage-by-purchase, according to which the wife is not a party to the divorce negotiations.

Sometimes both spouses are represented by their fathers, which stresses even more the customary character of the proceedings. Thus, in one case, the two fathers agreed upon customary *khulʿ*; the husband's father, as his son's *wakīl*, agreed to the conditions, saying: 'I have already divorced (*qad ṭallaqtu*) [the name of the wife] from her husband, my son [name], who is absent from the session of the court.'[8] In another case, in which the husband was represented by his father and the wife was herself a party to the negotiations,

6 AP:E4: p. 117, no. 114, 20.3.47; A:E104, p. 197, no. 335, 8.4.53; and AP:E3, p. 326, no. 355, 29.5.54, respectively Cf. Layish (1975: 160).

7 AP:E2, p. 182, no. 178, 8.1.48 and A:E102, p. 333, no. 567, 23.6.54, respectively.

8 A:E104, p. 226, no. 375, ?.7.53. See also KD59–73, K48: p. 82, no. 159, 28.3.61; K48: p. 178, no. 385, 19.8.63; K50: p. 20, no. 48, 14.7.65; p. 131, no. 269, 8.7.72.

it was stated that the husband's father had divorced his daughter-in-law, saying: 'The woman has redeemed herself [with] the specific dower, which she has delivered to him [to the husband's father], and he has entered to her debit [as compensation] the financial loss (*khasāra*) caused to him [the dower, gifts and a certain sum] …; when she finds a husband he shall pay that sum before the reading of *al-Fātiḥa* [the solemnization of the marriage].' It is not clear from this document whether the reference is to the loss caused to the husband or to the loss caused to his father as the person who financed the dower and the other expenses connected with the marriage. In one case, the wife was represented in customary *khulʿ* proceedings by her guardian. It was agreed between the husband and the guardian that the latter should pay the husband a certain sum out of his own money when the ward (*rabība*) married another man. The guardian also undertook to maintain her during the waiting period. It seems that the guardian, in accordance with the customary norm, treats the ward's dower as his own money, whence his readiness to compensate the husband upon her remarriage. It is also quite possible that the guardian holds succession rights of the ward and is therefore prepared to maintain her during the waiting period.[9] This phenomenon has also been observed in Northern Nigeria. Anderson notes that the wife is seldom able to raise funds of her own for her redemption; much more often her guardian or her family pays the dower to her husband, expecting to recoup themselves by an identical amount upon her remarriage or to collect it secretly from her new husband (Anderson, 1970: 209).

The particulars of the financial arrangement between the parties to a customary *khulʿ* are, as one may expect, settled outside the *Sharīʿa* Court on a voluntary basis. The arrangement is recorded in the *quṣṣa* or *quṣṣat al-marʾa*, literally: 'lock of hair' or 'wife's lock of hair'. This term, which has been found only in the *sijill* of Kufra, is a popular-customary expression. It describes a kind of promissory note drawn up to guard against the unexpected. Colucci explains that the father's obligation, 'written [on his daughter's] lock of hair', to pay the agreed amount to the husband upon the daughter's marriage to another man is contracted in case she dies before remarrying, lest the husband loses his financial right (Colucci, 1932: 43; idem, 1927: 26). The usual formula is: 'Entered (*kutiba*) [or: recorded (*sujjila*)] to her [the wife's] debit (*ʿalayhā*) the amount of … in her 'lock of hair' [as follows:] "When she marries another man,

---

9 KD59–73, K50: p. 131, no. 270, 11.7.62 and A:E103, p. 96, no. 178, 3.7.52, respectively. On the *al-Fātiḥa* see Layish and Shmueli (1979: 33) and the sources indicated there.

he shall pay the said amount".'[10] All the kinds of compensation which the wife owes to her divorcer – various jewelry, household effects, livestock, etc. – are sometimes specified, with an indication of their total monetary value; 'they are recorded in the arrangement until he who seeks her hand is caused to pay the said amount.'[11] It is sometimes expressly noted – again, apparently, for reasons of legal certainty – that the compensation shall be paid 'before the making of the marriage contract with her [by the new husband]' or – more frequently – 'before the public reading of [*ṣūrat*] al-Fātiḥa', which is – as mentioned above – equivalent to the formation of the marriage tie. In other words: the payment of the compensation is a condition of the woman's remarriage.[12] In one case, it was expressly noted that it was 'not permitted (*mā yajūz*) to anyone to read *al-Fātiḥa* before payment of the above-mentioned'.[13] Also among the Berbers in the Kabyle Mountains of Algeria, a woman divorced by customary *khulʿ* cannot marry another man before the former husband has been compensated (Bousquet, 1950: 75 ff.). The same phenomenon has also been observed in Israel (Layish, 1975: 160). In another case, it was said: 'If the *Fātiḥa* is read to her without this amount having been paid, he who reads it shall be regarded as a transgressor (*ḍālim*) [*ẓālim*, that is to say, there shall be a ground for a monetary claim against him under the rules of customary law], and he shall be compelled to pay that amount.'[14]

Moreover, there are those who – in the best tradition of customary contracts drawn up by arbitrators without statutory status or power of enforcement – demand a guarantee for the payment of compensation upon the woman's marriage to another man. Thus, in one case, it was said: 'Thirty pounds have been entered in her *quṣṣa* with the guarantee (*kafāla*) of her *wakīl*; upon her marriage to another man, the *wakīl* shall pay.' The *wakīl* delivered the power of attorney to the husband's father (who represented the husband in the *khulʿ* proceedings); only then did the husband divorce the wife. According to customary law, the *kafīl* (guarantor) is only required to pay out of his own pocket if the party he represents does not fulfill his obligation under the agreement.[15] In another

---

10 E.g., K59–73, K47: p. 196, no. 464, 16.6.64; p. 206, no. 496, 10.9.64; p. 217, no. 518, 26.12.64; p. 24, no. 56, 4.8.65; p. 207, no. 498, 7.8.65. Cf. Bousquet (1950: 76, 78).

11 E.g., KD59–73, K50: p. 10, no. 25, 14.4.65.

12 E.g., B2:KM38–43: T41–3, K6: p. 93, no. 247, 27.2.43; KD59–73; K50: p. 131, no. 269, 8.8.72, no. 270, 11.7.72; p. 20, no. 48, 14.7.65.

13 KD59–73, K48: p. 178, no. 385, 19.8.63.

14 KD59–73, p. 24, no. 56, 4.8.65. On the customary '*ẓālim*' see Layish (2011).

15 KD59–73, K48: p. 176, no. 382, 15.8.63. On the customary '*kafāla*' see Stewart; Stewart and Blanc.

case, the wife's maternal uncle (*khāl*) guaranteed for her.[16] Instances of security being given for the return of the dower in customary *khulʿ* have been observed among the Bedouin of the Judean Desert. In one case, arbitrators decided that the woman's father must, upon her remarriage, pay a certain amount of dinars in consideration of her divorce; if she did not remarry within ten months, her father must raise that amount from some other source. As security for the implementation of this award, all the property of the woman's father was pledged pending taking possession (*qabḍ*) of the dower. A well-known shaykh was appointed surety for the implementation of the award. In another case, an arbitrator decided that if the woman's father refused to return the dower to her husband, he must return his daughter to him 'and there will be no divorce until *Allāh* puts them out of their misery'. In Israel, it has been observed that the woman's father gave a promissory note, signed by him, payable on the date of her remarriage (Layish and Shmueli, 1979: 37 f.; Layish, 1975: 160 f.).

Finally, resort to the *Sharīʿa* Court for the putting into practice of an institution contrary to the *sharīʿa* is evidence of a desire to utilize a judicial power anchored in law to give 'teeth' to the compensation agreement, i.e. to enable it to be enforced in the event of one of the parties not fulfilling his part under its terms. Thus, in one case, it was noted that the parties had agreed on dissolution 'out of court'. The court confirmed that the wife must pay a certain sum of money upon her marriage to another man; only when she had done so did the husband divorce her in the presence of the court.[17] In other cases, it was stipulated in the wife's *quṣṣa*, upon the husband's demand, that the compensation should be paid, upon her remarriage, 'through the medium (*ʿalā yad*)' of the *Sharīʿa* Court.[18]

The *sijill* contains almost no information on the implementation of customary *khulʿ* agreements in everyday life, and it therefore seems that they were generally implemented faithfully, in both letter and spirit, without the parties seeking the intervention of the court. At the same time it is quite possible that, upon non-fulfillment of an obligation under such an agreement, the parties prefer to resort to arbitration (or to a civil court); but of this, obviously, there is no evidence in the *sijill*. There are some actual testimonies to the fulfillment of the terms of a customary *khulʿ*. Thus, in one case, a man divorced his wife by *khulʿ*, indicating in her *quṣṣa* a certain amount of money which her fiancé was to pay before the reading of *al-Fātiḥa*. The woman 'remarried, her new

16 AP:E3, p. 342, no. 582, 6.7.54. On the position of the *khāl* see Peters (1965: 135); Obermayer (1968: 125 f., 130), Oweidi (1982: 107 f.).

17 KD59–73, K48: p. 82, no. 159, 28.3.61.

18 See below, 4. *Qāḍīs and customary khulʿ*.

husband paid her debt (*khallaṣa mā ʿalayhā*) … and there is no more claim against her.' In another case, it is said that the wife 'returned thirty pounds, which had been entered in the *quṣṣa* to her debit, to the [former] husband after another man had married her.'[19]

Nevertheless, there are occasional hints at problems in connection with the implementation of a customary *khulʿ*. Thus, in one case, a woman told her new husband that the former husband 'claims from you, O Ibrāhīm, the price of my marriage (*thaman zawājī*'), i.e. her dower. The new husband admitted only that he owed her the deferred dower, and the wife did not succeed in proving that she had not yet received the prompt dower. From this, we may infer that the dower was not paid over to the first husband before the woman's remarriage. In another case, a woman claimed from her divorcer a certain sum as dower and clothing allowance, about one-quarter of it destined for a certain person; 'when he comes [to court] and demands it from this my husband, he shall pay it to him.' This certain person was not her father or an agnatic relative; he may have been her first husband, who had divorced her by customary *khulʿ* and had not yet been compensated in spite of her remarriage. Now that she had been divorced from her second husband, she wanted to realize her rights and may on this occasion have wished to pay her debt to her first husband. In another case, the woman's former husband appointed a *wakīl* to receive a certain sum of money 'from the husband of the principal's divorced wife'. The *wakīl* was given absolute power of attorney (*tafwīḍ*) and permitted 'to apply to all the other official agencies, *sharʿī* and civil', apparently in order to institute legal proceedings for the realization of the debt due to the first husband under the customary *khulʿ* agreement. In this and the preceding case, it was noted that the first husband claimed the debt from the second husband and not from the wife or her guardian, although the second husband was not a party to the customary *khulʿ* agreement.[20] Among the Berbers of the Kabyle Mountains, it is usual for the first husband to claim the compensation from the wife's father or second husband. The compensation is usually equal to the dower, but the husband sometimes demands an excessive compensation to revenge himself on the wife and make it more difficult for her to remarry; attempts to fight this practice by legislation have been unsuccessful (Bousquet, 1950: 76 ff.).

---

19 KD59–73, K50: p. 131, no. 269, 8.7.72 and K48: p. 50, no. 93, 4.12.65, respectively.

20 B2:KM38–43:EA, K4a: no. 1, 4.7.32; T41–3, K8: p. 21, no. 49, 24.9.41; and T43, K6: p. 37, no. 111, 28.12.43, respectively. Cf. '*thāmamth*' in Bousquet (1950: 77). On the 'customary' deferred dower payable after a specified number of years and not on widowhood or divorce see Layish, *Divorce* (iv, 3a (1)); Anderson (1970: 369).

## 3 The Causes of Customary *khulʿ*

Mohsen encountered customary *khulʿ* among the Awlād ʿAlī in the Western Desert in cases where a woman left her husband to marry her lover. A man whose 'patronage' she sought in order that he might persuade her husband to divorce her tried at the same time to persuade the future husband to pay to the present one the dower which the future husband was to have paid to her before marrying her. Mohsen found that in a number of cases the present husband was prepared to divorce his wife only after the future husband had promised to pay him the dower at the time of marrying her. In one such case, in which the *ʿumda* mediated, the latter tried at first to persuade the woman's father to return the dower to her husband and when he failed, he paid the husband a certain sum on account out of his own money and undertook that the remainder would be paid upon her marriage to her lover. Only then did the husband divorce her, and a week later she was married to her lover (Mohsen, 1970: 231; 1975: 117 f.). Customary *khulʿ* under similar circumstances has been observed by Anderson in several places in Africa. On the Gold Coast, for instance, if the wife elopes with her lover and refuses to return to the husband, the latter may demand that her father reimburse him for all the expenses incurred by him, and the father, in turn, will try to recoup himself from the lover, though not by formal litigation (Anderson, 1970: 272).

In the Libyan *sijill*, we have found no references to customary *khulʿ* following intimacy between the woman and her future husband. It may be that, for reasons of discretion or from reluctance to charge the wife with adultery (*zinā*), the Qurʾānic punishment for which is most severe (stoning in the case of a married woman), the *qāḍīs* refrain from specifying the circumstances of the divorce or from indicating the identity of the future husband. On the other hand, there are indications that the rationale of customary *khulʿ* may be financial distress of the wife or her agnatic relatives. Thus, in one case, the wife persuaded the husband to divorce her, 'asking him to grant her a delay (*imhāl*) for the payment [of compensation] because of her poverty (*li-faqrihā*)'. In another case, it was agreed that compensation should be paid 'later'.[21] In these cases, it was not expressly stated that the wife needed the delay in order to remarry. Colucci too explains that the father's obligation, written on the daughter's 'lock of hair', to pay an agreed amount to the divorcing husband originates in the father's inability to pay it at the time of the divorce (Colucci, 1932: 43). The money may be raised also from other sources, e.g., from agnatic relatives

21 AP:E4, p. 121, no. 118, 9.4.47 and KD59–73, K43: p. 47, no. 90, 27.6.60, respectively.

of the wife. Thus, in one case, it was agreed at the time of the *khulʿ* that the wife's grandfather should pay the divorcing husband a certain sum 'when his son [the wife's brother] returns from the [military?] service.'[22] Law No. 18 of 18 March 1973, enables the court to grant a delay for the payment of compensation in a *khulʿ* divorce where the wife is in financial straits and the husband refuses to divorce her out of spite and will not give her time to raise the money (Mayer, 1978: p. 39, n. 1; p. 41, n. 3).

Some documents dealing with instances of customary *khulʿ* suggest that *khulʿ* in these cases arises from financial distress of the wife and her agnatic relatives: the identity of the future husband is never stated, even in the context of security for the payment of the debt; the remarriage as such is shrouded in the mists of the future (although a divorced woman of child-bearing age does not find it difficult to remarry); and references to the wife's remarriage are cautious and subdued; blind fate or the will of *Allāh* are not challenged: 'When I am able to marry another man' (*ʿindamā yatayassar lī iqtirān bi-ghayrihi*) or 'When a fiancé comes her way' (*idhā atāhā khāṭib*).[23] The custom derives from the institution of marriage-by-purchase, under which the bride is the object of a sale; according to this concept, the seller of the bride (an agnatic relative) may compensate the first husband, following the cancellation of the transaction, by means of the consideration he receives upon her transfer to another husband. Authentic vestiges of this customary concept survive even after the adoption of the *sharʿī* concept, according to which the woman is a party to the marriage contract: since her competence to own property is limited, the only way open to her, except requesting assistance from her agnatic relatives, is to compensate her first husband by means of the dower she receives from the second. Similarly, among the Berbers of the Kabyle Mountains, the background of customary *khulʿ* is purely financial: the payment of compensation is deferred until the woman's remarriage, and she is forbidden to marry her lover (Bousquet, 1950: 77–8). In Israel too customary *khulʿ* is motivated by financial distress. It is an arrangement designed to ensure compensation to the divorcing husband at some other time, when the situation has improved. The woman's father undertakes that upon her marriage to another man he will satisfy her former husband out of the prompt dower (Layish 1975: 160).

---

22 KDP, K45: p. ?, no. 136, 26.11.60 (her brother).

23 E.g., AP:E4, p. 137, no. 127, 23.5.47; AP:E2, p. 182, no. 178, 8.1.48; KD59–73, K50: p. 131, no. 270, 11.7.62; p. 10, no. 25, 14.4.65.

## 4 *Qāḍīs* and Customary *khulʿ*

Making the remarriage of a woman divorced by customary *khulʿ* dependent on the transfer of the dower from the new husband to the divorcing husband, especially if the transfer is made through her agnatic relatives, without her being a party to the proceedings, is, as stated, in glaring contradiction to the *sharīʿa*. How do the *qāḍīs* react to this contradiction? They seem to be totally unaware of it. They treat customary *khulʿ* as *khulʿ* in all respects. They do not interfere in voluntary agreements between the parties, which were probably reached out of court and included in the wife's *quṣṣa*, but honour and confirm them as part of the *sharʿī* judgement. They are content if it is proved to their satisfaction that the financial arrangement was made by the free consent of the parties and that they were legally competent to give up rights and assume financial obligations, and they order the woman or her agnatic relative to fulfill his or her obligation upon her marriage to a third party. Thus, in one case, it is said in the judgement, following a statement of the conditions of the customary *khulʿ*: 'On the basis of what the parties have agreed between them of their own free will (*ṭawʿan*), at the session of the court … the *qāḍī* awards a *khulʿi ṭalāq* and orders the wife and her father to pay the compensation with which the latter redeems her by virtue of a power of attorney from her …'. In other cases, it is said: 'On the basis of what has been agreed between them – they being competent from a *sharʿī* point of view – and on the basis of a financial arrangement held by him to be sound, the *qāḍī* awards a *khulʿī ṭalāq* and debits the wife's father with what he has renounced and has undertaken to pay on his daughter's marriage to another man.'[24]

It seems that the *qāḍīs* regard customary *khulʿ* as a legitimate – since mutually agreed – deferment, prompted by financial distress of the woman or her agnatic relative, of the payment of compensation to the divorcing husband. We have mentioned above a case in which the wife, who had initiated the *khulʿ*, requested a 'deferment of the payment [of compensation] to the husband because of her poverty'. The husband granted the request. The *qāḍī* tried to prevent the dissolution, and when he did not succeed, he declared that the *khulʿ* and the deferment were valid owing to the husband's consent. When it is agreed between the parties that the period of deferment shall end upon the woman's marriage to another man, the *qāḍīs* are careful to note in the judgement that the debt shall be paid 'in due time, without subterfuge or

24 AP:E2, p. 182, no. 178, 8.1.48; A:E102, p. 30, no. 58, 21.9.51; and p. 333, no. 567, 23.6.54, respectively.

delay'.[25] The *qāḍīs* confirm the customary *khulʿ* agreement, even if it is found in the course of the proceedings that an explicit *sharʿī* norm has been ignored, viz. that the woman's father has undertaken to pay to the divorcer of his daughter, at the time of her marriage to another man, a certain amount of money which 'he received out of her dower'. The woman's father is ordered to fulfill his undertaking in disregard of the *sharʿī* norm that the dower is the property of the wife.[26] Although the *qāḍīs* also order the wife's agnatic relative or guardian to fulfill his obligation as regards her marital rights as a divorced woman, such as maintenance during the waiting period, they seem to be doing so not because these rights are anchored in the *sharīʿa* but because of the agreement between the parties or by virtue of a unilateral undertaking.[27]

The court confirms the security designed to ensure the implementation of the *khulʿ* agreements, e.g. the guarantee (*kafāla*), anchored in customary law, by the wife's relatives for the payment of compensation to the husband.[28] Moreover, the *qāḍīs* confirm such security even where, on the face of it, it is contrary to the *sharʿī* norm. We have seen above that the *khulʿ* agreement frequently stipulates that the compensation to the divorcing husband shall be paid before the reading of *al-Fātiḥa*, and sometimes it is even stated expressly that the wife must not remarry before the compensation has been paid.[29] A debt of a divorced woman to her first husband is not a *sharʿī* bar to her remarriage, but it may be a bar to it according to the customary concept of marriage-by-purchase. Moreover, the court is instrumental in upholding customary *khulʿ* agreements contrary to the *sharīʿa*. We have seen above that the parties resort to the court as a statutory judicial authority in the expectation that the compensation will be paid through it before the marriage contract is made, and they thereby turn the court into a full partner in a deviation from the *sharīʿa*. In fact, in one case, it was held that if the marriage was performed before payment of the compensation into court 'the person who reads the *Fātiḥa* is a transgressor [and shall be ordered] to pay the amount'.[30] The reader of the *Fātiḥa* may be the *maʾdhūn*, the person authorized on behalf of the *Sharīʿa* Court to perform marriages. The court thus gives *sharʿī* sanction to a customary punishment although the *maʾdhūn* would be acting within the

---

25 AP:E4, p. 121, no. 118, 9.4.47 and AP:E4, p. 137, no. 127, 23.5.47, respectively. See also p. 117, no. 114, 20.3.47; p. 121, no. 118, 9.4.47.

26 A:E104, p. 197, no. 335, 8.4.53.

27 E.g., A:E103, p. 96, no. 178, 3.7.52.

28 E.g., AP:E3, p. 342, no. 582, 6.7.54.

29 See above, p. 431.

30 KD59–73, p. 24, no. 56, 4.8.65. See also KD59–73, K50: p. 131, no. 270, 11.7.62; K51: p. 203, no. 490, 24.8.64; K50: p. 18, no. 42, 7.7.65.

*sharīʿa* if he refused to postpone the remarriage of the divorced woman for non-*sharʿī* reasons.

Similarly, the *qāḍīs* lend a hand in enforcing customary *khulʿ* agreements involving a deviation from the *sharīʿa*. We have seen above how a man who had divorced his wife by customary *khulʿ* empowered another man to receive a sum of money from her new husband and even to sue him before *sharʿī* and other authorities, as might be necessary. The *qāḍī* permitted (*ajāza*) this delegation of power (*tafwīḍ*) although the second husband was not a party to the *khulʿ* agreement and although the claim should have been addressed to the wife or her authorized representative. We have also seen above how a woman contended against her husband that her former husband claimed 'the price of my marriage'. The *qāḍī* did not dismiss the action *in limine* on the grounds that there was no legal connection between the two cases, but rejected the woman's claim solely because she had not succeeded in proving her contention: 'unless she brings [before the court] just, conclusive proof from [her first husband] …'. We have already noted a feature observed on the Gold Coast: a wife who elopes with her lover may dissolve her marriage by paying compensation to the husband. But the court claims the compensation from the *wife's father*, who, according to the customary concept, is a party to the marriage contract, and he, in turn, seeks to recover it from the new husband. Some Nigerian *sharīʿa* courts prohibit a wife who obtains her freedom with the encouragement, and perhaps the financial assistance, of her lover from marrying him,[31] probably because adultery of the wife is a serious offence according to the *sharīʿa*.

All the foregoing leads to the conclusion that the *Sharīʿa* Court feels bound to confirm agreements reached outside the *Sharīʿa* Court under the rules of customary law even if they conflict with the *Sharīʿa*, provided they were reached by free choice: 'The parties have become reconciled (*iṣṭalaḥā*) and the dispute (*shiqāq*) between them has ceased, and the *qāḍī* has permitted the reconciliation (*ṣulḥ*) arrangement.' In other cases of customary *khulʿ* in which the wife undertook to pay the husband a sum of money upon her marriage to another man, the court gave effect to the divorce and ordered the wife 'to fulfill her undertaking upon her remarriage' or saw to it that the sum was entered in her *quṣṣa* and paid when she remarried.[32] This attitude of the *qāḍīs* towards customary *khulʿ* is strikingly in line with the declared attitude of Muslim *qāḍīs* in Israel on the same issue, according to which the court does not interfere

31 B2:KM38–43:T43, K6: p. 37, no. 111, 28.12.43 and EA, K4a: no. 1, 4.7.32, respectively. Cf. Anderson (1970: 210, 272).

32 AP:E3, p. 326, no. 555, 29.5.54.

in voluntary agreements, holding that 'mutual agreement is stronger than the *qāḍī*' (*al-tarāḍī yaghlib al-qāḍī*); the court treats the undertaking to compensate the first husband upon the marriage of the divorced wife to another man like a promissory note that has to be honoured (Layish, 1975: 160 f., 198). The *qāḍīs* regard customary *khulʿ* as a *khulʿ* divorce also as to the legal effects of the dissolution. The divorce comes into force immediately and is not conditional on compensation to the husband. The *qāḍīs* pronounce dissolution and order the wife to observe the waiting period from the date of the judgement. Thus, in one case, when the parties had agreed on the amount to be paid to the husband upon the wife's remarriage, the husband divorced her by one minor irrevocable repudiation entailing a short separation (*bānat baynūna ṣughrā*), after which the wife 'is not permitted to him unless a new marriage contract is concluded and a new dower paid'; she was ordered to observe the waiting-period (*iʿtidād*) from the date of the judgement.[33] The *qāḍīs* serving among the Berbers of the Kabyle Mountains (as well as the French courts) also sometimes – though not frequently – treated customary *khulʿ*, as to its legal effects, like *sharʿī khulʿ* (Bousquet, 1950: 75).

## 5 Summary

Customary *khulʿ* as reflected in the Libyan *sijill* is another instance of the firm position of custom in North African society. The *qāḍī*, who, more than any other religious functionary, finds himself in direct daily confrontation with custom and is supposed to represent normative Islam, is prepared to go a long way to meet custom while preserving the nominal supremacy of the *sharīʿa*. The Mālikī school, probably because of the tribal environment in which it grew and consolidated in Medina, is likelier than any other orthodox school to compromise with custom. This trend was noticeable already in the Middle Ages in Mālikī judicial practice (*ʿamal*) (Schacht, 1966: 29, 61 f.; Coulson, 1964: 145 ff.; Milliot, 1953: 167–78; Berque, *EI*); but contrary to that tradition, the Libyan *sijill* does not suggest a systematic, sophisticated approach aimed at absorbing custom into the *sharīʿa*. Thus, e.g., no attempt is made to apply the principle of *maṣlaḥa* (public interest) for this purpose. The *fuqahāʾ* and *qāḍīs* have always used that principle as an efficient mechanism to bridge the gap between an ideal *sharīʿa* and an everyday practice dominated by custom (Coulson, 1964: 144; Layish, 1975: 332 ff.; Layish, 1987: 285). The *sijill* contains no significant

33 59–73, K50: p. 10, no. 25, 14.4.65. See also A:E104, p. 182, no. 314, 28.2.53; p. 197, no. 335, 8.4.53; KDP, K45: p. ?, no. 136, 26.11.60.

evidence of attempts by *qāḍīs* to enlist the *fuqahāʾ*, whose function is to adapt the *sharīʿa* to changing social conditions by means of legal opinions (*fatwā*); recourse to religious – legal literature is also rare.

It is difficult to gain from the *sijill* the impression that the *qāḍīs* are fully aware of the tension between custom and *sharīʿa*, though in matters embodying the essence of the ethical-religious philosophy of Islam, such as the legal effects of divorce, there are instances of rejection of custom and enforcement of the *sharīʿa*. The *qāḍīs* sidestep, or rather are spared, the problem by achieving an amicable settlement between the parties, which is thereupon automatically confirmed by the court as part of the judgement; if an actual decision is unavoidable, they resort to some brief stereotype. This state of things may be due to the personal social background and legal training of the *qāḍīs* in districts remote from the administrative centres (Layish 1991, ch. viii). A similar situation has been observed in other areas of Africa (Anderson, 1970; 140 f., 232, 292 f.; Coulson, 1964; 136 f.).

## Primary Sources

The *sijill* of the *Sharīʿa* Courts (in the alphabetical order of the abbreviations)

| | |
|---|---|
| A:E102 (–104) | *Sharīʿa* Court of Ajdābiya, Envelope 102 (–104) |
| AP:E1 (–4) | *Sharīʿa* Court of Ajdābiya – Puzzles, Envelope 1 (–4) |
| B2:KM38–43: T41–3 | BOX 2: *Sharīʿa* Court of Kufra – Marriages 1938–43: *Ṭalāq* 1941–3 |
| T43 | *Ṭalāq* 1943 |
| EA | Envelope A |
| KD59–73 | *Sharīʿa* Court of Kufra – Divorce, 1959–71, 1973 |
| KDP | *Sharīʿa* Court of Kufra – Divorce – Puzzles |

## Secondary Sources

Anderson, J.N.D. 1970. *Islamic law in Africa*. New impression. London: Cass.

Berque, J. "Amal', *EI* (2nd ed.), 427 f.

Bousquet, G.-H. [1945.] 'Islamic law and customary law in French North Africa.' A Special University Lecture delivered in the University of London, London.

Bousquet, G.-H. 1950. *Justice française et coutumes kabiles*. Alger: Imprimerie Nord-Africaine, S. Crescenzo.

Colucci, M. 1927. 'Il Diritto consuetudinario delle tribù della Cirenaica', *Rivista Coloniale*, Vol. 22: 24–37.

Colucci, M. 1932. 'Il Diritto consuetudinario della Cirenaica', *Revista Giuridica del Medio ed Estremo Oriente Giustizia Coloniale*, Vol. x, Fasc 1–2: 38–50.

Coulson, N.J. 1964. *A history of Islamic law*. (Islamic Surveys, 2.) Edinburgh: Edinburgh University Press.

Layish, A. 1975. *Women and Islamic law in a non-Muslim state: a study based on the decisions of the sharīʿa courts in Israel*. New York and Jerusalem: John Wiley & Sons.

Layish, A. 1987. 'Saudi Arabian legal reform as a mechanism to moderate Wahhābī doctrine', *JAOS*, 107/2: 279–92.

Layish, A. 2011. *Legal documents from the Judean desert. The impact of the Sharīʿa on Bedouin customary law*. Leiden: Brill.

Layish, A. 1991. *Divorce in the Libyan family: a study based on the sijill of the sharīʿa courts of Ajdābiya and Kufra*. New York: New York University Press.

Layish, A. and Shmueli, A. 1979. 'Custom and *sharīʿa* in the Bedouin family according to legal documents from the Judaean Desert', *BSOAS*, XLII, 1: 29–45.

Linant de Bellefonds, Y. 1965. *Traité de droit musulman comparé*. Vol. 2. Paris: Mouton.

Mayer, Ann. 1978. 'Developments in the law of marriage and divorce in Libya since the 1969 revolution', *Journal of African Law*, 22/1: 30–49.

Milliot, L. 1953. *Introduction à l'étude du droit musulman*. Paris: Recueil Sirey.

Mohsen, Safia K. 1970. 'Aspects of the legal status of women among Awlad ʿAli', in Sweet, Louise E. (ed.), *People and cultures of the Middle East*, I. Garden City, N.Y.: Natural History Press: 220–33.

Mohsen, Safia K. 1975. *Conflict and law among Awlad ʿAli of the Western Desert*. Cairo: National Center for Social and Criminological Research.

Peters, E.L. 1965. 'Aspects of the family among the Bedouin of Cyrenaica', in Nimkoff, M.F. (ed.), *Comparative family systems*. Boston, Mass.: Houghton Mifflin: 121–46.

Obermayer, G.J. 1968. *Structure and authority in a Bedouin tribe: the ʿAishaibat of the Western Desert of Egypt*. Ph.D. dissertation, Indiana University (University Microfilms).

Oweidi, Ahmad Saleh Suleiman. 1982. *Bedouin justice in Jordan: the customary legal system of the tribes and its integration into the framework of state policy from 1921 onwards*. Ph.D. thesis, Cambridge University.

Schacht, J. 1966. *An introduction to Islamic law*. Second impression. Oxford: Oxford University Press.

Stern, Gertrude. 1939. *Marriage in early Islam*. London: Royal Asiatic Society.

Stewart, F.H. *A Bedouin tribe and its law* [unpublished?]

Stewart, F.H. 1988. *Texts in Sinai Bedouin law. With the assistance of Haim Blanc and Salaamih Hseen. Part I: The texts in English translation; Part II: The texts in Arabic*. Wiesbaden: Harrassowitz.

CHAPTER 2

# Interplay between Tribal and *Sharʿī* Law: A Case of Tibbāwī Blood Money in the *Sharīʿa* Court of Kufra

## 1 The Relationship between Customary Law and *Sharīʿa**

*Sharīʿa* and custom are profoundly different legal systems. Broadly speaking, *sharīʿa* is based on divine revelation and is imposed on society from above, whereas custom is an unwritten law shaped by daily practice and therefore accommodated to changing circumstances. The *sharīʿa* has demonstrated its assimilative power in relation to custom ever since its formation and crystallization in the early ʿAbbāsid period. Although Islamic legal methodology (*uṣūl al-fiqh*) does not recognize custom as a source of law, the Mālikī school did incorporate custom into its legal doctrine in its later development in the Maghrib.

In contemporary Arab society, customary law continues to enjoy various degrees of autonomy alongside the *sharīʿa*, especially in tribal areas. Tribal courts and arbitrators apply customary law largely undisturbed by the central government; moreover, decisions of the *sharīʿa* courts are carried out only to the extent that the *sharʿī* norm is compatible with custom.

Normative Islam, with its beliefs, institutions, and law, does not play a central role in the shaping of a nomadic society although there are of course differences in this regard from one region to another. In North Africa, for example, tribesmen seem to be closer to normative Islam than their counterparts in the Middle East.[1] Popular religion, including saint worship and intercession, still predominates. Customary law survives even among tribesmen who have nominally adopted Islam. Bedouin throughout the Muslim world identify themselves as Muslims although their knowledge and practice of Islamic doctrine, worship, ethics and law is limited (this applies to the Cyrenaican Bedouin even

* Originally published in *Islamic Law and Society* 13/1 (2006), pp. 63–75. I wish to express my gratitude to the following colleagues and scholars: John Davis (Oxford University) for placing at my disposal a selection of decisions issued by the Sharīʿa Courts of Ajdābiya and Kufra (see Davis, *Note*); Frank Stewart for his careful reading of the essay and valuable suggestions; the anonymous readers for their comments and suggestions; David Powers for editorial suggestions (and more); Andrzej Zaborski (Jagellonian University, Cracow) for his philological comments on the document; and Yehuda Pardo for his assistance with the Italian literature.

1 This may be due to the prevalence of Ṣūfī orders in North Africa.

 | DOI:10.1163/9789004680920_004

after the Sanūsī revivalist movement was established in their midst). Their acceptance of Islamic law is partial and slow. Although the Islamization of the Bedouin has been going on for centuries, it has not yet been fully completed. At present, a kind of peaceful co-existence is maintained between customary law and the *sharīʿa*, with each legal system confining itself to a particular domain (Stewart, 891).

In North Africa, tribal law seems to be giving way to the *sharīʿa*. This is manifested, *inter alia*, in the increasing tendency, in the early 1970s, of Cyrenaican tribesmen to resort to *sharʿī* jurisdiction (although they continued to use the tribal courts).[2] This tendency is a result of several causes: the sedentarization of tribes and their physical proximity to urban, religious, and economic centers; the administrative, civil and economic exigencies of a modern state; the accelerated religious transformation of the Bedouin and the strengthening of their Islamic identity, as a result of the spread of religious education and modern means of communication; the imposition of *sharʿī* jurisdiction on the Bedouin together with the abolition of the officially recognized court system that administered customary law; the equality of all parties in the *sharīʿa* court, irrespective of tribe, origin, color, or legal position; and the executive power of the *sharīʿa* court, which seeks to ensure the legal and financial rights of the parties to a dispute. Consequently, in those domains in which the Bedouin apply to the *sharʿī* judicial system and its agents, their lifestyle has become closer to normative Islam in the areas of worship, religious duties, and law.

The relationship between *sharīʿa* and tribal custom may be divided into two spheres. In one, custom reigns supreme with only minor concessions to the *sharīʿa* and outside of its control. In the other, the *sharīʿa* exercises assimilative power over custom, and *qāḍīs* play a decisive role in bringing the Bedouin within the orbit of the *sharīʿa*. It is the *qāḍī*, rather than the *muftī*, who directly confronts the Bedouin, and his willingness to tolerate custom and make concessions to it, while adopting and absorbing it into the *sharīʿa*, may create a climate in which a custom-bound population will apply to a *sharʿī* judicial authority with increasing frequency. On the other hand, a *qāḍī* who attempts to enforce both the letter and spirit of the *sharīʿa* may deter the Bedouin from applying to his court.

To illustrate the relationship between the *sharīʿa* and tribal customary law, I translate below a legal document issued by the Sharīʿa Court of Kufra in July 1942, when Cyrenaica was under Italian administration. An addition to the document is dated October 1944 when Cyrenaica was under British Military Administration (Evans-Pritchard, 227; Pelt, 33).

---

2 On the advantages of tribal arbitration, see Khayrallāh, 169–70; Davis, *Koufra*, 558.

## 2 *Sharīʿa* Courts under Italian Rule (1932–42)

During the period of Italian rule, the jurisdiction of the *sharīʿa* courts in Cyrenaica was, in theory, limited to disputes pertaining to personal status issues (Del Boca, II, 122). In fact, the Sharīʿa Court of Kufra exercised wide jurisdiction: in addition to disputes relating to personal status, inheritance, and *waqf*, the *sijill* contains judgments and orders pertaining to civil claims, contracts, property, homicide and assault – matters formally within the jurisdiction of the civil courts. The wide jurisdiction of the Sharīʿa Court may have been a carryover from Ottoman rule; apparently, the Ottoman judicial reforms of the 1860s were not implemented in Kufra because of its remoteness from the political and administrative centers of Libya and its location in the midst of tribesmen.[3] When the Italians took control, they left intact the *sharīʿa* court's jurisdiction in personal status matters; moreover, the civil court was empowered to transfer civil claims by Libyan citizens to the *sharīʿa* courts (Cicchitti, 485–6). Davis reports that it was not unusual for civil claims to be brought before the Sharīʿa Court in Kufra, since the civil court system was not fixed and institutionalized.[4]

The Sharīʿa Court in Kufra was run by a *qāḍī*, assisted by a *nāʾib* (deputy), *masʾūl* ("person in charge"), *mufattish* ("inspector"), and *kātib* (scribe or court clerk).[5] In a *sijill* dating to the early 1960s, the Sharīʿa court is referred to as "the Department of the Sharīʿa" (*dāʾirat al-sharʿ*) in the district of Kufra;[6] this may indicate its incorporation into the civil judiciary system.

Italian policy in Libya was to exercise supervision over the *sharīʿa* courts, in accordance with Western standards (Cicchitti, 478). The effects of this policy may be seen in *sharʿī* judicial practice. Judgments issued by the Sharīʿa Court of Kufra in the early 1930s contain detailed summaries of the judgment, in Italian, followed by the remark, "Visto per l'esecuzione!" (Approved for implementation!) and the signature of the Military Governor of the Kufra Areas. This indicates that a judgment would not be executed unless it received official written confirmation.

---

3 Ibn Mūsā, 251–2; Anderson, *Reform*, 330–1. On the Ottoman policy and the plan to establish *kaymakamlık* (sub-district) in Kufra in the late nineteenth century and its motives, see Le Gall, 95, 100–1.

4 This was also the situation in the 1970s when Davis conducted field research in Kufra. Davis, *Koufra*, 558.

5 Layish, *Libyan Documents*, Name Index: Qāḍīs, Nāʾibs and Other Judicial Clerks, 103. The court archive (*sijill*) in Kufra starts in 1932. Davis, *Koufra*, 563.

6 See Layish, *Libyan Documents*, Glossary.

Parallel to the dual civil and *sharʿī* judicial system, there was a dual system of secular and religious law, which, until the limited reinstatement of Islamic law by Qadhdhāfī in the early 1970s, was applied in two different court systems: secular law in the civil system and religious law in the *sharʿī* system. The *sharīʿa* courts applied non-codified Mālikī law in matters within their jurisdiction. This too was a carryover from the Ottoman period when the central government nominated Mālikī *qāḍīs*.[7] The dual judicial system remained intact under British rule (the British presumably complied with the international law on the administration of occupied enemy territory (Anderson, *Libya*, 253), according to which they were required to retain the Italian legal system).

## 3 Kufra and the Tibbū[8]

Kufra is the name of a district center in the southern part of Libya that includes the oases of Rabiana, Buzaima and Tazarbu. Between 1895 and 1919 Kufra was the administrative center of the Sanūsiyya, a revivalist and reformist movement;[9] it was central to the expansion of Islam into the Sahel and was the command headquarters of resistance to French expansion. The dominant tribal group in Kufra are the Zwayya, who are clients (*mrābṭīn al-ṣadgān*) of the Maghārba.[10] Both are Arabic speaking.

Another Kufran tribe is the Tibbū, a small group numbering about 200 in the late 1920s and about 500 in the second half of the 1970s (Bertarelli, 514; Davis, *Koufra*, 551; Del Boca, II, 119). They claim descent from the original inhabitants of Kufra, those who lived there when the area was conquered first by the Jawāzī Arabs and later by the Zwayya. The Tibbū, who are black-skinned, speak both Arabic and a language of their own (unrelated to either Berber or Arabic). They have genealogical and political links between themselves and other Tibbū in Chad and in the Tibesti area of S.W. Libya. Some of them are nomads, others sedentary. They maintain their own social organization, culture and identity,

---

7 Ibn Mūsā, 66. For further details, see Layish, *Legal Documents*, 14–17.

8 Unless otherwise indicated, the data on Kufra and Tibbū are based on De Agostini, *Cufra*, 45–6, passim; Bertarelli, 514–17; Davis, *Libyan Politics*, 108, 111–12, 150–2; idem, *Kofra*, 547–8, 551–5, 561–3; idem, *Social Perspective*, 7; Chapelle, 5; Yver, *Tubu*, 580–1; idem, *Kufra*, 351–2; Evans-Pritchard, 21–2; Baroin, *La contestation*, 159–60.

9 See Evans-Pritchard, 21, 78, 102, 148; Vikør, 186–8; Triaud, 411–14, 429–38, 467–9, 471, 476–9 and passim; Hassanein, 160, 178, 181.

10 De Agostini, *Cirenáica*, 407; for a reference to the Zwayya, see ibid., 338; Evans-Pritchard, 52–3, 65–9; al-Ḥabbūnī, 201–7; Davis, *Libyan Politics*, 96; Albergoni, *Écrire la coutume*, 26, 27n., 43–4; cf. Albergoni, *Droit coutumier*, 126 (*mrābṭīn bi'l-baraka*).

and do not assimilate to the Zwayya, against whom, it is said, they frequently engage in reprisals.[11]

Generally speaking, the Tibbū do not observe all of the precepts of Islam. Their Islamic identity was strengthened after the emergence of the Sanūsiyya, and among the Tedda branch in the Tibesti area, attempts were made to codify tribal custom in an effort to bring the tribe closer to normative Islam. Within the framework of this legal reform, the Tibbū of Kufra have adopted *sharʿī* norms in matters relating to family, inheritance and blood money (*diya*). The Tibbūs' use of blood money to settle disputes – which was rare (Chapelle, 89–92, 320 n. 16, 323–8) – was an attempt to break the chain of vengeance between and among its groups (Triaud, II, 771; Baroin, *Anarchie,* 33). But the *sharʿī* norms are mitigated by concessions to custom. For example, *sharʿī* blood money rates have been introduced (100 camels for a male and 50 for a female),[12] but the killer is required to spend 3–4 years in exile – in accordance with custom – before he may initiate the procedure for settling the dispute by compensation, provided, of course, that no retaliation has taken place in the meantime.

## 4 The Blood Money Dispute

The document translated below deals with a Tibbāwī blood money dispute handled by the Sharīʿa Court of Kufra. In this case, a Tibbāwī was killed in tribal territory by a certain Warduqūh b. Būrī, whose name suggests (see below) that he too was a Tibbāwī. The dispute was resolved by payment of blood money in accordance with the "prevailing Tibbāwī customary law (*ʿurf*)."

This case is best seen against the background of the interaction between *sharīʿa* and customary law.[13] The blood money case was settled in the above-mentioned sphere in which the *sharīʿa* wields assimilative power over custom. An initial agreement was reached out of court, on the basis of a mixture of Tibbāwī tribal law and *sharīʿa*. It was apparently agreed that this settlement would be recorded later in the Sharīʿa Court. When this agreement was presented to the Qāḍī of the Sharīʿa Court of Kufra, he issued a judgment conferring *sharʿī* legitimacy on it.

---

11 Baroin, *Anarchie*, 74, 89, 140, 386–9; Hassanein, 129, 139–40, 151, 175; De Agostini, *Cufra*, 42.

12 Cf. Baroin, *Anarchie*, 163 (among the Tibbū of Air, the rates of *diya* are 100 cows for a male and 50 cows for a female).

13 For a full discussion of this issue, with references to the sources, see Layish, *The Qāḍī's Role*, 84–93; idem, *Sharīʿa and Custom*, Introduction.

The case highlights the interplay between Tibbāwī tribal law and Mālikī law: After spending several years in exile, the perpetrator returned to Kufra and, in its Sharīʿa Court, acknowledged his responsibility for the killing. In 1942 the killer and some of the victim's agnates made an agreement. The perpetrator undertook to compensate the victim's agnates – a brother, two sisters and six paternal cousins – with camels, livestock, and money. The parties also agreed that any member of the victim's group who subsequently killed or injured one of the perpetrator's kin would be personally liable for his act and would not be defended by his agnates. At a later date, another member of the Tibbū tribe, probably a uterine brother (maternal half-brother) of the victim, appeared and claimed his share of the blood money. According to the *sharīʿa*, blood money for a homicide becomes part of the victim's estate and, hence, is apportioned among the victim's relatives in accordance with the *sharʿī* rules of inheritance (a uterine brother – or sister – is entitled to one-sixth of the estate as a Qurʾānic heir).[14] Here, the victim's paternal brother and two sisters renounced one-sixth of the blood money paid to them in favor of the new claimant.

As noted, homicide and bodily harm were formally subject to the jurisdiction of the Libyan secular courts in the period under review. In practice, however, most claims were settled out of court by tribal arbitrators, by the *sharīʿa* court, or, as in this case, by a combination of the two. The parties apparently used the Sharīʿa Court in order to secure implementation of a settlement which was based upon a combination of tribal customary law and *sharʿī* norms.

## 5 Translation of the Court Decision[15]

[1] In the Sharīʿa Court of Kufra, presided over by the Qāḍī Shaykh Muḥammad Ṣāliḥ al-Bakrī. May Allāh the Exalted grant him success!

[2] A man called Bū Kinnī b. Madī [Maduw?] from the Mādhina lineage (*ʿāʾila*) of the Tibbū tribe (*qabīla*) appeared [in court] together with his paternal cousins,[16] ʿAbdallāh b. Jibrīl al-Sanūsī b. [3] Ḥasan, Madī [?] b. Ajī, Ibrāhīm Arduqūh, Qalamī b. Ūshiʾ, and Ḥasan b. Haranjī. The above-mentioned Abū [sic] Kinnī claimed that

14 See Ibn ʿĀṣim, 230, l. 1575; Ibn al-ʿAṭṭār, 452 ff.; Peters, *Criminal Law*, § 0.1.3.3.

15 For the facsimile reproduction of the original decision, see Layish, *Legal Documents*, Document 55. For a transcription of the document, see ibid., 72.

16 In Tibbāwī practice, vengeance generally is carried out by the victim's brothers or sons, and in their absence, by cousins (Chapelle, 323).

> Warduqūh b. Būrī, [4] who killed (*qatala*)[17] my brother[18] Ṣāliḥ in the territory (*diyār*) of the Tibbū tribe, several years ago, has now appeared in the town of Kufra.[19]

Warduqūh b. Būrī was accompanied by [I]b[n]. [5] Mḥammad Bū Bakr b. al-Mamī [?] and his son Aḥmad. Warduqūh acknowledged (*aqarra*) that he was the killer (*qātil*) of Ṣāliḥ. They agreed among themselves on the payment of blood money (*diya*) in accordance with the Tibbāwī tribal customary law (*ʿurf*) that prevails among them.[20] [6] He took upon himself the obligation (*alzama*)[21] to pay the blood money that is customary (*maʿrūfa*) among them, that is, four male camels, two *ḥawāyij*[22] of sheep and donkeys, and four *ḥawāyij* of *darāhim* (money). The slain man (*maqtūl*) [7] has two sisters[23] in Tibbū territory, and it was agreed that [the perpetrator] would pay them [out of the aforementioned blood money] two camels, one *ḥāja* of livestock, and one

17 Under both tribal customary and *sharʿī* law, homicide is classified as private law. The agreement between the parties does not make the distinction, essential in Islamic law, between deliberate (*ʿamd*) and accidental (*khaṭaʾ*) homicide. The Mālikī school adopted the broadest definition of deliberate homicide, a definition that absorbs the category of quasi-deliberate (*shibh ʿamd*) homicide (Anderson, *Homicide*, 820 ff.; Peters, *Criminal Law*, § 0.1.3). Under Tibbāwī tribal law, both deliberate and accidental homicide cases may be settled by vengeance (*thaʾr*) rather than compensation (Chapelle, 323).

18 They share at least the same father (Madī [?] al-Tibbāwī). See ll. 16–17 below.

19 See Chapelle, 327. In this case, the perpetrator seems to have fulfilled the full term of his exile, as required, before the dispute might be settled by payment of blood money. In a similar case, a woman claimed in court that her husband, a member of the Qawābil [Gabàil] tribe (De Agostini, *Cirenáica*, 405–6, index, s.v. Gabàil, which refers to several different Mrābṭīn groups), had killed a Tibbāwī man from Rabiana and taken his camel. The perpetrator then fled to his kinsfolk in the Western District (al-Jiha al-Gharbiyya – probably Fazzān), no doubt out of fear of blood revenge (Layish, *Legal Documents*, 48, doc. 29).

20 The reference is probably to the codified version of the law (Chapelle, 324 ff.). The terms "*ʿurf*" and "*maʿrūfa*" (ll. 5–6) refer to the customary amount of blood money among the Tibbū tribe, but it may well be that the reference here is to the Islamic version of blood money as adopted by the Tibbū (see above). It is impossible to determine whether these terms were used by the litigants or by the Qāḍī; in the latter case, the usage would reflect his awareness of the distinction between custom and *sharīʿa*.

21 According to Tibbāwī tribal law, full blood money for a male (100 camels or oxen) is paid collectively by the killer's agnates (Chapelle, 327).

22 The *ḥāja* (pl. *ḥawāʾij*) is a unit of payment of dower and blood money (*diya*) in kind (livestock, utensils, clothes, personal effects) or in cash (*darāhim*) (cf. de Premare, III, 264–5); see translation, ll. 7–9; Layish, *Legal Documents*, doc. 6: ll. 11, 14–15; doc. 13: ll. 6, 9–10; doc. 46: ll. 2–3. I have not been able to determine the size of this unit.

23 They must be either full sisters or paternal half-sisters. Note the apportionment of the blood money, as stated below.

*ḥāja* of *darāhim*.[24] He will [also] pay one *ḥāja* [8] of *darāhim* to the victim's male paternal cousins[25] [living] in the Tibbū tribal territory. He has now transferred one camel here [at this court session, as blood money] to Bū Kinnī, who received it from him. [He will also pay] one camel and two *ḥawāyij* of *darāhim* [9] and one *ḥāja* of livestock [viz., the remainder due to Bū Kinnī][26] which he [viz., Warduqūh] will bring here and deliver to Bū Kinnī and [with this] the dispute between them will be settled. Whoever kills or assaults [10] a member [of the killer's agnatic group in the future] will make only himself liable (*yulzim*)[27] [to vengeance] and he [alone] will be responsible (*mas'ūl*) [for the consequences of his action].[28]

[The Qāḍī ruled] that no further claim or demand exists between them, except for the aforementioned payment due as blood money. [11] Any person [from the victim's kin] who commits homicide hereafter thereby inflicts death on himself (*qatala nafsahu*).[29] This agreement was entered into voluntarily by

24 Each of the sisters takes one-half of the victim's paternal brother's share, with respect to the camels and the livestock (but one-eighth with respect to the *darāhim*). This proportion agrees with the doctrine of *taʿṣīb* as it applies to paternal sisters and brothers, that is, either full brothers and sisters or paternal half-brothers and half-sisters, under the *sharʿī* inheritance rules (Coulson, 34–5, 41–2, 69–70). Although Tibbū customary law probably does not make any provision for payment of blood money to the victim's female kin, the Tibbū adopted the Islamic law of inheritance and blood money, with some concessions to tribal law (see above).

25 Under *sharʿī* inheritance rules, paternal uncles (and their male issue) have no share in the deceased's estate in the presence of paternal brothers, because the latter belong to a higher class or parentela (*ṭabaqa*) of male agnates (on these classes, see Coulson, 33; cf. Colucci, 29–30). Here, however, one *ḥāja* of *darāhim* is apportioned equally between the cousins, presumably in accordance with Tibbāwī custom. Baroin (*Anarchie*, 282–3) reports that among the Tibbū of Air, the *sharʿī* inheritance rules give way to local inheritance practices.

26 As the closest male agnatic heir of the victim, and probably in the absence of issue, Bū Kinnī takes one-half of the entire amount of the blood money. Under the *sharīʿa*, he would have taken the residue of the blood money after the Qur'ānic heirs took their prescribed portions.

27 The Arabic original here has *"yalūm"* where *"yulzim"* is more appropriate (cf. *wa-alzama nafsahu* in l. 6 above; al-Ḥabbūnī, 33, 35). This may be a scribal error. If *"yalūm"* is intended, the translation would read, "will expose only himself to blame."

28 In other words, if one of the victim's relatives were to commit a violent act against the killer's relatives, in disregard of the terms of the settlement, the perpetrator would be held personally responsible for the consequences of his act; whereas under normal circumstances, the victim's agnates would defend him, in this case, he would not enjoy their protection; whoever killed him would not be the object of legitimate revenge by the victim's kin.

29 In other words, he will be personally responsible for the consequences of his acts, including liability for blood vengeance, with no protection from his agnates.

all parties concerned. The Qāḍī gave it the force of a judgment[30] and signed [the document in which the agreement is recorded].[12] This was done in the precincts where the Qāḍī's court is officially located on the 12th day of Rajab 1361, [corresponding to] July 26, 1942.

[13] The scribe (*kātib*) of the Sharīʿa Court
The Qāḍī of Kufra
Muḥammad Ṣāliḥ al-Bakrī
[14] Witnesses
[15] ʿAbdallāh b. Ūsī [Ūshī'?]
Slēmān Imrī [?] b. Lāmīn
al-Sanūsī Tūtī [?] b. Bakr [?]

[16] Aḥmad Rajab al-Tibbāwī appeared [in court] and claimed that he was entitled to one-sixth of the blood money due for Ṣāliḥ b. Madī [?] al-Tibbāwī. [17] He was paid [an amount equivalent to] one-half of this sixth in Kufra, which he received from Bū Kinnī b. [18] Madī [?]. He is to receive [the other] half of the sixth from his sisters in the Tibbū tribal territory (*dār*). One-half of the sixth which [19] they have already received will be paid to him.[31]

This [document] has been issued for this purpose on the date [20] of the 7th day of Dhū 'l-Qaʿda, [corresponding to] October 24, 1944.

30 The extent of the Qāḍī's involvement in securing the agreement is not clear. As noted above, it is highly likely that the agreement was initially reached out of court, in accordance with Tibbāwī law, as mitigated by *sharʿī* norms, and was later drawn up in the Sharīʿa Court. In validating the apportionment of blood money, the Qāḍī certainly was aware of the Mālikī norm, although there is no explicit indication of this in the document.

31 It is reasonable to assume that Aḥmad is a uterine brother (maternal half-brother) of the victim. Had he been a paternal brother, he would have been entitled to the same share as Bū Kinnī. This may be inferred from the fact that the Qur'ānic portion of a uterine brother under the *sharʿī* rules of inheritance is one-sixth. The victim's paternal brother and two sisters compensate the uterine brother, using the portion of the blood money that they received two years previously. This seems to be another instance of a compromise between the *sharīʿa* in its Mālikī version and tribal law, at the expense of the latter; under *sharʿī* inheritance rules, the Qur'ānic heirs take their portions first, leaving the residue to the agnatic heirs. We do not know whether the victim of the killing was married or not. If he was, his widow should have received her share in the blood money under the *sharʿī* inheritance rules, here one-quarter in the absence of children (no children are mentioned in the document); that no widow is mentioned in the text may indicate either (a) that he was not married when he died, or (b) that the *sharʿī* rule pertaining to the widow is being ignored.

## Bibliography

Items are listed in alphabetical order of the abbreviations used in the notes (disregarding the definite article *al-* in Arabic).

de Agostini, E. *Le Popolazioni della Cirenáica*. Benghazi: Governo della Cirenáica, 1922–1923.

de Agostini, E. *Notizie sulla regione di Cufra (el-Càfra)*. Benghazi: Governo della Cirenáica, 1927.

Albergoni, G. "Droit coutumier, ethos tribal et économie moderne: un ʿurf bédouin de 1970." *Annales Islamologiques*, 27 (1993), 109–36.

Albergoni, G. "Écrire la coutume. Une tribu bédouine de Cyrénaïque face à la modernité." *Études rurales*, 155–156 (2000), 25–50.

Anderson, J.N.D. "Homicide in Islamic Law." *Bulletin of the School of Oriental and African Studies*, 13 (1951), 811–28.

Anderson, Lisa. "Nineteenth-Century Reform in Ottoman Libya." *International Journal of Middle East Studies*, 16 (1984), 325–48.

Anderson, Lisa. *The State and Social Transformation in Tunisia and Libya, 1830–1980*. Princeton, New Jersey: Princeton University Press, 1987.

Baroin, Catherine. *Anarchie et cohésion sociale chez les Toubou. Les Daza Kécherda (Niger)*. Paris: Éditions de la Maison des sciences de l'homme, 1985.

Baroin, Catherine. "La contestation chez les Toubou du central." *Etudes Rurales*, 157–158 (2001), 159–72.

Bertarelli, L.V. (ed.). *Possedimenti e Colonie. Isole Egee, Tripolitánia, Cirenáica, Eritréa, Somália*. Guida d'Itália del Touring Club Italiano. Milano: Touring Club Italiano, 1929.

Chapelle, Jean. *Nomades noirs du Sahara*. Paris: Libraire Plon, 1957.

Cicchitti, Arnaldo. "Il problema religioso nella legislazione coloniale italiana." *Revista Coloniale*, 21 (1926), 474–96.

Colucci, Massimo. "Il diritto consuetudinario della tribù della Cirenaica." *Revista Coloniale*, 22 (1927), 24–37.

Coulson, N.J. *Succession in the Muslim Family*. Cambridge: Cambridge University Press, 1971.

Davis, J. "A Note on Some Libyan Archives in Canterbury." *Bulletin of the British Society for Middle Eastern Studies*, 9 (1982), 75–9.

Davis, J. "La Structure sociale de Koufra." *Annuaire de l'Afrique du Nord*, XXII (1983), 545–64.

Davis, J. *Libyan Politics: Tribe and Revolution*. London: I.B. Tauris, 1987.

Davis, J. "A Social Perspective." In Layish, *Legal Documents*, 7–13.

Del Boca, Angelo. *Gli Italiani in Libia*. 2 vols. Roma-Bari: Editori Laterza, 1988.

Evans-Pritchard, E.E. *The Sanusi of Cyrenaica*. Oxford: Clarendon Press, 1949.

al-Ḥabbūnī, ʿAbd al-Salām Ḥamad. *Ansāb qabāʾil al-ʿarab*. Cairo: Dār al-Zaynī li'l-Ṭibāʿa wa'l-Nashr, 1379/1960.

Hassanein Bey, A.H. *The Lost Oases*. London: Thornton Butterworth, 1925.

Ibn ʿĀṣim, [Abū Bakr Muḥammad b. Muḥammad] al-Mālikī al-Gharnāṭī. *al-ʿĀṣimiyya* ou *Tuḥfat al-ḥukkām fī nukat 'l-ʿuqūd wa'l-aḥkām*, ed., trans., and annot. L. Bercher. Algiers: Institut d'Études Orientales, Université d'Alger, 1958.

Ibn al-ʿAṭṭār, [Abū ʿAbd Allāh] Muḥammad b. Aḥmad [b. ʿUbayd Allāh b. Saʿīd] al-Umawī. *Kitāb al-wathāʾiq wa'l-sjillāt* (Formulario Notarial Hispano-Ârabe), ed. P. Chalmeta & F. Corriente. Academia Matritense del Notariado. Instituto Hispano-Ârabe de Cultura. Madrid: Raycar, 1983.

Ibn Mūsā, Taysīr. *al-Mujtamaʿ al-arabī al-lībī fī 'l-ʿahd al-ʿuthmānī. Dirāsa taʾrīkhiyya ijtimāʿiyya*. Tripoli: al-Dār al-ʿArabiyya li'l-Kitāb, 1988.

Khayrallāh, al-Ṭayyib al-Sharīf. *al-Qabīla bayna al-sharīʿa wa'l-qānūn*. Ṭubruq: Dār al-Hudā li'l-Nashr wa'l-Tawzīʿ, 2001.

Layish, A. *Legal Documents on Libyan Tribal Society in Process of Sedentarization. Part 1: The Documents in Arabic*. Mediterranean Language and Culture Monograph Series 14. Wiesbaden: Harrassowitz, 1998.

Layish, A. "The *Qāḍī*'s Role in the Islamization of Sedentary Tribal Society." In *Public Sphere in Muslim Societies*, ed. M. Hoexter, S.N. Eisenstadt and N. Levtzion, 83–107. Series in Near Eastern Studies. Albany: State University of New York Press, 2002.

Layish, A. *Sharīʿa and Custom in Libyan Tribal Society. An Annotated Translation of Decisions from the Sharīʿa Courts of Ajdābiya and Kufra*. Studies in Islamic Law and Society 24. Leiden: Brill, 2005.

Le Gall, Michel. "The Ottoman Government and the Sanusiyya: A Reappraisal." *International Journal of Middle East Studies*, 21 (1989), 91–106.

Pelt, A. *Libyan Independence and the United Nations. A Case of Planned Decolonization*. New Haven: Yale University Press, 1970.

Peters, R. "Criminal Law: A Survey for the Course 'Introduction to Islamic Law.'" Amsterdam: University of Amsterdam, Department of Arabic Studies, 1996 [unpublished].

de Premare, A.-L. et al. *Dictionaire Arabe-Français*. Langue et Culture Marocaines. 12 vols. Paris: Editions L'Harmattan, 1993–1999.

Stewart, F.H. "ʿUrf. 2. Arab Customary Law." *The Encyclopaedia of Islam*, 2nd ed., x (2000), 888–92.

Triaud, J.-L. *La légende noire de la Sanusiyya*. 2 vols. Paris: Éditions de la Maison des sciences de l'homme, 1995.

Vikør, K.S. *Sufi and Scholar on the Desert Edge: Muḥammad b. ʿAlī al-Sanūsī and his Brotherhood*. Series in Islam and Society in Africa. London: Hurst & Northwestern University Press, 1995.

Yver, G. "Kufra." *The Encyclopaedia of Islam*, 2nd ed., v (1986), 351–2.

Yver, G. "Tubu." *The Encyclopaedia of Islam*, 2nd ed., x (1999), 580–1.

CHAPTER 3

# *Shahādat naql* in the Judicial Practice in Modern Libya

*In memoriam* Jeanette A. Wakin

## 1 Introduction[1]

The cases under review were recorded in the Sharīʿa Court of Ajdābiya,[2] a district center in the plain near the Mediterranean coast. The people of this area are part of the Saʿādī confederation. The principal tribes of this confederation are the Maghāriba and Majābira (Davis 1987:7–8, 80ff., 84–5, 94, 169, 189; idem 1998: 7–13). Prior to the abolition of the *Sharīʿa* courts in Libya in the early 1970s, the local *sharīʿa* court had sole jurisdiction in matters of personal status, succession and *waqf*; and it also dealt with civil claims, contracts and property, homicide, assault, and more – matters that formally were amenable to the civil court. This extensive jurisdiction may have been a carryover from the period before the Ottoman reform of the judicial system. The material law applicable in the *Sharīʿa* court in the period under review was the uncodified *sharīʿa* in its Mālikī version (Layish 1991: 14–15; idem 1998: 14–20).

*Shahādat naql* (attestation of the conveyance of evidence) is a document, attested to before a qāḍī, that contains a statement of fact pertaining to matters such as conjugal rights, succession, and property. The qāḍī endorses the corroborating testimony of the witnesses. The proceeding is authenticated by the court notaries (*shuhūd al-ḥāl, ʿudūl*) and registered in the minutes of the *sharīʿa* court (*maḥāḍir*). A copy of the written testimony is given to the

1 Originally published in *Dispensing Justice in Islam: Qadis and their Judgements*, eds. Muhammad Khalid Masud, Rudolph Peters, and David Powers. Leiden, 2005, pp. 495–516. The Libyan documents were placed at my disposal by John Davis of Oxford University. I am most grateful to him. Wael Hallaq read an early version of this essay and made generous, valuable comments for which I express my profound gratitude. I am also indebted to Delfina Serrano for her comments and to Alexander Borg and David Powers for their expert editorial assistance. The research was supported by the Israel Science Foundation.

2 For this spelling, see Yāqūt (1866–76, 1:131–2).

 | DOI:10.1163/9789004680920_005

claimant so that it may be conveyed to a qāḍī of another locality for the purpose of accomplishing the legal proceedings required for handing down a decision, or (more often) so that the written testimony may be used by the claimant for any practical purpose at an unspecified future date as the need arises.

## 2 Written Documents in Doctrine and Practice[3]

The Qur'ān rules explicitly (2:282):

> When you contract a debt for a fixed term, record it in writing. Let a scribe record it in writing between you. ... Be not averse to writing down [the contract], whether [the amount] be small or great, with its term.

The *ḥadīth*, too, supports the use of written documents. The rulings of the Qur'ān and the *ḥadīth*, however, were reduced by doctrine to a recommendation rather than a binding injunction. Written documents (*ṣakk, wathīqa*) were nevertheless admitted, especially in the Mālikī school, as valid evidence once they had been attested by qualified witnesses.

Indeed, written documents proved so indispensable in practice that they remained in constant use, became a normal accompaniment of every transaction of importance, and gave rise to a highly developed branch of law with a voluminous literature of its own.[4] Formally, attestation of witnesses remained the ultimate requirement in classical Islamic legal theory; doctrine continued to reason as if there were no documents but only the oral testimony of witnesses, possibly supported by private records; practice, on the other hand, acted as if documents were essential and "witnessing" only a formality to make them fully valid. Professional witnesses (*ʿudūl*), whose integrity (*ʿadāla*) had been established by the court, came to exercise the functions of notaries public. They had legal training and were appointed and dismissed by the qāḍīs.[5]

---

3 Unless otherwise indicated, the following survey is based on: Wakin (1972:4–10); Schacht (1964:82–3, 193); Tyan (1960:239–41); idem (1986); Coulson (1964:125, 146, 173); Peters (1995:208); Toledano (1981:11 [and the reference to Tyan 1945], 13–14).

4 The branch of legal science that deals with documents is called the science of *shurūṭ*, "formularies," (or *wathāʾiq*, "documents," in the Mālikī school). See Schacht (1964:82 fn. 1; Wakin 1972:1 fn. 1, 13). On the relations between doctrine and practice, see Hallaq (1995).

5 Hallaq maintains that at least some notaries operated independently, drafting and authenticating documents for individuals outside the boundaries of the court (personal communication).

The authors of the manuals of legal formularies were specialists in *fiqh*; they provided forms of documents for all possible practical needs and safeguards against all contingencies; these had only to be "witnessed" in order to become legally valid.

In Andalusia, the judicial practice (*ʿamal*) was reflected in formulary manuals (*wathāʾiq*). Much of this material was later incorporated in *al-ʿĀṣimiyya* or *Tuḥfat al-ḥukkām* by Ibn ʿĀṣim (d. 829/1426) (See References. Cf. Serrano 2000), the Qāḍā al-Jamāʿa of Granada. The science of *wathāʾiq* was first and foremost a practical outcome of customary law in the Maghrib. The *wathāʾiq* works became closely connected with the judicial practice, the terms of the documents being drafted in accordance with this judicial practice (Wakin 1972:13–14; Toledano 1981:13–14).

In the modern period, during which the application of Islamic law and the organization of its tribunals have been modified by independent Islamic governments, written documents have been generally admitted as valid proof, and sometimes the competence of the qāḍīs has been restricted to cases in which documentary evidence is produced. The introduction of written documents (*tawthīq bi'l-kitāba*) in modern Egypt was approved by Muḥammad ʿAbduh (ʿAbduh 1900:34; Anderson 1976: Index, s.v. *ʿadam al-samāʿ*.).

The phenomenon of *shahādat naql*, as reflected in the Libyan *sijill*, appears to be a variation of, or deviation from, the institution of *kitāb al-qāḍī ilā 'l-qāḍī* (conveyance of testimony from one qāḍī to another) caused by the judicial practice and justified by considerations of public interest (*maṣlaḥa*). The communication of *kitāb al-qādī ilā 'l-qāḍī* took place when "a qāḍī of a particular locale writes to a qāḍī of a different locale regarding a person's right that he, the first qāḍī, established against another person, so that the receiving qāḍī might carry out the effects of the communication in his locale" (Hallaq 1999:438 and fn. 6 there). The *raison d'être* of this communication was to avoid the injustice that might be caused to the plaintiff due to geographical distance between the two locales, that is, the hardship involved in bringing witnesses, whose testimony is essential, to the court of the receiving qāḍī.[6]

It was probably as a result of this hardship that the Mālikī judicial practice, sometime during the eleventh century, deviated from the procedure regarding written communications. The Andalusī and Maghribī qāḍīs began to admit the validity of written instruments without the testimony of the witnesses. Instead, the authentication of the document by the attestation of the qāḍīs's handwriting (*al-shahāda ʿalā 'l-khaṭṭ*) was sufficient to validate it. If

6 Hallaq (1999, 444, 449, 451); Santillana (1938, 2:604–5 [*naql al-shahāda*:] and the reference to Khalīl in fn. 283).

the receiving qāḍī could not identify the handwriting of the sending qāḍī, he had to procure two just witnesses, experts in handwritten documents and knowledgeable of the handwriting of the qāḍī in question, to identify the handwriting in order to verify the authenticity of the document. Immediate registration and attestation of the document's validity is required for reasons of legal certainty that may arise in case the sending or the receiving qāḍī – or both – died. The new practice was justified on the basis of *ḍarūra* (necessity), the authoritative basis of which was found in the Q. 2:185 (Hallaq 1999:453–4, 457–8).

Evidence suggests that the institution of *shahādat naql* was adopted by Ibn ʿĀsim in his treatise *al-ʿĀṣimiyya* or *Tuḥfat al-ḥukkām,* commonly used by some of the Libyan qāḍās (Layish 1998:18 fn. 26). The *shahādat naql* is discussed in this treatise under the section *"Khiṭāb al-Quḍāt* and Related Matters."[7] The procedural similarities between *Khiṭāb al-Quḍāt* and *kitāb al-qāḍī ilā 'l-qāḍī* leave no doubt as to the source of the former, despite differences in details. The *Khiṭāb al-Quḍāt* is a mechanism whereby the sending qāḍī notifies the receiving qāḍī of the established facts in the case under review on the basis of a court decision. The key word in this context is *"aʿlama"* and its derivatives. *Al-ʿĀṣimiyya* states explicitly that "notification" by means of this word is legally admissible (*qabūl*) in "contemporary judicial practice" (*wa 'l-ʿamal al-yawm*) (line 86). If the sending qāḍī dies or is dismissed, his notification is unacceptable unless it has been registered (line 89). Registration implies that the notification has been properly authenticated by witnesses. A notification issued by a qāḍī of good reputation (*ʿadl*) by virtue of his judicial authority should be executed (line 91). Once the decision becomes executable, the qāḍī must register it upon the plaintiff's request (line 95). The qāḍī may perform the registration on his own initiative (line 96). At the plaintiff's request, the qāḍī may register documents, provided these are not disputable, as in the case of old charters of *waqf,* the handwriting of which can be authenticated by witnesses (line 97). Following the pronouncement of a decision, the plaintiff may request the qāḍī to rule that the defendant is prohibited from advancing any claim in the future (*taʿjīz*), subject to exceptions in matters relating to *waqf* (*ḥabs*), divorce (*ṭalāq*), paternity (*nasab*), homicide (*dam*), or manumission of a slave (*ʿitāq*) (lines 98–9).

7 See Ibn ʿAṣim (1958:14, 16 and the French translation and annotation).

## 3 *Shahādat naql* in Judicial Practice

*Shahādat naql* is a common practice in the Libyan *sijill*. The present study is based on a casual sample of a dozen documents, all issued by the Sharīʿa Court of Ajdābiya between 1951 and 1954.

The documents are usually written in stereotyped phraseology and formulaic language. The most common introductory formula is the utterance of an invocation and a prayer for the soul of the Prophet, his family and Companions, intended to invoke divine guidance in the processes of justice and to reinforce the validity and binding character of the qāḍī's legal pronouncements. Tribute is also paid to Muḥammad Idrīs al-Mahdī al-Sanūsī, the Emir of Barqa, the region of Eastern Libya (Cyrenaica), who was proclaimed king of independent Libya in 1951.

The introductory formulas are followed by the definition of the subject matter of the document: "*shahādat naql* in favor (*li-ṣāliḥ* or *li-maṣlaḥa*) of [so and so]," a reference to the page and number of the protocol in the court minutes (*maḥḍar*), the location of the Sharīʿa Court, and the name of the qāḍī or *nāʾib* presiding over the specific case, "may Allāh, the Exalted, grant him success."

Next the document provides details that accurately identify the claimant (Cf. Wakin 1972:50–1): his private name, the names of his father, grandfather (up to three generations), lineage (*ʿāʾila*), tribal affiliation (*qabīla*), age, place of birth and residence. Usually, it is stated that the claimant has been "identified by his person and name" (*maʿrūfan dhātan wa-isman*) (Layish 1998: e.g., doc. 48, line 6; doc. 57, line 5; doc. 61, line 5; doc. 67, line 5), a formula that refers to the *sharʿī* procedure of identification (*taʿrīf*). In one case there is a clear indication to this effect: *wa-baʿd maʿrifatihā ʿalā al-manhaj al-sharʿī* (Layish 1998, doc. 14, line 5). The possibility, however, that the claimant was identified by the qāḍī on the basis of personal knowledge cannot be ruled out. Thus, in one case, it was stated: *al-maʿrūf ladaynā* [i.e., the qāḍī] *isman wa-dhātan* (Layish 1998, doc. 58, lines 5–6).

Subsequently, the claimant presents his case before the qāḍī. Generally, the narrative is written in the past tense. The claim is cast in personal subjective style, quite often in first-person statements (Cf. Wakin 1972:42), at the end of which the claimant asks the qāḍī to summon his witnesses to the court and hear their testimony. The qāḍī complies and asks the claimant to produce witnesses who will corroborate the alleged facts of the case. Usually, the primary witnesses testify to a fact or event that they themselves witnessed or about which they had personal knowledge (Layish 1998, doc. 4, line 6; doc. 54, lines 9ff.; doc. 48, lines 11–12). Occasionally, witnesses testify on the basis of hearsay. Thus, in one case, the witnesses met the claimant's husband out of town and heard him say that he had divorced his wife sometime previously. In a case pertaining to an inheritance dispute, the witnesses' testimony was based on a "widespread rumor."[8]

In two cases the primary witnesses' credibility was tested (*tazkiya*) by the *imām* and *mukhtār* of the town and by *shaykhs* of the same tribe (Layish 1998, doc. 14, line 14; and doc. 57, line 12). The witnesses usually use formulas calculated to reflect their credibility. The most common formulas are: "[He] gave testimony [the truthfulness of which he deemed to be] beyond any shadow of doubt, corroborating in letter and spirit the statement of [...]" (Layish 1998, doc. 61, line 9. Cf. doc. 14, line 12; doc. 48, 11; doc. 67, line 10). The witnesses conclude their testimony with a pious expression: "This is our testimony. Let Allāh be our pledge [lit. agent] (*wakīl*) to what we have said."[9]

The qāḍī authenticates the content of the document. The usual formula for this purpose is: "On the basis of [the statement] endorsed by the aforementioned witnesses, both of whom were in a state of legal competence (*ḥāla jā'iza*) in *sharʿī* terms, as duly certified before the aforementioned judge, the latter endorsed (*ajāza*) this testimony, given on the account of both witnesses,[10] signed it, and had the undersigned [notaries] testify to it, and instructed that it be registered." Occasionally he makes the primary witnesses sign the witnessed document (Layish 1998, e.g., doc. 54, lines 22–4; doc. 58, line 14). In one case, the qāḍī added, as a gesture of credibility, that the testimony of the five witnesses to a testamentary *waqf* was "free from any hint of collusion (*tawāṭu'*) among them." Their signatures appear alongside those of the professional witnesses (Layish 1998, doc. 54, lines 17, 22–4).

The professional witnesses, that is, notaries, present in court sign the written testimony. Their names and court functions[11] are mentioned at the bottom of the document, their task being to witness the entire proceedings that transpired in court.

In fact, four kinds of witnesses may be distinguished in the witnessed documents: (1) witnesses required to identify (*taʿrīf*) the claimant or the primary

8 Layish (1998: doc. 14, lines 11–14; and doc. 67, lines 10–11, respectively). Hearsay evidence is admissible in court in litigations relating to inheritance. See Ibn ʿĀṣim (1958:28–9, lines 177ff.).

9 Layish (1998: doc. 4, line 13; doc. 48, lines 12–13; 48, lines 16–17; doc. 61, line 10; doc. 67, lines 11–12). Cf. Layish and Shmueli (1979:41).

10 Layish (1998: doc. 4, line 14; doc.14, line 16; doc. 48, line 14; doc. 57, line 11; doc. 61, line 11; doc. 67, line 13).

11 Ibid. (doc. 57, line 19 [*mubāshir*, court usher]; doc. 61, line 14 [*nā'ib*, deputy *qāḍī*]).

witnesses; (2) primary witnesses enlisted by the claimant for the purpose of corroborating his contention; their testimonies are expected to be based upon their knowledge of the facts; (3) witnesses required to ascertain the primary witnesses' credibility (*tazkiya*); and (4) court notaries (Cf. Wakin 1972:65–70).

The notaries' signatures are followed by the qāḍī's endorsement of the legal validity of the proceedings. The usual formula for this purpose is: "The matter is as indicated above." Upon the claimant's request, the qāḍī gives him a copy of the witnessed document (Cf. Wakin 1972:45–7) that bears the date of its registration, which usually coincides with the date on which the document was drawn up or witnessed. The date is recorded by the day, month, and year of the Hijrī calendar, followed by the corresponding Gregorian date (Cf. Wakin 1972:47–8).

*Case 1*[12]

I have come across only one instance in which *shahādat naql* corresponds to the procedure of *kitāb al-qāḍī ilā. 'l-qāḍī*. A small boy, Ismāʿīl, from the Maghāriba tribe was run over by a car and, as a result of the accident, his right leg was severely injured. The injury caused a highly visible physical disability. A date was set for a meeting, at the Sharīʿa Court of Benghazi, between the boy's agnates and the driver involved in the accident in order to determine the amount of financial compensation. Since the boy's father could not travel there, he asked the Sharīʿa Court of Ajdābiya to hear the testimony of his witnesses, who were tribal assessors, so that their testimony could serve as a factual basis for the court in Benghazi to determine appropriate compensation.

The Sharʿī Nā'ib granted his request and, after ascertaining the witnesses' credibility according to *sharʿī* procedures, ordered the assessors to testify regarding the injured leg. Their assessment appears to have been based on criteria pertaining exclusively to tribal customary law. The Nā'ib – without interfering with the principles underlying the assessors' procedures – gave the boy's father a certified copy of the testimony for his use at any eventual legal proceedings in Benghazi. The translation of this document follows:

> *Translation*
>
> [1] In the name of Allāh, the Merciful, the Compassionate. May Allāh bless our Lord Muḥammad, his family and Companions and grant them peace.

12 For the Arabic text, see Layish (1998: doc. 57). For an annotated translation of this document with introduction, see idem (2005: doc. 57). Cf. Hallaq (1999:441fn. 21).

[2] In the reign of his Excellency *sayyid*[13] Muḥammad Idrīs al-Mahdī al-Sanūsī, Emir of Barqa [Cyrenaica].

[3] ATTESTATION OF THE CONVEYANCE OF EVIDENCE (*shahādat naql*) IN FAVOR OF SHAYKH AL-LĀFĪ AL-MUFTĀḤ AL-ṢUBḤĪ

Entered in register no. 5/314, p. 5/214

[4] In the Sharīa Court of Ajdābiya, presided over by Muḥammad al-Mabrūk Abī Jāziya, the Nāʾib of his honor the *sharʿī*, Qāḍī, and in charge of the Qāḍī's Affairs. May Allāh the Exalted grant him success. [5] Shaykh al-Lāfī b. Muftāḥ from the al-Shaykhī lineage [*ʿāʾila*] of the Ṣubḥ [subtribe] (De Agostini 1922–23:323–4) belonging to Maghāriba tribe [*qabīla*], identified by name (*maʿrūf*) appeared [in court] accompanied by his son Ismāʿīl, [6] who is about 10 years [old], and made the following statement:

> Fifteen months ago, my son Ismāʿīl, present here, was run over by a car that crushed his right leg. [7] After [the bones] were set and medically treated, [the leg technically] healed but a highly visible physical defect due to permanent mutilation (*ʿadam*)[14] remained which reduced [the leg] to the state of utter disability; [8] [the leg] ceased to function as a healthy limb. Since a date has been fixed for a meeting between me and the perpetrator (*jānī*)[15] concerning my son and his kinsmen[16] before the Qāḍī of Benghazi, and since I am unable [9] to travel there with the child, I ask [the court] to hear the testimony of the witnesses

13 The title implies the status of a *sharīf*, that is, a descendant of the Prophet Muḥammad. Cf. Evans-Pritchard (1949:83, 117).

14 In determining the amount of compensation due for bodily injury, tribal law among the Awlād ʿAlī in the Western Desert makes a distinction between wounds that heal (*al-ḍarb al-salīm*) and wounds that cause permanent mutilation (*al-ḍarb al-ʿadīm*). The case under review belongs to the second category. See al-Ḥabbūnī (1960:31, 34); al-Jawharī (1961:187ff.); Maḥjūb (n. d.: 183, 200, 314–5, 318 [definition of *ʿadam*]); Mohsen (1975:149); Murray (1935:205); Stewart (2000:890–1); cf. Abū Ḥassān (1974:230); Ghayth (1990:137).

15 The unintentional nature of the motor accident does not exempt the perpetrator from the financial liability for the injury caused. Davis notes that the victim's agnates in road accidents receive double compensation: i.e., both from the state insurance company, and from the driver involved in the accident and his kinsmen in conformity with tribal law. This phenomenon has also been observed in Jerusalem. See Davis (1987:176, 223–4); Zilberman (1991:70).

16 The injured boy and his solidarity group (*ʿāqila*), i.e., male agnates up to a certain degree of relationship, share the financial compensation paid for the injury caused to him. Cf. al-Qusūs (1972:83–4).

> [present here] who are fully qualified[17] to testify to the fact that my son's leg has been reduced to a state [10] of disability.[18]

His request was granted and he was permitted to produce his witnesses. He brought Shaykh Muḥammad Bū al-Bughayyiḍ al-Zuwayyī al-Sudaydī[19] and Ḥājj [11] Yūnus b. Ṣāliḥ al-ʿĪdiyya of the aforementioned [Zuwayya] tribe, both of whom are known by name. Each of them gave testimony on his own account, corroborating his claim, [12] after due examination of the boy's leg, on the basis of their expertise. Subsequently, Shaykh Saʿīd b. Yūnus Shalabī and Shaykh [13] ʿAlī b. al-Fūl, both from the Hayba lineage of the Naṣr [subtribe] belonging to the Maghāriba (De Agostini 1922–23:316, 323) [tribe] were summoned for the purpose of ascertaining [the assessor's] credibility (*tazkiya*). They both testified that the aforementioned witnesses were persons of good reputation and that their testimony [14] completely corroborated the established facts. All this transpired and was registered on the date stated below, and upon his [i.e., the claimant's] request [the court] gave him a copy [of this document][20] bearing the date of the 21st day of Dhū [15] 'l-Qaʿda 1370 corresponding to August 23, 1951.

> [16] Witnesses to the proceedings (*shuhūd al-ḥāl*)
> [17] The Court ushers (*mubāshir*)
> [20] ʿImrān Manṣūr al-Magharī
> Muḥammad ʿAbd al-Salām[21]

---

17 Tribal assessors for bodily injuries are intended here. See Mohsen (1975:148ff.); cf. Stewart (1988:19, 83–5, 110–1 (*qaṣṣāṣ*), Index, s. v. injury assessors); idem (1990: Glossary, s.v. *qaṣṣāṣ*); Kressel (1996:79 [*qaṣṣāṣīn al-dam*]).

18 Attestation of conveyance is not admitted in Islamic criminal procedure (Schacht 1964:198); however, homicide and bodily injury are considered, under both *sharʿī* and tribal law, as instances of damages within the domain of private law.

19 In other words, he belongs to the Sudaydī branch of the Zuwayya tribe. See De Agostini (1922–23:407).

20 The qāḍī's role is here reduced to the hearing and registration of the testimonies of the assessors brought by the claimant without interfering with the principles of tribal law underlying the assessors' procedures. Under the *sharīʿa*, the qāḍī may resolve disputes of blood money (*diya*) in cases of unintentional injuries (*jirāḥ al-khaṭaʾ*). See Ibn ʿĀṣim (1958:232f. [the chapter on injuries, *jirāḥāt*]). Nonetheless, it is worth noting that the test of the assessors' credibility is carried out in accordance with *sharʿī* procedures. The registration of testimonies is intended to serve the interests of the boy and his kinsmen at proceedings pertaining to damages to be held in Benghazi.

21 He acts concurrently or intermittently in two capacities: as a court usher and as a notary or professional witness. See Layish (1998: Name Index, 103–4).

> [17] The matter being as indicated above
> [18] The Deputy-in-Charge of the Affairs
> of the Qāḍī of Ajdābiya,
> the Sharʿī Nāʾib
> [21] Muḥammad al-Mabrūk Abī Jāziya

Case 1 corresponds to the pattern of *kitāb al-qāḍī ilāʾl-qāḍī* in the sense that the written testimony is addressed to a certain *qāḍī*. All the other cases entitled "*shahādat naql* in favor of [...]" in the Libyan *sijill* deviate from this pattern in the sense that they can be classified – to use Hallaq's wording – as an "open communication," that is, a communication addressed to any qāḍī, even one in the same locale.[22] The original rationale for the written testimony, i.e., to avoid the hardship of enlisting witnesses caused by geographical distance – is replaced here by the desire to avoid the hardship of enlisting witnesses at some future unspecified date when their testimony may be required to ensure the realization of some right or goal. In other words, the dimension of distance as the cause of hardship is replaced by the dimension of time. The witnessed document before the qāḍī is deposited in his *sijill* for safekeeping (Cf. Wakin 1972:9 and the reference to Tyan 1945 in fn. 2); it is intended to achieve legal certainty on the spot so that it may be used for some purpose at some unspecified date in the future. As will be seen from the cases below, the qāḍīs implicitly justify the deviation from the normative pattern of written testimony on the basis of the doctrine of *maṣlaḥa* (public interest).

*Case 2*[23]
ʿAbd al-Karīm appeared in the Sharīʿa Court of Ajdābiya, presided over by Shaykh Muḥammad al-Aḥlāfī. He acted as his wife's proxy concerning her deceased father's estate. The couple belonged to the Zuwayya tribe. ʿAbd al-Karīm made the following statement:

> [6] The [property of the] late Ḥasan, father of [7] Balāʾil, whom I am representing, and of his brother Muḥammad [...], within their [joint] ownership, be it immovable property, livestock, merchandise convertible into cash [8] and [other] goods, was not divided (*qisma*)[24] between the

22 Hallaq (1999:452). Cf. *rasm istirʿāʾ* in Powers (1990:245 and fn. 97); idem (2002:31–7 [for definition, see 31 note 35] 43, 50, 120–1, 128, 130, 136, 221–2, 225, 227).

23 For the Arabic document, see Layish (1998: doc. 48). For annotated translation of the entire document, see idem (2005: doc. 48).

24 On the mechanisms for allotment (*qisma*) of immovable and other property in Mālikī law, see Ibn ʿĀṣim (1958:140–6).

> two before their successive deaths. They [continued] to own the entire [patrimony] that they left behind in al-Kufra and Jikharra [See Evans-Pritchard, map facing p. 35] oases and in Maṭrūḥ in equal shares until [9] the present.[25] I have brought with me a witness who will testify regarding what I have said; he is [...]. I ask [10] the noble Sharīʿa Court to question him, to register his testimony and to give it to me [so that it will be available to me] when the need arises (*ʿinda al-luzūm*).[26]

The *qāḍī* endorsed this testimony, affixed his signature thereto, had the notaries testify to this effect, and instructed that it be registered in the *sijill*.

The written testimony here was intended to facilitate the issuance of a court order enabling Balāʾil to secure her share of her father's estate. The fact that the estate of the two brothers remained undivided even after their deaths implies that Balāʾil was deprived of her personal share in the estate. The representation of a married daughter by her husband here suggests the possibility of exerting structural pressures in the division of the patrimony. As an outsider, the husband is not guided by concern for the integrity of the agnatic patrimony.

*Case 3*[27]

Two brothers, ʿAbdallāh and ʿAbd al-Qādir, from the Ibn al-Ruways lineage of the Qabāʾil tribe, worked a land in their joint ownership, with the understanding that they would equally share the expenses involved. Following a dispute between them, they appeared in the Shariʿa Court of Ajdābiya, presided over by Shaykh Muḥammad al-Sanūsī al-Ghazzālī. ʿAbdallāh made the following statement:

> [6] My brother ʿAbd al-Qādir and I own [in common] livestock and other movable property (*manqūlāt*). We have dissociated ourselves

25 In other words, no succession order was issued in regard to the estate that was inherited by the two brothers. Instead of dividing it between them as required by *sharʿī* apportionment, they chose to retain their joint ownership – a kind of family *mushāʿ* – and to administer the household on a cooperative basis.

26 I.e., when a succession order is issued in which his wife's *sharʿī* share in her father's estate will be secured. Although the written testimony here sounds like "open communication," it stands to reason that the document was meant to be delivered to the *qāḍī* of the Sharīʿa Court of Kufra when the time would be appropriate for issuing a succession order. As indicated in line 8, the entire patrimony of the two brothers was located in Kufra and other places while the witness and the claimant were residing in Ajdābiya. In this respect, the written testimony here is closer to the pattern of *kitāb al-qāḍī ilā ʾl-qāḍī*.

27 For the Arabic document, see Layish (1998: doc. 4). For annotated translation of the entire document, see idem (2005: doc. 4).

> from each other [with respect to the common property] (*tafāṣalnā*) (Cf. Lane 1984:2406ii) today in the presence of the witnesses who are present: [...] [7] I call upon the honorable Sharīʿa Court to register their testimony.

Two witnesses testified that ʿAbdallāh spent nothing on the purchase of the seeds and that it was ʿAbd al-Qādir who solely financed their purchase. Hence it was agreed that ʿAbdallāh should pay the sum of fifteen pounds to ʿAbd al-Qādir towards the end of the harvest period of that year.

> [12] ʿAbd al-Qādir had borne the responsibility for all their debts, except for that relating to the dower, [concerning which an agreement had already been reached to the effect that]: Each of them would pay his own dower independently [13] for his respective wife.[28] We have borne witness to this effect.

On the basis of what has been established, the qāḍī endorsed the testimony given, had the witnesses testify to its validity and registered their testimony.

It seems that the written testimony in the case under review was intended to safeguard the payment of fifteen pounds to ʿAbd al-Qādir at the end of the harvest, the settlement of debts against the family estate by ʿAbd al-Qādir and, most important, the payment of the dower independently by each of the brothers for his respective wife at an unspecified date in the future. The document precludes any attempt in the future on the part of either brother to obtain the dower out of the family estate.

*Case 4*[29]

Sālima bint Ṣāliḥ from the al-Harash lineage of the ʿUjaylāt tribe appeared in the Sharīʿa Court of Ajdābiya, presided over by Shaykh Ḥusayn Muḥammad al-Aḥlāfī. She made the following statement:

---

28 In other words, for the time being, until the patrimony is divided between the two brothers; they seem to run the joint estate on the basis of partnership (*shirka* or *mushāraka*). The exclusion of the dowers from the partnership is a significant indication of their intention to bring about a total division of the patrimony at some future date. See Colucci (1927:27 [The landed property remains united within the *bayt* even after the death of the head of the family], 29); Peters (1980:154). (The cooperative farm usually breaks after the brothers have married); cf. Rosenfeld (1968).

29 For the Arabic document, see Layish (1998: doc. 14). For an annotated translation of the entire document, see idem (2005: doc. 14). Cf. Sharīʿa Court of Ajdābiya, p. 27 no. 52 of September 8, 1951 (ill-treatment of a wife in a polygamous marriage); p. 218 no. 363 of July [?], 1953 (nonprovision of maintenance to a grandson).

> [6] A paternal cousin of mine called Maḥmūd al-Harash married me and [subsequently] divorced me about ten months ago. [7] I have brought witnesses with me who will testify to what I have stated concerning the divorce from my aforementioned husband. Their [names] are: […] [8] – all belonging to the ʿUjaylāt tribe. I ask the honorable Sharīʿa Court [9] to question them, to record their testimony, and to grant me permission to [re]marry and thus safeguard my honor (*karāma, sharaf*), since I am young and still a minor, and I am afraid [10] of falling into temptation (*ʿanat*).[30]

When the aforementioned witnesses were questioned, the first two said:

> We all met with [11] ʿAlī al-Kawnī, the Shaykh of our tribe, who told us: "I heard Maḥmūd al-Harash say that he had divorced his aforementioned wife Sālima [12] bint Ṣāliḥ." ʿAlī […] gave testimony, regarding which he had no doubt whatsoever, that he had definitely met the aforementioned Maḥmūd [13] al-Harash in the town of al-ʿUjaylāt, where the latter had told him: "I have divorced my wife Sālima bint Ṣāliḥ," and this meeting [14] with Maḥmūd occurred in the month of Muḥarram 1373. Afterwards, all [the witnesses] said: "This is what we know and testify to."

After the witnesses corroborated Sālima's claim regarding the divorce and their credibility had been established (*tazkiya*), the qāḍī endorsed the testimony given, had the witnesses testify to its validity and registered their testimony.

The written testimony here was meant to serve Sālima's interests by authenticating her marital status as divorcee, thus removing legal bars to any future remarriage. It is worthwhile mentioning in this connection that the wife's fear of committing adultery is a common ground for divorce in Libyan judicial practice (cf. Layish 1991:91–2). The sanctions against illicit intercourse (*zinā*) are very stringent, both in customary law (cf. Abū Ḥassān 1974:242; Kressel 1981) and *sharīʿa*.

*Case 5*[31]

The *shaykh* and administrator of Zāwiyat Sīdī ʿAbd al-Salām (a Ṣūfī saint) in Ajdābiya, Shaykh ʿAbdallāh al-Jīlānī from the Ben Gharīb lineage of the

30 Cf. D'Emilia (1946:25) (*yukhshā ʿalayhā al-fasād*); Mohsen (1975:116–9); Powers, *Dispensing Justice*. The woman's honor here should be evaluated in terms of her good name (*ʿird*), as understood by an agnatic society.

31 For the Arabic document, see Layish (1998: doc. 54); for an annotated translation of the entire document, see idem (2005: doc. 54).

Maṣwāna tribe, born in Benghazi and residing in Ajdābiya, appeared in the Sharīʿa Court of Ajdābiya, presided over by the Qāḍī, *sayyid*[32] Muḥammad al-Sanūsī al-Ghazzālī al-Khaṭṭābī. He made the following statement:

> [6] In my capacity as guardian of the Zāwiya[33] known as Zāwiyat Sīdī ʿAbd al-Salām[34] in Ajdābiya, [I have been informed] that the woman [7] called Mabrūka [...] bequeathed (*awṣat*) one-third[35] of her immovable property [in favor of a certain *zāwiya*; see below] in the presence of a group of Muslim witnesses, and subsequently died. I ask that the noble Sharīʿa Court [8] hear the testimony of the following witnesses: [...] [9], and register [their testimony] in favor of the aforementioned Zāwiya.

His request was granted. We [the qāḍī] questioned each of the five witnesses, who concurred that

> [10] Mabrūka [...] summoned us to her house, where [11] she held a session while in her bed, and had tea served to us and drank with us. Subsequently she said:
>
> > I am very ill and apprehensive concerning my health. You are my witnesses that I have no claim [12] against anyone; nor does anyone have a claim against me.[36] I own two goats, and I would like to have them slaughtered and given away as charity (*ṣadaqa*) [to the poor] after my

32 I.e., *sharīf*, a descendant of the Prophet Muḥammad.

33 The *shaykh* of the *zāwiya* fulfills both a spiritual-ritual function and an administrative one. Sometimes the founder of the *waqf* stipulates that the *shaykh* should also act as the *mutawallī* of the *waqf*. Mohsen (1975:73–4). Cf. Layish (1994:161–2).

34 The reference is to Sīdī ʿAbd al-Salām al-Asmar al-Fīṭūrī from Zliten; see Albergoni (1993:128); cf. Layish (2002:107n., 87, and the sources indicated there concerning saints' worship); al-Sūrī (1984:395–6).

35 The testamentary *waqf* is subject to the *ultra vires* doctrine which is meant to safeguard the legal heirs' *sharʿī* rights to the estate; it is not legally permissible to bequeath by will more than one-third of one's estate. See Ibn ʿĀṣim (1958:202, lines 1374, 1381); Coulson (1971:235–6). On testamentary *waqf*, see Layish (1983:2ff.).

36 In Mālikī law, a testamentary disposition within the limits of one-third of the estate is valid regardless of whether the testator is in good health or in a state of "death-sickness" (*maraḍ al-mawt*) (see Ibn ʿĀṣim [1958:202, line 1374]; Zaydān [1993, 10:383, § 11195]). Similarly, a *waqf* in death-sickness is valid provided it is within one-third of the estate and not in favor of a legal heir (see Zaydān [1993, 10:457–8, § 11403]). In contrast, a charitable gift made in death-sickness or where the object of the gift is subject to heavy debts – is not valid (see Ibn ʿĀṣim [1958:176, line 1191]; Zaydān [1993, 10:369, § 11159]; cf. Coulson [1971:269]). There is no information here as to whether the testamentary *waqf* and the

death.[37] I have a building complex bordering on [...]. [15] I have designated (*awqaftu*) [by means of testamentary disposition] one-third of my building complex as a *waqf* in favor of Zāwiyat[38] Sīdī ʿAbd al-Salām currently presided over by Shaykh ʿAbdallāh al-Jīlānī. The chest in the house is the private property of my husband Abī Bakr.

[16] This is her testimony and bequest of her own free will and choice and without coercion or compulsion. Though sick in body she was mentally in a state of a full legal capacity.[39]

On the basis of the testimony of the five witnesses, the qāḍī endorsed the witnesses' testimony relating to the testamentary *waqf* in favor of the Zāwiya, signed it, had the undersigned notaries testify thereto and instructed that it be registered [in the *sijill*].

The written testimony here was required to prevent any attempt in the future to invalidate the testamentary *waqf* on some legal grounds such as the testatrix's incompetence to engage in transactions or that her property was subject to debts.

*Case 6*[40]

ʿAlī b. Faraj from the Zuwayya tribe appeared in the Sharīʿa Court of Ajdābiya, presided over by the Qāḍī Ḥusayn Muḥammad al-Aḥlāfī. He claimed that fifty years previously his late mother, Fuṭayma, had purchased a female slave from ʿAlī b. Masʿūd from the same tribe, in return for a camel owned by her[41] He said:

---

charitable gift were made in death-sickness. There is, however, a clear statement to the effect that the woman's property was not subject to debts.

37 This pious gesture is performed by the testatrix in order to ensure the salvation of her soul; cf. Layish (1994:147); Reiter (1996:109). Sacrifice is practiced among the Bedouin of Cyrenaica. See Peters (1984:214); cf. Stewart (1998: Index, s.v. sacrifice).

38 On *waqf* in favor of a *zāwiya*, see Baer (1997:266–71); Reiter (1996:107). This form of pious activity is particularly common among women. See Layish (1994:156); Baer and Layish (1971:21). In Cyrenaica, the propensity for founding *waqf* in favor of *zāwiyas* was no doubt intensified on account of the special status enjoyed there by the Sanūsī order. See Layish (1991:5, 12, 16–17, 204–5, and the sources indicated there).

39 On the testator's legal capacity, see Coulson (1971:216–7).

40 For the Arabic document, see Layish (1998: doc. 61). For an annotated translation of the entire document, see idem (2005: doc. 61).

41 Under the *sharīʿa* a slave is considered as property (*māl*) that can be disposed of in a legal transaction provided that the owner's rights over the slave are not restricted in any way. On the sale of slaves in Mālikī law, see Ibn ʿĀṣim (1958:110, lines 737ff); Ibn al-ʿAṭṭār (1983:33ff.); on slaves in Libya see Davis (1987:111); cf. Abū Ḥassān (1974:255–6 [aggressors are liable to pay fines by giving slaves]).

> [7] I have brought with me two witnesses called [...], both [8] from the Zuwayya tribe. I [hereby] ask that the noble Sharīʿa Court question them [on this matter], register their testimony and give me [a document pertaining to] their testimony [that I can use] as the need arises.[42]
>
> When the aforementioned witnesses, identified in person and name, were questioned, [9] they both gave testimony [whose truthfulness the witness deemed to be] beyond any shadow of doubt, corroborating in letter and spirit the statement of the aforementioned ʿAlī b. Faraj.

The qāḍī sanctioned (*ajāza*) their testimony and instructed that it be registered in the *sijill*.

The reason for the written testimony is indicated explicitly in the document: It is to be used "as the need arises." As a legal heir ʿAlī was anxious to ensure that no one dispute his mother's ownership of the female slave. Since the sale of the female slave had taken place fifty years earlier, he felt that it was important to enlist the testimony of the witnesses to that sale before they died. Such a document would be necessary in the event of any transaction pertaining to the slave girl.[43]

*Case 7*[44]

A dispute arose concerning the estate of a deceased woman between Mabrūka, the deceased's daughter-in-law through her deceased son Ādam, and Maryam, daughter of the deceased, both of them belonging to the Sudaydī lineage of the Zuwayya tribe. The case was heard in the Sharīʿa Court of Ajdābiya, presided over by the Qāḍī Ḥusayn Muḥammad al-Aḥlāfī. Mabrūka, the claimant, denied Maryam's right to inherit a certain she-camel belonging to her mother since, according to the former, the mother had, in her lifetime, gifted (*wahabat*) this same camel to Ādam. In her version, since the time of the gift, Ādam

---

42 Such as in the event he decides to sell the female slave.

43 Cf. Sharīʿa Court of Ajdābiya, p. 224 no. 371 of July 15, 1953 (A woman belonging to the Maṣrāta tribe claimed that she, her father and sister together bought a house in Ajdābiya, each of them having one-third of the house; the claimant shared her portion with her late husband. She brought her father to testify to this effect, and asked the court to issue a "*shahādat naql* in my favor [to be used] when the need arises"); p. 230 no. 380 of July 23, 1953 (A man belonging to the Zuwayya tribe claimed that he owned a house in the Ajdābiya. He brought his witnesses to testify that he had built the house with his private money); p. 342 no. 581 of July 6, 1954 (*shahādat naql* pertaining to sale of land); p. 346 no. 590 of July 4, 1954 (sale of land).

44 For the Arabic document, see Layish (1998: doc. 67). For an annotated translation of the entire document, see idem (2005: doc. 67).

> [7] proceeded to dispose of it and of its issue, so that they [the camel and its issue] passed into his property (*milk*).[45] After the death of the mother[46] and her son [Ādam, [8] the camel and its issue] became part of his [Ādam's] estate [by virtue of the gift].[47] [...] I have produced witnesses to testify [to the truth] of my statement, and they are [...]. [9] I ask that the noble Sharīʿa Court interrogate them and register their testimonies.

Mabrūka's witnesses testified that according to "widespread" rumor that had reached them, the aforementioned camel had been transferred to Ādam by gift rather than intestate succession. The qāḍī endorsed their testimony and instructed that it be registered in favor of Mabrūka.

The written testimony was requested here because Ādam's right to the camel by virtue of the gift was contested by Maryam, daughter of the deceased, who had been deprived of her share in the camel and its issue by this gift as an instrument for circumventing the *sharʿī* rules of inheritance, and the qāḍī endorsed the transaction on the basis of hearsay evidence.[48]

Occasionally, the differences between a regular judicial decision and a *shahādat naql* are blurred. The same phraseology and legal formularies are used in both cases and the documents are intended to serve the same purpose, namely, to avoid the necessity of enlisting witnesses to a specific right or event when that necessity constitutes a hardship. In both cases the qāḍī appears to have been guided by the doctrine of *maṣlaḥa* (public interest).

*Case 8*[49]

Al-Sāʿidī, belonging to Julūlāt, a branch of the Zuwayya tribe, born and residing in Ajdābiya, appeared in the Sharīʿa Court of Ajdābiya, presided over by the Deputy Qāḍī, the Nāʾib Muḥammad al-Ṭālib al-Hammālī. Al-Sāʿidī claimed that his daughter Fawziyya, aged eight, while playing with her sister at home,

45 On gifts and other means for circumventing the *sharʿī* rules of inheritance, see Layish (1983); idem (1997); Powers (2002:207–10).

46 Mention of the mother's death is irrelevant in a case of a gift, since the camel did not constitute part of her estate. Cf. fn. 48 below.

47 The daughter-in-law bases her claim to the she-camel on her right to her husband's estate.

48 Cf. Sharīʿa Court of Ajdābiya, p. 344 no. 587 of July 11, 1954. (Shortly after the issuance of a *sharʿī* order of succession on her mother-in-law's estate, a woman claimed in court that three she-camels out of this estate had been given as a gift to her late husband by his mother thirty years earlier and that since then he had been disposing of the progeny of these she-camels freely as his own private property rather than part of his mother's estate. She asked the court to issue a *shahādat naql* in her favor.).

49 For the Arabic document, see Layish (1998: doc. 58). For an annotated translation of the entire document, see idem (2005: doc. 58).

fell down on the sharp handle of a handmill and, as a result, broke her hymen. A woman, probably a practitioner of popular medicine, examined the girl immediately after the accident, while she was still bleeding, and confirmed the girl's loss of virginity as a result of the accident. Al-Sāʿidī made the following statement:

> [10] [...] Since this accident has been ordained [11] by Allāh the Exalted, I [al-Sāʿidī] request that it be registered at the Sharīʿa Court so that I may resort to [the document] whenever the need arises and testify to its contents.[50]

All this occurred [12] in the presence of witnesses [i.e., the notaries] listed below.

On the basis of what has been established by the aforementioned al-Sāʿidī [...] while he was in a state of legal competence in *sharʿī* terms, as duly certified [13] in the presence of the aforementioned Nāʾib, the latter issued a judgment endorsing what has been established above, and had the undersigned [professional witnesses] testify to it. He then signed and endorsed it [14] and had it registered [in the *sijill*].

Because the accident occurred in the absence of witnesses, this legal document was meant to establish, at the time of Fawziyya's marriage, that her loss of virginity did not occur in circumstances liable to disgrace her agnates. Fully cognizant of the father's delicate predicament, the Nāʾib accepted the father's

50 Loss of virginity out of wedlock is tantamount to illicit intercourse which under customary law implies disgrace to the bride's agnates and may entail severe sanctions. Bedouin would stipulate in the marriage contract that the bride should be a virgin. If on the day of the marriage the virginity test shows that the bride is not a virgin the marriage may be canceled or (if concluded) revoked and the bride (or her father) be requested to return the prompt dower. Dissolution of the marriage under such circumstances seriously diminishes the woman's chances to remarry. Moreover, due to the disgrace caused to the bride's agnates she may be exposed to death threats. See Peters (1965:121–2 [virginity test], 129); D'Emilia (1946:38); Powers (*Dispensing Justice*); Mohsen (1975:107); Obermeyer (1968:122); Abū Ḥassān (1974:241–2). The *sharīʿa* takes a more lenient attitude in this matter. In the case under review, the girl's father was fully aware of the consequences under customary law of loss of virginity and this may well be the reason why he presented the case as an accident attributable to an irrevocable "act of God." In his distress he resorted to the Sharīʿa Court, rather than to tribal proceedings, to obtain a document certifying that the girl's ruptured hymen did not imply disgrace to her agnates. The recourse to the Sharīʿa Court rather than to tribal justice may have been prompted also by considerations of discreteness. This document would presumably serve to forestall misunderstandings with a future husband and the resort to severe sanctions on the part of the girl's agnates.

version without even requiring the testimony of the woman who had examined the daughter immediately after the accident. The expert's report may be regarded as circumstantial evidence. Formally, we have here a judicial decision. In practical terms, however, the procedure was equivalent to *shahādat naql*. The Nā'ib complied with al-Sā'idī's request to issue the document even though there were no witnesses to the event. He was probably motivated to do so by regard for Fawziyya's welfare.

## 4 Summary and Conclusions

Hallaq's main conclusions with respect to the institution of *kitāb al-qāḍī ilā 'l-qāḍī* are that the written instrument is indispensable in daily life and that practice, through the coercive power of custom and social reality, modified and redefined legal doctrine to the point of bridging the gap between doctrine and practice, the ideal and the real (Hallaq 1999:464–6). These conclusions seem to be valid also with respect to the institution of *shahādat naql*, although there are some differences deriving from the nature of the source which deals with the written testimony (legal treatises vis-à-vis judicial practice) and the period in which the written testimony took place (premodern vs. modern). The justification for both institutions lies in the need for written documents in daily social and economic life. In the case of Libya this is reflected in the qāḍīs' awareness of the necessity to adapt practical norms to the exigencies of changing circumstances. Naturally, the sophistication manifested by the qāḍī in his attempt to bring about a synthesis of orthodox *sharʿī* rules of evidence and day-to-day pressures is less evident here than it is in the *adab al-qāḍī* literature. This, however, does not detract from the qāḍīs' contribution to narrowing the gap between doctrine and practice. The qāḍīs seem to be motivated in the first place by pragmatic considerations. This approach displays itself also in their efforts to bring sedentary tribal society within the orbit of normative Islam (Layish 2002:90–3). The doctrine of *ḍarūra* (necessity) in *adab al-qāḍī* treatises (Hallaq 1999:457) has been replaced in the Libyan judicial practice by variants of *maṣlaḥa*, both being, in effect, two sides of the same coin. This trend manifests itself in the qāḍī's admitting into his court decisions the claimant's request to register his testimony so that the written testimony is issued in the claimant's favor to be used "when the need arises."

We have noted earlier that the Libyan qāḍīs do not often invoke the legal literature. It is, however, important to mention that some of them do refer to Ibn ʿAṣim's *al-ʿAṣimiyya*, which incorporates the judicial practice (*ʿamal*) of al-Andalus.[51] This suggests that the qāḍīs are aware of the power of custom as an informal source of law that molds legal norms in daily life and are ready to compromise with it, at the expense of the traditional rules of evidence.[52] In this respect we witness here a realistic form of Islamic jurisprudence, though the main burden in our case lies on the shoulders of the qāḍīs rather than those of the jurists (Cf. Coulson 1964:147).

The widespread practice of *shahādat naql* in the Libyan *sijill* is in conformity with the modern trend of admitting, by means of statutory legislation, written documents as valid proof (See above, 497). As already observed, the *raison d'être* of *kitāb al-qāḍī ilā 'l-qāḍī*, dating back to premodern times, remained intact. However, the hardship of enlisting witnesses has shifted from geographical distance, of less significance nowadays due to the modernization of communications, to legal certainty, which meets the requirements of present-day exigencies. From this perspective, written documents are regarded as an indispensable instrument for securing legal and financial rights in the unforeseen future. In this respect, *shahādat naql* may be regarded as an extension of the Mālikī judicial practice (*ʿamal*) that seeks to accommodate the *sharīʿa* to the present-day circumstances. All the qāḍīs in the abovementioned cases seem to share the same approach towards written documents.[53]

As noted earlier, all the cases of *shahādat naql* were registered in the Sharīʿa Court of Ajdābiya, a district center in the plain near the Mediterranean coast, and none in the Sharīʿa Court of Kufra, which is located in the southern tribal region of Cyrenaica, far from governmental administrative centers (Davis 1998:7). It seems that the process of integration of sedentary Bedouin into normative Islam is largely facilitated by the pragmatic judicial practice of the *sharīʿa* court as manifested *inter alia* in mechanisms such as *shahādat naql*.

---

51 See above, 498; Layish (1998: doc. 1, line 23; doc. 31, lines 25–6).

52 Cf. Layish (1984:41 {The Qāḍī of Bethlehem: "Since reconciliation is stronger than the qāḍī (*al- ṣulḥ yuqawwī al-qāḍī*), because it is based on agreement between the parties, it affects the *sharʿī* decision}).

53 Unfortunately, no information on the Libyan qāḍīs' *sharʿī* education and legal training is available to me.

CHAPTER 4

# Islamization of Custom as Reflected in Awards of Tribal Arbitrators in the Judaean Desert

*In memoriam*
*Dr. Avshalom Shmueli*

•••

*waṣiyyat irth baʿd al-wafāt ghayr sharʿiyya jāhiliyya*
MUḤAMMAD SĀLIM AL-DHUWAYB ʿASHĪRAT AL-SHARĀYIʿA AL-TAʿĀMIRA

•••

*diya muḥammadiyya ʿalā sharʿ al-islām*
AḤMAD ḤASAN ḤUMAYD ʿASHĪRAT AL-ḤAJĀḤIJA AL-TAʿĀMIRA

•••

## Introduction*

The purpose of this study is to describe and analyze the process of Islamization affecting the tribal customary law of a sedentary tribal society in the Judaean Desert on the basis of legal documents collected from the Bedouin in the Jerusalem-Bethlehem region during the 1970s.[1] The Bedouin in this region comprise a group of tribes: al-Sawāḥira (*c.* 6000 persons in the 1970s) east of Jerusalem, al-ʿUbaydiyya (*c.* 5,500) east of Bayt Sāḥūr, the 13 Taʿāmira tribes (*c.* 20,000) east of Bayt Sāḥūr in the north to Bayt Fajjār in the south, and al-Rashāyida (*c.* 500) south-east of Taqūʿa. Most of the tribes in question are said to have originated from Ḥijāz and Najd; they appeared in the region in

* Originally published in *Jerusalem Studies in Arabic and Islam*, 35 (2008), pp. 285–334.

1 On the interaction between custom and *sharīʿa* within the domain of personal status, see Layish and Shmueli, "Custom and *sharīʿa* in the Bedouin family," p. 29; Layish, "Challenges to customary law and arbitration," p. 206.

 | DOI:10.1163/9789004680920_006

small groups from the sixteenth century onwards, gradually developing into tribes, while absorbing local *fellahin*. Their most significant demographic expansion occurred in the twentieth century.

The sedentarization of these tribes began in the 1920s and was almost complete by the 1970s. It was furthered by proximity to religious, economic, and administrative centers and by the consolidation of internal security. Al-Taʿāmira tribes have established settlements of their own; some of them settled in existing Judaean villages and in suburbs of Bethlehem, and in the mid-1950s, under Jordanian rule, they began to migrate to Jordan and the oil-producing countries from where they sent considerable sums of money to their families which greatly accelerated sedentarization. As a result, the tribal structure began to dissolve into the constituent *ḥamūla*s (clans); the tribe ceased to function as a political unit, and the *shaykh* has, in most of the tribes, been replaced by the *mukhtār*. In the 1970s the Bedouin earned their livelihood outside the tribal areas, mainly as laborers in construction, industry, tourism, and as watchmen. Small stockbreeding and ground-crop farming diminished considerably.

Since the awards of a tribe's arbitrator (*ḥakam, muḥakkam*) or tribal judge (*qāḍī ʿashāʾirī*) enjoy some precedential value,[2] it seems right to maintain that the arbitrator shapes the customary law in the process of his adjudication. Some arbitrators from the Judaean Desert have acquired a fine reputation even outside their tribe and are resorted to also by members of other tribes and by sedentary rural and urban population, including Christians. This is not surprising when it is recalled that in the Mashriq, "a large part of the customary law of the sedentary population was adopted from the Bedouin."[3] Arbitration generally passes by inheritance within certain families. The economic position of the arbitrator is sound, for he is paid for his judicial work.[4]

The written document (*ṣakk, sanad, waraqa, wathīqa*) is not essential, in Arab customary law, for the establishment of the validity of a legal act or a contention, though it may be of some help. Broadly speaking, the most common recognized mode of proof is by oral witnesses. In some regions, as in central Sinai, the Bedouin almost entirely lack written documents.[5] As is known, written documents are ignored in Islamic legal theory.[6] It seems that the use of written documents increases with the progress of sedentarization; the main factors influencing this process are closer economic contacts with

2 Stewart, "Customary law among the Bedouin," p. 243.

3 *Ibid.*, p. 241.

4 For more details, see Layish and Shmueli, "Custom and *sharīʿa* in the Bedouin family," pp. 29–30.

5 Stewart, "The contract with surety," p. 173.

6 Schacht, *Introduction*, pp. 82–83; Layish, "*Shahādat naql*," pp. 496–99.

settled population and land transactions; the transition from tribal property to private ownership; the influence of *sharʿī* and civil justice; the exigencies of modern administration, and the spread of literacy.[7] Several hundreds of legal documents, including documents obtained by Bedouin from the *sharīʿa* courts of Jerusalem and Bethlehem, and data pertaining to Bedouin collected by the author from the *sijill* (records) of the Sharīʿa Court of Bethlehem in the author's possession deal with matters of procedure and evidence, personal status, succession, homicide and injury, land, obligations, and contracts. Most documents in the present collection date from the twentieth century; the rest are mostly from the last quarter of the nineteenth century. Some were written by paid scribes (*kātib*) from Jerusalem or Bethlehem and some by the arbitrators themselves or their assistants; the latter are in colloquial Arabic.[8] Needless to say, documents written by urban scribes well versed in *sharʿī* terminology tend to blur or obliterate the tribal customary norms by phrasing them in *sharʿī* terms,[9] whereas the documents written by arbitrators are more likely to reflect the authentic tribal customary norm.

Customary law and *sharīʿa* are two profoundly different kinds of legal systems, although they share common features. Thus both of them are systems of personal law in the sense that they are not bound by territory.[10] Broadly speaking, custom is unwritten law shaped by the praxis and collective experience of ordinary people, their acceptance of its norms over a long period of time having crystallized into a binding legal norm with respect to the place and subject matter to which it relates. *Sharīʿa,* on the other hand, is perceived as a divinely revealed law, as interpreted by its authoritative exponents, and imposed on society from above by means of religious and state sanctions. Unlike the *sharīʿa,* customary law is not vested with supernatural authority; hence a tribe can modify its laws usually through a consensus reached at a gathering of its leaders and, as noted, by tribal adjudication.

The co-existence of these two discrete legal systems dates back to the early ʿAbbāsī period, when the *sharīʿa* emerged as a full-fledged and crystallized system. The *sharīʿa* encoded the idealized religious norm, whereas customary law reflected the law of the tribes. The two systems co-existed side by side, not

7 In the present case, appeals were also made by the author to the arbitrators to commit their decisions to writing in order to enrich the documentation of this study.

8 Layish and Shmueli, "Custom and *sharīʿa* in the Bedouin family," pp. 30–31.

9 *Idem, sharīʿa and custom in Libyan tribal society*, p. xi.

10 Stewart, "Customary law among the Bedouin," p. 242; Layish, "Adaptation," p. 171. Unless otherwise indicated, this section draws freely on Layish, *Sharīʿa and custom in Libyan tribal society*, pp. 1–10; and Layish and Shmueli, "Custom and *sharīʿa* in the Bedouin family, p. 2.

always in a perfectly harmonious manner. For all that, customary law was to play a vital role in molding the *sharīʿa*.[11] The subsequent process of the intensive interaction and mutual fertilization of the two systems lasted for centuries; the *sharīʿa* displayed remarkable assimilative power culminating in far-reaching integration and Islamization of customary law.[12] Theoretically, the *sharīʿa* maintained its absolute sovereignty in every legal domain, including those that had long been assigned to the sphere of customary law. In day-to-day practical terms, however, a compromise was maintained between theory and practice.

In the contemporary Islamic world, customary law still enjoys varying degrees of autonomy alongside the *sharīʿa*, especially in regions with largely tribal communities; in some places, tribal courts and arbitrators continue to apply customary law with little if any interference by the central government. Furthermore, the *sharīʿa* courts' decisions are carried out in practice only to the extent that the *sharʿī* norm is compatible with custom. Stewart has found that "many, perhaps all, systems of Bedouin customary law have to some degree been influenced by Islamic law,"[13] though this seems to apply especially in North Africa, and to a lesser extent in Palestine and other parts of this region.[14] For the time being, however, a kind of peaceful coexistence is maintained between the two laws, each administrating its own judicial apparatus and confining itself to a particular domain of life.

One of the most serious methodological difficulties facing the scholar is how to distinguish, in tribal documents, between custom and *sharīʿa*. The main problem is that the legal terms in the two laws are, broadly speaking, fairly similar, especially in issues pertaining to personal status, succession, homicide and bodily injury; this is less so in the law of contracts and obligations.[15] In general, customary law in these domains was integrated into the *sharīʿa* in its formative period; the process involved moderation and mitigation of the customary norms by religious-ethical ones, occasionally to the extent that the substance of the terms underwent a radical change, though the terms themselves remained intact.

In modern times, the interaction between customary and Islamic law is in the opposite direction: Islamic legal terms and institutions penetrate increasingly into customary law as the Bedouin become sedentary and closer to

11 Abū Sinna, *al-ʿUrf wa-'l-ʿāda* (I am grateful to Prof. M.J. Kister for presenting me with a copy of this book); Libson, "Custom as a source of law," p. 131; *idem* "Urf," p. 887; Zysow, "Custom in Islamic law."

12 Cf. Schacht, *Introduction*, p. 84.

13 Stewart, "Customary law among the Bedouin," p. 245.

14 Stewart, "'Urf," p. 891ii; al-Salḥūt, *al-Qaḍāʾ al-ʿashāʾirī*, p. 71.

15 Cf. Schacht, *Introduction*, pp. 76ff.

normative Islam. The identification of the customary norm involves some difficulties where it varies from one region to another; i.e., fluid and changing in character, and not yet in a finalized state. So far, the Bedouin of the Judaean Desert have not codified their customary law[16] though, as noted below, some efforts in this direction have been made.

The present author proposes a socio-legalistic method for the distinction between custom and *sharīʿa*: where the two legal systems share the same technical terms, their connotations should be examined while paying regard to the social substance which may be quite different in some essential respects in the two laws. Where, as in central Sinai, under customary law the woman has no legal personality,[17] the dower (*ṣadāq, mahr*) belongs to her agnates, whereas under the *sharīʿa* the woman is a party to the marriage contract and the dower is therefore her property. When coming across dower in a document, in order to establish its customary or *sharʿī* identity it is necessary to examine who is entitled to receive it or, more exactly, who actually receives it.[18]

It is tempting to reconstruct the pre-Islamic tribal law on the basis of modern documents. Schacht argues that the customary law of the contemporary Bedouin deserves special attention "because, though influenced by Islamic law, it goes back in the last resort to the customary law of the pre-Islamic Arabs and enables us to control the information which literary sources give us on this last."[19] This objective, however, is beyond the scope of this study.

Normative Islam, with its system of beliefs, institutions, and laws, has a limited impact on nomadic society where folk religion, including the cult of saints and intercession, are still predominant. The Bedouin regard the *sharīʿa* as an auxiliary source of law and resort to it only in cases of lacunae in custom or when two customs contradict each other. Customary law has survived even in areas where its followers nominally adopted Islam. Bedouin in various parts of the Muslim world identify themselves as Muslims regardless of the state of their knowledge and practice of Islamic doctrine, worship, ethical and legal norms.[20] They regard tribal law as part of their Islamic heritage; in fact, they

16 Cf. Stewart, "Customary law among the Bedouin," p. 244; Oweidi, "Bedouin justice in Jordan," pp. 160–61, 203, 207, 210, 320; Ḥasanayn, *Niẓām al-masʾūliyya*, p. 170; Layish, Sharīʿa *and custom in Libyan tribal society*, p. 199, fn. 1, p. 200.

17 Stewart, "The contract with surety," p. 189.

18 Layish, *Divorce*, pp. 2–4; cf. Antoun, "The Islamic court," p. 456.

19 Schacht, *Introduction*, p. 77.

20 Al-ʿAbbādī, *al-Qaḍāʾ ʿinda al-ʿashāʾir al-urdunniyya*, pp. 163, 198–201; Bailey, "Bedouin religious practices," pp. 70, 85.

perceive *sharīʿa* being identical with tribal customary law[21] although some of their customs are inconsistent with the *sharīʿa.*[22]

The relationship between customary law and *sharīʿa* in tribal society has two dimensions. The first entails a situation in which tribal customary law reigns supreme and makes only minor concessions to the *sharīʿa.* The second dimension predominantly displays the impact of the *sharīʿa* on custom. Here, the *qāḍī* of the *sharīʿa* court plays a decisive role in shaping the consequences of the encounter between *sharīʿa* and tribal custom and thus contributes substantively to bringing the Bedouin population within the orbit of the *sharīʿa.*[23] The *muftī* too has a vital role in this regard.[24] This study is concerned with the interaction between custom and *sharīʿa* from the point of view of custom and the extent in which it is reflected in the tribal judiciary practice.

The sedentarization of the Bedouin in modern times brings them under the control of the central government, one aspect of which is the *sharīʿa* court. George Bisharat, who wrote his doctoral dissertation on the Palestinian legal profession in the West Bank in the mid-1980s, maintains that the role of the central government and the connections of the tribal legal system with the state legal system, rather than processes of sedentarization and modernization, and increasing contacts and identification with Islam, are the main driving forces behind the change in the tribal legal system.[25] Bedouin resort increasingly to the *sharīʿa* courts while resorting at the same time to tribal courts and arbitrators.[26] One of the reasons for this tendency is the power vested in the *sharīʿa* court to execute its judgements that secures realization of the legal and financial rights of the parties.[27] In modern times, the ability of the tribal arbitrator to keep the Bedouin within the orbit of the tribal legal system has declined. This is mainly due to the competition on the part of

21 Oweidi, "Bedouin justice in Jordan," pp. 177–78.

22 Cf. Schacht, *Introduction*, p. 77.

23 Layish, "The Islamization of the Bedouin family," p. 39; *idem, Women and Islamic law*, pp. 332–37; *idem*, "Shariʿa u-minhag," p. 377; *idem*, Sharīʿa *and custom in Libyan tribal society*, pp. 7–8; *idem*, "The *Qāḍī*'s role in the Islamization," p. 83; *idem*, "*Dār ʿAdl*", p. 198; *idem, Divorce*, pp. 185–208; *idem*, "Tajdīda," p. 488; *idem*, "Customary *Khulʿ*," p. 428; *idem*, "Blood money," p. 63; Peters, "Dakhla oasis," pp. 79, 87–88; Antoun, "The Islamic court," p. 455 (the *qāḍī* is a "culture broker"), pp. 465–66.

24 Layish, "The *Fatwā* as an instrument of Islamization," p. 449; *idem*, "The *Fatwā* as an instrument of accommodation," p. 270.

25 Bisharat's comments.

26 Stewart, "Customary law among the Bedouin," p. 274.

27 Antoun, "The Islamic court," pp. 458, 462; ʿAbd Allāh, *al-Mujtamaʿ al-rīfī fī 'l- ʿIrāq*, p. 53. For a full analysis of these reasons, see Layish, Sharīʿa *and custom in Libyan tribal society*, pp. 4–5.

*sharʿī* and the civil judiciary.[28] Bisharat points out that the tribal judge is fully aware of the fact that his judgments conforming with Jordanian civil law can be enforced only through the civil execution department charged with executing judgements and that he fears that if he does not resort to the statutory civil law his clients will resort to the state court system where the rulings will be enforced.[29] When the disputed parties finally resort to the *sharīʿa* court, the entire case is, of course, dealt with in accordance with the *sharʿī* substantive as well as the procedural and evidential law.

Thus, in one case, after the spouses, both belonging to al-Taʿāmira tribes, had been identified according to the *sharʿī* identification procedure (*taʿrīf*), the Qāḍī of Bethlehem explained to them that the wife was divorced by one absolute divorce (*bānat ... bi-.ṭalqa wāḥida*), that she was not permitted to return to her ex-husband save by a new matrimonial contract and dower, and that she was required to observe the *sharʿī* waiting-period (*ʿidda*).[30] In a case of homicide, the parties belonging to al-Taʿāmira tribes, the reconciliation contract (*ʿaqd muṣālaḥa*) took place in the presence of the *sharʿī* Qāḍī of Bethlehem and the Muftī of Hebron, probably with a view to adding a *sharʿī* sanction to the arbitrators' award.[31] It should be noted that blood money (*diya*), but not homicide, was within the jurisdiction of the *sharīʿa* court under the Jordanian law applicable in the West Bank in the period under review.[32] In other cases the parties, at the arbitrators' request, undertook to waive claims and rights in the civil courts. Thus, in one case, the agnates of the deceased renounced all their civil (*madaniyya*), penal (*jazāʾiyya*) and tribal (*ʿashāʾiriyya*) rights, that is, monetary and criminal claims (the latter on the prosecution's initiative) in civil court[33] and claims for vengeance (*thaʾr*) or alternatively for blood-money according to tribal customary law.[34]

---

28 Cf. Oweidi, "Bedouin justice in Jordan," pp. 188–92, 259, 281–82, 259, 321; Tsafrir, "Arab customary law in Israel," p. 76.

29 Bisharat's comments.

30 Layish, Archive of legal documents collected from tribal arbitrators in the Judaean Desert [hereafter: Layish, *Archive*] File Divorce, No 11, Sharīʿa Court of Bethlehem, Sijill 3, p. 176, no. 13, 12.3.1962.

31 Layish, *Archive*, Ṣulḥ, No. 4, [owner of the document] Muḥammad Sālim al-Dhuwayb [al-Dhuʾayb] ʿAshīrat al-Sharāyiʿa al-Taʿāmira, 12.5.1955; cf. Diya, No. 2, 31.3.1957 (*Diya Muḥammadiyya* was paid and a tribal *ʿaṭwa* [truce] ceremony was held in the presence of the Qāʾimaqām, the Sharʿī Qāḍī, and the Commander of the Muqāṭaʿa).

32 Layish, "Maḥkama," p. 32i.

33 Cf. Ḥasanyan, *Niẓām al-masʾūliyya*, p. 132.

34 Layish, *Archive*, Ṣulḥ, No. 2, Muḥammad Sālim al-Dhuwayb ʿAshīrat al-Sharāyiʿa al-Taʿāmira, 26.10.1967; Appointment of Arbitrators, No. 19, 24.8.1978; No. 18, 22.4.1976; cf. Divorce, No. 10, Sulaymān Sālim al-Taʿāmira, 20.10.1974.

There is ample evidence in the documents that the government encourages amicable settlement of disputes out of court. Thus, in a decision of a *manshad* (tribal judge dealing with violation of honor)[35] pertaining to breach of guaranteed truce (*ʿaṭwa*), the matter was settled without informing the authorities in light of the fact that "the Government welcomes reconciliation (*iṣlāḥ*)."[36] In another case, it was agreed between the two parties that "the award of the arbitrator shall be subject to approval by the Governor of the Bethlehem District, who shall have the right to appoint an umpire [to review his award] (*al-ḥaqq fī tamyīzihi*) as he may see fit." The award was executed in the presence of the Governor.[37]

## 1 Procedure and Evidence

The tribal customary law corresponds to a society that is not subject to central authority. In the Judaean Desert, arbitrators are not statutory bodies, but even in countries where arbitration judiciary is regulated by state law, the resort to the adjudication of arbitrators can take place only by voluntary agreement between the parties.[38]

A good notion of the procedure pertaining to the appointment of arbitrators and guarantors may be gathered from the following case which is in fact an agreement to resort to arbitration. Following the renewal of a blood dispute between the two parties, both of Ḥamūlat al-Marāshida of Bayt Sāḥūr, and in reliance on a document of tribal truce (*ṣakk al-ʿaṭwa al-ʿashāʾiriyya*), a meeting was held at the house of a well-known personality attended by the representatives of the parties, a number of prominent dignitaries (*wujūh*), the guarantors (*kufalāʾ*) and mediators (*wusaṭāʾ al-khayr*), for the purpose of completing the procedure of arbitration. Each party appointed an arbitrator (*muḥakkam*) of his choice, and it was agreed as follows:

1. The parties undertake to accept the award (*ḥukm*) handed down by the arbitrators as final and not open to objection or to appeal (*istiʾnāf*).
2. If the arbitrators disagree, the parties shall choose a third arbitrator as umpire (*mumayyiz*); his award shall be final and binding (*mulzim*).

---

35 Al-ʿĀrif, *al-Qaḍāʾ bayna al-badw*, p. 56.

36 Layish, *Archive*, Wajh, No. 7, Muḥammad Sālim al-Dhuwayb ʿAshīrat al-Sharāyiʿa al-Taʿāmira, 14.2.1975; cf. Oweidi, "Bedouin justice in Jordan," p. 238. On a guarantor for a "free truce," see Stewart, "The contract with surety," p. 255.

37 Layish, *Archive*, Appointment of Arbitrators, No. 10, Maḥmūd Musallam al-Burayjiyya ʿAshīrat al-Zawāhira al-Taʿāmira, 31.7.1966; cf. Oweidi, "Bedouin justice in Jordan," pp. 259, 270.

38 Stewart, "Customary law among the Bedouin," p. 262.

3. Each party shall submit, within one week, to the two arbitrators its pleadings (*ḥujja*, [*ḥijjih*]) in writing and all the documents (*wathāʾiq*) and the names of witnesses of good characters (*shuhūd ʿadl*); they may present the statements of the witnesses in writing.
4. The parties undertake to pay the fee (*atʿāb*) and expenses (*nafaqāt*) of the arbitrators and the umpire; the latter's is to be shared equally between the parties.
5. The two arbitrators may register the submission (*sanad taḥkīm*) and their award with the notary (*kātib ʿadl*) of the Court of Bethlehem.
6. The parties undertake to maintain quiet and to refrain from causing wrong (*iʿtidāʾ*) and provocation (*taḥarrush*) against any member of the other party, and each party shall be responsible for the behavior of every member of its *ʿāʾila*.[39]
7. Each party appoints two "guarantors of payment [of blood-money] and of restraint [from taking revenge, and instead accepting blood-money] (*kufalāʾ dafʿ wa-manʿ*);[40] each party is responsible to its guarantors for carrying out the provisions of this agreement and for carrying out the award of the arbitrators or the umpire.
8. If one of the parties fails to carry out any of the provisions of the agreement, the guarantors shall be bound to discharge (*wafāʾ*) the obligations (*iltizāmāt*) of that party at the expense of that defaulting or infringing party, and as a result, that party shall be liable to be sued by its guarantors for everything due in respect of damages (*ʿaṭal wa-ḍarar*) in addition to a fine (*gharāma*) of five hundred Jordanian dinars in favor of the second party.

The representatives of the parties and the guarantors signed the submission in the presence of witnesses.[41]

39 Since both parties belong to the same *ḥamūla* (clan), the framework of responsibility was reduced to the *ʿāʾila*, a smaller unit based on blood ties.

40 The same phrases appear also in Layish, *Archive*, Appointment of Arbitrators, No. 17, Muḥammad Sālim al-Dhuwayb, ʿAshīrat al-Sharāyiʿa al-Taʿāmira, 9.5.1977. In one case the document reads *kufalāʾ al-wafāʾ* (*al-dafʿ*) indicating that the terms are synonymous. Layish, *Archive*, Appointment of Arbitrators, No. 17A, Sharārī Muḥammad al-Aʿraj al-Sawāḥira, 11.10.1977. The customary phrases in Jordan and Central Sinai are *kufalāʾ al-wafāʾ* (payment) *wa-difʾ* (warmth in the sense of restraint); see al-Qusūs, *al-Qaḍāʾ al-badawī*, pp. 81–82; Stewart, "A Bedouin narrative," pp. 84–85; *idem*, *Texts*, pt. 1, p. 200.

41 Layish, *Archive*, Appointment of Arbitrators, No. 19, Muḥammad Sālim al-Dhuwayb, ʿAshīrat al-Sharāyiʿa al-Taʿāmira, 22.4.1976; cf. Layish and Shmueli, *Legal documents on the Bedouin of the Judaean Desert*, p. 43. In one case the parties chose one arbitrator for both of them. His award was subject to the approval of the Governor of the Bethlehem District who could appoint an umpire as he might see fit. Layish, *Archive*, Arbitration, No. 10,

This case reflects the adaptation of the arbitration institution to modern times. The agreement was recorded on a printed form with empty spaces for the names of the participants, such as the parties to the disputes, the guarantors and the witnesses, to be filled in in handwriting. The parties' pleadings and the witnesses' testimonies were required to be presented in writing. The registration of the submission and the award with the notary of the civil court was done probably with a view to benefiting from the department charged with executing judgments in the event that one of the parties fails to comply with the arbitrators' awards; this reflects the rising impact of the civil justice. The *sharīʿa* plays a minor role in this document, though the phrase *shuhūd ʿadl* seems to be inspired by the *sharʿī* notaries in the *sharīʿa* court.

As already noted, in modern times tribal arbitration is strongly exposed to competition from the *sharʿī* and the civil judiciary. Thus in an instrument of arbitration, the parties to the dispute, both of ʿArab al-Taʿāmira, agreed, at the arbitrators' request, to withdraw the claims filed by them with the *sharīʿa* court, both the claims for maintenance (*nafaqa*) filed by the wife and the claim for obedience (*ṭāʿa*) filed by the husband. Both parties undertook not to file claims with the [*sharʿī* or civil] courts unless the arbitrators failed to make an award (*qarār*).[42]

Occasionally, the procedure for settling a dispute starts with tribal arbitration and ends up in the *sharīʿa* court.[43] Thus in one case, the arbitrator decided that the husband should prepare a legal dwelling (*bayt sharʿī*) equipped with all the legal (*sharʿiyya*) accessories for his wife[44] (both being of ʿArab al-Taʿāmira) and treat her without impairing her rights and honor, and that the wife should obey (*ṭāʿa*) her husband and move into his new dwelling. The arbitrator stipulated that

---

Maḥmūd Musallam al-Burayjiyya ʿAshīrat al-Zawāhira al-Taʿāmira, 31.7.1966; cf. al-ʿĀrif, *al-Qaḍāʾ bayna al-badw*, pp. 57–58.

42 Layish, *Archive*, Appointment of Arbitrators, No. 1, Nimr ʿAwda al-Mubārak Nabāhīn ʿAshīrat al-Waḥsh, 29.9.1963; Layish and Shmueli, *Legal documents on the Bedouin of the Judaean desert*, p. 43.

43 *Quḍāt al-tamhīd*, judges whose function is to make the preliminary investigation as to the competent judicial instance to deal with a specific matter, have been enlisted to this end; Oweidi, "Bedouin justice in Jordan," pp. 230 ff., 271–72, 279; al-ʿAbbādī, *al-Qaḍāʾ ʿinda al-ʿashāʾir al-urdunniyya*, pp. 298–99; cf. Layish and Shmueli, "Custom and *sharīʿa* in the Bedouin family," p. 44.

44 The reference is to the Islamic *maskan sharʿī* (legal conjugal residence) though phrased in customary terms; on the Islamization of *al-bayt al-sharʿī*, see al-ʿAbbādī, *al-Jarāʾim al-ṣughrā*, pp. 76 ff.

> if the husband refuses to prepare a dwelling etc. as aforementioned, he shall divorce the wife by a *sharʿī* divorce (*yuṭalliquhā ṭalāqan sharʿiyyan*) since he will thus be deemed as failing (*muqṣiran*) to fulfill his obligation as to her rights [...] and the wife shall renounce what he owes her in the *sharīʿa* court.[45]

In another case, where no consummation of the marriage had taken place between the couples (both being minors), the arbitrators ruled that the girl should declare in the *sharīʿa* court:

> I have nothing left owing to me (*dhimma*) by [... my husband], such as prompt or deferred dower or accumulated maintenance or waiting-period maintenance (*nafaqat al-ʿidda*).[46]

And [her husband] should declare [in court]:

> I waive (*usāmiḥuhā*) all my rights and I shall never have any claim against her.[47]

It is interesting to note that although the renunciation divorce was scheduled to take place in the *sharīʿa* court, the boy's undertaking to waive his rights was guaranteed by his guarantor according to customary law.[48]

Where possible, the arbitrators' decisions are based on evidence, and in its absence, on individual or collective oaths.[49] Usually, the oath takes place in a tribal environment and the legal terms pertaining to the evidence have a purely tribal customary connotation totally unrelated to Islamic law. Thus, in one case, the arbitrator of ʿArab al-Sawāḥira, having declared "I pronounce

45 Layish, *Archive*, Divorce, No. 3, Ibrāhīm ʿAbd Allāh al-Darʿāwī, 26.8.1970.

46 Waiting-period maintenance is a reform introduced by Islamic law; cf. Oweidi, "Bedouin justice in Jordan," pp. 152–53 (the Bedouin do not observe the *ʿidda*); Shuqayr, *Taʾrīkh Sīnāʾ*, p. 418; ʿAbd Allāh, *al-Mujtamaʿ al-rīfī fī ʾl-ʿIrāq*, p. 61.

47 Layish, *Archive*, Divorce, No. 4, Muḥammad Maḥmūd Fakhkhār, 10.12.1966; cf. Divorce, No. 10, Sulaymān Sālim al-Taʿāmira, 20.10.1974 (the *shaykhs* of al-Taʿāmira decided that the husband should divorce [*yuṭalliq*] his wife in the presence of the *sharʿī* Qāḍī of Bethlehem).

48 Cf. Layish, *Archive*, Divorce, No. 10, Sulaymān Sālim al-Taʿāmira, 20.10.1974 (renunciation divorce with guarantors in the presence of the *sharʿī qāḍī*); Stewart, "The contract with surety," pp. 188–90.

49 Stewart, "Customary law among the Bedouin," p. 265.

(*anā min ʿindī*),[50] but only Allāh, may He be extolled and exalted, knows the truth (*ḥaqq*)," decided that the defendant charged with stealing sheep must swear (*yaḥlif al-yamīn*), in any place which the owner of the property, i.e., the sheep, may choose,[51] and declare that he did not steal the sheep and does not know who stole [them], and if he swears, with the honor (*wajh*) of the guarantor (*kafīl*) [the latter depositing his honor with the obligee, i.e., the plaintiff], he shall be free from guilt (*barīʾ*), but if he does not swear, he must pay the price of twenty sheep. The reason for this is that he [allegedly] stole (*saraqa*) from a place where he ate and stayed overnight.[52]

In other cases, *sharʿī* terminology is interspersed in tribal awards, though in actual fact this terminology reflects customary rather than *sharʿī* substance. Thus, in a dispute over the boundaries of land, one of the arbitrators used terms accompanied by derivatives from "*sharīʿa*" such as "to protect and safeguard the *sharʿī* oath (*yamīn*)." In one case, the purchaser who had infringed the award of the first arbitrator was requested to bring persons who would

> bear witness to the credibility of his demarcation [of the land] (*an yuzakkiya mā ḥaddadahu*) [...] by virtue of an oath [the truthfulness of which has been established] by virtue of religion and five persons (*bi-mūjib dīn wa-khamsa*) [...] If [the purchaser] refuses to take an oath (*yamīn*) and bring five witnesses to attest to the veracity of the oath (*muzakkūn*), he must accept the solution proposed by the seller of the land [as to the boundaries].[53]

In another case, a charge was brought against the defendant of using foul language against the daughter of the plaintiff; it was agreed to file a monetary

50 Stewart, *Texts*, pt. 1, p. 10, Text 4, lines 1 and 3 and fn. 4; *idem*, *Texts*, pt. 2, p. 16, Text 4, lines 3 and 8; Oweidi, "Bedouin justice in Jordan," p. 315; Shuqayr, *Taʾrīkh Sīnāʾ*, p. 422.

51 This may refer to a tomb of a *walī mashhūr* (renowned saint) which is a source for blessing (*baraka*). In Palestine, this may refer to holy places such as al-Ḥaram al-Sharīf, Qubbat al-Ṣakhra, and *maqāms* (tombs of saints) of various prophets; Salḥūt, *al-Qaḍāʾ al-ʿashāʾirī*, p. 89; cf. al-Qusūs, *al-Qaḍāʾ al-badawī*, p. 38; Bailey, "Bedouin religious practices," pp. 75–7; Oweidi, "Bedouin justice in Jordan," pp. 95, 306; Farīq al-Muzhir Āl Firʿawn, *al-Qaḍāʾ al-ʿashāʾirī*, p. 211.

52 Layish, *Archive*, Evidence and Procedure, No. 1, Muḥammad al-Aʿraj al-Sāḥūrī al-Sawāḥira, 1.4.1945; cf. Oweidi, "Bedouin justice in Jordan," p. 160.

53 Layish, *Archive*, Appointment of Arbitrators, No. 13, Mūsā Muḥammad ʿAwdat Allāh al-ʿAṣāt al-ʿUbaydiyya, 28.1.1966. On oathes concerning tribal boundaries, see Stewart, *Texts*, pt. 1, pp. 190–3. On *sharʿī* oathes and the procedure of *tazkiya*, see Peters, "Shāhid," p. 207ii.

claim in tribal proceedings rendering formal judgment (*ḥaqq*) before the tribal *qāḍī* of al-ʿUbaydiyya and that

> if the *qāḍī* decides that a *sharʿī* oath (*yamīn al-sharʿ*) must be taken concerning the charge, the plaintiff will have to pay the *qāḍī's* fee (*rizqa*) because the defendant is prepared to take the *sharʿī* oath *before* going to the [tribal] *qāḍī*, without any loss (*khasāra*)[54] or fee being incurred. The plaintiff may [...] choose between tendering the oath and litigating before the *qāḍī*.[55]

Occasionally, however, rules of evidence seem to clearly have been influenced by the *sharīʿa*. Thus in one case, the arbitrator began with a citation of a Qurʾānic verse: "O, believers, if ye judge between mankind, that ye judge justly" (Qurʾān 4:58), and proceeded by quoting a *ḥadīth* attributed to the Prophet concerning evidence:

> The onus of proof [by means of witnesses] is on the plaintiff and the oath-taking is on him who denies the charge (*al-bayyina ʿalā man iddaʿā wa-ʾl-yamīn ʿalā man ankara*).[56]

In some cases, the place where the oath takes place is of great religious significance. Thus, in one case, the representatives of the two parties appeared at al-Aqṣā Mosque. Each of the representatives of ʿUbaydiyya took the following oath (*yamīn*) in the presence of the *muzakkūn:*

> I swear by Allāh and by the truth (*ḥaqq*) of this al-Ḥaram al-Sharīf and by Allāh's precious book that neither I nor anyone else of al-ʿUbaydiyya [...] have murdered [...], that we do not know who killed him and know nothing either secret or open about his disappearance.[57]

---

54 That is, expenses involved in dispensing justice.

55 Layish, *Archive*, Evidence and Procedure, No. 18, Muḥammad Sālim al-Dhuwayb ʿAshīrat al-Sharāyiʿa al-Taʿāmira, 13.8.1974.

56 This is, with a minor variation (*al-bayyina ʿalā al-muddaʿī wa-ʾl-yamīn ʿalā al-muddaʿā ʿalayhi*), an Islamic rule of evidence phrased in a legal maxim. Wensinck, *Concordance*, p. 258ii; Layish, *Archive*, Assault, No. 8, Mūsā Muḥammad ʿAwdat Allāh al-ʿAṣāt al-ʿUbaydiyya, 9.4.1956; cf. al-Qusūs, *al-Qaḍāʾ al-badawī*, p. 32; al-Salḥūt, *al-Qaḍāʾ- al-ʿashāʾirī*, p. 87; al-Yamānī, *Sīnāʾ*, p. 224; Oweidi, "Bedouin justice in Jordan," p. 150; al-ʿAbbādī, *al-Qaḍāʾ ʿinda al-ʿashāʾir al-urdunniyya*, p. 200.

57 On oath of compurgation in Islam (*qasāma*), see Peters, "Crime and punishment," pp. 16ff.

The *muzakkūn*, who had been agreed upon, confirmed the representatives' credibility (*zakkāhum*), and the arbitrator decided that the sons of the victim had no right to lodge a claim (*ḥaqq*) against the people of al-ʿUbaydiyya.[58]

The term *tazkiya*, test of credibility, too, has a purely tribal customary connotation.[59] Thus, in a land dispute between al-Taʿāmira and al-ʿUbaydiyya, the representatives of al-Taʿāmira agreed

> to give the right of oath-taking (*ḥaqq ḥilf al-yamīn*) to [...] Darwīsh [...]; and five persons [...] all of the ʿUbaydiyya tribe, shall be duty-bound and compelled (*mukallafūn wa-majbūrūn*) to attest to the veracity of the oath (*yuzakkū ṣiḥḥat yamīn*) [that is, to the credibility of the principal oath-taker ...]; the purpose of the oath shall be to corroborate the boundaries of the land of the two tribes [...]. The oath-taking is to be announced by public notice [...] within everybody's sight and hearing. It is to be a well-known (*mashhūr*) kind of oath, the contents, form and written rendering of which are in accordance with custom (*ḥasab al-ʿurf wa-'l-ʿāda*) prevailing among the Bedouin tribes in regard to land and property (*amlāk*).

The representative of al-Taʿāmira undertook that in the event that Darwīsh's honorable record was established by the five persons performing the credibility test (*tazkiyat al-khamsa*), the land of al-ʿUbaydiyya tribe in the disputed lands and their boundaries should be in accordance with Darwīsh's determination with no objection on the part of al-ʿUbaydiyya.[60]

In another land dispute between two *ʿashīra*s, the tribal *qāḍī* decided that if no *sharʿī* witnesses (*shuhūd al-sharʿ*) are found, and if the plaintiff was unable to confirm through witnesses an allegation pertaining to the land he would have to swear an oath corroborated by five persons (*yamīn bi-khamsa*) to the truthfulness of his allegation; and if he failed to comply, he would be fined.[61]

---

58 Layish, *Archive*, Evidence and Procedure, No. 4, Mūsā Muḥammad ʿAwdat Allāh al-ʿAṣāt al-ʿUbaydiyya, 17.8.1954. Similarly, in a land dispute between ʿArab al-Sawāḥira and ʿArab al-ʿUbaydiyya it was decided that an oath by a representative of Ubaydiyya regarding payment will be taken in Jerusalem, possibly at al-Aqṣā Mosque; see Evidence and Procedure, No. 8A, Sulaymān Sālim Muḥammad Dār Ṣalāḥ al-Taʿāmira, 5.1.1976.

59 Cf. Abū Ḥassān, *Turāth al-badw al-qaḍāʾī*, p. 104; Farīq al-Muzhir Āl Firʿawn. *al-Qaḍāʾ al-ʿashāʾirī*, p. 69, fn. 1, p. 211.

60 Layish, *Archive*, Evidence and Procedure, No. 7, Muḥammad Sālim al-Dhuwayb ʿAshīrat al-Sharāyiʿa al-Taʿāmira, 4.4.1935. On *tazkiyat al-qasam bi-khamsa*, see al-Salḥūt, *al-Qaḍāʾ al-ʿashā-irī*, pp. 87–88.

61 Layish, *Archive*, Wajh, No. 1, Sulaymān Sālim Muḥammad Dār Ṣalāḥ al-Taʿāmira, 20.2.1972.

In yet another case, a man was accused of laying his hand on a woman in an isolated place in his field.[62] The tribal *qāḍī* decided to have the hand of the accused cut off (*tuqṭaʿ yaduhu*)[63] unless he

> takes a *sharʿī* oath (*yaḥlif al-yamīn al-sharʿī*) – after observing the oath-taking customs prevalent among the tribes (*muttabaʿa bayn al-ʿashāʾir*) – that the [woman's] allegations [...] are fabrications [...]. Then the veracity of his oath shall be confirmed (*yuzakkī yamīnahu*) by five men from among his relatives, who shall be chosen by [the woman's] full brother [...]; if [... the accused] avoids taking the *sharʿī* oath or if one of the five *muzakkūn* delays confirming the veracity of his [the accused's] oath, I shall invoke against him the right of "the woman who screams (*ṣāʾiḥa*)"[64] early in the morning [*ḍuḥan*] [... in which case] I shall decide that a truce (*ʿaṭwa*) of a "screaming woman" shall be arranged.[65]

## 2 Family

Under tribal customary law, the nuclear family does not function as a corporation. Males and agnates have priority over females and cognates, respectively; the woman is regarded as an object rather than a party to the marriage contract; only ties between husband and wife and between father and children, but not between mother and children, are recognized.[66] In the Bedouin documents, however, occasionally the *sharʿī* concept of the woman as a party to the marriage contract seems to have penetrated tribal arbitration. Thus in one case the "elders" (*ikhtiyāriyya*) and "youngsters" (*shabāb*) of the ʿArab al-Radāyida, al-Marāʿina and al-ʿAsāsiwa clans (*ḥamāʾil*) assembled and adopted the following protocol (*mazbaṭa* [*maḍbaṭa*]):

---

62 In the Mashriq, a sexual offense against a woman is generally viewed as an offense against the honor (*ʿirḍ*) of her agnates; Stewart, "Customary law among the Bedouin," p. 260.

63 Cf. Stewart, "Customary law among the Bedouin," p. 265; Oweidi, "Bedouin justice in Jordan," pp. 173–74, 218, 300–1. Under Islamic law amputation is reserved for theft (*sariqa*) and highway robbery (*qaṭʿ al-ṭarīq*).

64 A customary mechanism intended to clean a woman of a charge of immoral behavior. See al-Salḥūt, *al-Qaḍāʾ al-ʿashāʾirī*, p. 59; Oweidi, "Bedouin justice in Jordan," p. 287; al-ʿAbbādī, *al-Qaḍāʾ ʿinda al-ʿashāʾir al-urdunniyya*, pp. 85–86; Farīq al-Muzhir Āl Firʿawn, *al-Qaḍāʾ al-ʿashāʾirī*, p. 97; Ghayth, *Qāḍāʾ al-ʿashāʾir fī ḍawʾ al-sharʿ al-islāmī*, pp. 140–41.

65 Layish, *Archive*, Assault, No. 8, Mūsā Muḥammad ʿAwdat Allāh al-ʿAṣāt al-ʿUbaydiyya, 9.4.1956.

66 Stewart, "Customary law among the Bedouin," p. 261; al-Qusūs, *al-Qaḍāʾ al-badawī*, pp. 90–91.

> We […] have agreed upon the dower (*mahr*) payable between [… the clans], as follows: for a girl 45 pounds, for a widow (*ʿazba* [*ʿazbāʾ*]) 25 pounds, for a childless widow 30 pounds […]. A girl is credited with five pounds by her father; a widow is credited with three pounds by her guardian.[67]

The perception whereby the dower is the property of the woman reflects a *sharʿī* norm. In the case under review, the customary concept according to which the dower is the property of the woman's guardian seems to be still dominant but a degree of compromise can be noted here: the woman's right to the dower is recognized with regard to a small portion of the dower. In fact, the *maḍbaṭa* adopted by the tribal assembly may be regarded as an act of reform of tribal customary law which has been moderated to some extent in line with the *shar sharīʿa.*

A certificate addressed by the *mukhtār*s and *ikhtiyāriyya* of ʿArab al-ʿUbaydiyya to the Qāḍī of the Sharīʿa Court of Bethlehem reflects the extent to which *sharʿī* norms have infiltrated into customary tribal law. They attested that the suitor (*khāṭib*)

> is legally major (*bāligh*), and of sound mind (*ʿāqil*) and mature (*rashīd*), […] free from wives [single] and from wives in the waiting period of a revocable divorce (*muʿtaddāt min ṭalāq rajʿī*) desires to contract marriage (*zawāj wa-nikāḥ*) with a woman who is not a virgin […] for the two above-mentioned dowers: prompt (*muʿajjal*) […] and deferred (*muʾajjal*) […] and whereas there is no *sharʿī* or secular legal (*niẓāmī*) impediment (*māniʿ*) to the conclusion of the contract (*ʿaqd*) between them, and it [the contract] has the consent of the parties and the consent and the permission (*ijāza*) of the woman's *sharʿī* guardian (*walī*), viz. her father. […].[68]

In one case a couple, both of ʿArab al-Sawāḥira, contended in the Sharīʿa Court of Jerusalem that their marriage that had been concluded sixteen years previously in accordance with the custom (*ʿāda*) of ʿArab al-Sawāḥira and consummated (*dukhūl*) was valid (*ṣaḥīḥ*) under the *sharīʿa,* and requested its registration. In fact, they were asking for a declaratory judgment concerning the validity of the marriage. The Qāḍī of Jerusalem decided:

67 Layish, *Archive*, Marriage, No. 1, ʿAlī Ḥasan Muḥammad al-Radāyida ʿArab al-Taʿāmira, 24.6.1940.

68 Layish, *Archive*, Marriage, No. 2, Mūsā Muḥammad ʿAwdat Allāh al-ʿAṣāt al-ʿUbaydiyya, n.d.

> As the whole matter is certified by a petition (*maḍbaṭa*) signed by the Mukhtār and notables (*wujūh*) [...] and a statement (*ikhbār*) by the [two] aforementioned trustworthy identifiers (*muʿarrif*), and the acknowledgment (*iqrār*) of the parties was made while they were in a mental and physical state considered as *sharʿī*, we decide to register [the marriage].[69]

In other words, the Qāḍī retroactively validated the customary marriage as a *sharʿī* contract for any legal or practical purpose.

In a marriage contract concluded by a *sharʿī* solemnizer (*maʾdhūn*), both parties belonging to "Arab al-ʿUbaydiyya ʿAshīrat al-Radāyida, a *maḍbaṭa* of the Mukhtār and *ikhtiyāriyya* attested to the absence of *sharʿī* and secular-legal (*qānūnī*) impediments (*mawāniʿ*) to marriage. The witnesses to the contract and the agency (*wakāla*) were identified in accordance with the *sharʿī* procedure of identification (*taʿrīf*). The prompt dower and deferred dower payable "at the nearer of the two dates" (*li-aqrab al-ajalayn*), that is, on divorce or death of either parties, were stipulated in the contract, and the bride confirmed that she had received (*qabḍ*) the prompt dower. The woman's guardian permitted her to be married by the *sharʿī* Qāḍī of Bethlehem. The bride's father addressed the bridegroom saying:

> I married to you (*zawwajtuka wa-ankaḥtuka*) my principal (*muwakkila*), my daughter, for the prompt dower [...] and deferred dower [... and the bridegroom replied]: I accept (*qa-biltu*) the marriage (*zawāj wa-nikāḥ*) to your principal, thy daughter [...] for the said two dowers and I consent to it.

The *sharʿī maʾ dhūn* of ʿArab al-ʿUbaydiyya, a resident of Bayt Sāḥūr, probably not a Bedouin, drew up the contract after it had been established to his satisfaction that the *sharʿī* requirements had been met.[70] Hence the *maʾdhūn* proves to be a vital agent for the islamization of tribal society.

In one case, the parties to the agreement were Ṣafiyya and her two minor brothers and their mother Fāṭima, the minors' guardian (*waliyya*), as the First Party, and Aḥmad, Ṣafiyya's bridegroom (or husband?)[71] along with his brothers, as the Second Party. The two parties agreed that

69 Layish, *Archive*, Marriage, No. 4, Sharīʿa Court of Jerusalem, 4.8.1956.

70 Layish, *Archive*, Marriage, No. 3; Layish and Shmueli, *Legal documents on the Bedouin of the Judaean Desert*, p. 34, Sharīʿa Court of Bethlehem, Certificate (*qasīma*) No. 79393, 14.4.1958.

71 One possibility is that Aḥmad, Ṣafiyya's bridegroom had to raise the dower out of the family household (see next footnote). Another possibility is that Ṣafiyya died before the

> [Fāṭima] shall take 80 Jordanian dinars from Aḥmad […] as the dower of her daughter Ṣafiyya […]. This amount shall be paid in the form of half of a house jointly owned [by the brothers] (*mushtaraka*) and […] in cash.[72] The two parties agreed on this idea.[73]

This document attests to the woman's capacity to own and dispose of property and to act as guardian and representative of her children in accordance with the *sharīʿa.*

The following divorce case reflects the impact of the *sharīʿa* on the tribal arbitrators. The husband contended that his wife's parents, both parties belonging to ʿArab al-Taʿāmira, had not exerted pressure upon her to ensure her obedience. Since the parties were bent on reaching an understanding, the arbitrators decided

> in accordance with tribal custom (*al-ʿawāʾid al-ʿashāʾiriyya*): The husband shall fit out his house perfectly, equipping it with everything required for *sharʿī* residence (*buyūt sharʿiyya*) within the meaning of a statutory [the Jordanian Family Rights Law of 1951] provision (*al-manṣūṣ ʿalayhā*) accepted by the *sharīʿa* courts. If he refuses or is unable to do so […], he will have to divorce (*yuṭalliq*) his wife without any *quid pro quo* (*muqābil*) and to pay all the matrimonial rights (*ḥuqūq zawjiyya*) due to her […]; if the husband fails to carry out an obligation (*taqṣīr*) or is guilty of fraud, he shall divorce his wife Fāṭima without any *quid pro quo,* pay the matrimonial rights due to her and repudiate her by a *sharʿī ṭalāq.* If the parties agree of their own free will to be released (*khalāṣ*) from each other [that is, by divorce], we decide […] that the wife shall have no right to claim

---

dower (or the residue thereof) was paid to her, in which case it became part of Ṣafiyya's estate and had to be apportioned among her *sharʿī* heirs: her mother Fāṭima (who seems to be have been a widow), Safiyya's two minor brothers and her husband.

72 The jointly-owned house, that is, family *mushāʿ* (cf. al-ʿAbbādī, *al-Jarāʾim al-ṣughrā*, pp. 74–75; Farīq al-Muzhir Āl Firʿawn, *al-Qaḍāʾ al-ʿashāʾirī*, p. 149) is part of the estate left by the head of the family. Aḥmad seeks to raise the dower out of the family household before its division among the heirs (*ifrāz*). In another case, two brothers sharing immovable property through inheritance (a family *mushāʿ*) concluded an agreement for the purpose of financing the dowers of their respective wives out of the family household. Layish, *Archive*, Marriage, No. 8, Muḥammad Sālim al-Dhuwayb, ʿAshīrat al-Sharāyiʿa al-Taʿāmira, 16.8.1957. Cf. Layish, Sharīʿa *and custom in Libyan tribal society*, p. 28, Doc. 4.

73 It seems that the rest of the brothers had already raised the dowers for their wives out of the family household during their father's lifetime or after his death; this may explain why they did not resist the arrangement with respect to their brother Aḥmad. Layish, *Archive*, Marriage, No. 7, Mūsā Muḥammad ʿAwdat Allāh al-ʿAṣāt al-ʿUbaydiyya, 1.8.1955.

> from the husband anything whatsoever, such as [waiting-period] maintenance (*nafaqa*) and deferred (*mu'ajjal*) dower.[74]

In another case it became clear to the arbitrators and the umpire that no consummation of the marriage had taken place between the couple (both being minors), and after consultations with the parties they reached the conclusion that the perfect solution was divorce (*firāq*) of the disputants with a payment of 90 dinars as compensation (taʿ*wīẓ* [*taʿwīḍ*]) to the husband for the divorce (*talāq*), that is, *khulʿ* divorce. The arbitrators ruled that the wife should apply to the *sharīʿ a* court and declare:

> I have nothing left due to me (*dhimma*) from [... my husband], such as prompt or deferred dower or earlier [i.e., accumulated] maintenance or waiting-period maintenance (*nafaqat al-ʿidda*).

And the divorcing husband should declare:

> I waive (*usāmiḥuhā*) all my rights and I shall never have any claim against her.[75]

In yet another case, the divorced wife made the following declaration in the presence of tribal witnesses (*shāhid*) and identifiers (*muʿarrif*) [in charge of identification (*taʿrīf*) procedure in *sharīʿa* court]:

> I [...] of ʿArab al-Jaʿāfira, make complete renunciation (*ibrā'*) of, and release my husband [...] from liability (*dhimma*) for, all matrimonial claims (*ḥuqūq zawjiyya*), viz. waiting-period maintenance (*nafaqat al-ʿidda*) and deferred dower (*ṣadāq mu'akhkhar*) in return for the dissolution of my marriage tie (*infikāk ʿiṣmatī*) and for my divorce (*ṭalāqī*) from my husband.[76]

## 3 Inheritance

In the domain of inheritance, customary law seems to reign supreme: most of the estate, in particular the land, goes to the sons of the deceased, usually to

74 Layish, *Archive*, Divorce, No. 9, Sulaymān Sālim Dār Ṣalāḥ al-Taʿāmira, 11.5.1972.

75 Layish, *Archive*, Divorce, No. 4, Muḥammad Maḥmūd Fakhkhār [?], 10.12.1966; cf. al-ʿAbbādī, *al-Jarā'im al-ṣughrā*, pp. 239–40.

76 Layish, *Archive*, Divorce, No.14, Abū Ṭālib Khaḍr Muḥammad Ḥasan al-Jaʿfarī, 1.1.1948.

be shared equally between them or, in their absence, to paternal brothers and uncles, no matter how remote; the widow is totally deprived. This is usually the case also with respect to the daughters, the rationale being the desire to prevent the exclusion of their shares in the patrimony through their marriages to non-agnates; however, the daughters are entitled to maintenance out of the estate from their paternal brothers until they marry and receive their dowers.[77] Moreover, the issuance of a succession order by a *sharīʿa* court does not *ipso facto* guarantee that the order will be implemented in letter and spirit; renunciation of *sharʿī* rights in succession out of court seems to be a common practice though it indicates that Qurʾānic heirs are aware of their *sharʿī* portions. Thus in an instrument of renunciation (*waṣl tanāzul*) out of court, authenticated by witnesses, the deceased's daughter renounced her *sharʿī* share in her father's estate in favor of her paternal brother in return for some compensation; thereupon she declared:

> I [...], daughter of the late [...] of al-Sawāh.ira [...] affirm, acknowledge and attest that I have nothing left with my brother [...] of the property (*amlāk*) we inherited from our father and grandfather, viz. the following [six] parcels of land: [...]. In witness whereof I have given him and signed this instrument (*waṣl*) upon receiving all my above-mentioned rights in full and having nothing left in his possession (*dhimma*) that is mine (*haṣṣanī*) of [the estate of] my father, [...]. I gave him this instrument without anybody forcing me [to do so], of my own accord (*rāḍiya*), for the sake of peace (*mustarḍiya*) and in awareness of everything it implies.[78]

In one case, the succession order issued by the Sharīʿa Court of Bethlehem stated that the legal heirs were the deceased's paternal sister, his widow and his two paternal cousins, all of them residents of Bethlehem. The estate (*tarika*) consisted of a house and three parcels of land in Bethlehem. It seems that the paternal sister was not satisfied with the *sharʿī* division of the estate. Hence she applied to tribal arbitrators with a view to re-dividing the estate on the basis of a voluntary agreement. The arbitrators handed down the following decision (*qarār*):

77 Al-Qusūs, *al-Qaḍāʾ al-badawī*, 43–44; al-ʿAbbādī, *al-Jarāʾim al-ṣughrā*, pp. 71–72; Stewart, "Customary law among the Bedouin," p. 261.

78 Layish, *Archive*, Succession, No. 1, Sharārī Muḥammad al-Aʿraj Sawāḥira, 29.5.1956. For details, see Layish and Shmueli, "Custom and *sharīʿa* in the Bedouin family," p. 40.

> The widow[79] […] agrees to renounce (*tatanāzal*) what has been left to her by the deceased […] immovables and lands in favor of [… the deceased's paternal sister][80] in consideration of the sum of 1,650 dinars [… The deceased's two cousins[81]] agreed to renounce what had been left to them by the deceased […] in favor of [his paternal sister] or her successors in consideration of the sum of 300 dinars.[82]

The renunciation by the deceased's remote agnates in favor of his paternal sister is consistent with the *sharʿī* Jabarī's rule.[83]

In a similar case an agreement was reached between nine daughters of the deceased and their paternal uncle (*ʿamm*) regarding their father's estate. The daughters empowered (*wakkalna*) two of their members to represent them before the Land Registry in order to register their rights of ownership in their father s estate. It was agreed between the two parties that

> The abovementioned parcel shall be in the possession of their mother […], who shall cultivate it unchallenged. After the death of their mother […] the parcel shall be divided equally among the said heirs, and none of the heirs shall have the right to use any part of that parcel without the consent of the heirs [the daughters].[84]

It seems that the deceased had no sons. The widow apparently did not belong to his descent (judging by her name, which appears beside her fingerprint). She was entitled only to the usufruct of the parcel so long as she lived and was prohibited from performing any transaction involving the ownership of the land. The right to usufruct is tantamount to maintenance out of the estate.[85] The paternal uncle did not oppose the transfer of the estate to the daughters in

---

79 As a Qurʾānic heir, the widow takes one-quarter of the estate in the absence of a descendant; Coulson, *Succession*, p. 41.

80 In the absence of a daughter, paternal granddaughter or paternal brother, a paternal sister takes one-half of the estate as a Qurʾānic heir; Coulson, *Succession*, p. 68.

81 The paternal cousins take the rest of the estate as residuary heirs; they are not excluded by a paternal sister when she inherits as a Qurʾānic heir; Coulson, *Succession* pp. 77–78.

82 Layish, *Archive*, Succession, No. 11, Muḥammad Sālim al-Dhuwayb ʿAshīrat al-Sharāyiʿa al-Taʿamira, 3.11.1958.

83 According to this rule, a member of a higher parentela (paternal cousins) or class (*ṭabaqa*) with regard to the deceased (in this case, the paternal sister) totally excludes any member of a lower parentela; Coulson, *Succession*, pp. 33, 78.

84 Layish, *Archive*, Succession, No. 8, Sulaymān Sālim Muḥammad ʿAshīral al-Ṣalāḥ al-Taʿāmira, 11.3.1967.

85 Cf. Layish,"The family *waqf*," pp. 380–82.

the Land Registry, probably because he expected them to marry their agnates, such as first cousins, i.e., his sons, thus frustrating the disintegration of the paternal patrimony. [86]

The tribal customary law in the Judaean Desert does not seem to acknowledge the *sharʿī ultra vires* doctrine pertaining to testamentary disposition. Under this doctrine, it is prohibited to dispose by will of more than one-third of one's estate or in favor of a legal heir unless the consent of all the heirs is obtained after the testator's death. In one case, the testator, a Bedouin of al-Taʿāmira, who seems to have had no sons, made the following will:

> I [...] Ḥājj [...] al-Dhuwayb, make this will (*ūṣī*) while in good health and full possession of my mental faculties, under no constraint (*maqhūr*) or compulsion (*majbūr*) but of my own volition (*ṭawʿ*) and choice (*ikhtiyār*), wholeheartedly (*riḍan*), with love, gladness and good intent in the presence of distinguished persons. The latter I call to witness that I make disposition (*awṣaytu*) in favor of [...] my [five] daughters by my two wives, Ḥulwa [...] and Raḥma [...] al-Dhuwayb [...] in my custody (*dhimma*) [that is, lawful marriage].

He allocated to his daughters and wives complete (rather than proportional) shares in parcels of land (in some cases to be shared by two daughters and wives) bordering on agnates lands. His daughters, with the exception of one, were married to their agnates; this implies that their shares in the estate would not be excluded from the patrimony through their marriages. In this sense the case resembles the case of the Daughters of Zelophehad.[87] The case does not necessarily attest to women's capacity to own and dispose of property. With respect to the daughter who seems to have been married to an outsider, the testator stipulated: "If she does not receive the equivalent of the land in money [which implies a recommendation to sell the land to her agnates], she shall keep the land without anyone being permitted to dispute this disposition." The arbitrator who kept this will in his file was fully aware of the *sharʿī ultra vires* doctrine and hence he entitled the document "non-*sharʿī jāhilī* will."[88]

In another document entitled Instrument of Disposal of Inheritance (*maḍbaṭat ḥaṣr irth*), the owner of the property made the following statement:

---

86 In this sense the case resembles the case of the Daughters of Zelophehad (Num. 27); cf. Farīq al-Muzhir Āl Firʿawn, *al-Qaḍāʾ*. al-*ʿashāʾirī* pp. 118–19.

87 Num. 27.[307] *"non-sharʿī jāhilī will."[88]*

88 Layish, *Archive*, Succession, No. 2, Muḥammad Sālim al-Dhuwayb al-Taʿāmira, 27.4.1975. Cf. Layish and Shmueli, "Custom and *sharīʿa* in the Bedouin family," pp. 40–41. On customary will, see al-,ʿAbbādī *al-Jarāʾim al-ṣughrā*, p. 85.

> I, the undersigned [...] of ʿArab al-Taʿāmira ʿArab al-Shāwawira, leave (*warrathtu*) to my legitimate (*sharʿiyyāt*) [three] daughters [...] my house and all my property (*milk*) in my lifetime [...]. Their mother [...] shall be their guardian (*waliyya*) [...]. In witness thereof I have given and duly signed this [instrument of] inheritance (*wirātha*).

The *mukhtār*s of ʿArab al-Taʿāmira attested to the validity of the statement and that, except those daughters, there was no heir (*wārith*) or person entitled (*mustaḥiqq*) to a share in their father's estate (*tarika*). Although the phrase "in my lifetime" may suggest that we are dealing here with a distribution of the estate during the owner's lifetime, that is, an *inter vivos* gift, it seems that in fact this is a bequest in favor of the daughters, probably in the absence of sons; the will becomes operative after the testator's death. The verb *"warrathtu"* implies "after my death" rather than "in my lifetime." The mother is actually *waṣī mukhtār*, that is, executor of the will, which also demonstrates her capacity to dispose of property.[89]

In an instrument entitled "To Whom It May Concern," the owner of the property, of ʿArab al-Masāʿida, made the following statement:

> I, [...], in full possession of my mental and physical powers, affirm and acknowledge that I have renounced (*tanāzaltu*) in favor of [...] my minor (*qāṣir*) son by my lawful wife [...] of ʿArab al-Taʿāmira, [...] parcels [...] to finance his marriage (*badal zawājihi*). Let it be known to all and sundry that my [other] four sons [...] shall not claim the said land from their brother unless they marry him off.

The instrument was made with the guarantee (*kafāla*) of two well-known arbitrators and the *mukhtār*s of al-Taʿāmira tribe. This renunciation is actually a will (it becomes operative upon the father's death) in favor of a son who is a legal heir. At the moment, the legatee is a minor; when he comes of age (by which time his father may be dead) the parcels will be transferred to his ownership and possession. To this end the customary guarantors are required. However, if the grown-up sons marry off their young brother and provide the dower for his marriage out of the patrimony, they may have a claim to these parcels.[90]

---

89 Layish, *Archive*, Succession, No. 6, Rizq Saʿīd Rizq, ʿArab al-Taʿāmira, ʿArab al-Shawāwira, 18.11.1954; cf. Layish and Shmueli, "Custom and *sharīʿa* in the Bedouin family," p. 40

90 Layish, *Archive*, Succession, No. 7, Muḥammad Sālim al-Dhuwayb , ʿAshīrat al- Sharāyiʿa al-Taʿāmira, 20.6.1956; Layish and Shmueli, "Custom and *sharīʿa* in the Bedouin family," p. 40.

## 4 Homicide and Grievous Bodily Harm

Both tribal customary and Islamic law classify homicide (*qatl*) and grievous bodily harm (*jurḥ*) within the domain of private prosecution (or civil claims) rather than public-criminal law. In fact, Islamic law adopted the customary concept of revenge; the *sharʿī* right of retaliation (*qiṣāṣ*) is molded on the patterns of customary vengeance (*thaʾr*),[91] though mitigating it by religious ethical norms. Thus, the *sharīʿa* acknowledges only personal, rather than collective, liability for the offense, that is, revenge in kind can be taken only on the person of the offender, not his agnates; retaliation can be performed only after it has been authorized by a *sharʿī qāḍī*, and pardon or financial compensation, instead of retaliation, is recommended. Under Ḥanafī doctrine the option of retaliation is limited to cases of intentional (*ʿamd*) offenses.[92]

The tribal arbitrator's award (*taqrīr ḥukm ʿashāʾirī*) below reflects a mixture of *sharʿī* and tribal customary norms:

> Given in accordance with the discretion (*raʾy*) of the tribal judge (*qāḍī*): "A tooth for a tooth, an eye for an eye, and retaliation for wounds" (*al-sinn bi-'l-sinn wa-'l-ʿayn bi-'l-ʿayn wa-'l-jurūḥ qiṣās*).[93] [In this case, the accusation can be established on the basis of] eyewitnesses (*wa-'l-shuhūd ʿiyān*); [this is not a serious matter where the case should be decided in accordance with the tribal legal maxim]: "A charge of unchastity or homicide cannot be established on the basis of witnesses" (*wa-lā ʿayb ʿalayhi shuhūd wa-lā dam ʿalayhi wurūd*).[94]
>
> Every stab wound (*ghurza*) in the head of the attacked man rates two [Jordanian] dinars; a blow in the face rates thirty Jordanian dinars [for reasons of] honor and dignity (*wa-jāha wa-wajāha*),[95] the unsheathing of the dagger rates five Jordanian dinars; its return to the sheath another

91 Stewart, "Thaʾr," pp. 442–43; Oweidi, "Bedouin justice in Jordan," p. 300.

92 Peters, *Crime and punishment*, pp. 39–40; Ḥasanayn, *Niẓām al-masʾūliyya*, pp. 5–6.

93 Cf. Qurʾān 5:45. The last part of the verse which commends the replacement of retaliation by remission (*kaffāra*, atonement) is missing; within the Qurʾānic context, the phrase "*wa-'l-jurūḥ. qiṣāṣ*" should be translated: "wounds equal for wounds." Peters, *Crime and punishment*, p. 40, fn. 39. The tribal *qāḍī* follows suit; see al-Yamānī *Sīnāʾ*, p. 255; cf. Oweidi, "Bedouin justice in Jordan," p.300; Shuqayr, *Taʾrīkh Sīnāʾ*, p. 410.

94 A serious charge of this kind can be established only by the procedure of *bishʿa* or oath taking (*yamīn*) by the accused; Sulaymān Dār Ṣalāh (personal communication, 29.12. 1975) explains that it was just a case of *ṭawsha ʿumūmiyya*, general turmoil or quarrel; cf. al-Qusūs, *al-Qaḍāʾal-badawī*, p. 48; al-Yamānī, Sīnā-, p. 233.

95 Cf. Stewart, *Texts*, pt. 2, p. 278, Glossary, *wjh*.

> five dinars; and the attacker must kiss the head of the attacked man and appease him.[96]

In a case of a different kind, the avenge group (*ahl al-dam*) of the victim (*maghdūr*) of al-Taʿāmira tribe who had been run over by a car, met at the houses of arbitrators with a view to obtaining a reconciliation contract (*ʿaqd muṣālaḥa*). The *sharʿī* Qāḍī of Bethlehem and the Muftī of Hebron were also present at this meeting. The contract reads as follows:

> Since the parties had decided that the accident was an act of God – decreed by the fate (*qaḍāʾan wa-qadaran*) – the executors of the blood feud (*awliyāʾ al-dam*) of the dead man, [thanks to] their being endowed with Bedouin virtues (*taḥallaw bi-'l-akhlāq al-ʿarabiyya*) and [to] Bedouin generosity, disengaged themselves [i.e., granted forgiveness] and renounced (*asqaṭū*) the right to sue and claim (*ḥaqq al-murā-faʿa wa-'l-iddiʿāʾ*) civil (*madaniyya*) damages [under state law] or amends pertaining to the collective [of the blood group] (*ijtimāʿiyya*) [under tribal customary law.[97] resulting from that accident].[98]

The blood avengers in this case regard car accidents as a matter of fate being beyond human control and hence do not warrant vengeance.[99]Judging by the end result, this is equivalent to the category of unintentional homicide under the *sharīʿa.* Although the term "*khaṭaʾ*" is not mentioned explicitly in the document, having regard to the citation of the Qurʾānic verse pertaining to retaliation, the possibility that the *sharʿī* category concerning unintentional homicide served as a source of inspiration cannot be ruled out.[100] The arbitrators precluded any possibility of seeking resort in some state agency that will interfere with the terms of the contract of reconciliation.

---

96 Layish and Shmueli, *Legal documents on the Bedouin of the Judaean Desert*, p. 57; Layish, *Archive*, Assault, No. 1, ʿAlī, ʿĀyid Abū Ḥadīd, ʿArab al-Sawāḥira, 7.10.1956.

97 Under state law, homicide has two aspects: criminal and civil, i.e., compensation for damages caused. Both aspects, on personal level, are within the jurisdiction of civil courts (hence *madaniyya*); claims for amends incurred to the blood group as a collective (hence *ijtimāʿiyya*) are dealt with in tribal adjudication; cf. Ḥasanayn, *Niẓām al-masʾ ūliyya*, pp. 218–20.

98 Layish, *Archive*, Ṣulḥ, No. 4, Muḥammad Sālim al-Dhuwayb ʿAshīrat al-Sharāyiʿa al-Taʿāmira, 12.5.1955.

99 Cf. Abū Ḥassān, *Turāth al-badw al-qaḍāʾ ī*, p. 213.

100 Al-Sawāḥira's classification of the categories of homicide seems to be based exclusively on the *sharīʿa*; see al-Sawāḥira, *al-Mūjaz fī 'l-qaḍāʾ al-ʿashāʾ irī*, pp. 49–51.

The concept *diya muḥammadiyya*, Islamic blood money, is a clear illustration of the adoption of the *sharʿī* category of unintentional homicide (*qatl khaṭaʾ*) by tribal customary law that originally does not distinguish between intentional and unintentional homicide.[101] Abū Ḥassān maintains that the mere distinction between the two situations is an innovation brought about by the influence of Islam.[102] Stewart maintains that the amount of blood money due to the victim takes into consideration, *inter alia*, whether the deed of the perpetrator was intentional or not.[103] Under the *sharīʿa*, the absence of the element of intention mitigates the financial consequences of homicide. The normal blood money due in cases of unintentional homicide is one hundred camels of various specifications as to age and sex, whereas for intentional and semi-intentional (*shibh ʿamd*) homicide, the enhanced blood money (*diya mughallaẓa*) too is one hundred camels, but of a different, more valuable specification. Already in early Islam the blood money was given a monetary value of 1000 dinars. *Diya muḥammadiyya* reflects the normal blood money.[104]

In one case, a man murdered his brother's children and wife, the latter belonging to another *ḥamūla*. Soon after the killer was arrested, a member of the woman's *ḥamūla* went at night to the jail to avenge (*thaʾr*) his paternal cousin (*bint ʿamm*). When he opened fire on the criminal, he unintentionally (*khaṭaʾ*) shot and killed a policeman. The accident was regarded as destiny and fate (*qaḍāʾ wa-qadar*). A six months' truce (*ʿaṭwa*) was secured, and the killer's *ʿashīra* paid to the victim's family two hundred Jordanian dinars "in accordance with the customs embodied in Islamic *sharīʿa* law" (*ḥasab al-ʿurf wa-'l-ʿādāt fī qawānīn sharʿ al-islām*). Upon the termination of the *ʿaṭwa*, the notables of the two *ʿashīra*s went to the victim's family in a village in the District of Nablus. The kin of the dead man "put their handkerchiefs around the necks [of two relatives of the killer]" (*arkhaw al-maḥārim fī arqābihim [riqābihim]*)[105] and,

101 Ḥasanayn, *Niẓam al-masʾūliyya*, p. 4.

102 Abū Ḥassān, *Turāth al-badw al-qaḍāʾī*, p. 203; cf. Oweidi, "Bedouin justice in Jordan," p. 93; al-ʿAbbādī, *al-Qaḍāʾ ʿinda al-ʿashāʾir al-urdunniyya*, pp. 78, 84; Shuqayr, *Taʾrīkh Sīnāʾ*, p. 415.

103 Stewart, "Customary law among the Bedouin," p. 252.

104 Peters, *Crime and punishment*, pp. 50–52. In Jordan, the state adopted, by means of legislation, the current tribal legal conception that regards homicide caused by a car as implying unintentional homicide (provided the event was accidental and the driver had a valid license); in such cases the driver is liable to pay *diya muḥammadiyya* estimated at 330 Jordanian dinars; Oweidi, "Bedouin justice in Jordan," pp. 236–37; cf. Stewart, "Customary law among the Bedouin," pp. 272–73 (payment of blood money in motor vehicle accidents where the victim enjoyed employee insurance).

105 That is, to indicate that the relatives of the killer were now safe from vengeance. Cf. al-Qusūs, *al-Qaḍāʾ al-badawī*, pp. 82–83; Stewart, *Honor*, p. 96.

in the presence of the tribal *qāḍī*, granted forgiveness and remission (*ʿafw, musāmaḥa*) in accordance with custom (*ḥasab al-ʿurf wa-'l-ʿāda*). The *qāḍī*

> imposed compensation of 2,500 dinars sterling on the killer's family. Then [the victim's family, as a gesture of] forgiveness waived 1,000 dinars in honor of Allāh, the Prophet Muḥammad and the respected persons (*jāh*). The claim thus finally amounted to 1,500 dinars sterling, 1,000 thereof being Muḥammadan blood-money in accordance with the Islamic *sharīʿa* (*diya muḥammadiyya ʿalā sharʿ al-Islām*).[106]

In another case of homicide in which *diya Muḥammadiyya* was paid, the *sharʿī qaḍī* attended the tribal *ʿaṭwa* ceremonies (the Qā'imaqām too was present).[107] His presence seems to have enhanced the application of the *diya Muḥammadiyya*.

In a case of assault, ʿAlī hit Saʿīd on the head with a stone in the courtyard of the Muḥāfaẓa in the presence of government officials, the *mukhtār*s of the village and a gathering of village people. Hence the arbitrator decided:

> I consider it [this assault] tantamount to abominable (*munkar*)[108] murder (*ightiyāl*) [...] I hand down a decision against Mr. ʿAlī [...] in accordance with tribal law (*qānūn ʿashā'irī*) applying, prevailing and accepted among the tribes. As the injury to Saʿīd was deadly (*qātila*), humiliating (*muhīna*) unprovoked [lit. without any sin, *dhanb*] and inflicted without any good, clear reason, I decide – and the decision (*ḥukm*) is Allāh's, praised and exalted be He, as He said in His precious book: "Truth hath come and falsehood hath vanished. Lo! Falsehood is ever bound to vanish"[109] – as follows: In respect of the hitting with the stone inflicted on Saʿīd [...] by ʿAlī [...] in the center of the village, it being tantamount to murder (*ightiyāl*), I decide that the assailant's (*mughtāl*) hand shall be cut off (*qaṭʿ yad*), in accordance with tribal *ʿurf* and *ʿāda*, or, alternatively, in forgiveness (*bi-'l-ʿafwan* [*bi-'l-ʿafw*]) thereof, that one-third of [the value of]

---

106 Layish, *Archive*, Diya, No. 1, Aḥmad Ḥasan Ḥumayd, ʿAshīrat al-Ḥajāḥija, 2.8.1975; cf. Abū Ḥassān, *Turāth al-badw al-qaḍā'ī*, pp. 169–70.

107 Layish, *Archive*, Diya, No. 2, Muḥammad Sālim al-Dhuwayb ʿAshīrat al-Sharāyiʿa al-Taʿāmira, 31.3.1957.

108 The classification of the act as abominable is due to the fact that the victim was attacked from behind; the negative ethical expression "*munkar*" occurs also in Islamic law; cf. *makrūh* in *al-aḥKām al-khamsa* (Schacht, *Introduction*, pp. 120ff).

109 Qur'ān 17:81. The sanction of the Qur'ān is enlisted to enhance the validity of the tribal award.

> a person shall be paid, viz. one hundred dinars. And in respect of [Saʿīd's] falling to the ground [...] the injury being of a kind apt to be fatal, I award him fifty dinars.[110] [...] And the attacked man, Mr. Saʿīd, shall have the option of waiving or not waiving the cutting of the hand, and if he waives it, he will be a generous and compassionate person.[111]

As usual in obligations under customary law pertaining to homicide and grievous bodily harm, the fulfillment of which depends on a guarantee of a third party, the assailant was requested to provide a pledge of "honor," *wajh*, lit. "face." In other words, the guarantor, who undertook to the obligee (the plaintiff) that the principal (the defendant) would refrain from committing another assault, deposited his honor to secure the fulfillment of the obligation.[112] The stress laid on the stone with which the attack was carried out is in harmony with the *sharīʿa* which maintains that if the instrument is intrinsically likely to cause death, the presumption of intention exists and the act is deemed *qatl ʿamid*.[113] There is no explicit indication that the recommendation to opt for waiving amputation of the hand was inspired by Islam but such a possibility cannot be ruled out.[114]

## 5 Property

The Bedouin documents pertaining to land reflect a transitional period from the conception of land in terms of political control of territory to the conception of land in terms of private ownership and usufruct. This distinction is in harmony with the process of sedentarization that increases the attachment of the Bedouin to land within the framework of private households rather than an expression of tribal solidarity.

The conception of land in tribal political terms is manifested in Bedouin agreements pertaining to the partition of land in accordance with purely tribal

---

110 Usually a *gaṣṣāṣ* (expert) sets up the price for the injury caused; Stewart, *Texts*, pt. 1, p. 223; al-ʿAbbādī, *al-Qaḍāʾ ʿinda al-ʿashāʾir al-urdunniyya*, p. 288.

111 The option of choosing between retaliation and blood money exists in Islamic law only with respect to intentional (*ʿamd*) offense. In other categories blood money alone is permitted. See Peters, *Crime and punishment*, pp. 43–44.

112 Stewart, "The contract with surety," pp. 179–85; *idem*, "Customary law among the Bedouin," p. 267.

113 Peters, *Crime and punishment*, pp. 41–42; Anderson, "Homicide," p. 819.

114 Layish, *Archive*, Assault, No. 2, Ibrāhīm ʿAbd Allāh al-Darʿāwī ʿAshīrat al- Shawāwira al-Taʿāmira, 10.11.1973.

customary law.[115] In modern times, state law, rather than the *sharīʿa*, seems to have left a significant impact on these agreements. Bisharat maintains that central governments have a great interest in land as it is closely connected to taxes. Since parties to land disputes have to take into consideration the central authority (land settlement and registry), the domain of land ownership has become an entry point through which state legal principles enter the tribal legal system.[116]

In one case, the *shaykh*s, notables (*aʿyān*), heads of *ḥamūla*s (*wujūh*)[117] and leaders (*zuʿamāʾ*) of the *qabīla*s of al-Taʿāmira signed a general agreement (*ittifāq ʿumūmī*) regarding desert land (*arḍ barriyya*) they allegedly owned between the Dead Sea and the District of Bethlehem. All the desert land was to be divided among the three *ʿashīra*s, each *thulth* dividing its land among four *arbāʿ*,[118] and each *rubʿ* dividing its land among the members as agreed between them.

> Whoever is negligent in defense to secure confirmation of our ownership of the land, whether the negligence is caused by a physical act (*māddī*) or intention (*maʿnawī*),[119] shall lose his entitlement (*istiḥqāq*) to the land and be considered as seceding from the *ʿashīra*s of al-Taʿāmira, and his entitlement shall pass to the nearest *ʿashīra* in terms of agnatic relationship (*adnā ʿashīra taqrub aṣabiyyatahu*).[120]

The document reflects the point of transition from tribal land to private property.[121]

In a similar case, the *mukhtār*s and notables of the *ʿashīra*s of al-Ḥajāḥija, al-ʿUbayyāt, al-Maḥārida and al-Saʿada, ʿArab al-Taʿāmira, and ʿArab al-ʿUbaydiyya signed an agreement concerning the partition (*taqsīm*) of the land of al-Fashkha "which has been jointly (*bi-ʾl-ishtirāk*) owned and disposed of by us since ancient times." Each *ʿashīra* was entitled to receive one portion (*ḥiṣṣa*) out of

115 Cf. Stewart, *Bedouin boundaries*, p. 27.

116 Bisharat's comments.

117 Shmueli, *Hitnaḥalut ha-bedewim*, p. 34ii.

118 The original tribe of the al-Taʿāmira disintegrated (probably in the 19th century) into three politically independent tribes, *thulths*; each *thulth* consisted of four sub- tribes, *rubʿ*, headed by a *shaykh* in charge of the seasonal division of land and tax collection; Shmueli, *Hitnaḥalut ha-bedewim*, pp. 33–34.

119 Cf. Ḥasanayn, *Niẓām al-masʾūliyya*, pp. 30, 101, 136; *Farīq* al-Muzhir Āl Firʿawn, *al-Qaḍāʾ al-ʿashāʾirī*, pp. 211–12.

120 Layish, *Archive*, Land, No. 10, Sulaymān Sālim Muḥammad ʿAshīrat Ṣalāḥ al-Taʿāmira, 10.7.1935.

121 Cf. Shmueli, *Hitnaḥalut ha-bedewim*, p. 34i.

four. They undertook to pay all the fees and expenses proportionally owed on their respective portions,

> so as to protect our rights of ownership (*tamalluk*) and disposition in the above-mentioned lands of al-Fashkha before the land-settlement (*taswiya*) judge and all the civil (*niẓāmiyya*) judicial authorities in their respective grades and spheres of competence […]; and we undertake to make a concerted effort to submit the evidence (*bayyina*) required for registration of the land in the names of the aforesaid *ʿashīra*s in accordance with the above apportionment.

The instrument of agreement was made out in order that it might be possible to act upon it when necessary. [122]

Exchange of land (*tabādul*), unlike partition of land, is performed in accordance with the provisions of article 12 of the *Mejelle*, the Ottoman Civil Code of 1876. In a contract of agreement, the parties both of al-Taʿāmira, exchanged by way of offer (*ījāb*) and acceptance (*qabūl*) two parcels in the territory of al-Taʿāmira. The exchanged parcels passed to the ownership (*milk*) of the two parties. Each of them was entitled, in regard to cultivation, sowing, tilling and leaving untilled (*ʿamār wa-kharāb*), the demarcation of boundaries (*taḥdīd*), the planting of trees, the erection of structures, the digging of wells, sale and purchase, to deal with the land as full owners without outside interference:

> If either party defrauds (*iftirāʾ*), withdraws from (*nukūl*), acts corruptly (*fasād*) or cancels (*ibṭāl*) the exchange, he shall be guilty and shall have to pay […] to the other party as damages (*ʿaṭal wa-ḍarar*).[123]

In one case, the bride's mother received in trust (*amāna*) goats given as prompt dower. The case is dealt with in purely *sharʿī* terms. The woman of a sound mind (*ʿāqila*), in possession of all the required *sharʿī* and secular-legal (*qānūnī*) qualifications affirmed, acknowledged and attested

> that she had twenty-eight milch goats in trust (*amāna*) on behalf of her daughter […] – being property in full ownership (*milk*) [and part of her daughter's] private property as well as [part of] her prompt

---

122 Layish and Shmueli, *Legal documents on the Bedouin* of the Judaean desert, p. 111; Layish, *Archive*, Land, No. 4, Muḥammad Aḥmad Abū ʿĀmiriyya, ʿAshīrat al-Sharāyi,a, 12.11.1954; cf. Stewart, Bedouin boundaries, pp. 6–9. On division of land by means of qurʿa (lit. lot), see al-ʿAbbādī, *al-Jarāʾim al-ṣughrā*, pp. 172–73, 392, 412–13.

123 Layish and Shmueli, *Legal documents on the Bedouin of the Judaean Desert*, p. 12; Layish, *Archive*, Land, No. 8, Aḥmad Ḥasan Ḥumayd ʿAshīrat al-Ḥajāḥija al-Taʿāmira, 26.5.1962.

> dower – entrusted (*mawdūʿāt*) to her mother […] until she, the daughter, claimed it. [The mother] undertook to deliver the twenty-eight goats to her daughter on request or when necessary.[124]

*Rahn*, pledge of land as a security for a debt allowing the creditor the acquisition of the proceeds (*istighlāl*),[125] seems to be common practice among the Bedouin of the Judaean Desert. In all cases the pledges were effected strictly in accordance with *sharʿī* rules and terminology. The explicit prohibition of interest suggests that the pledgee (or rather the scribe?) was aware of the *sharʿī* prohibition, though the pledge is deemed one of the *sharʿī* devices for circumventing the prohibition on interest.[126] Thus, in one case, Ibrāhīm of ʿAshīrat Ṣalāḥ al-Taʿāmira attested as follows:

> I have pledged (*arhantu*), voluntarily and by my own choice, without duress and compulsion, my property [which passed into my ownership] by way of *sharʿī* inheritance (*irth*) […] in al-Taʿāmira territory […] to the bearer of this *sharʿī* document, Muḥammad […] of the said *ʿashīra*, in return for [… It was effected] by an absolute pledge (*rahn*) that must be observed (*marʿī*), which is free from deception (*ghabn*) and to which no corruption (*fasād*) attaches […] by making and taking *sharʿī* delivery (*taslīm, tasallum*), by consent (*riḍāʾ*), acceptance (*qabūl*), affirmation and acknowledgment, for I […] delivered the land to the pledgee and granted him the right to proceeds (*istighlāl*) thereof at will so long as it remained in his possession; he shall derive its proceeds until I pay him [the amount of the loan], whereupon he shall return the land to me without any deceit (*muḥāwala*);[127] […] the *darāhim* [the amount of the loan] shall bear no excess (*rabāʾ*).[128]

In a similar case, Adība, a widow of a Bedouin of ʿArab al-ʿUbayyāt al-Taʿāmira confirms that she received from Ḥasan of the same *ʿashīra* a sum of money by way of loan. In return

124 Layish and Shmueli, *Legal documents on the Bedouin of the Judaean Desert*, pp. 98–99; Layish, *Archive*, Trust and Deposit, Nos. 1–2, Sharārī [Abū Qāʾid] Muḥammad al-Aʿraj al-Saḥūrī al-Sawāḥira, 9.10.1934 and 9.8.1934 (deposit, *wadīʿa*, of the wife's dower with the husband); Stewart, *Texts*, pt. 1, p. 62 fn. 21; Schacht, *Introduction*, p. 157.

125 For a definition, see *Mejelle*, article 701; also article 1008 (reasons for preemption) ff.; cf. Schacht, *Introduction*, p. 142; *idem*, "Rahn," p. 400.

126 Schacht, *Introduction*, p. 79.

127 E.g., by leasing the land to a third party; see below.

128 Layish and Shmueli, *Legal documents on the Bedouin of the Judaean desert*, p. 97; Layish, *Archive*, Pledge, No. 1, Maḥmūd Fakhkhār of ʿAshīrat Ṣalāḥ al-Taʿāmira, 29.11.1952.

> I undertake to pay it back to him on demand, and I, on behalf of my children … and myself, have pledged (*arhantu*) to Ḥasan […] a parcel of land […] and allowed him to sow the parcel […] and derive the *sharʿī* benefit (*intifāʿ*) unopposed and unchallenged until the abovementioned sum is repaid when the land will return to its owner and the money to its owner. The money is given as an interest-free loan and the land is pledged without the pledgee having the right to lease it out (*māl bi-lā ribā wa-arḍ bi-lā ījār*) [to secure Adība's control of the estate].[129]

The document attests to the woman's capacity to own and dispose of real property which reflects a *sharʿī* rather than a customary norm.[130]

In a case of a different kind, ʿAwda of Ḥamūlat al-Rashāyida al-ʿUbaydiyya sells a certain plot allegedly in his ownership and possession (*ḥiyāza*) that he claims to have inherited from his ascendants, to some people of the ʿAshīrat al-ʿUbayyāt al-Taʿāmira in consideration of ninety-three French gold pounds. Actually we seem to be dealing here with a loan that had been given by ʿAwda's ascendants ninety-two years previously (in 1250/1834), against a pledge of the plot. Since the loan had never been returned, the pledged land seems to have passed to the ownership of the creditor.[131] Now ʿAwda, the heir of the pledgees, sells the pledged land back to the heirs of the pledger, the original owner of the land. It is claimed that the current sale is

> a definite (*bātt*), complete (*nājiz*) *sharʿī* agreement involving offer (*ījāb*) and acceptance (*qabūl*) […]. Seventy-five French pounds were received [in 1250] in the form of [i.e., against] a pledge (*bi-ṣūrat al-rahn*) [being considered now as the first installment on account of the sale], and I received eighteen French pounds on the date of the present document […]. In return, I have delivered the whole of the said land […] to the aforesaid purchasers; the act of receiving possession (*tasallum*) and alienation (*farāgh*) are legal and definite. They may dispose of it, the right of disposition (*taṣarruf*) being operative (*nāfidh*), absolute (*muṭlaq*), without contestation or challenge by anybody, as owners dispose of their property and holders of rights of their rights.[132]

---

129 Layish, *Archive*, Pledge, No. 2, al-Hājj Jūnus Abū Dayya ʿAshīrat al-ʿUbayyāt al-Taʿāmira, 11.7.1927.

130 Cf. al-ʿĀrif, *al-Qaḍāʾ bayna al-badw*, p. 239, article 28.

131 Cf. Schacht, "Rahn," p. 400i.

132 Layish, *Archive*, Pledge, No. 5, Nimr ʿAwda al-Mubārak Nabāhīn ʿAshīrat al-ʿUbayyāt al-Taʿāmira, 4th Dhū al-Qaʿda, 1345 AH [1926]. Cf. *bayʿ, bi-ʾl-wafāʾ*, sale with a right of redemption; Schacht, Introduction, pp. 78–79; Coulson, *History*, p. 142.

One of the witnesses, an agnate of the seller, acted as guarantor for the fulfillment of the seller's obligations undertaken under the contract, i.e., to transmit the plot on receipt of its entire price; in other words, we are dealing here with a tribal customary contract with surety, that is, a three-party (principal, obligee, and guarantor) contract of sale[133] merged with *sharʿī* terminology.

In a similar case it was agreed between the two parties, both of ʿAshīrat al-Waḥsh al-Taʿāmira, to conclude a contract of binding (*luzūm*) sale pertaining to a certain plot of land. It is stipulated in the contract that the purchaser may use (*yataṣarraf*) the plot so long as he does not return to the seller the money he has received for the plot. Once he returns the money, the contract of sale becomes void. On the face of it, we are dealing here with a sale with the right of redemption (*bayʿ bi-'l-wafāʾ*) whereby the option to repurchase the plot is reserved by the seller. However, from another stipulation in the contract of sale one may conclude that the plot had been pledged previously in return for a loan. Under the *sharīʿa*, the pledge (*rahn*) remains, by definition, in the ownership of the pledger; only the possession thereof is transferred to the pledgee.[134] Thus, it is stipulated that

> If the seller does not return the amount [to the purchaser] and objects to the pledgee (*mustarhin*) [i.e., the purchaser] using the land [as its owner], he shall pay a fine (*gharāma*) as damages (*ʿaṭal wa-ḍarar*) [… for the revocation of the transaction and in addition he shall have to return] the sum he had received beforehand [as a loan in return to the pledge].[135]

Schacht maintains that the concept of the right of pre-emption (*shufʿa*) was "eagerly adopted by popular custom."[136] The following cases demonstrate that the Bedouin of the Judaean Desert base the right of pre-emption on blood relationship, rather than on the *sharʿī* concept of neighborhood.[137] In one case, Ḥājja Khaḍra claimed, on behalf of herself and her minor children, permission to build a room at the front of the house of a certain Zaʿal on a plot jointly shared by the children's father (her husband) and their paternal uncle. The latter objected to her request. On the arbitrator's initiative, an agreement was

---

133 Stewart, "Customary law among the Bedouin," p. 268; for further details, see Stewart, "The contract with surety," p. 6.

134 Schacht, *Introduction*, pp. 138–40; Coulson, *History*, p. 142

135 Layish, *Archive*, Sale with Right of Redemption, No. 2, Aḥmad Ḥasan Ḥumayd ʿAshīrat Thulth al-Ḥajāḥija al-Taʿamira, 2.6.1933.

136 Schacht, *Introduction*, p. 78.

137 Cf. Coulson, *History*, pp. 49–50.

concluded under which the woman consented to the partition (*qism*) of the plot. The arbitrator decided that if the children's uncle

> sells his share (*ḥiṣṣa*) of the [... jointly-owned] land, then she, as the representative (*bi-'l-niyāba*) of the children of his brother [...], is worthier (*aḥaqq*) than anyone else to acquire the land at the current market price (*dārij*) or less. I [the arbitrator] have therefore permitted Ḥājja Khaḍra to build the room on the site adjoining (*mulāṣiqa*) the house of Zaʿal.

In a similar case, the purchaser decided to

> renounce [...] those *qīrāṭs* [...] which I bought from [the seller ...] since [the seller's] paternal cousins [his heirs] are worthier (*awlā*) as to those *qīrāṭs* than I am. Since they have reimbursed me for the sum which I paid to [the seller ...], I no longer have anything to do with those *qīrāṭs*, which have become the property of [the seller's paternal cousins].[138]

The renunciation here seems to be by virtue of the right of pre-emption based on blood relationship. In Palestine, the seller's blood relatives are first in order of priority (*awlawiyya*) for re-purchase and the neighbor is the last one though he is the worthiest for pre-emption (*aḥaqq bi-'l-shufʿa*).[139] In Jordan, the order of priority to the right of pre-emption is as follows: blood relatives (*aqārib*), partners (*shurakā'*), and the adjoining neighbor (*jār mulāṣiq*).[140] In Iraq, too, blood relationship (*qarāba*) precedes neighborhood; among the relatives, the closer in degree (*daraja*) to the deceased excludes the more remote.[141]

In an agreement for transfer of debt (*ḥawāla*) from the liability of one person to another (*ittifāqiyyat taḥwīl dayn*), the transfer was effected in a strictly *sharʿī* manner:[142]

---

138 Layish, *Archive*, Pre-emption, No. 1, Muḥammad Sālim al-Dhuwayb ʿAshīrat al-Sharāyiʿa al-Taʿāmira, 6.10.1965; and No. 2, Khaḍr [Abū Ṭālib] Muḥammad Ḥasan Jaʿfarī al-Sawāḥira, 20.8.1951, respectively.

139 Al-Salḥūt, *al-Qaḍā' al-ʿashā'irī*, pp. 36–37

140 Al-Qusūs, *al-Qaḍā al-badawī*, pp. 39, 41–42.

141 Ḥasanayn. *Niẓām al-mas'ūliyya*, p. 153; cf. Farīq al-Muzhir Āl Fir ʿawn, *al-Qaḍā al-ʿashā'irī*, p. 170 (it is forbidden to sell land outside the *ʿashīra*); Stewart, "Customary law among the Bedouin," p. 249 (when arable land is held by the individual, the territorial group usually has some control over its alienation to an outsider).

142 *Mejelle*, article 673 ff.; Schacht, *Introduction*, pp. 78, 148–49.

> I, the undersigned, Muḥammad […], refer (*ḥawwaltu*) my creditor, Ḥājj Khamās […] of al-Taʿāmira, to Ismāʿīl […] of ʿAshīrat al-Nabāhn al-Taʿamira […] considering that Ismāʿīl owes (*dayn, dhimma*) me seventy-six dinars and that I owe Hājj Khamīs one hundred and thirty-five dinars. I transfer to Ḥājj Khamīs the right to collect (*istilām*) the debt which Ismāʿīl […] owes me.[143]

## 6 Obligations and Contracts

Stewart writes that "commerce is not highly developed among the Bedouin, and as far as our knowledge extends, the contracts for transactions such as sale, hire and employment (for instance, of herdsmen or sharecroppers) are of no special legal interest,"[144] and that the three-party contract, which is essential for the implementation of obligations under arbitral decisions, is not generally used for commercial purposes.[145] Broadly speaking, these findings do not reflect the practice common among the Bedouin of the Judaean Desert, probably because the Bedouin there are in a fairly advanced stage of sedentarization – and for other reasons discussed below.

The Bedouin documents in our possession dealing with contracts and obligations are actually *sharʿī* documents almost in every respect because they seem to have been written by scribes well versed in the *sharīʿa*. The *sharʿī* law of contracts and obligations in its turn was ruled by a customary law which respected the main principles and institutions of the *sharīʿa*, but showed greater flexibility and adaptability, supplementing it in many respects.[146]

In specific areas, however, custom reigns supreme.[147] Thus in a contract of sale of an old thoroughbred mare (*faras aṣīla kuḥayla ʿajūz*), backed up by joint liability of the purchasers (*mutakāfilīn, mutaḍāminān*), the First Party of al-ʿUbaydiyya sold to the Second Party of al-Taʿāmira an eight-year-old cream-colored [?] (*ṣafrāʾ*) mare. The parties agreed that the price should be paid upon the expiration of two months, failure of which would entail the payment of twenty-five pounds as damages (*ʿaṭal wa-ḍarar*).

143 Layish, *Archive*, Ḥawāla, No. 1, Muḥammad Sālim al-Dhuwayb ʿAshīrat al-Sharāyiʿa al-Taʿāmira, 19.11.1968; cf. Shuqayr, *Taʾrīkh Sīnāʾ*, p. 418.

144 Stewart, "Customary law among the Bedouin," p. 266.

145 *Ibid.*, p. 268.

146 Schacht, *Introduction*, pp. 77–78, 144; cf. Petres, "Dakhla oasis," p. 81.

147 On the main features of the tribal customary sale, see al-Qusūs, *al-Qaḍāʾ al-badawī*, pp. 39–40.

> The First Party, the seller, stipulates with the Second Party, the purchasers, that the first and the second foals (*fāʾiẓ* [*fāʾiḍ*] [of the mare], if female, shall belong to the seller and if male, to the purchaser.[148] The Second Party undertakes that if it loses a foal of the mare, being a female, and thus does not deliver it to the seller, it will pay fifty pounds in current coin for this omission, being the non-delivery of the filly.[149]

There is evidence to the effect that already in the early 1830s, Bedouin concluded *sharʿī* contracts of sale.[150] Thus, in one case, two people of ʿArab al-Rashāyida, "Ottoman subjects," confirm that they sold to two brothers of ʿUrbān al-Taʿāmira ʿArab al-Nabāhīn a parcel of land situated in the territory of al-Rashāyida.

> [The transaction] is to be regarded as *sharʿī*, as an absolute (*bātt*) sale, completed (*nājiz*) and valid (*ṣaḥīḥ*) [...]. Receipt (*qabḍ*) [of the sum] and acknowledgment (*iʿtiraf*) [of receipt] are *sharʿī*. By virtue of all this, I release the said purchasers from all liability (*barītu* [*bariʾtu*] *dhimma*) for the specified price and from all amends (*jazā*[ʾ]*iyya*) responsibility [...]. be legally responsible (*ḍamān*) for it[151] as required under the *sharīʿa*. The undermentioned witnesses, voluntarily and by their own choice, have attested, that we, the sellers, have cleared the purchasers [...] of the responsibility to the charge of causing damages (*ḍarar*), and committing grave deception (*ghabn fāḥish*)[152] [...] we have therefore delivered into the possession of the purchasers [...] the whole of the object of sale [...] and have permitted them to dispose (*taṣarruf*) thereof at will [...] and we

---

148 Cf. al-ʿArif, *al-Qaḍā bayna al-badw*, pp. 144–45.

149 Layish, *Archive*, Absolute Sale, No. 41, Mūsā Muḥammad ʿAwdat Allāh al-ʿAṣāt al-ʿUbaydiyya, 11.6.1950. For a sale of the mare according to the custom relating to the horses (*ʿawāʾ id al-khayl*), see Layish, *Archive*, Absolute Sale, no. 41A Mūsā Muḥammad ʿAwdat Allāh al-ʿAṣāt al-ʿUbaydiyya, 4.7.1947; cf. al-ʿĀrif, *al-Qaḍāʾ bayna al-badw*, p. 145; al-Qusūs, *al-Qaḍāʾ al-badawī*, pp. 87–89; Oweidi, "Bedouin justice in Jordan," p. 152, n. 15.

150 Cf. Ḥasanayn. *Niẓām al-masʾ ūliyya*, pp. 150, 152.

151 Cf. *Mejelle*, articles 200, 416; Ḥasanayn, *Niẓām al-masʾ ūliyya*, p. 131; Layish, *Archive*, Liability for Damages, No. 1, Sharārī [Abū Qāʾid] Muḥammad al-Aʿraj al-Saḥūrī al-Sawāḥira, 11.7.1947 (it was agreed between the parties, both of ʿArab al-Sawāḥira, that "If a defect [*darak* or *tabiʿa*] as to ownership is found in this sale, the liability for the damages [*ḍamān*] shall be on the seller as required by the *sharīʿa*); cf. Schacht, *Introduction*, p. 139 (*darak*); *idem*, "Bayʿ," p. 111.

152 Cf. *Mejelle*, article 165; Schacht, *Introduction*, p. 117.

> undertake to appear before the Transactions Committee and to inform them of the sale.[153]

The following is a *sharʿī* contract of sale in every respect; yet remnants of tribal customary environment have been integrated into it. Maḥmūd of Thulth al-Ḥajāḥija al-Taʿāmira declares in the presence of eyewitnesses that he has sold, by an absolute *sharʿī* sale, a plot of land in al-Taʿāmira territory transmitted to him by way of *sharʿī* inheritance, to the bearer of this *sharʿī* document of Thulth al-Saʿada

> in accordance with the customs prevailing and established with us [...]. I have written this document in lieu of *kūshān tābū*, so that the purchaser may keep it until registration in the official land register is completed.[154]

The Bedouin are fully aware of the importance of the Land Registry as an instrument to safeguard their land rights. Thus in one case, both parties to a sale contract of ʿArab al-Sawāḥira, the sellers (consisting of 15 people including three sisters represented by a proxy) undertook to

> transfer the land to [the purchaser] at the Land Registry or register it at the Land Department or give him a power of attorney (*wakāla*) certified by the notary public (*kātib al-ʿadl*) of Jerusalem [...] to deliver the whole of the said parcel of land to the [purchaser] free of any sale, pledge, confiscation (*ḥajz*), pre-emption (*shufʿa*), contract of lease of agricultural land (*muzāraʿa*), priority (*awlawiyya*) right, and third-party right and from anything that might interfere with the registration [of the parcel] in the name of the [the purchaser].[155]

In the absence of land settlement, legal security seems to be the strongest incentive for reducing a *sharʿī* contract of sale in writing.[156] It is noteworthy

---

153 Layish, *Archive*, Absolute Sale, No. 12, Ibn ʿAwda al-Mubārak ʿAshīrat al-Nabāhīn al-Taʿāmira, 12.4.1247 AH [1831].

154 Layish and Shmueli, *Legal documents on the Bedouin of the Judaean Desert*, p. 81; Layish, *Archive*, Absolute Sale, No. 4, Sālim al-Zaḥlān Thulth al-Saʿada al- Taʿāmira, 27.4.1940. Cf. Absolute Sale, No. 32, ʿAlī Ḥasan Muḥammad ʿAshīrat al-Radāyida ʿArab al-Taʿāmira, 20th Jumāda 1321 AH [1903] (payment of damages in a *sharʿī* contract of sale "according to the regulations of the Sublime State [i.e., the Ottoman Empire] and Bedouin custom").

155 Layish, *Archive*, Absolute Sale, No. 33, Sharārī [Abū Qā'id] al-Aʿraj al-Sawāḥira, 17.10.1945.

156 External deed of sale in the absence settlement of titles (*taswiya*) is called *ḥujjat bay ʿkhārijiyya*; see Layish, *Archive*, Absolute Sale, No. 19A, Khaḍr [Abū Ṭālib] Muḥammad Ḥasan Jaʿafarī al-Sawāḥira, 28.2.1964.

that the First Party undertook to fulfill all his obligations under the agreement on the basis of mutual liability (*bi-'l-takāful wa-'l-taḍāmun*). Since no guarantor's name (*kafīl*) was mentioned, one may conclude that tribal solidarity was enlisted to strengthen a two-party contract under the *sharīʿa*.

The following sale attests to the principle of the separation of property between the spouses and to the woman's capacity to own and dispose of property; this capacity reflects *sharʿī* rather than tribal customary norms. ʿIwaḍ Allāh [...] al-Taʿāmirī ʿArab al-Zawāhira affirms:

> I have sold to my wife, Salma [...] al-Taʿāmirī [...] fifteen (15) head of small cattle in all [...] by absolute, final (*qaṭʿī*) sale, free from grave deception (*ghabn*) and corruption (*fasād*) [...]. I have accordingly delivered to the purchaser, my said wife, Salma [...], the whole of the object of sale [...], and permitted her to dispose (*taṣarruf*) of it at will, without hindrance, in any lawful way, as owners will dispose of their property and the holders of rights of their rights.[157]

In one case, the sale was performed by way of an exchange of land that seems to have been guided by economic considerations pertaining to cultivation. The parties of ʿAshīrat al-Sharāyiʿa and ʿAshīrat al- Ḥajāḥija, both belonging to al-Taʿāmira, contracted an agreement in which each party renounced to the other

> in exchange for the land he has received from the [other] party ...]. The renunciation is final and constitutes an absolute, final (*qaṭʿī*) sale by way of exchange (*tabdīl*), not open to revocation (*rujūʿ*) or withdrawal (*nukūl*) in any form whatsoever. At the same time, [each of the parties] permits the [other] party to receive his land and empowers him to take possession thereof, dispose thereof and enjoy the proceeds (*istighlāl*)[158] [. ... The transaction] involves no deceit (*ghabn*) or uncertainty (*gharar*).[159] Each party estimates the value of his land at one hundred Jordanian dinars and has received in exchange for it land worth just as much, neither more nor less.[160]

---

157 Layish, *Archive*, Absolute Sale, No. 3, Aḥmad Ḥasan Ḥumayd ʿAshīrat al-Ḥajāḥija al-Taʿamira, 28.3.1929.

158 Cf. Schacht, *Introduction*, p. 137.

159 Cf. *ibid.*, pp. 135, 146 ff.; Saleh, *Unlawful gain*, pp. 50 ff.; cf. Peters, "Dakhla oasis," p. 85.

160 Layish, *Archive*, Absolute Sale, No. 30, Muḥammad Sālim al-Dhuwayb ʿAshīrat al-Sharāyiʿa al-Taʿāmira, 16.8.1954.

The Bedouin of the Judaean Desert are not impressed by the *sharʿī* prohibition of interest.[161] Thus in a contract of sale, both parties belonging to ʿArab al- Ḥajāḥija, the seller undertook

> that if anyone should appear claiming to have a right (*mustaḥiqq*)[162] to all or part of the sold property (*mabīʿ*) and should sue the Second Party [purchaser], the First Party [seller] will […] return the full price of […] together with legal interest (*fāʾida qānūniyya*) from today's date until the date of the last payment, and damages.[163]

The following document demonstrates the use of the *sharʿī* authorization as an instrument for sorting out land transactions in the civil, *sharʿī* and tribal judiciary. It also attests to the capacity of women to own and dispose of property. Three brothers of ʿArab al-Sharāyiʿa al-Taʿāmira empowered someone by "authorization for specific purpose involving another person's right" (*wakāla dawriyya khuṣūṣiyya*)[164] to sell, by absolute sale, to Maryam a parcel of land in al-Taʿāmira territory which they had inherited from their father, in the Registers of the Property Tax, to take any necessary action at the Land Registry, and represent them before the civil (*niẓāmiyya*) and *sharʿī* courts in taking out a succession order (*iʿlām irth*). The agent was also authorized to

> represent us before any judicial authority […], appoint arbitrators, umpires and experts (*ahl khibra*) and oppose their election and decisions, submit evidence (*bayyiniāt*), tender oaths (*yamīn*), receive and serve process, level execution (ijrāʾ) and enforce judgments (*tanfīdh*), receive [money] (*qabḍ*), effect reconciliations (*ṣulḥ*), make acknowledgments (*iqrār*) and waive [rights] (*ibrāʾ*). We give this authorization in favor of a third party, the purchaser […] Maryam, as a power of attorney reverting to another person's right (*wakāla dawriyya*) [… This is an] authorization for a specific purpose (*khuṣūṣiyya*).[165]

---

161 Saleh, *Unlawful gain*, pp. 35 ff., 47–48.

162 Cf. Schacht, "Bayʿ," p. 1112ii.

163 Layish, *Archive*, Absolute Sale, no. 46, Aḥmad Ḥasan Ḥumayd ʿAshīrat al-Ḥajāḥija al-Taʿāmira, 10.10.1936; cf. Absolute Sale, no. 47, Muḥammad Abū Qāʾid al-Aʿraj al-Sāḥūrī al-Sawāḥira, 25.2.1944 (the seller undertook that if he infringed upon one of the sale contract's conditions, he should be required to return the price paid in addition to legal interest (*fāʾ-id qānūnī*) at the rate of nine per cent *per annum*); Shuqayr, *Taʾrīkh Sīnāʾ*, pp. 418–19.

164 *Mejelle*, article 1456.

165 Layish, *Archive*, Authorization, No. 2 [unsigned draft], Muḥammad Sālim al-Dhuwayb ʿAshīrat al-Sharāyiʿa al-Taʿāmira, n.d.

The terms of *muzāraʿa*, lease of a field, where the rent consists of a percentage of the produce, are in harmony with both *sharʿī* requirements[166] and the local practice among the Bedouin of the Judaean Desert though there are some variations. In a document of agreement as to the tenancy of agricultural land, both parties being residents of al-ʿUbaydiyya, it was agreed between the owner of three parcels of desert land and the tenant (*muzāirī*ʿ)-laborer (*ʿāmil*) for ploughing thereof and for planting various kinds of vegetables and cereals thereon, on the following conditions:

1. All the expenses [for cultivation, seeds, repairs, laborers and wages, etc.] shall be chargeable to the personal account of the tenant.
2. Partnership (*mushtarak* [*sharika*]) will be on the basis of one-third of the crop (*nātij*) going to [...] the owner of the land [. ... The tenant] may not give up any part of the land to another without prior consent from [the owner of the land].
3. If [the tenant becomes] unable to cultivate the land, he must vacate it at once and shall be fined [...] to be paid to [the owner] as damages [...]. The [owner] undertakes that if he withdraws from the contract [...] he shall be fined the same amount [...] as damages for the [tenant].
4. Delivery is made (*taslīm*) and taken (*tasallum*) with effect from the date on which this agreement comes into force until the end of the cereal planting season [of the sowing of the seeds] on [...]. The contract shall be renewed if the owner of the land so wishes.

In another agreement for the lease of land, people of ʿArab al-Nuṣay-rāt leased land to one of the Mukhtārs of al-ʿUbaydiyya for a whole year ending at harvest time. It was stipulated that

> The lessee may not lease the land to another. The lessors (*muʾajjirūn*) have no right to demand part of the crop because the land has been granted on lease (*ījār*) [...] and upon termination of the harvest at the end of this year the lessee shall restore possession of the land to the lessors.[167]

---

166 Schacht, *Introduction*, p. 155; cf. Donaldson, *Sharecropping*, pp. 60 ff.; Peters, "Dakhla oasis," pp. 79–91.

167 Layish and Shmueli, *Legal documents on the Bedouin of the Judaean desert*, p. 95; Layish, *Archive*, Partnership, No. 1, Yūsuf ʿAṭiyya ʿAliyyān, Mukhtār of al-ʿUbaydiyya, Ḥamūlat Rubayʿa, 13.9.1973; Lease, No. 3, Mūsā Muḥammad ʿAwdat Allāh al-ʿAṣāt al-ʿUbaydiyya, 18.8.1959, respectively; cf. Ḥasanayn, *Niẓām al-masʾūliyya*, p. 150; Layish, *Sharīʿa and custom in Libyan tribal society*, p. 243, doc. 65.

"The concept of corporation does not exist in Islamic law; only the *ʿāqila* can be regarded as a rudimentary form of corporation."[168] Schacht's observation seems to be still relevant in contemporary sedentary tribal society of the Judaean Desert. The cases below are formally defined as partnership, but there is indeed good reason to believe that the mechanism serving the functions of cooperation is strongly backed up by the notion of mutual responsibility and solidarity based on blood relationship.

In the first case, the whole ʿĀʾilat ʿAbd al-Qādir assembled with a view to building a road (*fatḥ ṭarīq*) next to the school of al-Sawāḥira al-Sharqiyya. They agreed upon the following conditions and signed them "willingly, of their own choice, without any coercion." The road was required for the transportation of sick persons, schoolchildren, water supply in times of shortage, and other essential public purposes (*maṣāliḥ*). The road was intended for all the members of ʿĀʾilat ʿAbd al-Qādir Ḥasan Jaʿfar (approximately three hundred), each sharing in the expenses in accordance with the number of the members of his ʿāʾila. All the participants (*mushtarikūn*) in the initiative were required to take action against the owners of the fences hindering the building of the road to the point of removing those fences. If anyone refused to pay towards the cost of the road, he should be forbidden (*yuḥram*) to derive any benefit from the road. In addition a complaint would be filed with the competent departments and the supreme authorities (*marājiʿ*).

> All the members of ʿĀʾilat ʿAbd al-Qādir shall sign this agreement and be bound by its conditions, and whoever infringes it shall be regarded as cut off (*mafṣūl*) from the *ʿāʾila*; the *ʿāʾila* shall not be responsible for his conduct and shall be prepared to publicly announce the dissociation (*barāʾa*) of its members from him and his doings.[169]

Strictly speaking, the *ʿāʾila* is not a legal person or entity in the conventional sense of the term; the association of its members for any specific purpose is not regulated by state law. Yet the enlistment of the members to the initiative of building a road by means of mutual responsibility and solidarity based on blood relationship and of social sanctions such as dissociation creates the notion of a rudimentary form of corporation.

168 Schacht, *Introduction*, pp. 155–56; cf. Stewart, "The contract with surety," pp. 194–6; *idem*, "Customary law among the Bedouin," pp. 247 ff.

169 Layish, *Archive*, Right of Way, No. 1, Khaḍr [Abū Ṭālib] Muḥammad Ḥasan Jaʿfarī al-Sawāḥira, 3.2.1965. Cf. Oweidi, "Bedouin justice in Jordan," p. 304; Stewart, *Texts*, pt. 1, Index, blood-money groups – disaffiliation.

In another case, the two parties who possessed "the utmost qualifications required under the *sharīʿa* to the validity of dispositions" (*akmal al-awṣāf al-muʿtabara sharʿan li-ṣiḥḥat al-taṣarrufāt*), have formed

> a partnership (*ishtaraka*) for the construction of a bridge leading to the water [of a spring?] after each of them has paid the amount agreed upon. All the amounts have been merged, as it were, into a single, indivisible fund (*māl*), and eventually, all the profits will belong to all of them, and each of them will be free to dispose of [his share of] the profits as he wishes. They undertake to adopt this arrangement out of fear of Allāh (*taqwā*), exalted be He, shunning embezzlement and complying with everything stipulated between them, each according to the number of his *qīrāts*; the loss (*khasrān*), too, shall be shared in this way [...]. If one of the persons named above deviates from an agreed stipulation, he shall have to pay the sum of [... as a fine].[170]

## 7 Conclusions

Tribal customary law in the Judaean Desert has been undergoing a process of Islamization the more the Bedouin become sedentary and the more they resort to the *sharīʿa* court. *Sharʿī* doctrines and legal terms infiltrate tribal law in the course of its adaptation to modern requirements through daily arbitration and occasional legislation in specific domains of law, as in the case of dower.

Tribal arbitrators become acquainted with the *sharīʿa* through their contacts with *sharʿī qāḍīs* and *muftīs*. Occasionally tribal arbitrations take place in their presence; moreover, the parties to the dispute are quite often advised by tribal arbitrators to have the tribal awards approved and sanctioned by *sharīʿa* courts. The *sharʿī maʾdhūn,* the solemnizer of marriages in tribal regions, is the *qāḍī*'s direct agent of Islamization of the tribal society. The scribe (*kātib*), who may be knowledgeable in the *sharīʿa* (he is not necessarily of Bedouin origin), contributes to the Islamization of tribal customary law by phrasing tribal documents in *sharʿī* terms.

The impact of the *sharīʿa* on tribal law differs from one domain of law to another. It is most profound in the domain of contracts and obligations,

170 Layish, *Archive*, Partnership, No. 3, ʿAlī Ḥasan Muḥammad al-Radāyida al-ʿUbaydiyya, n.d.; cf. Shuqayr, *Taʾrīkh Sīnāʾ*, p. 420 (partnership of agricultural purposes); Ḥasanayn, *Niẓām al-masʾūliyya*, p. 152 (*sharikat ʿudūla*, partnership for raising sheep and goats); Stewart, "The contract with surety," pp. 274–75.

especially sales. The contracts are based on the *sharʿī* conception of a two-party contract though occasionally it seems that a tribal pledge of honor, guarantee (*kafāla*), is enlisted to back it up. Sedentary Bedouin who are owners of land are anxious to have their property registered in the Land Registry or, in the absence of land settlement, secure their property rights by means of *sharʿī* documents based exclusively on the *Mejelle*; they realize that these documents are required to secure their rights in civil courts of all instances up to the Supreme Court whenever these rights are contested by a third party. Indeed, the oldest documents (dating back to the 1830s) available are contracts of sale pertaining to land and real estate.

Isolated instances of transfer of debt (*ḥawāla*) and authorization (*wakāla*) indicate that these too are based exclusively on the *sharīʿa*. This applies also to cases of tenancy contracts (*muzāiraʿa*): the terms of the contracts are in harmony with *sharʿī* requirements but there are some deviations having regard to local practice among the Bedouin of the Judaean Desert (such as lease of land for rent).

The impact of the *sharīʿa* is also manifested in documents dealing with pledge (*rahn*) though with some compromise with customary law. There is some indication that the fulfillment of obligations undertaken by the parties are ensured by guarantors which suggests that we are dealing here with tribal customary three-party contracts of sale merged with *sharʿī* terminology. The pledge is traditionally used as a device to circumvent the *sharʿī* prohibition on interest (*ribā*), but it may well be that the Bedouin are not fully aware of its religious-ethical aspect. Quite often the reference in the documents is to interest (*fāʾida*) in the secular, rather than *ribā* in the *sharʿī*, context.

The interaction between customary law and the *sharīʿa* has a special dimension in the domain of family law. Cases pertaining to marriage and divorce are dealt with concurrently by both tribal and *sharʿī* judiciaries. Sedentary Bedouin tend increasingly to resort to the *sharīʿa* court at the expense of tribal arbitrators. Moreover, it seems that tribal customary law is gradually yielding ground to the *sharīʿa* on its own soil. The two legal systems share some technical terminology and in spite of the methodological problems involved it seems safe to conclude that legal terms and doctrines pertaining to marriage and divorce should be conceived within *sharʿī*, rather than tribal, context. In matters concerning inheritance and wills, however, custom still reigns supreme; females and cognates are deprived of their *sharʿī* rights even after succession orders have been issued by the *sharīʿa* court. Renunciation of inheritance rights in favor of male agnates are occasionally backed up by guarantors, that is, by a third party. Nevertheless, there is significant evidence that daughters and wives do inherit real estate and enjoy the capacity to own and dispose of property; this *sharʿī* norm seems to reflect the status of women in rural and urban society.

In documents dealing with pre-emption (*shufʿa*) and partnership (*sharika*) there is a clear tendency to adapt the *sharʿī* institutions to norms of tribal society such as solidarity and corporation based on blood relationship. In such cases, one is tempted to conclude that the *sharīʿa* is maintained as far as terminology is concerned while the substance is purely customary.

The guarantors, who play an indispensable role in the procedure of tribal arbitration as a judicial system totally independent from the state, may be found occasionally in *sharʿī* legal documents. In the domain of evidence, tribal arbitrators use the same legal terminology, such as *yamīn* and *tazkiya*, as in the *sharʿī* judiciary. Usually the terminology seems to have a tribal customary connotation, but occasionally there seems to be some evidence connecting these terms to *sharʿī* context.

In the domain of homicide and grievous bodily harm, custom reigns supreme. Tribal awards are regulated and executed by a three-party contract; guarantors, rather than state execution department, are expected to enforce obligations undertaken by the parties. Close proximity to political and administrative centers, however, inevitably causes tribal arbitrators in the Judaean Desert to compete with the civil judiciary, the *sharīʿa* courts having no jurisdiction in these matters (except for blood money). Nevertheless, it seems that the *sharīʿa* leaves its imprint also on this domain. Tribal arbitrators seem to have mitigated and softened their approach to homicide; they make a distinction between intentional (*ʿamd*) and unintentional (*khaṭaʾ*) homicide as in the case of the motor vehicle accident, and in the latter case they recommend the *diya muḥammadiyya*.

Documents pertaining to the partition of desert land among the tribes are based during the period under review on pure tribal customary law with no reference whatsoever to the *sharīʿa*. The mere partition, however, reflects a transition from tribal land in territorial political terms to property in terms of private ownership. This conceptual transition brings the Bedouin law closer to the civil (and to a lesser extent to the *sharʿī*) legal system. Sales "according to the custom relating to horses" too are based on pure tribal customary law; they are backed up by a three-party contract.

The arbitrators in the Judaean Desert are highly pragmatic. They do not hesitate to resort concurrently to both *sharʿī* and civil law to the extent that this serves best the interests of the parties. The fact that they are committed to Islam and tend to identify customary law with the *sharīʿa* facilitates their rapprochement to the *sharʿī* legal system. At the same time the arbitrators need no ideological justification to adopt principles and mechanisms from the civil legal system; they are guided by pure practical considerations. The syncretism in the arbitrators' judicial practice resembles (with due reservations) the eclectic device (*takhayyur, talfīq*) in Middle Eastern and North African statutory legislation and judicial practice.[171]

Finally, these conclusions should be treated as an interim assessment since they are based on a small sample of the Bedouin documents in the author's possession. The conclusions are tentative awaiting further research on the basis of the entire corpus of the documents available; for the time being, their sole purpose is to outline some of the principal trends and mechanisms in the process of Islamization of tribal customary law of sedentary Bedouin in the Judaean Desert.

## Bibliography

### *Primary Sources*

Layish, A. Archive of legal documents collected from tribal arbitrators in the Judaean Desert.

### *Secondary Sources*

al-ʿAbbādī, Aḥmad ʿUwaydī. *Al-Jarāʾim al-ṣughrā ʿinda al-ʿashāʾir al-urdunniyya (1900–1986)*. Amman, 1408/1987.

al-ʿAbbādī, Aḥmad ʿUwaydī. *Al-Qaḍāʾ ʿinda al-ʿashāʾir al-urdunniyya*. Amman, 1988.

ʿAbd Allāh, ʿAbd ʿAlī Salmān. *Al-Mujtamaʿ al-rīfī fī 'l-ʿIrāq*. Baghdad, 1980.

Abū Ḥassān, Muḥammad. *Turāth al-badw al-qaḍāʾī*. Amman, 1974.

Abū Sinna, Aḥmad Fahmī. *Al-ʿUrf wa-'l-ʿāda fī raʾy al-fuqahāʾ: ʿarḍ naẓariyya fī 'l-tashrīʿ al-Islāmī*. Cairo, 1949.

Anderson, J.N.D. "Homicide in Islamic law." *BSOAS* 13 (1951): 811–28.

Antoun, Richard T. "The Islamic court, the Islamic judge, and the accommodation of traditions: a Jordanian case study." *IJMES* 12 (1980): 455–67.

al-ʿĀrif, ʿĀrif. *Al-Qaḍāʾ bayna al-badw*. Jerusalem, 1933.

Bailey, C. "Bedouin religious practices in Sinai and the Negev." *Anthropos, International Review of Ethnology and Linguistics* 79 (1982): 65–88.

Bisharat's comments = G. Bisharat's comments on the author's paper at the Princeton Conference on Customary Law, held at Princeton University, New Jersey on May 13–14, 2006, 2pp.

Coulson, N.J. *A history of Islamic law*. Edinburgh, 1964.

Coulson, N.J. *Succession in the Muslim family*. Cambridge, 1971.

171 Layish, "The transformation of the *Sharīʿa*," p. 102.

Donaldson, W.J. *Sharecropping in the Yemen. Study in Islamic theory, custom and pragmatism.* Leiden, 2000.

Farīq al-Muzhir Āl Firʿawn. *Al-Qaḍāʾ al-ʿashāʾirī.* Baghdad, 1941.

Ghayth, Muḥammad Ḥasan Abū Ḥammād. *Qāḍāʾ al-ʿashāʾir fī ḍawʾ al-sharʿ al-Islāmī.* 2nd ed. Jerusalem, 1410/1990.

Ḥasanayn, Muṣṭafā. *Niẓām al-masʾūliyya ʿinda al-ʿashāʾir al-ʿirāqiyya al-ʿarabiyya al-muʿāṣira.* Cairo, 1967.

Layish, A. "Adaptation of a jurists' law to modern times in an alien environment: the case of the *Sharīʿa* in Israel." *Die Welt des Islams* 46 (2006): 168–225.

Layish, A. "Challenges to customary law and arbitration: the impact of Islamic law upon settled Bedouin in the Judaean desert." *Tel Aviv University Studies in Law* 5 (1980–82): 206–21.

Layish, A. "Customary *Khulʿ* as reflected in the *Sijill* of the Libyan *Sharīʿa* courts." BSOAS 51.2 (1988): 428–89.

Layish, A. "*Dār ʿAdl* – symbiosis of custom and *Sharīʿa* in a tribal society in the process of sedentarization." JSAI 18 (1985): 198–213.

Layish, A. [331]*Divorce in the Libyan family. A study based on the* Sijill *of the* Sharīʿa *courts of Ajdābiya and Kufra.* New York & Jerusalem, 1991.

Layish, A. "The family *Waqf* and the *Sharʿī* law of succession in modern times." *Islamic Law and Society* 4 (1997): 352–88.

Layish, A. "The *Fatwā* as an instrument of Islamization of tribal society in process of sedentarization." BSOAS 54 (1991): 449–59.

Layish, A. [Revised] "The *Fatwā* as an Instrument of accommodation." In *Islamic legal interpretation. Muftis and their fatwas.* M.Kh. Masud, B. Messick and D.S. Powers, eds. Cambridge, MA., 1996, pp. 270–77.

Layish, A. "Interplay between tribal and *Sharʿī* law: a case of Tibbāwī blood money in the Sharīʿa court of Kufra." *Islamic Law and Society* 13 (2006): 63–75.

Layish, A. "The Islamization of the Bedouin family in the Judaean desert as reflected in the *Sijill*s of the *Sharīʿa* court." In *The changing Bedouin.* E. Marx and A. Shmueli, eds. New Brunswick, N.J., 1984, pp. 39–58.

Layish, A. *Legal documents on Libyan tribal society in process of sedentarization. A selection of decisions from the* Sijills *of the* Sharīʿa *courts of Ajdābiya and Kufra.* Pt. 1: *the documents in Arabic.* Wiesbaden, 1998.

Layish, A. "Maḥkama. 4. The Arab lands and Israel in the modern period." $EI^2$, s.v.

Layish, A. "The *Qāḍī*'s role in the Islamization of sedentary tribal society." In *The public sphere in Muslim societies.* M. Hoexter, S.N. Eisenstadt, and N. Levtzion, eds. New York, 2002, pp. 83–107.

Layish, A. "*Shahādat naql* in the judicial practice in modern Libya." In *Dispensing justice in Muslim courts: Qadis, procedures and judgments.* M.Kh. Masud, R. Peters and D.S. Powers, eds. Leiden, 2005, pp. 493–514.

Layish, A. Sharīʿa *and custom in Libyan tribal society. An annotated translation of decisions from the* Sharīʿa *courts of Ajdābiya and Kufra*. Leiden, 2005.

Layish, A. "Shariʿa u-minhag ba-mishpaḥa ha-muslimit be-yisraʾel (*Sharīʿa* and custom in the Muslim family in Israel)." *Hamizrah Hehadash* 23 (1974): 377–409.

Layish, A. "*Sharīʿa* and tribal custom in Libya: was Tajdīda married to two husbands?" *Archív Orientální* 63 (1995): 488–503.

Layish, A. "The transformation of the *Sharīʿa* from jurists' law to statutory law in the contemporary Muslim world." *Die Welt des Islams* 44 (2004): 85–112.

Layish, A. *Women and Islamic law in a non-Muslim state. A study based on the decisions of the* Sharīʿa *courts in Israel*. New York & Jerusalem, 1975.

Layish, A. and A. Shmueli. "Custom and *Sharīʿa* in the Bedouin family according to legal documents from the Judaean desert." *BSOAS* 42 (1979): 29–45.

Layish, A. and A. Shmueli. (eds.) *Legal documents on the Bedouin of the Judaean desert and the Negev. A selection of documents*. Jerusalem, 1975.

Libson, G. "On the development of custom as a source of law in Islamic law: *al-rujūʿu ilā al-ʿurfi aḥadu al-qawāʿidi al-khamsi allatī yatabannā ʿalayhā al-fiqhu*." *Islamic Law and Society* 4 (1997): 131–55.

Libson, G. "ʿUrf. 1. The status of custom in Islamic law." *EI*², s.v.

*Mejelle-i aḥkām-i ʿadliyye* [the Ottoman civil code of 1876].

Oweidi, Ahmed Saleh Suleiman. "Bedouin justice in Jordan." Ph.D. dissertation, Cambridge University, 1982.

Peters, R. *Crime and punishment in Islamic law: theory and practice from the sixteenth to the twenty-first century*. Cambridge, 2005.

Peters, R. "Shāhid." *EI*², s.v.

Peters, R. "Sharecropping in the Dakhla oasis: *sharīʿa* and customary law in Ottoman Egypt." In P. Bearman, W. Heinrichs and B.G. Weiss, eds. *The law applied. Contextualizing the Islamic* sharīʿa. *A volume in honor of Frank E. Vogel*. London, 2008, pp. 79–91.

al-Qusūs, ʿAwda. *Al-Qaḍāʾ al-badawī*, 2nd ed. Amman, 1972.

Saleh, N.A. *Unlawful gain and legitimate profit in Islamic law*. Cambridge, 1986.

al-Sawāḥira, Muḥammad Fahd Muḥammad al-Aʿraj. *Al-Mūjaz fī ʾl-qaḍāʾ al-ʿashāʾirī*. Jerusalem, 2003.

al-Salḥūt, Jamīl. *Al-Qaḍāʾ al-ʿashāʾirī*. Acre, 1987.

Schacht, J. "Bayʿ." *EI*², s.v.

Schacht, J. *An introduction to Islamic law*. Oxford, 1964.

Schacht, J. "Rahn." *EI*², s.v.

Shmueli, A. *Hitnaḥalut ha-bedewim shel Midbar Yehuda* (*Sedentarization of the Bedouin in the Judaean Desert*). Tel Aviv, 1970.

Shuqayr, Naʿʿūm. *Taʾrīkh Sīnīʾ*. Cairo, 1916.

Stewart, F.H. *Bedouin boundaries in central Sinai and the southern Negev. A document from the Aḥaywāt tribe*. Wiesbaden, 1986.

Stewart, F.H. "A Bedouin narrative from central Sinai." *Zeitschrift für Arabische Linguistik* 16 (1987): 44–92.

Stewart, F.H. "The contract with surety in Bedouin customary law." UCLA *Journal of Islamic and Near Eastern Law* 2 (2003): 163–280.

Stewart, F.H. "Customary law among the Bedouin of the Middle East and North Africa." *Nomadic societies in the Middle East and North Africa*. D. Chatty, ed. Leiden, 2006, pp. 239–79.

Stewart, F.H. *Honor*. Chicago, 1994.

Stewart, F.H. *Texts in Sinai Bedouin law*. Pt. 1. *The texts in English translation*. Wiesbaden, 1988.

Stewart, F.H. *Texts in Sinai Bedouin law*. Pt. 2. *The texts in Arabic*. Wiesbaden, 1990.

Stewart, F.H. "Tha'r." *EI*², s.v.

Stewart, F.H. "ʿUrf. 2. Arab customary law." *EI*², s.v.

Tsafrir, Nurit. "Arab customary law in Israel: *Ṣulḥa* agreements and Israel courts." *Islamic Law and Society* 13,1 (2006): 76–98.

Wensinck, A.J. *Concordance et indices de la tradition musulmane*. 8 vols. Leiden, 1992.

al-Yamānī, Sālim. *Sīnāʾ. Al-arḍ wa-'l-ḥarb wa-'l-bashar*. Cairo, 1975.

Zysow, A. "The under-theorization of custom in Islamic law." A paper submitted to the Conference on Customary Law held at Princeton University, New Jersey on May 13–14, 2006.

CHAPTER 5

# The *Qāḍī*'s Role in the Islamization of Sedentary Tribal Society

## 1 Introduction[*,1]

The discourse pertaining to such terms as *civil society* and *public sphere* is closely connected with the history of Western society and state.[2] This point should be borne in mind when attempting to translate these terms into the reality of Muslim society and state. In theory, there is no separation of state and "church" in Islam.[3] Although theocracy is not the commonest political system in modern Islam,[4] significant remnants of this religio-political system have survived in some contemporary Muslim countries. For instance, the 1980 Egyptian Constitution maintains that the *sharīʿa* (the non-codified Islamic law) is the main source of legislation (Article 2).[5] Muslim countries have adopted Western conceptions of political system, including the separation of powers – a principle totally alien to Islamic classical theory. However, it seems that the process of internalizing this principle has not so far been completed. Moreover, since the early 1970s there has been an increasing tendency toward the Islamization of the legal system in such countries as Libya, Iran, the Sudan, and Pakistan by means of statutory legislation and court decisions making the validity of statutory provisions conditional on their conformity to the *sharīʿa*.[6]

Taylor distinguishes three modes of civil society in the West: the first exists in societies where there are free associations, not under the tutelage of state power; the second (with a wider sense) exists where society as a whole can

---

* My colleagues Miriam Hoexter, David Powers, Frank Stewart, and Knut Vikør read an earlier version of this essay and made useful comments for which I am most grateful. [Originally published in Miriam Hoexter, Shmuel Eisenstadt, and Nehemia Levtzion (eds.), *The Public Sphere in Muslim Societies* (New York: State University of New York Press, 2002), pp. 83–107.

1 "Islamization" in this essay denotes the process of bringing tribal society closer to normative Islam, not conversion. Cf. Levtzion 1979a, 19, 21; 1981, 78.

2 See e.g. Taylor 1990; Calhoun 1992; Cohen and Arato 1992. I am indebted to Professor S.N. Eisenstadt for these references.

3 Mayer 1987, 130–39.

4 Layish 1984b; 1987.

5 Some Egyptian judges in civil courts, by invoking Article 2, refused to apply statutory provisions contradictory to the *sharīʿa*. See Layish and Shaham *EI*²b.

6 Mayer 1987, 150–66.

 | DOI:10.1163/9789004680920_007

structure itself and coordinate its actions through such associations, which are free of state tutelage; and the third (which is an alternative or supplement to the second) exists where the ensemble of associations can significantly determine or inflect the course of state policy.[7]

The premodern Muslim society seems to fit in with the first (the narrowest) mode of civil society. Prior to the integration of the *ʿulamāʾ* (sing, *ʿālim*; scholars of religious sciences) in the state establishment one could trace in the Muslim society substantial elements of civil society. Levtzion analyzes the *ʿulamāʾ*'s role as intermediaries between the rulers and their subjects to the extent that the *ʿulamāʾ* enter the definition of "free association, not under the tutelage of state power": on the one hand, they bestowed legitimacy using their religious prestige to secure the obedience of the masses to the ruler's authority; on the other hand, they acted as representatives of the masses communicating to rulers the popular grievances. The *ʿulamāʾ*'s attitude toward the political authorities was ambivalent: they recognized the need for a strong government to defend Islam from external and domestic threats; but as an independent (also in economic respects) class or association they considered almost every government by definition as oppressive and declined to cooperate with it or accept governmental nominations so as to avoid being corrupted. As guardians of the *sharīʿa* and the public morals it was their duty, they believed, to guide the political rulers, from outside, on how to apply the *sharīʿa* properly.[8] In this respect one may compare the role of the noninstitutionalized *ʿulamāʾ* to that of the intellectuals in Western civil society.

The process of integration of the *ʿulamāʾ* into the state establishment, which had started already in the Middle Ages, has been completed in the twentieth century. The *muftī* (a specialist in *sharīʿa* who gives authoritative legal opinions), perhaps the most important agency for the development of the *sharīʿa* and the preservation of its vitality, the *qāḍī* (the judge of a *sharīʿa* court), in charge of the application of the *sharīʿa* in day-to-day reality, and other religious functionaries have been incorporated into the civil service with a view to implementing the government's policy.[9] It goes without saying that the loss of independence from the political authority diminishes the *ʿulamāʾ*'s ability to fulfill their traditional role as intermediaries and guardians of the *sharīʿa* and the public morals. In this respect contemporary Muslim society has lost a vital element of civil society, though the function of the *ʿulamāʾ* may have been taken over by secular intellectuals and other associations.

---

7 Taylor 1990, 98.
8 Levtzion 1979b.
9 Layish 1989, 5.

## 2 The Function of the Sharīʿa in Sedentary Tribal Society

### 2.1 *The* Qāḍī's *Autonomy*

This chapter is concerned with the role of the *qāḍīs*, an essential part of the *ʿulamāʾ*, in contemporary Muslim society. To what extent is the *sharīʿa* court a "public sphere" in the sense that the *qāḍī* is capable of formulating norms of social, ethical, and legal behavior independently – that is, outside the control of the political authority – and of imposing them on Muslim society? An attempt will be made below to assess the *sharʿī qāḍī*'s autonomy and his impact on tribal society in the process of sedentarization in modern Libya (broadly speaking from the early 1930s to the early 1970s) and the Judean Desert (from the last quarter of the nineteenth century to the early 1970s) on the basis of legal documents collected from the *sharīʿa* courts of Ajdābiya and Kufra in Libya and of Bethlehem, and tribal arbitrators in the Jerusalem-Bethlehem region.[10] The case pertaining to denial of paternity, which appears at the end of this chapter is meant to provide an illustrative notion of the *qāḍī*'s scope of autonomy, which is significant in the context of the public sphere.

On the face of it the question seems to be irrelevant since the *qāḍī* is part of the state apparatus. He is a delegate of authority invested with the power of jurisdiction (*qaḍāʾ*). He is nominated either by the caliph himself (who, in theory, retains the power to exercise justice in person) or by his intermediate representatives (*wazīr*, governor of a province, etc.).[11] In other words, the ruler appoints the *qāḍī*, pays his salary, and dismisses him from office when he deems it necessary. One might be tempted to conclude that this pattern of delegation intrinsically does not allow the *qāḍī* a wide measure of autonomy.

Moreover, among the *ʿulamāʾ* and *fuqahāʾ* (sing.: *faqīh*; jurists, experts in *fiqh*, the science of the *sharīʿa*, the sacred law of Islam) it is the *muftī*, rather than the *qāḍī*, who best represents the class of (religious) intellectuals of premodern Muslim society. This assertion refers first and foremost to the original concept of the *muftī* dating back to the ʿAbbāsids (750–945), before he

10 The Libyan legal documents were placed at my disposal by Professor John Davis of Oxford University. The legal documents from the Judean Desert were collected with the assistance of my colleague, the late Dr. Avshalom Shmueli of Tel Aviv University. I am profoundly grateful to both of them. The findings and conclusions below are drawn freely from my previous research conducted on the basis of these material sources with a view to presenting them within an integrative thesis on *sharīʿa* and custom in tribal societies and within the context of public sphere.

11 The most authoritative source on the history and organization of the office of the *qāḍī* is Tyan 1960. See esp. 100ff. For a short survey see Tyan *EI*². Cf. Levtzion 1979b, *passim*.

became integrated into the political establishment.[12] Even today there are – alongside nominated *muftīs* – independent *muftīs* whose status is a function of their learned reputation.[13] Indeed, *muftīs*, not *qāḍīs*, were the creators and exponents of the *sharīʿa*, which is a set not only of legal norms but also of ethical values. The *sharīʿa* is a "jurists' law" – that is, a system of law that developed outside an official legislature and the control of the executive authority. All the efforts of rulers – during the formative period of the *sharīʿa* – to institutionalize the independent *fuqahāʾ* in order to shape the legal norm to suit political purposes were in vain. The *sharīʿa* did not undergo a formal process of codification until the late nineteenth century. The first codification was the *Mejelle*, the Ottoman Civil Code (1869–1876). From the strict *sharʿī* point of view, codification itself implies the transformation of the *sharīʿa* from a jurists' law to statutory law, with all the attendant consequences: departure from the religious-legal literature; disruption of the *sharʿī* legal methodology of sources of law (*uṣūl al-fiqh*); and collapse of the legal professional class of the *fuqahāʾ* and *muftīs*, the authorized exponents of the *sharīʿa*.[14]

On the other hand, the judicial practice of the *qāḍīs* was never regarded as a formal source of law. The historical contribution of *qāḍīs* to Islamic law took place during the Umayyad Empire (661–750), prior to the emergence of the class of *muftīs*. By using unrestricted personal reasoning or discretion (*raʾy*) and religious ethical norms derived from the Qurʾān, the *qāḍīs* succeeded in assimilating elements of foreign legal systems that gradually penetrated into legal practice. In this respect they laid the foundations for the creation of the *sharīʿa*; but case law – that is, law settled by precedent[15] – was never recognized by Islamic legal theory as a source of law. Islamic law developed as an expression of a religious ideal in contrast to practice.[16] A sophisticated legal methodology was created later by the *muftīs*. The "judicial practice" (*ʿamal*) that emerged in Morocco beginning in the late fifteenth century seems to be a single instance of a "realist" form of Islamic jurisprudence that was intended to bring custom within the orbit of Mālikī law. Its significance from the point of view of legal theory is, however, disputed by scholars.[17]

Although the *qāḍī* is subject to the ruler who appoints him to the office and can dismiss him at will, he nevertheless enjoys a measure of autonomy with

12 Masud, Messick, and Powers 1996b.

13 Layish 1996.

14 For details see Layish and Shaham *EI*²b.

15 Cf. Black 1990, 216.

16 Schacht 1964, 19–22; Coulson 1964, 28–35; Layish 1984a, 54. For a different view see Crone 1987, 15–16.

17 Milliot 1953, 156–69, 167–78; Berque *EI*²; Coulson 1964, 143ff.; Schacht 1964, 61–62; Serrano [Ruano] 1996; Layish 1984a, 55.

regard to the application of the non-codified *sharīʿa* in matters that are within the *sharīʿa* court's jurisdiction. The *qāḍī* is subject to the ruler only administratively; otherwise – that is, as far as the substantive law applicable in court is concerned – he is subject to the *sharīʿa* alone.[18] From the point of view of the *qāḍī*, codification implies subordination to legal norms shaped by earthly legislature outside the control of the *fuqahāʾ*. Thus, with regard to the *sharīʿa* courts of Ajdābiya and Kufra from the early 1930s to the early 1970s, the *qāḍī* was totally independent in this respect. The first codification of the law of personal status in Libya took place in 1972 (but unfortunately, its application is not reflected in the decisions available to me).[19] In case of doubt in any substantive or procedural matter the *qāḍī* might – though this happens quite rarely – consult any Mālikī *muftī* or a legal treatise, according to his free choice.[20] The ruler had no standing in this matter. Moreover, the ruler was concerned in the first place with the maintenance of public order (including cases of homicide or bodily injury, which are in fact within the domain of Islamic private rather than public law) and, as might be expected, matters of personal status were not usually of great concern, unless a certain legal norm disturbed public order.[21] On the other hand, the law applicable in the *sharīʿa* court of Bethlehem, under whose jurisdiction the Bedouin of the Judean Desert fall, underwent codification. The *sharīʿa* applying to matters of personal status was replaced by the Ottoman Family Rights Law of 1917 and by the Jordanian family laws of 1951 and 1976, successively.[22] The *qāḍī*'s autonomy in this court, as far as the material law is concerned, is less than that of the Libyan *qāḍī* in the period under review.

## 3 Sedentary Tribal Society, Custom, and *Sharīʿa*

The population of Cyrenaica and the Judean Desert, which is the object of this study, is different with respect to social, economic, and political conditions, and school of law and material law applicable in the *sharīʿa* courts. Moreover, substantial differences exist even within Cyrenaica itself between the regions

18 The *qāḍī*'s autonomy is greater than that of the civil judge, who is bound by statutory legislation and by precedents of the supreme court.

19 For further details see Layish 1991, 14–15; 1998, 19–20.

20 The Islamic legal treatises most commenly cited in the courts' record were written by Ibn ʿĀṣim (d. 829/1426) 1958, ʿIllaysh (d. 1299/1881–1882) n.d., and al-Ṣāwī (d. 1241/1825–1826) 1806. Cf. Powers 1994.

21 The Italians sought to retain a certain measure of normative supervision over the decisions of the *qāḍīs* in matters that were contrary to public policy. The "sleeping embryo" (*ḥaml nāʾim*) is a case in point. For details see Layish 1991, 5–6; 1998, 57 doc. 38.

22 Anderson 1976, 41; Layish and Shaham *EI*²a; Layish *EI*²c, *EI*²b, *EI*²a.

of Ajdābiya and Kufra. In spite of these differences, Cyrenaica and the Judean Desert share one fundamental feature: in both cases tribal societies in the process of sedentarization are being brought within the orbit of the *sharīʿa*.[23]

Ajdābiya, a district center in the cultivable plain near the Mediterranean coast, has always been an important center, owing to its location at a strategic junction of roads leading to Tripoli in the west, Benghazi, Alexandria, and Cairo in the east, and Kufra and Khartoum in the south. The town was the seat of the Sanūsī government during the short period of indirect rule under the Italians. The people in this area are part of the Saʿādī confederation of tribes, the principal tribes being the Maghāriba and Majābira. In the town of Ajdābiya, however, they are outnumbered by members of other tribes and clans. Kufra, far in the south, consists of oases and is also located on trade routes. Kufra was the administrative center for the Sanūsiyya and a command headquarters during the resistance to French expansion. The Zuwayya tribe is the largest population group and the dominant one; but there are other tribes, black-skinned and white-skinned, immigrant laborers from Chad and the Sudan; *Ikhwān* ("brothers" – that is, descendants of officials and servants of *zāwiyas* of the Sanūsī order who remained in Kufra after the abolition of the order); and emancipated slaves integrated into the Zuwayya genealogy. The tribes in these two regions are in different stages of sedentarization.[24]

The Bedouin in the Judean Desert are a group of tribes in the Jerusalem-Bethlehem region: al-Sawāḥira east of Jerusalem, al-ʿUbaydiyya east of Bayt Sāḥūr, the al-Taʿāmira tribes extending from Bayt Sāḥūr in the north to Bayt Fajjār in the south, and al-Rashāʾida southeast of Taqūʿa. The settlement of these Bedouin, which began in the 1920s and was almost complete by the 1970s, was accelerated by proximity to Jerusalem and Bethlehem and by domestic security policy. Al-Taʿāmira tribes have established settlements of their own in existing Judean villages and in the suburbs of Bethlehem. About half of these Bedouin no longer live within a tribal framework.[25]

As is known, normative Islam, with its system of beliefs, institutions, and laws, plays no central part in the shaping of a nomadic society.[26] Folk religion, including saint worship and intercession, still predominates. Moreover, in Cyrenaica vestiges remain of the Sanūsiyya, an instance of Ṣūfī order, adapted to the institutional and normative system of a tribal society – although the

23 Cf. Levtzion 1981, 80.

24 The assessment regarding sedentarization is disputed by J. Davis. See Davis 1998, 11. Cf. Layish 1991, 15–18 and the sources indicated there.

25 For further details see Layish and Shmueli 1979, 29.

26 Cf. Gellner 1969, 8ff., 135–36; 1984, 23–24, 30; Levtzion 1979a, 20; 1981, 79; Shaham 1993, 192–93 and the source indicated in n. 3.

Sanūsī establishment started to disintegrate after the Italian invasion in 1911.[27] Custom survived even when its followers had nominally adopted Islam. Western and Muslim scholars have observed that although Bedouin in various parts of the Muslim world consider themselves to be Muslims, their knowledge of Islamic doctrine, worship, and ethics is modest (this applies also to the Cyrenaican Bedouin even after the Sanūsī revivalist movement had become established in their midst). Thus, they are negligent in the carrying out of such religious obligations as performing public prayer in the mosque on Fridays, and customary law has the upper hand in its encounter with Islamic law. Their acceptance of Islamic law is partial and slow. Although the Islamization of the Bedouin has been going on for centuries it has not yet been completed in every respect.[28] As might be expected, the Bedouin are not fully aware of this process. They identify themselves as Muslims. They believe in Allāh and resort to him in various circumstances.[29] They regard tribal law as part of their Islamic heritage, although some of the customs are inconsistent with normative Islam.[30] The fact that the Bedouin identify their daily practice with the *sharīʿa* in every respect is naturally of great significance. The outside observer, however, cannot and should not stop at this point but rather must make a clear distinction, devoid of value judgment, between orthodox *sharīʿa* and tribal custom.[31] There is ample evidence to the effect that the Libyan *qāḍī*s themselves are fully aware of the distinction between *sharīʿa*, custom (*ʿāda*) and statutory law (*qānūn*). The *wakīl qāḍī* (the *qāḍī*'s deputy) of Bethlehem, Shaykh Muḥammad Saʿīd Jamāl al-Rifāʿī, maintains that "custom (*ʿurf, ʿāda*) is binding law (*ḥukm mulzim*), provided that it does not conflict with an explicit provision (*naṣṣ*) of the Qurʾān and the *sunna*."[32]

The sedentarization of the Bedouin in modern times brings them under the control of the central government, one aspect of which is the *sharīʿa* court. Under Italian rule the Bedouin of Cyrenaica applied to the *sharīʿa* courts only to a limited extent, preferring to settle their affairs according to tribal custom.[33]

27 Davis 1987, 110 n. 15.

28 Cf. Levtzion 1979a, 7, 19–20; 1981, 78.

29 For details see Layish and Shmueli 1979, 41–42.

30 For details see Layish 1991, 170–71; Gellner 1969, 47; 1981, 100; 1984, 38; Evans-Pritchard 1949, 62; Colucci 1927, 24; Milliot 1953, 157, 166; Layish and Shmueli 1979, 31; al-ʿAbbādī 1988, 163, 179–83, 198–99, 406–7, based on Oweidi 1982, 121, 134–37, 149, 321–22 and Coulson 1964, 135–36; Laoust 1939, 519ff.; 1965, 323, 324; Smith 1963, 48ff.; Goldziher 1981, 238ff.; Baer 1964, 132 and the sources indicated there; 1969, 13, 14; Henninger 1959, 125ff. and the sources indicated there (I am indebted to Professor M.J. Kister for this last reference).

31 Cf. Gellner 1969, 68, 105ff., 129ff., 135; Rosen 1995, 194–97, 201, 206; Davis 1998, 12.

32 For Libya see Layish 1991, 175–76, 185–91. For Bethlehem see Layish 1984a, 41–42.

33 Cf. Gellner 1969, 105ff.; Lewis 1984, 153.

In the early 1970s their recourse to the *sharīʿa* courts increased although they did not cease to apply concurrently to the tribal courts.

Researchers have suggested several explanations for the Bedouin's application to the *sharīʿa* courts:[34]

1. Sedentarization, which brings the Bedouin closer to normative Islam and hence increases their respect for the *qāḍī*'s moral and religious authority and his function as the nominal head of the school of law (*madhhab*).
2. The spread of religious education and modern means of communication.
3. Geographical proximity to urban, religious, administrative, and economic centers.
4. The imposition – on the initiative of the central government – of *sharʿī* jurisdiction on the Bedouin along with the abolition of statutory tribal jurisdiction (in the case of Jordan),[35] with a view to strengthening the Muslim establishment as a means to consolidate the government's position in tribal society. From the point of view of the central government, it is easier to rule through its control of institutionalized normative Islam rather than trying to control popular religion and customs that vary from one place to another and are dominated by indigenous leaders competing among themselves for power.
5. Administrative exigencies in a modern state. Thus, for example, confirmation of marriage by a *qāḍī* or a *sharʿī* solemnizer is required to ensure that no impediments to marriage exist between the parties that may render the marriage irregular (*fāsid*) or null and void (*bāṭil*). Registration of changes in marital status by the *sharīʿa* court is also required to secure social allowances and education and medical care for children, and a *sharʿī* order of succession is required to effect property rights and transactions in the land registers.

---

34 For details see Davis 1987, 223–25, 228; Layish 1991, 127, 182–83; 1984a, 39–40 and the sources indicated there. Cf. Levtzion 1979a, 21; 1979b; 1981, 79.

35 The statutes pertaining to the establishment of tribal courts, including the Tribal Court of Appeal of 1936, were abolished in 1976. Jordanian law still applies in the West Bank. See al-ʿAbbādī 1988, 114ff., 445. In Israel, the tribal courts in the Negev, which had been established during the British Mandate, were abolished though their judicial basis has been left intact. I have found no indication in Libyan *sharīʿa* courts of the existence of statutory tribal courts, but there is ample evidence that matters were settled out of *sharīʿa* courts in accordance with tribal law, most probably by tribal arbitrators on a voluntary basis and with the mutual consent of the parties, as is the case in the Judean Desert. Tribal arbitrators (with no formal status) in the Judean Desert deal with issues pertaining to matters of personal status and succession (in competition with the *sharīʿa* courts), penal matters (homicide and bodily injury), property, obligations, and contracts (in competiton with the civil courts).

6. Equality of all parties, regardless of their tribe, origin, color, or legal position in the *sharīʿa* court. (There is evidence of the rights of manumitted slaves being protected there).[36] True, the position of women and cognates under the *sharīʿa* is not equal to that of men and agnates, respectively. However, their position under the *sharīʿa* is much better than under tribal customary law. Indeed, some evidence suggests that the *sharīʿa* court is preferred especially by people whose position in traditional society is weak and who therefore cannot realize their rights under the tribal customary system. Thus, the *sharīʿa* court is applied to by divorced women who have been denied their financial rights or by heirs deprived of their share in the estate under customary law. The applicants expect the *sharīʿa* court to determine their rights under the *sharīʿa*.[37]
7. The executive power of the *sharīʿa* court provides legal security for the realization of legal and financial rights between the parties.

Although there can be no doubt that application by sedentary Bedouin to the *sharīʿa* court reflects to some extent a genuine religious transformation,[38] administrative exigencies and practical considerations are no doubt the main causes of this phenomenon. In any case, once the process of sedentarization starts, normative Islam gradually becomes a more binding lifestyle as regards worship, religious duties, and law in those domains with respect to which the sedentary Bedouin apply to the *sharʿī* judicial system and the exponents of the *sharīʿa* – namely, in matters of personal status and succession.

## 4 The *Qāḍī*, Custom, and *Sharīʿa*

From the *sijills* of the *sharīʿa* courts and the documents collected from tribal arbitrators, one may conclude that the more the Bedouin become sedentarized the closer they are brought within normative Islam.[39] The complex of relations between *sharīʿa* and tribal custom may be divided into two main

36 See Layish 1998, 78–79 doc. 62.

37 Cf. Shahar 1997, 24–25. Cf. Kressel 1992, 94–95, 166, 184.

38 There is evidence that already in the nomadic period Bedouin of the Judean Desert would visit the al-Aqṣā Mosque, the Dome of the Rock, and the markets of the old city of Jerusalem on Fridays. Layish 1980–1982, 220; 1996, 276 and the source indicated in n. 25. On the performance of religious obligations among the Bedouin of central Sinai see Stewart 1988, 7, 17, 44, 53n., 194; 1987, 53; Lewis 1984, 152–53. I have found no evidence in the *sijills* (court records) to the effect that the Bedouin resort to the *sharīʿa* court is inspired by their desire to belong to the Islamic body politic; such a possibility, however, cannot be ruled out.

39 Cf. Levtzion 1981, 78.

categories. In one custom reigns supreme, outside the control of the *sharīʿa*, with only minor concessions to the *sharīʿa*. Included in this category are "gift" (*ʿaṭāʾ*) marriages[40] that do not meet the *sharʿī* requirements for contractual validity (offer and acceptance, etc.) and other residual traces of customary marriage according to which a woman is not a party to the marriage contract, such as the marrying off of a girl by her guardian (*walī*) against her will (*wilāyat ijbār*), contrary to the Ḥanafī doctrine with respect to a girl who has reached maturity. Also in this category is exchange marriage (*tabādul zawjāt, shighār*) – that is, the mutual waiver of the payment of dower for the two brides, each of them representing the dower of the other;[41] customary legal maxims couched in rhyme pertaining to deferred dower payable upon divorce or death of one of the spouses;[42] *khulʿ* ("divestiture," divorce by agreement, by which the wife redeems herself from the marriage for a consideration), in which a promissory note (*quṣṣa*) in the amount of the dower is drawn up and made payable to the divorcing husband upon the marriage of the divorced wife to another man.[43] Other cases in this category are divorce by means of the archaic *ẓihār* oath, which renders the wife a blood relative within the forbidden degrees for marriage[44] and homicide and bodily injury regulated by pure customary law.[45]

The other category prominently displays the impact of the *sharīʿa* in areas in which it wields assimilative power over custom. In this category, the *qāḍī*s play a decisive role in bringing a Bedouin population within the orbit of the *sharīʿa*. Unlike the independent *muftī*, the *qāḍī* is directly and constantly confronted by the Bedouin; his ability to display a tolerant attitude toward custom, to compromise with it while adopting and absorbing it into the *sharīʿa*, may create a favorable climate in which a custom-bound population will apply to a *sharʿī* judicial authority. On the other hand, a *qāḍī*'s uncompromising effort to enforce the *sharīʿa* in letter and spirit, regardless of the modest Islamic knowledge of those applying to the court, may turn the Bedouin population away from its jurisdiction. It has been observed in various regions of the Islamic world that nomads accept the *sharʿī qāḍī*s' decisions only insofar as such decisions agree with the customary norm.[46]

---

40 For details see Layish 1995b; Cf. Nāṭūr 1991; Lewis 1984, 145–46, 152–54.

41 Layish and Shmueli 1979, 35–37. Cf. Kressel 1992, 226, 230 (waiver of *sharʿī* inheritance rights).

42 Layish 1998, 29–30 docs. 5–6.

43 Ibid., 45–46 docs. 25–27. Customary *khulʿ* has also been observed among Israeli Muslims. See Layish and Shmueli 1979, 37–38.

44 See Layish 1998, 38 doc. 15.

45 Ibid., 72–73 docs. 55–56; Layish 1980–1982, 211.

46 For additional details see Layish 1991, 185–86 and the sources indicated there; 1980–1982, 218, 221; Cf. 1975, 334; 1974, 407ff.; al-ʿAbbādī 1988, 123–25; Oweidi [al-ʿAbbādī] 1982, 88–89.

How do the *qāḍī*s react to the confrontation between the *sharīʿa*, which they are expected to apply, and tribal customary law dominant among the Bedouin? Do they uncompromisingly impose the *sharīʿa* on the Bedouin, thus risking the latter's withdrawal from the *sharīʿa* court? Do they submit to tribal custom, thus abusing their role as exponents of the *sharīʿa*? Or do they seek a golden path between the two and meet custom halfway, knowing this to be the only way to bring the Bedouin closer to the *sharīʿa*? Naturally, much depends on the education and professional training of the *qāḍī*, his religious and social backgound, and his personal motivation. Unfortunately, I have no such information regarding the Libyan *qāḍī*s.[47] There is no indication in their decisions that they were influenced or inspired by the legal methodology of the Grand Sanūsī. Although the Sanūsī belonged to the Mālikī school, he felt free to deviate from it with respect to some issues. Moreover, under the influence of Ibn Taymiyya he did not regard himself as bound by *taqlīd*, the established body of law, of the Mālikī school, and claimed for himself some freedom to exercise personal *ijtihād* (reasoning).[48] The *qāḍī*s of Bethlehem, who are bound by the Ḥanafī school of law, seem to have a formal and solid education in Islamic law, both codified and uncodified.

Several tendencies can be distinguished in the judicial practice: the *qāḍī*s' reconciliation with custom (as, with regard to customary *khulʿ*, reinstatement of the divorced wife unrestrictedly regardless of the waiting period and the quota of three divorces; the circumvention of the *sharʿī* rules of inheritance; and customary "*Jāhilī*" will) and enforcement of the *sharīʿa* while rejecting custom completely (as with regard to the legal consequences of divorce).[49] In Libya, *dār ʿadl*, a tribal arbitrator who has been incorporated in the *sharīʿa* court to the extent that he is treated by the *qāḍī* as a *sharʿī* notary (*ʿadl*) of the court, is a unique example of the symbiosis of custom and *sharīʿa* to which the *qāḍī* makes a vital contribution. This institution, which provides a mechanism for handling marital disputes, falls within the gray zone between custom and *sharīʿa*.[50] The *qāḍī*s of Bethlehem give retroactive effect to customary marriages of Bedouin not performed by a *sharʿī maʾdhūn* (solemnizer) and accept the testimony of Bedouin shaykhs certifying that the marriage was performed by a valid (*ṣaḥīḥ*) *sharʿī* union "in accordance with the custom of ʿArab al-Sawāḥira." This phenomenon has also been observed among some of the Israeli *qāḍī*s.[51]

---

47 For the name index of the *qāḍī*s and the *nāʾib*s (deputy *qāḍī*s) see Layish 1998, 103.

48 On the legal methodology of the Grand Sanūsī with special reference to *ijtihād* and *ijtihād fīʾl-madhhab* see Vikør 1994; 1995. See also Layish 1991, 204 and the sources indicated there.

49 For more details see Layish 1991, 172ff.; Layish and Shmueli 1979, 37ff.

50 For details see Layish 1995a.

51 Layish 1984a, 42; 1974, 398–99, 402–3.

Shaykh ʿAbd al-Qādir ʿAbd al-Muḥsin ʿĀbidīn, the *qāḍī* of the *Sharīʿa* Court of Bethlehem, would say: "Since reconciliation is stronger than the *qāḍī* (*al-ṣulḥ yuqawwī al-qāḍī*), because it is based on an agreement between the parties, it affects the *qāḍī*'s decision." Moreover, he would attest that an arrangement by mutual agreement (*bi'l-tarāḍī*) was frequently achieved with the help of tribal notables (*wujūh al-ʿashā'ir*), and that when a *qāḍī* was unable to solve a particular problem, he would refer the parties to an arbitrator. Among the Bedouin of the Judean Desert it has been observed that the parties appoint arbitrators to prepare the ground (*tamhīdan*) for the settlement of financial matters between them and then rush to the *sharīʿa* court to obtain *sharʿī* legitimation for the proposed settlement. There is ample evidence for the close cooperation between the customary arbitrator and the *sharʿī qāḍī*.[52] Customary substantive and procedural law still plays an important role in the Judean Desert.[53]

The *qāḍīs*' tendency to reconcile with custom may bring about deviations from orthodox *sharīʿa*, as in the case of a *khulʿ* agreement (endorsed by the court) in which it is stipulated that the divorced wife is prohibited from marrying someone before her ex-husband has been compensated by the dower of the future husband.[54]

The Mālikī school, like other Sunnī schools of law, does not recognize custom (*ʿāda, ʿurf*) as a formal source of law. Yet custom has a solid basis in the Mālikī corpus of law due to the fact that the Medinese practices (*ʿamal*) were incorporated into that school and granted the status of Prophetic *sunna*. In other words, custom has been absorbed into the oral traditions; hence its status as a formal source of law has ceased to be relevant.[55] This may explain why the Mālikī school applicable in Libya is more inclined than any other school to compromise with custom. The eclecticism of the Mālikī school found, since the fifteenth century, sophisticated expression in the judicial practice (*ʿamal*) of the *sharīʿa* courts in North Africa, which in the view of some observers became a source of law in its own right.[56]

---

52 I was present at a meeting in court between the *qāḍī* and a tribal arbitrator, who discussed ways of settling a family dispute that was to have been heard in court. For details see Layish and Shmueli 1979, 44; Layish 1984a, 41.

53 Layish 1980–1982, 211–12.

54 For details see Layish 1991, 186–99.

55 Libson 1997, 133–37.

56 See also p. 86 above and the references in n. 17. Cf. Layish 1991, p. 206. Ibn ʿĀṣim 1958 (see n. 20 above) incorporated in his *al-ʿĀṣimiyya* or *Tuḥfat al-ḥukkām* (see bibliography) the Andalusian judicial practice (*ʿamal*). The Libyan documents contain some evidence of the impact of the Mālikī judicial practice on day-to-day reality. See Layish 1998, e.g., 80 doc. 65 (*musāqāt*), 82 doc. 69 (*shahādat al-lafīf*).

The Libyan documents do not point to a sophisticated, systematic approach by the *qāḍīs* aimed at absorbing custom by the *sharīʿa*. Moreover, there is no significant evidence in our documents of the *qāḍīs*' recourse to religious-legal literature,[57] which may imply unwillingness on their part to invoke the *fuqahāʾ*, who are charged with the task of adapting the *sharīʿa* to changing social conditions by means of expert legal opinions (*fatwās*). On the other hand, some evidence in Libya suggests that the *qāḍī* is occasionally approached in his capacity not as a judicial authority but rather as a *muftī* competent to issue a legal opinion (*jawāb*) in matters pertaining to divorce, succession, validity of a conversion into foreign currency, and the apportionment of tax burden among the parties to a camel-hiring contract.[58] When acting in his capacity as a *muftī* the *qāḍī* functions by virtue not of his nomination by the ruler but rather of his reputation as an independent *faqīh*.

The *qāḍīs*' decisions in Libya are generally characterized by a formalistic approach.[59] Occasionally, however, while imposing the religious-legal consequences derived from any given act, they may reproach a party to a dispute who has violated a religious-legal norm. In one case, in which a husband divorced his wife by five repudiations at one session, the *qāḍī* ruled that the first three exhausted the husband's *sharʿī* quota and the rest made a mockery of the Qurʾānic verses.[60] This style of the *qāḍī* was meant to strengthen awareness of the *sharīʿa* in a custom-bound population applying to the *sharīʿa* court out of practical considerations.

As mentioned earlier, an agreement between the parties is "stronger than the *qāḍī*." However, in the absence of such an agreement, the *qāḍīs* of Bethlehem, charged with adjudicating matters of personal status and succession of the Judean Desert Bedouin, reject custom altogether and apply the *sharīʿa* in its codified version under Jordanian family law, even when they know this will involve intolerable hardship.[61] It is interesting to note in this connection that some of the Israeli *sharʿī qāḍīs* dissolved marital unions on the ground that they had been concluded according to tribal custom rather than the Ottoman Family Rights Law of 1917 (which was adopted in Palestine in 1919) and ordered the parties to conclude *sharʿī* marriages.[62] Deviation from statutory provisions of the family law would create grounds for appeal to the Sharīʿa Court of Appeal. The scope of judicial discretion available to the *qāḍīs* of Bethlehem

57 Layish 1998, 24 doc. 1, 49 doc. 31, 67 doc. 50; 1991, 145–46.
58 Layish and Davis 1988, 122 doc. no. 156, 123 doc. no. 157; Layish 1998, 84 docs. 71–72.
59 Layish 1991, 206–7.
60 Layish 1998, 55 doc. 36.
61 Layish 1984a, 41ff.
62 See Layish 1974, 399.

that could be used to bridge the gap between *sharīʿa* and custom was by the nature of things restricted to cases where there was no need to hand down a decision based on statutory provisions – that is, cases that were settled by mutual consent of the parties. Among the Bedouin of the Judean Desert, some evidence points to a kind of sophistication designed to facilitate the adoption of the *sharīʿa* by means of Shāfiʿī *fatwā*s – that is, outside the control of the *sharīʿa* court. This applies, for example, to cases of reinstatement of a triply divorced wife. Under the Ḥanafī doctrine, which is dominant in the Sharīʿa Court of Betlehem, the intent (*niyya*) of the husband to divorce his wife is irrelevant, and the triply divorced wife is therefore not legally permitted to her ex-husband unless an intermediate marriage to a third party has taken place. Under the Shāfiʿī doctrine, on the other hand, lack of intent to divorce the wife is taken into account (*muʿtabara*) and thus may spare the inconvenience involved in an intermediate marriage.[63] The Libyan *qāḍī*s use their discretion to invoke the principle of *maṣlaḥa* (public interest) to bridge the gap between *sharīʿa* and custom. In the twentieth century, the ability of the *sharīʿa* court to bring the Bedouin within the orbit of normative Islam has declined due not only to the codification of the *sharīʿa* but also to the competition of civil courts and the process of secularization.[64]

As noted earlier, in classical theory, the *qāḍī* is a delegate, either direct or indirect, of the caliph. The findings accumulated from the *sijill*s of the *sharīʿa* courts suggest, however, that the *qāḍī*s regard themselves rather as representatives of the Muslim community at large by virtue of their commission to apply the *sharīʿa*. Their moral integrity and inner conviction of fulfilling a public mission is in the best tradition of the *muḥtasib*, the Islamic inspector of the market, anchored in the religious command: "to promote good and discourage evil" (*al-amr biʾl-maʿrūf waʾl-nahy ʿan al-munkar*). In other words, the *qāḍī* regards himself as responsible for enforcing Islamic morals and behavior in the Muslim community. Such a function is incumbent on any individual who seeks to gain religious merit by his zeal for the *sharīʿa*, due to the limited role of the public authority in Muslim society (thus, there is no office of public prosecution in Islam).[65] It is interesting to note in this connection that in a

63 For further details see Layish 1996.

64 Layish 1984a, 55–56; 1980–1982, 221 and the references indicated there. Cf. Shaham 1993; Shahar 1997.

65 See Schacht 1964, 52, 207; Cahen and Talbi *EI*². Cf. Layish 1984b, 35–37. Similarly, conversion to Islam can take place by the mere recitation of the *shahāda* (Muslim creed) in the presence of witnesses without resorting to any public agency (Anderson 1970, 235, 374). It is significant to mention in this connection that the concept of public law is not

land dispute settled in a Sudanese court by mutual consent of the parties and made effective by judicial decision (*ḥukm riḍāʾī*), the court was inspired by the Qurʾānic commandment "to promote good and discourage evil." Later, one of the parties changed his mind, but the judicial decision was sustained by the court of appeal on the grounds that "the statutory law (*qānūn*) and the *sharīʿa* authorize [the *qāḍī*] to combine the office of the judge with the function of the *muḥtasib* (*al-jamʿ bayna waẓīfatay al-qaḍāʾ wa'l-ḥisba*)."[66]

## 5 Denial of Paternity – A Decision Handed Down by the *Sharīʿa* Court of Ajdābiya

### 5.1 *Summary*

The case discussed below[67] is meant to illustrate the *qāḍī*'s scope of autonomy to the extent of deviating from the strict *sharʿī* norm and adopting local customs and institutions. In doing so the *qāḍī* was inspired solely by the welfare of all the parties concerned. Yet he used his judicial discretion and religious authority to resolve the dispute within the boundaries of the *sharīʿa* court, thus bringing the sedentary Bedouin closer to normative Islam.

After a series of disputes between the spouses that resulted in the wife leaving her husband's house and moving to her father's house as "an angry woman," the court instructed the spouses to stay with a certain tribal notary (*dār ʿadl*) so that the latter might report to the court about their behavior. After some time it became apparent that the woman was pregnant. Her husband denied paternity of the child. The woman at first acknowledged that she was pregnant by a stranger. Later, however, she claimed that her husband had intimidated her into making this acknowledgment. She explained that while she had been "an angry woman" in her father's house, before moving to the *dār ʿadl*, her husband had continued to visit her in secret and have sexual relations with her at will; moreover, he had acknowledged having caused her pregnancy, and later on, while under the protection of the *ʿadl*, they had lived together in complete harmony until her father-in-law showed up and incited her husband against her.

---

developed in Islam. Thus homicide and bodily injury fall within the domain of torts – that is, private law to which the state is not a party (Schacht 1964, 75; Anderson 1951a, 811–28).

66 *al-Ṣaḥāfa*, 5 August 1984, 2.

67 Layish 1998, 60 doc. 41 (taken from the *sijill* of *Sharīʿa* Court of Ajdābiya, 189–91 no. [186/7], 16 February 1948).

The *ʿadl* confirmed in court that the couple's mutual relations had been normal until her father-in-law appeared on the scene, after which the husband denied his part in the pregnancy. After the wife had acknowledged that she was pregnant by a stranger, the *ʿadl* summoned her and, pointing at a saint's tomb, enjoined her to tell the truth. Recourse to the sanction of the holy man's tomb had its effect: the woman withdrew her first acknowledgment and attributed her pregnancy to her husband. The latter, however, persisted in denying paternity.

The *qāḍī* rejected the husband's denial, apparently on the grounds that the *liʿān* procedure had not taken place. According to this procedure, in cases of unproven charges of adultery against the wife it is possible to dissolve the marriage through a process of mutual imprecation; while paternity is denied, the parties are not subject to the Qurʾānic sanctions prescribed for adultery (*zinā*) and unproven charges of adultery (*qadhf*). The *qāḍī* ascribed paternity to the husband and enjoined him to return the wife to his house, to treat her well, restore her dower, her trousseau, and her jewelry, and pay her maintenance retroactively for the period during which he had neglected to do so.

## 5.2 *Legal Background*[68]

Denial of paternity, as in the case under review, is tantamount to an accusation of adultery (*zinā*). The offense can be established either by the wife's acknowledgment (four acknowledgments are required) or by the testimony of four eyewitnesses to the act of sexual intercourse. Once the offense has been established, the wife is liable to Qurʾānic punishment (*ḥadd*) – that is, death by stoning (*rajm*) – provided she is *muḥṣana* – that is, that the marriage has been consummated. If, however, the husband fails to establish the offense, he is liable to the Qurʾānic punishment for an unfounded accusation of adultery (*qadhf*), eighty lashes and removal of the right to testify until he repents.[69]

If the husband cannot prove his allegation but nevertheless continues to deny paternity, he is expected to initiate the procedure of *liʿān*. According to this procedure, which is based on the Qurʾān (24: 4, 6–9) and the *ḥadīth*, the husband must swear four oaths (by analogy to four witnesses required to

68 Unless stated otherwise, this survey is based on Shalabī 1973, 597–605; Ibn ʿĀṣim 1958, 76–79 lines 502–17, 246 line 1694; al-Ṣāwī 1806, vol. 1, 456–61; Mālik (d. 179/796) 1989, 228–30; ʿIllaysh n.d., vol. 2, 76.

69 Peters 1996.

establish adultery) in which he invokes the name of God to the effect that he is telling the truth, and a fifth oath to the effect that if he lies he will be liable to God's imprecation. If he fails to swear these oaths after having accused his wife of adultery, he will be liable for the *ḥadd*-punishment for *qadhf.* The wife must swear four oaths in which she invokes the name of God to the effect that her husband is lying and that she is innocent, and a fifth oath to the effect that if her husband is telling the truth she will be liable to God's anger. If she fails to swear these oaths she will be liable to the *ḥadd*-punishment for *zinā*. If the husband keeps silent while pregnancy becomes apparent, he is liable to the Qur'ānic *ḥadd* and may not resort to the *li'ān* procedure. The *ḥadd* applies also in the event that he retracts from his denial of paternity.

For the *li'ān* procedure to be effected, the marriage must be valid or presumed (*ḥukman*) to be valid. If the marriage is irregular (*fāsid*) the woman is regarded as a stranger. If both the husband and wife adhere to the *li'ān* procedure, then they are exempt from the Qur'ānic punishments – lashes and stoning, respectively (*li'ān* averts [*yadra'u*] the *ḥadd*); they are not allowed to have sexual relations with each other (*istimtā'*) even before the marriage is dissolved by the court. According to the Mālikī school the marriage is dissolved (*furqa*) by the act of mutual imprecation (*mulā'ana*), and the *qāḍī*'s decision is required only to make dissolution effective (*munaffadh*). *Li'ān* is regarded as judicial dissolution (*faskh*) rather than (as under Abū Ḥanifa's doctrine) irrevocable (*bā'in*) unilateral repudiation (*ṭalāq*); in fact, it is tantamount to eternal (*mu'abbad*) dissolution, which creates a permanent prohibition for marriage, as in the case of a prohibition on grounds of fosterage (*raḍā'*).

*Li'ān* precludes the husband's paternity of the child (the child is related only to his mother), and there exist no mutual rights of inheritance (but the child and his mother inherit each other) or maintenance. If the procedure of *li'ān* takes place before consummation, the wife is entitled to half of her dower. Nevertheless, some of the legal effects of paternity are left intact as a precaution in case paternity between the husband and child is established in the future: no option of retaliation (*qiṣāṣ*) exists if one of them causes the death of the other; they and their relatives are prohibited from marrying each other on grounds of affinity (*muṣāhara*). And finally, the child who is the object of the denial is not regarded as a child of unknown paternity and therefore may not be claimed for the purpose of paternity by a stranger.

### 5.3 *The* Qāḍī*'s Decision*

In this case, the *qāḍī* rejected the husband's denial of paternity and ruled that paternity should be attributed (*ilḥāq*) to him (court's decision, line 33). There is a clear indication to the effect that the *qāḍī* was aware of the *liʿān* procedure, and one wonders why he did not mention it explicitly. After having established the validity (*thubūt*) of the marriage between the spouses, their intimate association (*muʿāshara*), and their legal marital relations (*khulṭa*), the *qāḍī* drew attention to the fact that the husband had not invoked the procedure especially laid down in the *sharīʿa* for the denial of paternity (*nafy al-ḥaml*) (lines 31–32). There can be no doubt that he was referring to *liʿān*.

As noted, denial of paternity is tantamount to an accusation of adultery, and if it is not proven either by four acknowledgments or by eyewitnesses – as in the present case – a ground is created for the *ḥadd* punishment for *qadhf* – that is, eighty lashes. Yet the *qāḍī* totally ignored the Qurʾānic sanction without attempting to explain his omission. One possible explanation is that the *sharīʿa* court in contemporary Libya has no jurisdiction over matters pertaining to *sharʿī* penal sanctions (*ḥudūd*)[70] However, this does not provide a fully satisfactory explanation. Paternity and its denial are matters of personal status within the sole jurisdiction of the *sharīʿa* court,[71] although this court may not affect the attendant penal sanction if the husband cannot prove his accusation. One would expect the *qāḍī* to draw attention to the *sharʿī* legal norm involved, or at least to make some value judgment regarding the fact that the husband has violated the Qurʾānic prohibition of *qadhf*. Nothing of the kind is to be found in the judgment.

A more satisfactory explanation is that the *qāḍī* was motivated by the interests of the wife and, even more so, the yet-to-be-born child. He was fully convinced that the wife was pregnant by her husband and hence there was no reason, in his mind, to dissolve the marriage. As a result, he decided to concentrate on rehabilitation of the marriage in spite of the husband's continued denial of paternity. It goes without saying that the *liʿān* procedure was not helpful to this end. Moreover, an accusation of adultery, even if unproven, may cause severe damage to the reputation of the wife in addition to the dissolution of the marriage. Similarly, denial of paternity may affect the child's right to receive maintenance from his father and to inherit from his estate. Instead, the *qāḍī* enjoined the husband to take his wife back to the conjugal dwelling, restore all her financial rights and personal effects, and pay her maintenance

70 Layish 1991, 4ff.

71 Cf. Powers 1994; Shaham 1997, 158–59.

retroactively. One should bear in mind that maintenance includes *maskan sharʿī* – that is, legal conjugal dwelling "in the neighborhood of virtuous persons" (*bi-jiwār qawm ṣāliḥīn*)[72] rather than in a desolate dwelling (line 1) – which may have been the initial cause of the dispute between the spouses. If this explanation is correct, we have to do here with a clear instance of applying the principle of *maṣlaḥa*, public interest, in judicial practice.

The *qāḍī* here does not regard himself as being bound by the *sharʿī* norms pertaining to the denial of paternity. In fact, he seems to be guided purely by pragmatic considerations. He has no inhibitions whatsoever about resorting to a tribal notary (*dār ʿadl*) for handling this particular marital dispute. As explained elsewhere, *dār ʿadl* is a tribal customary institution that became incorporated in the *sharīʿa* court. The *sharʿī qāḍī* makes a decisive contribution to this end in his efforts to bring tribal society within the orbit of normative Islam.[73] The *ʿadl*, on his part, enlists the sanction of a holy man's tomb[74] to cause the wife to withdraw her first acknowledgment according to which she was pregnant by a stranger. The *qāḍī* does not seem to be disturbed by this procedure while assessing the accumulating evidence for rejecting the husband's denial of paternity. Indeed, the court's decision demonstrates the consolidated status of tribal custom and popular religion in the daily life of a tribal society in the process of sedentarization.

The case under review illustrates the extent of the *qāḍī*'s judicial discretion to accommodate the *sharīʿa* to social reality. In theory, he is bound by the *sharīʿa* in its Mālikī version. In practice, he uses his own discretion to bridge the gap between idealistic *sharīʿa* and custom. Unless a violation of public order is anticipated as a result of the *qāḍī*'s decision, no intervention on the part of the ruler is expected. Such an intervention is unlikely in matters of personal status. Hence, one may conclude that the *sharīʿa* court fulfills a vital role in the public sphere in the sense that the *qāḍī* is capable of formulating norms of social, ethical, and legal behavior independently – that is, outside the control of the political authority.

72 See below, n. 78.

73 See Layish 1995a, 198ff.

74 On the saint's role as an agent of Islamization in tribal society see Gellner 1969, 9ff. 135; 1984, 38; Morsy 1984, 48; Levtzion 1979a, 16ff.

## Appendix. The Court's Decision and Its Translation

### *The Arabic Text*

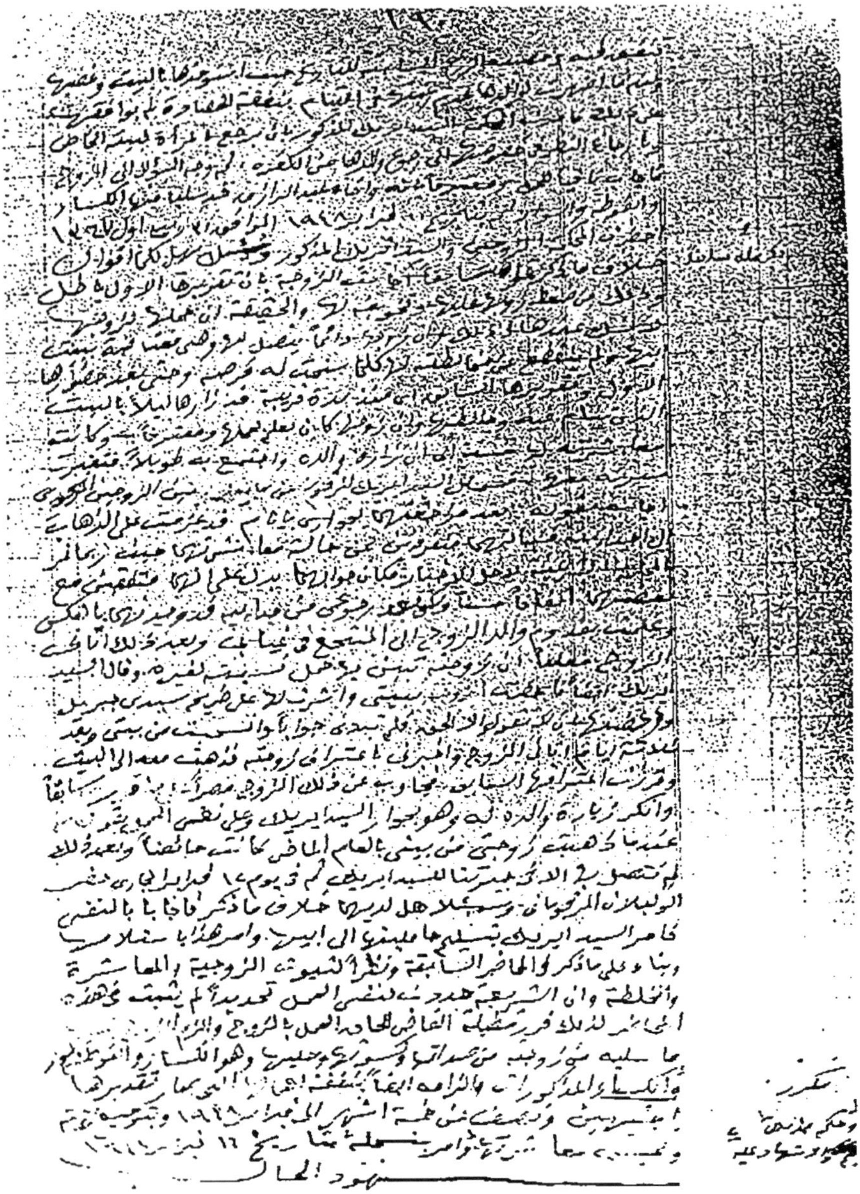

FIGURE 5.1 The court's decision

[١][...][1] تنفق طيه في حصيدة الزرع السابقة للتاريخ حيث استوحدها بالبيت وغصبها [٢]وعندما اظهرت لوالدها عدم رغبتها في القيام بنفقة الحصادة لم يوافقها [٣]على ذلك فامرت المحكمة السيد ابريك المذكور بان يرجع بالمراة لبيته الخاص [٤] وبارجاع النظر في خصوصها الى رجوع والدها من الكفرة. ثم وجه السؤال الى الزوج [٥] فاجاب نافيا للحمل ومعترفا بانه واخاه عبد الرازق قد سلبا منها الكساء [٦]والفوطة والسوار. ثم بتاريخ ١١ فبراير ١٩٤٨ الموافق ٣٠ ربيع اول ١٣٦٧ [٧]احضرت المحكمة الزوجين والسيد ابريك المذكور وسئلا بهل لكما اقوال [٨]خلاف ما ذكرتماه سابقًا[2] اجابت الزوجة بان تقريرها الاول باطل [٩] وذلك من ضغط زوجها عليها وتخويفه لها والحقيقة ان حملها لزوجها [١٠]لا شك عندها في ذلك وان زوجها دائمًا يتصل بها وهي مفتاضة [مفتاظة] ببيت [١١]ابيها ولم ينقطع عن مخالطته لها كلما سنحت له فرصة وحتى بعد حضورها [١٢]الاول وتقريرها السابق اي منذ مدة قريبة قد زارها ليلاً بالبيت[١٣]الذي تنام فيه وخالطها وان زوجها كان يعلم بحملها ومعترفًا به وكانت [١٤] معاشرته لها حسنة الى ان زاره والده واجتمع به طويلاً فتغيرت [١٥] سيرته معها فسئل السيد ابريك المرقوم في ما يعلمه بين الزوجين المذكورين [١٦] اجاب بقوله بعد مراجعتهما بجواري بايام قد عزمت على الذهاب [١٧] الى اجدابية فسألتهما منفردين عن حالة معاشرتهما حيث ربما نمر[3][١٨] بالمحكمة الشرعية لاجل الاخبار فكان جوابهما يدل على انهما متفقين مع [١٩] بعضهما اتفاقًا حسنًا ولكن بعد رجوعي من {ا} جدابية قد وجدتهما بالعكس [٢٠]وعلمت بقدوم والد الزوج الى المنتجع في غيابي وبعد ذلك اتاني [٢١] الزوج معلنًا ان زوجته تبين بها حمل نسبته لغيره. وقال السيد [٢٢] ابريك ايضًا فاحضرت الزوجة ببيتي واشرت لها على ضريح سيدي جبريل [٢٣]ووعظتها بان لا تقول الا الحق فلم تبدي جوابًا وانسحبت من بيتي وبعد [٢٤]ثلاثة ايام اتاني الزوج واخبرني باعتراف زوجته فذهبت معه الى البيت [٢٥]وقررت اعترافها السابق فجاوب عن ذلك الزوج مصراً على ما قرره سابقًا [٢٦] وانكر زيارة والده له وهو بجوار السيد ابريك وعلى نفي الحمل بقوله [٢٧] عندما ذهبت زوجتي من بيتي بالعام الماضي كانت حائضًا وبعد ذلك [٢٨]لم نتصل بها الا في جيرتنا للسيد ابريك ثم في يوم ١٢ فبراير الجاري حضر [٢٩]الوكيلان المرقوماني وسئلا هل لديهما خلاف ما ذكر فاجابا بالنفي [٣٠] فامر السيد ابريك بتسليم حاميتها < حمايتها> الى ابيها وامر هذا باستلامها

[٣١] وبناء على ما ذكر في المحاضر السابقة ونظراً لثبوت الزوجية والمعاشرة [٣٢]والخلطة وان الشريعة حددت لنفي الحمل تحديداً لم يثبت في هذه [٣٣]المحاضر لذلك قرر فضيلة القاضي الحاق الحمل بالزوج والزم الزوج بترجيع [٣٤] ما سلبه من زوجته من صداقها وكسوتها وحليها وهو الكساء[4] والفوطة والسوار [٣٥] المذكورات والزامه ايضًا بنفقة اهمالها التي صار تقديرها [٣٦] باجنيهين ونصف عن خمسة اشهر الى فبراير ١٩٤٨ وبترجيع زوجته [٣٧]وبحسن معاشرتها وحكم بذلك وامر بتسجيله والاشهاد عليه[5] بتاريخ ١٦ فبراير ١٩٤٨.

[٣٨]شـــــهـــــود الـــــحـــــال[6]

{[٣٩]الامر كما ذكر فيه

[٤٠]قاضي اجدابية

[٤١]رافع عبد الرحمن القاضي}

[Notes to the Arabic transcription of the document:]

1 Regrettably, the beginning of this document is not available for inclusion here. However, on the basis of a preceding document, it is possible to conclude that the matter was decided by Shaykh Rāfiʿ ʿAbd al-Raḥmān al-Qāḍī, the Qāḍī of the Sharīʿa Court of Ajdābiya. See Layish and Davis 1988, 89, no. 115 (taken from the *sijill* of Sharīʿa Court of Ajdābiya, p. 188, no. 185 of 12 February 1948).

2 The words ذكر تماه سابقا; have been corrected in the document and appear in the margin of the document.

3 The grammatical form of the imperfect verb with *n*- in the first person singular reflects spoken usage in the Maghrib. For further details see Blanc 1974, 206 and 209.

4 This word was copied twice in the original, the second time at the beginning of line 35. A note to this effect (مكرر) is mentioned in the margin of the document, which implies that the repetition is cancelled.

5 Some words were omitted from line 37 in its original version. This line has here been reconstructed on the basis of corrections in the margin of the document.

6 The conclusion to this document is not available to me. See fn. 1 above.

### *Translation*[75]

[1] [...][76] [the wife had claimed in court that she] was supporting herself (*tunfiq*) on gleanings from the harvest of a field from the [season] that preceded the date,[77] due to the fact that [her husband] had lodged her in a

75 Lines are not numbered in the original text. Numbers in [ ] brackets have been introduced in both the Arabic printed text and the English translation in order to facilitate comparison between the two. Omitted words in the facsimile production have been reconstructed and inserted in { } brackets. In cases in which a particular word appears to have been written incorrectly, thereby yielding a meaning incompatible with the context, a corrected version has been suggested in < > brackets. My student Muḥammad Ṭāṭūr read the document and made some useful suggestions for which I am most grateful.

76 The missing beginning of the document seems to include some details on the dispute between the spouses, a reference to a previous court meeting in which the wife acknowledged that she was pregnant by a stranger, the *qāḍī*'s appointment of Ibrīk as a notary (*dār ʿadl*) to examine the issue, and the *qāḍī*'s instruction that the spouses stay with this notary. See below, lines 7–8, 11–12, 15ff.

77 The reference is probably to the date on which she proclaimed herself "an angry woman" and moved to her father's house. See below, line 10.

desolate dwelling (*istawḥadahā*)[78] and unlawfully seized [her belongings] (*ghaṣabahā*).[79] [2] When she revealed to her father her unwillingness to support herself (*nafaqa*) on the harvest, he did not agree with her [3] on this point.[80] Then, the court instructed the aforementioned *sayyid* Ibrīk to return the wife [from the conjugal dwelling] to his own private home[81] [4] and to reexamine the case on her father's return from Kufra. Afterwards, the [*qāḍī*] addressed a question to the husband [5] who responded by denying (*nāfiyan*) the pregnancy [paternity] (*ḥaml*),[82] and acknowledging that he and his brother ʿAbd al-Rāziq had taken away from her by force (*salabā*) [her] garment, [6] her apron, and [her] bracelet. Subsequently, on 11 February 1948, which corresponds to the 30th of Rabīʿ Awwal 1367, [7] the court summoned the two spouses and the aforementioned *sayyid* Ibrīk, and both [spouses] were asked: "Do you want to make statements (*aqwāl*) [8] that contradict what you have previously said [in court]?"[83] To this, the wife answered that her first statement (*taqrīr*) was null and void (*bāṭil*) [9] because it had been given under pressure (*ḍaghṭ*) and intimidation from her husband, and that in reality, she had been made pregnant by her husband. [10] She had no doubt concerning that fact because her husband continued to maintain contact with her during the period when she was "an angry woman" (*mughtāḍa*) [*mughtāẓa*][84] in her father's [11] house, and he did not cease having sexual relations (*mukhālaṭa*) with her whenever the occasion allowed; indeed, even after her first appearance [12] [in court] and her recent preceding statement, he visited her at night in the room [13] in

78 Instead of lodging her "in the neighborhood of virtuous persons" (*bi-jiwār qawm ṣāliḥīn*) or "in the midst of virtuous trustworthy neighbours" (*wasṭ jīrān ṣāliḥīn maʾmūnīn*) within the meaning of "legal conjugal dwelling" (*maskan sharʿī*). See Layish 1995a, 205–6 and Shalabī 1973, 436, respectively. "Virtuous neighbors" are needed so that the wife does not feel lonely (*lā tastawḥish*) and lose her sanity. See Meron 1971, 210–11. Another possible translation of *istawḥadahā:* "sought to isolate her" or "sought to be alone with her."

79 See Ibn ʿĀṣim 1958, 218, lines 1498ff. Cf. lines 5–6 below. *ghaṣabahā* means also "raped her," but this connotation does not fit the present context.

80 In other words, the woman expressed her desire to leave the conjugal dwelling but her father discouraged her from doing so.

81 It appears that the couple had already stayed in the same *dār ʿadl*, whose function is to observe the couple's behavior and submit his report to the court. See Layish 1995a. Cf. *dār amīn* in Fierro 1985, 86ff.

82 As we shall see later, this is a case of a pregnancy begun while the woman was "angry" living in her father's house before moving to *dār ʿadl*.

83 This seems to refer to the wife's first admission that she was pregnant by a stranger.

84 The status of "an angry woman" seems to be common practice in Cyrenaica. See, e.g., Sharīʿa Court of Ajdābiya, 176 no.172 of 30 October 1947 (*mughāḍaba*); 27 no. 52 (date not available); Mohsen 1975, 114. Cf. Layish 1975, 98 n. 66 and the references indicated there.

which she slept and had sexual relations with her (*khālaṭahā*). [She also said that] her husband knew about her pregnancy and acknowledged it [14] and that he had lived in harmonious intimacy (*muʿāshara*) with her [after having moved to the *dār ʿadl*] until his father visited him and they had a long meeting; whereupon [15] his behavior toward her changed.[85]

The aforementioned *sayyid* Ibrīk was asked [to state] what he knew [concerning the relations] between the aforementioned couple. [16] He answered, saying: "A few days after they resumed their conjugal relations (*murājaʿatihimā*) under my protection (*jiwār*),[86] I decided to go [17] to Ajdābiya, and I asked each of them separately concerning their intimate association (*muʿāsharatihimā*), since there was a possibility that I might pass by [18] the Sharīʿa Court in order to report information (*ikhbār*) [concerning the spouses under his protection]. Their answers indicated that there was complete harmony between them. [19] However, on my return from Ajdābiyya I found the two of them in an opposite frame of mind, [20] and I was informed that in my absence the husband's father had come to the pasturage. Subsequently, the husband came to me [21] to inform me of his wife's pregnancy, which she attributed to someone else." *Sayyid* [22] Ibrīk also said: "I brought the wife to my home and, pointing to the tomb (*ḍarīḥ*) of Sīdī Jibrīl, [23] I exhorted her to say nothing but the truth.[87] However, she left my house without saying a word. [24] Three days later, her husband came to me and informed me that his wife acknowledged (*iʿtirāf*) [that her pregnancy was by him]. I accompanied him home [25] and the wife confirmed what she had previously acknowledged [that she was pregnant by her husband]. To this her husband responded by insisting on what he had previously declared [viz., that the pregnancy was not by him]." [26] He [viz.,

85 Due to the fact that the intimate relations between the spouses (while the wife was living in her father's house) were kept secret, the father may have convinced his son that the wife's pregnancy would be attributed to a stranger and that it was appropriate for his son, to safeguard family reputation and honor, to deny paternity. Had it not been for the status of "the angry woman" the presumption would have been that "paternity belongs to lawful wedlock" (*al-walad li'l-firāsh*). See Coulson 1971, 23; Peters 1980, 126–27, 145.

86 For details on *jiwār* see Layish 1995a, 206–8.

87 The Bedouin believe that holy men and their tombs are sources of *baraka*, divine blessing. The *ʿadl* here enlists the sanction of the local Ṣūfī saint's tomb as a means of deterring the wife from lying about her pregnancy; the expedient proved successful. Cf. Layish 1998, 71 doc. 54 (Sīdī ʿAbd al-Salām al-Asmar); Layish 1995a, 204 and the references indicated there; Davis 1987, 146–47; Mohsen 1975, 57–59 (according to the customary law [*darāʾib*] of Awlād ʿAlī in the Western Desert, if the defendant refuses to take an oath at the saint's tomb he loses his case in favor of the claimant); al-Sūrī 1984, 395–96; Gellner 1969, 9ff.; 1984, 28; Evans-Pritchard 1949, 8–9, 65, 82–83, 117; Levtzion 1979a, 17–18; Hart 1996, 360; Morsy 1984, 49; Ginat 1987, 84, 120.

the husband] denied [in court] that his father had come to visit him while under *sayyid* Ibrīk's protection (*jiwār*). [He persisted in his] denial (*nafy*) of the pregnancy [paternity] saying: [27] "When my wife left my home last year [and moved to her father's house as "an angry woman"] she was menstruating (*ḥā'iḍ*). After that [28] I had no contact with her until [we placed ourselves] under *sayyid* Ibrīk's protection (*jīra*)."[88]

Afterwards, on the 12th of the month of February of the current [year], [29] the two aforementioned proxies (*wakīlān*)[89] appeared [in court], and they were asked if they had [anything to say] that contradicted what had been stated. They answered negatively. [30] *Sayyid* Ibrīk was ordered to transfer (*taslīm*) her protection (*ḥāmiyatihā*) <*ḥimāyatihā*>[90] to her father and the latter was ordered to accept (*istilām*) it [viz., the protection].[91]

[31] On the basis of what had been said in the preceding depositions (*maḥāḍir*) and with due regard to the certification (*thubūt*) of the marriage contract, the spouses' intimate association (*muʿāshara*),[32] their sexual intercourse (*khulṭa*), [and also with due regard to the fact that] the *sharīʿa* established a procedure (*ḥaddadat ... taḥdīdan*) for the denial of pregnancy [paternity] (*nafy al-ḥaml*) – no proof of which had been produced [showing that this procedure had been carried out][92] in these [33] dispositions – [on the basis of all these,] his honour the Qāḍī ruled that the pregnancy should be attributed (*ilḥāq*) to the husband,[93] and he obliged him to restore [34] to his wife everything he had taken by force: her dower, her clothing and her jewelry which are her garments, her apron, and her bracelet which have been mentioned. [35] He likewise obligated him to provide [arrears] maintenance from the time that he had neglected to pay it (*nafaqat ihmālihā*). This was valued [36] at two and a half pounds for a period of five months until February 1948. [He also obliged him] to take his wife back [37] and to treat her well. He duly handed down [the verdict], instructed that it be entered, and required [the witnesses] to testify (*ishhād*) to it on 16 February 1948.

---

88 Cf. *jiwār*, lines 16, 28 above; al-Qusūs 1972, 57; Layish 1995a, 207–8.

89 Their identity may have been mentioned in the missing beginning of the document.

90 Cf. al-Qusūs 1972, 57.

91 The *ʿadl*'s function ends after he has reported to the *qāḍī* concerning the essence of the dispute between the spouses and their respective responsibilities vis-à-vis the dispute. The wife returns to her father's house before the *qāḍī*'s verdict is put into effect.

92 It appears that the *qāḍī* here is referring to the procedure of *liʿān*.

93 Cf. Sharīʿa Court of Kufra, no. 23 of 14 April 1933 (the *Qāḍī* attributed the pregnancy of a divorced woman to her ex-husband on the basis of the testimony of witnesses); no. 28 of 18 July 1933 (a woman claimed to have been raped by a stranger; the *Qāḍī* refused to attribute her pregnancy to this stranger because she had failed to notify someone of the rape immediately after its occurrence).

[38] Witnesses to the proceedings (*shuhūd al-ḥāl*).
[39] The matter being as indicated above
[40] the Qāḍī of Ajdābiya
[41] Rāfiʿ ʿAbd al-Raḥmān al-Qāḍī

## Works Cited

al-ʿAbbādī, Aḥmad ʿUwaydī. 1988. *Al-Qaḍāʾ ʿinda al-ʿAshāʾir al-Urdunniyya. Silsila man hum al-Badu?* Ph.D. dissertation, Cambridge University.

Anderson, J.N.D. 1951a. "Homicide in Islamic Law." *Bulletin of the School of Oriental and African Studies* 13: 811–28.

Anderson, J.N.D. 1970. *Islamic Law in Africa*. London: Frank Cass.

Anderson, J.N.D. 1976. *Law Reform in the Muslim World*. London: Athlone Press.

Baer, G. 1964. *Population and Society in the Arab East*. London: Routledge & Kegan Paul.

Baer, G. 1969. *Studies in the History of Modern Egypt*. Chicago: Chicago University Press.

Berque, J. EI² "ʿAmal." In *Encyclopaedia of Islam*, new edition. Leiden: Brill.

Black, H.C. et al. 1990. *Black's Law Dictionary*, 6th ed. St. Paul, Minn.: West Publishing Co.

Blanc, H. 1974. "The nekteb-nektebu Imperfect in a Variety of Cairene Arabic." *Israel Oriental Studies* 4: 206–26.

Cahen, C., and M. Talbi. EI² "Hisba." In Encyclopaedia of Islam, new edition. Leiden: Brill.

Calhoun, C. 1992, 1994. "Introduction." In *Habermas and the Public Sphere*, ed. C. Calhoun. Cambridge, MA: MIT Press, 1–48.

Cohen, J.L. and A. Arato. 1992. *Civil Society and Political Theory*. Cambridge, MA: MIT Press.

Colucci, M. 1927. "Il diritto consuetudinario della tribù della Cirenaica." *Revista Coloniale* 22: 24–37.

Coulson, N.J. 1964. *A History of Islamic Law*. Edinburgh: Edinburgh University Press.

Coulson, N.J. 1971. *Succession in the Muslim Family*. Cambridge: Cambridge University Press.

Crone, P. 1987. *Roman, Provincial and Islamic Law*. Cambridge: Cambridge University Press.

Davis, J. 1987. *Libyan Politics: Tribe and Revolution*. London: I.B. Tauris.

Davis, J. 1998. "A Social Perspective." In *Legal Documents on Libyan Tribal Society in Process of Sedentarization*, ed. A. Layish. Wiesbaden: Harrassowitz, 7–13.

Evans-Pritchard, E.E. 1949. *The Sanusi of Cyrenaica*. Oxford: Clarendon Press.

Fierro, M.I. 1985. "Los Malikies de Al-Andalus y Los Dos Àrbitros (*al- Ḥakamān*)." *Al-Qantara* 6: 79–102.

Gellner, E. 1969. *Saints of the Atlas*. Chicago: Chicago University Press.

Gellner, E. 1981. *The Muslim Society*. Cambridge: Cambridge University Press.

Gellner, E. 1984. "Doctor and Saint." In *Islam in Tribal Societies*, ed. S.A. Akbar, and D.M. Hart. London: Routledge and Kegan Paul, 21–38.

Ginat, J. 1987. *Blood Disputes among Bedouin and Rural Arabs in Israel: Revenge, Mediation, Outcasting and Family Honor*. Pittsburgh: University of Pittsburgh Press.

Goldziher, I. 1981. *Introduction to Islamic Theology and Law*. Trans. A. Andras and R. Hamori. Princeton: Princeton University Press.

Hart, D.M. 1996. "Murder in the Market: Penal Aspects of Berber Customary Law in Precolonial Moroccan Rif." *Islamic Law and Society* 3: 343–71.

Henninger, J. 1959. "La religion bédouine préislamique." *L'antica Società Beduina, Studi Semitici* 2: 115–40.

Ibn ʿĀṣim, Muḥammad b. Muḥammad al-Mālikī al-Gharnāṭī (d. 829/1426). 1958. *Al-ʿĀṣimiyya ou Tuḥfat al-Ḥukkām fi 'l-ʿUqūd wa 'l-Aḥkām*. Ed. L. Bercher. Alger: La Typo-Litho.

ʿIllaysh, Muḥammad b. Aḥmad (d. 1299/1881–1882). n.d. *Fatḥ al-ʿAlī al-Mālik fi 'l-Fatwā ʿalā Madhhab al-Imām Mālik*, 2 vols. Cairo: Dār al-Fikr.

Kressel, G.M. 1992. *Descent through Males. Mediterranean Language and Culture Monograph Series* 8. Wiesbaden: Harrassowitz.

Laoust, H. 1939. *Essai sur les doctrines sociales et politiques de Taḳī al-Dīn Aḥmad b. Taimīya*. Cairo: Institut Français d'Archéologie Orientale.

Laoust, H. 1965. *Les schismes dans l'Islam; introduction à une étude de la religion musulmane*. Paris: Payot.

Layish, A. 1974. "*Shariʿa* u-Minhag ba-Mishpaḥa ha-Muslimit bi-Yisraʾel." *Hamizrah Hehadash* 23: 377–409.

Layish, A. 1975. *Women and Islamic Law in a Non-Muslim State*. Jerusalem: Israeli Universities Press; New York: Wiley.

Layish, A. 1980–82. "Challenges to Customary Law and Arbitration: The Impact of Islamic Law upon Settled Bedouin in the Judaean Desert." *Tel Aviv University Studies in Law* 5: 206–21.

Layish, A. 1984a. "The Islamization of the Bedouin Family in the Judaean Desert as Reflected in the *Sijill* of the *Shariʿa* Court." In *The Changing Bedouin*, ed. E. Marx and A. Shmueli. New Brunswick, NJ: Transaction Books, 39–58.

Layish, A. 1984b. "*ʿUlamāʾ* and Politics in Saudi Arabia." In *Islam and Politics in the Modern Middle East*, ed. M. Heper and R. Israeli. London: Croom Helm, 29–63.

Layish, A. 1987. "Legal Reform in Saudi Arabia as a Mechanism to Moderate Wahhabi Doctrine." *Journal of the American Oriental Society* 107: 279–92.

Layish, A. 1989. "Islamic Law in the Contemporary Middle East." *Occasional Papers* 3, Centre of the Near and Middle Eastern Studies, University of London. London: School of Oriental and African Studies.

Layish, A. 1991. *Divorce in the Libyan Family*. New York: New York University Press; Magnes Press.

Layish, A. 1995a. "*Dār ʿAdl* – Symbiosis of Custom and *Sharīʿa* in a Tribal Society in the Process of Sedentarization." *Jerusalem Studies in Arabic and Islam* 18: 198–213.

Layish, A. 1995b. "*Shariʿa* and Tribal Custom in Libya: Was Tajdīda Married to Two Husbands?" *Archív Orientální* 63: 488–503.

Layish, A. 1996. "The Fatwa as an Instrument of Accommodation." In *Islamic Legal Interpretation. Muftis and Their fatwas*, ed. M.K. Masud, B. Messick, and D.S. Powers. Cambridge: Harvard University Press, 270–77.

Layish, A. 1998. *Legal Documents on Libyan Tribal Society in Process of Sedentarizaion.* Pt 1: *The Documents in Arabic. Mediterranean Language and Culture Monograph Series* 14. Wiesbaden: Harrassowitz.

Layish, A. *EI*²a "Maḥkama." In *Encyclopaedia of Islam*, new edition. Leiden: Brill.

Layish, A. *EI*²b "Mīrāth." In *Encyclopaedia of Islam*, new edition. Leiden: Brill.

Layish, A. *EI*²c "Ṭalāḳ." In *Encyclopaedia of Islam*, new edition. Leiden: Brill.

Layish, A. and J. Davis. 1988. *Libyan Society: A Selection of Documents from the sijills of the Sharīʿa Courts of Ajdābiya and Kufra*. Jerusalem: Acadamon.

Layish, A. and R. Shaham. *EI*² "Nikaḥ." In *Encyclopaedia of Islam*, new edition.

Layish, A. and R. Shaham. *EI*² "Tashrīʿ." In *Encyclopaedia of Islam*, new edition. Leiden: Brill.

Layish, A. and A. Shmueli. 1979. "Custom and *Sharīʿa* in the Bedouin Family according to Legal Documents from the Judaean Desert." *Bulletin of the School of Oriental and African Studies* 42: 29–45.

Levtzion, N. 1979a. "Toward a Comparative Study of Islamization." In *Conversion to Islam*, ed. N. Levtzion. New York and London: Holmes & Meier, 1–23.

Levtzion, N. 1979b. "The ʿUlamāʾ as Officials and as Popular Leaders." Paper submitted to the conference on Hierarchy and Stratification in the Middle East, under the auspices of the Joint Committee on Near and Middle East, Social Science Research Council, and the American Council of Learned Societies, Mt. Kisco, New York, 9–12 May 1979.

Levtzion, N. 1981. "Shariʿa u-Minhag be-Tahalikhei Hitʾaslemut ve-Hitnahalut." *Cathedra* 20: 78–80.

Lewis, I.M. 1984. "Sufism in Somaliland: A Study in Tribal Islam." In *Islam in Tribal Societies*, ed. Akbar S. Ahmed and D.M. Hart. London: Routledge & Kegan Paul, 127–68.

Libson, G. 1997. "On the Development of Custom as a Source of Law in Islamic Law." *Islamic Law and Society* 4: 131–55.

Mālik, Abū ʿAbd Allāh b. Anas (d. 179/796). 1989. *al-Muwatta of Imam Malik ibn Anas*. Trans. Aisha Abdurrahman Bewley. London: Kegan Paul International.

Masud, M.K., B. Messick, and D.S. Powers. 1996b. "Muftis, Fatwas, and Islamic Legal Interpretation." In *Islamic Legal Interpretation. Muftis and Their Fatwas*, ed. M.K. Masud, B. Messick, and D.S. Powers. Cambridge, MA: Harvard University Press, 3–32.

Mayer, A.E. 1987. "Law and Religion in the Muslim Middle East." *The American Journal of Comparative Law* 35: 127–84.

Meron, Y. 1971. *L'obligation alimentaire entre époux en droit musulman hanéfite*. Paris: R. Pichon et R. Durand-Auzias.

Milliot, L. 1953. *Introduction à l'étude du droit musulman*. Paris: Recueil Sirey.

Mohsen, Safia Kassem. 1975. *Conflict and Law among Awlad 'Ali of the Western Desert*. Cairo: National Center for Social and Criminological Research.

Morsy, M. 1984. "Arbitration as a Political Institution: An Interpretation of the Status of Monarchy in Morocco." In *Islam in Tribal Societies*, ed. Akbar S. Ahmed and D.M. Hart. London: Routledge and Kegan Paul, 39–65.

Nāṭūr, Aḥmad. 1991. "Shari'a u-Mihhag ba-Mishpaḥa ha-Bedevit ba-Negev 'al pi ha-Pesiqa shel Beit ha-Din ha-Shar'i bi-Be'ersheva." *Hamizrah Hehadash* 33: 94–111.

Oweidi [al-'Abbādī], A.S.S. 1982. "Bedouin Justice in Jordan." Ph.D. dissertation, Cambridge University.

Peters, E.L. 1980. "Aspects of the Bedouin Bridewealth among Camel Herders in Cyrenaica." In *The Meaning of Marriage Payments*, ed. J.L. Comaroff. London: Academic Press, 25–60.

Peters, R. 2005. *Crime and Punishment in Islamic Law. Themes in Islamic Law* 2. Cambridge: Cambridge University Press.

Powers, D. 1994. "Kadijustiz or Qadi-Justice? A Paternity Dispute from Fourteenth-Century Morocco." *Islamic Law and Society* 1: 332–66.

al-Qusūs, 'Awda. 1972. *al-Qaḍā' al-Badawī*, 2nd ed. Amman: al-Maṭba'a al-Urduniyya.

Rosen, L. 1995. "Law and Custom in the Popular Legal Culture of North Africa." *Islamic Law and Society* 2: 194–208.

al-Ṣāwī, Aḥmad (d. 1241/1825–1826). 1806. *Bulghat al-Sālik li-Aqrab al-Masālik*, 2 vols. [Cairo]: al-Maktaba al-Tijāriyya al-Kubrā.

Schacht, J. 1964. *An Introduction to Islamic Law*. London: Clarendon Press.

Serrano [Ruano], D. 1996. "La práctica legal (*'amal*) en al-Andalus a través de los Madhahib al-hukkam fi nawazil al-ahkam de Muhammad Ibn 'Iyad." *Qurtuba* 1: 171–92.

Shaham, R. 1993. "A Woman's Place: A Confrontation with Bedouin Custom in the Shari'a Court." *Journal of the American Oriental Society* 111: 192–97.

Shaham, R. 1997. *Family and the Court in Modern Egypt*. Leiden: Brill.

Shahar, I. 1997. "Trilemma be-Diyunei Beit ha-Din 'al-Maḥkama al-Shar'iyya' bi-Be'ersheva ki-Nequdat Mifgash shel Shalosh Ma'arachot Ḥoq: Ḥuqei ha-Medina, ha-Ḥoq ha-Shar'i veha-'Urf ha-Bedevi." *Jamā'a* 1: 11–35.

Shalabī, Muḥammad Muṣṭafā. 1973. *Aḥkām al-Usra fī 'l-Islām. Dirāsa Muqārana bayna Fiqh al-Madhāhib al-Sunniyya wa 'l-Madhhab al-Jaʿfarī*. Beirut: Dār al-Nahḍa al-ʿArabiyya.

Smith, W.C. 1963. *Islam in Modern History*. New York: New American Library.

Stewart, F.H. 1987. "A Bedouin Narrative from Central Sinai." *Zeitschrift für Arabische Linguistik* 16: 44–92.

Stewart, F.H. 1988. *Texts in Sinai Bedouin Law. Pt. 1. The Texts in English Translation. Mediterranean Language and Culture Monograph Series* 5. Wiesbaden: Harrassowitz.

Stewart, F.H. 1990. *Texts in Sinai Bedouin Law. Pt. 2. The Texts in Arabic. Mediterranean Language and Culture Monograph Series* 5. Wiesbaden: Harrassowitz.

al-Sūrī, Ṣalāḥ al-Dīn Ḥasan. 1984. "Lībyā wa 'l-Ghazw al-Thaqāfī al-Īṭālī." In *Buḥūth wa-Dirāsāt fī 'l-Ta'rīkh al-Lībī 1911–1943*, ed. Ṣalāḥ al-Dīn Ḥasan al-Sūrī and Ḥabīb Wadāʿa al-Ḥusnāwī. vol. 2. Tripoli: n.p., 393–431.

Taylor, C. 1990. "Modes of Civil Society." *Public Culture* 3: 95–132.

Tyan, E. 1960. *Histoire de l'organisation judiciare en pays d'islam*. Leiden: Brill.

Tyan, E. *EI2* "Ḳaḍī." In *Encyclopaedia of Islam*, new edition. Leiden: Brill.

Vikør, K.S. 2006. "The Shaykh as *Mujtahid*: A Sufi Conception of *Ijtihād*?" In *El Sufismo y las normas del Islam*, ed. Alfonso Carmona. Murcia: Editora Regional de Murcia, 351–75.

Vikør, K.S. 1995. *Sufi and Scholar on the Desert Edge: Muhammad b. Ali al-Sanusi and His Brotherhood*. London: Hurst.

CHAPTER 6

# *Dār ʿadl* – Symbiosis of Custom and *Sharīʿa* in a Tribal Society in Process of Sedentarization

## 1 Introduction*

The *sijill* of the Sharīʿa Court of Ajdābiya[1] in northern Cyrenaica contains a number of references to an institution providing a mechanism for handling marital disputes. This institution, called *dār ʿadl*,[2] is not known in classical Islamic law, although the term *ʿadl* is not alien there. One gains the impression that these references concern an institution in the ill-defined zone between custom and *sharīʿa* or, more precisely, a tribal institution which became incorporated in the *sharīʿa* court in a synthesis with *sharʿī* elements. The *sharʿī qāḍī* makes a decisive contribution to this synthesis in his efforts to bring tribal society within the orbit of normative Islam. The references are from the early 1950s, when the tribal society of Ajdābiya had reached an advanced stage of sedentarization.[3] Following are the main findings from the *sijill* in their original form, and an attempt to identify the institution, describe its function and establish its sources of inspiration.

---

* My profound thanks go to Professor John Davis of Oxford University, who placed at my disposal a rich selection of legal documents which he collected and photographed in the course of his anthropological research from the *sijill* of the Sharīʿa Courts of Ajdābiya and Kufra. My teacher and colleague, Professor Pessah Shinar, has assisted and inspired me over the years, and has my sincere gratitude. Professor Frank Stewart of the Hebrew University read the manuscript and offered valuable comments. [Originally published in *Jerusalem Studies in Arabic and Islam*, 19 (1995), pp. 198–213.]

1 For this unusual spelling (Ajdābiya rather than Ajdābiyya) see Yāqūt, *Muʿjam al-buldān*, s.v. I owe this reference to Dr. Yasin Dutton, Oxford.

2 Not connected with the *dār al-ʿadl* relating to the justice of the *maẓālim* in the Mamluk state. See E. Tyan, *Histoire de l'organisation judiciaire en pays d'Islam*, 2nd ed. (Leiden, 1960), pp. 279, 425, 502, 511, 625. See also p. 224 (*iftāʾ dār al-ʿadl*). On the practical functioning of that institution see: Faḍl Allāh al-ʿUmarī, *Masālik al-abṣār fī mamālik al-amṣār*, ed. Dorothea Krawulsky, (Beirut, 1986), pp. 100–02. See also P.M. Holt, *The Age of the Crusades: the Near East from the Eleventh Century to 1517* (London, 1986), pp. 45, 73, 144–45, 150; D. Ayalon, "The Great Yasa of Chingiz Khan. A Reexamination," pt. C2, *Studia Islamica*, 38 (1973), pp. 124–27; J.S. Nielsen, *Secular Justice in an Islamic State. Maẓālim under the Baḥrī Mamlūks 662–789/1264–1387* (London, 1985). I am indebted to my colleague Dr. Reuven Amitai-Preiss for drawing my attention to al-ʿUmarī's book and the recent literature on this subject.

3 J. Davis, *Libyan Politics: Tribe and Revolution* (London, 1987), pp. 7–8, 80 ff., 84–85, 93, 169, 189; A. Layish, *Divorce in the Libyan Family* (Jerusalem and New York, 1991), pp. 15–16.

 | DOI:10.1163/9789004680920_008

## 2 The Findings

In one case, a lengthy dispute arose between spouses, flaring up again after reconciliation and leading them time and again to court. The wife claimed that her husband ill-treated her without a *sharʿī* reason while the husband accused her of refusing to have intercourse with him. After discussing their mutual financial rights – an indication that divorce may have been considered – the couple agreed to dwell (*suknā*) in the neighbourhood (*jiwār*) of a well-known *faqīh* from another tribe, so that his house might "serve as a house of a virtuous person testifying [to the court] to what was going on between them on the basis of his personal observation" (*li-yakūn dār ʿadl yashhad baynahumā bi-mā yarāhu minhumā*). The *qāḍī*, the degree of whose involvement in reaching the agreement is not known, gave it the form of a *sharʿī* judgement and directed the couple to reside beside (*ṭaraf*) the *faqīh*.[4]

In another case, the spouses were at odds over the husband's taking control of the wife's property and her dissatisfaction with her living conditions. The husband was ready to lodge her in the vicinity (*jiwār*) of a certain person. The wife rejected his proposal on the ground that this individual was unacceptable to her as an *ʿadl*. As both parties clung to their positions, the *qāḍī* summoned them for further consideration concerning "a place in the neighbourhood of virtuous persons who would testify as to her [the wife]" (*maḥall bi-jiwār qawm ṣāliḥīn li-yashhadū ʿalayhā*). Meanwhile the wife continued to live in the vicinity of a certain neighbour (*jār*), who testified in court that the husband acted as transgressor (*ẓālim*) toward her by accusing her of misconduct, that his behaviour was dishonourable, that he caused her injury by speaking coarsely to her and beating her until she was forced to complain to the police and resort to court several times. She demanded that the husband be required to place her in a *dār ʿadl* or, alternatively, to supply her with adequate maintenance, since she was prejudiced by living in a place where, apart from the neighbourhood (*jīra*), she had no ties of consanguinity (*ṣila min al-qarāba*). The court supported the wife's demand and required the husband to accommodate her in a place (*maḥall*) where there was an *ʿadl*. The husband categorically rejected the wife's demand on the ground that he was poor and a stranger (*gharīb*) to the place. After all the *qāḍī*'s efforts to settle the dispute peacefully had failed and after the wife had proved through witnesses that damage (*ḍarar*) had been caused to her by her husband, the *qāḍī* presented the wife with the choice of

4 A. Layish and J. Davis, *Libyan Society: A Selection of Documents from the Sijills of the Sharīʿa Courts of Ajdābiyya and Kufra* (Jerusalem, 1988), doc. 24, p. 20. For the document and its translation see Appendix at the end of the article.

continuing the marriage in its present form or dissolving it. The wife opted for *ṭalāq* and divorced herself.[5]

In a similar case the wife contended, inter alia, that the husband had lodged her in an isolated residence (*istawḥadahā bi 'l-bayt*) and had stolen her personal belongings. On an earlier occasion, the court had directed the couple to move to the private (*khāṣṣ*) house of a certain person. Later, it summoned them together with their host and asked him what he knew about relations between them. To this he replied, "After their resorting (*murājaʿa*) to my neighbourhood (*jiwār*), I questioned each of them separately, several days before my departure for Ajdābiya, as to their intimate association (*muʿāshara*), for I frequently have occasion to visit the *sharīʿa* court to give information (*ikhbār*) [about persons in my house]. Their replies confirmed that they were in full agreement with each other. However, after my return from Ajdābiya I found them in a totally different situation. I learnt that during my absence the husband's father had appeared in the pasturage (*muntajaʿ*). Thereafter the husband came to me and told me that he had noticed a state of pregnancy in his wife which she attributed to another man." The husband wished to deny his paternity. In her first statement, the wife confirmed that she had conceived out of wedlock, but in her second statement in court she withdrew the first one. She explained that it had been given because of pressure and intimidation on the part of her husband and that in fact, while she was an "angry woman" (*mughāḍiba*) at her father's house, before moving to the host's house, her husband continued to have marital relations with her at every available opportunity. According to her, the husband had admitted to impregnating her and they had lived together harmoniously until her father-in-law appeared and incited her husband against her. At this stage the host entered the scene, summoning the wife and warning her, pointing at the tomb of Sīdī Jibrīl, to speak nothing but the truth. The fear of the saint indeed had its effect: the wife retracted her original statement and ascribed her pregnancy to her husband. The court rejected the husband's denial of paternity on the ground that the *sharʿī* procedure required under such circumstances had not been upheld – the reference is apparently to the *liʿān*[6] – and ascribed paternity to the husband. The host terminated his function and was ordered to release the wife from his protection (*ḥāmiyatuhā* [*ḥimāyatuhā*]) and to hand her over (*taslīm*) to her father.[7]

5 Sharīʿa Court of Ajdābiya, pp. 133 ff. no. [126] (two pages and the end of the document are missing). Cf. Layish, *Divorce*, pp. 144 ff.

6 J.N.D. Anderson, *Islamic Law in Africa*, 2nd ed. (London, 1970), Glossary, s.v. *liʿān*.

7 Layish and Davis, doc. 101, p. 73.

Further scraps of information on *dār ʿadl* may be obtained from other cases. In one case, the spouses became reconciled after the husband had, inter alia, undertaken to lodge his wife in a dwelling (*manzil*) in the vicinity (*jiwār*) of the *ʿadl*, a tribal *shaykh*, on whom they had agreed "in order that he be a witness as to the measure of kindness which they displayed towards each other in living together" (*li-yakūn shāhidan ʿalā al-ḥusn minhumā ilā al-ākhar fīʾl-muʿāshara*).[8] In the second case, each of the estranged spouses requested *dār ʿadl*, but eventually they became reconciled and domestic peace was restored.[9]

## 3 *Dār ʿAdl* – Identification and Function

Two of the five cases described above contain indications apparently connecting *dār ʿadl* with *maskan sharʿī*, the legal conjugal dwelling according to *sharʿī* requirements. In one of them, the *qāḍī* used the expression "a place in the neighbourhood of virtuous persons" (*maḥall bi-jiwār qawm ṣāliḥīn*), and in the other case the wife claimed, before moving to the appointed *dār ʿadl*, that her husband had lodged her in an isolated dwelling (*istawḥadahā bi ʾl-bayt*). She seems to have meant that her expectations of a dwelling "in the neighbourhood of virtuous persons" had not been fulfilled. A dwelling "in the midst of virtuous neighbours who can be relied upon" (*wasaṭ jīrān ṣāliḥīn maʾmūnīn*) or a dwelling in which "her [the wife's] person and property are safe" (*taʾman fīhā ʿalā nafsihā wa-mālihā*) is known to be an important element of the conjugal residence according to the *sharīʿa*. The principle underlying this concept of residence according to all schools of law (with slight variations) is that the husband must not establish his residence in the vicinity of persons of dubious morality or persons who may cause injury to the wife, just as she must not be lodged in an isolated place, far from the neighbourhood of virtuous persons. If the husband nevertheless lodges her among dishonest persons or persons in whose proximity she is not safe, she has the right to demand to be moved elsewhere and the husband must comply with her demand. If he does not do so, she will be entitled to relief from the court. Other elements of the *maskan sharʿī* are separate living quarters, including kitchen and conveniences, within the patrilocal dwelling unit, or, if the husband is a man of means, separate living quarters outside that unit. The same applies when the man has more than one wife: each is entitled to separate living quarters as distant as possible from those of her rival in order to prevent quarrels between them. The husband may

8 Sharīʿa Court of Ajdābiya, p. 22, no. 43, 29 August 1951.

9 Ibid., p. 174, no. 803, 14 February 1953.

not lodge his relatives, not even children by an earlier marriage, in those quarters unless they are below the age of discrimination (*mumayyiz*). The wife, on the other hand, may take in her small children only with her husband's permission. Lastly, the dwelling must also include all the furniture required for the upkeep of a normal household and the cosmetics needed by the wife. If these conditions are not fully complied with, the wife is entitled to leave the conjugal dwelling without being declared rebellious, that is to say, without losing her right to maintenance.[10] There is, in fact, express evidence in the *sijill* of claims concerning dwellings which do not meet the above conditions. In one case, a wife demanded that her husband "lodge her in a separate dwelling with all that this implies" (*suknāhā bi-mufradihā bi-kāffat mā yulzimuhā*) and her husband undertook to do so, but, on the other hand, he demanded that the wife not lodge there her minor son by an earlier marriage. In another case, the husband undertook to lodge his wife in his house (*bayt*) "by herself" (*li-waḥdihā*), that is to say, in a separate dwelling within the patrilocal dwelling unit, and to supply her with household utensils and accessories as required of him under the *sharīʿa*.[11]

However, a careful examination of the findings from the *sijill* reveals that in spite of the terminological resemblance between the *bijiwār qawm ṣāliḥīn* and some of the conditions of the *maskan sharʿī*, we have here two fundamentally different institutions. While *maskan sharʿī* refers to a *permanent* conjugal dwelling anchored in Islamic law, *dār ʿadl* is a *temporary* residential arrangement which, as we shall see below, originates in customary tribal law and is intended to serve as a mechanism for handling disputes between spouses in matters not necessarily connected with residence. Functionally, its whole purpose is to make it possible to ascertain the cause of the dispute and the degree of responsibility of each of the spouses. This information is necessary in determining the financial consequences at the time of the settlement of the dispute, whether within the marriage or upon its dissolution. For instance, in one such case described above, the *qāḍī* decided that damage (*ḍarar*) had been caused to the wife and he gave her the option to divorce herself. When she exercised that option the *qāḍī* ordered the husband to pay her the remainder of her dower and other financial rights.[12] *Dār ʿadl* therefore signifies residence *outside* the

10 Y. Linant de Bellefonds, *Traité de droit musulman comparé*, vol. 2 (Paris, 1965), pp. 259–60; Muḥammad Muṣṭafā Shalabī, *Aḥkām al-usra fī 'l-islām* (Beirut, 1973), p. 436; Muḥammad Muḥyī al-Dīn ʿAbd al-Ḥamīd, *Al-aḥwāl al-shakhṣiyya fī 'l-sharīʿa al-islāmiyya* (Cairo, 1942), p. 266; Muḥammad Abū Zahra, *Al-aḥwāl al-shakhṣiyya*, 3rd ed. (Cairo, 1957), p. 284.

11 Sharīʿa Court of Ajdābiya, p. 172, no. 300, [?] February 1953 and p. 321, no. 544, 22 May 1954, respectively.

12 Cf. Layish, *Divorce*, pp. 144 ff.

permanent conjugal dwelling, in the neighbourhood of the *ʿadl* if not actually in his house; when the *ʿadl* has fulfilled his function, the spouses return to their permanent residence or, if the dispute has not yet been settled, the wife moves to her father's house. Thus, in the case where the husband accused his wife of having conceived by another man while staying at the house of a certain person, doubtless a *dār ʿadl*, upon settlement of the dispute the *ʿadl* was requested to release the wife from his control and return her to her father's house. In another case, where a dispute between spouses was settled even before the *dār ʿadl* mechanism had been applied in accordance with their original demand, the spouses remained in their permanent conjugal dwelling.

From the above findings, it appears that the function of the *ʿadl* is to serve as an eyewitness, to gain an impression of the relations between the spouses (*li-yakūn dār ʿadl yashhad baynahumā bi-mā yarāhu minhumā* or *li-yakūn shāhidan ʿalā al-ḥusn minhumā ilā al-ākhar fī ʾl-muʿāshara*) and to report to the court accordingly. *ʿAdāla* signifies moral and religious integrity. In public law this quality is required of holders of public office, such as *qāḍīs*, but the concept has become particularly developed in private law. *ʿAdāla* is required of a witness (*shāhid*) and of anyone likely to be called upon to testify in certain circumstances, such as a court secretary or registrar.[13] According to the Mālikī jurist Ibn ʿĀṣim (d. 829/1426), a witness is required, inter alia, to avoid major sins (*kabāʾir*), some of which entail Qurʾānic punishments (*ḥudūd*), and minor ones (*ṣaghāʾir*).[14] False testimony is regarded as a serious sin disqualifying the sinner from serving as a witness. In one case mentioned above, a woman rejected a person proposed by her husband as an *ʿadl* apparently because he did not possess the qualities expected of the bearer of this function. In Mālikī legal literature, *ʿadāla* is required also of the customary arbitrator. Accordingly, in Ibn ʿĀṣim's treatise where the damage (*ḍarar*) caused to the wife is at issue, we find the *ʿadl* both as a witness in the usual sense, testifying to the damage done to her, and as an arbitrator deciding the dispute according to customary law. Where it cannot be proved that damage has been caused to the wife, two arbitrators (*ḥakamān*) are to be appointed as required by the Qurʾānic provisions. These arbitrators must be *ʿadlān* – if possible, relatives of the parties – and their decision shall be binding.[15]

---

13 For more detail see Tyan, *Histoire*, pp. 166, 226, 242, 248, 256; idem, art. "ʿAdl," *EI*², p. 209. Cf. C. Bailey, "A Note on the Bedouin Image of ʿAdl as Justice", *Muslim World* 66 (1976), pp. 133–35.

14 Abū Bakr Muḥammad b. Muḥammad Ibn ʿĀṣim al-Mālikī al-Gharnāṭī, *Matn al-ʿĀṣimiyya al-musammā bi-Tuḥfat al-ḥukkām fī nukat al-ʿuqūd wa ʾl-aḥkām*, ed. and trans. L. Bercher (Algiers, 1958), lines 103 ff., pp. 16 ff., 261 n. 77.

15 See Ibn ʿĀṣim, lines 446, 451–54, pp. 68–69.

However, what characterizes *dār ʿadl* as reflected in the *sijill* is its functioning as a mechanism for handling disputes between spouses without resort to arbitrators; or, more precisely, the *ʿadl*, himself possessing the qualities of an arbitrator, replaces the institution of arbitration. Being an agent of the *qāḍī*, he no longer represents either of the parties. Anderson has likewise found that in various localities in Africa, in cases where the wife claimed that she had suffered damage, the courts, contrary to expectation in such circumstances, tended not to resort to arbitration at all in order to solve the dispute between the spouses.[16] In one specific instance (from Zanzibar) the court, in such circumstances, resorted to the services of an *amīn* (a "reliable person"). His function, similar to that of the *ʿadl*, is to closely monitor the behaviour of the spouses and to report his findings to the court.[17] In other words the *amīn*, like the *ʿadl*, is a kind of professional witness on behalf of the court in the best tradition of the professional witness or notary.[18] In Islam the *amīn*, as the agent of the *sharīʿa* court, is associated with the *amīn al-ḥukm*, who is also an instrument of the court, responsible on its behalf for the care and management of the property of minor orphans. This institution was observed in Egypt in the Middle Ages.[19]

There is express evidence that the *ʿadl* is well acquainted with saint worship. In the case in which the husband accused his wife of having been impregnated by a stranger, the *ʿadl* invoked the sanction of a local saint (Sīdī Jibrīl) to persuade the wife to reveal the father's true identity. The sanction produced the desired effect, demonstrating the unshaken position of saint worship in the sedentarizing tribal society of Ajdābiya.[20] Can we hence conclude that the *ʿadl*, among his other qualities, enjoys magic powers which help him carry out his task? The anthropologist Mohsen, who conducted research among the Awlād ʿAlī (they, too, adherents of the Sanūsī order) in the Western Desert on the Cyrenaican border, observed the invocation of saints by arbitrators and mediators in connection with the fulfilment of their task. They were all convinced of the ability of the *murābiṭūn bi 'l-baraka* who – as their adherents believe, have connections with supernatural powers – to harm those who insult them. Mohsen describes a murder case tried before a *shaykh* of the *murābiṭūn* whom everybody treated with respect and fear, believing that after his death he would

16 E.g., Anderson, pp. 20, 25, 32.

17 Ibid., pp. 73–74.

18 Tyan, *ʿAdl*, pp. 209–10.

19 Tyan, *Histoire*, pp. 259–60.

20 Cf. E.E. Evans-Pritchard, *The Sanusi of Cyrenaica* (Oxford, 1949), pp. 8, 10, 65, 67, 82.

become a saint (*walī*). Oaths were taken at the tombs of saints in the hope of using their powers to enhance the integrity of the swearers.[21]

In a case referred to above, the *qāḍī* suggested lodging the wife in "the neighbourhood of virtuous persons" (*bi-jiwār qawm ṣāliḥīn*). Is it possible that the term *ṣāliḥ* refers to the *ʿadl*'s being a saint in the popular meaning of the term? The term *ṣulaḥāʾ* is known in medieval literature as a synonym for saints.[22] Although this possibility cannot be ruled out, further evidence is required to support it, for it seems that the *qāḍī* in this case made use of an expression familiar to him from religious-legal literature in the context of *maskan sharʿī*, that is to say, a dwelling in the neighbourhood of virtuous persons. At any rate, this issue will concern us further on when dealing with the origin of the term *maskan sharʿī*.

## 4 The Sources of Inspiration of *Dār ʿAdl*

Most of the evidence in the *sijill* suggests that the *ʿadl* is a functionary of the *sharīʿa* court and that his function is to observe directly the behaviour of the couple living near him, and then to assist the *qāḍī* in reaching a decision by providing the necessary information on the nature of the dispute and the party responsible for it. Moreover, the term *ʿadl* has a normative Islamic connotation: the informant reporting to the court is essentially an eyewitness and is therefore expected, like a professional witness or notary attached to the court, to possess integrity, hence the designation *ʿadl*. Nevertheless, some evidence exists in research literature as well as in the Libyan *sijill* indicating that the institution of *dār ʿadl* originated in customary tribal law. It seems to have been established in the judicial practice of the Cyrenaican *qāḍī*s in the manner set out below.

Mohsen describes a procedure based on an ancient custom among the Awlād ʿAlī in the Western Desert which can be identified without difficulty as *dār ʿadl*, although it has no connection with the *sharīʿa* court. Among these Bedouin on the Cyrenaican border impotence is grounds for dissolution of

21 For more detail see Safia K. Mohsen, *Conflict and Law among Awlad ʿAli of the Western Desert* (Cairo, 1975), pp. 25–26, 58–59, 131–32, 136–37. Cf. Layish, *Divorce*, pp. 189–90 and the sources indicated there.

22 ʿAbd al-Ḥaqq b. Ismāʿīl al-Bādisī, *Al-maqṣad al-sharīf wa ʾl-manzaʿ al-laṭīf fī dhikr ṣulaḥāʾ al-rīf*. The book was written in 722/1322. It includes a list of some forty saints. See E. Levi-Provençal, *Les historiens des chorfa* (Paris, 1922), p. 221 ff. I owe these references to Professor P. Shinar, to whom I am also indebted for suggesting the possible linkage between *ʿadl* and saint.

the marriage on the wife's initiative without her having to return the dower to the husband. However, if the husband denies the claim that he is impotent while the wife insists that she is right, each of them may demand to undergo a test of the *bayt al-shanāʿa*, "the house of dreadful deeds." According to one version, the couple lives in a tent whose cloth is rolled up so that anyone can see what goes on inside. According to a more frequent version, the relevant one in our case, the spouses move their tent into the vicinity of "a respectable man whose word is believed and honoured." This honourable man is expected to keep track of the spouses by listening or watching at the openings in the tent. His impression determines the fate of the marriage and the financial consequences of the settlement of the dispute. If he ascertains that the husband is impotent, he compels him to divorce his wife while renouncing the dower. If, on the other hand, it appears that the husband is not impotent, he will instruct him to divorce her, and the husband will be entitled to receive not only the dower already paid, but also compensation for the damage done to his good name.[23]

If *dār ʿadl* in fact originates in customary law, the expression *bi-jiwār qawm ṣāliḥīn* will have to be reevaluated within a customary context. In the religious-legal literature, the expression *bayna jīrān ṣāliḥīn* appears in the context of *maskan sharʿī*, "legal conjugal dwelling." According to this concept, as we have seen above, the husband must lodge his wife in a dwelling situated in the neighbourhood (*jiwār*) of virtuous neighbours (*jīrān*) of undoubted integrity. Meron, who studied the historical development of the *maskan sharʿī* on the basis of Ḥanafī legal literature, notes that initially, before final consolidation of the law, the requirement of the wife's residence "in the midst of virtuous neighbours" had a procedural purpose: two virtuous witnesses were required whom the *qāḍī* could question if the wife complained that the husband had beaten her without a *sharʿī* justification. In the 15th century this requirement was accompanied by a psychological element: the "virtuous neighbours" were needed in order that the wife not be lonely (*lā tastawḥish*) and lose her mind. Only in the 16th century was the presence of "virtuous neighbours" raised to the degree of a principle: "a dwelling without [virtuous] neighbours does not fulfil the requirements of a *sharʿī* conjugal dwelling."[24]

---

23 Mohsen, *Conflict*, p. 112; idem, "Aspects of the Legal Status of Women Among Awlād ʿAlī," in *People and Cultures of the Middle East*, vol. 1, ed. Louise E. Sweet (New York, 1970), pp. 227–28. Cf. Layish, *Divorce*, p. 23.

24 Y. Meron, *L'obligation alimentaire entre époux en droit musulman hanéfite* (Paris, 1971), pp. 210–11.

It seems to us, however, that the roots of *jīrān ṣāliḥīn* (*ṣāliḥ* in the sense of saint?) should be sought in the period preceding the institutionalization of *maskan sharʿī* in Islamic law. The Libyan *sijill* may be very helpful in this respect. In all the evidence from that source relating to *dār ʿadl* the term *jiwār*, not *jīrān*, is used. The former term has two connotations, established by Lecerf, one being "neighbourhood" and the other "protection" in the sense of customary tribal law.[25] While "neighbourhood" is the connotation that became institutionalized in the late doctrine of *maskan sharʿī* in religious-legal literature, "protection," the original early sense, is the connotation preserved in the tribal society of Ajdābiya in the context of *dār ʿadl*. In other words, the estranged spouses come under the protection of the *ʿadl* and live in his geographic vicinity – if not actually his home – in order that he may closely watch their conduct. It seems that the term *jiwār* in the sense of protection appears in the *sijill* also in contexts other than *dār ʿadl*. For example, in one case where after her husband's death a woman wished to remain in her children's company, the claimant, the woman's son by the deceased, declared that his mother had remained at her house – actually meaning his house – for several months before marrying another man. By staying at the house she had been "*bi-jiwārinā*"; it seems that the reference was not to neighbourhood, for the children remain in their father's house, but to the protection of the agnates of the deceased.[26]

Support for the assumption that the term *jiwār* in the context of *dār ʿadl* should be understood as "protection" may be found in two of the cases dealt with above. In the case where a husband abused his wife in word and deed until she was forced to complain to the police and apply to the court, the term *jīra*, more commonly used for "protection," appears. The wife claimed that she preferred the proximity of blood relations to protection (*jīra*) by a particular individual who was not able to safeguard her from damage inflicted by her husband.[27] The support provided by the second case is even more explicit. There, where the husband accused the wife of having been impregnated by a stranger during her stay in the *dār ʿadl*, the *qāḍī*, relying on the *ʿadl*'s opinion, rejected the denial of paternity. When the *ʿadl*'s task had come to an end, the *qāḍī* directed him to release the woman from his protection (*ḥāmiyatuhā* [*ḥimāyatuhā*]) and to hand her over (*taslīm*) to her father.[28] Al-Qusūs, whose

25 J. Lecerf, art. "Djiwār," *EI*², pp. 558–59. Cf. Patricia Crone, *Roman, Provincial and Islamic Law: The Origins of the Islamic Patronate* (Cambridge, 1987), pp. 51 ff. and the sources indicated in notes 90–92; E.W. Lane, *Arabic – English Lexicon*, vol. 1 (Cambridge, 1984), p. 483, col. 3 (s.v. *jār*); Qurʾān, 8:48.

26 Layish and Davis, doc. 102, p. 71.

27 See p. 199, above.

28 See p. 200, above.

book on Bedouin law is considered authoritative, explains: "*jīra* means protection (*ḥimāya*), e.g.: 'somebody granted protection (*ajāra*) to someone else,' that is to say, defended him (*ḥamāhu*) and extended his protection (*jiwār*) over him."[29] Protection, as we know, is a fundamental institution in tribal law, and a violation of protection (*qaṭʿ al-jīra*) entails a sanction the gravity of which is determined in accordance with the social standing of the guarantor of the protection. In addition the offender must propitiate the injured party.[30] The relationship between the *ʿadl* and the couple is thus primarily one between the guarantor of protection and its recipient. This relationship has an inner logic in tribal society. During the period of observation of their conduct by the *ʿadl* the spouses are outside their protected natural environment based on agnatic blood relationship. The protection by the *ʿadl* is thus vital in order to provide them an alternative defence against damage to their persons and property during that period.[31] When the *ʿadl* has concluded his task, the spouses return to their natural environment and the protection is no longer required. The *ʿadl* is therefore expected to be – to use Mohsen's mode of speech – "a respectable person whose word is believed and honoured" or, in other terms, a person whose protection is to be regarded as an honour because of his status and prestige in tribal society.

## 5 Summary

The *dār ʿadl* reflected in the *sijill* is a combination of a customary tribal institution with the *sharīʿa*, a synthesis characteristic of a Bedouin society at an advanced stage of sedentarization resorting to a *sharʿī* judiciary. The mechanism of the protection-granting notable, originally a tribal arbitrator handling disputes between spouses, is harnessed by the *sharīʿa* court; the arbitrator is replaced by the *ʿadl*, a professional witness, a notary, who now acts on the *qāḍī*'s behalf and no longer on his own. His task is to testify about the conduct of the couple committed to his charge for a period of observation and to report his impressions and findings to the *sharīʿa* court, so that the latter, not he, may decide upon an appropriate solution to the dispute.

Islamization of the institution is complete when the *qāḍī* identifies it, if only implicitly, with *maskan sharʿī*. The expression *bi-jiwār qawm ṣāliḥīn*, which

29 ʿAwda al-Qusūs, *Al-qaḍāʾ al-badawī*, 2nd ed. (ʿAmmān, 1972), p. 57.

30 Ibid., pp. 57–58.

31 Ibid., p. 59 (*al-tajāwuz ʿalā al-dakhīl*); F.H. Stewart, *Texts in Sinai Bedouin Law*, pt. 2 (Wiesbaden, 1990), Glossary, s.v. *dxl*. Cf. Layish and Davis, doc. 137, p. 118 (*dakhl al-bayt*).

creates an immediate association with the term *bayna jīrān ṣāliḥīn* from the context of the *maskan sharʿī*, is here the meeting point of custom and *sharīʿa*. In formulating in *sharʿī* terms the arguments of the parties, nurtured on customary tribal law, the *qāḍī* makes a decisive contribution to the Islamization of customary institutions. It is doubtful whether he is conscious of the process.[32] His decisions contain neither manifestations of sophistication nor references to Mālikī legal literature in support of the integration of custom within the *sharīʿa* or of compromise between the two legal systems, be it only to preserve the nominal sovereignty of the *sharīʿa*. The Mālikī school's tolerant attitude towards custom and its readiness to meet it halfway are impressively demonstrated by the "judicial practice" (*ʿamal*) of the *sharīʿa* courts in North Africa in the Middle Ages, as reflected by Milliot.[33] The origin of this tolerance probably lies in the fact that the Mālikī school developed and was initially formulated in the tribal society of Medina.[34] It is very likely that the *qāḍī* identified *dār ʿadl* with *maskan sharʿī* in good faith, but this does not detract from the importance of his contribution to the Islamization of tribal institutions.[35] The circle is completed when the *qāḍī* appoints a *faqīh* to the function of *ʿadl*, for the *faqīh* represents normative *sharīʿa*, as distinct from the arbitrator who represents the customary tribal law. Of course, in this particular case it may be reasonably assumed that the *faqīh* in question was not an expert in orthodox *fiqh* in the formal sense of the term, but rather in the popular meaning of the term. His title was most likely conferred upon him by his tribal community rather than some institution for religious legal studies.

Lastly, it is significant that the evidence concerning *dār ʿadl* was found in the *sijill* of the Sharīʿa Court of Ajdābiya in northern Cyrenaica. The tribal society of that region is at an advanced stage of sedentarization and Islamization

32 While here mutual consent of the parties and approval by the *qāḍī* are prerequisites for the *ʿadl*'s involvement, normative Islam disapproves of prying into someone else's intimacy. See Qur'ān, 49:12; Abū Ḥāmid al-Ghazālī, *Iḥyāʾ ʿulūm al-dīn*, book no. 19 (*al-amr bi 'l maʿrūf wa 'l nahy ʿan al-munkar*), pt. II, book 9, *rukn* 2 (*mā fīhi al-ḥisba*), *sharṭ* 3 (*an yakūn al-munkar ẓāhiran li 'l-muḥtasib bi-lā tajassus*). I am indebted to my colleague Professor Hava Lazarus-Yafeh for drawing my attention to this point and to the relevant literature. Concerning *tajassus* see also al-Ṭabarī, *Annals of Kings and Prophets*, Arabic text, ed. De Goeje, Prima Series, vol V (Leiden, 1960), p. 2743. I owe this reference to my student, Eliyahu Stern.

33 L. Milliot, *Introduction à l'étude du droit musulman* (Paris, 1953), pp. 156–69; J. Berque, art. "ʿAmal," *EI*[2], pp. 427–29; Layish, *Divorce*, pp. 206, 207 and the sources indicated there.

34 Layish, *Divorce*, p. 206.

35 Ibid., pp. 205 ff.

owing to its proximity to administrative and government centers.[36] Contrarily, no evidence of *dār ʿadl* was found in the *sijill* of the Sharīʿa Court of Kufra in southern Cyrenaica on the fringe of the desert. The population of that region still preserves the character of a tribal society and is less exposed to processes of sedentarization and Islamization than that of Ajdābiya.

## Appendix. A Document Concerning *Dār ʿAdl* and its Translation[37]

[١] بسم الله الرحمن الرحيم و صلى الله على سيدنا محمد وآله وصحبه وسلم
[٢] في عهد الملك محمد ادريس الاول ملك المملكة اللّيبية المتحدة حفظه الله تعالى
[٣] حكم بدار عدل
بين عبد الله علي رجب و حواء عبد الكريم
ضبط برقم ٦/١٨١ صحيفة ١٢٠
[٤] بمحكمة اجدابية الشّرعية بين يدي قاضيها الشّيخ محمد السّنوسي الغزالي
الخطابي اصلح الله احواله آمين
[٥]حضر كل من الزّوجين عبد الله بن علي بن رجب قبيلة زوية عائلة
سديدي المولود بواحة الكفرة البالغ من العمر [٦]ثلاثين سنة وحواء بنت عبد
االكريم بن سعود من القبيلة والعائلة المذكورتين المولودة بواحة الكفرة البالغة
[٧] من العمر عشرين سنة المقيمان في اجدابية المعروفان ذاتا واسما قرّرت
الزّوجة حواء المذكورة قائلة لقد [٨]تزوجني عبد الله هذا بعقد شرعي سجّل
بهذه المحكمة منذ عام وشهرين ودخل بي من تاريخ العقد على صداق معلوم
اوفاني[٩] ببعضه ولكن العلاقة الزّوجية لم تنتظم بيننا وقد حصل بيننا
سوء تفاهم ادى الى ان وصلنا الى هذه[١٠] المحكمة فاصطلحنا بتاريخ ٢٨
يناير سنة ١٩٥٣ تحت رقم ٤/٢٨٨ ودائما يسيء اليّ وينا زعني بدون[١١]
سبب شرعي فصادقها زوجها عبد الله المذكور على جميع ما ذكرته من الزّوجية
والصداق والمعاشرة وانكر اساءته[١٢] لها ونسب الاساءة اليها واضاف قائلا لم
تعاشرني معاشرة الازواج المطلوبة بين الزوجين شرعا[١٣] وبعد اخذ ورد

---

36 Layish, *Divorce*, p. 177; A. Layish and A. Shmueli, "Custom and *Sharīʿa* in the Bedouin Family According to Legal Documents from the Judaean Desert," *BSOAS*, vol. XLII, pt. 1 (1979), pp. 31, 41.

37 See Layish and Davis, doc. 24, p. 20 (The Sharīʿa Court of Ajdābiya, p. 184, no. 317, 5 March 1953).

فيما يتعلق بالحقوق الزّوجية وتوابعها بين الزوجين آل الامر بينهما الى ان اتّفقا
على السّكنى [١٤] بجوار المدعو الفقيه بو [كذا] بكر بن عتيقة القبائلي
ليكون دار عدل يشهد بينهما بما يراه منهما وقد رضيا [١٥] به معا عن طيب
نفس واطمئنان جرى ذلك بمحضر الشهود الآتي ذكرهم.
فبناء على ما تقرّر بين الزوجين [١٦] وهما بحالة جائزة شرعا وثبوت ذلك
لدى الحاكم المذكور حكم على الزّوجين عبد الله وحواء المذكورين [١٧]
بان يسكنا طرف الفقيه ابا [كذا] بكر بن عتيقة القبائلي ليكون دار عدل بينهما
حسبما اتّفقا عليه وفهمهما بذلك بالمجلس [١٨] حكما شرعيا فامضاه وارتضاه
واشهد عليه من يوقع ادناه جرى ذلك بتاريخ ١٩ جمادى الثاني سنة ١٣٧٢
[١٩] الموافق ٥ مارس سنة ١٩٥٣.

ا مضاء الزّوج بصمة الزوجة

[٢٠] شهود الحال

الامر كما ذكر فيه
قاضي اجدابية
محمد السنوسي الغزالي

[٢١] بو بكر عبد الكريم الزوي
محمد عبد السلام
محمد الطالب الهمالي

[1] In the name of Allāh, the Merciful, the Compassionate, may Allāh bless our Lord Muḥammad, his family and companions, and grant them salvation![38]
[2] In the reign of King Muḥammad Idrīs I, sovereign of the United Kingdom of Libya, may Glorious Allāh preserve him![39]
[3] SENTENCE PERTAINING TO THE HOUSE OF A VIRTUOUS PERSON (*dār ʿadl*) [IN THE DISPUTE BETWEEN THE COUPLE] ʿABDALLĀH ʿALĪ RAJAB AND ḤAWĀʾ ʿABD AL-KARĪM
Entered in register no. 6/181, p. 120

38 The utterance of invocation is designed to add – through enlistment of religious sanction – more respect to the *sharīʿa* court and to reinforce the validity of the *qāḍī*'s decision.

39 King Idrīs ruled in Libya from the declaration of its independence in 1952, until the coup d'état headed by Qadhdhāfī in 1969.

[4] In the Sharīʿa Court of Ajdābiya, presided over by the *Qāḍī* Shaykh Muḥammad al-Sanūsī al-Ghazālī al-Khaṭṭābī, may Allāh prosper him! [5] The couple ʿAbdallāh b. ʿAlī b. Rajab from the Sdīdī *ʿāʾila* of the Zuwayya *qabīla*, born in the al-Kufra oasis, [6] now 30 years of age, and Ḥawāʾ bint ʿAbd al-Karīm b. Saʿūd from the aforementioned *ʿāʾila* and *qabīla*, born in the al-Kufra oasis, [7] now 20 years old. Both live in Ajdābiya and have been identified (*maʿrūfān*) by person and name.[40] The wife Ḥawāʾ stated: [8] "ʿAbdallāh present here wedded me by means of a *sharʿī* marriage contract (*ʿaqd*), registered in this court one year and two months ago, and consummated the marriage (*dakhala bī*) at the conclusion of the contract against payment to me of part of a specified dower (*ṣadāq*).[41] [9] However, our marital relations (*muʿāsharat al-azwāj*) were not harmonious, and our incompatibility in this matter made it necessary for us to resort to [10] this law court. On January 28, 1953 we went through a conciliation (file no. 4/288), but he persisted in his misconduct towards me, and quarreled with me on no justifiable [11] grounds as recognized by the *sharīʿa*." Her husband, the aforementioned ʿAbdallāh, endorsed everything she said concerning the marriage, the dower, and their marital intimacy, but denied having ill-treated her, [12] and held her responsible for the deterioration in their relations, adding: "She did not have sexual relations with me as required between spouses according to the *sharīʿa*."[42] [13] After a discussion relating to the matrimonial rights of the married couple and matters relating to dower (*tawābiʿ*), the upshot was that the parties agreed on dwelling (*suknā*) [14] under the protection (*jiwār*) of a certain individual called the *faqīh* Abū Bakr b. ʿAtīqa al-Qabāʾilī, in order that his house should become *dār ʿadl*, that is, the house of a virtuous person appointed to testify [to the court] concerning their [the couple's] conduct on the basis of his personal observation. The couple

40 The reference is to the *sharʿī* procedure of identification through witnesses (*taʿrīf*).

41 The fact that the marriage was consummated indicates that payment of the remainder of the dower was deferred by mutual agreement of the parties to some later stage in the course of the marriage. This is the customary deferred (*muʾajjal*) dower, as distinct from the normative dower paid under circumstances of divorce or death of one of the spouses. See Layish, *Divorce*, pp. 48–49, 175–76, 187. The connection (*ʿalā*) made here between consummation of the marriage and payment of the dower seems to be a remnant of the customary concept of the marriage institution in which the wife is not a party to the marriage contract. Cf. Linant, pp. 200–201, 233.

42 Cohabitation, when no *sharʿī* inhibition is present, is an element of the wife's duty of obedience towards her husband. According to the *sharīʿa*, cohabitation is the raison d'être of marriage, and all schools excepting the Ḥanafī claim that a wife's refusal to have intercourse with her husband deprives her of her right to maintenance even when she does not leave the conjugal dwelling. See Linant, pp. 289–90; Anderson, Glossary, s.v. *ṭāʿa*.

agreed [15] to his [appointment] and did so quietly and with good grace. All this transpired in the presence of the witnesses indicated below.

On the basis of the agreement reached by the spouses [16] while they were both in a state of legal competence (*ḥāla jā'iza*) in *sharʿī* terms as duly certified (*thubūt*) by the aforementioned judge (*ḥākim*), the latter ruled that the aforementioned spouses, ʿAbdallāh and Ḥawā', [17] should reside in the vicinity (*ṭaraf*) of the *faqīh* Abū Bakr b. ʿAtīqa al-Qabā'ilī, in order that [his house should serve as] *dār ʿadl* in their regard, in accordance with the agreement reached between the two of them. [The judge] explained this to them at the court session.

[18] [Issued as a] *sharʿī* sentence. The judge signed and endorsed it, and obtained the testimony of the undersigned [witnesses]. This took place on the 19th day of Jumādā al-Thānī 1372, [19] corresponding to March 5, 1953.

Husband's signature — Wife's fingerprint

[20] Witnesses to the proceedings (*shuhūd al-ḥāl*)[43]

The matter being as indicated above
The *Qāḍī* of Ajdābiya
[21] Muḥammad al-Sanūsī al-Ghazālī

Abu Bakr ʿAbd al-Karīm al-Zuwayy[ī]
Muḥammad ʿAbd al-Salām
Muḥammad al-Ṭālib al-Ḥammālī

43 Intended here are professional witnesses, notaries. See Tyan, *ʿAdl*, pp. 209–10.

CHAPTER 7

# The *fatwā* as an Instrument of the Islamization of a Tribal Society in Process of Sedentarization

## Introduction[1]

The *fatwā* is the legal opinion of a jurist not institutionalized in the classical sense: it is intended to elucidate, at the request of an inquirer, the position as to a legal issue; it is not binding on the inquirer or anyone else; unlike the judgement of a *qāḍī*, it is not enforceable. The *fatwā* that is the object of this paper belongs to a collection of legal documents gathered from tribal arbitrators in the Judean Desert and from the archives of *sharīʿa* courts. Those documents deal with various legal matters: personal status, torts (homicide and assault), contracts and property, land, etc.; most date from the twentieth century and some from the last quarter of the nineteenth. The collection has been used in research on the Islamization of tribal society in the Judean Desert in process of sedentarization.[2]

The applicant for the legal opinion, ʿAlī Ḥasan, belongs to a *ḥamūla* of the al-Radāʾida ʿArab al-ʿUbaydiyya. That tribe is located east of Bayt Sāḥūr in the Jerusalem – Bethlehem region. According to an account current in the region, that tribe and the neighbouring al-Taʿāmira and al-Sawāḥira tribes originate from the Ḥijāz and Najd. The three tribes appeared in the region in the sixteenth century and absorbed local *fallāḥī* elements. The sedentarization of the Bedouin began in the 1920s and is now almost complete. They settled on the outskirts of Jerusalem and Bethlehem, but a part of them emigrated to the east bank of the Jordan and to the oil states. The sedentarization of the Bedouin

1 This article is based on a paper presented at an international conference on 'The making of a *fatwā*' held at the Centre for Islamic Studies, Granada, on 11–14 January 1990, under the auspices of the Social Science Research Council (New York). My colleague, Professor Frank H. Stewart, read the manuscript and made valuable comments for which I am most grateful. Needless to say, I alone am responsible for any mistakes that may have remained. [Originally published in *Bulletin of the School of Oriental and African Studies*, 54/3 (1991), pp. 449–459.]

2 The documents were collected with the assistance of the late Dr. Avshalom Shmueli of the Department of Geography of Tel Aviv University. The research was conducted under the auspices of the Harry S. Truman Institute for the Advancement of Peace of the Hebrew University of Jerusalem, and supported by the Fund for Basic Research administered by the Israel Academy of Sciences and Humanities.

 | DOI:10.1163/9789004680920_009

was facilitated by their close proximity to urban, religious and economic centres. Following sedentarization, the tribes dissolved into their constituent *ḥamūlas*.[3]

The purpose of this paper is to examine a *fatwā* not from the point of view of legal theory but as an instrument of the Islamization of a tribal society in process of sedentarization. It is known that orthodox Islam, with its system of beliefs and institutions, plays no central role in shaping a nomadic Bedouin society. Though Bedouin are Muslims, their Islamization is incomplete; they do not fulfill ritual precepts properly or regulate matters of personal status or succession in accordance with the *sharīʿa*. As sedentarization progresses, they draw closer to normative Islam. It gradually becomes their binding life-style as regards worship, pious duties and law, and increasing attachment is felt by them for Islamic institutions and for religious functionaries as the guardians, exponents and practitioners of the *sharīʿa*.

The relationship between custom and *sharīʿa* in the Judean Desert is determined by the successive stages of the transition from a nomadic to a sedentary society. In the early stages of sedentarization, custom still enjoyed a supremacy unfettered by *sharʿī* control. Many legal institutions of the Bedouin, though equated with corresponding *sharʿī* institutions, retained the connotation they had before they were incorporated into Islamic law. There have been many instances when intimate arbitration, whose norms were familiar to the Bedouin, were preferred to institutionalized *sharʿī* justice, which was too formal and rigid for their taste. Sometimes the parties resorted to arbitrators even after the proceedings in the *sharīʿa* court had already begun.

Though the influence of Islam on Bedouin law dates back many centuries, there can be no doubt that the more sedentarization advances, the stronger is the impact of the *sharīʿa* upon the Bedouin. This finds expression in the appearance, in arbitral awards, of elements reflecting a belief in the oneness of God and the mission of the Prophet Muḥammad, and of Qurʾānic passages, as well as in the penetration of *sharʿī* institutions into substantive tribal law; oaths, either by their style or as part of the evidential proceeding, assume a more and more orthodox Islamic character. Sometimes the arbitrators themselves, to complete a proceeding begun by them, refer the litigants to the *sharīʿa* court, and sometimes the arbitral proceeding is a 'preparation' (*tamhīd*) for a *sharʿī* proceeding, it being expected that the *qāḍī* will give *sharʿī* sanction

3 A. Layish and A. Shmueli, 'Custom and *Sharīʿa* in the Bedouin family according to legal documents from the Judean Desert', *BSOAS*, XLII, 1, 1979, 30.

to an arrangement arrived at by arbitration. A *ṣulḥ*, an amicable settlement of a dispute, takes place in the presence of religious functionaries.[4]

There can be no doubt that the *sharʿī qāḍī* bears the brunt of the enforcement of the *sharīʿa* upon a tribal society in process of sedentarization. The court is the meeting-place *par excellence* of *sharīʿa* and custom. The *qāḍī* is in perpetual, daily confrontation with a tribal population nurtured on customary law. The results of that confrontation depend on the degree of the *qāḍī*'s orthodoxy, his religious and general education, his social philosophy and the measure of his understanding of the Islamization processes of a tribal society. The *Sharīʿa* Court of Bethlehem demonstrates the important part played by the *qāḍī* in the Islamization of the Bedouin either by accepting the existence of custom while seeking to absorb and assimilate it into the *sharīʿa* or by enforcing the *sharīʿa* while ousting custom completely.[5] Similarly, the Cyrenaican *qāḍī* plays a vital part in bringing the Bedouin-in-process-of-sedentarization closer to normative Islam, mainly by going a long way to meet custom while according a merely nominal supremacy to the *sharīʿa*.[6]

Yet not only the *qāḍī* but also the *muftī* plays an important part in winning the Bedouin over to the *sharīʿa*. He replaces the *qāḍī* where the exigencies of the latter's office and of the school of law to which he belongs tend to keep the Bedouin outside the orbit of the *sharīʿa*. The *muftī*'s main function in this context is to enlist passages from religious-legal literature in support of a mitigation of the *sharīʿa* and a reduction of its severity to a degree enabling the Bedouin to absorb it into their lifestyle without detracting from the customary norms and rules to which they are used.

## 1 The Institutional Setting

In formal respect, the Bedouin of the Judean Desert are subject to the jurisdiction of the *Sharīʿa* Courts of Jerusalem and Bethlehem. Since the annexation of the West Bank by the Kingdom of Jordan, the Jordanian law of personal status

---

4 For more details see Layish – Shmueli, 32–42; A. Layish, 'Challenges to customary law and arbitration: the impact of Islamic law upon settled. Bedouin in the Judean Desert', *Tel Aviv University Studies in Law*, V, 1980–82, 206–21.

5 For more details see A. Layish, 'The Islamization of the Bedouin family in the Judean Desert as reflected in the *sijill* of the *sharīʿa* court', in E. Marx and A. Shmueli (ed.), *The changing Bedouin* (New Brunswick, N.J., 1984), 41–50.

6 A. Layish, 'Customary *khulʿ* as reflected in the *sijill* of the Libyan *sharīʿa* courts', BSOAS, LI, 3, 1988, 435–8; *idem, Divorce in the Libyan family: a study based on the sijill of the sharīʿa courts of Ajdābiyya and Kufra* (Jerusalem and New York, 1991), 185 ff.

has applied in these courts, which are competent in matters of personal status, succession, *waqf*, and blood money (*diya*). Alongside them, tribal arbitrators act without any statutory status. In the East Bank, tribal courts anchored in statute acted until their abolition in 1976.[7] The Bedouin of the Judean Desert, who are at an advanced stage of sedentarization, resort to the *sharʿī qāḍī* and the tribal arbitrator at one and the same time. In matters of personal status, the arbitrator has gradually been superseded by the institutionalized *sharʿī qāḍī*, whose position is reinforced by execution proceedings and by civil exigencies prompting Bedouin to resort to the court.

It seems that Shaykh ʿAlī Ḥasan chose to apply to the *muftī* because he surmised that he could not expect the *sharīʿa* court to extricate him from the predicament into which he had stumbled. He had divorced his wife by an oath of suspended repudiation intended to emphasize his determination in a matter that had nothing to do with his wife;[8] he had repeated the oath several times. The condition of the repudiation was fulfilled, and it was pointed out to him that his wife was now divorced by three successive repudiations though he had not intended to divorce her at all. It seems that the shaykh was aware of the position of the *sharīʿa* in this matter, according to which the only way to rehabilitate his marriage was by an intermediate marriage of his wife to a third party and her subsequent divorce by the latter.[9] The *sharīʿa* court was bound by the Ḥanafī doctrine, which attaches no importance to the element of intent (*niyya*). In other words, the wife was divorced though there had been

7 A.A.S. Oweidi [ʿAbbādī], 'Bedouin justice in Jordan. The customary legal system of the tribes and its integration into the framework of the state policy from 1921 onwards.' Ph.D. thesis, University of Cambridge, 1982, 85 f.

8 The *sharʿī* mechanism of suspended repudiation distinguishes between repudiation intended to ensure the wife's obedience to the husband, and repudiation involving an oath lending additional weight to some utterance of the husband in which case there is no intention of divorce. In both cases the divorce becomes effective upon the fulfillment of the condition or contingency mentioned in the oath. See A. Layish, *Women and Islamic law in a non-Muslim state* (Jerusalem and New York, 1975), 137 f. and 156 f.; N. Anderson, *Law reform in the Muslim world* (London, 1976), 123 f. On the *ḥarām* oath, see J.N.D. Anderson, *Islamic law in Africa*, new impression (London, 1970), 362–3.

9 All the schools agree that the intermediate marriage must be contracted in good-faith and must be consummated before it can be dissolved; the woman can only remarry her former husband upon the expiration of the waiting period (*ʿidda*). However, there are differences between the schools as to the application of that principle. The Ḥanafī school holds that the intermediate marriage is valid even with the (unexpressed) intention to render the woman lawfully permitted again to her former husband (*bi-qaṣd al taḥlīll*), while other schools hold that such a marriage is null and void, short of the requirements of an intermediate marriage. See Layish, *Divorce in Libya*, 99–100 and the sources mentioned in note 2; Layish, *Women*, 173 f.

no intention to divorce her. Under these circumstances, the shaykh sought a remedy which would spare him the need to separate from his wife and to surrender her, though only temporarily, to another.

The Jordanian Law of Personal Status of 1951, in reliance on the position of jurists outside the Ḥanafī school (*takhayyur*), prescribes that a triple divorce effected at one session is to be considered one revocable divorce, whereby the legislator intended to mitigate the legal consequences of a triple divorce. But on the other hand, he aggravated the legal position by prescribing that after the third repudiation the marriage cannot be restored by an intermediate marriage even where the intention of making the woman lawful again to her former husband (*bi-qaṣd al-taḥlīl*) is not expressed; this, too, is contrary to the position of the Ḥanafī school. In other words, an intermediate marriage, to be valid, must be *bona fide* to the full satisfaction of the *qāḍī*; the silence of the parties as to the purpose of the marriage is not by itself sufficient proof of good faith.[10] It is doubtful whether the shaykh was aware of those positions of the law when seeking a remedy for his problem outside the *sharīʿa* court.[11]

In Jordan, there are *muftīs* linked to geographical *sharīʿa* court districts. As far as we can judge from staff-lists and salaries, it seems that the *muftī*'s formal status in the *ʿulamāʾ* hierarchy is lower than that of the *qāḍī* in the same district. On the other hand, the *muftī*'s public status may be higher than the *q̄aḍī*'s, depending on the former's personality and legal and moral authority. By the side of the appointed *muftīs*, there are *ʿulamāʾ* and *fuqahāʾ* serving as *muftīs* without appointment. They are not integrated in the establishment; their status is based on their personal authority and they regard themselves as competent to decide, at the request of members of the public, all matters to which the *sharīʿa* applies, not only matters within the jurisdiction of the *sharīʿa* court. Although there are professional and social relations between the *qāḍī* and the (appointed or unappointed) *muftī*, there is a latent rivalry between them for positions of public and political power. This rivalry was used by the Jordanian royal house to strengthen its position with the religious-political élite in Jerusalem and the West Bank by conferring honours and appointments on functionaries at religious institutions of a legal, executive or economic character who were to replace the Supreme Muslim Council of the British Mandate period.[12]

---

10 Anderson, *Legal reform*, 73 and 124.

11 The legal opinion is not dated; the case may have occurred before the enactment of the Personal Status Law of 1951.

12 For more details see A. Layish, 'Ha-Mimsad ha-dati ha-Muslimi ba-Gada ha-Maʿaravit ba-Tequfa ḥa-Yardenit', *Medina, Mimshal Wiḥasim Benleumiyim*, 11, 1977, 97–108.

The *ʿālim* who signed the *fatwā* is unknown to the author, who has no information as to his education, but the legal opinion itself and some references to religious-legal literature permit the assumption that he has had a sound traditional *sharʿī* training. The author knows no other *fatwā* of that *ʿālim* and so cannot say whether this *fatwā* agrees with any others he may have written. In any case, it seems that the *ʿālim*, who defines himself as a Shāfiʿī, is not a *muftī* by appointment. His opinion is not written on official stationery and is not dated, which indicates that he is not institutionalized but is a private person. His authority derives from his generally recognized learning and probably also from his reputation as a pragmatist who straightens out legal situations involving unbearable hardship. This independent *muftī* gives an opinion to every comer in the best classical tradition. He probably receives a fee for his trouble. The decision to apply to the *muftī* was in this case based on the wish to take advantage of the differences between the Ḥanafī doctrine prevailing in the courts (a heritage from Ottoman rule in the region) and the Shāfiʿī doctrine followed by the local Muslim population in matters other than personal status.

## 2 Style and Reasoning of the *fatwā*

The shaykh probably asked his question orally in colloquial Arabic, in non-technical language, as he was not familiar with Islamic law and technical terminology, whereas the *ʿālim* framed (and wrote down)[13] the question in sober technical language, in the third person and very succinctly, adding introductory and closing formulas interspersed with religious elements, as usual under such circumstances.

The *muftī*'s approach in seeking a remedy to extricate the shaykh from his predicament was based on three alternative legal solutions: (1) lack of intent to divorce where suspended repudiation was used, which means that the marriage remained valid as if nothing had happened; (2) the mitigation of the legal consequences of the divorce by placing it on a par with a revocable divorce, which does not dissolve the marriage immediately and enables the husband to reinstate the wife within the waiting-period; and (3) the man's admission that the original marriage had not conformed with the niceties of the *sharīʿa* but was based on tribal custom; this conception of the matter indeed made it necessary for the shaykh to separate from his wife and to remarry her in

13 Although the size and spacing of the letters are different in the question and the responsum, the handwriting is the same; it is probably that of the Shāfiʿī *ʿālim*.

accordance with *sharʿī* requirements but it did not involve heavy legal costs because the couple's children would be considered legitimate on the strength of their being acknowledged, and, most importantly, the wife would not have to contract an intermediate marriage in order to be permitted again to the husband.[14]

The *fatwā* does not engage in rhetoric; its style is professional and matter-of-fact. The three solutions are formulated very succinctly (eight lines) but so as to be intelligible only to those familiar with Islamic law and Islamic legal literature. The authority of a famous *ʿālim* is invoked, probably in order to lend greater weight to the legal opinion. The *fatwā* concludes with religious formulas expressing, *inter alia*, humility and praise to Allāh as the source of all wisdom.

## 3 Assessment of the *fatwā* as an Instrument of Islamization

The *muftī*'s legal opinion is binding on no one, neither on the person who commissions it nor on the *sharīʿa* court; its acceptance is purely voluntary. In the present case, the shaykh obtained full satisfaction. His wife was not divorced and his Muslim conscience was set at rest (because the *sharīʿa* was left intact). There was no reason to apply to another *muftī* or to ask the *sharīʿa* court to confirm the *fatwā*. If the shaykh had applied to the court (before the enactment of the Personal Status Law of 1951), the *qāḍī* would have rejected the *fatwā*, deciding that the wife must separate from the husband, marry another man and be divorced by him before she was again permitted to her first husband. The *fatwā* was not confirmed or registered by any *sharʿī* or state institution. It was deposited with the man who commissioned it as evidence that his marriage was valid notwithstanding the three successive repudiations.

Although the legal opinion is adapted to the particular circumstances of the shaykh, it is also of use to the general public since it is couched in general terms and not limited either personally or territorially. Reliance on the legal opinion of an *ʿālim* not officially appointed as a *muftī* is in itself an indication that the formal status is not particularly important in the view of the people. What matters, first of all, is the *ʿālim*'s recognized personal authority. This approach fits the institution of the independent *muftī*, unconnected with any official agency of the classical period.

14 For a detailed analysis of the three alternative solutions, with an explanation of the legal mechanisms, see the notes on the translation of the *fatwā*.

The *fatwā* sets no new legal norms. At the same time, it is very important as an instrument to bring the Bedouin closer to normative Islam in the sense that it bridges the gap between the formalistic *sharīʿa* in its Ḥanafi version and customary tribal law. The religious transformation of the Bedouin proceeds in several channels: *sharʿī* indoctrination carried out through religious education in schools and mosques, modern communication media, the marriage solemnizers and, of course, the *sharʿī qāḍīs*. Though the Bedouin may to some extent be conscious of this process,[15] it seems that it is essentially the result of pressures forcibly directing the Bedouin towards the orthodox Muslim way of life. Such pressures are the strengthening of the central authority, which, in turn, strengthens the religious establishment; the abolition of the tribal courts and the subjection of the Bedouin to *sharʿī* justice; and the geographical proximity of the Bedouin to religious, administrative and economic centres.

The readiness of the Bedouin to accept Islam as a way of life is conditional on its not being markedly contradictory to the way of life determined by the customary law to which they are used; in other words: the *sharīʿa* is observed not for its own sake but to the extent that it is consistent with custom.[16] The requirement of an intermediate marriage after three successive repudiations or triple repudiation at one session which according to the formalistic Ḥanafī school has to be met under any circumstances – though the marriage may have been contracted with the (unexpressed) intention to render the woman lawful once again to her former husband (*bi-qaṣd al-taḥlīl*) – is a hardship which the Bedouin community cannot bear. The Shāfiʿī *fatwā*, which takes the element of intention into account, makes it possible to render religious law more flexible, to mitigate it to such a degree that the community can digest and absorb it. Paradoxically, a patently *sharʿī* institution such as the *fatwā* is enlisted by the Bedouin to uphold custom while maintaining a merely nominal supremacy of the *sharīʿa*. The Shāfiʿī *muftī* uses the legal opinion mechanism as a sort of legal device to soften harsh precepts with which the community cannot live. It is known that such devices (*ḥiyal*) were used by *fuqahāʾ* in the Middle Ages as

---

15 Frank Stewart, who studied the tribal law of the Aḥaywāt in central Sinai, claims that the Bedouin there were very conscious agents of Islamization, e.g., when in town they would see the *shaykh al-dīn* and obtain from him all kinds of information about proper Muslim practice, which they would then transmit to their fellow tribesmen. Sometimes they would record his answers on tape so as to be sure to get them right. They were actively searching for information that would allow them to live a proper Muslim life. (Stewart's letter to the author of 10 October 1989.)

16 Cf. Layish, *Divorce in Libya*, 205, and the source indicated in n. 50.

standard means to bridge the gap between a doctrinaire *sharīʿa* and social and economic reality.[17]

The enlistment of the *fatwā* as an instrument of Islamization took place on the personal, not the state level. As aforesaid, the Jordanian government preferred to deal with the issue of triple repudiation and intermediate marriage by means of legislation (in the same way it assumed the role of guardian of religious-public ethics by anchoring the duty of the fast of Ramaḍān in a statutory penal sanction). Personal resort to Shāfiʿī *muftīs* to avoid the painfulness of an intermediate marriage after three repudiations, or a triple repudiation at one session, is a usual practice attested also by the *sijill* of the *Sharīʿa* Court of Bethlehem, to which the Bedouin of the Judean Desert are amenable.[18] This practice is quite natural because the Bedouin are unaware of the differences between the schools of law and so, obviously, do not regard themselves as tied to a particular school. The advantage of resorting to the Shāfiʿī *ʿālim* rather than the *sharīʿa* court to avoid an intermediate marriage seems to have been discovered by them empirically after failing to obtain relief from the court; they had no notion of the doctrinal differences between the schools represented by the *qāḍī* and the *muftī*, respectively.[19]

It is easy to imagine that the *qāḍīs* of the *sharīʿa* courts, supposed to apply the *sharīʿa* in matters of personal status (with the changes required by statutory legislation), do not look favourably upon the Bedouin's resort to Shāfiʿī *fuqahāʾ*, which detracts from the court's status as the sole authority for the application of the *sharīʿa*. An inevitable consequence of simultaneous resort to the *sharīʿa* court and the *fuqahāʾ* is perplexity and confusion due to reference to different legal norms (reflecting differences between schools) which in part are anchored in state-imposed sanctions and enforceable, and in part are derived from the religious-legal authority of the *fuqahāʾ* and not capable of enforcement. However, this situation is not new; in fact, it has always existed as a result of the development of Islamic law through *fuqahāʾ* outside the establishment. The legal opinions of *muftīs* are sought also within the *sharīʿa* court; each of the parties may obtain an opinion supporting his position, and the *qāḍī* may commission the legal opinion of a third *muftī* if he is uncertain as to the law applicable to the case. However, none of these opinions is binding, whereas the *qāḍī*'s decision is binding and enforceable.

---

17 J. Schacht, *An introduction to Islamic law* (2nd ed., Oxford, 1966), 78 ff.

18 See Layish-Shmueli, 52 f.; cf. F. Ziadeh, 'Fatawa and legal systems', a paper presented to the Granada conference (see n. 1 above), 13.

19 See Layish – Shmueli, 54.

*The fatwā*

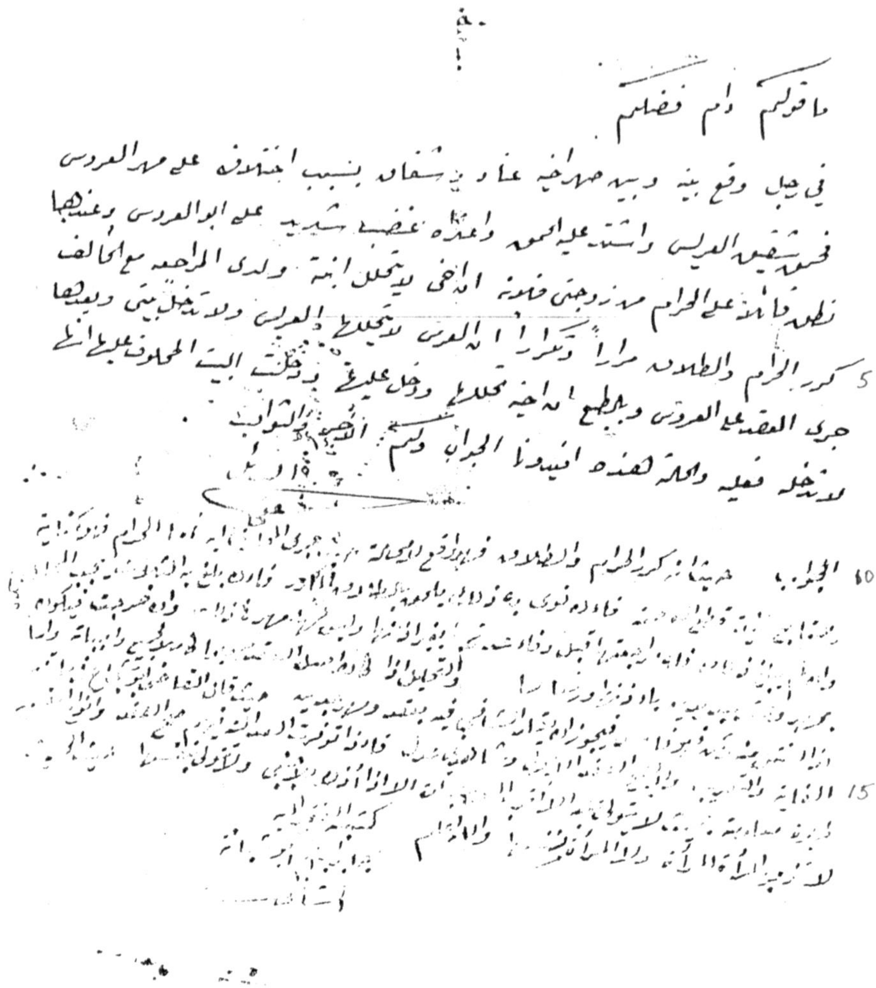

FIGURE 7.1 The *fatwā*

١ ما قولكم دام فضلكم

٢ في رجل وقع بينه وبين صهر اخيه عناد وشقاق بسبب اختلافه على مهر العروس.

٣ فحمق شقيق العريس واشتد عليه الحمق واعتداه غضب شديد على ابو العروس وعندها

٤ نطق قائلاً: "عليَّ الحرام من زوجتي فلانة ان اخي لا يتحلل ابنته." ولدى المراجعة مع الحالف

٥ كرر الحرام والطلاق مرارًا وتكرارًا: "ان العر[و]س لا يتحللها العريس ولا تدخل بيتي." وبعدها

٦ جرى العقد على العروس وبالطبع ان اخيه تحللها ودخل عليها ودخلت البيت المحلوف عليها انها

٧ لا تدخله. فعليه والحالة هذه افيدونا الجواب ولكم الاجر والثواب.

٨ السائل

٩ علي [محمد] حسن

١٠ الجواب
حيث انه كرر الحرام والطلاق فهو واقع لا محالة حيث جرى المحلوف عليه. اما الحرام فهو كناية

١١ يحتاج لنية قطع العصمة، فإن نوى به ذلك يلحق بالطلاق المكرر فإن بلغ به الثلاث يجب المحلل،

١٢ وان لم يبلغ ذلك فله مراجعتها قبل وفاء عدتها بغير اذنها وليس لها مهر في ذلك. وان خرجت فيكون

١٣ بمهر وعقد جديدين بإذنها ورضاها. والتحليل اذا كان اصل العقد صحيحًا كاملاً لجميع واجباته. واما

١٤ اذا اختل منه ركن فهو فاسد فيجوز ان يقلد الشافعي فيه بعقد ومهر جديد[ين] حيث قال القاضي ابو شجاع في شأنه

١٥ [في] الغاية والتقريب: "ولا يصح العقد [عقد النكاح] إلا بوَلي وشاهدَيْ عدل،" فاذا توفرت العدالة فيهم صح العقد وانواع الفسق

١٦ كثيرة معلومة، بحيث لا يتولى عليه إلا اقرب العصبات إلا اذا أذن للاجنبي. ولا تتولى بنفسها حيث الحديث:

١٧ "لا تزوج المرأة المرأه ولا المرأة بنفسها" والله اعلم.

كتبه الفقير لله

١٨ جابر ابراهيم ابوشبانة[؟]

١٩ الشافعي

Translation of the *fatwā*

[*Request for a legal opinion*]

1. May your excellence endure! What is your opinion (*mā qawlukum dāma faḍlukum*)[20]
2. concerning a man between whom and whose brother's son-in-law [or brother-in-law] (*ṣihr*) ill-feeling and conflict arose because of the former's objection to the [amount of the] dower of the bride?
3. The germane brother of the groom lost his temper. His temper got the
4. better of him; he became very angry at the bride's father || and said: '[I swear that] my wife, so-and-so, shall be forbidden to me (*ʿalayya al-ḥarām*); my brother shall not marry (*yataḥallal*) that man's daughter'.[21] When [people] approached the one who swore the oath, [trying to persuade
5. him to desist from speaking as he did], || he repeated the oath of prohibition (*ḥarām*) and the *ṭalāq* again and again: 'The groom shall not marry the
6. bride; she shall not enter my house.'[22] Afterwards || the contract (*ʿaqd*) with the bride was made[23] and, of course, his brother married her and consummated the marriage and the bride entered the house concerning which an

20 A formula usual in requests for a formal legal opinion (*istiftāʾ*). When Bedouin of the Judean Desert present an oral pleading (*ḥujja*), to an arbitrator-judge, they usually employ the formula *aysh qawlukum* or *aysh raʾyukum*, which means a request for a judgement. On the similarity between a request for the legal opinion of a *muftī* and the *ḥujja* in a customary proceeding see A. Layish, *Bedouin of the Judean Desert: Islamization of a tribal society: a study based on legal documents of arbitrators and sharīʿa courts* (in preparation). That formula is usual also in requests for legal opinions of *sharʿī qāḍīs* in Cyrenaica. See A. Layish and J. Davis, *Libyan society: a selection of documents from the sijill of the Sharīʿa Courts of Ajdābiyya and Kufra*, Academon (Jerusalem, 1988), Document no. 158, 124.

21 Although this formula would seem to consist of two independent sentences, it should be construed as a suspended repudiation involving an oath, intended to emphasize the man's determination to prevent his brother's marriage because of an amount of dower regarded as excessive; cf. Layish, *Women*, 114, 138 and 235); the literal meaning of *taḥallala* is 'to render [the daughter] lawfully permitted', which should here be interpreted in the context of marriage. Confirmation of this view may be obtained from the responsum, the legal opinion of the Shāfiʿī *ʿālim*; see below.

22 Under Islamic law of obedience the wife is expected to join her husband at the place of residence chosen by him; as the brother lived in the same house, the bride's entry into the shaykh's house indicates that she has indeed married his brother. This formula, too, should be understood as referring to a suspended repudiation involving an oath.

23 The suspended repudiation seems to have made an impact upon the bride's father: he agreed to reduce the dower to an amount acceptable to the other party, thus removing the obstacle to the marriage.

7. oath had been taken || that she should not enter it. Under these circumstances, we beg you to direct us by a responsum (*afīdūnā al-jawāb*[24]), and yours are the wages and the reward (*wa-lakum al-ajr wa'l-thawāb*).[25]
8. The inquirer[26]
9. *ʿAlī Ḥasan*[27]
10. *Responsum* (*jawāb*) As he has repeated the oath of prohibition and the *ṭalāq*,[28] the repudiation has become a fact (*wāqiʿ*). This conclusion is inescapable because the condition to which the oath relates [the marriage and the entry of the bride into the house] has been fulfilled. As regards the oath, it is an implicit
11. (*kināya*) declaration || which, to be effective, requires [the ascertainment of] the intent (*niyya*)[29] to dissolve the marriage (*qaṭʿ al-ʿiṣma*). If he had such an intent,[30] that declaration entailed repeated (*mukarrar*)[31] repudiation, and if he uttered it three times, the one who renders her [again] lawfully permitted

24 *Jawāb*, in this document, is synonymous with *fatwā*. This use of the term is common among the Bedouin and occurs also in the *sharīʿa* courts. See Layish, *Divorce in Libya*, 184. Cf. Layish, *Bedouin of the Judean Desert*.

25 The closing passage, a typically Islamic element, refers to wages and reward in the next world. This embellishment for *sharʿī* indoctrination purposes is usual also among the Cyrenaican Bedouin as a closing formula in requests for a religious legal opinion. See, e.g., Layish – Davis, Documents nos. 156/2–3 on p. 122. Frank Stewart claims that, though *ajr* and *thawāb* may be typically Islamic elements, they are long-established among the Bedouin. He often heard the words himself in formulas the Bedouin used in the context of sacrifices, and Musil (*Arabia Petraea*, III, Wien, 1908), from the beginning of the century, cites them more than once (e.g., pp. 452 f.) (Stewart's letter to the author of 10 October 1989.)

26 I.e. the person requesting the legal opinion.

27 Of the Ḥamūlat al-Radāʿida 'Arab al-ʿUbaydiyya. This tribe lives east of Bayt Sāḥūr in the Jerusalem – Bethlehem area. I am indebted to the late Shaykh ʿAlī Ḥasan for placing this document at my disposal.

28 I.e. repeated the suspended repudiation involving an oath.

29 See Schacht, *Introduction*, 116.

30 The affirmative implies the negative: if he did not intend to divorce the wife when using the oath of prohibition, then she is not divorced. This may be said to be a hinted instruction as to how the shaykh may extricate himself from his predicament: all he has to do is to declare that he did not intend to divorce his wife.

31 A *ṭalāq mukarrar* entails the legal consequences of a revocable (*rajʿī*) divorce, which enables the wife to be reinstated without a new marriage or dower (see below) after each of the first two repudiations.

12. (*muḥallil*) [to her former husband][32] is required, ‖ but if he did not utter that declaration three times, he may reinstate (*murājaʿa*) the wife without her permission before the expiration of the waiting-period (*ʿidda*) and without her being entitled to a dower.[33] If she has left [the conjugal home],[34] he may

13. [reinstate her] by means of ‖ a new dower and a new contract with her permission and consent. An intermediate marriage designed to render the divorced woman lawfully permitted [to her former husband] (*taḥlīl*) is required where the nature (*aṣl*) of the [original] contract was valid (*ṣaḥīḥ*),

14. fulfilling all the legal conditions (*wājibāt*);[35] ‖ where one of the essential elements (*rukn*) [of marriage] was infringed, the marriage is defective (*fāsid*)[36] and it is permissible to follow [the Imām] al-Shāfiʿī,[37] [who, under these conditions, prescribed] a new contract and dower.[38] In this connection,

---

32 I.e. somebody who will contract an intermediate marriage with her, and then divorce her, in order that she may be permitted to her former husband again.

33 A revocable (*rajʿī*) divorce does not dissolve the marriage immediately. The husband may reinstate the wife during the waiting-period without her consent and without a new marriage or dower; the reinstatement is effected by an express verbal utterance or by meaningful conduct. The requirement of the waiting-period applies where the marriage has been consummated; the waiting-period is three menstrual periods or, where the woman is pregnant, lasts until she gives birth or miscarries (Schacht, *Introduction*, 166; Anderson, *Legal reform*, 101 and 102; Layish, *Women*, 177 and 178). This, too, is a possible way of remedying the situation if it is found that the husband indeed intended to divorce the wife but pronounced the oath of prohibition only twice.

34 If she completes the waiting-period without the husband having exercised the option of reinstating her, the divorce becomes irrevocable (*bāʾin*) with all the legal consequences attending dissolution. See Layish, *Women*, 173.

35 Conditions of the validity of a marriage are offer and acceptance (*ījāb wa-qabūl*), the use of terms expressly relating to marriage and the presence of witnesses at the session of the marriage contract. Cf. Schacht, *Introduction*, 121 and 161.

36 In the case of a defective marriage, the couple must at once be separated. If the marriage has been consummated, some of the numerous legal consequences of a valid (*ṣaḥīḥ*) marriage apply, such as the payment of dower, legitimacy of the children, and the waiting-period. See Schacht, *Introduction*, 163.

37 Muḥammad b. Idrīs al-Shāfiʿī (d. 204/820), regarded as the founder of the school of law named after him.

38 Here the *ʿālim* probably hints at a further possibility of extricating the shaykh from his quandary. If it is found, as is very likely, that the shaykh did not marry his wife in accordance with all the niceties of the *sharīʿa* or, in other words, if the marriage was performed according to tribal custom, i.e. was a marriage by *ʿaṭāʾ* or *hiba*, very common among the Bedouin of the Judean Desert (see Layish – Shmueli, 35 ff. and the sources indicated

15. the *Qāḍī* Abū Shujāʿ wrote in his ‖ *al-Ghāya wa ʾl-Taqrīb*:[39] 'A contract [of marriage] is not fully valid unless it is made through a guardian (*walī*) and in the presence of two witnesses of good character (*ʿadl*)'; if the requirement of good character (*ʿadāla*) has been met, the contract is valid. The kinds of

16. sinfulness (*fisq*)[40] are ‖ many and well known. No one but the nearest agnate (*ʿaṣabāt*) may assume the office of marriage-guardian unless a stranger has been permitted [by the court] to assume it.[41] Nor may the woman herself act

17. as a guardian, for the *ḥadīth* says: ‖ 'a woman may not give a woman away in marriage, and a woman may not give herself away in marriage.'[42] And it is Allāh who knows.[43] Written by the poor man [who resorted] to Him [God].[44]

---

there), then all that was required to legalize it was to separate the couple and to reunite them by a flawless *sharʿī* marriage. This procedure of course involves some unpleasantness (*inter alia*, the court must affiliate the children to their father, which will no doubt be done in reliance on his acknowledgement), but considering the alternative of an intermediate marriage it offers vast relief.

39 Abū Shujāʿ Aḥmad Ḥasan Aḥmad (b. 434/1042–43), a famous Shāfiʿī jurist and *qāḍī*, whose family originated from Isfahan. He wrote a compendium of Islamic law entitled *al-Ghāya fī ʾl-Ikhtiṣār* or *al-Mukhtaṣar* or *al-Taqrīb* which promoted the spread of the Shāfiʿī school. It is the subject of many commentaries. For an interpretation of the quotation from his treatise occurring in the *fatwā*, see, for instance, *Sharḥ al-ʿallāma al-shaykh Muḥammad b. Qāsim al-Ghazzī al-musammā Fatḥ al-qarīb al-mujīb ʿalā al-kitāb al-musammā biʾl-Taqrīb liʾl-imām al-ʿallāma Aḥmad b. al-Ḥusayn al-shahīr bi-Abī Shujāʿ* (2nd ed., Cairo, 1927), 41–2. On questions relating to divorce by an implicit (*kināya*) declaration – whose validity is contingent on the factor of intent (*niyya*) – or to revocable (*rajʿī*) divorce, see ibid., 44–5. Cf. Aḥmad al-Ṣāwī, *Bulghat al-sālik li-aqrab al-masālik ʿalā al-Sharḥ al-ṣaghīr liʾl-quṭb al-shahīr sīdī Aḥmad al-Dardīr*, [Mālikī] (Cairo, n.d.), I, 348–9.) See J. Schacht, 'Abū Shudjāʿ', *EI*, 2nd ed., 150 f.; C. Brockelmann, *Geschichte der arabischen Litteratur* (2nd ed., Leiden, 1943), I, 492. I am indebted to my colleague, Professor Michael Schwartz, for drawing my attention to Abū Shujāʿ's treatise.

40 *Fisq* is the opposite of *ʿadāla* for the purposes of testimony. See Schacht, *Introduction*, 125.

41 Marriage-guardians – like other guardians over someone's person or property – are natural guardians by virtue of blood relationship, in a fixed order according to the degree of their relationship to the ward. The court may, under certain circumstances, appoint a non-relative as guardian.

42 According to the Ḥanafī School, a fully competent woman may marry without a marriage guardian. However, the marriage guardian may oppose the marriage if the intended husband does not meet the conditions of equality in marriage (*kafāʾa*). See Schacht, *Introduction*, 162.

43 An expression of modesty and piety on the part of the *ʿālim*.

44 The *ʿālim* modestly ascribes his wisdom to Allāh.

18. Jābir Ibrāhīm Abū Shabāna [?]
19. al-Shāfiʿī[45]

*Note*

The translation of the document is as literal as possible, with additions to elucidate the subject-matter and the technical terms. Short additions appear in the body of the text, in square brackets, and more detailed explanations in footnotes.

45 It seems that the word 'al-Shāfiʿī' is not part of the *ʿālim*'s name but indicates his affiliation with the Shāfiʿī school, a fact of particular importance in relation to the legal opinion. The references to Shāfiʿī sources reinforce this assumption.

# PART 2

## *Legal Methodologies in Sudan*

CHAPTER 8

# The Sudanese Mahdī's Legal Methodology and its *Ṣūfī* Inspiration

## 1 Introduction[1]

Muḥammad Aḥmad b. ʿAbdallāh, the Sudanese Mahdī, headed a movement for the revival and reform of Islam in the late 19th century, strongly influenced by the *salafiyya*, with a view to bringing about the restoration of the theocracy of the Prophet and the "Righteous Caliphs."[2] The Mahdī's legal methodology provided him with almost unlimited authority to accommodate the *sharīʿa* to his political, social and economic requirements.

The Mahdī ignored all schools of law (*madhāhib*).[3] He acknowledged three sources of law: the Prophetic *sunna*, the Qurʾān, and the Prophetic inspiration (*ilhām*) transmitted to him by means of vision or colloquy (*ḥaḍra*).[4] From this

---

1 Most of the material for this research was collected at the University of Bergen. I would like to thank both Prof. R. Seán O'Fahey and Prof. Knut S. Vikør for the warm hospitality extended to me. The late Prof. P.M. Holt, Dr. Bernd Radtke, Prof. Vikør, Prof. Ella Landau-Tasseron and Prof. Gabriel Warburg read early drafts and made valuable comments and suggestions for which I am most grateful. I am also indebted to Prof. Holt and Prof. P. Shinar for intellectual inspiration over the years. Thanks are also due to Prof. Yohanan Friedmann for clarifying issues pertaining to the *ḥadīth*. The first draft of this essay was presented at the IV International Conference on Islamic Legal Studies: "Law and Sufism" held in Murcia (Spain) on May 8–10, 2003. I am grateful for the participants' comments and suggestions. This is a revised version of an essay published in Hebrew in Ami Ayalon and David J. Wasserstein (eds.), *Madrasa; Education, religion and state in the Middle East.* Studies in honor of Michael Winter (Tel Aviv: The Moshe Dayan Center for Middle Eastern and African Studies, 2004), pp. 109–28.

The essay is based on a small sample from the Mahdī's documents arranged according to subject matter (see Layish, *Selection from the Mahdī's documents*); hence, the conclusions should be regarded as tentative. The research on the Mahdī's legal methodology is supported by a grant from the Israel Science Foundation.

[Originally published in *Jerusalem Studies in Arabic and Islam*, 33 (2007), pp. 279–308.]

Unless otherwise indicated, the introduction is based on Layish, "Issues in marriage and divorce" and Layish, "Mechanism for adapting the *Sharīʿa*."

2 Holt, *Mahdist state*, pp. 19ff.; *idem*, "al-Mahdiyya," pp. 1247ii ff.; Abū Salīm, *al-Ḥaraka*, p. 164; O'Fahey, "Sudanese Mahdi," pp. 276–77; cf. Mustafa, "The common law," p. 38.

3 Mālik, *al-Muqāwama*, pp. 151, 153; Sulaymān, *Dawr al-Azhar*, p. 82; Ibrāhīm, *al-Taʿlīm*, p. 332.

4 Holt suggests "colloquy" for *ḥaḍra* since the emphasis is not on the visible appearance of the Prophet, but on the message he communicates. The usual Arabic term for "vision," *ruʾyā*, is not used in the Mahdī's documents (*Mahdist state*, p. 105, fn. 1), but is used elsewhere; also *ibid.*, p. 128; cf. Kister, "The struggle against Musaylima," pp. 4, 7, 13ff., 16. On *ḥaḍra*, see below.

 | DOI:10.1163/9789004680920_010

order it may be inferred that he regarded the *sunna* as more important than the Qur'ān, and indeed, he did not rule out the possibility that a *ḥadīth* may abrogate (*yansakh*) a Qur'ānic provision.[5] He preferred the literal, external (*ẓāhir*) interpretation of the textual sources.

The Mahdī replaced analogical reasoning (*qiyās*) with Prophetic inspiration (*ilhām*),[6] which ranks even higher than the *ḥadīth* since it is impossible to refute its authenticity. Hence, the legal norm shaped by the Mahdī was final, irrevocable and infallible (*maʿṣūm min al-khaṭa'*).[7] The enlistment of Prophetic sanction was apparently meant to allow the Mahdī to dispense with the mechanism of the consensus of the *ʿulamā'* (*ijmāʿ*), thus placing him outside the reach of public criticism. The abrogation of the *madhāhib* too seems to have served the same purpose.[8] This procedure conferred upon the Mahdī a degree of discretion greater than that allowed by analogical reasoning. The Mahdī derived his legitimacy from his claim to be recognized as heir (*wārith*) to, and successor of, the Prophet,[9] and as the "Expected Mahdī."

There is ample evidence in the Mahdī's documents that his decisions and *fatwās* were heavily dependent upon the Qur'ān, the *ḥadīth*, and *ilhām*, which occasionally resulted in *ijtihad*.[10] The Mahdī also instructed the *umarā'* (military commanders commissioned by the Mahdī with *jihād*), *khulafā'* (deputies of local heads, *shaykh*s, of Ṣūfī orders) and *nuwwāb* (judicial deputies) to hand down their decisions on the basis of the textual sources.[11] The application of his

5 This is an ancient concept in orthodox Islam: "Sunna and Koran were considered as of entirely equal importance" due to the divine origin of the *sunna*; see Goldziher, *Muslim Studies*, p. 31 and the source cited there.

6 Occasionally the Mahdī requests the inspiration directly from God or by means of the "Angel of Inspiration": *Al-Āthār*, vol. 3 (1991), no. 341, p. 111 (*astaʿīn bi-llāhi ... wa-astawhibuhu 'l-ilhām*); *ibid.*, vol. 4 (1992), no. 776, p. 94 (*fa-min hādhā al-khabar al-nabawī ʿalimtu anna 'lladhī yulhimunī allāh bihi bi-wāsiṭat malak al-ilhām*); cf. Radtke, "Sufism in the 18th century," p. 350; see below footnote 9.

7 Cf. Radtke, "Sufism in the 18th century," p. 359.

8 Cf. Abū Salām, *al-Ḥaraka*, p. 83, 179; Mālik, *al-Muqāwama*, p. 151.

9 Cf. Kister, "The struggle against Musaylima," p. 13; Goldziher, *Muslims studies*, p. 266.

10 Layish, "Mechanism for adapting the *Sharīʿa*", e.g., p. 223 (Qur'ānic verses pertaining to a divorced woman's waiting period, and to inheritance), p. 226 (Qurānic verse concerning spoils), p. 229 (Prophetic *ḥadīth* regarding prohibition of marriage on grounds of fosterage), p. 233 (Qur'ānic verses related to amputation of a thief's hand, and to the sanction prescribed for *qadhf*), p. 235f. and fn. 48 (*ilhām* pertaining to reinstatement of triply-divorced wife and to polygamous marriage); Maḥmūd, *al-Fikr al-ṣūfū.*, p. 101; al-Qaddāl, *al-Mahdū*, p. 143; Trimingham, *Islam in the Sudan*, p. 155. The Mahdī, however, denied having exercised *ijtihād*; he attributed his pronouncements to the inspiration from the Prophet or the Angel of Inspiration. Holt, *Mahdist state*, p. 122 fn. 2, p. 128.

11 Khālid, *al-Fajr al-kādhib*, pp. 21, 293; Mustafa, *The common law*, p. 39.

legal methodology enabled the Mahdī to introduce innovative reforms, some of which were far-reaching deviations from orthodox *sharīʿa*.[12] These brought the Mahdī into conflict with the Turco-Egyptian-oriented "*ʿulamāʾ* of the evil" (*sūʾ*), some of whom were graduates of al-Azhar.[13] The Mahdī's claim to be the "Expected Mahdī" was also severely criticized by the *ʿulamāʾ*.[14]

In his defense against the *ʿulamāʾ*'s contention that the Mahdī was not qualified for *ijtihād*,[15] al-ʿAbbādī claims that the Mahdī was above *ijtihād* since he derived rules while in a state of wakefulness (*yaqẓatan*) directly from the Angel of Inspiration[16] and the Prophet; moreover, he was infallible. Hence, those initiated into mystical knowledge (the *ʿārifūn*) claimed that the Mahdī could deduce rules from the textual sources without making recourse to reasoning (*raʾy*) and analogy (*qiyās*), and without being bound by the *taqlīd*. Al-ʿAbbādī enlists Ibn al-ʿArabī (d. 638/1240) and ʿAbd al-Wahhāb al-Shaʿrānī (d. 973/1565) in his defense, and concludes that the Mahdī's communion with the Prophet fully qualifies him for *ijtihād* even if he lacks some of the required qualifications. The *ʿulamāʾ* rejected *ilhām* and the vision of the Prophet (*ruʾyā*; see below), on the grounds that they, the *ʿulamāʾ*, were bound by the textual sources and the *sharīʿa*. The Mahdī, on the other hand, contended that the will of God is above the textual sources which may be abrogated by *naskh*.[17]

Abū Salīm maintains that the Mahdī's *ijtihād* was exercised within the framework of Salafī Islam, totally detached from any school or jurist and that he was the supreme legal authority (*al-marjaʿ al-aʿlā*); since he received inspiration directly from the Prophet, he alone was able to deduce valid rules. Hence, the *ʿulamāʾ* had no alternative but to abide by his *ijtihād*.[18]

---

12 On the Mahdī as a divinely-guided reformer and *mujaddid*, see O'Fahey, "Sudanese Mahdi," p. 273.

13 Holt, *Mahdist state*, p. 116; al-Mahdī, "al-Mahdiyya," p. 225; Mālik, *al-Mqāwama*, p. 123; al-Qaddāl, *al-Mahdī*, pp. 94–95; Sulaymām, *Dawr al-Azhar*, pp. 83ff. Cf. Goldziher, *Muslim studies*, p. 267.

14 Holt, *Mahdist state*, pp. 107–10.

15 Al-ʿAbbādī, *al-Anwār*, pp. 230–36; *idem, Ṣafḥa min khilāf al-ʿulamāʾ*, pp. 28–29, 114–16; al-Mahdī, *al-Mahdiyya*, p. 223; for details on al-ʿAbbādī's treatise (*al-Anwār*), see *ibid.*, pp. 5ff.; O'Fahey, *Arabic literature of Africa*, pp. 334–35; Abu Shouk, *A bibliography of the Mahdist state*, pp. 134–35; Abū Salīm, *al-Ḥaraka*, pp. 65–66; Mālik, *al-Muqāwama*, p. 131.

16 Layish, "Issues in marriage and divorce," pp. 49, 60; cf. Radtke, "Sufism in the 18th century," p. 359.

17 Al-Mahdī, "al-Mahdiyya," p. 225; Ibrāhīm, *al-Ṣirūʿ*, p. 41.

18 Abū Salīm, *al-Ḥaraka*, pp. 165, 168, 189–90. Khalīfa ʿAbdullāhi, the Mahdī's successor, regarded the Mahdī as the last of the *mujaddidūn*; *ibid.*, p. 89 fn. 4. Cf. *al-Āthār*, vol. 5 (1992), no. 944, p. 367 (the Mahdī: *wa-innī mujaddid mā 'ndarasa min al-sunan wa-tafsār al-Qurʾān*); al-Qaddāl, *al-Mahdī*, p. 140.

The Mahdī's legal opinions, circulars (*manshūrāt*), proclamations, orders, decisions, warnings etc. were in fact sources of law;[19] these governmental instruments established the Mahdī's position as the custodian of public morality with a view to superseding and abolishing Ṣūfī orders and bringing the Sudanese society within the orbit of the Mahdist state.[20] The legal reforms in matters of personal status significantly improved the status of women.

The Mahdī left no treatise in which he presented his legal methodology and its sources of inspiration. Hence, this study is an attempt to reconstruct his methodology on the basis of the documents issued by, or attributed to, him.[21] In the documents consulted so far there is no explicit or direct evidence as to the Mahdī's sources of inspiration and the evidence is mainly circumstantial: references to Ṣūfīs with whom the Mahdī had contacts during various stages of his life, mediators who served as links between the Mahdī and doctrines expressed by founders of *ṭarīqa*s. Pragmatic and practical considerations undoubtedly played a role in shaping the Mahdī's legal thinking since he did not live in a vacuum. Due attention should therefore be given to the intellectual environment in which the Mahdī was brought up and in which his spiritual world view was molded. Undoubtedly, the Ṣūfī tradition was the dominant formative factor in this environment. It is worth noting that Muḥammad Aḥmad was a Ṣūfī shaykh before his manifestation as a Mahdī and that he mobilized the Ṣūfī networks in the Sudan to promote his cause.[22]

Most of the revivalist and reformist movements in Arabia and the Maghreb during the 18th and 19th centuries were linked one way or another with a Ṣūfī tradition.[23] Hence, there seems to be causal connections, through doctrinal links in Arabia and the Maghrib, between the Mahdī's legal reformism and his Ṣūfī background. Naturally, one can identify Ṣūfī mechanisms and terminology in the Mahdī's legal methodology.[24] Some acquaintance with the legal doctrines of the founders of *ṭarīqas* who may have shaped the Mahdī's legal thinking is therefore indispensable. An attempt will be made below to trace the Mahdī's

19 Abdullāhi would instruct newly nominated *qāḍīs* to hand down their decisions on the basis of the Qur'ān, the *sunna* and the Mahdī's *manshūrāt*. ʿAlī, *Azmat al-Islām al-siyāsī*, p. 41; Mālik, *al-Muqāwama*, p. 151; Sulaymān, *Dawr al-Azhar*, p. 82; Rayāḍ, *Mūjaz ta'rīkh al-sulṭa al-tashrīʿiyya*, p. 16.

20 Holt, *Mahdist state*, p. 21. Cf. Voll, "Sudanese Mahdī," pp. 162ff.

21 For a bibliography of his documents and other items, see O'Fahey, *Arabic literature of Africa*, pp. 306ff.; Abu Shouk, "A bibliography of the Mahdist state," pp. 145ff., 163ff.

22 Karrar, *The Sufi brotherhoods*, p. 4.

23 For the 18th century Neo-Sufism, see Voll, "Hadith," pp. 264, 267ff.; *idem*, "Mizjaji family," p. 87; Letzion and Voll, *Renewal and reform*, p. 8; al-Qaddāl, *al-Mahdī*, p. 90.

24 *Al-Āthār*, vol. 1 (1990), no. 15, p. 77, fn. 6 (the Prophet in a *ḥaḍra nabawiyya*: "Your *shaykh* is the Mahdī").

sources of inspiration by means of comparative and textual (where available) analysis of the legal methodologies of dominant Ṣūfīs regarding whom there is circumstantial evidence linking them to the Mahdī.

The Mahdī's educational and Ṣūfī background is, of course, of special importance. His family claimed to be *ashrāf*, descendants of the Prophet. He attended *khalawāt*, Qur'ān schools, and studied with local holy men and *fakīs* (a dialect-form of *faqīh*s), religious teachers propagating Islam; he also received a religious education in a state school. Unlike some of his colleagues, he did not proceed to al-Azhar, but rather preferred a life of asceticism and mystic experiences within the discipline of a Ṣūfī order. He spent seven years with Shaykh Muḥammad Sharīf Nūr al-Dā'im, the grandson of Shaykh Aḥmad al-Ṭayyib al-Bashīr, who had introduced the Sammāniyya *ṭarīqa*, a branch of the Khalwatiyya, into the Sudan;[25] he gained a reputation for extreme asceticism, and was given an *ijāza* to teach as a shaykh of the Sammāniyya.[26] After having moved to Abā Island, a crisis with his master caused his subsequent expulsion from the order. Muḥammad Aḥmad professed allegiance to Shaykh al-Qurashī wad al-Zayn, a rival head of the Sammāniyya. When the latter died, his followers recognized Muḥammad Aḥmad as the new leader of the Sammāniyya.[27]

According to Abū Salīm, Muḥammad Aḥmad read treatises by al-Ghazālī, Ibn al-ʿArabī, Ibn Idrīs, and Aḥmad Ṭayyib al-Bashīr. At some time he joined the Tijānī order in Berber. He also had a good knowledge of the Qur'ān, *ḥadīth*, *tafsīr* and *fiqh*. He was inclined to the Mālikī school in matters pertaining to substantive law, to the Shāfiʿī school in matters of *ʿibādāt*, and to the Ḥanbalī school in matters concerning theology (*tawḥīd*) and penal law. Ibrāhīm suggests that the Mahdī intended to unite all the schools by means of the eclectic method (*ikhtiyār*). The Mahdī never left the Sudan and seemed to lack orientation in issues facing Islam outside its borders.[28]

---

25 Holt, "A Sudanese saint," pp. 108–15; Holt, *Mahdist state*, pp. 21, 45–49; O'Fahey, *Arabic literature of Africa*, pp. 304–5; Trimingham, *Islam in the Sudan*, pp. 93–95, 226–27; Karrar, *The Sufi brotherhoods*, pp. 43–47; O'Fahey, "Sudanese Mahdi," pp. 268ff.

26 *Al-Āthār*, vol. 1 (1990), no. 1, pp. 1ff.; al-Qaddāl, *al-Mahdī*, pp. 37ff., 44ff.; Shaked, *The life of the Sudanese Mahdi*, pp. 56–57; Sulaymān, *Dawr al-Azhar*, p. 83; Trimingham, *Islam in the Sudan*, p. 93; O'Fahey, "Sudanese Mahdi," p. 270.

27 Holt, *Mahdist state*, pp. 21, 45–50; *idem*, "A Sudanese saint," pp. 114–15; Trimingham, *Islam in the Sudan*, p. 227; O'Fahey, *Enigmatic saint*, p. 35; *idem*, "Sudanese Mahdi," pp. 269–271; Abū Salīm, *al-Ḥaraka*, pp. 93–94; Maḥmūd, *al-Fikr al-ṣūfī*, pp. 93ff.

28 Abū Salīm, *al-Ḥaraka*, pp. 79, 83–84, 95–97 Ibrāhīm, *al-Fikr*, p. 31. Cf. Mālik, *al-Muqāwama*, p. 154; al-Mahdī, "al-Mahdiyya," pp. 180, 192; O'Fahey, "Sudanese Mahdi," pp. 274–76; al-Qaddāl, *al-Mahdī*, p. 53.

## 2 The Sammānī Tradition

It stands to reason that the Sammāniyya order, into which Muḥammad Aḥmad was initiated in his early formative period, had an immediate impact on his spiritual and mystical life. According to Karrar, the Sammāniyya was introduced into the Sudan as a "reformist" *ṭarīqa* with an emphasis on aspects of worship, such as *dhikr* and *madīḥ* (songs of praise), and on the (Ṣūfī) philosophy.[29] Although Muḥammad b. ʿAbd al-Karīm al-Sammān (d. 1775) is not mentioned in the Mahdī's documents,[30] there is some substantial evidence that links the Mahdī to al-Sammān's doctrines. In his writings, al-Sammān elaborates themes connected with the *ṭarīqa Muḥammadiyya*, such as his own visionary experiences regarding the *nūr Muḥammadī* and the "external" appearance of the Prophet and his *sunna* which the mystic is required to follow. Al-Sammān distinguishes between a physical (*ṣūrī*) and spiritual (*maʿnawī*) imitation of the Prophet, the latter consisting of visualizing the Prophet's appearance in its physical reality (*istiḥḍār ṣūratihi*). Moreover, at a higher stage, one is capable of visualizing the light of the *ḥaqīqa Muḥammadiyya* itself and becoming extinguished in it. Visions of this kind were experienced and recorded by al-Sammān himself. He regards association with the Prophet as an established practice for the enlightened mystic (i.e., one who has experienced *faṭh*, illumination) who may speak with the Prophet, as did the Companions (thus becoming a *ṣaḥābī*), and consult him about legal issues.[31]

The notion of encounters with the Prophet (*ḥaḍrat al-rasūl*) seems indeed to have been well established in the Sammāniyya order. Both Muḥammad b. ʿAbd al-Karīm al-Sammān and Aḥmad al-Ṭayyib al-Bashīr conceived of praying (*taṣliya*) for the Prophet as a prelude to encountering him, either in one's sleep or in a state of wakefulness.[32] Aḥmad al-Ṭayyib al-Bashīr had a vision confirming that his real master in Medina was Muḥammad b. ʿAbd al-Karīm al-Sammān, and another vision in which the Prophet declared Muḥammad Sharīf Nūr al-Dāʾim as Ahmad al-Ṭayyib's successor.[33]

29 Holt, *Mahdist State*, p. 21; Karrar, *The Sufi brotherhoods*, pp. 45, 48; Trimingham, *Islam in the Sudan*, pp. 226–27.

30 Muḥammad ʿAbd al-Karīm al-Sammānī mentioned in the Names Index of *al-Āthār*, vol. 7 (1994), p. 349, is the Mahdī's paternal cousin and agent (*ʿāmil*) in the Province of Sinnār.

31 Radtke, "Sufism in the 18th century," pp. 332, 355, 357. On the *faṭh*, see *ibid.*, p. 358; Radtke *et al.*, "Two Ṣūfī treatises," p. 158 (al-Sammān refers to angelic thought as *ilhām*). Cf. Goldziher, *Muslim studies*, p. 162.

32 Karrar, *The Sufi brotherhoods*, p. 177 (Glossary); Obeid, "The history of the Sammāniyya *Ṭarīqa*," p. 141, ch. 2.4; see below.

33 Karrar, *The Sufi brotherhoods*, pp. 45–48.

As already noted, the encounter with the Prophet or *ḥaḍra*[34] was instrumental in the Mahdī's procedure of legislation. The encounter provided him with the opportunity to seek inspiration (*ilhām*) from the Prophet or, occasionally, from the "Angel of Inspiration" in order to solve legal problems. Inspiration thus became a source of law in the Mahdī's legal methodology.

Nūr al-Dā'im provides some information on Aḥmad al-Ṭayyib al-Bashīr's Ṣūfī doctrine which may have some legal relevance. He makes a distinction between internal knowledge (*ʿilm al-bāṭin*) and external knowledge (*ʿilm al-ẓāhir*). The former is manifested in *al-ḥaqīqa*, "true reality," which seems to imply that it is accessible only to the initiated into a Ṣūfi *ṭarīqa*. The latter is manifested in the *sharīʿa*, which seems to imply that the literal interpretation of the textual sources is accessible to the uninitiated. He cites in this context ʿAbd al-Wahhāb al-Shaʿrānī who strongly supports this distinction.[35] As we shall see below, al-Bashīr's doctrine is largely identical with that of Ibn Idrīs.[36] It may well be that the Mahdī was exposed to Ibn Idrīs' literal interpretation of the textual sources through Muḥammad Sharīf Nūr al-Dā'im. Nūr al-Dā'im further maintains that fear of God (*taqwā*) is one of six principles of al-Bashīr's Ṣūfī doctrine. There is no indication that this principle was transformed by the Mahdī into a legal source, as in Ibn Idrīs' *Risālat al-radd*.[37]

Abū Salīm argues that the decision to abrogate the *madhāhib* with a view to bringing about the unification of the Muslim world occurred already at a very early stage of Muḥammad Aḥmad's formative period, and that in fact this issue was one of the main causes of the break with Shaykh Muḥammad Sharīf Nūr al-Dā'im. The first indication in the Mahdī's documents of his departure from the *madhāhib* preceded his manifestation (*ẓuhūr*) as the Mahdī.[38] It is worthwhile mentioning in this connection that in al-Sammān's view, mere adherence to one of the four schools of law is a self-evident truth;[39] in other words, he admits the legitimacy of all the *madhāhib*. Al-Ṣādiq al-Mahdī argues that initially, prior to his rejection of school fanaticism (*taʿaṣṣub*), the Mahdī had a tolerant approach towards the Imāms of the *madhāhib*; he changed his mind,

34 See footnotes 4 and 6, above. Cf. Radtke, "Ibrāziana," pp. 121–23; Radtke, "Sufism in the 18th century," pp. 356–59; Hofheinz, "Transcending the Madhhab," p. 244, fn. 48 (*ḥaḍra* [Prophetic or Divine] presence); Trimingham, *Islam in the Sudan*, pp. 95, 151–52; Maḥmūd, *al-Fikr al-ṣūfī*, pp. 100–1; al-Zākī, *"al-Islām wa-ḥayātunā al-tashrīʿiyya,"* p. 148. See below.

35 Nūr al-Dā'im, *Azāhīr al-riyāḍ*, pp. 187ff., 252–54. Cf. Massignon-Radtke, "*Taṣawwuf*," p. 314; Radtke, "Sufism in the 18th century," pp. 335–36; Radtke *et al.*, *The Exoteric*, p. 15, fn. 40 and the references mentioned there.

36 Cf. Muḥammad ʿAlī Yūsuf's Appendix to *Azāhīr al-riyāḍ*, pp. 383ff.

37 Nūr al-Dā'im, *Azāhīr al-riyāḍ*, p. 83; see below.

38 Abū Salīm, *al-Ḥaraka*, p. 86.

39 Radtke, "Sufism in the 18th century," p. 338.

according to al-Qaddāl, when he realized that the pluralism of *madhāhib* and legal literature were a cause of confusion in religion.[40]

Muḥammad Aḥmad was taught the Sammānī litanies (*awrād*), and after obtaining the *ijāza* was authorized to teach them to his followers.[41] There is evidence in the Mahdī's documents that it was Muḥammad Sharīf Nūr al-Dā'im who exposed him to the notion of the Expected Mahdī.[42] As we shall see below, ʿAbdullāhi al-Dufārī who provided the doctrinal link between Ibn Idrīs and the Mahdī, had earlier visited the centre of Aḥmad al-Ṭayyib b. al-Bashīr. Karrar observes that al-Dufārī kept up the tradition of close ties with the Sammāniyya followed by all those influenced by Ibn Idrīs.[43]

From the above evidence one may conclude that the Sammāniyya may have played some role in the Mahdī's early formative period, especially with respect to the doctrine of encounters with the Prophet which is an essential element in the structure of the Mahdī's legal methodology.

## 3 The Idrīsī Tradition

Textual analysis of Aḥmad Ibn Idrīs al-Fāsī's writings suggests that he was Muḥammad Aḥmad's most influential teacher even before his manifestation as the Mahdī. Although Ibn Idrīs did not establish his own *ṭarīqa*, he initiated a tradition that gave rise to several reformist Ṣūfī orders.[44] In the Mahdī's documents, Ibn Idrīs plays a dominant role in the vision of Muḥammad Aḥmad as the "Expected Mahdī" and the Prophet's Successor; Ibn Idrīs, whom the Mahdī regards as an authority for authenticating the validity of *ḥadīth* (*muḥaqqiq*), is enlisted to testify to the Mahdī's genuine Mahdiship.[45]

Moreover, there is evidence of an indirect intermediary, Shaykh ʿAbdallāhi ʿAbd al-Ḥafīẓ al-Dufārī (d. 1908), who provided a doctrinal link between Ibn Idrīs and Muḥammad Aḥmad. Al-Dufārī, who studied with Ibrāhīm al-Rashīd (d. 1874), a disciple of Ibn Idrīs, in the Ḥijāz, taught Muḥammad Aḥmad Ibn

40 Al-Mahdī, *al-Mahdiyya*, pp. 164, 170–71, 234; and al-Qaddāl, *al-Mahdī*, p. 140.

41 Obeid, "The history of Sammāniyya *Ṭarīqa*, p. 141, ch. 2.4.

42 *Al-Āthār*, vol. 1 (1990), no. 153, p. 421; and vol. 3 (1991), no. 328, p. 87f.; Abū Salīm, *al-Ḥaraka*, p. 23.

43 Karrar, *The Sufi brotherhoods*, p. 111.

44 Holt, *Mahdist state*, pp. 19–21; O'Fahey, *Enigmatic saint*, pp. 9ff.; O'Fahey and Karrar, "The enigmatic Imam," p. 205f.; Levtzion and Weigert, "Religious reform in eighteenth-century Morocco," p. 194.

45 *Al-Āthār*, vol. 1 (1990), no. 115, pp. 336ff.; O'Fahey, *Enigmatic saint*, pp. 178–79; *idem*, "Sudanese Mahdi," p. 275; O'Fahey and Karrar, "The enigmatic Imam," p. 213; Aḥmad, *Ibn Idrīs*, p. 8.

Idrīs' litanies (*awrād, aḥzāb*) which may symbolize a doctrinal integration with the latter's Ṣūfī tradition. Hence, it is hardly surprising that according to some sources, al-Dufārī gave Muḥammad Aḥmad an *ijāza* to teach Ibn Idrīs' doctrines and litanies.[46]

The reconstruction of Ibn Idrīs' views on the *madhāhib* is based on a textual analysis of his *Risālat al-radd ʿalā ahl al-raʾy bi'l-ṣawāb li-muwāfaqat al-sunna wa-'l-kitāb.* He categorically denies the *madhāhib* any authority whatsoever; likewise, he denies the founders of the schools, along with the Companions, the virtue of infallibility. Moreover, adherence to the *madhādhib* amounts to *shirk* because the schools are not anchored in the authority of God. Consequently, the layman may not follow an *ʿālim* unless the latter has based his judgment exclusively on revelation (i.e., the Qurʾān and the *ḥadīth*). He further maintains that the adherence to the *madhāhib* should be replaced by fear of God (*taqwā*), by means of which an individual can arrive at a higher form of discrimination (*furqān*) that will enable him to conceive of God's commands solely on the basis of the textual sources, without having resort to the legal literature of the *madhāhib.* Fear of God is requested from those who have not been initiated in the mystic path and whose grasp of God's commands is hence based on intuitive rather than intellectual understanding. On the other hand, those who have been initiated in the mystic path are expected to be guided by the *ṭarīqa Muḥammadiyya* which combines Ṣūfism and law and provides a state of illuminated consciousness.[47] Needless to say, this approach, though less sophisticated, is shared by the Mahdī.[48] O'Fahey, on the other hand, argues that Ibn Idrīs tolerated all the schools, especially the Ḥanbalī, and hence rejected school fanaticism on the grounds that Muslims form one religious community. The Mahdī too initially did not regard himself bound exclusively by any of the schools.[49]

---

46 Karrar, *The Sufi brotherhoods*, pp. 97, 110–114; O'Fahey, *Enigmatic saint*, pp. 178–79; Ibrāhīm, *Ibn Idrīs*, pp. 384–85; Aḥmad, *Ibn Idrīs*, pp. 6, 8; Radtke, "Sufism in the 18th century," p. 334. Cf. Hofheinz, "Internalising Islam," p. 184.

47 O'Fahey and Radtke. "Neo-Sufism reconsidered," pp. 65–71; Radtke *et al., The Exoteric*, pp. ix–x, 12, 25–26 (Vikør, who is one of the co-authors of *The Exoteric*, does not share the view that *taqwā* should be regarded as inspiration from God; see Vikør, "The Shaykh as *Mujtahid*"); Radtke, "Sufism in the 18th century," pp. 338–39, 355; *idem, "Ijtihād* and Neo-Sufism," p. 919 (rejection of *taʿaṣṣub al- madhāhib*); Ibrāhīm, *Ibn Idrīs*, pp. 108–9, 229; cf. Vikør, "Jihād," p. 155; Levtzion and Voll, *Renewal and reform*, pp. 9–10; O'Fahey, *Enigmatic saint*, p. 134. On the concept of *ṭarīqa muḥammadiyya*, see Radtke, "Projection," pp. 72–74, 77 fn. 18; *idem*, "Ibrīziana," p. 114ff. On Qurʾān and *furqān* in Ibn al-ʿArabī's teachings, see Chittick, "Taṣawwuf," pp. 317ii–18.

48 Layish, "Issues in marriage and divorce," p. 39; cf. Khālid, *al-Fajr al-kāadhib*, p. 293.

49 O'Fahey, *Enigmatic saint*, pp. 34, 75–76, 108; Abū Salīm, *al-Ḥaraka*, pp. 165–66; above.

The *Risāla* provides a clear notion of Ibn Idrīs' legal methodology.[50] The legal methodology consists of the Qur'ān and the *sunna* which are tantamount to revelation (*waḥy*).[51] Hence, the textual sources alone constitute authoritative proof (*ḥujja*) (sections 1–3). Ibrāhīm maintains that Ibn Idrīs' *uṣūl* consists of a third textual source – *qawl al-ṣaḥābī*, i.e., legal opinion or judgment of a Companion, which may be resorted to in case of a lacuna (*faqd al-naṣṣ*) in the former two textual sources.[52]

Ibn Idrīs categorically rejects all forms of human reasoning (*ra'y, qiyās, fikr*) for deriving rules from the textual sources because they give rise to differences; the scholar is not immune from error (*maʿṣūm*) unless he follows the Prophet, that is, adheres to the *sunna*. Section 6 of the *Risāla* prohibits personal judgment on the basis of reason (*al-qawl bi'l-ra'y ḥarām*) and systematic analogy (*qiyās*) for deducing legal rules unless the textual sources of the Qur'ān and the *sunna* have been totally exhausted. In the event of "silence" (*sukūt*) or a lacuna in the textual sources (cf. sections 16, 25, 33) about a particular act, the act is regarded as being permissible (*jā'iz, mubāḥ*) or pardonable (*ʿafw*) in the legal sense (sections 33–34).[53]

The ability of the Qur'ān and the *sunna* to provide all the necessary rules for conducting one's life is subject to one being in fear of God (*taqwā*) (section 5). In other words, Ibn Idrīs replaces scholastic knowledge based on reasoning with pietism, which enables him to derive God's commands by means of intuitive knowledge based solely on the textual sources (section 14). Proper understanding (*fahm*) of the Qur'ān and the *sunna* cannot be achieved intellectually, but rather intuitively on the basis of one's fear of God.[54]

The same concept can be traced in the Mahdī's documents. While discussing the application of Qur'ānic punishments, the Mahdī states categorically that the derivation of rules (*ikhrāj al-aḥkām*) from the Qur'ān should be based exclusively on pietism (*bayān ikhrāj al-aḥkām min al-kitāb al-taqwā*) which implies a rejection of any form of reason (*ra'y* or *qiyās*). This statement is supported by Qur'ān 2:282 and 65:2.[55] In response to a question, the Mahdī replied: "Our *madhhab* is the Book, the *sunna*, and trust (*tawakkul*) in God ... [instead of] the reasoning of the founders of the *madhāhib* (*ra'y al-mashāyikh*)." In a

---

50 Radtke *et* al., *The Exoteric*, pp. ix–x, 7–13, 23–24. For the Arabic text of the *Risāla*, see *ibid.*, pp. 47–80; cf. Aḥmad, *Ibn Idrīs*, p. 21.

51 Cf. Radtke *et* al., "Two Ṣūfī treatises," p. 158.

52 Ibrāhīm, *Ibn Idrīs*, pp. 222–25.

53 The mystic alone is capable of exercising *qiyās* because he understands the inner cosmos; O'Fahey and Radtke. "Neo-Sufism reconsidered," p. 60; cf. O'Fahey, *Enigmatic saint*, pp. 25–26.

54 Radtke, "*Ijtihād* and Neo-Sufism," p. 919.

55 *Al-Āthār*, vol. 3 (1991), no. 452, p. 352.

Ṣūfī context, *tawakkul* means a mystic state of abandonment into God's hands. Legally, the term seems to be close to *taqwā*.[56]

In the *Risāla*, Ibn Idrīs does not refer at all to consensus (*ijmāʿ*) which seems to imply that he does not recognize it as a source of law. Abū Salīm and Aḥmad argue that Ibn Idrīs acknowledges only the *ijmāʿ* of the *ṣaḥāba*, not that of later jurists.[57] Needless to say, this restriction diminishes the operative significance of *ijmāʿ*.

Both Ibn Idrīs and the Mahdī share recognition of the Qurʾān and the *sunna* as sources of law while totally denying *qiyās* and implicitly also *ijmāʿ*. *Ilhām*, the third source of law in the Mahdī's legal methodology, may perhaps be identified, in terms of procedure and substance, with revelation (*waḥy*) in Ibn Idrīs' writings, though the reference there is to the revelations of Allāh to the Prophet: only by means of this revelation is the Prophet authorized to make things permissible (*taḥlīl*) or prohibited (*taḥrīm*) in a legal sense (section 24 of the *Risāla*).[58] The possibility that the Mahdī extended the scope of this procedure to cover revelation from, rather than to, the Prophet out of practical considerations cannot be ruled out, though no direct evidence to this effect is available in the Mahdī's documents.[59]

In the *Risāla*, Ibn Idrīs refers implicitly to the *ẓāhirī* interpretation of the textual sources: "Whatever is clearly stated [in scriptural revelation]… is not in need of further clarification (*al-mubayyan mubayyan … wa-lā yaḥtāj ilā bayān ākhar*)" (section 34).[60] A more explicit reference is found in his debate with the jurists of ʿAsīr:

> We construe the texts in accordance with their external meanings (*ẓawāhir*) in the Arabic language and we are of the opinion that attention to the external interpretation is indispensable, for there can be no hope of arriving at the internal meaning without first establishing the external sense (*wa-narā anna al-ʿināya bi-'l-tafsīr al-ẓāhir lā budda minhu, idh lā maṭmaʿ fī 'l-wuṣūl ilā al-bāṭin qabla iḥkām al-ẓāhir*).[61]

56 Al-Mahdī, *al-Mahdiyya*, pp. 172, 173; cf. Trimingham, *Ṣūfī orders*, Glossary, s.v. *tawakkul*.

57 O'Fahey, *Enigmatic saint*, p. 25; Ahmad, *Ibn Idrīs*, p. 22.

58 Cf. Radtke, "*Ijtihād* and Neo-Sufism," p. 913.

59 Cf. Aḥmad, *Ibn Idrīs*, pp. 18–19. On the differences between *ilhām* and *waḥy*, see Macdonald, "Ilhām," pp. 1119–20; Lazarus-Yafeh, *Studies in Ghazzālī*, pp. 304–6; al-Mahdī, "Mustaqbal," pp. 87, 389, 409.

60 Radtke *et al.*, *The Exoteric*, pp. 10, 65 (the Arabic text). Cf. Levtzion and Voll, *Renewal and reform*, p. 9.

61 Radtke *et al.*, *The Exoteric*, p. 41 ("precondition for internal interpretation of the Qurʾān is one's capability to exercise external [*ẓāhirī*] interpretation"), p. 163, no. (29) (the Arabic text), p. 198. Cf. Radtke, "*Ijtihād* and Neo-Sufism," p. 912; O'Fahey, *Enigmatic saint*, p. 195.

In *al-ʿIqd al-nafīs*, Ibn Idrīs distinguished between the inner dimension (*baṭn*), which is revealed only to the intellectual elite (*khawāṣṣ*), and the external dimension (*ẓahr*), revealed through the science (*ʿilm*) of the *sharīʿa*; this seems to imply that the conventional literal interpretation of the Qurʾān is accessible to the uninitiated into the mystic path.[62] According to Ibrāhīm, Ibn Idrīs maintains that only in cases where it is impossible to fully comprehend the meanings (*maʿānin*) of the Qurʾān by adhering to a *ẓāhirī* interpretation, is one permitted to resort to the knowledge of the divine grace (*al-ʿilm al-fayḍī*), which implies *bāṭinī* interpretation.[63]

The Mahdī resorted to a *ẓāhirī* interpretation of the textual sources. We discussed elsewhere instances of literal interpretation of a Prophetic *ḥadīth* pertaining to the prohibition to marry on grounds of fosterage (*yaḥrumu min al-riḍāʿ mā yaḥrumu min al-nasab*), and of the Qurʾānic verse 5:38 pertaining to the amputation of the thief's hand (*wa-ʾl-sāriq wa-ʾl-sāriqa fa-ʾqṭaʿū aydiyahumā jazāʾan bi-mā kasabā nakālan min allāh …*).[64] The tension between the Mahdī and the *ʿulamāʾ* is articulated in terms of a conflict between the Ṣūfīs representing the *ahl al-bāṭin*, i.e., the initiated into the mystic path (*al-khāṣṣa*), and the *ʿulamāʾ* representing the *ahl al-ẓāhir* (*al-ʿāmma*).[65] *Kashf*, revelation, divine *ilhām*, and colloquy (*ḥaḍra*) with, or vision (*ruʾyā*) of, the Prophet – vital mechanisms in the Mahdī's doctrine – are conceived in the best Ṣūfī tradition as *karāmāt* within the domain of *ʿilm al-bāṭin*, and hence outside the control of the *ʿulamāʾ*.[66]

Ibn Idrīs seems to have been the Mahdī's source of inspiration also with respect to the precedence of the Prophetic *sunna* over the Qurʾān. This seems to be a shortcut to abrogation (*naskh*) of Qurʾānic verses by *sunna*. Section 3 of the *Risāla* reads:

> Moreover, every legal rule is in the Qurʾān, the *sunna* being identical with it – in fact the *sunna* is its [authoritative] interpretation (*bal al-ḥukm kulluhu fī ʾl-kitāb idh al-sunna ʿaynuhu fa-innahā bayānuhu*).[67]

62 O'Fahey, *Enigmatic saint*, p. 196. For the Arabic text, see Ibn Idrās, *al-ʿIqd*, pp. 245–46; cf. Radtke, "Sufism in the 18th century," pp. 339–40; O'Fahey and Radtke, "Neo-Sufism reconsidered," p. 60; O'Fahey and Karrar, "The enigmatic Imam," p. 208.

63 Ibrāhīm, *Ibn Idrīs*, p. 228.

64 Layish, "Mechanism for adapting the *Sharīʿa*," pp. 229 and 233, respectively. Cf. Voll, "Sudanese Mahdī," pp. 149–52.

65 Ibrāhīm, *al-Ṣirāʿ*, p. 45; al-Qaddāl, *al-Mahdī*, pp. 90, 94; *idem*, "al-Ruʾyā," p. 78

66 Mālik, *al-Muqāwama*, p. 121; al-Mahdī, *al-Mahdiyya*, pp. 186–87.

67 Radtke *et al.*, *The Exoteric*, pp. 96–97. For the Arabic text, see *ibid.*, p. 49. Cf. Burton, "Naskh," p. 1010i.

Aḥmad reasserts that Ibn Idrīs interpreted the Qur'ān in the light of Prophetic *ḥadīth*s,[68] the actual result of which may be tantamount to abrogation of the interpreted verses.

We noted elsewhere that in the Mahdī's legal methodology, the Prophetic *sunna* precedes the Qur'ān in importance. The Mahdī rules: "… *ḥadīth* abrogates (*yansakh*) Qur'ān."[69] One may perhaps trace the source of this deviation to Ibn Idrīs' view regarding the identification of the Qur'ān with the *ḥadīth*, though the Mahdī seems to proceed beyond this point.

Generally speaking, Ibn Idrīs does not seem to approve of *ijtihād* other than that of the *ṣaḥāba*. He considers their legal views (*qawl*) a third source of law (*aṣl, maṣdar lil-uṣūl*) because their knowledge is derived directly from the Prophet. However, these views may be resorted to only in a necessity (*ḍarūra*), that is, in cases of lacunae (*faqd al-naṣṣ*) in the Qur'ān and the *ḥadīth* and provided they do not contradict the textual sources.[70]

The Mahdī, on the other hand, had no inhibitions about engaging in *ijtihdād*, probably because of his pretension to have direct contact with the Prophet, much like the *ṣaḥāba*. Needless to say, his version of *ijtihād* is not compatible with classical theory. He actually replaced *qiyās*, the systemic analogy from the textual sources, with Prophetic *ilhām*, the validity of which is not subject to the consensus of contemporary *ʿulamāʾ*.[71]

Ibn Idrīs seems to be the Mahdī's source of inspiration with respect to legislation. In matters pertaining to public morality, both Ibn Idrīs and the Mahdī forbade women to expose themselves to male strangers and the latter imposed heavy sanctions on those who violated this stricture.[72] The Mahdī's reformist legislation intended to improve the status of women within the family fits in with Ibn Idrīs' *fatwā* to the effect that women should be treated equally, be consulted, etc.[73]

The encounter with the Prophet is a salient feature of Ṣūfism. Moreover, the Ṣūfis conceive of the Prophet as being alive; they regard illumination (*fatḥ*) as the final goal which confers upon the individual the capacity to perceive,

---

68 Aḥmad, *Ibn Idrīs*, p. 13; cf. Radtke, "*Ijtihād* and Neo-Sufism," p. 918.

69 Layish, "Issues in marriage and divorce," pp. 39–40.

70 Ibrāhīm, *Ibn Idrīs*, pp. 109, 225–228. Cf. O'Fahey, *Enigmatic saint*, p. 199 (Ibn Idrīs seems to have exercised absolute [*muṭlaq*] *ijtihād*).

71 Layish, "Issues in marriage and divorce," pp. 40–42.

72 Radtke *et al., The Exoteric*, p. 183; Layish, "Mechanism for adapting the *Sharīʿa*," p. 235; Voll, "Sudanese Mahdī," pp. 156f.; al-Mahdī, *al-Mahdiyya*, pp. 198ff.; al-Qaddāl, *al-Mahdī*, pp. 147ff.

73 Aḥmad, *Ibn Idrīs*, p. 23; and Layish, "Mechanism for adapting the *Sharīʿa*," p. 237; cf. Radtke, "Sufism in the 18th century," p. 344 (the Khalwatiyya admits women into its order).

while awake rather than when dreaming, the Prophet himself in flesh and blood and to keep company with him (*ruʾyat al-nabī yaqẓatan, ruʾyat dhātihi* or *ijtimāʿ bi-ʾl-nabī yaqẓatan*). Whoever attains this state is regarded as an absolute legal authority. Claims for such authority were made by both Ibn Idrīs, and the Mahdī.[74] In *Kunūz al-jawāhir*, Ibn Idrīs distinguishes between two forms of revelation: revelation of sleep (*waḥy al-manām*) and revelation of random illusion or divine inspiration.[75] Ibn Idrīs claims to have met the Prophet in the presence of al-Khaḍir. The Prophet instructs al-Khaḍir, a legendary figure, to teach Ibn Idrīs the *dhikr*s. Moreover, the Prophet himself taught him additional invocations.[76] Some of the visionary meetings (*ijtimāʿ ṣūrī*) are regarded by Ibn Idrīs as miracles (*karāmāt*).[77] In the *Risāla*, Ibn Idrīs argues that recourse to God and the Prophet is tantamount to recourse to the sacred textual sources of the Qurʾān and the *sunna*, since the textual sources are the embodiment of God and the Prophet, respectively. Since it is not possible for everyone to have direct contact with God (*fa-laysa kull wāḥid minnā maftūḥan baynahu wa-bayna ʾllāh taʿālā bāb al-mukhāṭaba*) or to have encounters with the Messenger in this world, people who disagree (*muntaziʿūn*) in a matter of law can refer to the Prophet (sections 4, 15), by means of *ṭarīqa Muḥammadiyya* that leads one to a direct encounter with the living Prophet. Such an option, however, is only left for the mystic who has attained illumination (*fatḥ*).[78]

The encounter with the Prophet in which the Mahdī was nominated as *khalīfat rasūl Allāh* took place while the Mahdī too was "in a state of wakefulness (*yaqẓatan*)." However, al-Ṣādiq al-Mahdī explains that it was a "spiritual contact" (*ittiṣāl rūḥī*), not carnal (*jasadī*); the Mahdī did not pretend to have seen the Prophet alive, and may have derived this notion from al-Ghazālī.[79]

---

74 Radtke *et al.*, *The Exoteric*, p. 25; al-ʿAbbādī, *Ṣafḥa min khilāf al-ʿulamāʾ*, p. 20. On the conception of *fatḥ*, see Radtke, "*Ibrīziana*," p. 123; Hofheinz, "Internalising Islam," pp. 504ff.

75 O'Fahey, *Enigmatic saint*, p. 137; cf. Radtke, "*Ibrīziana*," p. 122; Radtke *et al.*, "Two Ṣūfī treatises," p. 158 (two forms of revelation: 1. dreams; 2. *khaṭar* or *ilhām*). On the distinction in Ṣūfism between a real encounter with the Prophet, and a physical encounter with him after his death in another form of physical existence, i.e., "in flesh and blood," see Radtke *et al.*, *The Exoteric*, p. 18; see also *ibid.*, p. 19.

76 Radtke *et* al., "Two Ṣūfī treatises," pp. 145–46, 161–62 (*ijtimāʿan ṣūriyyan*, in wakefulness and in sleep).

77 O'Fahey, *Enigmatic saint*, p. 14.

78 Radtke *et al.*, *The Exoteric*, pp. 7 and 9, respectively. For the Arabic text, see *ibid.*, pp. 49 and 56, respectively. For the English translation, see *ibid.*, pp. 97 and 105, respectively.

79 *Al-Āthār*, vol. 1 (1990), no. 115, p. 338; al-Mahdī, *al-Mahdiyya*, pp. 226–27. On the issue of union with the Prophet, see Radtke, "Sufism in the 18th century," pp. 360–62; Radtke *et al.*, "Two Ṣūfī treatises," p. 158.

Al-Khaḍir was also present, along with the Prophet, as he was in the aforementioned vision of Ibn Idrīs.[80] Ibrāhīm al-Rashīd claims to have seen in his dream Ibn Idrīs and through him to behold also the four caliphs along with the Prophet. We noted earlier that Ibrāhīm al-Rashīd had studied with ʿAbdullāhi al-Dufārī, the doctrinal link between Ibn Idrīs and Muḥammad Aḥmad, the Mahdī.[81] However, there is no evidence in the Mahdī's documents as to his view regarding the notion of union with the spirit of the Prophet, rather than God; this doctrine was advocated by Ibn Idrīs.[82]

The Mahdī's encounters with the Prophet were meant not only to facilitate innovative legislation, but also to legitimize and consolidate his position as a divinely-guided leader in a Ṣūfī-oriented society. This may explain the inclusion in the visions of famous Ṣūfīs, such as Ibn al-ʿArabī, Ibn Idrīs, Muḥammad al-Mahdī al-Sanūsī, and ʿAbd al-Qādir al-Jīlānī.[83]

Finally, the Mahdī's own *awrād* and the manual of litanies and devotional exercises (*rātib*) frequently mentioned in his documents[84] resemble in many respects Ibn Idrīs' *awrād*.[85]

## 4 The Sanūsī Tradition

Was Muḥammad b. ʿAlī al-Sanūsī (d. 1859),[86] the most famous of Ibn Idrīs' disciples, another link between Ibn Idrīs and Muḥammad Aḥmad, or perhaps a source of inspiration in his own right? Al-Sanūsī was strongly influenced by Ibn Idrīs. Thus all prayers in the Sanūsī rituals as well as the spiritual content of his concept of Ṣūfism originate with Ibn Idrīs.[87] However, it is argued that the

80 Radtke, "Sufism in the 18th century," p. 357; O'Fahey, *Enigmatic saint*, p. 203, also p. 108; *Al-Āthār*, vol. 1 (1990), no. 115, p. 336; Levtzion and Weigert, "Religious reform in eighteenth-century Morocco," p. 194.

81 O'Fahey, *Enigmatic saint*, pp. 157–58; see above.

82 O'Fahey, *Enigmatic saint*, p. 4; Voll, "Sudanese Mahdī," 155; *idem*, "Mizjaji family," p. 87.

83 *Al-Āthār*, vol. 5 (1992), no. 993, pp. 457, 460.

84 See, e.g., *ibid.*, vol. 4 (1992), no. 451, p. 192; vol. 5 (1992), no. 944, p. 367. For definition of *awrād*, see *ibid.*, vol. 7 (1994), Glossary, p. 399; al-Mahdī, *Rātib al-imām al-mahdī*; Trimingham, *Islam in the Sudan*, p. 156; for extensive analysis, see al-Mahdī, *al-Mahdiyya*, pp. 204ff.; Voll, "Sudanese Mahdī," p. 154; O'Fahey, *Arabic literature of Africa*, pp. 328–30; al-Qaddāl, *al-Mahdī*, p. 152.

85 O'Fahey, "Sudanese Mahdi," pp. 276–77; Radtke, "Sufism in the 18th century," p. 334; Aḥmad, *Ibn Idrīs*, p. 14; cf. Voll, "Hadith," p. 270.

86 For his biography, see Vikør, *Sufi and scholar*. Cf. O'Fahey, *Enigmatic saint*, pp. 130ff.

87 Vikør, *Sufi and scholar*, pp. 200, 270–71.

*Risālat al-radd* which is attributed to Ibn Idrīs, may actually have been written by al-Sanūsī.[88]

Al-Sanūsī rejects blind fanaticism to any particular school (*taʿaṣṣub al-madhhab*), including his own, the Mālikī: a jurist may resort to any school; moreover if he has solid knowledge in a school other than his own, he may issue rulings within the doctrine of that school.[89] Thus al-Sanūsī deviates from the Mālikī practice in some aspects of *ʿibādāt* in favor of the Shāfiʿī practice. We noted earlier that the Mahdī too was not bound by any particular school.[90]

Al-Sanūsī regards the Qurʾān and the *sunna* as one entity, though preference is given to the *ḥadīth* which he ranks as revelation; moreover, he argues that a "weak Tradition is preferred to analogy and individual opinion," and that the textual sources should be preferred to the view of any fallible *mujtahid*. He further argues that under all circumstances Muslims must follow the Qurʾān and the *sunna*, even in a case in which a textual source has been disregarded by an Imām of any given school. Peters concludes that such views amount to a total rejection of the *madhāhib*. Ostensibly, al-Sanūsī acknowledges the authorities of the four Imāms; in actual fact, however, he reserves for himself the right to deviate from their doctrines in favor of a tradition that he prefers.[91] Vikør claims, on the basis of ʿIllaysh, that there is evidence to the effect that al-Sanūsī was influenced by the Ẓāhirīs which implies that he was inclined to literal interpretation of the textual sources.[92]

Al-Sanūsī uses *ijtihād* and *ittibāʿ*, deriving and seeking (lit.: following) respectively, rules in the textual sources as synonyms.[93] He distinguishes between full (*muṭlaq*) and partial (*juzʾī*) *mujtahids*. In the first category, a distinction should be made between independent (*mustaqill*) and dependent (*muntasib*) *mujtahids*. Only the most knowledgeable scholars are qualified for the former *ijtihād* and hence capable of creating their own schools (this option ceased to be available following the closure of the gate of *ijtihād* in the full sense of the term though al-Sanūsī seems to claim this right for himself). The other scholars must limit themselves to *ijtihād* within the boundaries of a particular school (*ijtihād fī ʾl-madhhab*).[94]

---

88 Radtke *et al.*, *The Exoteric*, pp. vii, 2–3, 99 n. 24, p. 100 n. 28; Vikør, *Sufi and scholar*, pp. 221–23.

89 Vikør, *Sufi and scholar*, p. 111; *idem*, "Madhhab," pp. 10–11.

90 Vikør, *Sufi and scholar*, p. 224; *idem*, "*Ijtihād*"; *idem*, "*Jihād*," p. 155; see above.

91 Peters, "*Ijtihād* and *taqlīd*," pp. 136–37, 142–43; Radtke *et al.*, *The Exoteric*, pp. 14, 23–24.

92 Vikør, *Sufi and scholar*, p. 255. Radtke contends that no evidence of a Ẓāhirī influence has been provided. Personal communication, e-mail of 7.4.2003.

93 Vikør, "*Jihād*," p. 155.

94 Vikør, "*Madhhab*," pp. 9–10, 12; *ibid.*, "*Ijtihād*."

The Mahdī too ranks the *ḥadīth* above the Qur'ān and is inclined to a literal interpretation of the textual sources. Although he declares that he totally ignores the *madhāhib*, in actual fact his *fatwā*s and rulings are compatible with legal norms of various schools without being bound by any of them.[95] This practice amounts in fact to a rejection of school fanaticism. The Mahdī's legal methodology is undoubtedly less sophisticated than that of al-Sanūsī. No distinction has been noted in his documents between various kinds of *ijtihād*. Moreover, he denies allegations that he reserves for himself the right of *ijtihād*, although he actually practices this mechanism in his legislation.

Al-Sanūsī too claims to have experienced direct encounters with the Prophet and to have sought the Prophet's illumination.[96] Both al-Sanūsī and the Mahdī prohibit dancing (as well as singing, musical instruments, smoking etc.) during ritual gatherings.[97]

The Mahdī offered Muḥammad al-Mahdī al-Sanūsī, the son and successor of Muḥammad b. ʿAlī al-Sanūsī, nomination as th successor of the Khalīfa ʿUthmān, named after the third "rightly guided" *khalīfa* (*al-Khalīfa dhī 'l-nūrayn*) with a view to enlisting Muḥammad al-Mahdī al-Sanūsī to his cause.[98] This offer (which was ignored) does not, in itself, prove any ideological debt to Muḥammad b. ʿAlī al-Sanūsī; however, it seems safe to assume that the Sudanese Mahdī's initiative, even though it may have been motivated by pragmatic considerations, was greatly facilitated by doctrinal compatibility between the two parties. Still, the question of whether Muḥammad b. ʿAlī al-Sanūsī was an independent source of inspiration or merely a link between Ibn Idrīs and the Sudanese Mahdī remains unresolved for the time being.

---

95 Layish, "Mechanism for adapting the *sharīʿa*," e.g., p. 228 (prohibition of matrimonial coercion in conformity with the Ḥanafī school), p. 231 (*khulʿ* in respect to legal consequences constitutes *faskh*, dissolution by legal proceedings, rather than repudiation, in conformity with Ibn ʿAbbās' view).

96 Vikør, *Sufi and scholar*, pp. 233ff.; *ibid.*, "*Madhhab*," pp. 11–12; O'Fahey, *Enigmatic saint*, pp. 108, 134, 137–39; Levtzion and Weigert, "Religious reformism in eighteenth-century Morocco," p. 195.

97 Vikør, *Sufi and scholar*, p. 200; Holt, *Mahdist state*, p. 131; Layish, "Mechanism for adapting the *sharīʿa*", pp. 234–35. The practice of dancing is prohibited by other orders as well.

98 *Al-Āthār*, vol. 1 (1990), no. 115, p. 334ff.; Holt, "Outside world," pp. 278–79; *idem, Mahdist state*, pp. 107, 113; *idem*, "al-Mahdiyya," 1249i; O'Fahey, "Sudanese Mahdi," p. 281; Abū Salīm and Vikør, "The man who believed in the Mahdi," pp. 31–32, 48–49; Vikør, *Sufi and scholar*, pp. 120, 154–56; Evans-Pritchard, *The Sanusi of Cyrenaica*, pp. 19–27; Ziadeh, *Sanūsīya*, pp. 51–65.

## 5 The Majdhūbiyya Tradition

During his brief stay in Mecca the Sudanese Ṣūfī and scholar Muḥammad Majdhūb (d. 1831) was deeply inspired by Ibn Idrīs. Was Majdhūb a source of the Mahdī's legal methodology or a link to Ibn Idrīs' doctrine?[99] Unlike the Mahdī, Majdhūb did not abrogate the *madhāhib* altogether, but he did consider himself unbound to any particular school. Although the *madhhab* affiliation of his ancestors was Mālikī, in daily practice he did not hesitate to adopt the position of the Shāfiʿī school on various matters, probably due to the influence of the learned milieu during his formative period in Medina. He suggested replacing affiliation to a school with adherence to the example of the Prophet.[100]

Majdhub's legal methodology consists of employing only the two textual sources: the Qur›ān and the *ḥadīth*. However, similarly to the Mahdī, he too underscored the importance of the Prophetic *ḥadīth* to the extent that the Qur'ān should be interpreted in its light. In his writings, Majdhūb ignores systematic analogy (*qiyās*) altogether, and limits the scope of *ijmāʿ* to the consensus of the Prophet's Companions (*ijmāʿ al-ṣaḥāba*), thus diminishing its operative significance. Needless to say, Majdhūb's legal methodology was a fundamental departure from the classical *uṣūl al-fiqh*.[101] As already noted, the Mahdī replaced these mechanisms with inspiration (*ilhām*), with a view to placing himself outside the reach of the *'ulamā'*'s criticism.

The encounter with the Prophet plays a vital role in Majdhūb's legal methodology. He claims to have experienced direct communication with the Prophet in a dream or vision (*ru'yā, kashf*) where he could pose questions and receive answers.[102]

Majdhūb prohibited consumption of tobacco, gambling, illicit sexual intercourse (*zinā*) etc. Similarly, the Mahdī sought to uproot, by means of criminal sanctions, practices such as the consumption of tobacco, wine-drinking, and games of hazard.[103] Needless to say, the prohibition of consumption of tobacco, wine-drinking, and games of hazard was also shared by other orders. The

99 For a short biographical background, see Hofheinz, "Transcending the Madhhab," pp. 230–32; *idem.*, "al-Madjādhīb," pp. 555–56; cf. Trimingham, *Islam in the Sudan*, pp. 224–26.

100 Hofheinz, "Transcending the Madhhab," p. 234; *idem*, "Internalising Islam," pp. 181ff., 192, 321–22, 398.

101 Hofheinz, "Transcending the Madhhab," pp. 243, 245.

102 *Ibid.*, p. 244; *idem*, "Internalising Islam," pp. 158, 265, 401–2, 548, 555.

103 Hofheinz, "Internalising Islam," pp. 518ff.; Holt, *Mahdist state*, p. 131; Trimingham, *Islam in the Sudan*, p. 156.

consumption of intoxicants and tobacco was also prohibited by the Wahhābīs, but we have no evidence of any link between them and the Mahdī.[104]

There is no solid evidence indicating that Muḥammad Aḥmad, the later Mahdī, was inspired by Majdhūb's legal doctrines.[105] One of Muḥammad Aḥmad's teachers during his early formative period at Berber was Shaykh Muḥammad ʿAbdallāh Khōjalī, best known as Muḥammad al-Khayr and the *amīr* of Berber. Hofheinz, however, categorically maintains that Muḥammad al-Khayr was not affiliated to the Majdhūbiyya.[106]

Muḥammad Majdhūb, however, seems to have been influenced by the intellectual currents of his time, first and foremost by Ibn Idrīs.[107] Hence, since we have strong evidence linking the Mahdī to Ibn Idrīs, it seems safe to conclude that the latter, rather than Muḥammad Majdhūb, is the Mahdī's main source of inspiration. There is also evidence connecting the Majdhūbiyya with other traditions. Thus, according to Nūr al-Dāʾim, Aḥmad al-Ṭayyib al-Bashīr, who had introduced the Sammāniyya into the Sudan, stayed for some time at al-Dāmar with Ḥamad b. Muḥammad al-Majdhūb, whose grandson Muḥammad al-Majdhūb later became a prominent Sammāniyya leader. Likewise, it is claimed that the Tijānī missionary, Muḥammad b. Mukhtār b. ʿAbd al-Raḥmān al-Shinqīṭī, known as Abū 'l-Āliya, initiated into his *ṭarīqa* in Berber many followers, including Muḥammad al-Khayr.[108]

## 6 The Tijānī Tradition

Was Aḥmad al-Tijānī (d. 1815), the founder of the Tijāniyya order,[109] another possible source for the Mahdī's legal methodology? Al-Tijānī denies the

104 O'Fahey, *Enigmatic saint*, pp. 98–99; O'Fahey and Radtke, "Neo-Sufism reconsidered," pp. 57–58; Layish, "Mechanism for adapting the *sharīʿa*," pp. 234–35; *idem*, "Saudi Arabian legal reform," p. 282; Cf. Voll, "Sudanese Mahdī," p. 156; al-Qaddāl, *al-Mahdī*, pp. 143, 149ff. Ibn Idrīs and the Wahhībīs shared also rejection of the cult of tombs of saints; Radtke *et al.*, *The Exoteric*, p. 43; Aḥmad, *Ibn Idrīs*, p. 19; cf. Hofheinz, "Internalising Islam," p. 188.

105 Cf. Trimingham, *Islam in the Sudan*, p. 151.

106 Communication with Gabriel Warburg, December 30, 2002. Cf. Holt, *Mahdist state*, pp. 19, 98; Karrar, *The Sufi brotherhoods*, pp. 95–96.

107 Hofheinz, "Transcending the Madhhab," p. 230; *idem*, "Internalising Islam," p. 166; Holt, *Mahdist state*, p. 19.

108 Karrar, *The Sufi brotherhoods*, p. 46 and the sources mentioned in n. 17, and pp. 121–22, respectively.

109 Radtke, "Sufism in the 18th century," p. 333 and the sources indicated in the footnotes; Trimingham, *Islam in the Sudan*, pp. 236–37.

orthodox legal methodology and the law elaborated by the founders of the *madhāhib* on the grounds that only the Prophet was capable of properly comprehending the *sharīʿa* since he derived his knowledge directly from God.[110] Al-Tijānī further advocates *ijtihād* in matters of doctrine, provided the jurist is fully qualified.[111] Al-Tijānī claims to be descended from the Prophet, to have received guidance directly from him, and to have been raised by him to the same level as himself – the "seal of sainthood" alongside the "seal of prophethood" (*khatm al-nubuwwa*) – and hence his pretension to infallibility (*ʿiṣma*).[112]

Al-Tijānī too experienced visions of the Prophet on many occasions; in fact, the emergence of his *ṭarīqa* is connected with such an experience: The Prophet appeared to him "while he was awake," informed him that he was the *khatm al-awliyāʾ* (or *al-wilāya*) and the *quṭb al-aqṭāb* (the highest rank in the hierarchy of the Ṣūfī saints), and personally taught him the unique *awrād* of his new independent *ṭarīqa*.[113]

The Sudanese Mahdī shares with al-Tijānī the rejection of the classical legal methodology and *madhāhib*. Al-Tijānī's personal communion with the Prophet and his infallible authority seem to have provided him with the justification for deriving inspiration from the Prophet, similar to *ilhām* in the Mahdī's case. Hence, one may infer that al-Tijānī denied reasoning as a source of law. Both al-Tijānī and the Mahdī were engaged in *ijtihād* either in theory or in practice. Moreover, al-Tijānī met both Muḥammad b. ʿAbd al-Karīm al-Sammānī and Muḥammad b. ʿAlī al-Sanūsī.[114] *Awliyāʾ* and *aqṭāb*, who play a role in al-Tijānī's teachings, appear frequently in the Mahdī's visions, in the company of the Prophet Muḥammad and other prophets, angels, al-Khaḍir, and the four orthodox Caliphs.[115]

---

110 Abun-Nasr, *The Tijaniyya. A Sufi order*, pp. 163–64; cf. Radtke, "*Ijtihād* and Neo-Sufism," p. 918 (the view of al-Ḥājj ʿUmar b. Saʿīd al-Fūtī [d. 1864], the most famous follower of Ahmad al-Tijānī, on the *madhāhib*).

111 Abun-Nasr, *The Tijaniyya. A Sufi order*, p. 56; Levtzion and Weigert, "Religious reform in eighteenth-century Morocco," p. 193. Al-Ḥājj ʿUmar al-Fūtī (see n. 110) recognizes *ijtihād* as a source of law alongside the Qurʾān and the *sunna*; see Radtke, "*Ijtihād* and Neo-Sufism," p. 917; *idem*, "Rimāḥ."

112 Abun-Nasr, *The Tijaniyya. A Sufi order*, 34–35; *idem*, "al-Tidjānī," p. 463; Vikør, *Ṣūfī and scholar*, p. 58.

113 Abun-Nasr, *The Tijaniyya. A Sufi order*, pp. 19, 31ff., 37–38; *idem*, "al-Tidjānī," pp. 463–64; *idem*, "al-Tidjāniyya," pp. 464–65; Vikør, *Sufi and scholar*, p. 58; Levtzion and Weigert, "Religious reform in eighteenth-century Morocco," pp. 193–95. On al-Tijānī's cosmological system, see Radtke, "Sufism in the 18th century," pp. 352–53 (*ḥaqīqa muḥammadiyya*); Radtke, "*Ijtihād* and Neo-Sufism," pp. 914–16.

114 Levtzion and Weigert, "Religious reform in eighteenth-century Morocco," p. 193; Vikør, *Sufi and scholar*, pp. 58–60 (some claim that al-Sanūsī was initiated into the Tijāniyya).

115 *Al-Āthār*, vol. 1 (1990), no. 58, p. 190; no. 115, 336; vol. 5 (1992), no. 993, p. 457.

Nevertheless, there is no indication in the Mahdī's documents of al-Tijānī's influence on him, whether explicit or implicit. We do have evidence of some differences as regards technical terms. Thus the term *ḥaḍra*, which in the Mahdist context has the connotation of colloquy with the Prophet, denotes *dhikr* in the Tijānī *ṭarīqa* in accordance with the practice of the Khalwatiyya. *Ḥaḍra* takes place on Friday after the performance of *ṣalāt al-ʿaṣr.* Moreover, dancing (*raqṣ*) which is prohibited by the Sudanese Mahdī, is allowed by the Khalwatiyya as part of the *ḥaḍra.*[116]

## 7 Summary and Conclusions

There can be no doubt that the Mahdī's legal methodology was inspired first and foremost by Ṣūfī traditions that formed the social and intellectual background of his formative period. The textual sources, especially *ḥadīth*, and concepts and mechanisms closely related to the procedure of deriving law can be very easily traced in Ṣūfī practices. The concept of *ṭarīqa muḥammadiyya* which provides a link between Ṣūfism and law is a case in point. This "path" leads the enlightened mystic by means of illumination (*fatḥ*), to a direct encounter with the living Prophet who personally provides solutions to legal issues.[117] By virtue of the same token, the physical sensation caused by this encounter can be identified with the ecstatic experiences (*aḥwāl*).[118] In Ibn al-ʿArabī's teachings, the role of *sharīʿa* (*aḥkām*) is phrased in Ṣūfī terms: to bring about the return to God in a mode that guarantees felicity (*saʿāda*).[119]

Moreover, Levtzion suggests that the link between Ṣufism and *ḥadīth* in pre-modern Islam brought about the rejection of *taqlīd* and, by implication, the renewal of *sharīʿa* by means of *ijtihād*:

> Many of the *ʿulamāʾ* in the network in Mecca and Medina in the 18th and 19th centuries were committed to both *ḥadīth* and *taṣawwuf.* The combination of the exoteric and the esoteric teachings, of formalistic authority and charismatic leadership, of strict scripturalism and mystical intuition, pointed the way to the liberation from *taqlīd.*[120]

---

116 Abun-Nasr, *The Tijaniyya. A Sufi order*, pp. 50–54; *idem*, "Tidjāniyya," p. 465ii; Trimingham, *Ṣūfī orders*, Glossary, s.v. *dhikr, ḥaḍra.*

117 Radtke *et al.*, The *Exoteric*, p. 97 fn. 16 and the sources indicated in note; *ibid.*, p. 24; Radtke, "*Ijtihād* and Neo-Sufism," pp. 914–16, 920; O'Fahey and Radtke, "Neo-Sufism reconsidered," pp. 65–71.

118 Trimingham, *Sufi orders*, index, s.v. "ecstasy." Cf. Voll, "Sudanese Mahdī," p. 154.

119 Chittick, "Taṣawwuf," p. 318ii.

120 Levtzion, "The role of *Sharīʿa*-oriented Sūfī *Ṭuruq*."

In other words, it was natural for the Ṣūfī leaders to affiliate themselves with the *ḥadīth* because of the central role played by the Prophet in their traditions. Direct inspiration from the Prophet had become the main source for deriving law thus making sources of law based on human reasoning (*raʾy, qiyās*) and discretion based on consensus (*ijmāʿ*) superfluous. The transformation of the Prophet's inspiration and illumination into the main source of law facilitated the accommodation of the *sharīʿa* to contemporary requirements.[121] Needless to say, the encounter with the Prophet (*ḥaḍra*) was also instrumental in bringing the community within the orbit of the Mahdist movement.

There is no evidence in the Mahdī's documents to suggest that he was inspired directly by the writings of the founders of specific Ṣūfī traditions; rather, he seems to have been exposed to their doctrines through mediators. Nor is there evidence of a highly intellectual, sophisticated discussion of these doctrines[122] though one should bear in mind that the documents were issued for practical rather than scholarly purposes. The Mahdī's doctrinal and ideological rapprochement to Ṣūfī *ṭarīqa*s seems to have been prompted by political considerations. Thus the very dominant role of Ibn Idrīs in the vision of the Mahdī's manifestation could have been an attempt on the part of the Mahdī to assert superiority over the widespread and influential Khatmiyya *ṭarīqa*. Similarly, the Mahdī's offer to place Muḥammad al-Mahdī al-Sanūsī in the Mahdist hierarchy by designating him as successor (*khalīfa*) of ʿUthmān with a view to enlisting him to *jihād* against Egypt,[123] could have played a role in shaping the Mahdīi's legal practice if al-Sanūsī's acceptance of the offer necessitated some doctrinal (and political) adaptation. It seems that the Mahdī's Ṣūfī experience trained him to cope with these doctrines on the level of mystical intuition with due regard to political, economic and social considerations.

In matters pertaining to *madhāhib*, legal methodology, and *ijtihād*, it is possible to identify similarities, in one way or another, between the Mahdī's approach and those of the founders of specific *ṭarīqa*s. These similarities are even more evident in matters closely related to Ṣūfī tradition, such as the encounter with the Prophet (*ḥaḍra, ruʾyā*) and litanies (*awrād*), among other things. On the basis of the extant legal literature, it seems safe to conclude

---

121 *Mawlid al-nabī* is a another illustration of the Prophet's role in Ṣūfī tradition; see Shinar, "Traditional and reformist *mawlid* celebrations," pp. 373, 377, 394, 401. It should, however, be borne in mind that veneration of saints was originally alien to Islam; only later Muslims sought to create, through the concept of saints, mediators between themselves and an omnipotent Godhead; see Goldziher, *Muslim studies*, pp. 258–59.

122 Cf. Voll, "Mizjaji family," p. 82.

123 Holt, "Outside world," pp. 278–79; personal communication from Prof. Holt, 20.3.2003

that Ibn Idrīs was the Mahdī's most important source of inspiration. We have evidence to the effect that ʿAbdullāhi al-Dufārī provided the doctrinal link between Ibn Idrīs' doctrines and the Mahdī. This link is further supported by a textual analysis of Ibn Idrīs' writings. Finally, one should bear in mind that the founders of other *ṭarīqa*s with whom the Mahdī was acquainted were linked in one way or another to the Idrīsī tradition.

## Bibliography


Al-ʿAbbādī, *al-Anwār* = Al-ʿAbbādī, al-Ḥasan b. Saʿd b. Muḥammad. *Al-Anwār al-saniyya al-māḥiya li-ẓalām al-munkirīn ʿalā al-ḥaḍra al-mahdiyya*. Lithographic edition. Omdurman, 1888.

Al-ʿAbbādī, *Ṣafḥa min khilāf al-ʿulamdāʾ* = Al-ʿAbbādī, al-Ḥasan b. Saʿd b. Muḥammad. *Ṣafḥa min khilāf al-ʿulamāʾ ḥawla al-mahdiyya wa-imāra fī ʾl-ʿAtabāy*. Muḥammad Ibrāhīm Abū Salīm, ed. (unpublished MS).

Abū Salīm, *al-Ḥaraka* = Abū Salīm, Muḥammad Ibrāhīm. *Al-Ḥaraka al-fikriyya fī ʾl-mahdiyya*, 3rd ed. Khartoum, 1989.

Abū Salīm and Vikør, "The man who believed in the Mahdi." = Abū Salīm, Muḥammad Ibrāhīm and Knut S. Vikør. "The man who believed in the Mahdi." *Sudanic Africa* 2 (1991): 29–52.

Abu Shouk, "A bibliography of the Mahdist state." = Abu Shouk, Ahmed Ibrahim. "A bibliography of the Mahdist state in the Sudan (1881–1898)." *Sudanic Africa* 10 (1999): 133–68.

Abun-Nasr, Jamil M. "al-Tidjānī." *EI*², s.v.

Abun-Nasr, Jamil M. "Tidjāniyya." *EI*², s.v.

Abun-Nasr, Jamil M. *The Tijaniyya. A Sufi order in the modern world*. London, 1965.

Aḥmad, *Ibn Idrīs* = Aḥmad, Ḥasan Makkī Muḥammad. *Al-Sayyid Aḥmad b. Idrīs al-Fāsī (1837–1860). Manhajuhu fī ʾl-daʿwa wa-fikruhu al-siyāsā*. Al-Markaz al-Islāmī al-Ifrīqī bi-ʾl-Kharṭūm. Shuʿbat al-Daʿwa. Usbūʿ al-Daʿwa al-Thānī, 1407 /1986. [Khartoum], n.d.

ʿAlī, *Azmat al-Islām* = ʿAlī, Ḥaydar Ibrāhīm. *Azmat al-Islām al-siyāsī. Al-Jabha al-islāmiyya al-qawmiyya fī ʾl-Sūdān namūdhajan*. Markaz al-Dirāsāt al-Sūdāniyya. [Cairo], 1991.

*Al-Āthdār* = *Al-Āthār al-kāmila li-l-Imām al-Mahdī*. 7 vols. Muḥammad Ibrāhīm Abū Salīm, ed. Khartoum, 1990–94.

Burton, "Naskh" = Burton, J. "Naskh." *EI*², s.v.

Chittick, "Taṣawwuf" = Chittick, W.C. "Taṣawwuf. 2. Ibn al-ʿArabī and after in the Arabic and Persian lands and beyond." *EI*², s.v.

Evans-Pritchard, E.E. *The Sanusi of Cyrenaica*. Oxford, 1949.

Goldziher, *Muslim studies* = Goldziher, I. *Muslim studies*. S.M. Stern, ed.; C.R. Barber and S.M. Stern, trans. Vol. 2. London, 1971.

Hofheinz, "Internalising Islam" = Hofheinz, A. "Internalising Islam. Shaykh Muḥammad Majdhūb, scriptural Islam, and local context in early nineteenth-century Sudan." Ph.D. Thesis. University of Bergen, 1996.

Hofheinz, A. "Al-Madjādhīb." *EI*², s.v.

Hofheinz, "Transcending the Madhhab" = Hofheinz, A. "Transcending the Madhhab – in practice: the case of the Sudanese Shaykh Muḥammad Majdhūb (1795/6–1831)." *ILS* 10.2 (2003): 229–48.

Holt, *The Mahdist state* = Holt, P.M. *Mahdist state in the Sudan 1881–1898*. 2nd ed. Oxford, 1970.

Holt, P.M. "Al-Mahdiyya." *EI*², s.v.

Holt, "Outside world" = Holt, P.M. "The Sudanese Mahdia and the outside world: 1881–9." *BSOAS* 21.2 (1958): 276–90.

Holt, "A Sudanese saint" = Holt, P.M. "A Sudanese saint: Aḥmad al-Ṭayyib b. al-Bashīr (1155–1239/1742–1824)." In R. Veselý, ed. *Threefold wisdom – Islam, the Arab world and Africa*. Praha, 1993, pp. 107–15.

Ibn Idrīs, *al-ʿIqd* = Ibn Idrīs, Aḥmad. *Al-ʿIqd al-nafīs fī nuẓum jawāhir al-tadrīs*. [Cairo], 1315AH.

Ibn Idrīs, *Risālat al-radd* = Ibn Idrīs, Aḥmad. *Risālat al-radd ʿalā ahl al-raʾy bi-ʾl-ṣawāb li-muwāfaqat al-sunna wa-ʾl-kitāb*. Published with annotated translation in Radtke et al., *The exoteric* (see below), pp. 47–80, 95–130.

Ibrāhīm, *al-Fikr* = Ibrāhīm, Muḥammad al-Makkī. *Al-Fikr al-sūdānī. Uṣūluhu wa-taṭawwuruhu*. 2nd ed. n.p., 1989.

Ibrāhīm, *Ibn Idrīs* = Ibrāhīm, Yaḥyā Muḥmmad. *Madrasat Aḥmad b. Idrīs al-Maghribī wa-athāruhā fī ʾl-Sūdān*. Beirut, 1413/1993.

Ibrāhīm, *al-Ṣirāʿ* = Ibrāhīm, ʿAbd Allāh. *Al-Ṣirāʿ bayna al-Mahdī wa-ʾl-ʿulamāʾ*. 2nd ed. n.p., 1994.

Ibrāhīm, *al-Taʿlīm* = Ibrāhīm, Yaḥyā Muḥmmad. *Taʾrīkh al-taʿlīm al-dīnī fī ʾl-Sūdān*. Beirut, 1407/1987.

Karrar, *The Sufi brotherhoods* = Karrar, Ali Salih. *The Sufi brotherhoods in the Sudan*. London, 1992.

Khālid, *al-Fajr al-kādhib* = Khālid, Manṣūr. *Al-Fajr al-kādhib. Numayrī wa-taḥrīf al-sharīʿa*. Beirut, [1986].

Kister, "The struggle against Musaylima" = Kister, M.J. "The struggle against Musaylima and the conquest of Yamāma." *JSAI* 27 (2002): 1–56.

Layish, "Issues in marriage and divorce" = Layish, A. "The legal methodology of the Mahdī in the Sudan, 1881–1885: issues in marriage and divorce." *Sudanic Africa* 8 (1997): 37–47.

Layish, "Mechanism for adapting the *sharīʿa*" = Layish, A. "The legal methodology of the Mahdi in the Sudan as a mechanism for adapting the *Sharīʿa* to political and social purposes." *Mahdisme et millénanrisme en Islam*. Mercedes García-Arenal, ed. *Revue des Mondes Musulmans et de la Méditerranée*. Série Histoire 91–92–93–94 (2000): 221–38.

Layish, "Saudi Arabian legal reform" = Layish, A. "Saudi Arabian legal reform as a mechanism to moderate Wahhābī doctrine." *JAOS* 107.2 (1987): 279–92.

Layish, *Selection from the Mahdī's Documents* = Layish, A. *The Mahdī's legal methodology and its application in the Sudan. A selection from the Mahdī's documents (1881–1885)*. Jerusalem, 1996.

Lazarus-Yafeh, *Studies in Ghazzālī* = Lazarus-Yafeh, Hava. *Studies in Ghazzālī*. Jerusalem, 1975.

Levtzion, "The role of *Sharīʿa*-oriented Ṣūfī *Ṭuruq*" = Levtzion, N. "The role of *Sharīʿa*-oriented Ṣūfī *Ṭuruq* in the reform movements of the 18th and 19th centuries." In N. Levtzion, *Islam in Africa and the Middle East: Studies on Conversion and Renewal*. M. Abitbol and A. Nadan, eds. *Variorum*. Aldershot, Hampshire, 2007, chapter XV, pp. 1–31.

Levtzion and Voll, *Renewal and reform* = Levtzion, N. and J.O. Voll. *Eighteenth-century renewal and reform in Islam*. Syracuse, N.Y., 1987.

Levtzion and Weigert, "Religious reform in eighteenth-century Morocco" = Levtzion, N. and G. Weigert. "Religious reform in eighteenth-century Morocco." *JSAI* 19 (1995): 173–97.

Macdonald, D.B. "Ilhām." *EI*², s.v.

Al-Mahdī, *Rātib al-imām al-mahdī* = Al-Mahdī, Muḥammad Aḥmad, *Rātib al-imām al-mahdā*. Lithographic edition. n.p., n.d.

Al-Mahdī, "Mustaqbal" = Al-Mahdī, al-Ṣādiq. "Mustaqbal al-Islām fī 'l-Sūdān." In *al-Islām fī 'l-Sūdān. Buḥūth mukhtāra min al-mu'tamar al-awwal li-Jamā-ʿat al-Fikr wa-'l-Thaqāfa al-Islāmiyya, November 27–30, 1982*. Muddathir ʿAbd al-Raḥīm and al-Ṭayyib Zayn al-ʿĀbidīn, eds. Khartoum, 1987, pp. 375–425.

Al-Mahdī, *al-Mahdiyya* = Al-Mahdī, al-Ṣādiq. *Yas'alūnaka ʿan al-mahdiyya*. Cairo, 1975.

Maḥmūd, *al-Fikr al-ṣufī* = Maḥmūd, "Abd al-Qādir. *Al-Fikr al-ṣūfī fī 'l-Sūdān. Maṣādiruhu wa-tayyārātuhu wa-alwānuhu*. Cairo, 1968–69.

Mālik, *al-Muqāwama* = Mālik, Muḥammad Maḥjūb. *Al-Muqāwama al-dākhiliyya li-ḥarakat al-mahdiyya (1881–1898)*. Beirut, 1407/1987.

Massignon, L.-[B. Radtke]. "Taṣawwuf. 1. Early Development in the Arabic and Persian Lands." *EI*², s.v.

Mustafa, *The common law* = Mustafa, Zaki. *The common law in the Sudan. An account of 'justice, equity, and good conscience.'* Oxford, 1971.

Nūr al-Dā'im, *Azāhīr al-riyāḍ* = Nūr al-Dā'im, ʿAbd al-Maḥmūd. *Azāhīr al-riyāḍ fī manāqib al-ʿārif bi-'llāh taʿālā al-ustādh al-shaykh Aḥmad al-Ṭayyib*. Muḥammad al-Hādī Qarīballāh and Ṭāhā Muḥammad al-Mubārak, eds. Cairo, 1954.

Obeid, "The history of the Sammāniyya *Ṭarīqa*" = Obeid, Amani. "The history of the Sammāniyya *Ṭarīqa*", M.Sc. Thesis, University of Khartoum, 1993 [?].

O'Fahey, *Arabic literature of Africa,* = O'Fahey, R.S. *Arabic literature of Africa. Vol. 1. The writings of Eastern Sudanic Africa to c. 1900*. Leiden, 1994.

O'Fahey, *Enigmatic saint* = O'Fahey, R.S. *Enigmatic saint. Aḥmad Ibn Idris and the Idrisi tradition*. London, 1990.

O'Fahey, "Sudanese Mahdi" = O'Fahey, R.S. "Sufism in suspense: The Sudanese Mahdi and the Sufis." In F. De Jong and B. Radtke, eds. *Islamic mysticism contested. Thirteen centuries of controversies and polemics*. Leiden, 1999, pp. 267–82.

O'Fahey and Karrar, "The enigmatic Imam" = O'Fahey, R.S. and Ali Salih Karrar. "The enigmatic Imam: the influence of Ahmad Ibn Idris." *IJMES* 19 (1987): 205–20.

O'Fahey and Radtke, "Neo-Sufism reconsidered" = O'Fahey, R.S. and B. Radtke. "Neo-Sufism reconsidered." *Der Islam* 70 (1993): 52–87.

Peters, "*Idjtihād* and *taqlīd*" = Peters, R. "*Idjtihād* and *taqlīd* in 18th and 19th century Islam." *WI* 20.3–4 (1980): 132–45.

Al-Qaddāl, *al-Mahdī* = Al-Qaddāl, Muḥammad Saʿīd. *Al-Imām al-Mahdī. Muḥammad Aḥmad b. ʿAbd Allāh 1844–1885*. Beirut, 1412/1992.

Al-Qaddāl, "al-Ru'ya" = Al-Qaddāl, Muḥammad Saʿīd. "Al-Ru'ya al-thawriyya fī fikr al-Mahdī." In *Dirāsāt fī ta'rīkh al-mahdiyya*. Khartoum, 1982, pp. 74–97.

Radtke, "*Ibrīziana*" = Radtke, B. "*Ibrīziana*: themes and sources of a seminal Ṣūfī work." *Sudanic Africa* 7 (1996): 113–58.

Radtke, "*Ijtihād* and Neo-Sufism" = Radtke, B. "*Ijtihād* and Neo-Sufism." *Asiatische Studien* 48 (1994): 909–21.

Radtke, "Projection" = Radtke, B. "Between projection and suppression. Some considerations concerning the study of Sufism." In F. de Jong, ed. *Shīʿa Islam, sects and Sufism*. Utrecht, 1992, pp. 70–82.

Radtke, "Rimāḥ" = Radtke, B. "Studies on the sources of the Kitāb Rimāḥ ḥizb al-raḥīm of al-Ḥājj ʿUmar." *Sudanic Africa* 6 (1995): 73–113

Radtke, "Sufism in the 18th century" = Radtke, B. "Sufism in the 18th century. An attempt at a provisional appraisal." *WI* 36.3 (1996): 326–64.

Radtke *et al.*, *The exoteric* = Radtke, B., O'Kane, J., Vikør, K.S. and O'Fahey, R.S. *The exoteric Aḥmad Ibn Idrīs. A Ṣūfī's critique of the Madhāhib and the Wahhābīs. Four Arabic texts with translation and commentary*. Leiden, 2000.

Radtke *et al.*, "Two Ṣūfī treatises" = Radtke, B., O'Fahey, R.S. and O'Kane, J. "Two Ṣūfī treatises of Aḥmad ibn Idrīs." *Omens* 35 (1996): 143–78.

Rayāḍ, *Mūjaz ta'rīkh al-sulṭa al-tashrīʿiyya* = Rayāḍ, Henrī. *Mūjaz ta'rīkh al-sulṭa al-tashrīʿiyya fī 'l-Sūdān*. Beirut and Khartoum, 1967.

Shaked, H. *The life of the Sudanese Mahdi*. New Brunswick, N.J., 1978.

Shinar, "Traditional and reformist *mawlid* celebrations" = Shinar, P. "Traditional and reformist *mawlid* celebrations in the Maghrib." In M. Rosen-Ayalon, ed. *Studies in memory of Gaston Wiet*. Jerusalem, 1977, pp. 371–413. Reprinted in P. Shinar, *Modern Islam in the Maghreb*. Jerusalem, 2004, V.

Sulaymān, *Dawr al-Azhar* = Sulaymān, Muḥmmad. *Dawr al-Azhar fī 'l-Sūdān*. n.p., 1985.

Trimingham, J.S. *Islam in the Sudan*. London, 1965.

Trimingham, *Sufi orders* = Trimingham, J.S. *The Sufi orders in Islam*. London, 1973.

Vikør, "*Ijtihād*" = Vikør, Knut S. "The conception of *Ijtihād* in a 19th-century debate: Muḥammad b. ʿAlī al-Sanūsī's *Īqāẓ al-wasnān*." EURAMES, Inaugural Conference, Warwick 8–11 July 1994.

Vikør, "*Jihād*" = Vikør, Knut S. "*Jihād, ʿilm* and *taṣawwuf* – two justifications of action from the Idrīsī tradition." *Studia Islamica* 90 (2000): 153–76.

Vikør, "*Madhhab*" = Vikør, Knut S. "Opening the Mālikī school: Muḥammad b. ʿAli al-Sanūsī's views on the *Madhhab*." *The Journal of Libyan Studies* 1 (2000): 5–17.

Vikør, "The Shaykh as *Mujtahid*" = Vikør, Knut S. "The Shaykh as *Mujtahid*: A Ṣūfī conception of *Ijtihād*?" submitted to the Fourth International Conference on Islamic Legal Studies, Law and Sufism, Murcia, 7–10.5. 2003. [Since then published as "The shaykh as mujtahid: A Sufi conception of ijtihad?", in A. Carmona (ed.), *El Sufismo y las normas del Islam* (Murcia, 2006), 129–56/351–75.]

Vikør, *Sufi and scholar* = Vikør, Knut S. *Sufi and scholar on the desert edge. Muḥammad b. ʿAlī al-Sanūsī and his brotherhood*. London, 1995.

Voll, "Hadith" = Voll, John O. "Hadith scholars and Tariqahs: an Ulama group in the 18th century Haramayn and their impact in the Islamic world." *Journal of Asian and African Studies* 15.3–4 (1980): 264–73.

Voll, "Mizjaji family" = Voll, John O. "Linking groups in the networks of eighteenth-century revivalist scholars. The Mizjaji family in Yemen." In Levtzion and Voll, *Renewal and reform*, pp. 69–92.

Voll, "The Sudanese Mahdī" = Voll, John O. "The Sudanese Mahdī: frontier fundamentalist." IJMES 10 (1979): 145–66.

Al-Zākī, Ḥāfiẓ al-Shaykh. "Al-Islām wa-ḥayātunā al-tashrīʿiyya." In *Al-Islām fī 'l-Sūdān. Buḥūth mukhtāra min al-muʾtamar al-awwal li-jamāʿat al-fikr wa-'l-thaqāfa al-islāmiyya, 27–30 November 1982*. Khartoum, 1987.

Ziadeh, N.A. *Sanūsīyah. A study of a revivalist movement in Islam*. Leiden, 1968.

CHAPTER 9

# The Legal Methodology of the Mahdi in the Sudan, 1881–1885: Issues in Marriage and Divorce

Muḥammad Aḥmad b. ʿAbd Allāh (Muḥammad al-Mahdī) headed a religious-political movement for the revival and reform of Islam (the Mahdiyya) with a view to restoring, on the basis of the Qurʾān and the Sunna, the Islamic theocracy that prevailed in the days of the Prophet Muḥammad and the 'Righteous Caliphs' (*al-khulafāʾ al-rāshidūn*).* The idea of Mahdism had manifested itself in the Sudan as early as the seventeenth century. The Mahdist movement was motivated by eschatological expectations whose source of inspiration can be traced to Egypt in the eighteenth and nineteenth centuries. In its initial stages, the Mahdist movement had many features of a social and political protest movement. Its main causes were as follows: the conquest of the Sudan by Egypt under Muḥammad ʿAlī; the decline of the socio-political status of the indigenous religious functionaries and their replacement by orthodox *ʿulamāʾ*

---

* The purpose of this study is to describe and analyse, from the standpoint of the Sharīʿa, the Mahdi's legal methodology, its sources of inspiration, and its actual application on the basis of a rich variety of proclamations (*manshūrāt*), rulings (*aḥkām*), warnings (*indhārāt*), visions (*ḥaḍrāt*), etc. issued by the Mahdi from the time of his manifestation (*ẓuhūr*) in 1881 until his death in 1885. A great deal of this material pertains to religious legal issues par excellence, including legal opinions (*fatwās*) and judicial decisions. These documents appeared in various editions, in lithograph press and printing. The hypothesis presented in the introduction and the conclusion are tentative pending revision in the course of research. This research is supported by a grant from the Israel Science Foundation.

Most of the material for this research has been collected at the University of Bergen. I would like to thank Professor R.S. O'Fahey of the Department of History; Dr. Knut S. Vikør, Director, and Mrs. Sylvia Liland, Secretary of the Centre for Middle Eastern Studies, for the warm hospitality extended to me during my visits to the Centre in 1995, 1996 and 1997. I am also grateful to Professor P.M. Holt who graciously placed his personal collection of the Mahdi's documents at my disposal during my sabbatical stay in Oxford in 1993 and commented on my research proposal. Professor G.R. Warburg (University of Haifa), my collaborator in research on the revival of Islamic law in the Sudan under Numayrī, has initiated me into the field of Sudanese studies and whetted my curiosity with respect to the Mahdi's legal methodology, for which I am most grateful. I am also grateful to Professor Pessah Shinar for his guidance and inspiration and to Professors Etan Kohlberg, David Powers and Dr Ahmad I. Abu Shouk who read the manuscript and made important comments. I would also like to thank the editors of *SAJHS*, and especially Professor John O. Hunwick, Dr. Vikør, and Dr. Stefan Reichmuth, for their generous assistance and valuable comments and suggestions.

[Originally published in *Sudanic Africa* 8 (1997), pp. 37–66.]

 | DOI:10.1163/9789004680920_011

who were supported by the Turco-Egyptian regime; the annexation of Darfur to Egypt in the last quarter of the nineteenth century; and the attempts to put an end to the slave-trade with the assistance of Christians (Europeans and Americans), attempts that antagonised Sudanese vested interests.[1] In the following, I shall present briefly the hypothesis of the study and some of its findings and conclusions on the basis of part of the documentation.

Sudanese society was well entrenched in tribal customary law (and identified by its affiliation with popular Sufi *ṭarīqas*). P.M. Holt maintains that a distinction should be made between the more sophisticated settled riverain tribes and the nomadic tribes of the interior, especially the West. The former group provided most of the personnel of the Mahdist bureaucracy, financial administration and judiciary, while the latter formed the revolutionary army and (under the Khalifa) the Taʿāīshī ruling elite.[22] The success of the Mahdi's endeavour to consolidate a radical theocracy in such a society was dependent on the mitigation of the orthodox Sharīʿa to the extent that was necessary to meet custom halfway (while maintaining strict uncompromising puritanism in matters pertaining to morality and ethics), and enabling a charismatic leader enough scope of manœuvre to solve daily political and social problems arising within a theocracy. For this purpose the Mahdi created a unique legal methodology that provided him with unlimited authority to enact positive rules without any institutional restriction on the part of orthodox *ʿulamāʾ*.

The Mahdi's legal methodology, though simple and unsophisticated, seems to have been effective in enabling him to achieve his goals. He ignored all schools of law (*madhāhib*)[3] and disregarded their legal literature, thus releasing himself from the burden of *taqlīd*,[4] and the positive law as consolidated within these schools.

The Mahdi acknowledged in his rulings three sources of law, although he did not present them as a consolidated legal methodology. These sources, according to the order of their presentation, are: the Prophetic Sunna, the Qurʾān, and

1 The most authoritative source on the Mahdist state is P.M. Holt, *The Mahdist State in the Sudan, 1881–1898*, 2nd edn, Oxford 1970; in particular pp 19ff.; *idem*, 'al-Mahdiyya', *EI*(2), V, 1247 ii ff.

2 Holt's letter to the author of 25 March 1996.

3 For a general review see Jeanette A. Wakin, 'Islamic Law', in Joseph R. Strayer (general ed.), *Dictionary of the Middle Ages*, New York 1986, 485–9.

4 Sec Muḥammad Ibrāhīm Abū Salım (ed.), *al-Āthār al-kāmila li'l-Imām al-Mahdī*, Khartoum 1990–4, I, 164, 190; III, 319–20; IV, 485; V., 367; *cf.* Muḥammad Ibrāhīm Abū Salīm, *al-Ḥaraka al-fikriyya fī 'l-mahdiyya*, 3rd edn, Khartoum 1989, 86; 'Abd Allāh 'Alī Ibrāhīm, *al-Ṣirāʿ bayna al-Mahdī wa'l-ʿulamāʾ*, 2nd edn, n.p.: Dār Nūbār, 1994, 34; H. Shaked, *The Life of the Sudanese Mahdi*, New Brunswick, NJ 1978, 59, 219, and J. Schacht, 'Taḳlīd', *EI*(1), VIII, 630–1.

the inspiration (*ilhām*) transmitted to him by the Prophet Muḥammad.[5] From this order it may be inferred that the Sunna as a source of law is more important than the Qurʾān. This conclusion is sustained by the Mahdi's understanding of *naskh*, that is, abrogation of one textual provision (*naṣṣ*) by another textual provision. This procedure was intended to identify God's will in case of doubt arising from contradictions in the textual sources. One first had to exhaust the substantive material before resorting to the mechanism of *ijtihād*. According to the classical procedure, accepted by most of the *fuqahāʾ*, a Qurʾānic provision cannot abrogate a *ḥadīth*, and *vice versa*.[6] The Mahdi's understanding of *naskh* appears to have vacillated. Thus, in one case, he categorically maintained that a valid *ḥadīth* abrogates a valid *ḥadīth*, and a Qurʾānic verse abrogates a Qurʾānic verse.[7] In another case, however, he maintained that 'Qurʾān abrogates (*yansakh*) Qurʾān and *ḥadīth* abrogates Qurʾān'.[8] He also seems to have favoured adherence to the literal, external (*ẓāhir*) meaning of the textual sources, in conformity with Ibn Ḥazm's Ẓāhirī school of law, originally founded by Dāwūd b. ʿAlī b. Khalaf (d. 270/883).[9]

The Mahdi denied allegations that he reserved for himself the right of *ijtihād*. In one case he was asked to issue a decision in a matter of *khulʿ* divorce, that is, the release of a woman by her husband in return for compensation (such as handing back of the dower). The issue was whether such a divorce should be counted as one of the three repudiations after which an intermediate marriage was required in order that the woman might legally remarry her first husband. The Mahdi ruled that if the husband did not pronounce the word *ṭalāq* then the *khulʿ* should not count as a divorce and the husband may

---

5 On inspiration from God and the Prophet, see D.B. Macdonald, 'Ilhām', *EI*(2), III, 1119–20.

6 There were jurists, however, who maintained that it was possible to abrogate a Qurʾānic provision by a *ḥadīth* and a *ḥadīth* by a Qurʾānic provision, but this view was disputed by the *fuqahāʾ*. Al-Shāfiʿī, driven by his intention to promote the Sunna to the status of a major source of law, along with the Qurʾān, rejected this view altogether; see J. Burton, 'Naskh', *EI*(2), VII, 1009ff., and N.J. Coulson, *A History of Islamic Law*, Edinburgh 1964, 58, 76.

7 Abū Salīm, *al-Āthār al-kāmila*, I, 338.

8 *Manshūrāt al-Imām al-Mahdī*, repr. Khartoum 1963–64, III: al-Aḥkām wa'l-ādāb, 101.

9 *Ibid.*, 19. A case in point is the prophetic *ḥadīth* to the effect that prohibition of marriage on grounds of fosterage is regulated in parallel fashion to the prohibition on grounds of kinship (*yuḥram min al-riḍāʿ man yuḥram min al-nasab*). The orthodox schools maintain that this is not applicable in circumstances where the link producing prohibition on grounds of fosterage is not common to all blood relatives. Thus, the foster mother or sister of one of two blood brothers is not prohibited from marrying the other brother (see Muḥammad Muṣṭafā Shalabī, *Aḥkām al-usra fī 'l-islām. Dirāsa muqārana banya fiqh al-madhāhib al-sunniyya wa'l-madhhab al-Jaʿfarī wa'l-qānūn*, Beirut 1393/1973, 178–9, 182). The Mahdi, on the other hand, ruled that according to the literal meaning of that *ḥadīth*, this prohibition should be absolute with no exception; see Abū Salīm, *al-Āthār al-kāmila*, III, 33–5.

restore the wife without resorting to intermediate marriage unlike in the case where he pronounced *ṭalāq*. The Mahdi explained that in giving this ruling he did not make use of his personal legal discretion (*raʾy* or *ijtihād*), since he resorted to the established rule as manifested in the aforementioned three sources. In another case the Mahdi ruled, in a matter pertaining to the distribution of booty (*ghanīma*), that a *ḥadīth* abrogates a Qurʾānic provision. The Mahdi argued, with regard to this issue, that had his critics believed in his doctrine they would not have accused him of being a *mujtahid*.[10] The Mahdi's version of *ijtihād* is not compatible with the classical theory.[11] Similar to the Salafī concept common among revivalist and reformist movements preceding the Mahdiyya (such as the Wahhābiyya and the Sanūsiyya),[12] the Mahdi, too, emphasized the Qurʾān and the Prophetic Sunna[13] as sources of law.[14] However, *qiyās*[15] or analogical reasoning based on the textual sources of the Qurʾān and the Sunna was apparently replaced by the Mahdi with direct inspiration (*ilhām*) from the Prophet Muḥammad.[16] It should be mentioned in this connection that the Mahdi regarded himself as heir (*wārith*) to, and successor of, the Prophet Muḥammad (*khalīfat rasūl Allāh*),[17] and that he claimed the ability to communicate with the Prophet by means of visions (*ḥaḍrāt*).[18] The enlistment of Prophetic sanction was apparently meant to place him outside public criticism, that is, outside the control of the *ʿulamāʾ*. In other words, the positive rulings established by means of Prophetic inspiration were not subject to the consensus (*ijmāʿ*)[19] of the jurists, as required by the classical theory of Islamic law. This situation resembles the competition, dating back to the formative period of Islamic law, between *ahl al-raʾy*, who emphasized legal reasoning as a method for the creation of positive law, and *ahl al-ḥadīth*, who mobilized the Prophet's authority by means of *ḥadīth*s attributed to him in

10 Abū Salīm, *al-Āthār al-kāmila*, III, 119, and *Manshūrāt al-Imām al-Mahdī*, III, 101, respectively. *Cf.* Holt, *The Mahdist State*, 122n.

11 See J. Schacht and D.B. MacDonald, 'Idjtihād', *EI*(2), III, 1026–7.

12 See Holt, *The Mahdist State*, 19–20, and Knut S. Vikør, *Sufi and Scholar on the Desert Edge: Muḥammad b. ʿAlī al-Sanūsī and his Brotherhood*, London 1995, 218ff.

13 See J. Robson, 'Ḥadīth', *EI*(2), III, 23–28.

14 See, e.g., Abū Salīm, *al-Āthār al-kāmila*, III, 351–2.

15 See M. Bernard, 'Ḳiyās', *EI*(2), V, 238–42.

16 See e.g., Abū Salīm, *al-Āthār al-kāmila*, III, 119.

17 For a description of the Mahdi's installment as caliph see Abū Salīm, *al-Āthār al-kāmila*, IV, 491; V, 448.

18 See, e.g., Abū Salīm, *al-Āthār al-kāmila*, IV, 442 (*atatnā al-waṣiyya min al-ḥaḍra*); V, 449ff. (*ḥaḍra nabawiyya*).

19 See M. Bernard, 'Idjmāʿ', *EI*(2), III, 1023–6.

order to impose their views in legal disputes between jurists.[20] Moreover, it seems that *ilhām* ranks even higher than *ḥadīth* since, contrary to the *ḥadīth*, it is impossible to doubt its authenticity by means of the procedure of *al-jarḥ wa'l-taʿdīl*, that is, by disparaging and declaring a transmitter of *ḥadīth*s as untrustworthy.[21]

In the Mahdi's legal methodology to the extent that it can be reconstructed on the basis of his rulings, there is no explicit mention of custom (*ʿāda, ʿurf*) although in Sudanese society tribal custom reigns almost supreme in many domains. This is not unusual, since even in the classical theory of Islamic law custom has no status as a formal source of law in spite of its important contribution to the material development of Islamic law. This is due to fact that the classical theory was interested not in the historical but rather the systematic aspect of Islamic law.[22] As might be expected, the *fuqahāʾ* were not ready to place custom, which is determined from below by patterns of social behaviour binding in virtue of themselves, on the same level as the eternal textual sources of the Qurʾān and the Sunna. Moreover, recognition of custom as a formal source of law would have placed the development of the legal norm outside of the *fuqahāʾ*'s control and undermined the nature of Islamic law as a jurists' law. At the same time, it is likely that custom did not disappear completely from the Sharīʿa in its Mahdist version, as was the case with the orthodox Sharīʿa, where custom was assimilated by the mechanism of *ijtihād*. In other words, new legal rules were created by the jurists on the basis of legal precedents in the textual sources while taking into consideration social pressures from below. Similarly, it stands to reason that the impact of custom on positive law as shaped by the Mahdi in the light of political and social requirements, can be discerned in proclamations, rulings, judgments and decisions handed down by him, as well as in sayings (*aqwāl*) attributed to him after his death.[23] This phenomenon

20 J. Schacht, 'Ahl al-ḥadīth', *EI*(2), I, 258–9, and Coulson, *A History of Islamic Law*, 52, 56, 61. *Cf. ahl al-sunna* in Abū Salīm, *al-Ḥaraka al-fikriyya fī 'l-mahdiyya*, 164.

21 See J. Robson, 'al-Djarḥ wa'l-Taʿdīl', *EI*(2), II, 462. I owe this assessment to Etan Kohlberg.

22 See J. Schacht, *An Introduction to Islamic Law*, Oxford 1964, 62.

23 See, e.g., Abū Salīm, *al-Āthār al-kāmila*, V, 457–60. In this document the following sayings are attributed to the Mahdi: his nomination as *khalīfa* by God, in the presence of the Prophet and ʿAbd al-Qādir al-Jīlānī; confirmation from God, through angels, prophets and saints, of the appearance of the Mahdiyya; accusation of infidelity (*takfīr*) of anyone who does not believe in the Mahdi; obtaining permission from God and the Prophet to fight the Turks, 'the unbelievers who corrupt on the earth'; the Messenger of God tells the Mahdi, by means of a Prophetic vision, that after he has conquered al-Ubayyiḍ and performed the prayer in its mosque, he will pray in (i.e., having conquered) the mosques of Khartoum, Berber, Mecca, Egypt, Jerusalem, Iraq and Kūfa; two thirds of the people will die by sword or otherwise, and the last third will apply to God (i.e., believe in the

resembles the Prophetic Sunna, that is, normative custom as reflected in the sayings and behaviour of Muḥammad.[24]

To sum up, we are dealing here with a unique version of personal *ijtihād* bound by the textual sources not by *qiyās*, as required by the classical theory, but rather by *ilhām*. This kind of *ijtihād* confers upon the Mahdi a degree of discretion wider than allowed by analogical reasoning. Moreover, the legal norm shaped in this way by the Mahdi was, contrary to the mechanism of classical *ijtihād*, final and irrevocable rather than a tentative rule or conjecture (*ẓann*) awaiting the consensus (*ijmāʿ*) of the *ʿulamāʾ*.[25] Indeed, it seems – as was maintained by one of the Mahdi's advocates – that the Mahdi's authority was infallible (*maʿṣūm min al-khaṭaʾ*) due to the direct inspiration obtained from the Prophet.[26]

The Mahdi's legal methodology no doubt was inspired by revivalist and reformist movements in Arabia (Wahhābiyya) and North Africa (Sanūsiyya) dating back to the eighteenth and nineteenth centuries, respectively, as well as by various *ʿulamāʾ* whom he may have met and from whom he may have derived his knowledge in his formative period. It is likely that the inspiration was transmitted through intermediaries. Thus, e.g., ʿAbdullāhi al-Dufānī provided a link between Aḥmad b. Idrīs, the famous Moroccan mystic, and the Mahdiyya, since he taught the Sufi litanies (*awrād* and *aḥzāb*) of Ibn Idrīs to Muḥammad Aḥmad before the latter was proclaimed *mahdī*. Ibn Idrīs plays a vital role in Muḥammad Aḥmad's visions (*ḥaḍrāt*) announcing his manifestation as the 'Expected' (*muntaẓar*) *mahdī*.[27] This issue will be clarified in the light of the Mahdi's *sharʿī* legal education and training.

The Sufi background of the Mahdi may also have contributed to his legal reformism, as most of the revivalist movements of the eighteenth and early nineteenth centuries were associated in one way or another with a *ṭarīqa* tradition. There seems to be a causal connection between the Mahdi's legal

---

Mahdi); the Prophet's will to the effect that the Mahdi and his adherents cover themselves with loincloths, and put crowns and turbans on their heads; three things cause damage to a human being: envy, deceit and negligence of prayer; warning against stealing spoils (*ghanīma*), and a call to repent and restore the spoils [to the *bayt al-māl*].

24 *Cf.* G. Libson, 'On the Development of Custom as a Source of Law in Islamic Law: *al-Rujūʿu ilā al-ʿurfi aḥadu al-qawāʿidi al-khamsi allatī yatabannā ʿalayhā al-fiqhu*', *Islamic Law and Society*, iv, 2, 1997, 131–55.

25 *Cf.* Coulson, *History of Islamic law*, 78.

26 Al-Ḥasan b. Saʿd b. Muḥammad al-ʿAbbādī, *al-Anwār al-saniyya al-māḥiya li-ẓalām al-munkirīn ʿalā 'l-ḥaḍra al-mahdiyya*, Omdurman 1305 [1888], 233–4.

27 R.S. O'Fahey, *Enigmatic Saint: Ahmad Ibn Idris and the Idrisi Tradition*, London 1990, 178–9, and Abū Salīm, *al-Āthār al-kāmila*, I, 336.

reformism and his association with a Sufi *ṭarīqa*, the Sammāniyya.[28] The new Sufi *ṭarīqas* put special emphasis on adherence to the Prophet's virtues (*al-takhalluq bi-akhlāq al-nabī*) and even claim to have met the Prophet in person, as in the case of the Mahdi,[29] which may perhaps explain the growing interest in the study of Prophetic *ḥadiths* characteristic of revivalist movements.[30] In this connection it is significant to recall that the Mahdi regarded himself as the Prophet's successor and that he received direct inspiration from him. A satisfactory answer to this issue will be possible only after acquaintance with the legal methodology of revivalist movements and *ʿulamāʾ* that may have shaped the Mahdi's spiritual world.

The application of the Mahdi's legal methodology, which – to the best of my knowledge – was never formulated in one comprehensive legal treatise,[31] enabled the Mahdi to legislate without any restriction and introduce innovations, some of which were far-reaching deviations from the orthodox Sharīʿa. For instance, the Mahdi announced on various occasions that the Ottomans (against whom he had declared war) had rejected Islam (*takfīr*) in every respect.[32] This is why he did not hesitate to rule that if a woman stayed in Mahdist territory while her husband was left behind in Turkish territory, the marriage bond between them was null and void regardless of whether or not the wife had initiated dissolution by legal proceedings (a Muslim woman cannot be married to a non-Muslim). The Mahdi found support for this view in Qurʾān 10:60 which deals with the status of emigrating women (*muhājirāt*).[33] The 'infidel' husband's property was deemed, naturally, as spoils (*ghanīma*).[34] The Mahdi also abrogated the validity of a suspended divorce by means of an oath (*ʿalayya 'l-ṭalāq* or *ʿalayya 'l-ḥarām*, '[my wife] shall be forbidden to

28 Holt, *Mahdist State*, 21.

29 *Cf.* Bernd Radtke, '*Ibrīziana*: Themes and sources of a seminal Sufi work', *SAJHS*, 7, 1996, 121–3. I am indebted to my colleague Prof. Hava Lazaus-Yafeh and the editors of *SAJHS* for clarifying this issue.

30 John O. Voll, 'Linking Groups in the Networks of Eighteenth-Centuries Scholars. The Mizjaji Family in Yemen', in N. Levtzion and John O. Voll (eds.), *Eighteenth-Century Renewal and Reform in Islam*, Syracuse 1987, 86–7, and N. Levtzion and G. Weigert, 'Religious Reform in Eighteenth-Century Morocco', *Jerusalem Studies in Arabic and Islam*, XIX, 1995, 179.

31 *Cf.* Ahmad Ibrahim Abu Shouk [Abū Shūk], '*Minhajiyyat al-tashrīʿ al-mahdawī bayn al-ẓāhir wa'l-bāṭin*', a paper submitted to the conference on Sufi studies held at the University of Khartoum 28 October 1995. I am indebted to Dr Abu Shouk for letting me read the typescript; see also Rudolph Peters, '*Idjtihād* and *Taqlīd* in 18th and 19th Century Islam', *Die Welt des Islams*, XX, 3–4, 1980, 133 n. 4.

32 See e.g., Abū Salīm, *al-Āthār al-kāmila*, V, 417.

33 See e.g., Abū Salīm, *al-Āthār al-kāmila*, II, 94; III, 70; *Manshūrāt al-Imām al-Mahdī*, III, 5.

34 See e.g., Abū Salīm, *al-Āthār al-kāmila*, III, 163.

me') intended to reinforce a pronouncement made by the husband in a matter not necessarily connected with the wife, that is to say, the element of intent (*niyya*) to divorce is absent here – this too in reliance on the Qur'ān and the Prophetic Sunna.[35] Suspended divorce, which is valid under all schools of law, was abrogated by statutory legislation in some countries only in the twentieth century.[36] The Mahdi acted as a legislator in circumstances of political, social and personal exigencies. In this respect, too, there is a strong resemblance to the legislative activity of the Prophet Muḥammad. The Mahdi also introduced various prohibitions that were intended to regulate public morals, especially in regard to women's chastity.[37] The Mahdi's deviations from normative positive law brought him into conflict with orthodox *ʿulamāʾ* who backed the Turco-Egyptian regime, for which reason he designated them *ʿulamāʾ al-sūʾ* (scholars of evil).[38]

The Mahdi's legal opinion on several issues pertaining to divorce and polygamy, which is the primary subject of this short essay, is intended to serve as a tangible illustration of the application of the Mahdi's unique legal methodology and as an instructive example of the adaptation of the Sharīʿa to his requirements.

## 1 The Background of the Legal Opinion

The legal opinion under review was intended to solve problems created during the initial stages of the expansion and consolidation of the Mahdist movement. Since the Mahdi deemed the Turks to be unbelievers, a question emerged regarding the legal status of families some of whose members stayed in Mahdist territory while others were left behind the Turkish lines. Should the latter be treated as Muslims who are bound in matters of personal status (and otherwise) by the Sharīʿa? The Mahdi answered in the negative. This legal

---

35 *Manshūrāt al-Imām al-Mahdī*, III, 11–12, and Muḥammad Ibrāhīm Abū Salīm (ed.), *Manshūrāt al-Mahdiyya*, Beirut 1969, 200. *Cf.* A. Layish, *Divorce in the Libyan Family*, New York and Jerusalem 1991, 31, 100, 107–8.

36 N. Anderson, *Law Reform in the Muslim World*, London 1976, 123–4, and A. Layish, 'Ṭalāḳ', *EI*(2) (forthcoming).

37 See e.g., Abū Salīm, *al-Āthār al-kāmila*, II, 263–4 (women are required to use a veil, *ḥijāb*); III, 109–12 (greeting a woman entails a sanction, women are prohibited from assuming masculine manners, *mutarajilla*).

38 *Cf.* Abū Salīm, *al-Āthār al-kāmila*, IV, 481–2, and Holt, *Mahdist State*, 116; *idem*, 'al-Mahdiyya', 1248 i.

opinion was also intended to solve the Mahdi's personal problems in matters of divorce and polygamy.

The four Sunnī schools of law make a clear distinction between a revocable repudiation (*ṭalāq rajʿī*) and an irrevocable (*bāʾin*) repudiation. The former does not dissolve the marriage instantly, provided it has been consummated. The husband may resume marital relations with his wife, even without her consent, during the waiting period (*ʿidda*) of the divorce which – according to the Mālikī school – lasts for three periods of legal purity. If the husband does not reinstate his wife during this period, the revocable repudiation becomes irrevocable. Irrevocable repudiation dissolves the marriage instantly with all its legal and financial consequences. The husband may reinstate his divorced wife, but only with her consent and by means of a new marriage contract and dower. After the third repudiation – whether revocable or irrevocable – the divorced woman cannot be legally restored to her former husband unless she has married another man, that marriage has been dissolved, and the waiting period has been observed. The Mālikī school does not acknowledge a fictitious intermediate marriage intended to render the woman lawfully permitted to her first husband. In other words, the marriage of the divorced woman to a third party and her divorce by the latter should be in good faith. The waiting period, introduced by the Qurʾān, was intended to remove any doubt as to the paternity of a child, whereas the intermediate marriage was intended to avoid a hasty divorce by the husband. The latter purpose was frustrated by the *fuqahāʾ*'s recognition of triple divorce at one and the same session.[39]

The type and number of divorces are thus of the utmost significance in daily life. Disregard of the number of divorces, as well as the mere existence of a *sharʿī* marriage in circumstances in which one of the spouses remained in Turkish territory, created legal uncertainty regarding the marital status of the spouses, and the parties concerned resorted to the Mahdi with a view to extricating them from the predicament. As is evident from the legal opinion, the issue was of concern to the Mahdi himself since he had exhausted the quota of three repudiations with regard to some of his wives. In at least one instance the Mahdi wished to restore his divorced wife without her having to go through the embarrassing procedure of intermediate marriage.

The issue pertaining to polygamy concerns only the Mahdi. The orthodox Sharīʿa permits a man to marry up to four wives on condition that he treat them equally and justly (*ʿadl*) with respect to matters that can be measured in

---

39 See Layish, *Divorce in the Libyan Family*, 97–101 and the sources there. On intermediate marriage by means of *al-muḥallil min al-ṭalāq*, 'the one who renders [a triply divorced woman] lawfully permitted [to her former husband]'; see A. Layish, *Women and Islamic Law in a Non-Muslim State*, New York and Jerusalem 1975, 132, 173–5.

quantitative terms (such as maintenance and conjugal rights), although not in matters pertaining to sentiment (*mayl al-qalb*), in which area a human being cannot be expected to maintain equality between his wives.[40] From the legal opinion presented here it is clear that the Mahdi sought permission for himself to maintain more than four wives.

The Mahdi's legal opinion, which deviates substantially from the orthodox Sharīʿa, is based on Qurʾānic verses and *ḥadīth*s, as interpreted in the light of direct inspiration (*ilhām*). This inspiration was received during revelations and visions (*ḥaḍrāt*), occasionally entailing sharp physical sensation, manifested to the Mahdi by the Prophet or the 'angel of inspiration' whose identity the Mahdi fails to disclose.[41] In other words, the Mahdi did not, in regard to the interpretation of the textual sources, deem himelf bound to either the classical theory of the sources of law (*uṣūl al-fiqh*) or the positive law of the Sharīʿa. Moreover, it seems that the Mahdi sought support for his personal problems in precedents from the Prophet Muḥammad concerning the solution of some of the Prophet's problems in matters pertaining to marriage and divorce, namely, the option to maintain concurrently more than four wives and to restore his triply divorced wife without having recourse to an intermediate marriage.

The Mahdi's legal opinion is not a mere instrument for clarifying religio-legal doctrine on issues which have no solution under Islamic positive law. Rather, it is a political instrument – similarly to a circular (*manshūr*), order, decision (*ḥukm*), or warning (*indhār*) – intended to impose the legal norm, inspired by the Mahdi's political, economic and social considerations, on a society subject to his rule. Contrary to the regular legal opinion of a *muftī*, the acceptance of which is a matter of personal choice of the individual who requests it (*mustaftī*), the Mahdi's legal opinion was incumbent not only on the *mustaftī* but also on the entire community; it was tantamount to a statutory provision anchored in the sanction of a ruler who did not hesitate to excommunicate, by declaring him infidel (*takfīr*), any individual who did not submit himself to the Mahdi's doctrine. According to the normative conception, Islam does not recognize a hierarchy of degrees among independent *muftī*s. However, the Mahdi was not only a supreme political-military leader; he also placed himself as the supreme religio-legal authority. The integration of all these functions in his personality provided a coercive dimension to his legal opinion.[42]

---

40 Q 4:3, 129; Muḥammad ʿAbduh, *Tafsīr al-qurʾān al-ḥakīm al-shahīr bi-tafsīr al-Manār*, ed. Muḥammad Rashīd Riḍā, 3rd edn, [Cairo] 1367h, 348–51.

41 Usually, the 'Angel of Inspiration' is identified with Gabriel (I owe this clarification to Etan Kohlberg). *Cf.* ʿAbbādī, *Al-Anwār al-saniyya*, 233–4. See below, the legal opinion.

42 *Cf.* Muhammad Khalid Masud, Brinkley Messick and David S. Powers (eds.), *Islamic Legal Interpretation. Muftis and Their Fatwas*, Cambridge: Harvard University Press 1996, 3–32.

## 2 The *fatwā*[43]

بسم الله الرحمن الرحيم
الحمد لله الوالى الكريم والصلاة على سيدنا محمد وآله مع
التسليم

وبعد، فمن عبد ربه محمد المهدي بن السيد عبد الله·
انه قد كثر التضرر والتشكى اليّ وطلب الغوث من الانصار
الحاصل منهم الطلاق قبل زمن المهدية، ولا يخلى ذلك من
الضيق واحرج منهم ومن نسائهم، وقد تابوا والى الله انابوا،ا
وللألفة والاجتماع في دين الله طلبوا، ومرارا اعرض عن ذلك
واقول: أ ليسوا كانوا مؤمنين؟ وافتي للبعض ان عدم الحسبة
في الطلاق لاهل القيقر والنساء اللاتي لم يكن مؤمنات
لانهن لا عصم لهن فلا يكن لهن حسبة طلاق، حتى كثر
التضرر في ذلك والتردد فاهتممت بذلك وتضرعت
وابتهلت الى الله في ذلك ليحصل فرقان من كتاب الله تعالى
لانه سبحانه قد وعد بالفرقان والمحرخ للمتقين
وفوضت الامر الى الله وتركته حتى ورد عليّ وارد في آخر
ورد الراتب· وقد كان هذا الامر خارجا من بالي، فوردت
لي هذه الآية وهي قو له تعالى: وما جعل عليكم في
الدين من حرج مع الالهام انها المحرخ من ذلك التضرر
الحاصل في الطلاق قبل المهدية
وان الطلاق قبل المهدية لا يحسب لمن تمت الثلا ثة ولو بعد
المهدية، وسبق طلاق قبل المهدية. وبعد الهد ية لا تكون

الفتاوى التي كان العلماء يفتون بها في مطلقة الثلاث وقد
وقع في قلبي حينئذ - اعنى في وقت ذلك[44]

---

43 The legal opinion, together with the footnotes of the editor appears in Abū Salīm, *al-Āthār al-kāmila*, IV, 192–6. The legal opinion was copied from this source in A. Layish (ed.), *The Mahdī's Legal Methodology and its Application in the Sudan: A Selection from the Mahdī's Documents (1881–1885)*, Jerusalem: Academon 1996, 55–9.

44 *Al-Āthār al-kāmila* (iv, 193) inserts a dash here (neither dash appears in the *Manshūrāt*). For a better reading this has been moved to ﷺ.

الوارد لنا من
رسول الله ﷺ - اننا لما نخرج من ابا الى الغرب فالناس
يدخلون في دين الاسلام جد يدا عليّ او كما قال
وقد وقع لبعض نسائي تمام عدد الطلاق، وقد وقع بعضها
قبل المهدية وقد تضرروا بانفسهم وباهلهم بعض الاصحاب
وامرتهم بان يتزوجوا فلم يرتضوا حتى ورد الخبر بمنع ذلك
بالخصوصية التي ياتي ذكرها. ولا زالوا يتضررون فقلت لا
سبيل الى ذلك الا بشيء ياتي لنا من الله ورسوله ﷺ مع
وقوع بعض حضرات في حسبتها من نسائي ووقوفها معهم
في التصفية، وبعض حضرات حصل فيها الامر برجوعها مع
كثير من رآوي صالحة في حسبتها من نسائي
وبكل ذلك كنت اجد في نفسي الحرج من الرجوع لها مع
تمام حسبة الطلاق حتى وردلي الوارد فيها مع ذلك الوارد
التقدم ذكره، وهو قوله تعالى: لكيلا يكون عليك
حرج وكان الله غفورا رحيما الآية. فلا ادري الا وقد
انفرج ما بي من ذلك الخوف وانشرح لها صدري بغير ما

اعهده والامر لله، ولله تعالى في كل وقت شان. وقد جاء
الاخبار من رسول الله ﷺ ان ملك الالهام من الله يسددني
وعينه[45]
فمن هذا الخبر النبوي علمت ان الذي يلهمني الله
به بواسطة ملك الالهام لوكان رسول الله ﷺ حاضرا لفعله:
وقد وردلي مرارًا الخصوصية التي كانت له ﷺ في نسائه مع
التوصية منه ﷺ ان تنزل نسائي كمنزلة نسائه ﷺ ولما
اهديت اليّ النساء مع الوارد لي من رسول الله فيهن اخذ ني
خجل من ربي سبحانه في امرهن. وانا في ذلك فجاءني[46]
سلام سمعته بجميع جسدي من غير حرف ولا صوت ولا
سر ولا جهر ولا قرب ولا بعد. ولا اقدر على تكييف شيء
منه، فدلني على اسرار كثيرة، ولله المثل الاعلى، وتعالى الله

45 Thus in *Manshūrāt* and *al-Āthār al-kāmila*, *sc.* ويعينني.
46 See *al-Āthār al-kāmila*, iv, 194 n. 3, *sc.* وبينما انا

عن كل ما يخطر ببال، وامر ذلك مفوض الى الله تعالى
ولكن ما حصل لي، مع ذلك الالهام الذي يحصل لي
فانشرح لي به الصدر وانحل قلبي مما كنت مهتما به
وحصلت لي اسرار كثيرة يغمض فهمها . وقد حصل لي
مثل واقعة هذا السلام شيء يشبه ذلك في كيفية بعض
النساء بشارة نسبتها مع تسمية الولد والبنت الذين[47]
يجعلهما الله تعالى منها ،فسمعته بسائر جسمي باطنًا وكل
بالنساء ولا ابرئ نفسي الا[48] ذلك بحول الله وفضله لا لشغف
ان يزكيني ربي، وعلم حالي عند ربي، واعلم ان ظن
الؤمنين بي حسن ولكن ااخوف دخول الشيطان على من
ضعف قلبه مع العلم ان خلافتي لرسول الله ﷺ لا كخلافة
ااخلفاء السابقين. وسأبين بعض النصوص المذكورة في بعض
التفاسير في قوله تعالى لا يحل لك النساء من بعد
لينحل قلب بعض الاخوان الذين تقع في قلوبهم عداوة
الشيطان بسبب النساء اللاتي ارادهن لي ربي سبحانه ، وانما
الشيطان يجري من ابن آدم مجري الدم. فاذا فقد العبد
كثرت[49] انوار المحبة واليقين بالحقيقة التي نحن عليها اخاف
ان يضره الشيطان
قال عكرمة والضحاك: لا تحل لك النساء من بعد، اي: الا
اللاتي احللنا لك وهي قوله : انا احللنا لك ازواجك
اللاتي اتيت اجورهن الآية. ثم قال لا تحل لك النساء من

بعد، اي اللاتي احللنا لك بالصفة التي تقدم ذكرها. وقيل
لابي بن كعب: لو مات نساء رسول الله ﷺ أكان يحل له
ان يتزو ج؟ قال: وما يمنعه من ذلك؟ قيل: قوله تعالى:
لا يحل لك النساء من بعد قال انما احل الله ضربا من
النساء فقال تعالى يا ايها النبي انا احللنا لك ازواجك
الآية ، ثم قال: لايحل لك النساء من بعد وبين

47 *Ibid.*, 193 n. 4.
48 *Ibid.*, n. 5.
49 *Manshūrāt*: كثرة

بعضهم في هذا المقام انه ﷺ تجوز له ثلاثمائة امرأة. وقال
مجاهد ما معناه: لا تحل لك اليهوديات ولا النصرانيات بعد
المسلمات. ولا ان تبدل بهن من ازواج، يقول: ولا
ان تبدل المسلمات غيرهن من اليهود والنصارى. يقول لا
تكون ام المؤمنين يهودية ولا نصرانية، ولو اعجبك
حسنهن الا ما ملكت يمينك. احل الله له ما ملكت يمينه
من الكتابيات ان يتسرى بهن، وروي عن الضحاك: ولا أن
تبدل بهن من ازواج، يعني: ولا ان تبدل بازواجك اللاتي
هن في حبالك ازواجا غيرهن بان تطلقهن فتنكح غيرهن
فحرم عليه طلاق اللواتي كن عنده وحرمهن على غيره حين
اخترنه فاما نكاح غيرهن فلم يمنع عنه. وغيرذلك من نحو
هذا

اقول: وبعد هذا قد حصلت لي في هذا المعنى اسرار كثيرة
يطول ذكرها، والحمد لله على خاصيتنا برسول الله ﷺ
وعنايته بنا ودعائه لنا قديما وحديثا، فان شرف التابع من
شرف المتبوع، والسلام
١٨ ربيع اول سنة ١٣٠٢

## 3 Translation of the Legal Opinion[50]

In the name of God, the Beneficent, the Merciful.

Praise be to God, the Noble Ruler, and may God bless our Lord Muḥammad, and his family and grant them peace.

Now to our topic. Issued by the slave of his Lord,[51] Muḥammad al-Mahdī b. *al-sayyid*[52] ʿAbd Allāh.

50 The translation is as literal as possible, in an effort to preserve the original style of the *fatwa* to the extent that it does not cause any difficulty in understanding the text. Short explanations appear in the body of the translation in square brackets.

51 Quite often the Mahdi uses the formula 'the slave who is in need (*al-muftaqir*) of God'; Abū Salīm, *al-Āthār al-kāmila*, IV, 192 n. 2.

52 That is, a descendant of the Prophet Muḥammad (*sharīf*, pl. *ashrāf*). Muḥammad Aḥmad b. ʿAbd Allāh adopted this status after the announcement of his manifestation (*ẓuhūr*)

An increasing number of complaints pertaining to damage caused and asking for help have reached me from the *anṣār*[53] who have repudiated their wives by means of a unilateral divorce (*ṭalāq*) in the period preceding [the manifestation of] the Mahdiyya. This caused them and their wives distress and anguish, even after they had turned to God in repentance, seeking love and union in God's religion. Repeatedly I refrained [57] from dealing with this issue, wondering: 'Were they not believers?' but I gave some of them a formal legal opinion (*uftī*) to the effect that it is not required to take into account (*ḥisba*) [the number of] divorces with regard to the inhabitants of the [Turkish] fortified camps (*al-qayqar*)[54] and women who were not [regarded as] believers, because they were not subject to matrimonial authority [that is, not married]. Therefore, no account should be taken of the number of divorces.[55] When the complaints regarding damage in this matter increased and recurred, I paid attention to the matter and beseeched and supplicated God in this matter in the expectation of some evidence (*furqān*) from the Book of God [the Qur'ān], Exalted is He, since He, praise be to Him, had promised a *furqān* and way out to the Godfearing.

[Subsequently] I left the matter in God's hand and refrained from dealing with it until an insight reached me (*warada ʿalayya wārid*)[56] while performing the last devotion (*wird*) of *al-Rātib*.[57] This matter had escaped my mind. This verse reached me, and this is the word of God, Exalted is He, '[God] hath not laid upon you in religion any hardship' [Q 22:78],[58] together with a [Prophetic]

as *mahdī*; see Abū Salīm, *al-Āthār al-kāmila*, I, 339 (his message to Muḥammad al-Mahdī al-Sanūsī).

53 The Mahdi's supporters. The term is derived metaphorically from the Prophet's *anṣār*, see Holt, *Mahdist State*, 56n., and W. Montgomery Watt, 'al-Anṣār', *EI*(2), I, 514–15.

54 *Cf.* '*al-qaqra*' in Abū Salīm, *al-Āthār al-kāmila*, VII, Glossary, 398.

55 In other words, the mere presence of of a woman in Turkish territory renders her a non-Muslim, thereby invalidating her marriage from a *sharʿī* point of view, with the result that the question of the number of her divorces ceases to be relevant.

56 The insight being both the Qurʾānic verse that came to his mind and the solution to the divorce problem that came by inspiration; see Abū Salīm, *al-Āthār al-kāmila*, VII, Glossary, 399, '*al-wāridāt*'.

57 *Rātib al-Imām al-Mahdī*, the devotional manual compiled by the Mahdi (lithograph press, n.d., n.p.); see Holt, *Mahdist State*, 165; J. Spencer Trimingham, *The Sufi Orders in Islam*, Oxford 1971, Glossary, and *ALA*, I, 328.

58 In other words, God provides solutions for any given problem. The translation of this and the following verses is based on M.M. Pickthall, *The Meaning of the Glorious Koran*, New York 1953.

inspiration (*ilhām*)[59] [58] that this might provide a way out from that hardship resulting from the divorces which took place before the Mahdiyya.

The divorces which took place before the Mahdiyya should not be taken into account [within the *sharʿī* quota of divorces] even if someone completed three after the Mahdiyya, provided that [at least] one of the divorces preceded the Mahdiyya.[60] After the Mahdiyya no [validity is attached] to any legal opinion issued by the jurists [of evil][61] concerning a triply divorced woman [repudiated before the Mahdiyya].[62] And it came to my heart at that time [I mean at the time of that insight to us from the Messenger of God], may God bless him and grant him peace, that when we go forth from Abā[63] to the West, people would newly enter into the religion of Islam through my intervention,[64] or words [of the Prophet] to that effect.

One of my wives has completed the quota of divorces,[65] some of which had occurred before the Mahdiyya.[66] Some [59] of the adherents (*aṣḥāb*)[67] suffered hardship in regard to their persons and families, and I told them to [feel free] to marry [this divorced wife of mine], but they did not agree to this.[68] Then

59 According to Abū Salīm, the resort to inspiration indicates that the Mahdi intended to hand down a valid decision in *sharʿī* terms as if it had been issued by the Prophet; see Abū Salīm, *al-Āthār al-kāmila*, IV, 193 n. 2.

60 In other words, the enumeration of the divorces begins only after the manifestation of the Mahdiyya. Any divorce that preceded the Mahdiyya – a period that is tantamount, in the Mahdi's eyes, to the Jāhiliyya – has no significance from a *sharʿī* point of view, and should therefore not taken into account. *Cf.* Abū Salīm, *al-Āthār al-kāmila*, IV, 193 n. 4.

61 See above, n. 38.

62 It seems that what is meant here are *fatwā*s requiring a woman to resort to an intermediate marriage with a view to rendering her legally permitted to her first husband.

63 An island on the White Nile. It was here in March 1881 that the Mahdi first announced secretly to his disciples his manifestation as the 'Expected (*al-muntaẓar*) *mahdī*'. See Holt, *Mahdist State*, 46ff.; *idem*, 'al-Mahdiyya', 1248 ii-1249 i.

64 This implies that everything that precedes the Mahdiyya belongs to the period of heresy; see Abū Salīm, *al-Āthār al-kāmila*, IV, 192 n. 6.

65 That is, they were repudiated three times.

66 According to Abū Salīm, the Mahdi refers here to his wife Fāṭima bt. Ḥājj, his paternal cousin. He married her in Khartoum. Then he repudiated her prior to the manifestation of the Mahdiyya and reinstated her [without resorting to an intermediate marriage] in the period of the Mahdiyya. In what follows he deals with the circumstances of her reinstatement because of its *sharʿī* significance; see Abū Salīm, *al-Āthār al-kāmila*, IV, 192 n. 7.

67 Synonym of *anṣār*, this too – by analogy from the Prophet's *aṣḥāb*; see Abū Salīm, *al-Āthār al-kāmila*, V, 455 (the Prophet said to the Mahdi: 'Your adherents are like my adherents').

68 In other words, according to the Sharīʿa, after the quota of three divorces has been exhausted the divorced wife must marry somebody else in an intermediate marriage before she is rendered legally permissible to her first husband, that is, in the case under

came the [divinely inspired] message forbidding that, owing to the exclusivity (*khuṣūṣiyya*)[69] [of the divorced wives to the Mahdi] which will be mentioned [later]. When they continued to suffer hardship,[70] I said, 'There is no way out with respect to this matter except by something coming to us from God and His Messenger, may God bless him and grant him peace, upon the occurrence of some visions (*ḥaḍrāt*) concerning her being counted among my wives and her standing with them, solving this matter'.[71] Some visions [occurred], in which came the instruction of her reinstatement [60] [to the Mahdi without an intermediate marriage] in addition to many appropriate visions concerning counting her among my wives.

However, in spite of all this I was distressed with respect to her reinstatement [without an intermediate marriage] after having completed the number of divorces, until there came to me an insight (*al-wārid*) concerning her, along with the aforementioned one.[72] This is His word, Exalted is He, 'That thou mayst be free from blame, for Allah is Forgiving, Merciful' [Q 33:50], (to the end of the verse).[73]

Suddenly, the fear within me was driven away, and my heart was opened up to her in a manner never experienced before. The matter is left in God's hands, and God – Exalted is He – is at every moment engaged in [some new] task.[74] Reports from the Prophet, may God bless him and grant him

---

review, the Mahdi. The *anṣār*, however, did not want the Mahdi's divorced wives to marry someone else beside him, thus making it easier for him to reinstate them without resorting to an intermediate marriage. *Cf.* Abū Salīm, *al-Āthār al-kāmila*, IV, 193 n. 8. An alternative reading of this paragraph, assuming an influence of Sudanese colloquial usage to refer to a single wife [Fāṭima] in the plural, would read: 'I ordered them [Fāṭima] to marry [somebody else in intermediate marriage] but they [she] did not consent'.

69 On the exclusive status (*khuṣūṣiyya*) of the Prophet Muḥammad with regard to women, such as marriage with no dower, or marriage with more than four women concurrently; see Shalabī, *Aḥkām al-usra fī 'l-islām*, 108.

70 Due to fact that Fāṭima could not marry because of the legal uncertainty.

71 In other words, the Mahdi's legal opinion was meant to solve a general problem of women who had been triply divorced prior to the manifestation of the Mahdi.

72 In the edition of *Manshūrāt al-Mahdiyya* the text reads *al-mutaqaddim*.

73 This verse relates in its original context to polygamy. (See Abū Ja'far Muḥammad b. Jarīr al-Ṭabarī [d. 310/923], *Jāmi' al-bayān 'an ta'wīl āyāt al-Qur'ān*, 2nd edn, [Cairo] 1373/1954, XXII, 24, ll. 8–14). It seems, however, that the Mahdi attempted to adapt it to the purpose of reinstatement of his triply divorced wife without resorting to an intermediate marriage that would render her legally permitted to him. This privilege, among others, was granted to the Prophet Muḥammad; see Q 33:51; *The Korān*, trans. G. Sale, London [n.d.], 416 n. 1.

74 This may be an oblique reference to Qur'ān 55:29, '*Kull yawm huwa fī sha'n*', which Sufis interpret to mean that God is continually displaying Himself in new ways, or is always preoccupied with some new task (*sha'n*). See William C. Chittick, *The Sufi Path of Knowledge: Ibn al-'Arabī's metaphysics of imagination*, Albany, NY 1989, 96. I am indebted to John

peace, have reached [me] to the effect that the Angel of Inspiration (*malak al-ilhām*),[75] on behalf of God, shows me [61] the right way and assists me. From this Prophetic report I learned that what the inspiration that God conferred upon me (*yulhimunī*) by means of the Angel of Inspiration, if the Messenger of God, may God bless him and grant him peace, had been present [at this very moment] he would have conducted himself in like manner.

I was repeatedly approached [by means of visions] by the notion of the exclusivity which the Prophet, may God bless him and grant him peace, enjoyed as regards his wives, together with a recommendation by the Prophet that the status of my wives be similar to the status of his wives, may God bless him and grant him peace. When wives were conferred upon me, in accordance with the *wārid* that had reached me from the Messenger of God with regard to them, I was seized by [a sense of] shame concerning them from my Lord, Sublime is He. And while being preoccupied with this matter, I was approached by a sense of serenity which I heard with the entirety of my body, without a word or a voice, without secrecy or publicity, without [a sensation of] proximity or remoteness. I cannot describe the quality of anything thereof.[76] [The Qurʾānic verse] guided me toward many secrets, 'and Allah's is the Sublime Similitude' [Q 16:60], and God shall ascend above anything that comes to one's mind. This matter is entrusted to the hands of God, Exalted is He.

However, what occurred to me, by means of that inspiration I received, is that I became happy and relieved in regard to the matter with which I was preoccupied.[77] Many secrets, whose understanding was unclear, were vouchsafed to me. Similar to the occurrence of this serenity, I experienced something resembling it in regard to the appearance of a certain woman, an announcement of joyous news[78] which I connected with the naming of a son and a daughter which God would [62] bestow upon me from her. I heard it with my whole body in an inward fashion.[79] And all of that was through the power of

---

Hunwick for drawing my attention to the Qurʾānic verse and to source indicated in the reference.

75 The Mahdi does not disclose the identity of the Angel of Inspiration in the Circular of Propagating his Mission (*manshūr al-daʿwa*) and in the Vision of his Nomination (*ḥaḍrat al-tanṣīb*) as a *khalīfa*. In this context al-Khiḍr and ʿAzrāʾīl are mentioned; see Abū Salīm, *al-Āthār al-kāmila*, IV, 193 n. 2, and Holt, *Mahdist State*, 106. See n. 41 above.

76 This is clear evidence of the confusion of senses that the Mahdi experienced during the vision of revelation and inspiration.

77 It seems that the Mahdi refers here to the number of his wives.

78 Assuming the alternative *bi-bishāra*, as suggested by Abū Salīm (see n. 47, above).

79 The Mahdi is excusing himself for being captivated by the beauty of a woman who was not his wife just as the Prophet was captivated by Zaynab. He made his feelings obvious to his companions and then had to explain this away. He says that he received an inspiration

God and His grace, not through passion for women. I do not absolve myself from guilt, still my Lord vindicates me. My Lord is well acquainted with my situation. I know that the believers think well of me.[80] However, it is feared that Satan will dominate those whose hearts became weak due to the message that my status as the successor (*khalīfa*) of the Messenger of God, may God bless him and grant him peace, is not the same as the status of the successorship of the former caliphs.[81] I shall clarify some of the texts (*nuṣūṣ*) mentioned in some of the commentaries pertaining to God's saying, Exalted is He, 'It is not allowed thee to take (other) women henceforth' [Q 33:52],[82] in order that relaxation be imposed [63] on some of the *ikhwān* whose hearts are dominated by the hostility of Satan, due to the women whom my Lord, praise be to Him, wanted to be under my matrimonial authority. Yet, Satan flows in man as blood in the veins.[83] If a human being loses the abundance of the lights of love and the certainty of reality in which we exist,[84] I am afraid Satan might cause him harm.[85]

ʿIkrima[86] and al-Ḍaḥḥāk[87] said, '[Concerning the verse] "It is not allowed thee to take (other) women henceforth", that is, "save those whom We declared

that he would marry her and have children from her, thus seeking in some way to legitimize his passion. I owe this explanation to John Hunwick.

80 In spite of his deviation from the quota of four women who are legally permitted to other Muslims.

81 Abū Salīm explains that the caliphate of the Mahdi is different from that of the 'Rightly-guided Caliphs' (*al-khulafāʾ al-rāshidūn*) in the sense that the Mahdi could afford to ignore the schools of law due to the guidance received through the Mahdist inspiration, which singled him out from the rest of the people; see Abū Salīm, *al-Āthār al-kāmila*, IV, 195 n. 1.

82 See Abū Salīm, *al-Āthār al-kāmila*, IV, 195 n. 2. The commentators disagree over the meaning of this verse. Some maintain that it was meant to prohibit Muḥammad from marrying women in addition to the nine women already under his matrimonial authority, disregarding the quota of four women permissible to other Muslims. Other commentators maintain that Muḥammad was prohibited from marrying any woman in place of one of the women that might die or be divorced. And some maintain that Muḥammad was prohibited from marrying any woman save those belonging to the four categories specified in verse 50 (See Sale, *The Korān*, 416, n. 2). For more details see al-Ṭabarī, *Jāmiʿ al-bayān*, XXII, 28ff., and Abū ʿAbd Allāh Muḥammad b. Aḥmad al-Qurṭubī, *al-Jāmiʿ li-aḥkām al-Qurʾān*, Cairo 1387/1967, XIV, 141.

83 In other words, the presence of Satan, which here embodies the jealousy due to the permission the Mahdi availed himself of to marry more than four wives, in the heart of human being, is – according to the Mahdi – natural and self explanatory.

84 This may be regarded as a recommendation that people resign themselves to the idea that the Mahdi is entitled to marry more than four wives.

85 The Mahdi seems to be worried that some of the people might find it difficult to overcome their jealousy due to the permission that he availed himself of.

86 Qurʾān commentator, died 105/723–24; see J. Schacht, 'ʿIkrima', *EI* (2), III, 1081–2.

87 Qurʾān commentator, died 723.

legally permissible to you", who are, in God's words, "[O Prophet! Lo!] We have made lawful unto thee thy wives unto whom thou hast paid their dowries" (to the end of the verse)'.[88] Subsequently 'Ikrima said, '"It is not allowed thee to take (other) women henceforth", that is, "save those whom We declared legally permissible to you in the above-mentioned manner"'. Ubayy b. Kaʿb[89] was asked, 'If the wives of the Messenger of God, may God bless him and grant him peace, die, is it legally permissible to him to marry?' Ubayy asked, 'What prevents [64] him from doing so?' He was answered, '[What prevents him is] the saying of God, Exalted is He, "It is not allowed thee to take (other) women henceforth".' Ubayy said, 'God permitted [polygamous marriage] only with respect to a certain category of women [as specified in verse 50], since He, Exalted is He, said, "O Prophet! Lo! We have made lawful unto thee thy wives" (to the end of the verse)'.[90] Then He said, "It is not allowed thee to take (other) women henceforth".[91] One of them clarified with regard to this point that the Prophet, may God bless him and grant him peace, was legally permitted [to marry] three hundred women. Mujāhid[92] gave an interpretation the meaning of which is, 'It is not legally permissible for you [to marry] Jewish or Christian women after Muslim women', [citing the Qurʾān:] 'nor that thou shouldst change them for other wives' [Q 33:52].[93] Mujāhid said, 'neither to replace Muslim women by other – Jewish and Christian – women', and said, 'The "Mother of the Believers" cannot be a Jewish or a Christian[94] woman'. [As to the verse] 'even though their beauty pleased thee, save those whom thy right hand possesseth' [i.e., female slaves; Q 33:52], [Mujāhid said], 'God made permissible for him to take as concubines what his right hand possessed from women of the revealed religions'.[95] It was transmitted from al-Ḍaḥḥāk, '[With respect to the verse] "nor that thou shouldst change them for other wives", that is, "nor [is it permissible to you] to replace your wives who are tied to [65] you by strings [i.e., by marriage contract] by other women, namely, by repudiating

---

88 Q 33:50. The rest of the verse mentions female slaves that one hand is able to possess from one's share in the booty, paternal and maternal cousins that immigrated with Muḥammad from Mecca to Medina, but not others; see Sale, *The Korān*, 415 n. 4.

89 Qurʾān commentator, died *c.* 29–34/649–54.

90 *Cf.* al-Ṭabarī, *Jāmiʿ al-bayān*, XXII, 29, ll. 18–22.

91 *Cf.* al-Dārimī, *Sunan*, Nikāḥ 44 (edn 2 vols, Beirut n.d., II, 154). I owe this reference to Dr Vikør.

92 Died *c.* 100–04/718–22.

93 That is, by divorcing a wife and marrying another woman in her stead. Some maintain that what is meant here is the exchange of women between married couples, a common practice among the pagan Arabs; see Sale, *The Korān*, 419 n. 3; al-Qurṭubī, *al-Jāmiʿ li-aḥkām al-qurʾān*, XIV, 142.

94 See al-Qurṭubī, *al-Jāmiʿ li-aḥkām al-qurʾān*, XIV, 141–3.

95 *Cf.* al-Ṭabarī, *Jāmiʿ al-bayān*, XXII, 31, ll. 5–6.

them and subsequently marrying other women'.[96] God forbade him to repudiate those women who were at his disposal [i.e., in his matrimonial authority] and rendered them prohibited to others when the women had chosen him. As regards marriage with other women than them, he was not prevented from doing this', and other related issues.

I say: Subsequently there came to me many secrets of a like kind whose specification might take too long. Praise be to God for entitling me [to benefit from the same privilege] that was reserved for the Messenger of God,[97] may God bless him and grant him salvation, and for his [the Prophet's] concern for us and his praying for us in former and latter times. The honour of the adherent (*tābiʿ*) derives from the honour of the leader, and let it be done with that.

18 Rabīʿ I 1302 [5 January 1885].

## 4 Conclusion

This legal opinion illustrates very clearly the Mahdi's unique style of deviating from positive Islamic law and the classical theory of the jurisprudence in an effort to replace them with new methodological elements, the most important of which is Prophetic inspiration, promoted here to the status of a source of law in its own right, while displacing analogical reasoning (*qiyās*) from the textual sources. In the alternative legal methodology of the Mahdi there is no room for the consensus (*ijmāʿ*) of the *fuqahāʾ*. The Mahdi's attempt in matters of personal status to avail himself of the options that were available to the Prophet coincides with his efforts to consolidate himself as *khalīfat rasūl Allāh*, a status which ranks higher than that of the 'Righteous Caliphs'.[98]

[66]It is likely that the Mahdist state was one of the most important sources of inspiration for president Numayrī who initiated the revival of Islamic law in the Sudan in the early 1980s. The modern Sudanese experiment is not an anomalous historical development nor a break in the process of secularizing Islamic law which has been taking place in the Muslim world since the middle of the nineteenth century; it is rather a reflection of latent desires, since the suppression of the Mahdist rebellion in the late nineteenth century, to revive the theocratic state. Surely, the reinstatement of Islamic law in modern Sudan presents a strange synthesis of Islamic law with English law in its

96 *Cf. ibid.*, XXII, 31, ll. 10–11.

97 That is, the option to marry more than four women concurrently.

98 See Abū Salīm, *al-Āthār al-kāmila*, IV, 494; *Manshūrāt al-imām al-mahdī*, III, 97; *Manshūrāt al-mahdiyya*, 303.

Anglo-Muhammadan version, precedents of national courts, local custom, and above all – the right of civil judges to exercise *ijtihād* to shape legal norms on the basis of all these sources.[99] However, what is common to Numayrī's experiment and to the Mahdi's legal methodology is the emphasis placed on the Qur'ān and the Sunna. Moreover, Warburg has demonstrated that a wide range of Mahdist elements and symbols, such as *bayʿa* (vow of allegiance), *jihād* (holy war against the infidels), *bayt al-māl* (public treasury), *ghanīma* (booty), and *ṣadaqa* (charitable gift) have been adapted to the conditions of modern Sudan.[100]

The Mahdi's attempt to establish a theocracy in tribal and sedentarized tribal society, regulated by the Qur'ān and the Sunna, resembles in some respects the experience of the Prophet Muḥammad himself. Finally, the acquaintance with the interaction between the Sharīʿa (in the Mahdi's unique version) and tribal law may facilitate the understanding of the Islamization process at work within tribal societies.

---

99 See A. Layish and G.R. Warburg, *The Revival of Islamic Law in Sudan under Numayrī: Background, Methods, Application, Assessment and Repercussions* (in progress).

100 See G.R. Warburg, 'From Revolution to Conservatism: Some Aspects of Mahdist Ideology and Politics in the Sudan', *Der Islam*, lxx, 1, 1993, 88–111, and *idem*, 'Mahdism and Islamism in the Sudan', *International Journal of Middle East Studies*, xxvii, 1995, 219–36.

CHAPTER 10

# Ḥasan al-Turābī (1932–)

## 1 Life and Times[1]

Ḥasan ʿAbdallāh al-Turābī was born in Kasala, on the border between Sudan and Ethiopia, in 1932. His family came from a deep-rooted Sufi background. One of his ancestors, Shaykh Ḥamad al-Naḥlān b. Muḥammad al-Budayrī (d. 1705), was a well-known Sufi. Ḥasan al-Turābī received both an Islamic orthodox and Sufi education; the latter may well have affected his legal thought, although there is no evidence that he was affiliated with a Sufi tradition. Moreover, while engaged in launching his plan for an Islamist state in Sudan, al-Turābī did not hesitate to confront the Sufi orders. In his view, Sudanese adherence to the Sufi orders is one of the reasons for the failure of the movement of renewal (*tajdīd*) in Islam.[2]

Ḥasan al-Turābī received a traditional Muslim education from his father, a *qāḍī* in a *sharīʿa* court, and this may be the main source of his knowledge of Islamic law. It seems that al-Turābī never attended a religious institution, nor did he have close contacts with contemporary *ʿulamāʾ*; he was an autodidact in Islamic studies. Al-Turābī received a standard modern education at the Ḥantoub secondary school alongside other personalities in Sudanese politics who later became famous, such as Jaʿfar al-Numayrī and Muḥammad Ibrāhīm Naqḍ, Secretary General of the Sudanese Communist Party. Al-Turābī was influenced at an early age by members of the Society of Muslim Brothers (*jamʿiyyat al-ikhwān al-muslimīn*) who had fled from Egypt in order to avoid legal prosecution. In 1949 the Muslim Brothers founded a branch at the Gordon Memorial College, which later became the highly influential University College of Khartoum, affiliated with the University of London. The Muslim Brothers had a profound influence on the students of University

1 This essay is a revised and extended version of an argument initially presented in Layish and Warburg, *Reinstatement*, 79–94, here provided with a biographical introduction and excerpts from al-Turābī's works. I thank my colleague Gabriel Warburg for introducing me to Sudanese studies.

[Originally published in David Powers, Susan Spectorsky, and Oussama Arabi (eds.), *Islamic Legal Thought: A Compendium of Muslim Jurists* (Leiden, 2013), pp. 513–532; Ḥasan al-Turābī died in 2016.]

Unless otherwise indicated, this section is based on Weissbrod, *Turabi*, 13–22; Warburg, *Islam, Sectarianism and Politics in Sudan*, 179–83; Burr and Collins, *Revolutionary Sudan*, xiii–xv, 5–6; Layish and Warburg, *Reinstatement*, 14–17; Woodward, "Ḥasan al-Turābī."

2 Al-Turābī, *Tajdīd al-fikr*, 98.

 DOI:10.1163/9789004680920_012

College.[3] In 1955 (alternatively, 1952; Burr & Collins) al-Turābī graduated from Khartoum University College. Al-Ṣādiq al-Mahdī, the Acting Imām of the Anṣār (an activist, revivalist, Islamic movement) and Head of the Umma party, was one of his contemporaries at the College, and both of them later studied abroad. Their relationship was strengthened after al-Turābī married al-Ṣādiq's sister.[4] Al-Ṣādiq seems to have been al-Turābī's closest colleague, and there are substantial similarities between their legal methodologies.[5] In 1957 (alternatively, 1961; Burr and Collins, al-Turābī received his Master of Law degree from London University. After spending some time in Sudan, he studied in Paris, where he received his doctorate in law from the Sorbonne. His dissertation was on the emergency powers of the executive according to English and French constitutional law. Al-Turābī has a good command of both English and French.

As a student at Khartoum University, al-Turābī joined the Islamic Liberation Movement (ILM) (*ḥarakat al-taḥrīr al-islāmiyya*) and was subsequently elected to its executive. His reputation as a Western-oriented professor of law and Dean of the Law Faculty at Khartoum University College served his political career. His entrance into national politics coincided with General ʿAbbūd's downfall. Since 1964 al-Turābī has been the leader of the Muslim Brothers, and he was the unofficial ideologue of the 1989 Islamist military coup.

In 1965, al-Turābī founded the Islamic Charter Front (ICF) (*jabhat al-mīthāq al-islāmī*), which comprised several Islamic organizations and movements, first among them the Muslim Brothers. The ICF promoted the idea of an Islamic constitution for Sudan and al-Turābī was its secretary general until 1969, when it was disbanded, alongside other political parties in Sudan, following Jaʿfar Numayrī's military coup. Subsequently al-Turābī was arrested and spent several years in jail, where he wrote his first two books, *al-Ṣalāt ʿimād al-dīn* (1972) and *al-Īmān wa-athāruhu ʿalā ḥayāt al-insān* (1974). Following the "National Reconciliation" between the Muslim Brothers and Numayrī in 1977, which resulted in the former's entering the government, al-Turābī filled several public positions, most of them of a legal nature. In 1977 Numayrī appointed him to preside over a committee charged with the task of proposing a "revision of the laws so as to make them compatible with the *sharīʿa*" (*lajnat murājaʿat al-qawānīn li-tatamashshahā maʿa al-sharīʿa*). Between 1979 and 1982 al-Turābī was the Attorney General, and in 1983 he was the President's Adviser on Foreign and Legal Affairs. He was dismissed from this office in March 1983

3 For further details, see Lowrie, *Islam, Democracy, the State and the West*, 11; Abdelmoula, "Ethnicity, Religion, and Human Rights in the Sudan," 43ff.

4 As a reflection of a political alliance, in the 1960s, between the Umma party and the Islamic Constitutional Front, al-Turābī's party.

5 See Layish and Warburg, *Reinstatement*, 87–9.

when Numayrī dissolved his political alliance with the Muslim Brothers, and he was imprisoned shortly before Numayrī was overthrown in April 1985.

After Numayrī's downfall, al-Turābī established the National Islamic Front (*al-jabha al-islāmiyya al-qawmiyya*), which, between December 1988 and March 1989, was part of the coalition under al-Ṣādiq al-Mahdī. During that period al-Turābī served in several official positions (Attorney General, Minister of Justice and Minister for Foreign Affairs). In 1996 al-Turābī was elected Speaker of the Parliament. In May 2000 he was removed from his position as Secretary-General of the Popular National Congress (*al-mu'tamar al-sha'bī al-waṭanī*), and in August 2000 he founded his own PNC.[6]

Al-Turābī has played a central role in the pan-Islamic movement. In 1991 he founded the Arabic-Islamic Popular Conference (*al-mu'tamar al-sha'bī al-'arabī al-islāmī*), an international pan-Islamic organization that combines Islamic and Arab political movements, especially those that are in opposition to orthodox Islam (the Egyptian and Saudi Arabian movements did not join the organization), and since then has been its general secretary.

Al-Turābī was a key figure behind the Numayrī regime's experiment with Islamist legislation. The 1977 committee for the revision of the Sudanese statutes with regard to their compatibility with the *sharī'a*, under al-Turābī's chairmanship, drafted several bills. In 1983 Numayrī appointed a new commission headed by 'Alī 'Uthmān Ṭāhā. The acts drafted by this commission (the "September Laws") were profoundly influenced by al-Turābī's ideas on Islamic law and legal methodology. This is particularly the case with the Judgments (Basic Rules) Act, 1983, apparently drafted by al-Turābī himself. This statute, which provides the court with "the order of priorities" to be applied in cases of lacunae in the Islamist legislation, reflects in detail al-Turābī's legal methodology. Al-Turābī also drafted the new penal code of 1999.[7]

Al-Turābī is the leader of an Islamic political movement that operates on both the national and international levels, and he is one of the most important and original Islamic thinkers and ideologues of his generation. He is a prolific writer who has published an impressive number of books and articles, in Arabic and English, on a variety of subjects, such as the Islamic heritage, Islamic society and state, renewal and reform in Islam, Islamic law and methodology, Islam and democracy, secularism, Islam and the West, and the status of women.[8]

The present essay examines al-Turābī's contribution to the development of a contemporary Islamic legal methodology. The intellectual movement

6 See further Burr and Collins, *Revolutionary Sudan*, 277–80.

7 Cf. Layish and Warburg, *Reinstatement*, 75–9, 91–2, 284–6, 296, 302.

8 For a list of his publications, see Weissbrod, *Turabi*, 171f.;Layish and Warburg, *Reinstatement*, 314f.; see also Hallaq, *History*, 226 fn. 45.

initiated by al-Turābī may be defined as a liberal reformist (*iṣlāḥī*) attempt to find solutions for Sudanese problems through a modern version of the doctrine of *tawḥīd*,[9] a new legal methodology (*uṣūl al-fiqh*) and a corpus of positive law (*furūʿ*).[10]

Al-Turābī's literary style is direct and to the point, and his presentation is based on rational arguments stated in simple language and devoid of embellishments; he seldom resorts to citations from Qurʾān or *ḥadīth* to support his arguments. The style and exposition of al-Turābī's English lectures and publications have been drafted for a Western audience, with a view to securing its empathy.[11] His most famous books are *Tajdīd al-fikr al-islāmī* (The renewal of Islamic thought) (1985) and *al-Ḥaraka al-islāmiyya fī 'l-sūdān* (The Muslim [Brothers'] movement in the Sudan) (1991). Although al-Turābī is not an *ʿālim*, he seems to be well versed in the *sharīʿa*. Lack of a formal *sharʿī* education, however, may account for his practice of not providing references to legal treatises in his work.[12]

Al-Turābī's project to modernize legal methodology seems to have been inspired by both Islam and the West. He derives inspiration from both classical and modern Islam; and he has been exposed to literature on Qurʾān and *sunna*, the exegesis (*tafsīr, shurūḥ*) of all schools of law, Islamic popular culture – including the celebration of the Prophet's birthday – and the Forefathers (*al-salaf*) and mysticism. He claims to have been influenced by modern Islamic schools of thought, reformist *salafī* movements across the Muslim world, in particular the Egyptian Muslim Brothers (such as Ḥasan al-Bannāʾ, Muḥammad al-Ghazālī, Sayyid Quṭb) and the Pakistani Sayyid Abul-Ala Maudoodi.[13] He views Khumeini's revolution as "perhaps the greatest event in contemporary Islamic political history."[14]

9 *Tawḥīd*, a theological term that signifies the unity of God, has been extended by al-Turābī to the mundane-political sphere (the unity of the Muslim community) and to the legal sphere. For details, see al-Turābī, *Qaḍāyā al-tajdīd*, 33, 274; idem, *Manhajiyyat al-fiqh*, 10–11; idem, *Islamic State*, 241, 243, 247; El-Affendi, *Turabi's Revolution*, 169–70; Moussalli, "Hasan al-Turabi's Islamist Discourse," 55–62; Weissbrod, *Turabi*, 35; Sidahmed, *Politics and Islam in Contemporary Sudan*, 128.

10 Al-Turābī has recently begun writing a new commentary on the Qurʾān, based on *ijtihād* and his doctrine of *tawḥīd*, in which he seeks to bring the understanding of the text into conformity with modern conditions. See Layish and Warburg, *Reinstatement*, 79–80.

11 Cf. Burr and Collins, *Revolutionary Sudan*, 94–5.

12 This may be due also to the fact that his publications are based on lectures. See, e.g., al-Turābī, *Qaḍāyā al-tajdīd*, 149 (Chapter 3: Renewal of Islamic Thinking).

13 Al-Turābī, *al-Ḥaraka*, 153–4, 204, 225–6, 239–41. Cf. Abdelmoula, "Sudan: Islamic Fundamentalism," 16ff.; El-Affendi, *Turabi's Revolution*, 152–3; Wiessbrod, *Turabi*, 138 fn. 60; Mitchell, *The Society of the Muslim Brothers*, Index; Hourani, *Arabic Thought in the Liberal Age*, 37, 149, 230.

14 Al-Turābī, *al-Ḥaraka*, 242.

Al-Turābī does not seem to have been influenced by Muḥammad Aḥmad al-Mahdī's legal methodology. The Mahdī rejected consensus (*ijmāʿ*) and analogy (*qiyās*) and replaced them with the Prophet's inspiration (*ilhām*), and he ignored all schools of law (*madhāhib*).[15] In fact, the Mahdī is hardly mentioned in al-Turābī's writings, and his references to the Mahdī occur mainly in a political context.[16]

Al-Turābī also has been inspired by several European trends of thought, religious and non-religious, ranging from democratic, liberal and rational philosophy to materialist and Communist ideas and ideologies.[17] He maintains that the time is ripe for ideological transformation, since the present generation of young Islamic elite has received a Western education.[18] Moreover, some of the *ʿulamāʾ* have gone so far as to adopt foreign and even left-wing, ideas.[19] At the same time, al-Turābī is ambivalent toward the West; he accuses Western imperialists of causing the destruction of Muslim institutions and replacing the *sharīʿa* and the theory of Islamic law with statutory (*waḍʿiyya*) legislation and Western legal methodology. He would prefer a reopening of the door of *ijtihād* rather than the adoption of Western legal systems. The Muslim response the Western "cultural assault,"[20] he declares, has culminated in an Islamic awakening that seeks to bring about the emergence of a reformist movement which, in al-Turābī's view, can be compared to the Reformation in Christianity.[21]

## 2 Legal Methodology[22]

Al-Turābī maintains that a new legal methodology is required for an Islamic renaissance:

> The need for a legal methodology (*manhaj uṣūlī*) as an instrument for launching an Islamic renaissance (*nahḍa*) has become today an absolute necessity. It is our conviction that the traditional (*taqlīdī*) science of legal

15 Layish, "The Legal Methodology of the Mahdī in the Sudan, 1881–1885."

16 Al-Turābī, *al-Ḥaraka*, 22, 150, 236.Cf. El-Affendi, *Turabi's Revolution*, 152–3; Jacobs, "The Sudan's Islamization," 206.

17 Al-Turābī, *al-Ḥaraka*, 204, 217, 226, 242–3; Abdelmoula, "Sudan: Islamic Fundamentalism," 41, 45–6; El-Affendi, *Turabi's Revolution*, 49.

18 Al-Turābī, *Ḥiwārāt fī 'l-islām*, 37.

19 Al-Turābī, *al-Ḥaraka*, 152–3.

20 Cf. Layish, "The Contribution of the Modernists," 273.

21 Al-Turābī, *Ḥiwārāt fī 'l-islām*, 26–7, 43–4; idem, *al-Ḥaraka*, 18–22; idem, *Qaḍāyā al-tajdīd*, 204, 246; idem, *Tajdīd al-fikr*, 98; idem, *Manhajiyyat al-fiqh*, 5. Cf. al-Ghannūshī and al-Turābī, *al-Ḥaraka al-islāmiyya wa'l-taḥdīth*, 15.

22 For a short critical analysis of al-Turābī's legal methodology, see Hallaq, *History*, 226–30.

> methodology (*ʿilm al-uṣūl*), in which we seek guidance, is no longer sufficient to meet our modern requirements, since it reflects the historical circumstances in which it developed and crystallized, and the nature of the legal issues that [formerly] preoccupied legal research.[23] [...] Our ancient legal methodology, having flourished commendably [in past centuries], has ended up in a state of futile stagnation (*jumūd*) as a result of the deterioration of genuine religious life; no science of law (*fiqh*)has [since then] developed or emerged.[24]

In al-Turābī's view, zealous adherence to the schools of law was the main cause for the failure of a movement of renewal (*tajdīd*) in Islam.[25] Since the consolidation of classical legal methodology, circumstances have changed and the boundaries of human knowledge have expanded considerably.[26] Al-Turābī maintains that the *sharīʿa* displays a remarkable measure of flexibility, such that Islam can be accommodated to any time and place.[27] Moreover, he advocates the utilization of European experimental, social and natural sciences and, in particular, European legal methodologies (*manāhij al-fiqh*).[28] By adhering to the body of legal treatises (*mutūn*), commentary (*shurūḥ*) and super-commentary (i.e., marginal gloss) (*ḥawāshin*) of the schools of law, traditional *fiqh* detached itself from its origins and consequently failed to adapt itself to the goals (*maqāṣid*) of life.[29]

According to al-Turābī, historical *fiqh* has stagnated, resulting in the closing of the door of independent legal reasoning (*ijtihād*). It is commonly accepted that no one after the generation of the Forefathers (*al-salaf*) is authorized to propose an independent view, the assumption being that free exercise of the mind will generate errors and cause division among the people. At all events, the stagnation of legal methodology has caused serious damage to Islamic substantive law (*furūʿ*).[30] Hence, reopening the gate of *ijtihād* is essential for adapting traditional *sharīʿa* to changing conditions.

---

23 Al-Turābī, *Qaḍāyā al-tajdīd*, 195.

24 Ibid., 201; cf. idem, *Manhajiyyat al-fiqh*, 5.

25 The other cause was adherence to the Sufi orders; see al-Turābī, *Tajdīd al-fikr*, 98.

26 Al-Turābī, *Qaḍāyā al-tajdīd*, 191.

27 Cf. Muḥammad Shaḥrūr ("[the *sharīʿa* is] *ṣāliḥ li-kull makān wa-zamān*"); cited in Hallaq, *History*, 248.

28 Al-Turābī, *Ḥiwār*, 22; idem, *Qaḍāyā al-tajdīd*, 272. Cf. El-Affendi, *Turabi's Revolution*, 172–3; Abdelmoula, "Sudan: Islamic Fundamentalism," 43; Moussalli, "Hasan al-Turabi's Islamist Discourse," 53.

29 Al-Turābī, *al-Ḥaraka*, 210.

30 Ibid., 216; idem, *Qaḍāyā al-tajdīd*, 231ff., 242; idem, *Manhajiyyat al-fiqh*, 5. Cf. El-Affendi, *Turabi's Revolution*, 171.

> [Due to the West's impact on the Islamic world], broad cracks have developed in our life that make it incumbent on the contemporary jurists of Islam to undertake a new *ijtihād* with a view to devising new legal rules (*aḥkām*) or adjusting the ancient rules formulated by the jurists of past generations [to the contemporary generation]; the adjustment should be in conformity with place and time.[31]

In fact, al-Turābī maintains that Muslims were never inhibited about exercising a measure of *ijtihād*.[32] In his view, the new *ijtihād* will operate on same level as legal methodology (*uṣūl al-fiqh*) and substantive law (*furūʿ al-aḥkām*),[33] and it will serve as a means for bringing about a renewal that will constitute a genuine legal revolution (*thawra fiqhiyya*).[34]

The concern that personal *ijtihād* will result in legal innovations that have no basis in earlier doctrine[35] points to the need for striking a balance between *taqlīd* and *ijtihād*.[36] Al-Turābī makes a clear distinction between legal rulings that are the product of human (*basharī*) *ijtihād*, and basic principles (*uṣūl*) that constitute the "mothers" of the definite, enduring meanings of religion" (*ummuhāt maʿānī al-dīn qaṭʿiyyāt muḥkamāt*). The former can be accommodated to the requirements of the present, whereas the latter are eternal and immutable.[37] In the domain of religious practices and personal status, the extant legal rules leave sufficient scope for adaptation to modern times without resorting to *ijtihād*. By contrast, a comprehensive *ijtihād* is mandatory in the domain of public law.

> An extremely wide-ranging *ijtihād* is essential today. […] Broadly speaking, this *ijtihād* should address the domain of public life [i.e., public law], which has previously been neglected. In the domain of religious rites (*ʿibādāt→shaʿāʾiriyya*), for instance, the extant legal material (*al-mādda al-fiqhiyya*) [that is, substantive law] allows us sufficient scope [for

31 Al-Turābī, *Naẓarāt*, 156. Cf. Peters, "*Idjtihād* and *Taqlīd*," 139f.

32 Al-Turābī, *Ḥiwār*, 6; Lowrie, *Islam, Democracy, the State and the West*, 85; al-Ghannūshī and al-Turābī, *al-Ḥaraka al-islāmīya wa'l-taḥdīth*, 56; cf. Hallaq, *History*, 230; Abdelmoula, "Sudan: Islamic Fundamentalism," 43; Sidahmed, *Politics and Islam in Contemporary Sudan*, 128–9.

33 Al-Turābī, *al-Ḥaraka*, 216.

34 Al-Turābī, *Qaḍāyā al-tajdīd*, 218; idem, *Manhajiyyat al-fiqh*, 5 (*thawrat al-ijtihād*). Cf. El-Affendi, *Turabi's Revolution*, 170–2.

35 Al-Turābī, *Qaḍāyā al-tajdīd*, 217; idem, *Tajdīd al-fikr*, 93.

36 Al-Turābī, *Qaḍāyā al-tajdīd*, 269–71.

37 Al-Turābī, *Manhajiyyat al-fiqh*, 7. This distinction was made previously by Muḥammad Rashīd Riḍā; see Hallaq, *History*, 216.

> maneuvering without resorting to *ijtihād*] [...] Our main efforts should be addressed to the domain of public life [i.e., public law] and to the development of basic legal principles (*uṣūl fiqhiyya*) that will be in harmony [with the modern requirements of public law], starting with principles of interpretation (*uṣūl tafsīriyya*) [that do not change substantive law and continuing] down to the broad principles of *ijtihād*.[38] [...] Domains pertaining, e.g., to the political system (*ḥukm*), the economy and foreign relations, have been neglected by them [i.e., the Muslims of past centuries]. Our main concern should be to address these issues, with a view to formulating legal rules and deriving (*istinbāṭ*) substantive rules (*aḥkām farʿiyya*).[39]

The qualifications for exercising *ijtihād* include, in addition to a good knowledge of the *sharīʿa*, a command of the Arabic language, acquaintance with the Muslim legacy and familiarity with the natural and social sciences. For this purpose al-Turābī recommends the founding of a research institute for *ʿulamāʾ*. The qualifications required of the modern *mujtahid* differ from those required of the conventional *ʿālim*; what is needed at present is a kind of Western-inspired intellectual engaged in deriving law from the sources by using modern methods of research.[40]

Al-Turābī's legal methodology (*manhaj al-aḥkām* or *uṣūl al-fiqh*) is based on the following sources, in this order:[41]

*Qurʾān and sunna*

The heritage of legal methodology (*al-turāth al-uṣūlī*) consists first and foremost of the basic legal sources of substantive law (*aṣl al-uṣūl liʾl-aḥkām*): the *sharīʿa*, as embodied in Qurʾān and *sunna*, the "mother" of all legal sources, designated as *uṣūl waḍʿiyya*, the legal sources of *sharʿī* positive law[42] that are shared by the entire community. Al-Turābī maintains that social conditions in Sudan call for a radical change in worldview that will bring about a comprehensive "cultural revolution," yet without infringing on the legal sources and

38 Al-Turābī, *Tajdīd al-fikr*, 97; cf. ibid., 75–6.

39 Al-Turābī, *Qaḍāyā al-tajdīd*, 202. Cf. Hallaq, *History*, 227.

40 Al-Turābī, *Qaḍāyā al-tajdīd*, 212, 214, 216, 222; idem, *Tajdīd al-fikr*, 93. Cf. Hallaq, *History*, 230.

41 Al-Turābī, *Qaḍāyā al-tajdīd*, 272–4. Cf. Moussalli, "Hasan al-Turabi's Islamist Discourse," 54–5; Abū Jābir, *Ḥasan al-Turābī*, 66ff.; Sidahmed, *Politics and Islam in Contemporary Sudan*, 128.

42 Not to be confused with the technical term *waḍʿiyya*, which signifies statutory law (*waḍʿ al-bashar*); see al-Turābī, *Qaḍāyā al-tajdīd*, 249–50; see below.

positive law derived from them.[43] The *mujtahid*, in seeking a solution to any given problem, should start with the textual sources and proceed with the rules of interpretation. His goal should be to expand the scope of the options available to him in the process of deriving law. Statutory laws (*qawānīn waḍʿiyya*) adopt the literal (*ẓāhir*) interpretation of the text while ignoring the intentions (*niyyāt*), incentives (*dawāfi*) and goals (*maqāṣid*) that underlie those laws. Sufism (*taṣawwuf*), by contrast, adopts the inner (*bāṭin*) meaning of the text. These two approaches, al-Turābī suggests, must be brought into balance with one another:

> The sound methodology (*manhaj*) is the doctrine of unity (*tawḥīd*) and a balance between the exoteric (*ẓāhir*) and the esoteric (*bāṭin*), between the letter of the legal text (*ḥarf al-naṣṣ al-ḥukmī*) and its spirit [inner essence] (*rūḥ*).[44]

The balance envisioned here is in fact one of the manifestations of al-Turābī's doctrine of *tawḥīd*;[45] his reference to the Sufi doctrine in a legal context suggests that Sufism has been a source of inspiration for his legal thinking.[46] Al-Turābī maintains, however, that the positive law embedded in the textual sources (*nuṣūṣ*) dealing with daily life is limited in scope, and the principles of exegesis (*qawāʿid tafsīr*) are inadequate for providing solutions for all eventualities.[47]

*Consensus*

Al-Turābī maintains that since Qurʾānic verses of a legal nature are "quite rare," the substantive law should be formulated by means of consensus (*ijmāʿ*). In historical perspective, *taqlīd* and *jumūd* (stagnation) lie at the basis of zealous adherence to the law schools, and this in turn has hampered the individual's freedom and blocked his creative *élan* for the development of law.[48] The doctrine of *ijmāʿ* embodies the notion of sovereignty (*sulṭān*) of the Muslim community (*jamāʿa*) by means of its representatives, the *ʿulamāʾ*. *Ijmāʿ* is the

---

43 Al-Ghannūshī and al-Turābī, *al-Ḥaraka al-islāmīya wa'l-taḥdīth*, 74.

44 Al-Turābī, *Qaḍāyā al-tajdīd*, 201, 258–9; see also ibid., 272–4; idem, *al-Ḥaraka*, 22; Abdelmoula, "Sudan: Islamic Fundamentalism," 39. Cf. Schacht, *Introduction*, Glossary.

45 For other manifestations of this doctrine within a legal context, see al-Turābī, *Manhajiyyat al-fiqh*, 10–22.

46 Elsewhere al-Turābī notes that *sharʿī* legal methodology severed its connection with Sufi doctrine as well as with *kalām*or scholastic theology; al-Turābī, *Qaḍāyā al-tajdīd*, 274.

47 Al-Turābī, *Qaḍāyā al-tajdīd*, 203–4.

48 Ibid., 272; idem, *Ḥiwārāt fī 'l-islām*, 45–6; idem, *Ḥiwār*, 5; cf. al-Ghannūshī and al-Turābī, *al-Ḥaraka al-islāmīya wa'l-taḥdīth*, 61, 72; Abdelmoula, "Sudan: Islamic Fundamentalism," 43.

culmination of a process of consultation (*shūrā*). In fact, al-Turābī regards *shūrā*, consultative assembly, as a mechanism for reconciling differences of opinion (*yajmaʿ aṭrāf al-khilāf*), resembling the function of *ijmāʿ*. Once agreement has been reached on a certain point, this becomes a binding (*lāzim*) legal rule. In actuality, *ijmāʿ* has become a synonym for *shūrā*. According to al-Turābī, *ijmāʿ* is essentially a form of democracy. Indeed, he treats *"shūrā"* and "democracy" as synonyms, although he admits that there are essential differences between the two, the most important being that in Islam democracy cannot be separated from religion.[49]

Al-Turābī's understanding of consultation as a democratic process and of consensus as an instrument for expressing the will of the people may have been inspired by Riḍā.[50] In any case, his definition of democracy is not compatible with liberal democracy, since it lacks such vital elements as freedom of religion (as in the case of apostasy). At best, we are dealing here with "illiberal democracy." In al-Turābī's own words: "I do not refer to Western democracy, but rather to democracy in the literal sense, namely the rule of the people."[51] The traditional mechanism of *ijmāʿ* rests on the consensus of the jurists within each of the Sunnī schools rather than on that of ordinary people.[52]

*Analogical Reasoning*

Because the scope of positive law in Qurʾān and *sunna* is limited, al-Turābī maintains, traditional analogy (*qiyās*), that is, the derivation of new rules from textual sources, cannot meet the requirements of a modern society that has been exposed to the "cultural assault" of the West. In classical doctrine, *qiyās* is based on the effective cause (*ʿilla*) or *ratio legis* that lies behind the original ruling in the textual sources.[53] Although this procedure may be appropriate for updating marriage law, morals and religious rites, for the broad domains of religion – apparently referring to public law – a more expansive type of *qiyās*, one that takes the general public interest into consideration without being restricted by or bound to Qurʾān and *sunna*, is required:

---

49 Al-Turābī, *Qaḍāyā al-tajdīd*, 193; idem, *al-Shūrā*, 11–15; idem, *Tajdīd al-fikr*, 71; idem, *Islamic State*, 243–4; Hallaq, *History*, 229–30; Weissbrod, *Turabi*, 34–6; Abū Jābir, *Ḥasanal-Turābī, Riḍā, al-Khilāfa*, 53.

50 See Riḍā, *al-Khilāfa*, 57–61 (*ahl al-ḥall wa'l-ʿaqd*), 80 (*majlis al-shūrā al-ʿāmma*); cf. Hourani, *Arabic Thought in the Liberal Age*, 6, 144 (Muḥammad ʿAbduh), 234 (Rashīd Riḍā), 300; Hallaq, *History*, 216 (Riḍā), 223 (Khallāf), 261; Layish, "The Contribution of the Modernists," 226.

51 Al-Turābī, *Ḥiwārāt fī 'l-islām*, 45.

52 Cf. Zakaria, "The Rise of Illiberal Democracy," 22ff.; Weissbrod, *Turabi*, 23ff.; *EI*², s.v. "Idjmāʿ" (M. Bernard); Schacht, *Introduction*, 60ff.; Coulson, *A History of Islamic Law*, 76–7.

53 See Hallaq, *Sharīʿa*, 504, 506–7.

> Broadly speaking, traditional analogy does not meet our requirements since it operates under the oppressive impact of deceptive logical norms imposed on Muslims during the first cultural assault (*al-ghazwal-thaqāfī al-awwal*);[54] it left a profound impression on Muslims that can only be compared to contemporary modes of modern [Western] thinking. [...] The restricted [classical] analogy [by the textual sources] may be appropriate, in terms of perfection, to the basic principles of interpretation (*uṣūl tafsīriyya*) for elucidating [i.e., updating] marriage law, morals (*ādāb*) and religious rites (*shaʿāʾir*). However, for the broad domain of religion [that is, the domain of public law, classical analogy] is hardly useful; a natural (*fiṭrī*) *qiyās* independent of the stipulations [set by traditional *qiyās*, i.e., dependence on the textual sources] is required.[55]

*Secondary Mechanisms*

Al-Turābī maintains that once the textual sources and the rules of interpretation have been exhausted, the *mujtahid* should use (1) *maṣlaha*, public interest, and (2) *istiṣḥāb*, a secondary principle of legal evidence recognized by the Shāfiʿī school according to which the validity of a legal norm stands so long as there is a presumption of continuity of the state of affairs that gave rise to its underlying rationale.[56] Regarding the former, al-Turābī refers to the *al-maṣāliḥ al-mursala* within the context of expansive *qiyās:*

> As to [the method of] expansive (*ijmālī*) analogy [...] or analogy based on public interest (*qiyās al-maṣāliḥ al-mursala*),[57] it ranks higher [than traditional *qiyās*] in terms of research into the object [i.e., the essence] of the law (*manāṭāt al-aḥkām*). Thus if the totality of religious law is related (*mansūba*) to [i.e., confronted with] the totality of reality (*al-wāqiʿ*), then the [former has to] give way to the [latter, which leads one] to conclude that [the renunciation took place due] to general public interest (*maṣāliḥ ʿāmma*).[58]

---

54 The reference seems to be to Greek philosophy, especially logic, during the formativeperiod of Islamic law; cf. Layish and Warburg, *Reinstatement*, 85.

55 Al-Turābī, *Qaḍāyā al-tajdīd*, 204, 205, respectively.

56 Ibid., 208–9, 262–3; on *istiṣḥāb*, see further Hallaq, *History*, 113–15; idem, *Sharīʿa*, 120–1; Coulson, *A History of Islamic Law*, 92–3.

57 Al-Turābī, *Tajdīd al-fikr*, 83–4; cf. Hallaq, *History*, 228–9. On *maṣāliḥ mursala*, see Kerr, *Islamic Reform*, 70.

58 Al-Turābī, *Qaḍāyā al-tajdīd*, 207.

In his view, the combination of *istiṣḥāb* and *maṣāliḥ mursala* provides a comprehensive legal methodology for introducing reforms, presumably through statutory legislation, in the domain of public law.

Of course, the equation between *qiyās* and *al-maṣlaḥa al-mursala* effectively diminishes the importance of traditional analogical reasoning as a legal source for deriving law by way of *ijtihād*, on the one hand, and provides the *mujtahid* with a vital instrument to introduce reforms without being bound to Qurʾān and *sunna*, on the other.

Al-Turābī attempts to transform *istiṣḥāb* into an instrument for adapting the *sharīʿa*, especially in the domains of family law and religious practices, to the requirements of modern society. In traditional law the principle is applicable to specific cases. Al-Turābī broadens its scope – *istiṣḥāb wāsiʿ* – in an effort to transform it into a general principle.

> According to the doctrine of *istiṣḥāb*, the guiding principle is that all things and acts are [presumed to be] permitted, that legal obligation is not mandatory (*barāʾa min al-taklīf*), that everything a Muslim is capable of doing is [presumed to be guided by his] intention to act for the sake of God by way of acceptable worship (*ʿibāda*), that whatever one derives from the pleasures of this worldly life is [presumed] to be forgiven (*ʿafw*), left behind as a heritage (*matrūk*) [i.e., counted] in his favor or against him. [All these presumptions are valid] unless they contradict a textual source (*naṣṣ*), in which case the forgiveness or allowance with respect to any specific act is rejected [i.e., is deemed null and void].[59]

Other mechanisms mentioned by al-Turābī in this context are a decree by the ruler (*amr al-sulṭān*), probably referring to the doctrine of *siyāsa sharʿiyya*; a discretionary opinion inconsistent with strict analogy (*istiḥsān*); and necessity (*ḍarūra*), which he deems indispensable as a "social instrument" – in the event of difference of opinion – for the adjustment of legal norms to changing circumstances.[60] The reference to the ruler's decree points to al-Turābī's intention to introduce reforms by means of statutory legislation. *Siyāsa sharʿiyya* is needed to legitimize this course of action in *sharʿī* terms. The doctrine of *ḍarūra* is virtually synonymous with *maṣlaḥa*.[61] Al-Turābī also invokes the

---

59 Al-Turābī, *Tajdīd al-fikr*, 84–6. The citation is from p. 85; cf. Hallaq, *History*, 228–9.

60 Al-Turābī, *Qaḍāyā al-tajdīd*, 262–3; idem, *Naẓarāt*, 152. Cf. Hallaq, *History*, 230–1; Schacht, *Introduction*, Glossary, s.v. *siyāsa sharʿiyya*; *EI*², s.v. "Siyāsa, pt. 3" (Vogel).

61 Cf. Hallaq, *History*, 218. On *maṣlaḥa* and *istiṣlāḥ* in modernist theories, see Hallaq, *History*, 214–17 (Riḍā), 221 (Khallāf), 225 (al-Fāsī), 233 (ʿAshmāwī), 261.

doctrine of intention (*niyya*) as an instrument for interpreting Qurʾān and *sunna*, thus stressing his preference for "the spirit of religion" over the literal meaning of the text.[62]

*The Humanities and the Experimental Social and Natural Sciences*

Al-Turābī lays special emphasis on the adoption of Western legal methodologies. To this end he advocates initiating a comparative analysis of legal methodologies that will take into consideration Islamic values (*qiyam*) and norms (*sunan*).[63] In his view, such a synthesis has a precedent in Islamic history. Thus he maintains that traditional *qiyās* was strongly inspired by the "first cultural assault," i.e., Greek philosophy.[64]

According to al-Turābī, Sudan can benefit greatly from the legal experience of the West in dispensing justice. He regards international law as an essential part of the *sharīʿa*, and he strongly recommends the integration of Western social and comparative legal methods into the new Islamic legal methodology. Statutory legislation (*tashrīʿ*) requires, in his view, a thorough knowledge of the social and natural sciences.[65]

> It is possible to benefit from the human experience (*tajārib bashariyya*) [of the West] and its [legal] practices (*aʿrāf*) in dispensing justice.[66] [...] I strongly believe that to some extent Muslims already followed that course in the past even though we do not share [the views] expressed by Orientalists. [...] Whatever the case may be, the world today is interlocked (*mawṣūl*); societal patterns (*anmāṭ*) will converge before long, and [Western] comparative law inevitably will become integrated within our legal methodology; we shall firmly establish its [i.e., Western comparative law's] adoption [...]. The pursuit of *sharʿī* law (*fiqh al-aḥkām*) and statutory legislation (*tashrīʿ*) requires also an acquaintance with the modern world [...]; hence it is required that a [Muslim] jurist (*faqīh*) obtain

62 Al-Turābī, *Manhajiyyat al-fiqh*, 6.

63 Al-Turābī, *Qaḍāyā al-tajdīd*, 273. Cf. El-Affendi, *Turabi's Revolution*, 173.

64 Al-Turābī, *Qaḍāyā al-tajdīd*, 202–4. Cf. Weissbrod, *Turabi*, 36; Schacht, *Introduction*, 19–22; Coulson, *A History of Islamic Law*, 27ff.

65 Al-Turābī, *Qaḍāyā al-tajdīd* 253, 255, 257; idem, *Ḥiwārāt fī ʾl-islām*, 53. Cf. Viorst, "Sudan's Islamic Experiment," 53.

66 It is interesting to note that al-Turābī uses legal terms pertaining to justice that have different connotations in a Western and an Islamic milieu. While discussing *istiṣḥāb*, he refers to *ʿadl, qisṭ* and *wijdān mukhliṣ* in a Qurʾānic context (see al-Turābī, *Tajdīd al-fikr*, 85). The Sudanese Judgments (Basic Rules) Act, 1983, absorbs the English-inspired terms "justice" (*ʿadl*), "equity" (*qisṭ*) and "good conscience" (*wijdān salīm*); see Layish and Warburg, *Reinstatement*, 133–7.

> education in psychology and the social and natural sciences to an extent that will enable him to derive divine law (*tanzīl al-aḥkām*) [from Qurʾān and *sunna*] while being fully attentive [to the Western sciences].[67]

Al-Turābī does not, however, provide concrete suggestions as to how the social and natural sciences can shape the legal norms.[68]

Reforms based on the new legal methodology, al-Turābī maintains, should be carried out by means of statutory legislation with the cooperation of qualified *ʿulamāʾ*:

> [Changing circumstances] require [the exercise of] revolutionary *ijtihād* by means of jurists (*ijtihād fiqhī*). This task, however, is not incumbent on Muslim jurists alone; it should be entrusted simultaneously to the state; in order to obtain extensive *ijtihād* the state must be involved. To this end the state should make available a sizeable number of *mujtahids* and *ʿulamāʾ* capable of teaching and inculcating the methods (*mawāzīn*) of the *sharīʿa*.[69]

*The Sharīʿa State*

According to al-Turābī, a "*Sharīʿa* state" is one in which the *Sharīʿa* is applicable. In such a state, the legislature has no absolute authority with respect to formulating the state's laws, since the source of legal authority is vested exclusively in the *Sharīʿa* which, in turn, represents the sovereignty of God and hence constitutes of the state's basic norm. This implies that the legislator is subject to the normative control of the *sharīʿa*, in the sense that to be valid, a legislative act must be compatible with the *sharīʿa*. For this reason the *ʿulamāʾ* should be called in as advisers in the process of legislation. The *ʿulamāʾ*, however, should be familiar not only with the *sharīʿa* but also with the social and natural sciences and philosophy.

> A legal norm (*ḥukm*) [in the state] is absolutely bound by the *sharīʿa*, as is manifest in the constitution.[70] There is, however, a difference [between the *sharīʿa* and the constitution], in that the former is a kind of detailed and elaborated constitution (*dustūr mufaṣṣal*). Since *shūrū* is one of the

---

67 Al-Turābī, *Qaḍāyā al-tajdīd*, 253 and 257, respectively.

68 On the reinterpretation of Qurʾān and *ḥadīth* in light of the natural sciences in Muḥammad Shaḥrūr's legal methodology, see Hallaq, *History*, 245–6.

69 Al-Turābī, *Naẓarāt*, 157; cf. Hallaq, *History*, 230, 253 (Shaḥrūr).

70 The reference is to the *sharīʿa* as a source of law in the constitution.

> basic foundations (*arkān*) of the *sharīʿa*, anyone desiring to attain a key position [in the country] cannot do it otherwise than through the channel of the *sharīʿa*. The basic difference between *shūrū* and democracy [...] is that the *sharīʿa*'s comprehensiveness and completeness does not leave the legislator much scope to complement [the *sharīʿa* by means of statutory legislation]. Since this is the case, the power of the legislative authority in the *sharīʿa* state – be it an assembly (*majlis*), a parliament or the like – is not absolute in its legislative function because the decisive influence with respect to formulating a legal norm rests with the *sharīʿa*, not with human beings. Nevertheless, besides clear, unambiguous (*ṣarāḥa*) legal rules that permit of no interpretation, there are other [ambiguous] rules that [may be developed] by means of *ijtihād*.[71]

Al-Turābī identifies *ahlal-ḥaqq* [*al-ḥall*] *wa'l-ʿaqd*, jurists authorized to issue religio-legal permissions and prohibitions,[72] with *ahlal-shūrā*, representatives of the *umma*. In his view, the latter's functions should be fulfilled at the present time by a parliament or consultative council. However, a distinction should be made between the powers of consultative bodies and those that have been delegated to rulers by virtue of their constitutional and administrative rank.[73] He seems here to be referring to *siyāsa sharʿiyya*, the ruler's power to resort to administrative measures within the boundaries of the *sharīʿa*. He does not rule out the possibility that legal issues decided by a consensus of Muslims will be submitted for endorsement by "legislative consensus" (*ijmāʿ tashrīʿī*). In other words, this amounts to an attempt to integrate *ijmāʿ* into statutory legislation.[74] Such an institutionalized *ijmāʿ* obviously would not be the same as the classical *ijmāʿ* of independent jurists. Al-Turābī argues that it was the absence of a governmental agency charged with unifying the legal system that caused the closing of the door of *ijtihād*.[75] He adds that statutory legislation based on sound legal opinions and sanctioned by the ruler, which implies statutory *ijtihād* to the exclusion of individual *ijtihād*, is an appropriate solution for those who fear – referring here to orthodox *ʿulamā'* – that uncontrolled *ijtihād* will bring about methodological chaos and severe differences of opinion within the schools, as well as innovations incompatible with the doctrine of the Forefathers (*al-salaf*):

---

71 Al-Turābī, *Ḥiwārāt fī 'l-islām*, 45; cf. idem, *Islamic State*, 242, 245.

72 Cf. Riḍā, *al-Khilāfa*, 70, 79; Layish, "The Contribution of the Modernists," 265ff.

73 Al-Turābī, *Qaḍāyā al-tajdīd*, 225; Turabi, *Islamic State*, 243, 248.

74 Al-Turābī, *Tajdīd al-fikr*, 87.

75 Turābī, *Islamic State*, 246.

> One might claim that this state of affairs [...] is a source of severe danger. If we promote freedom of *ijtihād* within the relatively broad scope of those who are qualified and if we [moreover] add to the established principles of interpretation (*uṣūl tafsīriyya*) broad principles relating to *ijtihād* such as *maṣāliḥ* and *istiṣḥāb*, this will cause further differences of opinion among the schools. For this reason, we have already provided an unequivocal answer to this issue by clarifying that the role of the leader of the community (*sulṭān al-mujtamaʿ*) is to rely on sound personal opinions and to sanction them as statutorily binding (*qānūn mulzim*) to the exclusion of the rest of individual *ijtihād*. True, alertness with respect to the consequences of [unrestrained] freedom of *ijtihād* has been fairly well established among us. This is evident from the fact that even in circles favorable to opening the door of *ijtihād*, one can find people whose anxiety is extreme when they come across a new personal opinion not traceable to one of the Forefathers.[76]

Al-Turābī opposes the idea of establishing an institutionalized council for issuing *fatwās* (*majlis iftāʾ*) and prefers to see the *ʿulamāʾ* integrated into a parliament and participating in the process of legislation.[77] He notes that, in any case, *qāḍī*s and jurists prefer to apply statutory provisions rather than resort to personal opinion.[78]

The main function of *shūrā*, according to al-Turābī, is to incorporate – through the work of jurists – legal doctrines culled from various schools and jurists into statutory codification (*taqnīn*). In other words, the *ʿulamāʾ* should participate in the process of state codification and legislation.[79]

> Never mind the abundance of sources of law (*uṣūl fiqhiyya*) applied [in legislation], or that the legal opinions pertaining to substantive law (*fatāwin farʿiyya*) deriving [from these sources] are profoundly different from one another; the abundance of options available to the *shūrā* of the Muslims and the mass of the [legal] material at their [i.e., the *ʿulamāʾ*'s] disposal in the process of preparing their legal rulings [i.e., statutory provisions] indicate that a clear public interest (*maṣlaḥa*) is involved.[80]

---

76 Al-Turābī, *Qaḍāyā al-tajdīd*, 216–17; cf. idem, *Manhajiyyat al-fiqh*, 6.

77 Lowrie, *Islam, Democracy, the State and the West*, 39.

78 Al-Turābī, *Qaḍāyā al-tajdīd*, 267.

79 Ibid., 193, 211, 215; idem, *Tajdīd al-fikr*, 90; idem, *Islamic State*, 246; Weissbrod, *Turabi*, 47; cf. Hallaq, *History*, 222 (Khallāf), 253 (Shaḥrūr).

80 Al-Turābī, *Qaḍāyā al-tajdīd*, 211. This statement suggests that the variety of legal views is a blessing; see below.

Al-Turābī maintains that literary texts (*muṣannafāt*), such as private compilations of legal rules for practical purposes, *fatwās* and exegetical treatises, articulated in clear language, are equivalent to a modern corpus of statutes (*mudawwanāt qānūniyya*) [sic!]. His recommendation that the ruler of the country should monitor the *sharʿī* system[81] seems to imply imposing a codified *sharīʿa* on the state and society by virtue of the doctrine of *siyāsa sharʿiyya*. Al-Turābī further recommends the eclectic expedient (*takhayyur*), widely practiced in modern reformist legislation, as the main method for codifying the *sharīʿa* by means of statutory legislation. He argues that although the Mālikī school is dominant among the *ʿulamāʾ*, the tolerance of the Sudanese people and their open-mindedness toward other schools makes them ready to treat them equally and without zealous adherence to a particular law school:

> The people of Sudan, due to their school tolerance (*tasāmuḥ madhhabī*), accept Shāfiʿī and Ḥanafī legal authorities [in matters pertaining] to *jihād*, Sufi orders and the appointment of *qāḍīs* and *muftīs*; they have at the present time abandoned zealous adherence to a law school (*ʿaṣabiyya madhhabiyya*); Sunnī *fiqh* has spread among them all [without distinction between the schools].[82]

Differences of opinion between the schools should be regarded as a blessing, since the variety of legal options and the abundance of legal material available to the *shūrā* and the jurists can be used for the public benefit.[83] Al-Turābī advocates launching a comparative study of all schools with a view to reaching an authentic perspective on the legal methodology of the *sharīʿa*.[84]

## 3 Conclusion

In order to bring about an Islamic renaissance, al-Turābī proposes a new legal methodology that combines classical Islamic legal theory and Western legal principles. This methodology should be applied by means of legislative *ijtihād* (*tashrīʿ ijtihādī*), in which the doctrine of public interest, unaddressed in the textual sources of Qurʾān and *sunna* (*maṣlaḥa murṣala*), has been elevated

81 Al-Turābī, *Qaḍāyā al-tajdīd*, 215–16. Cf. Fadel, "The Social Logic of *Taqlīd* and the Rise of the *Mukhtaṣar*."

82 Al-Turābī, *al-Ḥaraka*, 152. Cf. Peters, "*Idjtihād* and *Taqlīd*," 141, 143.

83 Al-Turābī, *Qaḍāyā al-tajdīd*, 211.

84 Al-Turābī, *al-Ḥaraka*, 215; Lowrie, *Islam, Democracy, the State and the West*, 83.

in practice, though not formally, to an independent source of law. Specific domains of the *sharīʿa*, especially public law, are to be accommodated to changing conditions by means of statutory codification, the main instrument being the eclectic expedient (*takhayyur*), and imposed on society by means of *siyāsa sharʿiyya*. In order to legitimize this reform al-Turābī expects the *ʿulamāʾ* to serve as advisers in the process of *ijtihād* and even to join the parliament and form a kind of statutory consensus (*ijmāʿ*), which implies that they may veto any legislative initiative on the grounds of incompatibility with the *sharīʿa*.

Al-Turābī's legal methodology is not a crystallized and comprehensive theory of law; it is articulated in vague terms, leaving much room for speculation; no references to the textual sources of Qurʾān and *sunna*, or to classical and contemporary modernist legal literature are provided to support his thesis or to identify his sources of inspiration.[85]

Broadly speaking, al-Turābī has succeeded in putting his legal methodology into practice. The reinstatement of Islamic law in Sudan under Numayrī is based on al-Turābī's legal methodology. Various domains of the *sharīʿa* have undergone statutory codification, and the Judgments (Basic Rules) Act, 1983, probably drafted by al-Turābī, guides the courts, in the event of a lacuna in the Islamist statutes, on how to exercise *ijtihād* on the basis of Islamic and Western sources and legal principles, in a specified order.[86]

Hallaq distinguishes between two basic types of legal methodology: religious utilitarianism and religious liberalism. Methodologies of the first type use the doctrine of *maṣlaḥa*, public interest, as the main instrument for reform, while those of the second adopt a rational approach that takes into account changing circumstances in time and place.[87] According to Hallaq, al-Turābī's legal methodology belongs to the first type, due to his theological debt to ʿAbduh's doctrine and to his legal theory, which combines basic Islamic values with a modern version of substantive law couched in terms of public interest.[88]

---

85 Cf. Hallaq, *History*, 229, 231; an-Naʿim, *Toward an Islamic Reformation*, 39–40.

86 Thus Section 3(b)(vi) of the Judgments (Basic Rules) Act, 1983 provides that in the event of a lacuna in the law the judge shall take custom into account in transactions in a manner not contravening *sharʿī* rules or the principles of natural justice (*ʿadāla fiṭriyya*). Subsection (vii) provides that the judge shall consider the notion of justice as prescribed by human laws and the rules of equity (*qisṭ*) enshrined in good conscience (*wijdān salīm*). Subsection (v) provides that the judge, in the absence of a provision in Qurʾān and *sunna* and after having exhausted *ijtihād*, may resort to judicial precedents (*sawābiq al-ʿamal al-qaḍāʾī*) in Sudan, as long as they are not in contradiction of the *sharīʿa* or *sharʿī* legal opinions and principles. For further details, see Layish and Warburg, *Reinstatement*, 136, 138.

87 For further details, see Hallaq, *History*, ch. 6.

88 Ibid., 214, 228.

One wonders, however, whether al-Turābī's legal methodology merits evaluation within a *sharʿī* context. First, al-Turābī is not an *ʿālim,* and he holds that anyone with an academic degree in the natural or social sciences who possesses an adequate knowledge of the Islamic heritage and the *sharīʿa,* and has a good command of the Arabic language, is qualified for *ijtihād.* In fact, al-Turābī presents a liberal interpretation of Islam[89] from the viewpoint of a Western-oriented legal expert and social scientist capable of reflecting on Islam simultaneously from within and from outside. The inclusion of Western sources of law, such as natural justice (to be distinguished from God's justice) and legal precedent (in the state judiciary), in al-Turābī's legal methodology, as embodied in the aforementioned 1983 Act, is incompatible with orthodox *sharīʿa.* Al-Turābī mobilizes traditional Islamic mechanisms in an effort to obtain *sharʿī* legitimacy for his reformist legal theory. Considering his legal education, there can be no doubt that al-Turābī is fully aware that statutory codification of the *sharīʿa* entails its transformation from a jurists' law into statutory law, with all the consequences that follow.[90] However, he does not make this distinction between *sharīʿa* and statutory law, probably for tactical reasons. He strongly believes that codified *sharīʿa,* based on a synthesis of Islamic and Western principles of law and sanctioned by newly recruited *ʿulamāʾ,* is the only remaining option for triggering a renaissance in Muslim society.

In some respects al-Turābī's legal methodology resembles the legal theory of Zia Gökalp (d. 1924), an outstanding Turkish thinker in modern times. Gökalp regards Islam as a historical phenomenon subject to changing social circumstances. He uses rational and sociological tools for the purpose of introducing reforms in Islam by means of secular legislation.[91] In his theory of the *şeriat,* Gökalp distinguishes between two sources of law: (a) *nas* (*naṣṣ*) – the divine revelation in the Qurʾān – and *sunna,* neither of which is subject to change under any circumstances; and (b) *örf,* the custom of the Muslim community, which is subject to change. He advocates the promotion of a science of "the social roots of the theory of sources of law" (*içtimaî usul-ü fikih*) and the introduction of extensive reforms in family law.[92] Al-Turābī makes a similar distinction

89 Woodward, "Ḥasan al-Turābī," 241; cf. Weissbrod, *Turabi,* 129–30.

90 Cf. Layish, "The Transformation of the *Sharīʿa* from Jurists' Law to Statutory Law."

91 Heyd, *Foundations of Turkish Nationalism,* ix, 82–3; Berkes, *The Development of Secularism in Turkey,* 383.

92 Heyd, *Foundations of Turkish Nationalism,* 85–8, 94ff.; Berkes, *The Development of Secularism in Turkey,* 383. However, Gökalp went furthest by suggesting the separation of religion and state with a view to transforming Islam into a purely ethical religion; see Heyd, *Foundations of Turkish Nationalism,* 82, 85, 87, 101; Berkes, *The Development of Secularism in Turkey,* 383.

between religious practices (*ʿibādāt*) and personal status (probably because of their intensive treatment in the Qurʾān) on the one hand, and public law on the other. While the former can be accommodated to changing conditions only by means of interpretation, that is, without infringing on the substantive law, the latter is amenable to reform by means of "legislative *ijtihād*." Al-Turābī calls for the foundation of a research institute to train *ʿulamāʾ* to carry out reforms. Both al-Turābī and Gökalp have Islamic and Western backgrounds, and both were influenced by Sufism during their formative period. One can't help wondering whether the Sufi experience affected their legal methodologies by promoting a humanistic approach to law.[93]

It is doubtful that al-Turābī's legal methodology has had any impact on the theory of Islamic law, for the simple reason that he is acting outside the framework of the *sharīʿa*. On the other hand, there is no question that al-Turābī is the living spirit behind the legal experiment in Sudan under Numayrī which has had a major effect on the *status* of Islamic law in that country.[94]

The introduction of legal methodologies by figures other than qualified *ʿulamāʾ* indicates that the *ʿulamāʾ* have lost control of *sharʿī* discourse and that the issue of modernizing Islamic law and adapting it to changing circumstances has become the concern of various sectors of society. Because such a discourse lacks *sharʿī* legitimacy, it cannot be regarded as a development within Islamic law.

93 Cf. Heyd, *Foundations of Turkish Nationalism*, 23, 82.

94 For an assessment of the legal experiment, see Layish and Warburg, *Reinstatement*, ch. 5.

# PART 3

# *Modern Trends in Islamic Law*

CHAPTER 11

# The Transformation of the *Sharīʿa* from Jurists' Law to Statutory Law in the Contemporary Muslim World

*In memoriam* Hava Lazarus-Yafeh

## 1 Introduction*

In this short essay I want to present the thesis that the codification of the *sharīʿa* by Muslim legislatures, since the middle of the nineteenth century,

* The essay concentrates on the Middle East (including Egypt and the Sudan) and North Africa. I here attempt to draw an outline and some tentative conclusions with a view to promoting public discussion on what seems to be one of the most controversial issues among contemporary scholars. My approach to the subject matter is from the viewpoint of a socio-legal historian.

A first draft of this essay was presented at the Joseph Schacht Conference on Theory and Practice in Islamic Law, Leiden & Amsterdam, October 1994. A revised version of the essay was presented at the École des Hautes Études en Sciences Sociales in Paris on December 9, 1999. Baber Johansen kindly offered helpful comments on the text. I am most grateful to him and to La Maison des Sciences de l'Homme for the warm hospitality extended to me.

Wael B. Hallaq from McGill University, Gideon Libson and Ron Shaham, both from the Hebrew University, Nimrod Hurvitz from Ben Gurion University, Nathan J. Brown from the George Washington Universty also made valuable comments for which they deserve my profound gratitude. Thanks are also due to Stefan Reichmuth and the anonymous readers for their useful suggestions. It goes without saying that I alone bear the responsibility for the content of this essay.

I owe my colleague, the late Professor Hava Lazarus-Yafeh from the Hebrew University, much encouragement in embarking on this issue. She quite often expressed the idea that comparative research on Islamic law and Jewish law in modern times is extremely important. Hava's curiosity extended beyond the academic aspect. In both cases the question as to whether a theoretically immutable eternal law can adapt itself to changing conditions is of utmost practical importance. She strongly believed that contemporary exponents of Jewish law may greatly benefit from the experience gained by the codification of Islamic law since the mid-nineteenth century. This essay is dedicated to her memory.

[Originally published in *Die Welt des Islams*, 44/1 (2004), pp. 85–113.]

 | DOI:10.1163/9789004680920_013

brought about the transformation of the *sharīʿa* from "jurists' law," that is, a law created by independent legal experts, to "statutory law," in other words, a law promulgated by a national-territorial legislature. This transformation entails profound implications the most important of which is the deprivation of the *fuqahāʾ* of their "legislative" authority and its investment in secular legislature.

The *sharīʿa* is, broadly speaking, a product neither of legislative authority nor a case law; there is no binding precedent in the Western connotation of the term.[1] The *sharīʿa* is a jurists' law in the sense that it was created and developed by *fuqahāʾ* (jurists) and *muftīs* who in the formative period were not integrated as a professional class in the establishment.[2]

The characteristics of the *sharīʿa* are manifested in the textual sources, legal methodology, and the authority for sanctioning legal rules. The legal methodology (*uṣūl al-fiqh*) of the *sharīʿa* consists of four sources of law: the Qurʾān and the Prophetic *ḥadīth* or *sunna* (custom, normative way of life) that make up the material sources; the analogical deduction (*qiyās*) which is the method of deriving legal rulings from the above-mentioned sources; and the consensus (*ijmāʿ*) of the *fuqahāʾ* of each of the schools of law (*madhāhib*) which substantiates the new rulings.[3] This legal methodology did not leave the political ruler any leeway, except by means of administrative decrees (see below), to control the formulation of the legal norm in spite of all his efforts to the contrary.

It is interesting to note in this connection that Ibn al-Muqaffaʿ (d. 140/757), Secretary of State, suggested to the Caliph al-Manṣūr, while the *sharīʿa* was still in its formative period, that the latter enact, by an administrative decree, a comprehensive codification out of different doctrines of the main schools with a view to bringing about uniformity in the law, and have the codification imposed on the *sharīʿa* courts. This code was to be revised by successive caliphs.[4] Had the suggestion been adopted, the development of the *"sharīʿa"* could have taken a totally different course incompatible with jurists' law. The suggestion, however, did not materialize, and it seems that this course of events was not a coincidence. As Schacht rightly points out, "orthodox Islam

1 That is, the formation of positive law by means of cases handed down by the highest judicial court authorized to interpret statutes, regulations, and constitutional provisions. See Black, *Law Dictionary*, s.v. "Case Law."Cf. Johansen, *Truth and Validity of the Qāḍī's Judgment*.

2 For a detailed discussion of *fiqh* as a sacred law, see Johansen, *Contingency*, Introduction. On the role of *muftīs* in the development of Islamic law, see Hallaq, *Iftāʾ and Ijtihād*.

3 On the legal methodology, see Schacht, *Introduction*, 58ff.; Coulson, *History*, 55ff. For a detailed discussion of Islamic legal theory, see Zysow, *The Economy of Certainty;* Hallaq, *Legal Theories*.

4 Schacht, *Introduction*, 55–56; Coulson, *History*, 52. On Islamic historical precedents concerning codification of the *fiqh* by act of the ruler, see Vogel, *Saudi Arabia*, 313–336.

refused to be drawn into too close a connection with the state."[5] In other words, by then, the schools of law had already consolidated their autonomy and the *fuqahā'* had strengthened their status as the exclusive identifiers of the will of God on earth.[6]

The dominant view until recently was that the "door of *ijtihād*" had been closed early in the tenth century, and since then it has been impossible to derive new legal rules from the textual sources of the *sharīʿa* by means of the method described above. Notwithstanding the closure of the door of *ijtihād*,[7] the *sharīʿa* was developed and elaborated by independent *fuqahā'* and occasionally had significant original creative achievements within the framework of the *taqlīd*, the *fuqahā'*'s adherence to the consolidated orthodox schools of law.[8]

The *sharīʿa* is not a positive law, in the conventional sense, of a legislature. Rather, it is first and foremost a system of religious ethical commandments and precepts some of which were translated over the years into legal terms with specified sanctions (as in the case of usury).[9] In certain domains, such as criminal law entailing Qur'ānic punishments, damages entailing retaliation and blood money (homicide and bodily harm), land law and taxes, the *sharīʿa* was a fully applied system. The legal opinion (*fatwā*) of the noninstitutionalized *muftī* is not binding; its validity depends on his personal religious legal authority.[10]

The *sharīʿa* is a law of eternal divine revelation imposed on society and state from above. Yet, enough scope is left to human reason to identify God's will upon earth. The development of the *sharīʿa* is a rational process, and the abundance of qualified jurists to identify God's will was always regarded as a source of blessing. The maxim that disagreement in the community of Muslims (*ikhtilāf al-umma*) is a sign of divine indulgence, in the sense that diversity of doctrine brings about plurality of opinions, was enlisted to this end.[11] The

---

5 Schacht, *Introduction*, 56

6 Cf. Coulson, *History*, 52.

7 This is a controversial issue among contemporary scholars. No attempt will be made here to exhaust the issue. Suffice it to say that the debate has been focused so far on the level of legal methodology (*uṣūl al-fiqh*) rather than the body of law (*furūʿ*). See, e.g., Meron, *Legal Thought*; Hallaq, *Ijtihād Closed?*

8 See Schacht, *Introduction*, 71; Coulson, *History*, 81; Fadel, *Taqlīd and Mukhtaṣar*.

9 For a socio-anthropological approach to this issue, see, e.g., Dupret, *Legal Pluralism and Normative Plurality*.

10 See Masud, Messick, & Powers, *Islamic Legal Interpretation*.

11 Cf. Schacht, *Introduction*, 67; Coulson, *History*, 86; Hallaq, *Authority, Continuity and Change*, 57, 125, 158.

jurisconsult (*muftī*) and the author-jurist were the main agents for accommodating the *sharīʿa* to changing circumstances.[12]

In theory, legislative authority is alien to Islam. Nevertheless, temporal legislation by ʿAbbāsī caliphs and rulers based on the doctrine of *siyāsa sharʿiyya* (the ruler's prerogative to issue administrative orders provided they do not contradict the *sharīʿa*) was practiced to some extent in various domains of law, such as taxes, land and criminal law. This doctrine, however, was applied within the framework of a theocracy, the underlying concept of which was the sovereignty of the *sharīʿa* to the extent that everyone, including the ruler, was bound by it.[13] The Ottoman *qānūn* apparently intended to supplement the *sharīʿa*, actually amounted to superseding it especially with regard to discretionary punishments (*taʿzīr*). In many respects, the Ottoman *qānūn* may be regarded as secular legislation.[14]

In modern times far-reaching changes have been introduced, under the impact of the West, in the process of developing the legal norm: the adoption of the institution of legislative authority and the mechanism of codification (*taqnīn*). Parliaments were established that incorporated variants from the *sharīʿa* into statutory codes (hence *tashrīʿ*). The codes were imposed on society by means of state apparatus sanctions. Broadly speaking, the impetus for *tashrīʿ* was the desire to adapt the legal norm which until then was shaped by the *sharīʿa*, to changing social requirements and to bring about modernization under European influence.

The Young Ottomans, the first Islamic constitutional movement, introduced these innovations in the second half of the nineteenth century, and the trend with respect to codification, though not statutory codification, was followed in Egypt by the liberally-oriented modernist movement founded by Muḥammad ʿAbduh in the late nineteenth century. ʿAbduh advocated that the *ʿulamāʾ* (rather than the legislature) codify the *sharʿī* law pertaining to *muʿāmalāt*, transactions among human beings (with special reference to matters of personal status and *waqf*) with a view to imposing it on the *sharīʿa* courts by the state, by means of *siyāsa sharʿiyya*. Yet it was Western-trained jurists who took the leading role in advancing ideas such as statutory legislation, codification along European patterns, and modernization of the court system. As will be seen below, the *ʿulamāʾ*'s cooperation was required in order to provide the *sharʿī* juristic basis, and hence legitimacy, for *tashrīʿ*.[15]

---

12 Hallaq, *Authority, Continuity and Change*, chaps.5–6.Cf. Paret, *Innerislamischer Pluralismus*, 523.

13 Schacht, *Introduction*, 54; Coulson, *History*, 129; Vogel, *Siyāsa sharʿiyya.*

14 Schacht, *Introduction*, 90–91; İnalcik, *Ḳānūn*, 560–61.

15 Layish & Shaham, *Tashrīʿ*.

## 2 Codification of the *Sharīʿa*

Legal reform in the nineteenth-century Ottoman Empire started with adoption of European codes in specified domains in their entirety, but soon shifted to codification of various domains of the *sharīʿa*. The most important codification enacted in the nineteenth century was the Mejelle, the Ottoman civil code (1869–1876) which in respect of legal material was based exclusively on the Ḥanafī school, by means of the eclectic expedient (*takhayyur*), that is, adoption of legal doctrines of that school on the basis of their conformity to the requirements of the state and society. Towards the end of the nineteenth century, the Egyptian jurist Muḥammad Qadrī Pasha compiled three codes pertaining to obligations and contracts, personal status, and *waqf*. Similarly to the Mejelle, these too were based on the eclectic expedient exercised within the boundaries of the Ḥanafī school. In contrast to the Mejelle, however, they were not endorsed officially as state laws.[16]

Since the beginning of the twentieth century, codification has been extended to matters of personal status and succession (which are the core of the *sharīʿa*), and to *waqf* which, unlike civil, criminal, commercial and other domains of law, were never subject to Western-imported codes. Following the Ottoman Family Rights Law of 1917, most Middle Eastern and North African countries have promulgated reformist statutes in these domains. The impetus for the reforms was the desire to adapt *sharʿī* norm to the features of the nuclear family and to strengthen the position of women within the family.[17]

New civil codes were compiled in Egypt and other countries in which the dominance of the *sharīʿa* was more modest, with the exception of those codes that were inspired directly or indirectly by the Mejelle. The living spirit of this legislation was the Egyptian jurist ʿAbdal-Razzāq al-Sanhūrī.[18]

16 Coulson, *History*, 182–217.

17 Layish & Shaham, *Nikāḥ*; Layish, *Ṭalāḳ*; idem, *Mīrāth*; idem, *Wakf*; cf. Ebert, *Das Personalstatut arabischer Länder*.

18 He compiled the Egyptian civil code of 1948 which was based on the French-inspired Egyptian codes of 1875 and 1883, on national court decisions, and (to a less extent) on the *sharīʿa*. In the case of a lacuna, the court will decide the matter in accordance with (1) customary law, (2) adequate principles of the *sharīʿa*, and (3) the principles of equity. The Egyptian civil code was adopted with some variations by Syria (1949) and Libya (1954). Al-Sanhūrī was also the architect of the civil code of Iraq (1953), which is strongly inspired by the Mejelle, and that of Kuwait (1961). The Sudanese Transactions Act of 1984 is based mainly on the Jordanian Civil Code of 1976, which in turn is based on the Mejelle. The Iranian Civil Code of 1939 is a combination of *sharʿī* and French legal principles. The same is true of the Tunisian Code of Obligations and Contracts of 1906. See El-Sanhoury, *Le Code civil égyptien*; Anderson, *Law Reform*, 86–100; Bechor, *Contractual Justice in the*

The juristic basis for accommodating the *sharīʿa* via statutory legislation and codification was provided by a wide range of methods, some of which were proposed by the modernists, such as the eclectic device (*takhayyur* and *talfīq*), administrative orders provided they do not contradict the *sharīʿa* (*siyāsa sharʿiyya*), public interest (*maṣlaḥa*) and reinterpretation of the textual sources, the Qurʾān, and the *ḥadīth* (the so-called *neo-ijtihād*).[19]

No legislature in the strict sense of the term has so far been introduced in Saudi Arabia. The King's power to issue administrative orders (*marsūm* rather than *qānūn*) is in the best tradition of *siyāsa sharʿiyya*. In the wake of Ibn Saʿūd's unsuccessful attempt to codify the *sharīʿa*, six books by well-known Ḥanbalī jurists were designated as authoritative sources to be relied upon (in a specified order) in the *sharīʿa* courts.[20]

## 3 Evaluation of the Codification of the *Sharīʿa*

Western scholars are divided as to whether the codification of the *sharīʿa* and wide range of methods and mechanisms designed for the application of the codified *sharīʿa* since the mid-nineteenth century should be assessed in terms of development within or outside the *sharīʿa*. It is worth mentioning in passing that some would refute the legitimacy of such an agenda on grounds of political correctness.[21] As we shall see below, some scholars maintain that this development is an expression of the *sharīʿa*'s vitality and ability to renovate itself, to internalize Western inspiration and to adapt itself to changing conditions. Others (including this writer) maintain that codification reflects

---

*Egyptian Civil Law*; idem; *The Egyptian Civil Code*; Hill, *Al-Sanhuri and Islamic Law*; Shalakany, *Between Identity and Redistribution*; Layish & Warburg, *Sudan*, 114.

19 Anderson, *Law Reform*, 42–48; Coulson, *History*, 182–217. For further details on these methods, see below.

20 Layish, *Saudi Arabia*, 280ff.; cf. Vogel, *Saudi Arabia*, 94.

21 Thus, e.g., Ann Mayer (from the University of Pennsylvania) maintains that "non-Muslims cannot decide on the legitimacy of the conversion of the *sharīʿa* into statutes or whether the developments are inside or outside the *sharīʿa*. Such determinations are exclusively for Muslims to make. [...] It is acceptable for Westerners to examine critically the theories of legitimacy that Muslims put forward about statutes/codes being in conformity with the *sharīʿa* Islamic jurisprudence and to judge their coherence, etc" (Mayer, *Transformation of Islamic Law*). Needless to say, the issue at stake here is not the legitimacy of the codification of the *sharīʿa* but rather the significance and repercussions of this process from the viewpoint of orthodox *sharīʿa* as interpreted by its authorized exponents. In my view, outside observers may participate in this discourse provided no value judgment is involved.

a process of detachment from the *sharīʿa* and even its "secularization" by the creation of an alternative of statutory version of the *sharīʿa.*[22]

Some of the methods employed in the codification of the *sharīʿa* undoubtedly reside outside the *sharīʿa.* This applies to: (1) Reception of complete codes from Europe. (2) Statutory codification, along Western patterns, of various domains of the *sharīʿa.* As we shall see below, codification is not just a technical matter; rather, it has far-reaching repercussions. (3) The procedural expedient: refusal of legal relief (*ʿadam al-samāʿ*) to parties who disregard a particular reformist provision, such as the age of competence for marriage. This method is based on the ruler's right to restrict the jurisdiction of the court (*takhṣīṣ al-qaḍāʾ*). (4) Criminal legislation which, while its sanctions are supposed to deter potential violators of reformist provisions, does not derogate from the substantive validity of the *sharīʿa.* Thus polygamy has been prohibited in some countries by penal sanction; if someone marries another woman without a court permission he is liable to imprisonment but the polygamous marriage is valid. (5) Application of the *sharīʿa* in civil courts, by judges with secular legal training, in the light of national and foreign principles of law.

As far as traditional *sharʿī* mechanisms are concerned, there is a strong temptation to assess their application as a development within the *sharīʿa.* Support for this inclination may be obtained from the fact that these mechanisms were developed and elaborated by the modernists of Muḥammad ʿAbduh's school, whose religious-legal authority was generally acknowledged.[23] In my view, the relevant criterion for orthodoxy is not the *sharʿī* mechanism in itself but rather the religious-legal authority of the person who applies it. Statutes, even if based on mechanisms with traditional *sharʿī* connotations, are first and foremost legislative acts of sovereign parliaments and hence cannot be assessed as a development within the *sharīʿa.*

Moreover, the extensive recourse to traditional *sharʿī* mechanisms has quite often culminated in deviation from the *sharīʿa.* Thus, for instance, the *siyāsa sharʿiyya* doctrine has been used by the sovereign, *inter alia,* to restrict the jurisdiction of the *sharīʿa* courts to the point of their complete abolition (in some countries). As a result, the *sharīʿa* is undergoing a process of secularization due to its exposure to secular – national and foreign – principles of law in

22 See, for instance, Botiveau, *Loi islamique et droit,* 144–145. In order to remove any doubt, it is essential to clarify that the term "secularization" signifies the process of incorporating *sharʿī* rules and principles into statutory legislation; the *sharīʿa* as a jurists' law remains intact. Thus, e.g., it retains full sovereignty in determining the legal norm by means of legal opinions (*fatāwā*) of independent *muftīs.*

23 Kerr, *Islamic Reform,* chapters IV, VI; Layish, *Modernists,* 263–267.

the course of its application in civil courts.[24] Moreover, the *siyāsa* doctrine is being used to impose substantive legislation, the *sharʿī* basis of which is occasionally quite superficial. Thus, for instance, a woman who has been divorced arbitrarily after consummation of the marriage is entitled in some countries, such as Syria and Egypt, to compensation in the form of maintenance beyond the waiting period. This reform is based ostensibly on the Qurʾānic verses pertaining to *mutʿa,* consolatory compensation (2:37, 241). According to the Ḥanafī doctrine, this compensation is due in an unconsummated marriage where no dower has been stipulated in the marriage contract.[25]

Similarly, the *maṣlaḥa* (public interest) doctrine though regarded by some *fuqahāʾ* as "the ultimate purpose of the *sharīʿa,*" and yet never recognized as a source of law[26] has been extended by the legislator to the point that the link with the Qurʾān and *ḥadīth* (through the mechanism of the *qiyās*, the analogical reasoning) has been totally severed. The *maṣlaḥa* has thus become a pure concept of utility extensively applied in statutory legislation. The social incentive *per se* has become a source of law. The legislator resorted to this doctrine where no support for a reform could be found in the *sharīʿa.* This is the case with regard to "obligatory bequest" in favor of orphaned grandchildren – that is, their parent predeceased the praepositus, which was meant to correct a distortion (from the point of view of the grandchildren) anchored in the *sharʿī* law of inheritance (lack of the principle of representation). Hallaq regards *maṣlaḥa,* as used by modern reformers, a secularizing device.[27]

The eclectic expedient (*takhayyur*) was the major mechanism for reformist legislation. This expedient has been stretched to the point that the legislator does not hesitate to patch together (*talfīq*) contradictory doctrines, incompatible with each other, from various schools and jurists into one statutory provision with a view to providing a desirable solution to some specific problem. A case in point is the Egyptian *waqf* law of 1946 which introduced an innovative reform on the basis of contradictory views between jurists as to ownership in *waqf* property. The family *waqf* was to be abolished after a specified duration on the basis of the view held by a small minority of jurists. *Waqf* in favor of a mosque was deemed perpetual on the basis of the view shared by the majority of jurists. As to *waqf khayrī* – that is in favour of charity, other than a mosque, it was to be either temporary or perpetual on the basis of views held by the

24 Naveh, *Application of the sharīʿa in Civil Courts*, Chapter 7; idem, *The Tort of Injury*. 16–21.
25 Coulson, *History*, 209; Layish, *Ṭalāḳ*, 156–157.
26 Khadduri, *Maṣlaḥa.*
27 Hallaq, *The Transformation of Islamic law*, {7}; idem, *Legal Theories*, 214 ("The religious utilitarianists"); Coulson, *History*, 203–207.

respective jurists.[28] The Egyptian jurist Chafiq Chehata maintains that each of the schools is an independent entity in terms of historical background and legal thinking, and that it is inconceivable to mix up doctrines and concepts of one school with those of another school. Even Noel Coulson, who tends to evaluate the reformist legislation as a development within the *sharīʿa*, views *talfīq* as "juristic opportunism."[29] By means of this expedient, the legislator adopted appropriate variants from the Shīʿa that fit in with the reformist norms, as in the case of a bequest in favour of a legal heir in glaring contradiction to the Sunnī *ultra vires* doctrine, or even the entire Shīʿī law of inheritance based on blood relationship (*qarāba*) which does not distinguish between agnates (relatives through males, *ʿaṣaba*) and cognates (relatives through females, *dhawū al-arḥām*). Legislators in Arab countries went so far in this direction that scholars, such as Anderson and Coulson, maintain that the dividing line has been blurred not only between the four Sunnī schools but also between these schools and the Shīʿī law, and that this technique culminated finally in reforms with no basis in the *sharīʿa*, the rationale of which was pure public interest.[30]

In the process of the codification of the *sharīʿa* by means of the method of *tashrīʿ*, the legislator took the liberty to resort directly to the Qurʾān and the *ḥadīth* and to interpret them independently with a view to adapting the *sharīʿa* to present-day requirements having regard to contemporary needs, as in the cases of prohibition of polygamy, curtailment of the husband's freedom of repudiation, and compensation to the divorced wife. The legislator's direct approach to the textual sources of the *sharīʿa* bears a certain resemblance to classical *ijtihād*. This resemblance, however, is purely technical; there are material differences with respect to the mode of resorting to the textual sources (replacement of the deductive *qiyās* by the *maṣlaḥa*) and to the sources of inspiration and motivation for the reforms (Western ideas, and pressures arising from a disturbance of balances in Muslim society as a result of modernization and Westernization). Moreover, the possibility that the door of *ijtihād* will be reopened (assuming for the time being that the door was closed – an issue beyond the scope of this essay[31]) through judicial practice of national courts, as in the case of the Sudan under Numayrī, is problematic in view of the fact that judges applying the *ijtihād* lack appropriate *sharʿī* education (see below).

---

28 Anderson, 58; Hallaq, *Talfīḳ*; Krawietz, *Talfīq*; Layish, *Talfīḳ*; cf. Layish & Warburg, *Sudan*, 122–123 (Section 253 of the Penal Code, 1983).

29 Coulson, *History*, 221; Chehata, *Droit musulman*, 94–95.

30 Anderson & Coulson, *Islamic Law in Contemporary Cultural Change*, 86, 90; Coulson, *Conflicts*, 33ff.; Paret, 527–529.

31 See above, fn. 7.

In the process of codification of the *sharīʿa* the legislator has extended the *qāḍī*'s discretion with respect to matters which are within his jurisdiction probably with the expectation that the *qāḍī* use his discretion to accommodate the *sharīʿa* to the structural changes in the Muslim family and bear personal responsibility, publicly, for any possible deviation from the consolidated law of the orthodox schools. Thus in some countries, such as Syria and Iraq, polygamy has been prohibited unless permitted by the *qāḍī* who must be satisfied that the husband is financially capable of maintaining more than one wife, that he will treat his co-wives with equal justice or that there is some benefit (*manfaʿa*) in such a marriage. Under the strict orthodox *sharīʿa* such a permission is not required and therefore restricts the husband's freedom of marriage. In some countries a formula of unilateral divorce pronounced out of court has no validity unless effected by judicial decree, this too – contrary to the *sharīʿa* that recognizes unilateral divorce not entailing legal proceedings. The expansion of the *qāḍī's* discretion by the legislator has strengthened his function as the guardian of public morals in the best tradition of the *muḥtasib*.[32]

Statutory codification of various domains of the *sharīʿa* along Western patterns is not merely a technical-formalistic affair. Although materially the codes are based on the *sharīʿa*, from a strictly orthodox *sharʿī* point of view, the very Western-inspired codification implies the transformation of the *sharīʿa* from jurists' law to statutory law.[33] Statutory provisions have an autonomous existence based on state-imposed sanctions. In other words, the mere codification brings about the nationalization of the *sharīʿa* (*tamṣīr al-qānūn* in an Egyptian context).[34] The *sharʿī* variants incorporated in the statutes are to be interpreted strictly within the framework of the national-territorial statutes. On the level of the basic norm (which represents the primary legal norm in any given country), codification results in a complete departure from the religious-legal literature (unless, in the case of a lacuna, the *qāḍī* is instructed by the legislator to resort to the uncodified *sharīʿa*). On the level of interpretation, however, the *qāḍī* is not debarred from consulting religious-legal literature (or any other source) provided he does not contradict statutory provisions. Moreover, codification brings about total disruption of the *sharʿī* legal methodology (*uṣūl al-fiqh*), of the body of the *sharʿī* law as consolidated in each of the schools, and

32 Cf. Layish and Warburg, *Sudan*, 222–23, 266, 271, 280–81. On the Libyan Qāḍī's role as a *muḥtasib*, see Layish, *Qāḍī's Role*, 93. On the revival of the *ḥisba* in Egypt with special reference to the Abu Zayd case, see Jörn Thielmann, *Abu Zaid.*

33 Mayer, *Methodology or Substantive Rules?*, 184.

34 Botiveau, *Loi islamique*, 148, 191.

of the status of the *fuqahāʾ* and *muftīs* as the exclusive authorized exponents of the *sharīʿa*.

A clear distinction should be made between the orthodox *sharīʿa* and the *sharīʿa* that has undergone codification. Beyond the resemblance between the two systems in terms of the legal material they have nothing in common. The codified *sharīʿa* in its statutory version is a totally new entity; it is not bound by the classical legal methodology. Thus its provisions are sanctioned by the legislature, not by the consensus (*ijmāʿ*) of the *fuqahāʾ* as in the case of *sharʿī* rules. Actually, the status of the *sharīʿa* in statutory legislation has been reduced to the level of a symbol.[35] A similar situation existed in the formative period of Islamic law regarding the interrelations between the *sharīʿa* and custom, the former displaying assimilative power with respect to the latter. Specified domains in the *sharīʿa*, such as matters of personal status, inheritance, homicide and grievous injury derived their legal material (mitigated and softened by Islamic ethical norms) from custom (*ʿāda, ʿurf*), either pre-Islamic Arab custom or "provincial" practice – to use Patricia Crone's wording.[36] However, from the very moment that custom was absorbed by the *sharīʿa*, it lost its original identity to the extent that it was never formally, though not always in practice, until the nineteenth century, recognized as a source of law in the *sharʿī* legal methodology.[37] The orthodox *sharīʿa*, in contrast, in spite of its deprivation by statutory legislation, still maintains for the time being its status as a source of law. Thus in several countries, in the event of a lacuna in any given law, the court is guided to resort to the *sharīʿa* (see below).

The process of legislation in modern Arab countries is a function of social, economic, and political pressures the regulation of which has nothing to do with the traditional methodology of *uṣūl al-fiqh*, legislature in itself being totally alien to the *sharʿī* legal theory. Moreover, legislation seems to derive its inspiration from Western precepts. In some Arab countries, parliament is

35 Ibid., 192.

36 Crone, *Roman, Provincial and Islamic Law*, 11–17.

37 Ibn ʿĀbidīn raised, through the device of necessity (*ḍarūra*), universal custom (*ʿurf ʿāmm*) and local (*khāṣṣ*) custom to the status of legal source; the former is binding on the entire Muslim community, while the latter is binding in the locale in which it prevails. Shortly after Ibn ʿĀbidīn, custom was recognized in the Ottoman Empire as an independent source of law when the *sharʿī* civil law underwent a formal codification, namely the Mejelle. See Hallaq, *Ibn ʿĀbidīn on Custom and Legal Change*; Johansen, *Coutumes locales et coutumes universelles*; Libson, *Custom as a Source of Law*. The later Mālikī "judicial practice"(*ʿamal*) in North Africa should not be confused with customary law; it took some account of custom – in cases where the strict theory could not be implemented in practice – but without recognizing custom as an official source of law. See Schacht, *Introduction*, 61–62.

bound by the "Constitutional Provision" which provides that the *sharīʿa* is *a* (or *the*) main source for legislation. Any claim with respect to a statutory provision being contradictory to the *sharīʿa* should be decided by the Supreme Constitutional Court rather than *sharīʿa* or regular civil court (see below). Legislation of a constitutional nature is of course superior to regular legislation. The parliament, however, is the declared source of sovereignty; it is parliament that sets bounds to the *sharīʿa* rather than the other way around. It seems that the constitutional provision is first and foremost a symbol intended, within the domestic policy, to pacify the radical religious circles struggling for the Islamization of the state.

The constitutional provision reflects a paradox of legal pluralism. Several models have been suggested to define this paradox: (1) the *sharīʿa*'s normative control of statutory legislation; (2) interpenetration of the two legal systems, the *sharʿī* and the statutory; and (3) coexistence, side by side, of the *sharīʿa* and the statutory law as two autonomous legal systems.[38] It seems that the first model is the closest to reality although for the time being the impact of the *sharīʿa*'s normative control of the legislation should not be exaggerated. Thus, for instance, to date, the Supreme Constitutional Court in Egypt rejected all attempts to abolish statutory provisions by virtue of the constitutional provision (Article 2). The rejection was on the ground that Article 2 was not applicable to legal enactments in force prior to the adoption of the 1980 Constitution.[39] As to the future, much depends on the role of the *sharīʿa* in shaping the legal and social philosophy of the judges in various levels of the judiciary. In Egypt and the Sudan, the impact of judges striving to bring about Islamization of the law is discernible in lower courts up to courts of appeal (but not in the Supreme Court).[40] There is some evidence to the effect that *sharʿī qāḍīs* and civil judges sought to ignore statutory provisions not compatible with the *sharīʿa* and applied instead the uncodified *sharīʿa*.[41]

The parliaments' intention to carry out their secular reformist policy by means of *tashrīʿ* and traditional mechanisms prepared by the modernists, is inspired by national and tactical considerations: the creation of the impression that the reforms are a kind of internal renovation of the *sharīʿa*. The *sharīʿa* is

---

38 Bälz, *The Secular Reconstruction of Islamic Law*, 231–233.

39 Brown & Sharif, *Inscribing sharīʿa in Constitutional Law*, 6, 12 (It was claimed in the Supreme Constitutional Court that charging the University of al-Azhar interest on commercial debt violated the *sharʿī* prohibition on usury, *ribā*).

40 Lombardi, *Islamic Law as a Source of Constitutional Law* , 118–119; Layish and Warburg, *Sudan*, 263ff.

41 The phenomenon was observed in the Sudan ten years prior to the promulgation of the "September laws" (of 1983); see Layish & Warburg, *Sudan*, 174–180, 267, 276–277.

presented as part of the Arab national-cultural heritage with a view to preventing the creation of an ideological debt and subjection to the West ("*istiʿmār qānūnī*", legal colonialism).[42] Reference to the modernists of the school of Muḥammad ʿAbduh is intended to facilitate acceptance of the reforms by the *ʿulamāʾ*, conservative circles, and the *sharʿī* judiciary. The legislator's attitude is practical and pragmatic rather than theoretical: he is concerned first and foremost with achieving actual results in such a way that arouses the least amount of public criticism.

Since the early 1970s there has been an increasing tendency towards the Islamization of various domains of law, especially penal law, in countries such as Libya, Iran, Sudan, and Pakistan. This tendency too has been implemented by means of codification and statutory legislation with all the attendant consequences, the most important of which is the transformation of the *sharīʿa* from jurists' law to statutory law.[43] A good notion of the repercussions of the reinstatement of the *sharīʿa* by means of codification can be gathered from a recent study on the Sudanese experiment under Numayrī.[44] *Sharʿī* norms have been incorporated into statutes dealing with various domains of law. The main method chosen to this end was the eclectic expedient (*takhayyur*). The Islamist statutes reflect a synthesis of variants from the Sudanese English-inspired statutory law, and the *sharīʿa*. Quite often no compatibility exists between the *sharʿī* term and its definition in the statute. In cases of lacunae, the Sudanese civil court may apply the uncodified *sharīʿa* and even exercise *ijtihād* on the basis of the four *sharʿī* sources of law, as well as English principles of law, such as "justice, equity and good conscience," legal precedents (*sawābiq qaḍāʾiyya*), and custom (*ʿurf, ʿāda*). It goes without saying that, from the point of view of the strict *sharīʿa* as interpreted by its authorized exponents, such a mixture of sources of law is intolerable.[45]

The transformation of the *sharīʿa* from jurists' law to statutory law also left its imprint on the Muslim family which, in the process of codification, is gradually losing its traditional features. Underlying the Muslim family is the concept

42 Cf. Brown, *Law and Imperialism*; Mayer, *Methodology or Substantive Rules?*, 182; Layish & Warburg, *Sudan*, 36, 40.

43 Peters, *Islamization of Criminal Law*; Mehdi, *Pakistan*; Mayer, *Methodology or Substantive Rules?*, 182. It may be argued, in parenthesis, that the mere desire to reinstate the *sharīʿa* substantiates the contention that statutory law succeeded in impinging on the traditional, uncodified *sharīʿa*. Cf. Botiveau, *Loiislamique*, 277.

44 Layish & Warburg, *Sudan*, 94–98, 275ff.

45 Usury (*ribā*), which is a purely civil matter under the *sharīʿa*, has become a criminal offence in the Sudanese court. On the impact of the reinstatement of Islamic law on economy with special reference to prohibition of usury and the Islamization of the banking system, see ibid., 243–48, 292.

of the superiority of men over women and of agnates over cognates. Reforms such as the prohibition, not to speak of abolition, of polygamy, curtailment of the husband's freedom of unilateral divorce with a view to replacing it by judicial dissolution, and equality between the sexes in succession, undermine the patrilineal structure of the Muslim family as embedded in the *sharʿī* personal status rules. The legal norm adjusts itself to the nuclear family, to the weakening of the patriarchal authority of the head of the family and the supremacy of agnates, and to the consolidation of the capacity of women for any legal act and disposition of property. The legislator is the avant-garde of the reform, although undoubtedly he, in turn, is influenced by the changes taking place in his environment. These changes are clearly in conformity with the norms of Western-inspired urban society.[46]

## 4 The Attitudes of the *ʿUlamāʾ* and Judiciary towards Codification of the *Sharīʿa*

One may discern among the *ʿulamāʾ* two fundamentally different attitudes that cannot be reconciled: On the one hand, conservative *ʿulamāʾ*, to the extent that they can express their views freely, strongly protest against the *tashrīʿ* which they consider a means of secularizing the *sharīʿa*.[47] On the other hand, conformist *ʿulamāʾ* support the technique of the *tashrīʿ* with various degrees of enthusiasm and even provide specific proposals for legislation.

Several explanations have been suggested for the cooperation between the *ʿulamāʾ* and the state: the *ʿulamāʾ* are bound up with the regime and the establishment and fear to compromise their economic, social and political position;[48] they suspect that the alternative to a moderate reformist policy may be a radical one outside their supervision and control, or even the complete separation of religion and state, as in Turkey; the reforms are not carried out in the name of a declared anti-religious ideology; the integration of the *ʿulamāʾ* in the political establishment enables them to better understand the interests of the state and to cooperate from inner conviction; they identify the good of the state with their own good and are therefore interested in the maintenance of the *status quo*. In Saudi Arabia, cooperation between the

46 Layish, *Family*; Moors, *Public Debates on Family Law Reform*.

47 Cf. Brown, *Sharīʿa and State*, 366. On the Saudi *ʿulamāʾ*'s attitudes towards codification, see Vogel, *Saudi Arabia*, 357ff.

48 In Arab countries that had undergone military coup d'état the status of the *ʿulamāʾ* has been severely affected by the emergence of a new social and political stratification consisting, inter alia, of army officers, bureaucrats and secular trained jurists.

*ʿulamāʾ* and the *umarāʾ* has a theoretical basis in the political doctrine of Ibn Taymiyya (d. 1328), according to which the *sharīʿa* depends on the ruler for its application while the state needs the *sharīʿa* for its legitimation.[49]

The *ʿulamāʾ* do not seem to realize the full significance in the long run of the introduction of reforms by means of *tashrīʿ*.[50] Muḥammad Rashīd Riḍā criticizes the *ʿulamāʾ* of al-Azhar for not opposing the government's initiative to introduce a formal codification, based on state sanctions, of rules pertaining to matters of personal status; this same initiative would moreover seek to abolish the *sharīʿa* courts. He rightly anticipates that such an initiative would in the long run cause damage to the *ʿulamāʾ*'s economic status and reputation. Riḍā further claims that by this omission they became responsible, alongside the "Europeanized" (*mutafarnijūn*), for the loss of the state's Islamic character.[51] Broadly speaking, the *ʿulamāʾ* have not come forward with a constructive proposal for legal reform that would redefine the relations between the *sharīʿa* and the national state. Such an omission seems to have facilitated the government's effort to bring the *ʿulamāʾ* within the orbit of the secular policy of the regime.[52]

The success of Western-inspired reforms introduced through codification of the *sharīʿa* in the domain of personal status, succession and *waqf* depends, to a decisive extent, on the *qāḍīs* and judges charged with their application in *sharīʿa* and civil courts, respectively. In Egypt, Ron Shaham has found a gamut of grades in the *qāḍīs*' jurisprudence up to the abolition of the *sharīʿa* courts in 1955: Some *qāḍīs* who had inhibitions about applying reforms contradictory to their traditional religious and social philosophy, interpreted reformist provisions in a restrictive manner. There were also cases where the uncodified *sharīʿa* was applied instead of statutory provisions. Some contented themselves with formalistic application of the reforms in the best tradition of obedience to the ruler – or out of genuine support for the reforms. Most of the *qāḍīs*, however, especially in Cairo, identified themselves with the goals of the reformist legislation, occasionally even beyond the legislator's expectations, and made full

---

49 Layish, *Saudi Arabia*, 289ff. Cf. Heyd.

50 On the other hand, the awareness of the transformation of the *sharīʿa* from jurists' law to national, positive statutory law seems to have increased gradually among Muslim and Western scholars. See, e.g., An-Naʿim, *Sharīʿa and Positive Legislation*; Botiveau, *Loi islamique*, 192 fn. 3.

51 Riḍā regards family law as part of the category of *ʿibādāt*, religious observances or duties between man and God, due to Allāh's prohibitions of and permissions to marriage and divorce anchored in Qurʾānic verses pertaining to matrimonial rights. Riḍā, *Madaniyyat al-qawānīn*, 540–543.

52 Layish, *Modernists*, 274.

use of the discretion given them to promote the reforms. Generally speaking, it seems that many *qāḍīs* were attentive to social change and found encouragement in the statutory legislation to adopt a more innovative legal approach. As a whole, they did not obstruct the application of the reforms.[53]

Emanuel Naveh has found that the Egyptian national courts, whose jurisdiction has been extended to matters of personal status since the abolition of the *sharīʿa* courts, apply reformist statutory provisions without inhibitions. In cases of lacuna, however, they do not hesitate to adopt legal norms of the Ḥanafī or any other school of law. They apply Ḥanafī, alongside civil, rules of evidence and procedure. A few Egyptian judges of the civil courts, invoking Article 2 of the 1980 Constitution (according to which the *sharīʿa* is *the* main source of legislation), refused to apply statutory provisions contradictory to the *sharīʿa*, usually referring the case to the Supreme Constitutional Court to obtain a ruling with regard to the constitutionality of the provisions concerned.[54]

## 5 Summary and Conclusions

The liberally-oriented modernist movement in Islam, founded by Muḥammad ʿAbduh, is perhaps the most important attempt so far to reshape the *sharīʿa* from within, by its authorized exponents, with a view to adapting it to the requirements of modern society. The modernists attempted to bring about the reopening of the door of *ijtihād* by creating a new legal methodology in which the *maṣlaḥa* doctrine played a vital role; their attempts, however, failed. Moreover, the ideological foundation and traditional mechanisms created by the modernists for the renovation of the *sharīʿa* caused, on the one hand, the disruption of traditional legal theory and, on the other hand, prepared the ground for *tashrīʿ*.[55] As noted above, Muḥammad Rashīd Riḍā accused the *ʿulamāʾ*, the intellectuals of Muslim society, of betraying their duty to adapt the *sharīʿa*, of their own initiative and outside the control of the establishment, to the changing circumstances.

Since the failure of the modernists there were sporadic attempts to shape new legal methodologies amalgamating the traditional legal theory of the *sharīʿa* with Western legal methodologies. In the following I shall concentrate

53 Shaham, *Family and the Courts*, 230–235.

54 Naveh, *Application of the sharīʿa in Civil Courts*, Chapter 7 (Summary); Layish & Shaham, *Tashrīʿ*, 354. Cf. Brown, *sharīʿa and State*, 372; Botiveau, *Loi islamique*, 239. See above, fn. 39.

55 Layish, *Modernists*, 267; Hallaq, *Legal Theories*, 214ff. On *ijtihād* in the eighteenth and nineteenth centuries, see Peters, *Ijtihād and Taqlīd*.

very briefly on two of these attempts in order to give some notion of the trends and their consequences in modern times.[56]

The Egyptian Qāḍī Aḥmad Muḥammad Shākir (d. 1958) suggests three sources of law for guiding the *sharīʿa* court in its jurisprudence: the orthodox *sharīʿa*, statutory legislation, and justice (*ʿadl*). The statutory legislation in this combination applies also to the *sharīʿa* that has undergone codification. Since he did not deem himself bound by any particular school, Shākir seems to have supported the application of the eclectic expedient (*takhayyur*) from legal doctrines culled from the four Sunnī schools and earlier jurists provided these doctrines are compatible with the textual sources (the Qurʾān and the *sunna*). Justice as a source of law, to be distinguished from Allāh's justice, reflects the Western-inspired concept of natural justice.[57] Although Shākir does not treat the three guiding sources in terms of systematic, consolidated legal methodology, it seems that we are here dealing with three sources of law comprising a genuine legal methodology. It goes without saying that the combination of these sources suggested by an *ʿālim* acting as a *qāḍī*, deviates from the classical theory of the *sharīʿa*.

The Sudanese jurist and political scientist Ḥasan al-Turābī, who was the living spirit behind the experiment of reinstating the *sharīʿa* under Numayrī, suggests a new legal methodology to this end which in fact consists of a synthesis between the classical legal theory – the Qurʾān and the *sunna*, *ijmāʿ* and *qiyās*, as well as traditional mechanisms, such as *istiḥsān* (preference of considerations of public interest within the framework of deductive analogy) and *ḍarūra* (necessity) – and Western-inspired legal methodologies (*manāhij al-fiqh*). Support is derived also from the sciences of humanities, and social and natural sciences. He recommends reinstatement of the *sharīʿa* by means of statutory codification based mainly on the eclectic device (*takhayyur*). This legal methodology is strictly applied in the Judgments (Basic Rules) Act (*qānūn uṣūl al-aḥkām*), 1983, the Sudanese law of interpretation for the Islamist statutes. This Act authorizes the judge – in the event of lacuna in any given Islamist statute and the textual sources of the Qurʾān and the *sunna* – to exercise *ijtihād* on the basis of legal sources and principles in the following order: *ijmāʿ*, *qiyās*, *maṣlaḥa*, legal precedents (of the Sudanese national courts), and custom, provided they do not contradict the *sharīʿa* and natural justice (to be distinguished from God's justice), as well as the English-inspired principles of justice, equity and good conscience. Needless to say, this combination of

56 For integrative analysis of new legal theories, see Hallaq, *Legal Theories*, Chapter 6; Cf. Mayer, *Methodology or Substantive Rules?*, 186.

57 Shaham, *Qāḍī Aḥmad Shākir*, 443–451. On God's justice, see Johansen, *Contingency*, 16–19.

sources of law is inconceivable from the viewpoint of the authorized exponents of the orthodox *sharīʿa*.[58]

It is interesting to note, in this connection, that Noel Coulson suggests that Muslim jurists make use of researches carried out by Western scholars with a view to redefining the vital principles of the *sharīʿa* and creating a modern legal philosophy that will replace the classical legal theory and facilitate the accommodation of the *sharīʿa* to the requirements of a modern society. He offers his services as a historian of the *sharīʿa* although on the doctrinal – not the practical – level, the historical dimension is totally alien to the *sharīʿa* being a jurisprudence based on revelation.[59] Coulson probably meant to create a philosophical juristic basis for the transformation of the *sharīʿa* from jurists' law to statutory law.

In the spirit of Coulson's suggestion, the judges of Supreme Constitutional Court in Egypt strive, on the basis of Muslim historical heritage, to create a new legal philosophy which consists of elements of legal methodology par excellence. Regarding Article 2 of 1980 Constitution (the "Constitutional Provision"), they make a distinction between fundamental principles and the body of detailed rules. The fundamental principles, which ought to be accepted by all the *ʿulamāʾ*, are anchored in the classical theory of the *sharīʿa* (*uṣūl al-fiqh*), in each of the four orthodox schools of law, in muʿtazilite theories of law, and in the thought of Western-oriented modernists in Islam. The basic principles are immutable, eternal, unequivocal legal norms. The detailed rules, on the other hand, may be adjusted, by means of interpretation, to changing conditions of time and place. Contrary to Islamist circles that reserve to the *ʿulamāʾ* alone the ability to identify the basic principles of the *sharīʿa* and to apply them, the Supreme Constitutional Court maintains that *sharʿī* training is not an indispensable qualification to this end. In the absence of basic principles which may provide solutions to incidental problems, it is possible to resort to legislative and judicial *ijtihād* inspired by public interest. Thus, for instance, the Supreme Constitutional Court rejected in 1994 a claim to cancel a court ruling obligating a husband to pay the maintenance of his child retroactively from the day he had ceased to pay them on the ground that the ruling was contradictory to the Ḥanafī doctrine. The Supreme Constitutional Court ruled that retroactive obligation was in conformity with a *sharʿī* basic principle seeking to avert hardship (*mashaqqa*) from society. Similarly, the Supreme Constitutional Court rejected in 1996 the contention that the Minister of Education's instruction forbidding

58 Layish & Warburg, *Sudan*, 79–94. On judicial *ijtihād* in Saudi Arabia, see Vogel, Saudi *Arabia*, chapters 3–4.

59 Coulson, *History*, 6–7.

school girls to cover their faces with a veil (*niqāb, ḥijāb*) was contradictory to the *sharīʿa*. The Supreme Constitutional Court ruled that the provisions in the Qurʾān (24:31; 33:59) and the *ḥadīth* pertaining to unchastity of a woman (*ʿawra*) are not unequivocal and undisputable between the schools – hence, this was not a case of basic principle –, and most importantly, that the veil is deemed a hardship for society. The conclusion emerging from the above-mentioned is that the vagueness of the basic principles provides the necessary flexibility for adjusting the *sharīʿa* to the conditions of modern times. And finally, the Supreme Constitutional Court ruled that statutory legislation was also a very important layer in this legal methodology.[60]

It is doubtful whether the codification of the *sharīʿa* through the application of *sharʿī* principles and mechanisms is likely to bring about the adaptation of the *sharīʿa* to the changing requirements of a modern society. The *tashrīʿ* is first and foremost a legislative act of a sovereign parliament or ruler that decides which of the *sharʿī* principles are worthy of being adopted within the framework of statutes. Although some of the members of parliaments are qualified jurists with modern legal training, they are by no means the authorized interpreters and exponents of the *sharīʿa*; nor are they bound by the *sharʿī* legal methodology. As soon as they resort to statutory legislation and codification, they sidestep the framework of the *sharʿī* legal system.

Under these circumstances, it is also doubtful whether the present encounter of Islam with Western civilization will lead to the Islamization of foreign legal concepts and institutions, administrative practices etc. in contrast to what occurred during the formative period of the *sharīʿa*, when Islam was at the peak of its political, military and cultural success and the *sharīʿa*, by means of its assimilative power (the development of the *ḥadīth* was instrumental to this end), was able to absorb foreign elements and provide legal solutions to incidental problems of an incessantly expanding empire.[61] Hallaq maintains categorically that "the [classical] *sharīʿa* has no chance to be revived [...] the *sharīʿa* has gone with no return." In his view, the only relevant question left to be discussed is whether it is possible to anchor modern law in Islamic principles and sources. His answer is that "the ultimate test of Islamicizing the law lies in vindicating a defensible dialectic between the authoritative sources and the law." For this purpose, he maintains, an alternative theory to *uṣūl al-fiqh*, a theory of contextual analysis, is required similar to that initiated by the

60 Lombardi, 81, 90ff., 103ff., 115ff.; Peters, *Divine Law or Man-Made Law?*, 231–243; Brown & Sharif, *Inscribing sharīʿa*, 12ff. Cf. Johansen, *Contingency*, 7ff.; Layish & Warburg, *Sudan*, 124 (*mashaqqa*), 169–170 (*qawāʾid uṣūliyya*).

61 Schacht, *Introduction*, 19ff.; Coulson, *History*, 27ff.

Pakistani scholar Fazlur Rahman and the Egyptian jurist Muḥammad Saʿīd ʿAshmāwī. For the time being, he argues, most of the reforms introduced in the Muslim world by means of statutory legislation "have no authoritative textual source to sustain them. Nor do they have any prospect of acquiring an Islamic identity." Moreover, Hallaq claims, it is impossible to Islamize the entire body of European codes that have been adopted by Muslim countries.[62]

Middle Eastern and North African countries that recently achieved their political independence, are still struggling to release themselves from the cultural impact of the West, law being one of its manifestations, and are searching for their identity. In this connection, the *sharīʿa* (notwithstanding its codification) still has a symbolic value.

The transformation from jurists' law to statutory law is an ongoing process rather than an accomplished fact. We noted earlier that here were *qāḍī*s as well as civil judges who resort to the uncodified *sharīʿa* even in cases where there is no lacuna in any given statute. This seems to be a lost battle in which participants have yet to internalize the significance of the nationalization of the *sharīʿa* by means of codification and statutory legislation. Under these circumstances the last stronghold of the *sharīʿa* is the domain of *ʿibādāt*, but it seems that this domain too is gradually giving way to the intervention of statutory legislation and sanctions.[63]

The renovation of the uncodified *sharīʿa* in modern times depends on independent orthodox *ʿulamāʾ* outside the establishment. Gibb argues that

> It is the task of the Muslims to find the way and to reformulate their principles of belief and action accordingly, a task which will not be completed for many generations and probably not without conflict [...].[64]

62 Hallaq, *The Transformation of Islamic Law*. For further details on the trend of "religious liberalism" (to be distinguished from "religious utilitarianism") in connection with the attempts, in the contemporary Muslim world, to reformulate legal theories in a manner that combines the basic religious values of Islam with legal norms compatible with the needs of modern society, see Hallaq, *Legal Theories*, 214, 231–253.

63 Thus, for instance, in several states, such as Saudi Arabia and Sudan, the *zakāt*, the *sharʿī* obligatory payment of alms tax which in the course of time became a voluntary charity, has been anchored in statute (see Zysow, *Zakāt*, 418ff.; Schacht, *Introduction*, 105; Layish & Warburg, *Sudan*, 250–251). In Jordan, the violation of the fast of the month of Ramaḍān is a statutory criminal offense, not a matter of individual conscience. Cf. Johansen, *Contingency*, 34ff.

64 Gibb, *Modern Trends in Islam*, 6–7.

Gibb further argues that

> The future of Islam rests where it has rested in the past – on the insight of the orthodox leaders and their capacity to resolve the new tensions as they arise by a positive doctrine which will face and master the forces making for disintegration.[65]

A "positive doctrine" in the context of this essay means a new legal methodology closely connected with the classical one that will enable the accommodation of the *sharīʿa*, by means of *ijtihād*, to the changing requirements of modern society. If contemporary *ʿulamāʾ* deem this end worthy of achieving, then they are required to display intellectual vitality, creativity, integrity, and courage necessary for articulating and redefining a legal methodology without deviating from the nature of the *sharīʿa* as a jurists' law. In the absence of such an initiative, the forecast development in the foreseeable future in countries outside the control of radical Islam, is an increasing tendency towards nationalization of the *sharīʿa* by means of codification and statutory legislation and further detachment from the orthodox *sharīʿa*. In that case, the *sharīʿa* will survive solely as a domain for the intellectual activity of *ʿulamāʾ* with no practical relevance within the curtailed boundaries allocated to it by the state.[66] Which course – renovation of the *sharīʿa* by its authorized exponents or nationalization of the *sharīʿa* by the state – is the most appropriate to be adopted?[67] The choice between these two alternatives entails a value judgment and hence should be left exclusively to the discretion of Muslims; the historian is spared this dilemma.

---

65 Ibid., 122.

66 Muftīs, however, are not bound by statutory legislation and codification; they may apply the uncodified *sharīʿa* at the request of individuals with a view to solving personal problems but, as already noted, their legal opinions are not binding. Cf. Layish, *Fatwā*.

67 Hallaq's main conclusions in this respect are that "the traditional theory of *uṣūl al-fiqh* is no longer sufficient to deal with the exigencies of modern life, even if we assume against all odds – that a professional legal class, qualified to harness it, can be resurrected. This theory is essentially literalist, paying heed to the lexical and technical meanings of the revealed texts. In some cases, central to society and economy, no amount of interpretation can change the dictates of certain revealed texts. This theory has therefore no chance of any revival [...] Yet, it is only the state which can bring about a revival of Islamic law, but not without the full participation of Muslim intelligentsia and, more importantly, not while the present regimes remain in power." Hallaq, *Can the Shariʿa be restored?*, v. I am most grateful to Wael Hallaq for allowing me to consult his forthcoming essay prior to its publication.

## Bibliography

Anderson, N. *Law Reform in the Muslim World*. London 1976.

Anderson, N. and N.J. Coulson, *Islamic Law in Contemporary Cultural Change*. München 1967.

Bälz, K. "The Secular Reconstruction of Islamic Law: The Islamic Supreme Constitutional Court and the 'Battle over the Veil' in State-Run Schools." In B. Dupret, M. Berger and L. al-Zwaini (eds.), *Legal Pluralism in the Arab World*. The Hague, London, Boston 1999, 229–243.

Bechor, G. "The Egyptian Civil Code: In Search of Social Order, 1939–1949." Ph.D. thesis. Tel Aviv University 1998 (in Hebrew with English summary).

Bechor, G. "'To Hold the Hand of the Weak': The Emergence of Contractual Justice in the Egyptian Civil Law." *Islamic Law and Society* 8 (2001), 179–200.

Black, H.C., et al. *Black's Law Dictionary*. 6th ed. St. Paul, Minn. 1990.

Botiveau, B. *Loi islamique et droit dans les sociétés arabes. Mutations des systems juridiques du Moyen-Orient*. Paris 1993.

Brown, N. "Law and Imperialism: Egypt in Comparative Perspective." *Law and Society Review* 29 (1995), 103–125.

Brown, N. "Shariʿa and State in the Modern Muslim Middle East." *International Journal of Middle East Studies* 29 (1997), 359–376.

Brown, N.J. and A.O. Sherif, "Inscribing Shariʿa in Arab Constitutional Law." Washington (unpublished).

Chehata, Ch. *Droit musulman: Application au Proche-Orient*. Paris 1970.

Coulson, N.J. *Conflicts and Tensions in Islamic Jurisprudence*. Chicago 1969.

Coulson, N.J. *A History of Islamic Law*. Edinburgh 1964.

Crone, P. *Roman, Provincial and Islamic Law. The Origins of the Islamic Patronate*. Cambridge 1987.

Dupret, B. "Legal Pluralism, Normative Plurality, and the Arab World." In B. Dupret, M. Berger and L. al-Zwaini (eds.), *Legal Pluralism in the Arab World*. The Hague, London, Boston 1999, 29–40.

Ebert, H.-G. *Das Personalstatut arabischer Länder: Problemfelder, Methoden, Perspektiven. Ein Beitrag zum Diskurs über Theorie und Praxis des islamischen Rechts*. Frankfurt a.M. 1996.

Fadel, M. "The Social Logic of *Taqlīd* and the Rise of the *Mukhtaṣar*." *Islamic Law and Society* 3 (1966), 193–233.

Gibb, H.A.R. *Modern Trends in Islam*. New York 1972.

Hallaq, W.B. *Authority, Continuity and Change in Islamic Law*. Cambridge 2001.

Hallaq, W.B. "Can the Shariʿa Be Restored?" in *Islamic Law and the Challenges of Modernity*, ed. Yvonne Yazbeck Haddad and Barbara Freyer Stowasser (Lanham, MD, 2004), 21–53.

Hallaq, W.B. "Comments for the Panel: 'The Transformation of Islamic Law from Jurists' to Statute Law and Its Repercussions.'" *The Joseph Schacht Conference on Theory and Practice in Islamic Law*, Leiden & Amsterdam 1994.

Hallaq, W.B. *A History of Islamic Legal Theories*. Cambridge 1997.

Hallaq, W.B. "Ifta' and Ijtihad in Sunni Legal Theory: A Developmental Account." In Masud, Messick & Powers, *Islamic Legal Interpretation*, 33–43.

Hallaq, W.B. "A Prelude to Ottoman Reform: Ibn ʿĀbidīn on Custom and Legal Change." In I. Gershoni, H. Erdem and U. Woköck (eds.), *Histories of the Modern Middle East. New Directions*. Boulder & London 2002, 37–61.

Hallaq, W.B. "Talfīk. 1. In Classical Islamic Law." *The Encyclopaedia of Islam*. New ed., X (1998), 161.

Hallaq, W.B. "Was the Gate of Ijtihad Closed?" *International Journal of Middle East Studies* 16 (1984), 3–41.

Heyd, U. "The Ottoman 'Ulemā and Westernization in the Time of Selīm III and Maḥmūd II." In U. Heyd (ed.), *Studies in Islamic History and Civilization*, Scripta Hierosolymitana IX. Jerusalem 1961, 63–96.

Hill, E. "Al-Sanhuri and Islamic Law." *Arab Law Quarterly* 3 (1988), 33–64, 182–218.

İnalcık, H. "Ḳānūn. iii. Financial and Public Administration." *The Encyclopaedia of Islam*. New ed., IV (1997), 558–62.

Johansen, B. *Contingency in a Sacred Law: Legal and Ethical Norms in the Muslim Fiqh*. Leiden 1997.

Johansen, B. "Coutumes locales et coutumes universelles aux sources des règles juridiques en droit musulman Hanefite." *Annales Islamologiques* 27. Institute Français d'Archéologie Orientale du Caire. Cairo 1993, 29–35. Reprinted in Johansen, *Contingency*, 163–171.

Johansen, B. "Truth and Validity of the Qadi's Judgment: A Legal Debate among Muslim Sunni Jurists from the 9th to the 13th Centuries." *Recht van de Islam* 14. Maastricht 1997, 1–26.

Kerr, M.H. *Islamic Reform. The Political and Legal Theories of Muḥammad ʿAbduh and Rashīd Riḍā*. Berkeley & Los Angeles 1966.

Khadduri, M. "Maṣlaḥa." *The Encyclopaedia of Islam*. New ed., VI (1991), 739.

Krawietz, B. "Cut and Paste in Legal Rules: Designing Islamic Norms with Talfīq." *Die Welt des Islams* I 42,1 (2002), 3–40.

Layish, A. "The Contribution of the Modernists to the Secularization of Islamic Law." *Middle Eastern Studies* 14 (1978), 263–277.

Layish, A. "The Fatwa as an Instrument of Accommodation." In Masud, Messick & Powers, *Islamic Legal Interpretation*, 270–77.

Layish, A. "Mīrāth. 2. In the Modern Islamic Countries." *The Encyclopaedia of Islam*. New ed., VII (1993), 111–113.

Layish, A. "The *Qāḍī*'s Role in the Islamization of Sedentary Tribal Society." In M. Hoexter, S.N. Eisenstadt and N. Levtzion (eds.), *The Public Sphere in Muslim Societies*. New York 2002, 83–107.

Layish, A. "Reformist Matrimonial Legislation and the Collapse of the Muslim Patrilineal Family." *Awrāq* 2003, 57–80.

Layish, A. "Saudi Arabian Legal Reform as a Mechanism to Moderate Wahhābī Doctrine." *Journal of the American Oriental Society* 107 (1987), 279–292.

Layish, A. "Ṭalāḳ, II. Reforms in the Modern Middle East and North Africa." *The Encyclopaedia of Islam*. New ed., IX (1998), 155–157.

Layish, A. "Talfīḳ. 2. In Modern Islamic Legislation." *The Encyclopaedia of Islam*. New ed., X (1998), 161.

Layish, A. "Waḳf, Section 5: In the Modern Middle East and North Africa," *The Encyclopaedia of Islam*. New ed., vol. XI (2000), 78–81.

Layish, A. and R. Shaham, "*Nikāḥ*. II. In the Modern Islamic World. 1. The Arabs, Persian and Turkish Lands of the Middle East." *The Encyclopaedia of Islam*. New ed., VIII (1995), 29–32.

Layish, A. and R. Shaham, "*Tashrīʿ*." *The Encyclopaedia of Islam*. New ed., X (1999), 353–354.

Layish, A. and Warburg, G.R. *The Reinstatement of Islamic Law in Sudan under Numayrī. An Evaluation of a Legal Experiment in the Light of Its Historical Context, Methodology, and Repercussions*. Leiden 2002.

Libson, G. "On the Development of Custom as a Source of Law in Islamic Law: *al-rujūʿu ilā al-ʿurfi aḥadu al-qawāʾidi al-khamsi allatī yatabannā ʿalayhā al-fiqhu*." *Islamic Law and Society* 4 (1997), 131–155.

Lombardi, C.B. "Islamic Law as a Source of Constitutional Law in Egypt: The Constitutionalization of the Sharia in a Modern Arab State." *Columbia Journal of Transnational Law* 37 (1998), 81–123.

Masud, M.K., B. Messick & D.S. Powers (eds.), *Islamic Legal Interpretation. Muftis and their Fatwas*. Cambridge/Mass. and London 1996.

Mayer, A.E. "Outlining Comments for Panel: 'The Transformation of Islamic Law from Jurists' to Statute Law and Its Repercussions.'" *The Joseph Schacht Conference on Theory and Practice in Islamic Law*, Leiden & Amsterdam 1994.

Mayer, A.E. "The Sharīʿa: A Methodology or a Body of Substantive Rules?." In N. Heer (ed.), *Islamic Law and Jurisprudence: Studies in Honor of Farhat J. Ziadeh*. Seattle and London 1990, 175–198.

Mehdi, R. *The Islamization of the Law in Pakistan*. Surrey 1994.

Meron, Y. "The Development of Legal Thought in Ḥanafī Texts." *Studia Islamica* 30 (1969), 73–118.

Moors, A. Theme Issue: "Public Debates on Family Law Reform: Participants, Positions, and Styles of Argumentation in the 1990s." In A. Moors (Guest ed.). *Islamic Law and Society* 10, no. 1 (2003).

An-Naʿim, A.A. "Shariʿa and Positive Legislation: Is an Islamic State Possible or Viable?" In *Intellectual Property Laws of the Arab Countries*, ed. Abu-Ghazaleh Intellectual Property (TMP Agents). The Hague, London, New York 2000, 29–41.

Naveh, E. "Application of the *Sharīʿa* in Civil Courts in the Twentieth Century: A Comparative Study Based on Decisions of Civil Courts in Matters of Personal Status and *Waqf* of Muslims in a Muslim State (Egypt) and in a Non-Muslim State (Israel)." Ph.D. thesis, the Hebrew University. Jerusalem 1997 (in Hebrew with English summary).

Naveh, E. "The Tort of Injury and the Dissolution of Marriage at the Wife's Initiative in Egyptian *Maḥkamat al-Naqd*." *Islamic Law and Society* 9 (2002), 16–41.

Paret, R. "Innerislamischer Pluralismus." In U. Haarmann and P. Bachman (eds.), *Die Islamische Welt zwischen Mittelalter und Neuzeit. Festschrift für Hans Robert Roemer zum 65 Geburtstag*. Beirut: Beiruter Texte und Studien 1979, 523–529.

Peters, R. "Divine Law or Man-Made Law? Egypt and the Application of the shariʿa." *Arab Law Quarterly* (1988), 231–253.

Peters, R. "*Idjtihād* and *Taqlīd* in 18th and 19th Century Islam." *Die Welt des Islams* 30 (1980), 131–145.

Peters, R. "The Islamization of Criminal Law: A Comparative Analysis." *Die Welt des Islams* 34 (1994), 246–274.

Riḍā, M.R. "Madaniyyat al-qawānīn (wa-saʿy al-mutafarnijīn li-nabdh baqiy-yat al-sharīʿa wa-hadm al-dīn)." *al-Manār* 23 (1922), 539–548.

El-Sanhoury, A. "Le droit musulman comme élément de refonte du Code civil égyptien." In *Introduction à l'étude du droit comparé. Recueil d'études en l'honneur d'Édouard Lambert*, tome II, III^ème^ partie, Paris 1938, 621–642.

Schacht, J. *An Introduction to Islamic Law*. Oxford 1964.

Shaham, R. "An Egyptian Judge in a Period of Change: Qāḍī Aḥmad Muḥammad Shākir (1892–1958)." *Journal of the American Oriental Society* 119 (1999), 440–455.

Shaham, R. *Family and the Courts in Modern Egypt. A Study Based on Decisions by the Sharīʿa Courts, 1900–1955*. Leiden 1997.

Shalakany, A. "Between Identity and Redistribution: Sanhuri, Genealogy and the Will to Islamise." *Islamic Law and Society* 8 (2001), 201–244.

Thielmann, J. *Nasr Hamid Abu Zaid und die wiedererfundene hisba. Shariʿa und Qanun im heutigen Ägypten*. Würzburg 2003.

Vogel, F.E. *Islamic Law and Legal System: Studies of Saudi Arabia*. Leiden 2000.

Vogel, F.E. "Siyāsa. 3. In the Sense of *Siyāsa Sharʿiyya*." *The Encyclopaedia of Islam*. New ed., IX (1997), 694–696.

Zysow, A. "The Economy of Certainty: An Introduction to the Typology of Islamic Legal Theory." Ph.D. thesis. Harvard University. Cambridge Mass. 1984. U.M.I. Dissertation Services, 1995

Zysow, A. "Zakāt." *The Encyclopaedia of Islam*. New ed., XI (2001), 406–422.

CHAPTER 12

# Islamic Law in the Modern World: Nationalization, Islamization, Reinstatement

The purpose of this essay is to provide a general account of some of the main changes in Islamic law in the Middle East since the late 19th century, with special attention to its position in the state legal system.* The main issues discussed are the transformation of the *sharīʿa* from a jurists' law to a statutory law and the displacement of the *ʿulamāʾ* as the exclusive interpreters of the *sharīʿa*, to the point that they have lost control of *sharʿī* discourse; and the secularization and nationalization of Islamic law through the judicial practice of the Supreme Constitutional Court and the civil courts applying *sharʿī* personal law in Egypt. Other issues discussed include the impact of the West on Islamic law, the abolition of the *sharīʿa* in Turkey and its reduction to the status of custom, the collapse of traditional family law and the institution of *waqf*, the Islamization of customary law in tribal societies, and the application of the *sharīʿa* in a non-Muslim state (Israel). In the conclusion, I assess the chances of reinstating the *sharīʿa* as a jurists' law and Islamizing the statutory legal corpus, based on the experience of Iran, the Sudan, and Egypt (since the 2011 Arab Spring). The issues discussed reflect three different alternatives regarding the source of authority and the position of Islamic law in the state legal system: (1) secularization and nationalization of Islamic law; (2) Islamization of statutory law; and (3) reinstatement of Islamic law as a jurists' law.

Throughout the essay, I make occasional references to Jewish law – a jurists' law of a transcendental nature that experienced "closure of the door of law" – its integration in the Israeli legal system, its nationalization and the prospects

* The essay is based on a paper presented at the International Workshop on "Islamic Law Facing the Challenges of the 21st Century" held at the Van Leer Jerusalem Institute on 19–21 October 2009. I am grateful to friends and colleagues for their comments and suggestions on earlier drafts of this essay: Giora Eliraz, Miriam Hoexter, Adam Hofri-Winogradow, Nimrod Hurvits, Ze'ev Maghen, Roni Shaham, Nurit Tsafrir and Aron Zysow. Thanks also to the two anonymous reviewers for their useful comments and suggestions, to David Powers for his editorial assistance and much more, and to Daniel Lev for his technical assistance. I alone am responsible for the views expressed in this essay.

[Originally published in *Islamic Law and Society*, 21/3 (2014), pp. 276–307.]

 | DOI:10.1163/9789004680920_014

for its reinstatement, in an effort to provide better insight into the status of the *sharīʿa* in modern times.[1]

## 1 The Impact of the West

Since the late 19th century, Islamic law has experienced dramatic changes, many of them no doubt caused by the impact of the West. These changes have been so profound that Wael Hallaq, one of the most prominent and influential scholars of Islamic law in our generation, concludes categorically that "traditional *sharīʿa* can surely be said to have gone without return."[2] Apparently, Hallaq rules out the possibility of restoration of Islamic law as a jurists' law. Indeed, the legal impact of the West has been so great that Muslims call it "legal colonialism" (*istiʿmār qānūnī*).[3] Of course, other, internal factors have also affected Islamic law in modern times, although the Western impact has been the strongest incentive for change. For instance, Saudi Arabia, which emerged from the Wahhābiyya, a puritan revivalist movement in the late 18th century, never experienced colonial rule; the Wahhābī movement regards the first century of Islam as a model to be imitated. Yet even the Saudi Arabian effort to adapt Islamic law to modern conditions has been influenced to a very large extent by its increasing contacts with the West.[4]

Broadly speaking, the profound impact of Western law on the Muslim world persisted even after the physical withdrawal of the Western powers. This applies to Anglo-Muhammadan Law, *droit musulman algèrien*[5] and Dutch colonial law,[6] following the withdrawal of Britain, France and the Netherlands from their respective colonies. The indirect impact of the West may be observed on the level of ideology in such matters as constitutional movements, secular nationalism, separation of powers, natural justice, equality before the law and legal precedent. Its direct legal impact can be detected in the Capitulations and the mixed courts; the importation of Western codes (modified to accommodate indigenous conditions) and methods of codification. Other manifestations of direct legal impact include the establishment, alongside the

1 On Jewish law, see Englard.
2 Hallaq 2004, 42; cf. Shaham, 190–1.
3 E.g., Shalabī, 3, 183.
4 Layish 1987, 292 col. 2.
5 On the first two legal systems, see Hallaq 2009, 377–9, 432–8; Schacht, 94–9; Coulson 1964, 171–2.
6 Hallaq 2009, 493–6; Hooker, 270–3.

government, of a legislature and a judiciary modeled on Western patterns – such as a hierarchal appellate system, the collegial composition of the court, and the constitutional court.[7] The desire – not yet fully satisfied – to eliminate Western influence plays a considerable role in the policy of nationalization of the law in independent Arab states. A Western-inspired legal system continues to function in some Arab countries.[8]

## 2 Abolition of the *Sharīʿa* in Turkey

The "Young Ottoman" constitutional movement and the ideological struggle between the Westernist, Islamist and Turkish schools of thought of the "Young Turk" movement in the 19th century – both under the impact of the West – prepared the ground for the complete abolition of *sharīʿa*.[9] In 1928, secularism was established as a fundamental principle in the Constitution of the new republic. The *sharīʿa* and *sharīʿa* courts were abolished altogether, and radical reforms were introduced in the political system, *waqf*, language and education. The goal of these reforms was to replace the Islamic cultural heritage, of which the *sharīʿa* constitutes a central component, with Western civilization. In 1926 the Swiss Civil Code was adopted and applied in matters of personal status, and in 2001 the principle of equality between spouses was introduced in Article 41 of the Constitution.[10]

Kemalism succeeded in removing Islam from the political establishment but failed to transform Islam into a personal belief system. It seems that not all Turks have internalized the secular revolution. Social norms and practices usually lag behind legal reforms imposed from above. Thus many Turks in both rural and urban areas continue to marry (including polygamous unions) in accordance with the *sharīʿa*, and the government has been compelled over time to legitimize millions of children born of marriages performed according to the *sharīʿa*.[11] In other words, the *sharīʿa* has been reduced to the status of custom.[12] Until recently, the status of *sharīʿa* in Turkey was strongly affected by the country's European orientation and by the army's position as guardian of the secular constitution. The referendum of 12 September 2010 endorsed the government's proposal to amend the Turkish constitution in an effort to

7 Cf. Anderson, 34–8, 86–100; Coulson 1964, 149ff.; Layish 1991b.
8 Cf. Layish & Warburg, 78, 281.
9 Berkes, 201–18, and 337–46, respectively.
10 Yilmaz, 118ff.; Koçak, 263.
11 Dirks, 34ff., 77–8; Hallaq 2009, 498; Yilmaz, 121–7; Koçak, 263.
12 Cf. Peters 2003, 91.

achieve two goals: (1) to prevent the army from interfering in politics; and (2) to strengthen Parliament's control of the Supreme Court. This amendment was intended to enable the government to continue with its Islamist policy and, paradoxically, to increase Turkey's chances of admission to the European Union.[13] In fact, by replacing the old military command with a new one, the government severely limited the army's ability to interfere in politics, thereby reducing the Kemalist secular legacy. There is evidence of increasing Islamization of the public sphere in education and religious ritual.[14] At present, the main debate in Turkey is about the expansion of freedom of religion in the public sphere.[15] It is likely, however, that the more Turkey moves away from Europe, the more concessions will be granted to the *sharīʿa*.

## 3 The Transformation of the *Sharīʿa* from a Jurists' Law to a Statutory Law

The secularization of some Muslim states in the 20th century caused the *sharīʿa* to lose its most salient features as a jurists' law. Parliaments employ a variety of methods to introduce legal reforms. These include procedural and criminal legislation that does not affect *sharʿī* substantive law; the eclectic expedient (*takhayyur*, selection, or *talfīq*, combining elements from various sources), according to which all schools of law are treated as one common source; and reinterpretation of the textual sources on the basis of utilitarian principles such as "public interest" (*maṣlaḥa*) and "necessity" (*ḍarūra*).[16] By using these methods, parliaments seek to create the impression that the state is renewing the *sharīʿa* from within without changing its traditional features. However, the application of these methods through state codification comes at a very high price: it has resulted in the transformation of the *sharīʿa* from a jurists' law to a statutory law.[17] Although the actual substance of the codes is based on the *sharīʿa*, the statutory provisions have an autonomous existence that is based on state-imposed sanctions and – if applied in national or state courts – is subject to civil rules of evidence, procedure and interpretation.[18]

13 *Haaretz*, 13 September 2010.
14 Taşpınar; Atlas.
15 Koçak, 247, 267–8.
16 Hallaq 2009, 447–9; Lombardi, 81ff.; Anderson, 42–82; Layish 1978, 263–77; Layish 2004, 90–1.
17 Peters 2003, 88ff.
18 Cf. Hallaq 2009, 449.

Codification has contributed to the nationalization of the *sharīʿa*. Statutes are valid only within the framework of individual national-territorial states. Codification results in a complete departure from the *fiqh*, unless there is a provision to the effect that the doctrine of a specific *madhhab* may be invoked in the event of a gap in a statutory provision (see below). Over time, codification inevitably disrupts the *sharʿī* legal methodology (*uṣūl al-fiqh*) and positive law (*furūʿ*), as consolidated in each of the schools.

Another result of codification is the decline of religio-ethical sanctions as a method for shaping legal norms. A religio-ethical commandment with a sanction in the next world is irrelevant in a statute; it has no legal consequence unless it has been incorporated in criminal legislation.[19] In fact, sections of the *sharīʿa* that have undergone codification have become the domain of the secular professional lawyer rather than that of the traditional religious scholar.[20]

## 4 Dispossessing the *ʿUlamāʾ* of their Historic Role as Interpreters of the *Sharīʿa*

As a result of codification, religious scholars have lost their historic role as the authorized interpreters and exponents of the *sharīʿa* as well as their exclusive monopoly on the formulation of the law. The decline of the *ʿulamāʾ* has been accelerated by the nationalization of *waqf* properties that sustained their religious, political, economic and social status, as well as by the emergence of a new secular class of lawyers.[21]

As a result of the decline of the *ʿulamāʾ*'s interpretive authority, the domain of *sharʿī* interpretation has become widely accessible to individuals with no formal *sharʿī* education. *Fiqh* academies have emerged in the Middle East, and, recently, in Europe and the United States. In these academies, conservative jurists and modernist reformers attempt to create a new type of legal authority to promote their agendas. The resulting juristic discourse has contributed to a new globalism in Islamic law.[22] From the traditional *sharʿī* perspective, laymen may not participate in *sharʿī* discourse. In many Muslim countries, however, the *sharʿī* establishment seems to have lost control of *sharʿī* discourse.[23] Of course, the participation of laymen in *sharʿī* discourse should be viewed as a

19 Layish & Warburg, 220ff.; Layish 1978, 264.
20 Cf. Coulson 1969, 100.
21 Peters 2003, 93; Hallaq 2009, 500, 547; Cardinal; Baer, 91–2.
22 Cf. Ukeles.
23 Cf. Peters 2003, 91, 93–5; Hallaq 2004, 22; Layish 2013, 531; Vikør, 256–7, 261–2.

very important social and cultural development; such a discourse may promote the equality of women by exerting pressure on parliaments to initiate liberal progressive legislation in the domain of family law. However, the modern interpretation of the *sharīʿa* by laymen affects neither Islamic positive law nor its legal methodology.

## 5 Collapse of Traditional Muslim Family Law

The attempt to improve the status of women by means of the codification of family law has contributed to the conceptual collapse of traditional Muslim family law. The prohibition or abolition of polygamy and the curtailment of a husband's freedom of unilateral divorce, e.g., by transforming divorce into judicial dissolution, has undermined the patriarchal structure of Muslim family law. In 1963, Iraq introduced the Shīʿī system of order of priorities in succession, based on relationship (*qarāba*) with the deceased, according to which any lineal descendant – regardless of agnatic or cognatic affiliation – totally excludes all collaterals. The goal of the reform was to strengthen the rights of heirs within the nuclear family at the expense of heirs in the extended (or "outer") family.[24] This reform, together with the obligatory bequest in favor of orphaned grandchildren – which is inconsistent with the Islamic rule of degree[25] – was introduced in several countries, and has undermined the patrilineal pattern of Muslim family law. Due to the sporadic nature of reformist legislation, which is clearly inspired by Western norms, the traditional balance in Muslim family law between the rights and duties of spouses has been altered without achieving a new balance suited to the conditions of modern society.[26]

## 6 Privatization and Nationalization of the *Waqf*

The *waqf* or religious endowment, one of the most important institutions of traditional Muslim society, has undergone radical changes since the 19th century. Traditionally, the family (*dhurrī* or *ahlī*) *waqf* was a means to prevent the fragmentation of the agnatic patrimony through inheritance; and the

24 Coulson 1971, 108–10, 141–2.

25 Among relatives of the same class (*ṭabaqa*), the nearer in degree to the deceased excludes the more remote; thus any surviving son excludes the orphaned grandchildren of any other son who predeceased the grandfather (Coulson 1971, 33–4).

26 Layish, 2000a; cf. Hallaq, 2009, 450–71.

charitable (*khayrī*) *waqf* was the main vehicle for the provision of public services such as social welfare and religious education by the ruling elite (sultans and local governors). Broadly speaking, in the absence of state regulation in this domain (beyond care for the poor by means of the *zakāt* system), it was the elite who established *waqf*s, using their own private property to this end. The reforms sought to restore full ownership of endowed property to the private and public economic spheres.[27] The family *waqf* was abolished in Syria, Egypt and Libya. In Egypt, agricultural lands that had been endowed for charitable purposes were nationalized and allocated to the peasants within the framework of agrarian reform.[28]

## 7 The Islamization of Custom

Custom (*ʿāda, ʿurf*) has made an important contribution to the development of Islamic law, both as a source that provides legal norms for Islamic positive law and as an independent material source (*aṣl*) for creating legal norms. Although Muslim jurists never formally recognized custom as a source of law, it approximated this status in the Ḥanafī school.[29] By invoking the idea of necessity (*ḍarūra*), the Ḥanafī jurist Ibn ʿĀbidīn (d. 1836) elevated both universal and local custom to the status of a legal source. In this way he prepared the ground for the recognition of custom as a source of law in the Mecelle (1876), which, though based on Ḥanafī doctrine, is a product of statutory codification.[30]

Bedouin customary law has been very strong not only in tribal societies but also among peasants.[31] The earliest *qāḍī*s in the Umayyad administration filled local practices and customs with Islamic religious and ethical norms[32] (for example, collective accountability of the blood-money group, *ʿāqila*, for homicide was replaced with individual accountability of the perpetrator). The Islamization of tribal customary law has continued in modern times. It is most pronounced in the domains of private property, marriage and family, but also in inheritance, contracts and obligations, homicide, and bodily harm. The main agents of Islamization are the *qāḍī*, the marriage solemnizer (*maʾdhūn*), the *muftī*, and the civil court that applies the Mecelle (or a civil code based on

---

27 All schools of law (with the exception of the Mālikīs) hold that an endowment is inalienable in perpetuity; see Peters 2000, 67.

28 Layish 2000b; Hallaq 2009, 471–3.

29 Libson, 887b.

30 Hallāq 2002, 53, 55, 61.

31 Cf. Stewart 2000; Stewart 2012.

32 Schacht, 27.

the Mecelle). Tribal customary law is yielding ground to Islamic law on *its own territory*, i.e., in the domain of the tribal *qāḍī* (*ḥakam, muḥakkam*). However, the Islamization of tribal custom has not left a mark on either Islamic law or its methodology; its only result has been the emergence, in the tribal judiciary, of a hybrid version of a realistic, pragmatic Islamic-customary law, outside the control of the *ʿulamāʾ*. This development, in turn, has been instrumental in bringing the Bedouin within the orbit of conventional Islam.[33]

## 8 Modernists and New Legal Methodologies

Classical legal methodology (*uṣūl al-fiqh*) has survived almost intact into modern times. Since the late 19th century, the *ʿulamāʾ* increasingly have worked to update legal methodology so that Islamic law might be adapted to contemporary conditions. There have been sporadic attempts to create new legal methodologies. Hallaq classifies these legal methodologies into two major categories: religious utilitarianism and religious liberalism. This division is based on content analysis, regardless of the religious or secular background of the promoter of the methodology: Religious utilitarians use the doctrine of *maṣlaḥa* or "public interest" as the main instrument for reform, while religious liberals interpret textual sources in the light of changing circumstances.[34]

The Western-oriented Modernist movement, headed by Muḥammad ʿAbduh (d. 1905), is perhaps the most important attempt to date to reshape the *sharīʿa* from within and to adapt it to changing conditions. Muḥammad Rashīd Riḍā (d. 1935), a scholar of Syrian origin and ʿAbduh's disciple, assumed that this goal could be achieved by applying the doctrine of *al-maṣāliḥ al-mursala*, lit. "benefits that are set free, independent", in the sense that they are not addressed in the Qurʾān or *sunna*. According to this doctrine, in the absence of rulings in the Qurʾān or *sunna* for adapting the *sharīʿa* to modern conditions, new rules may be derived by means of analogical reasoning (*qiyās*) that takes into account public interest considerations. To this end it is necessary to extend the criterion of unattested suitability (*munāsaba mursala*), a method that identifies the "efficient cause" (*ʿilla, ratio legis*) on the basis of an unambiguous argument. In other words, it is necessary to identify in the textual sources the attribute that is common to both the new case and the original case.[35] The doctrines of

33 Layish & Shmueli; Layish 1991a; Layish 2002; Layish 2005; Layish 2008b; Layish 2011; cf. al-Atawneh 2009, 221ff.

34 Hallaq 1997, ch. 6.

35 Hallaq 1997, 83–4, 88–9,112; cf. Opwis 2005, 210–11. For further discussion, see below.

"necessity" (*ḍarūra*) and "ease" or "leniency" (*yusr*) also play an important role. The Modernists failed, but they contributed, albeit unintentionally, to the disintegration of traditional legal theory, on the one hand, and to the preparation of the ground for statutory codification of the *sharīʿa*, on the other.[36]

## 9 Article 2 of the Egyptian Constitution and a Theory of Islamic Law

Is the attempt by the Egyptian Supreme Constitutional Court [SCC] to "Islamize" statutory law a unique phenomenon in Islamic contemporary legal history? Lombardi argues that Article 2 of the 1971 Constitution was adopted in an attempt to forge "an official theory of Islamic law" that would bolster the government's legitimacy in the face of Islamist opposition. The Article provides, *inter alia*, that "the principles of *sharīʿa* shall be *a* [*the*, according to the 1980 Constitution] chief source of legislation (*maṣdar raʾīsī li'l-tashrīʿ*)." The goal of this article is to ensure that statutory legislation is compatible with *sharʿī* norms. Article 2 does not establish any criteria for identifying and implementing *sharʿī* norms,[37] thus creating legal uncertainty when the validity of a statutory provision is challenged on the ground of incompatibility with non-codified *sharīʿa*.[38]

Referring to SCC judicial practice,[39] Lombardi argues that the Court has developed a new liberal theory of Islamic law that combines the vocabulary and concepts of classical and modernist doctrines. According to this theory, the legislature and the SCC are required to identify both "universal roots" (*al-uṣūl al-kulliyya*), the authenticity and meaning of which are definitive and may never be violated, and "general goals (*al-maqāṣid al-ʿāmma*) of the *sharīʿa*," that is, public interest and necessities, such as the protection of religion, life, reason, progeny and property, support for which may be found in the *ḥadīth*. *Ijtihād* is permitted only in cases in which the authenticity and meaning of the "universal roots" are presumptive (*ẓaniyya*). The SCC is authorized to review the Parliament's legislation in light of the aforementioned principles. Lombardi concludes that SCC interpretation of the *sharīʿa* has reinforced liberal constitutional doctrine, particularly in the area of women's rights; moreover, it has

36 Kerr, 67ff., ch. 6, esp. 195ff.; Layish 1978; Hallaq 2009, 501–8; Opwis 2005, 220–2; Lombardi, 73–6; cf. Peters 1988, 231; Vikør, 58–60, 67–9.
37 Lombardi, 123–5, 129, 135; cf. Hallaq 2009, 479–80; Peters 2003, 91.
38 Cf. Peters 1988, 236.
39 Lombardi, Ch. 11, 200ff.; cf. Bälz, 231–73; Dupret, 136–43; Peters 1988, 240ff.

succeeded in shaping an official legal methodology applied by liberal justices who are "committed to democracy and human rights."[40]

Both the SCC and the Supreme Administrative Court [SAC] interpret the "principles of the *sharīʿa*" restrictively: rules explicitly derived from textual sources cannot be subjected to new interpretation; other rules may be subjected to new interpretation, provided the result is consistent with the goals of the *sharīʿa*. The SCC ruled that consistency with the *sharīʿa* should not apply retroactively to laws promulgated prior to 1980. To date, only family law has been "Islamized" by means of codification of the *sharīʿa*; in other domains, the law is regarded as "Islamic" by virtue of a statement that it is "not contradictory to *sharīʿa* principles."[41]

The SCC's public policy is based on a purely secular doctrine.[42] The judges assume that their application of Article 2 is in conformity with Egyptian constitutional law. The judges are trained in civil and constitutional law and, for the most part, have no formal education in *fiqh*. The SCC issued a decision specifying that any civil judge presiding in a national court may derive general principles from *sharʿī* sources.[43] Apparently, even a judge who is not trained in the *sharīʿa* may interpret the *sharīʿa*. From the traditional *sharʿī* point of view, a layman may not interpret the *sharīʿa*.

The Islamization of statutory legislation by means of codification of the *sharīʿa* in the light of liberal constitutional principles is clearly an important landmark in Egyptian legal history; it has been very helpful in creating a national consensus and legitimacy for the Egyptian government.[44] However, this legal experiment has taken place outside the framework of the history of Islamic legal theory. Although the *ʿulamāʾ* of al-Azhar participate in the preparation of draft codes for legislation,[45] there can be no doubt that Parliament is the source of sovereignty that determines the basic legislative norms and defines the space allowed for the application of the *sharīʿa*.

---

40 Lombardi, 140–1, 174, 178–80, 184, 188–92, 195, 272, 274; cf. Shaham, 176–7.

41 Berger & Sonneveld, 52, 64, 70, 73, 84–5.

42 Lombardi, 128.

43 Ibid., 183, 188; Hallaq 2009, 480–1; cf. Peters 1988, 242; Dupret, 129ff., 136–43.

44 The 1980 Israel Law of Legal Foundations provides that in the event of a gap in a statutory provision, the judiciary must apply the "heritage of Israel" (i.e., Jewish law), alongside universal principles such as freedom and justice. This provision is intended to satisfy the religious parties. The insertion of *halakhic* doctrines (*ḥaqiqa datit*, literally, "religious legislation") into Knesset legislation is fairly common; Jewish law, however, has undergone no statutory codification. In Orthodox religious discourse, the integration of Jewish elements into statutory legislation is mostly regarded as a distortion of Jewish law.

45 Lombardi, 135; cf. Shaham, 182–4.

## 10 Nationalization of *Sharʿī* Personal Law through Civil Judicial Practice

Another important landmark in modern legal history was the application of family law in civil courts following the abolition of the *sharīʿa* courts in Egypt, Tunisia, Libya, and Sudan. In Egypt, the *sharīʿa* courts (as well as Christian and Jewish religious courts) were abolished in 1955; their jurisdiction in matters of personal status (and *waqf*) was transferred to national civil courts, operating under the supervision of the Court of Cassation. Some *qāḍīs* were integrated into the national civil courts, mainly in lower instances. The civil courts now apply codified *sharʿī* personal law in accordance with civil rules of evidence, procedure, and interpretation. If there is a gap in a statutory provision, the civil judges, most of whom have no *sharʿī* education, base their decisions on the prevailing Ḥanafī doctrine. The judicial practice of the Court of Cassation in matters pertaining to *sharʿī* doctrines provides neither legal reasoning nor reference to decisions of the *sharīʿa* courts or *fiqh* doctrine. Doctrines of schools other than the Ḥanafī are not mentioned, unless these doctrines have been incorporated in a statutory code.[46]

The application of *sharʿī* personal status law, whether codified or uncodified, by civil courts is an important development in Egyptian legal history that has contributed to the nationalization of the *sharīʿa*. Civil adjudication takes place under the supervision of the SCC and outside the control of the *ʿulamāʾ*. Hence it should be evaluated in an extra-*sharʿī* context.

## 11 Reinstatement of the *Sharīʿa*

Beginning in the last quarter of the 20th century the *sharīʿa*, particularly criminal law, has been reinstated in several Muslim countries. In the early 1970s Libya was the first country to introduce Qurʾānic punishments (*ḥudūd*) for usury and for the consumption and/or sale of wine.[47] In what follows, we will consider two different models of reinstatement.

The example of the Islamic Republic of Iran is unique.[48] The 1979 Constitution combines democratic and theocratic principles and institutions. The freely elected Parliament and presidency are subordinate to the clerical establishment. The clergy, as the official interpreters of the Constitution and

46 Naveh 1997, 374, 384–8, 398; Naveh 2002, 16–21.

47 Layish 1991a, 10–12, and the references to Ann Mayer's articles.

48 Unless otherwise indicated, this section is based on Hallaq 2009a, 486–93.

the *sharīʿa*, have had a broad mandate to manage state affairs, especially after Khomeini's death.[49]

Khomeini's interpretation of the concept of the "Guardian Jurist" (*vali-ye faqih*) is the theoretical foundation of governance in the Islamic Republic. As the representative of the "hidden Imām," the Guardian Jurist is the "Chief Jurist" (*marjaʿ-i taqlid*, literally, the "source of imitation"), who functions as both the political and the religious ruler. He is the ultimate legal expert in charge of *ijtihād* and his legal opinions are binding.[50] Article 2 of the Constitution vests sovereignty in God alone and declares that divine revelation or God's justice is *the* source of legislation. The Parliament operates under the strict supervision of a statutory body of authorized interpreters of the *sharīʿa*. The validity of legislative acts is subject to approval by the Council of Guardians, which is composed of twelve jurists, six of whom are appointed by the Supreme Leader, the highest Shīʿī authority in the country (he is appointed by the Assembly of Experts), while the other six are laymen nominated by the head of the judiciary and approved by Parliament.[51] The Council may veto a statute on the grounds of incompatibility with the Constitution or the *sharīʿa*, in which case the statute returns, though not automatically, to the Expediency Discernment Council, an administrative assembly that, since 1988, has served as an advisory body to the Supreme Leader. If there is a gap in a legislative provision, the judge's decisions must conform to the *fatwā*s of learned jurists (Art. 167 of the Constitution). There is evidence that legal treatises and opinions issued by Khomeini and his disciples, jurists such as Hussein-Ali Montazeri, Seyyed Mohammad Hosseini Beheshti, and Morteza Motahhari, have led to changes in Shīʿī public law. These jurists used *maṣlaḥa* as the main instrument for reforms.[52]

Statutes promulgated before 1979 that were not in conformity with the *sharīʿa*, such as the Family Protection Law of 1967, were rescinded. However, for pragmatic reasons, most of the existing legal corpus has survived intact. On the other hand, statutes restoring *sharʿī* legal norms have been enacted. For example, usury was prohibited and Qur'ānic punishments (*ḥudūd*) and discretionary punishments (*taʿzīr*) were reinstated.[53]

---

49 Mir-Hosseini, 332–4, 364; Otto, 629.

50 In 1989, the constitution was amended so that the Guardian Jurist would no longer be the Chief Jurist, nor would he be the only individual tasked with exercising *ijtihād*. I am grateful to Ze'ev Maghen for this clarification.

51 Mir-Hosseini, 333.

52 I am grateful to Ze'ev Maghen for this information. Cf. Hallaq 2009a, 489, 492.

53 Cf. Vikør, 269–73.

To sum up, Islamization of the law in Iran has two dimensions: statutory codification of the *sharīʿa* under the control of the *ʿulamāʾ*, who enjoy veto power, and, to a lesser extent, renovation of the *sharīʿa* by independent jurists. This combination makes the Iranian model unique in the Muslim world; at present such a combination is not found in any Middle Eastern country.

A second model for reinstating the *sharīʿa* is found in the Sudan. This model is based on Ḥasan al-Turābī's legal methodology, which synthesizes classical legal theory and Western-inspired legal principles. The *sharīʿa* has been reinstated through statutory codification, based mainly on the eclectic device (*takhayyur*). If there is a gap in an Islamic statute or in the Qurʾān or *sunna*, the Sudanese Judgments (Basic Rules) Act, 1983 authorizes the civil judge (*sharīʿa* courts have been abolished) to exercise *ijtihād* on the basis of legal sources and principles, in the following order: consensus, analogical reasoning, public interest, judicial precedents (*sawābiq al-ʿamal al-qaḍāʾī*) in the Sudanese national courts, custom, and the English principles of natural justice (based upon moral rather than legal considerations or sanctions) and 'justice, equity and good conscience.'[54]

During Numayrī's reign (1969–85), most judges in the civil courts interpreted statutory provisions of Islamic codes in a manner consistent with the *sharīʿa*. Moreover, they consulted the Qurʾān and the *sunna* in cases in which explicit statutory provisions dealing with the case under review were available. The Sudanese version of judicial *ijtihād*, based on a mixture of Islamic and Western legal sources and principles, was reduced to judicial discretion. The doctrine of public interest was elevated, in practice, albeit not formally, to an independent source of law. Especially in lower instances, judges associated with the Muslim Brotherhood expedited the process of "Islamization" of the subject matter and public morality. The Supreme Court was attentive to the judicial practice of Western countries.[55]

## 12 Application of the *Sharīʿa* in a non-Muslim Territory

Applying the *sharīʿa* in a non-Muslim territory involves ethical and legal hardship because of the traditional dichotomy between "Abode of Islam" and "Abode of War."[56] Following the collapse of the Ottoman Empire and

---

54 Layish & Warburg, 76–7, 79ff. 199, n. 166 (definitions of the legal terms); Layish 2013, 518ff.

55 Layish & Warburg, 263–74.

56 Cf. Abou El Fadl 1994.

the establishment of the British Mandate, Palestine ceased to be part of a Muslim territory.

Israel is a unique instance of the application of the *sharīʿa* in a non-Muslim territory.[57] The Knesset (Parliament) has attempted to replace both the Ottoman-Muslim and the English legal heritage with legislation that is inspired not only by universal liberal, humanistic and democratic values, but also by Jewish law.[58] Until 2001, the Ottoman *millet* system remained virtually intact in domains pertaining to communal organization and the judiciary. Thus *sharīʿa* courts retained exclusive jurisdiction in virtually all matters of personal status (excluding succession) and *waqf*, while Rabbinical and Christian courts enjoyed exclusive jurisdiction only in matters of marriage and divorce. Since 2001 the civil family courts have had the same jurisdictional authority as that of the *sharīʿa* courts, except in matters relating to marriage and divorce, which have been left within the latter's exclusive jurisdiction.[59] The 1917 Ottoman Family Rights Law, based mainly on Ḥanafī doctrine, is still applicable. The Knesset has intervened, through substantive legislation, in matters such as custody, guardianship, property relations between the spouses, and maintenance for relatives other than the spouse and minor children. However, in matters pertaining to *sharʿī* permission for, or prohibition of, marriage and divorce, the Knesset has used criminal sanctions that do not affect *sharʿī* substantive law. The *sharʿī* judiciary has been integrated into the state judicial system and is subject to the supervision of the Supreme Court [SupC] in its capacity as the High Court of Justice [HCJ]; if a *qāḍī* ignores a statute explicitly addressed to religious courts, the HCJ is authorized to intervene.

In the absence of official *muftīs*, *qāḍīṣ* in Israel adapted the *sharīʿa* to changing conditions by holding periodic conferences (until the early 1970s) to discuss reform in judicial practice, mainly by enlisting elements from schools other than the Ḥanafī, and by handing down liberal decisions based mainly on the doctrine of public interest and by judicial decrees (*marsūm qaḍāʾī*) issued by the President of the Sharīʿa Court of Appeals [ShCApp].[60] The ShCApp has been heavily influenced by the SupC's jurisprudence. Thus it has adopted the concepts of "natural justice," "the best interest of the child" and "the right of standing in court", while attempting to Islamize these concepts by enlisting support for them in *sharīʿa*.

57 Unless otherwise indicated, this section is based on Layish 2006.

58 Layish 2008a, 129ff., 144–5.

59 Shahar, 205, 207, 211.

60 Ibid., 200–1.

The *sharīʿa* is applied in the civil courts in the light of Israeli principles of law and rules of evidence and procedure. As a result an Israeli version of Islamic law has emerged that resembles in some respects the Anglo-Muhammadan Law in British India (which existed from 1772 until 1950). The SupC has created new civil legal norms that are not consistent with Islamic law, such as "civil paternity" based on DNA testing (1995).

Until the early 1970s *qāḍīs* did not hesitate to apply Knesset legislation. Some *qāḍīs* relied on it explicitly in their decisions, adopting its legal norms even when these were not consistent with *sharʿī* norms. Thus some *qāḍīs* displayed a keen awareness of the Knesset prohibition on divorce against the wife's will or the prohibition of polygamy, and they would warn the husband not to commit a criminal offense by divorcing his wife against her will or by taking a second wife or, if he did, would alert the wife to her right to bring a criminal charge against her husband. Some *qāḍīs* welcomed Knesset penal legislation in matters of marriage and divorce, on the assumption that penal sanctions would reinforce *sharʿī* norms grounded in ethical sanctions. Moreover, some *qāḍīs* boldly called for secular legislation of a substantive nature to ensure the material support of a divorced woman, on the basis of the doctrine *siyāsa sharʿiyya*, which, under certain circumstances, acknowledges the ruler's right of legislation.[61]

Since the early 1990s, however, there has been an increasing tendency in the ShCApp to avoid applying Israeli statutes, even if explicitly addressed to religious courts, and to base the *sharīʿa* courts' decisions on Qurʾān, *sunna* and *fiqh* doctrine. This tendency is inspired by the Islamic Movement, which calls for self-governance of the Israeli Palestinians in an attempt to regulate Muslim affairs independently of the state legal system.[62]

## 13 Is There Any Possibility of Restoring the Authority of the *Sharīʿa*?

Abdullahi Ahmed An-Naʿim argues that the transformations occasioned by European colonialism are so profound and so deeply entrenched that restoration of the traditional *sharīʿa* is not a realistic option. In his view, "*Sharīʿa*

61 Layish 1975, 334–7. For further details on *siyāsa sharʿiyya*, see further below, 293. Support for the "jurisprudence of minorities" (*fiqh al-aqalliyyāt*), an ideology designed to facilitate the integration of Muslims in non-Muslim states, is found in the Qurʾān, the *ḥadīth*, and legal doctrines such as public welfare, necessity, governance in accordance with the *sharīʿa*, the goals of the *sharīʿa* and facilitation (*taysīr*) of *fiqh* (March; Abou El Fadl 2005, chs. 10–11).

62 Shahar, 210; Abou Ramadan, 84; cf. Stern 2007, 35.

principles can and should be a source of public policy and legislation, subject to the constitutional and human rights of all citizens, men and women, Muslim and non-Muslim, equally and without discrimination."[63] As noted, Hallaq categorically rejects the possibility of the reinstatement of traditional *sharīʿa*. In his view, the only relevant question today is whether it is possible to Islamize the entire body of European codes that have been adopted by Muslim countries. To this end, he argues, an alternative legal methodology is required, similar to the methodologies developed by the Egyptian jurist Muhammad Saʿīd ʿAshmāwī and the Pakistani scholar Fazlur Rahman (d. 1988).[64]

In my view, "Islamization" of Western-inspired codes is promoted for the sake of the state's internal, secular policies rather than for the sake of God or religion; the state enlists the symbolic value of the *sharīʿa* as part of the Islamic and national cultural heritage[65] to satisfy the Islamist opposition. The main problem is that Islamization is carried out by agents other than the *ʿulamāʾ*. Thus ʿAshmāwī, although well-versed in the *sharīʿa*, reflects on it from outside as a lawyer. The same holds for Fazlur Rahman, who took into account the social, economic, and political conditions of Arabia at the time of the emergence of Islam. Hence, one cannot escape the conclusion that the legal methodologies for the Islamization of the statutory legal corpus developed by ʿAshmāwī and Rahman are not relevant from the point of view of the *sharīʿa*.

It is too early, however, to conclude that the *sharīʿa* is doomed to extinction. The survival or revival of the *sharīʿa* depends on the ability of highly motivated, determined *ʿulamāʾ* to formulate a new legal methodology, to exercise *ijtihād* and to Islamize the legal corpus.[66] The issue is not only the *technique* used for exercising *ijtihād* but also, and mainly, the *source of authority and legitimacy* – God or human beings – that sanctions the use of this technique. In other words, from a traditional *sharʿī* perspective, only qualified *ʿulamāʾ*, as authorized interpreters of the will of God, are endowed with legitimacy to propose new legal methodologies; the secular legislator and the civil court are not qualified either to exercise "*ijtihād*" or "Islamize" the legal corpus, even if they enlist *sharʿī* doctrines to this end; from the *sharʿī* point of view, such legal experimentation is meaningless.[67]

---

63 An-Naʿim, 334, 337.

64 Hallaq, 2009, 522, 527; cf. Shaham, 190–1.

65 Cf. Dupret, 126ff.

66 Layish 2004, 108.

67 Prof. Izhak Englard, former Director of the Institute for Jewish Law at the Hebrew University and retired Justice of the Israeli Supreme Court, categorically dismisses the possibility of the revival of Jewish law within the state legal system (personal communication, 5 January 2010). Prof. Yedidia Stern of Bar Ilan University Law School and Vice

The ability of contemporary *ʿulamāʾ* to Islamize foreign laws is limited in comparison to that demonstrated by *ʿulamāʾ* during the formative period (between the mid-8th and late 9th centuries CE). The very existence of a well-established legal theory that has developed gradually over centuries restricts the scope of maneuver in modern times. However, there may be still enough space for contemporary *ʿulamāʾ* to demonstrate legal creativity. Whereas Muhammad ʿAbduh was part of the religious establishment, his successor as leader of a revival movement may well emerge from outside that establishment, in the best tradition of Islam. Although higher institutions for *sharʿī* studies, such as al-Azhar, have lost their monopoly over *sharʿī* learning,[68] there are still independent *ʿulamāʾ*, such as Yūsuf al-Qaraḍāwī, whose legal authority and charisma are fully accepted across the Muslim world. The possibility that someone will come forward with a coherent and comprehensive legal methodology, in an attempt to adapt the *sharīʿa* to modern conditions, cannot be ruled out.[69]

The main tools available for the revival of the *sharīʿa* as a jurists' law, and for the *ʿulamāʾ* to Islamize the statutory legal corpus, are the two related doctrines of *maṣlaha mursala* and *siyāsa sharʿiyya.*[70]

(1) Public interest (*maṣlaḥa mursala*)[71] can provide a justification for any reform needed to adapt the *sharīʿa,* in the domain of private and personal law,[72] to modern conditions, provided the reform does not explicitly contradict fundamental principles of the *sharīʿa.*[73] In the teachings of Modernists, *maṣlaḥa mursala* is vague and abstract with no criteria for its application. On the face of it, Riḍā's doctrine of *maṣlaḥa mursala,* based on natural law, which guides human conduct independently of any source of law, has been reduced to pure utilitarianism.[74] This, however, does not imply that any benefit under any circumstance is justified. For instance, *maṣlaḥa mursala* may not be applied in matters of worship and religious ritual,[75] nor may it contradict the

President of Research at the Israel Democracy Institute, suggests that a group of independent jurists who are recognized as outstanding scholars in Jewish law should adapt Jewish law to present-day conditions; he hopes that the Knesset and the state judiciary will apply the adapted Jewish law *voluntarily* (Stern 2007, 52–6).

68 Cf. Shaham, 182–3.

69 Cf. ibid., 180–1, 184.

70 Friedman, 215; cf. al-Atawneh 2001, 61.

71 For a definition, see above, [284].

72 Cf. Friedman, 218.

73 Khadduri; Opwis 2005, 197ff.; Opwis 2010, Index, s.v. legal change; cf. Layish 2013, 524–5.

74 Hallaq 1997, 214ff.; cf. Layish 1978, 270–1; Shaham, 176.

75 Hallaq 1997, 218–19.

"goals (*maqāṣid*) of the *sharīʿa*" (such as the protection of religion and life). The discretionary right to apply the doctrine is vested in the judiciary. One assumes that *qāḍīs* will define *maṣlaḥa* in positive terms or set limits to its application in accordance with *sharʿī* principles of law and in accordance with their social philosophy, which guides them in daily practice, subject to the aforementioned reservations.[76]

(2) The classical doctrine of *siyāsa sharʿiyya* (lit. "governance in accordance with the *sharīʿa*") acknowledges the ruler's right, in the event of a gap in the Qurʾān, *sunna* or *fiqh* doctrine,[77] to supplement the *sharīʿa* with his own legislation, taking into account public interest.[78] In fact, the doctrine provides *sharʿī* legitimacy for statutory legislation. Since early ʿAbbāsid times administrative justice has derived its legitimacy from this doctrine.[79] At the present time, the doctrine can be used to adapt the *sharīʿa* to changing circumstances and to Islamize the legal corpus that has accumulated since the second half of the 19th century, especially in the areas of criminal and fiscal law. Statutes that are compatible with the *sharīʿa*, or at least not explicitly repugnant to it, can be absorbed within the *sharʿī* corpus. The *sharʿī* domain of *muʿāmalāt* (pecuniary transactions), which has a technical, secular nature, can easily be reconciled with statutory legislation.

There is ample evidence to suggest that public interest and *siyāsa sharʿiyya*, alongside other doctrines and *sharʿī* mechanisms, play a substantial role in contemporary legal history. Saudi Arabia is a case in point. Article 1 of the 1992 Basic Ordinance provides that the Qurʾān and the Prophetic *sunna* are the constitution of the kingdom and that the *sharīʿa* is the basis of its legal system. The king may promulgate regulations (*niẓāms*) in the event of a gap in the *sharīʿa*. This authority, based on Ibn Taymiyya's theory of *siyāsa sharʿiyya*, is conditional upon the legislation's serving the public good and complementing, rather than contradicting, the textual sources.[80] The monarchy appears to be fully aware of the necessity to moderate Wahhābī doctrine in order to promote its political and economic relations with the West. Until recently, the *sharīʿa* in Saudi Arabia had not undergone codification. Instead, the king designated six treatises by well-known Ḥanbalī jurists as authoritative sources to be relied on

---

76 In those countries in which *sharīʿa* courts have been abolished, some kind of supervision is required to ensure that the doctrine of public welfare is properly applied in the light of the principles of the *sharīʿa*.

77 Friedman, 218ff.

78 Vogel 1997, 694ff.; cf. Schacht, 54.

79 Schacht, 54.

80 van Eijk, 140, 157–8, 172.

and to be applied in a specific order in *sharīʿa* courts.[81] The *ʿulamāʾ*, who serve in the political establishment, exercise control over the drafting of laws; they are consulted and often enjoy veto power.[82] They are expected to provide the royal family with *sharʿī* legal opinions to legitimize the adaptation of the law to modern challenges.[83]

In practice, the doctrine of public interest has been elevated to the status of a source of law.[84] Principles or legal maxims (*qawāʿid*) such as "no harm and no causing of harm" (*lā ḍarar wa-lā ḍirār*) guide *qāḍīs* in their decisions.[85] As Muhammad al-Atawneh has recently observed, the doctrines of public interest and necessity – two sides of the same coin – provide the theoretical basis for the legitimization of innovations in the fields of medicine and technology.[86]

At present, the doctrine of *siyāsa sharʿiyya*, as transmitted to Wahhābī jurists from Ibn Taymiyya and Ibn Qayyim al-Jawziyya, provides legitimacy for hundreds of royal regulations issued in the event of a gap in a textual source.[87] Article 55 of the 1992 Basic Regulation stipulates that the King shall conduct the affairs of the state by *siyāsa sharʿiyya*, in accordance with the rules of Islam.[88] This implies that *siyāsa sharʿiyya* is an independent source of law. Al-Atawneh argues that Saudi authorities use the traditional doctrine of *siyāsa sharʿiyya* as a "most important instrument for the preservation of the theocratic-legal nature, mainly the Wahhābī, of the country, simultaneously with the accommodation of the institutionalized normative system of a theocracy to the conditions of the country facing the challenges of modernity."[89]

Saudi *ʿulamāʾ* claim that the door of *ijtihād* was never closed.[90] However, innovative reforms, based on *ijtihād*, including judicial *ijtihād* by direct engagement with Qurʾān and *sunna*, have been rare.[91] It is noteworthy that already at the beginning of the 11th century, *fiqh* specialists applied *siyāsa sharʿiyya* as an alternative to *ijtihād* in an effort to adapt Islamic law, especially public law,

81 Layish, 1987, 280b; Vogel, 2000, 94; cf. Peters 2003, 87.

82 Vogel 2000, 175, 357–8. In 1992, Saudi Arabia codified its constitutional law in the Basic Ordinance; in 2001, it codified its criminal procedure law (Otto, 629).

83 Cf. Peters 2003, 90ff. Some *ʿulamāʾ* decline to issue the required legal opinions. Thus in the wake of the *qāḍīs*' tendency to ignore the King's regulations, other tribunals have been established to enforce these regulations (Vogel 2000, 175–6).

84 Vogel 2000, 343–4; Layish 1987, 285. Cf. Opwis 2005, 222.

85 Vogel 2000, 134–5.

86 Al-Atawneh 2010, 63–4, 139–40, 144; al-Atawneh 2011, 348f., 354–5.

87 Vogel 2000, 124, 173–5, 341.

88 Ibid., 295–6; Layish 1987, 284b.

89 Al-Atawneh 2001, 57.

90 Vogel 2000, 78; al-Atawneh 2010, 64ff.

91 Vogel 2000, 122–3; Layish 1987, 292; van Eijk, 161.

to the requirements of the contemporary Muslim community.[92] As Vogel has observed, for the time being, the replacement of *ijtihād* with *siyāsa sharʿiyya* is being carried out without the cooperation of the *ʿulamāʾ*; this, in turn, may result in a shift in the primary agency determining law from the *ʿulamāʾ* to the political ruler, with all that this implies.[93]

The freedom of Saudi *qāḍīs* to exercise *ijtihād* without being constrained by the doctrine of the Ḥanbalī school makes it possible for them to base their decisions on views favorable to innovative reforms derived from other schools, although this option has been applied only on a moderate scale.[94] Quite often the aforementioned doctrines and mechanisms are applied by means of collective *fatwās* issued by Saudi *ʿulamāʾ* operating on behalf of state institutions. This is a clear indication of the institutionalization of the *muftī* in modern times.[95]

There is some evidence that *maṣlaḥa* and *siyāsa sharʿiyya* are being applied in Iran. In a *fatwā* issued in 1984, Khomeini authorized the Parliament to initiate legislation on the basis of necessity and public interest. He expressed his view that the Supreme Leader, who, according to the Constitution, is the highest Shīʿī authority, may suspend prayer or pilgrimage if he deems it to be in the public interest.[96] In cases in which legislative provisions are not consistent with the *sharīʿa*, the Expediency Discernment Council seeks pragmatic solutions on the basis of public interest.[97]

## 14 The Muslim Brotherhood and the Reinstatement of the *Sharīʿa*

The Muslim Brotherhood [MB], originally an activist group, represents not only a wide range of liberal professions, businessmen and teachers, but also some low-ranking *ʿulamāʾ* of al-Azhar. Most members are not trained in the traditional disciplines and do not have a clear, common legal methodology. Their interpretation of the Qurʾān and Prophetic *sunna* is influenced by the social and natural sciences, in an attempt to adapt Islamic law to modern conditions and to insure that religious morality lies at the center of the social order.[98]

92 Friedman, ch. 4.
93 Vogel 2000, 342.
94 Ibid., 107, 126; al-Atawneh 2010, 148.
95 Cf. Layish 1978, 265.
96 Mir-Hosseini, 335, 338, and the reference there to Arjomand.
97 Schneider.
98 Hallaq 2009, 475–8.

Ḥasan al-Huḍaybī, a lawyer with almost no *sharʿī* education, was elected as the Guide (*murshid*) of the Brotherhood in 1951. He advocated an Islamic state that would abolish all symbols of secular identity.[99] Unlike Ḥasan al-Bannāʾ and Sayyid Quṭb, he did not approve of a radical, activist policy against the regime, probably for pragmatic reasons. He argued that following the abolition of the caliphate in 1924, the concept of an Islamic state responsible for the collective application of Islamic law (*farḍ al-kifāya*) was replaced by the concept of individual responsibility for fulfilling *sharʿī* obligations (*farḍ al-ʿayn*). This implies that the *sharīʿa* can be applied without invoking the state's executive authority.

Al-Huḍaybī promoted Islamic governance (*ḥukūma*) and the re-establishment of the caliphate, with the *sharīʿa* as its fundamental law, under the leadership of the *imām* or the ruler (*walī al-amr*). It is mandatory – he claimed – that the *imām* be well-versed in *sharʿī* studies and qualified to engage in *ijtihād*. Whereas the domain of religious observances (*ʿibādāt*) is immutable, that of pecuniary transactions (*muʿāmalāt*) may be adapted to changing conditions. He probably regarded the *shūrā* or consultative body as an alternative to a parliamentary system. Al-Huḍaybī's suggestion to subject state legislation to the control of a religious authority bears a resemblance to Khomeini's concept of the Guardian Jurist.

Yūsuf al-Qaraḍāwī's program for the adaptation of Islamic law to modern conditions is reflected in his views on *ijtihād*. Although he argues that the *sharīʿa* is appropriate to any time and place, contemporary scientists and intellectuals agree that *ijtihād* is essential in order to update the *sharīʿa*.[100] He quotes Sayyid Quṭb, who argued that contemporary Muslims are bound by the legal methodology of the *sharīʿa* rather than by the positive law (*aḥkām*) and principles (*qawāʿid*) of ancient times.[101] *Ijtihād* is not only permissible (*jāʾiz*) on the personal level, but also a collective duty, the fulfillment of which by a sufficient number of individuals exempts the rest of the Muslim community from the obligation to perform this duty.[102]

Al-Qaraḍāwī distinguishes between selective (*intiqāʾī*) *ijtihād* and creative (*inshāʾī*) *ijtihād:* A jurist who engages in selective *ijtihād* uses the eclectic device (*talfīq*) from the legal heritage of *fatwā*s and the judicial practice of all Sunni schools. A jurist who engages in creative *ijtihād* deduces (*istinbāṭ*)

99 The following survey is based on Zollner, 21, 104, 112, 116–18, 121–4, 127–30, 144–6, 151; and al-Huḍaybī, 73–4, 129–30, 133, 143ff.

100 Al-Qaraḍāwī 1998a, 10, 92.

101 Ibid., 128.

102 Ibid., 16, 23, 103.

unprecedented and innovative rules.[103] Al-Qaraḍāwī is probably referring here to the distinction between *ijtihād* applied within a school of law and *ijtihād* that is absolute or independent (*muṭlaq*). He maintains that *ijtihād* may be applied on three levels: (1) legal opinion; (2) legal research (*baḥth*) conducted in universities and scientific conferences and published in academic journals; and (3) parliamentary codification (*taqnīn*). On all three levels, the *mujtahid* must be a qualified jurist who meets the "generally recognized *sharʿī* learning conditions" – at least those required for applying partial (*juzʾī*) *ijtihād* that does not relate to the entire case under review, as distinct from absolute *ijtihād*.[104] In other words, in addition to professional *ʿulamāʾ*, independent academicians and legislators may also exercise *ijtihād*, on the condition that they possess the necessary *sharʿī* qualifications. *Ijtihād*, however, is not permitted in cases in which the *sharʿī* rules are of a definitive (*qaṭʿiyya*) nature, unless all other options for deriving law have been exhausted.[105]

Al-Qaraḍāwī strongly recommends applying the doctrine of *maṣlaḥa mursala* at all levels of legislation (both private and public, including religious observances), legal opinion (*iftāʾ*) and adjudication (*qaḍāʾ*). He finds support for this position in textual sources, *sharʿī* principles and the "goals of the *sharīʿa*" that serve the public interest.[106] Moreover, he recommends that the *sharīʿa* should be codified without being bound to any particular school of law, as suggested by the doctrine of *siyāsa sharʿiyya*. To this end he invokes Ḥasan al-Bannāʾ, who argued that the opinion of a ruler is binding in the following cases: (1) to fill a gap in a textual source, (2) to interpret a text that has more than one interpretation, and (3) to address matters of public interest not dealt with in the Qurʾān or *sunna*.[107] In other words, al-Qaraḍāwī advocates statutory codification of the *sharīʿa* as a legitimate instrument for adapting the *sharīʿa* to present-day conditions, provided that the legislators are qualified *ʿulamāʾ*.

In recent years, the MB in Egypt has attempted to reinstate the *sharīʿa* within the framework of a civil-law state. A draft of the Brotherhood's program of 25 August 2007 suggests re-constituting the Committee of Senior ʿUlamāʾ [CSU] as an independent advisory body to be elected from among the *ʿulamāʾ* and assisted by experienced, knowledgeable advisers, who also possess expertise in the secular sciences. The *sharīʿa* is to be applied in accordance with the will of the nation as expressed by members of a freely elected parliament.

---

103 Ibid., 24, 26, 27, 37.
104 Ibid., 46, 50.
105 Ibid., 98–9.
106 Hallaq 2009, 104; see above, 285.
107 Al-Qaraḍāwī 1998b, 104–6.

The parliament or, in its absence, the president of the state, must consult the CSU before promulgating a legislative act. If the *sharʿī* validity and meaning of a matter are equivocal, the parliament may ignore the CSU's view, provided that the parliament's decision is based on an absolute majority and takes into account public interest. However, if a *sharʿī* rule based on Qurʾān or *sunna* is unequivocal, the CSU's view is binding on the parliament.

While senior leaders of the Brotherhood regard the CSU as an advisory body whose sole purpose is to ensure the application of the *sharīʿa* in accordance with Article 2 of the Egyptian Constitution, critics treat the program as an attempt to establish a religious Islamist state modeled on Iran.[108]

In the wake of the 2011 Egyptian revolution and the fall of Ḥusnī Mubārak, the MB was legalized by the new regime and allowed to participate in the democratic process. In the general elections of June 2012, the Brotherhood's Ḥizb al-Ḥurriyya wa'l-ʿAdāla emerged as the dominant party in the country, and, together with the ultraconservative Salafīs, Islamists now hold a large majority in the parliament. Muḥammad Mursī, chairman of the Brotherhood's party, is the first president after the fall of the old regime.

The new constitution, which was approved in a referendum on 25 December 2012, is more Islamic than any previous constitution in Egypt.[109] The articles pertaining to the *sharīʿa* reflect a compromise between liberals and Salafīs. Al-Azhar, whose independent status has been considerably strengthened by the constitution, is expected to supervise the application of Article 2 by the SCC. President Mursī has publicly committed himself to fully implementing the *sharīʿa*. In practice, the MB has adopted a pragmatist stance – partial implementation of the *sharīʿa* and compromise on matters of ideology – in order to maintain stability. Senior MB officials have declared that full implementation of the *sharīʿa* will begin once the public has been prepared for this. In January 2012, al-Qaraḍāwī suggested that the *sharīʿa* should be implemented gradually and that "in the first five years there should be no chopping off of hands." In his view, during this transitional period the public should be instructed about the detailed laws of the *sharīʿa* and the economic and social problems of Egyptian society should be addressed and solved.[110]

Article 2 of the draft constitution reasserts that "the principles of Islamic *sharīʿa*" are "*the* main source of legislation," as in the 1980 Constitution. However, Article 219 clarifies: "[The expression] the principles of Islamic *sharīʿa*' includes the entirety of legal indicants (*adilla*), principles pertaining

108 MEMRI, 25 November 2007.

109 Unless otherwise indicated, the survey of the draft constitution is based on Lavi.

110 Al-Qaraḍāwī 2012.

to legal methodology, *fiqh* doctrine and valid textual sources recognized by the Sunni schools of law and the [Muslim] community." The function of this article is to prevent a narrow reading of Article 2 by the SCC. Article 4 recognizes al-Azhar as the supreme religious body in Egypt, independent of the regime. CSU is to be consulted (*yu'khadh ra'y*) in matters pertaining to the *sharīʿa* – a reference to the SCC's duty to consult with CSU before rendering its decisions. The formulation of this article suggests that the opinion of al-Azhar's scholars is not binding. In other words, the SCC has the discretion either to accept or reject the CSU's advice. At the same time, this article is meant to placate Salafīs who want the *sharīʿa as a complete legal system* to be the main source of legislation, with al-Azhar having the final say in determining whether statutory laws are consistent with the *sharīʿa*.[111]

Article 5 states that "sovereignty is for the people," who are the "source of authority." This formulation is contrary to the position of the Salafīs, who insist that sovereignty is for the Lord. Article 6 states that "the political system is based upon the principles of democracy and *shūrā* [the classical consultative institution]." This formulation represents an attempt to please both liberals and Salafīs.[112]

On 2 June 2013, the SupC dissolved the Shūrā Council (the upper house of Parliament) on the ground that it was elected illegally. The SupC also dissolved the committee that had drafted the constitution.[113] Early in July 2013, when this essay was submitted, the Egyptian army stripped President Mursī of his power and suspended the new Constitution. General ʿAbd al-Fattāḥ Khalīl al-Sīsī, Minister of Defense, called for presidential and parliamentary elections, the establishment of a panel to review the constitution, and a national reconciliation committee. ʿAdlī Maḥmūd Manṣūr, President of the Supreme Constitutional Court, was sworn in as an interim president to conduct the affairs of state until a new president is elected. On July 9, Dr. Ḥāzim ʿAbd al-ʿAzīz al-Bablāwī, a former finance minister, was named Egypt's prime minister, and Dr. Muḥammad al-Barādhiʿī, the former head of the International Atomic Energy [IAEA], was named Egypt's vice president for foreign affairs.

It has been reported that the interim President Manṣūr is considering the dissolution of the upper house of the parliament and the preparation for new elections for the presidency and the parliament. He has declared that Egypt

111 Abdel Kouddous.

112 For an English translation of the draft constitution, published in *Egypt Independent*, 8 December 2012, see http://www.egyptindependent.com/news/egypt-s-draft-constitution-translated. For analysis of Article 219, see Lombardi & Brown.

113 *Haaretz*, 3 June 2013; http://www.euronews.com/2013/07/03/egypt-constitution-suspended/.

will be a secular democratic state with no discrimination on grounds of religion and sex although the status of the *sharīʿa* as a source of law in the Constitution will remain intact. Clearly, it is too early to assess the changes in the position of the *sharīʿa* in Egypt.[114]

Ḥamās has been strongly influenced by the Egyptian MB.[115] The experience it has accumulated in Gaza since 2007 may provide a notion as to what might have been expected with regard to the reinstatement of the *sharīʿa* in Egypt had the Muslim Brothers managed to rule the country.[116] While taking into consideration the secular agenda of the Palestinian national movement, Ḥamās has adopted a pragmatic policy, opting for the gradual Islamization of Gaza's legal system. Thus Yūsuf Rizqa, political advisor to Ismāʿīl Haniyya, senior political leader of Ḥamās and Prime Minister of the Gaza Strip since 2006, announced (May 2010): "The government believes in a political spectrum without the imposition of Islamic rule on the people. Our task is not to establish an Islamic state. There is no strategic plan to implement *sharīʿa*, either gradually or comprehensively. The time is not right, and [when it is] the matter should be decided by a public referendum."[117] However, there is ample evidence that Ḥamās is moving rapidly toward reinstatement of the *sharīʿa:* Islamic norms have been introduced into statutory legislation, a section of the judiciary that is based on arbitration is undergoing a process of Islamization, and judges are instructed to ignore English and Israeli statutes and to apply the *sharīʿa* instead. Islamic banks and insurance companies that do not charge interest have been established, and *zakāt* tax is collected from business companies.[118] Both the *daʿwa*, the missionary arm of Ḥamās, and the religious volunteers (*mutaṭawwiʿīn*), strive to enforce observance of religious commandments and public morality. The League of Muslim Scholars is in charge of issuing *fatwā*s on daily problems.[119]

---

114 For further details, see *Ahram Online*, 2, 3, 6, 7 and 9 July 2013; *Haaretz*, 4, 7, 8 and 10 July 2013; CBS/AP 3 July 2013.

115 Unless otherwise indicated, this section is based on Pelham 2009.

116 Suffice to say that Egypt's new constitution reflects in large measure the agenda of the MB and Salafists, and that President Mursī dismissed the Attorney General and caused the untimely retirement of some 3000 judges in an attempt to replace them with judges associated with Islamist groups, thus preparing the ground for taking control of the SCC (Tzoreff). The reasons for the MB's political failure are beyond the scope of this article.

117 Pelham 2011, 15.

118 In 2009, the Parliament considered introducing amputation as punishment for theft; see Issacharoff 2009.

119 In recent years, Orthodox Jews in Israel have endeavored to strengthen the position of Jewish law in the state legal system. Since 2005, statutory courts of arbitration for resolving financial disputes in accordance with Jewish law operate alongside the state

## 15 Summary and Conclusion

If the *sharīʿa* is to be reinstated, several conditions must be met: An authoritative religious scholar well-versed in the *sharīʿa*, fully qualified to exercise *ijtihād*, capable of drafting a new legal methodology, highly motivated, determined, and enjoying the support of both the political authority and the public. If these conditions are met, one may expect a new version of the *sharīʿa* totally different from the traditional one. Created by qualified scholars (*ʿulamāʾ*), it will continue to be a "jurists' law," but its image as a divine law will probably be diminished because of the application of human doctrines or mechanisms, such as public welfare and "governance in accordance with the *sharīʿa*," alongside traditional sources of law. The possibility that the Iranian model for reinstating the *sharīʿa* will be adopted by Sunni states cannot be ruled out.[120] *Ijtihād* by qualified *sharʿī* scholars within a parliamentary framework will most likely serve as the main instrument for the elaboration of the law, although the development of the *sharīʿa* by independent scholars outside the establishment cannot be ruled out. Moreover, statutory *ijtihād* will enable scholars to Islamize the existing legal corpus, either by bringing it into conformity with fundamental principles of the *sharīʿa* or by applying *sharʿī* mechanisms in statutory legislation.

If the aforementioned conditions are not met, most Middle Eastern countries will experience an increasing tendency toward nationalization of the *sharīʿa*, in which case Islamic law will cease to be a jurists' law. Indeed, even the last stronghold of the *sharīʿa* – religious observance – is gradually giving way to reform legislation.[121] Domains of the *sharīʿa* that do not undergo codification will continue to engage *muftīs* and jurists intellectually, though probably with little practical effect in daily life.[122]

The choice between the reinstatement of the *sharīʿa* by its authorized exponents and its nationalization by the state involves a value judgment and hence should be left exclusively to the discretion of the Muslim community.[123]

---

judiciary (Hofri-Winogradow, 65 and *passim*). In 2010, a bill extending the jurisdiction of the Rabbinical courts to financial disputes, subject to the parties' consent, was submitted to the Knesset. Stern strongly believes that this may bring an end to the monopoly of the state courts in civil claims, the privatization of the civil law and, in its wake, the disintegration of the social fabric in Israel (Stern 2010). In 2009, former Justice Minister Prof. Yaʿakov Neeman expressed (in a closed forum) the hope that Torah law (the Law of Moses) will gradually be binding in the State of Israel (*Haaretz*, 8 December 2009).

120 Cf. Hatina.

121 Cf. Peters 2003, 93–4.

122 Cf. ibid., 91.

123 Cf. ibid., 92f.

## Bibliography

Abdel Kouddous, Sharif. 2012. "Will Egypt's New Constitution Take the Country Backwards?" *The Nation*, October 9, 2012.

Abou El Fadl, Khaled. 1994. "Islamic Law and Muslim Minorities: The Juristic Discourse on Muslim Minorities from the Second/Eighth to the Eleventh/Seventeenth Centuries." *Islamic Law and Society* 1:2, 141–87.

Abou El Fadl, Khaled. 2005. *The Great Theft. Wrestling Islam from the Extremists*. New York: Harper One.

Abou Ramadan, Moussa. 2008. "Notes on the Anomaly of the *Sharīʿa* Field in Israel." *Islamic Law and Society* 15:1, 84–111.

Anderson, Norman. 1976. *Law Reform in the Muslim World*. London: The Athlone Press.

Al-Atawneh, Muhammad. 2001. "*Sharīʿa* and Politics in Saudi Arabia: *Siyāsa sharʿiyya* as a Mechanism for Stabilization of Government and Society." *Jamāʿa* 8, 54–83 (Hebrew).

Al-Atawneh, Muhammad. 2009. "Reconciling Tribalism and Islam in the Writings of Contemporary Wahhabi 'Ulama'." In *Guardians of Faith in Modern Times: 'Ulama' in the Middle East*. Ed. Meir Hatina. Leiden: Brill, 211–27.

Al-Atawneh, Muhammad. 2010. *Wahhābī Islam Facing the Challenges of Modernity. Dār al-Iftāʾ in the Modern Saudi State*. Leiden: Brill.

Al-Atawneh, Muhammad. 2011. "Wahhābī Legal Theory as Reflected in Modern Official Saudi *Fatwās*: *Ijtihād, Taqlīd*, Sources, and Methodology." *Islamic Law and Society* 18:3–4, 327–55.

Atlas, Duygu. 2012. "Turkey Faces Creeping Islamization in the Public Sphere." *Tsomet Hamizrah Hatikhon* 2:9. Tel Aviv University, The Moshe Dayan Center (Hebrew).

Baer, Gabriel. 1969. *Studies in the Social History of Modern Egypt*. Chicago: The University of Chicago Press.

Bälz, Kilian. 1999. "The Secular Reconstruction of Islamic Law: The Egyptian Supreme Constitutional Court and the 'Battle over the Veil' in State-Run Schools." In *Legal Pluralism in the Arab World*. Ed. Baudouin Dupret, Maurits Berger and Laila al-Zwaini. The Hague: Kluwer Law International, 229–43.

Berger, Maurits and Nadia Sonneveld. 2010. "Sharia and National Law in Egypt." In *Sharia Incorporated. A Comparative Overview of the Legal Systems of Twelve Muslim Countries in Past and Present*. Ed. Jan Michiel Otto. Leiden: Leiden University Press, 51–88.

Berkes, Niyazi. 1964. *The Development of Secularism in Turkey*. Montreal: McGill University Press.

Cardinal, Monique C. "Islamic Legal Theory Curriculum: Are the Classics Taught Today?" *Islamic Law and Society* 12:2, 224–72.

Coulson, Noel J. 1964. *A History of Islamic Law*. Edinburgh: Edinburgh University Press.

Coulson, Noel J. 1969. *Conflicts and Tensions in Islamic Jurisprudence*. Chicago: University of Chicago Press.

Coulson, Noel J. 1971. *Succession in the Muslim Family*. Cambridge: Cambridge University Press.

Dirks, Sabine, 1969. *La famille musulmane turque*. Paris: Mouton.

Dupret, Baudouin. 2003. "A Return to the Shariah? Egyptian Judges and Referring to Islam." In *Modernizing Islam. Religion in the Public Sphere in Europe and the Middle East*. Ed. John L. Esposito and François Burgat. London: Hurst, 125–43.

Englard, Izhak. 2009. "Der Einfluss religiösen Rechts auf das Rechtssystem in Israel." In *Der Einfluss der Weltreligionen auf die Rechtssysteme der Länder*. Ed. L. Simon & R. Lauda. Frankfurt am Main: Schriften der Rechtsanwaltskammer Frankfurt am Main, 147–60.

Friedman, Yehoshuʿa. 2007. "Public Law in Islam in the Perspective of *siyāsa sharʿiyya*" Ph.D thesis. Bar-Ilan University, Ramat-Gan (Hebrew).

Hallaq, Wael B. 1997. *A History of Islamic Legal Theories*. Cambridge: Cambridge University Press.

Hallaq, Wael B. 2002. "A Prelude to Ottoman Reform: Ibn ʿĀbidīn on Custom and Legal Change." In *Histories of the Modern Middle East. New Directions*. Ed. Israel Gershoni, Hakan Erdem and Ursula Woköck. Boulder: Lynne Rienner Publishers, 37–61.

Hallaq, Wael B. 2004. "Can the *Sharīʿa* Be Restored?" In *Islamic Law and the Challenge of Modernity*. Ed. Yvonne Y. Haddad and Barbara F. Stowasser. Lanham, MD, 21–53.

Hallaq, Wael B. 2009. *Sharīʿa: Theory, Practice, Transformations*. Cambridge: Cambridge University Press.

Hatina, Meir. 2010. "An Earlier Sunnī Version of Khomeini's Rule of the Jurist: Muṣṭafā l-Sibāʿī on *ʿUlamāʾ* and Politics." *Arabica* 57, 455–76.

Hofri-Winogradow, Adam. 2010. "A Plurality of Discontent: Legal Pluralism, Religious Adjudication and the State." *Journal of Law and Religion* 26:1, 57–89.

Hooker, M.B. 1984. *Islamic Law in South-East Asia*. Oxford: Oxford University Press.

Al-Huḍabyī, Ḥasan Ismāʿīl. 1977. *Duʿāt lā quḍāt. Abḥāth fīʾl-ʿaqīda al-islāmiyya wa-manhaj al-daʿwa ilā allāh*. Cairo: Dār al-Ṭibāʾa waʾl-Nashr al-Islāmiyya.

Issacharoff, Avi. 2009. "Under the Supervision of the Jewish [Religious] Court of Justice, Gaza." *Haaretz*, 4 December 2009 (Hebrew).

Kerr, Malcolm. 1966. *Islamic Reform. The Political and Legal Theories of Muḥammad ʿAbduh and Rashīd Riḍā*. Berkeley: University of California Press.

Khadduri, Madjid, 1991. "Maṣlaḥa." *Encyclopaedia of Islam*, 2nd ed., VI, 738–40.

Koçak, Mustafa. 2010. "Islam and National Law in Turkey." In *Sharia Incorporated. A Comparative Overview of the Legal Systems of Twelve Muslim Countries in Past and Present*. Ed. Jan Michiel Otto. Leiden: Leiden University Press, 231–72.

Lavi, L. 2012. "An Examination of Egypt's Draft Constitution Part I: Religion and State – The Most Islamic Constitution in Egypt's History." MEMRI Inquiry and Analysis 904, December 3, 2012. http://www.egyptindependent.com/news/egypt-s-draft-constitution-translated.

Layish, Aharon. 1975. *Women and Islamic Law in a Non-Muslim State. A Study Based on the Decisions of the Sharīʿa Courts in Israel.* New York: John Wiley & Sons.

Layish, Aharon. 1978. "The Contribution of the Modernists to the Secularization of Islamic Law." *Middle Eastern Studies* 14:3, 263–77.

Layish, Aharon. 1987. "Legal Reform in Saudi Arabia as a Mechanism to Moderate Wahhābī Doctrine." *Journal of the American Oriental Society* 107:2, 279–92.

Layish, Aharon. 1991a. *Divorce in the Libyan Family. A Study Based on the* Sijill *of the* Sharīʿa *Courts of Ajdābiya and Kufra.* New York: New York University Press.

Layish, Aharon. 1991b. "Maḥkama, pt. 4. The Arab Lands and Israel in the Modern Period." *Encyclopaedia of Islam*, 2nd ed., VI, 22–38, 40–42.

Layish, Aharon. 2000a. "Reformist Matrimonial Legislation and the Collapse of the Muslim Patrilineal Family." *Awrāq* 21, 57–80.

Layish, Aharon. 2000b. "Waḳf, pt. 5: In the Modern Middle East and North Africa." *Encyclopaedia of Islam*, 2nd ed., XI, 78–81.

Layish, Aharon. 2002. "The *Qāḍī*'s Role in the Islamization of Sedentary Tribal Society." In *The Public Sphere in Muslim Societies*. Ed. Miriam Hoexter, Shmuel N. Eisenstadt, and Nehemia Levtzion. New York: SUNY, 83–107.

Layish, Aharon. 2004. "The Transformation of the *Sharīʿa* from Jurists' Law to Statutory Law in the Contemporary Muslim World." *Die Welt des Islams* 44:1, 85–112.

Layish, Aharon. 2005. Sharīʿa *and Custom in Libyan Tribal Society. An Annotated Translation of Decisions from the* Sharīʿa *Courts of Ajdābiya and Kufra*. Leiden: Brill.

Layish, Aharon. 2006. "Adaptation of a Jurists' Law to Modern Times in an Alien Environment: The Case of the *Sharīʿa* in Israel." *Die Welt des Islams* 46:2, 168–225.

Layish, Aharon. 2008a. "The Heritage of Ottoman Rule in the Israeli Legal System: The Concept of *umma* and *millet* System." In *The Law Applied: Contextualizing the Islamic Sharīʿa. A volume in honor of Frank E. Vogel.* Ed. Peri Bearman, Wolfhart Heinrichs, and Bernard G. Weiss. London: I.B. Tauris, 128–48.

Layish, Aharon. 2008b. "Islamization of Custom as Reflected in Awards of Tribal Arbitrators in the Judaean Desert." *Jerusalem Studies in Arabic and Islam* 35, 285–334.

Layish, Aharon. 2011. *Legal Documents from the Judean Desert: The Impact of the Sharīʿa on Bedouin Customary Law.* With the assistance of Mūsā Shawārbah and including his linguistic essay. Leiden: Brill.

Layish, Aharon. 2013. "Ḥasan al-Turābī (1932–)." In *Islamic Legal Thought: A Compendium of Muslim Jurists*. Ed. Oussama Arabi, David S. Powers and Susan A. Spectorsky. Leiden: Brill, 513–32.

Layish, Aharon and Avshalom Shmueli. 1979. "Custom and *Sharīʿa* in the Bedouin Family according to Legal Documents from the Judaean Desert." *Bulletin of the School of Oriental and African Studies* 42:1, 29–45.

Layish, Aharon and Gabriel R. Warburg. 2002. *The Reinstatement of Islamic Law in Sudan under Numayrī. An Evaluation of a Legal Experiment in the Light of Its Historical Context, Methodology, and Repercussions*. Leiden: Brill.

Libson, Gideon. 2000. "ʿUrf, pt. 1. The Status of Custom in Islamic Law." *Encyclopaedia of Islam*, 2nd ed., x, 887–88.

Lombardi, Clark B. 2006. *State Law as Islamic Law in Modern Egypt. The Incorporation of the* Sharīʿa *into Egyptian Constitutional Law*. Leiden: Brill.

Lombardi, Clark and Nathan J. Brown. 2012. "Islam in Egypt's New Constitution." *Foreign Policy*, December 13, 2012, published in http://mideast.foreignpolicy.com/posts/2012/12/13/islam_in_egypts_new_constitution.

March, Andrew F. 2009. "Sources of Moral Obligation to non-Muslims in the 'Jurisprudence of Muslim Minorities' (*Fiqh al-aqalliyyāt*)." *Islamic Law and Society* 16:1, 34–94.

MEMRI, The Middle East Media Research Institute, Jerusalem.

Mir-Hosseini, Ziba. 2010. "*Sharīʿa* and National Law in Iran." In *Sharia Incorporated. A Comparative Overview of the Legal Systems of Twelve Muslim Countries in Past and Present*. Ed. Jan Michiel Otto. Leiden: Leiden University Press, 319–71.

An-Naʿim, Abdullahi Ahmed. 2008. "Shariʿa in the Secular State. A Paradox of Separation and Conflation." In *The Law Applied: Contextualizing the Islamic Shariʿa. A volume in honor of Frank E. Vogel*. Ed. Peri Bearman, Wolfhart Heinrichs, and Bernard G. Weiss. London: I.B. Tauris, 321–41.

Naveh, Immanuel. 1997. "Application of the *Sharīʿa* in Civil Courts in the Twentieth Century: A Comparative Study Based on Decisions of Civil Courts in Matters of Personal Status and *Waqf* of Muslims in a Muslim State (Egypt) and in a Non-Muslim State (Israel)." Ph.D. thesis. The Hebrew University, Jerusalem (Hebrew).

Naveh, Immanuel. 2002. "The Tort of Injury and Dissolution of Marriage at the Wife's Initiative in Egyptian *Maḥkamat al-Naqḍ* Rulings." *Islamic Law and Society* 9:1, 16–41.

Opwis, Felicitas. 2005. "*Maṣlaḥa* in Contemporary Islamic Theory." *Islamic Law and Society* 12:2, 182–223.

Opwis, Felicitas. 2010. Maṣlaḥa *and the Purpose of the Law. Islamic Discourse on Legal Change from the 4th/10th to 8th/14th Century*. Leiden: Brill.

Otto, Jan Michiel. 2010. "Towards Comparative Conclusions on the Role of the Sharia in National Law." In *Sharia Incorporated. A Comparative Overview of the Legal Systems of Twelve Muslim Countries in Past and Present*. Ed. Jan Michiel Otto. Leiden: Leiden University Press, 613–54.

Pelham, Nicolas. 2009. "The Legal System in Gaza under Ḥamās." A paper submitted to the International Workshop on "Islamic Law Facing the Challenges of the

21st Century" held at the Van Leer Jerusalem Institute on 19–21 October 2009 (unpublished).

Pelham, Nicolas. 2011. "How Islamists Govern: Lessons from Gaza." A TIDA Synthesis Report. January 2011. Published in http://www.academia.edu/2983727/How_Islamists_Govern_Lessons_from_Gaza.

Peters, Rudolph. 1988. "Divine Law or Man-Made Law? Egypt and the Application of the Shariʿa." *Arab Law Quarterly* 3, 231–53.

Peters, Rudolph. 2000. "Waqf, pt. 1. In Classical Islamic Law." *Encyclopaedia of Islam*, 2nd ed., XI, 59–63.

Peters, Rudolph. 2003. "From Jurists' Law to Statute Law or What Happens When the Shariʿa is Codified." *Mediterranean Politics* 7 (Special issue on Shaping the Current Islamic Reformation. Ed. B.A. Roberson), 82–95.

Al-Qaraḍāwī, Yūsuf. 1418/1998a. *Al-Ijtihād al-muʿāṣir bayna al-inḍibāṭ wa'l-infirāṭ*. 2nd ed. Beirut: Al-Maktab al-Islāmī.

Al-Qaraḍāwī, Yūsuf. 1419/1998b. *Al-Siyāsa al-sharʿiyya fī ḍaw' nuṣūṣ al-sharīʿa wa-maqāṣidihā*. Cairo: Maktabat Wahba.

Al-Qaraḍāwī, Yūsuf. 2012. Interview with Yūsuf al-Qaraḍāwī aired on *Al-Nahar TV*, MEMRI, 26 January 2012.

Schacht, Joseph. 1964. *An Introduction to Islamic Law*. Oxford: The Clarendon Press.

Schneider, Irene. 2010. "Polygamy and Legislation in Contemporary Iran: An Analysis of the Public Legal Discourse." An expanded version of a paper submitted to the International Workshop on "Islamic Law Facing the Challenges of the 21st Century" held at the Van Leer Jerusalem Institute on 19–21 October 2009 (unpublished).

Shaham, Ron. 2009. "Western Scholars on the Role of the *'Ulama'* in Adapting the Shariʿa to Modernity: A Critical Review." In *Guardians of Faith in Modern Times: 'Ulama' in the Middle East*. Ed. Meir Hatina. Leiden: Brill, 171–92.

Shahar, Ido. 2007. "Legal Reform, Interpretive Communities and the Quest for Legitimacy: A Contextual Analysis of a Legal Circular." In *Law, Custom, and Statute in the Muslim World. Studies in honor of Aharon Layish*. Ed. Ron Shaham. Leiden: Brill.

Shalabī, Muḥammad Muṣṭafā. 1960. *Al-Fiqh al-islāmī bayna al-mithāliyya wa'l-wāqiʿiyya*. Beirut: Dār al-Jamʿiyya.

Stern, Yedidia Z. 2007. "What is Jewish in Israeli Law?" In *The Jewishness of Israel*. Ed. Aviezer Ravitzky and Yedidia Z. Stern. Jerusalem: The Democracy Library, 13–60 (Hebrew).

Stern, Yedidia Z. 2010. "View Article: Legal Autonomy to the Religious Sectors." *Yediʿot Aharonot*, 2 February 2010 (Hebrew).

Stewart, Frank H. 2000. "ʿUrf, pt. 2. Arab Customary Law." *Encyclopaedia of Islam*, 2nd ed., X, 888–92.

Stewart, Frank H. 2012. "Tribalism." The *Encyclopaedia of Islamic Political Thought*. Princeton: Princeton University Press, 563–67.

Taşpınar, Ömer. 2012. "Turkey: The New Model?" http://www.brookings.edu/research/papers/2012/04/24-turkey-new-model-taspinar.

Tzoreff, Mira. 2013. "The People's Life is Entrusted in Their Hands and the President is Nothing but Their Servant." *Tzomet HaMizrach haTichon*. Moshe Dayan Center for Middle Eastern and African Studies, Tel Aviv University. 8:3 (7 July 2013) (Hebrew).

Ukeles, Raquel M. 2009. "When Law is Personal: The Authority of *Fiqh* in Western Muslim Debates Regarding Women Imams." A paper submitted to the International Workshop on "Islamic Law Facing the Challenges of the 21st Century" held at the Van Leer Jerusalem Institute on 19–21 October 2009 (unpublished).

van Eijk, Esther. 2010. "Sharia and National Law in Saudi Arabia." In *Sharia Incorporated. A Comparative Overview of the Legal Systems of Twelve Muslim Countries in Past and Present*. Ed. Jan Michiel Otto. Leiden: Leiden University Press, 139–80.

Vikør, Knut S. 2005. *Between God and the Sultan. A History of Islamic Law*. London: Hurst.

Vogel, Frank E. 1997. "Siyāsa, pt. 3. In the sense of *siyāsa sharʿiyya*" *Encyclopaedia of Islam*, 2nd ed., IX, 694–96.

Vogel, Frank E. 2000. *Islamic Law and Legal System: Studies of Saudi Arabia*. Leiden: Brill.

Yilmaz, Ihsan. 2002. "Secular Law and the Emergence of Unofficial Turkish Islamic Law." *Middle East Journal* 56, 113–31.

Zollner, Barbara H.E. 2009. *The Muslim Brotherhood. Hasan al-Hudaybi and Ideology*. London: Routledge.

# PART 4

# Waqf, *Testamentary* Waqf *and Bequests*

CHAPTER 13

# *Waqf*s of *Awlād al-Nās* in Aleppo in the Late Mamlūk Period as Reflected in a Family Archive

This article focuses on an Arabic scroll kept in the Staatsbibliothek Preussischer Kulturbesitz in Berlin, which contains a chronological registration of 32 transactions concluded in rural and urban estates belonging to descendants of a Mamlūk amīr in Aleppo.[*,1] The scroll contains two registers (*sijill*): the first comprises 25 transactions and the second 7. These transactions were concluded over a period of more than 100 years, from the late fourteenth century to the beginning of the sixteenth century CE. The registers contain records of various kinds of legal transactions,[2] but in this essay I will concentrate on five

* This essay is based on a paper submitted to the conference on *Waqf* Law held at Harvard Law School, Cambridge, Mass. on May 26–8, 2006. An earlier draft of the paper was read at a conference held at the Hebrew University of Jerusalem on "Society, Culture and Law in the Muslim World – the Maghrib and Mashriq" organized under the auspices of the Institute of Asian and African Studies, the Nehemia Levtzion Center for the Study of Islam, and the Harry S. Truman Research Institute for the Advancement of Peace on 15 May 2005 on the occasion of Prof. Miriam Hoexter's retirement. For a couple of years, Miriam and I have been running a seminar on the *Waqf* for graduate students at the Hebrew University of Jerusalem; it therefore gives me great pleasure to dedicate this essay to her. I am most grateful to Miriam and to my colleagues Reuven Amitai, Amalia Levanoni, David Powers, Michael Winter, and the anonymous reviewer who read earlier drafts of this essay with a critical eye and offered most valuable comments and suggestions. Thanks are also due to my colleague Miriam Rosen-Ayalon and my students Muḥammad Ṭāṭūr and Nikolaus Wildner for their assistance. I would like to thank Dr. Maurits van den Boogert for the generous editorial comments and suggestions.

[Originally published in *Journal of the Economic and Social History of the Orient*, 51/2 (2008), pp. 287–326.]

1 The manuscript in question is 20 meters long and 30 centimeters wide, and comprises 120 pages. My profound thanks are due to the Staatsbibliothek Preussischer Kulturbesitz, Berlin, for providing me with a photocopy. For an annotated edition of 24 of the documents from the late fourteenth century to the middle of the fifteenth century, see Souad Saghbini, *Mamlukische Urkunden aus Aleppo: Die urkundensammlung (ǧāmiʿ al-mustanadāt) der mamlukisch-aleppinischen Familie Uġulbak* (Hildesheim, Zürich & New York, 2005): 11–2, who did not include two of the five *Waqfiyya*s discussed in this article. I am grateful to Dr. Johannes Pahlitzsch for drawing my attention to this publication. The references to the *Waqfiyya*s in this essay are to the original manuscript (*Sijill*).

2 We find documents relating to sale; inheritance; *intiqāl*, the transfer of property; *istibdāl*, the exchange of *Waqf* property; *ājār*, lease, or rent; and *tamlīk*, transfer of ownership. The *tamlīk* is executed by means of *sharʿī* offer and acceptance (*ījāb wa-qabūl*) and delivery and taking

 | DOI:10.1163/9789004680920_015

extensive *waqfiyyas*, deeds of pious endowments founded by descendants of the Mamlūk amīr, Ughulbak b. ʿAbdallāh b. Sulaymān al-Jāshankīr, over a period of four generations. Although limited in number, these *waqfiyyas* provide us with a rare opportunity to trace sections of Aleppo's society in the period during which the Mamlūks, originally a military elite, became a civil elite.

The present study focuses on legal praxis rather than theoretical discussion. Besides legal points pertaining to the process of endowment, the *waqfiyya* reflects the founder's wish regarding the apportionment of entitlement to the proceeds of the *waqf* among the beneficiaries and the order of administrators of the *waqf*. Within this context, the main issue emerging from the documents is that of the social and economic pressures of daily life. An attempt will be made to evaluate the repercussions of these pressures within the context of legal and social history. Because of the limited number of documents and the specific time span they cover, this study should be regarded as a sketch of the major trends in judicial practice, and its conclusions as tentative.

## 1 The Sources

In his study of dozens of *waqfiyyas* and properties of Mamlūks registered in the Ottoman *defters* in the mid-sixteenth century, M. Winter has observed the significance of *waqf* and *milk* documents for the study of the social and economic history of al-Shām (the District of Damascus) in the late Mamlūk period.[3] In many cases the original *waqfiyyas* did not survive and the Ottoman clerks had no choice but to draw up a summary, based on the record (*maḥḍar*) of the *sharīʿa* court.[4] The *waqf* documents under examination here are copies

delivery (*taslīm wa-tasallum*); *Jāmi al-mustanadāt al-ʿāʾid li-ʿāʾilat Ughulbak al-ḥalabiyya al-mamlūkiyya*. Annotated edition of 24 documents in Arabic. In Saghbini, *Mamlukische Urkunden aus Aleppo* [hereafter: Arabic documents]: 73, last paragraph. Cf. B. Johansen, *The Islamic Law on Land Tax and Rent: The Peasants' Loss of Property Rights as Interpreted in the Hanafite Legal Literature of the Mamluk and Ottoman Periods* (London, 1988): 27; C.F. Petry, *Protectors or Praetorians? The Last Mamlūk Sultans and Egypt's Waning as a Great Power* (Albany, 1994): 196; C.F. Petry, "The Estate of al-Khuwand Fāṭima al-Khasṣbakiyya: Royal Spouse, Autonomous Investor." In *The Mamluks in Egyptian and Syrian Politics and Society*, eds. M. Winter and Amalia Levanoni (Leiden, 2004): 280–1; D.P. Little, *A Catalogue of the Islamic Documents from al-Ḥaram al-Sharīf in Jerusalem* (Beirut, 1984): 299.

3 M. Winter, "Mamluks and their Households in Late Mamluk Damascus: A *Waqf* Study." In *The Mamluks in Egyptian and Syrian Politics and Society*, eds. M. Winter and Amalia Levanoni (Leiden, 2004): 297. Winter is presently engaged in a comprehensive study on Damascus on the basis of these documents.

4 Winter, "Mamluks and their Households in Late Mamluk Damascus": 306, 315.

of the originals that had been recorded in the *sijill* dozens of years after the founders' decease. Thus, for example, one document concludes with the statement that the *qāḍī al-quḍāt* (chief judge-cum-administrator) of Aleppo "confirmed (*thubūt*) the original *waqfiyya* along with a verbatim copy that had been made from the original (*maʿa aṣlihi al-manqūl minhu ḥarfan bi-ḥarfin*)."[5] The authenticity of the *waqfiyya*'s was confirmed only after an extensive hearing of high-ranking witnesses (*qāḍī al-quḍāt*s from different schools of law) who testified that the property in question had been rightfully in the full possession of the founder of the *waqf*. These testimonies and the court's authentication precede the text of the copies of the *waqfiyyas*.

The original *waqfiyyas* were probably kept in the private family's archive, along with other legal documents, from which they were copied, in chronological order, onto the scroll.[6] The last document of the first register (no. 25) describes the procedure of the comparison (*muqābala*) of the documents registered on the scroll with the originals, and ends with the identification of the scribe in the following words: "The collector of the documents [in the family register, including] … the original [documents] from which [the documents in the family register] were copied and recorded (*jāmiʿ al-mustanadāt … bi-uṣūlihi allātī nuqila ʿanhā wa-nusikha minhā*)".[7] Technically, registration of the *waqfiyya* is not required for its validation, but in practice it may have added legal security.[8] In some cases, up to 80 years passed between the foundation of the *waqf* and its registration in the *sijill* of the *sharīʿa* court.

## 2 Aleppo's Administration in the Mamlūk Period

During the Mamlūk period Syria comprised two major provinces, Damascus and Aleppo. The jurisdiction of the latter extended over Ḥims, Ḥamā, Ṭarābulus, and the towns of southeastern Anatolia. The sultan, who resided in Cairo, delegated extensive powers to the viceroys of Damascus and Aleppo. Most of them were promoted to the rank of *muqaddam* before they assumed

5 *Sijill* 1, Waqf 1, p. 15, lines 8–9. The name of the clerk who copied the *Waqfiyya* appears in line 16.

6 In one case, the original *Waqfiyya* was ratified along with four copies and it seems that a copy of all these documents was given to the founder's family. *Sijill* 1, Waqf 3, p. 24, line 13 – p. 25, line 4.

7 *Sijill* 1, Muqābala, p. 71, line 13.

8 Cf. Muḥammad Qadrī, *Kitāb Qānūn al-ʿadl wa-l-inṣāf lil-qaḍāʾ ʿalā mushkilāt al-awqāf*. 3rd edition (Cairo, 1320/1902): art. 2; W. Heffening, "Waḳf." In *Encyclopaedia of Islam*, 1st edition: 1096ii.

their offices in Syria, which suggests that they presided over large households and small armies of their own.[9]

Sultan Baybars appointed four chief *qāḍī*s in both Cairo and Damascus, i.e. one for every Sunnī school of law, but the chief *qāḍī* of the Shāfiʿī school held the most senior position. He had exclusive jurisdiction in matters pertaining to the Public Treasury (*bayt al-māl*) and the property of orphans. In the second half of the fourteenth century, four chief *qāḍī*s were appointed in Aleppo as well. The sultan nominated the chief *qāḍī*s from among prominent representatives of the local *ʿulamāʾ*. The new judicial system, which continued until the Ottoman conquest, was aimed at creating a uniform, but flexible legal system. Uniformity was obtained by restricting the scope of the *qāḍī*s discretion to the dominant (*mashūr*) view within the relevant school, i.e. by promoting *taqlīd*, while flexibility was achieved by giving the four schools an equal status, thus offering optimal maneuverability of the individual between the schools.[10] For instance, when members of the military elite, predominantly affiliated with the Ḥanafī school, wished to record the alienation of a *waqf* property, they would apply to the Ḥanbalī *qāḍī*, the school which permitted the exchange of property (*istibdāl*) if the endowed property has been damaged or destroyed. Contrary to the Ḥanafī school, the Ḥanbalī scholars permitted this course of action even if the founder of the *waqf* had not stipulated such an option for the administrator in the *waqfiyya*, and even without obtaining prior approval of the alienation from the *qāḍī*. It seems that the military elite and the judiciary acted in harmony here, keeping in mind the public interest.[11]

---

9 Petry, *Protectors or Praetorians?*: 35.

10 Y. Rapoport, "Legal Diversity in the Age of *Taqlīd*: The Four Chief *Qāḍī*s under the Mamluks." *Islamic Law and Society* 10.2 (2003): 210–3; J. Drory, "Founding a New Mamlaka: Some Remarks Concerning Safed and the Organization of the Region in the Mamluk Period." In *The Mamluks in Egyptian and Syrian Politics and Society*, eds. M. Winter and Amalia Levanoni (Leiden, 2004): 182–3; M. Winter, "Inter-*Madhhab* Competition in Mamlūk Damascus: al-Ṭarsūsī's Counsel for the Turkish Sultans." David Ayalon Memorial Volume, *Jerusalem Studies in Arabic and Islam* 25 (2001): 196; Petry, *Protectors or Praetorians?*: 36.

11 R. Peters, "Waḳf. I. In the Classical Islamic Law." *Encyclopaedia of Islam*, 2nd edition: XI: 62ii; cf. Rapoport, "Legal Diversity in the Age of *Taqlīd*": 222, 227–8. There is ample evidence that Shāfiʿī *qāḍī*s transmitted cases involving charges of heresy to Mālikī *qāḍī*s to ensure execution (Ibid: 223ff.); cf. Winter, "Inter-*Madhhab* Competition in Mamlūk Damascus": 203; Abdul-Karim Rafeq, "The Application of Islamic Law in the Ottoman Courts in Damascus: The Case of the Rental of *Waqf* Land." In *Dispensing Justice in Islam: Qadis and their Judgments*, eds. Muhammad Kh. Masud, R. Peters and D. S. Powers (Leiden, 2006): 415.

## 3 The Doctrinal Basis of the *Waqfiyyas*

It seems that all the *waqf*s examined for this article were formulated according to Ḥanafī doctrine. This can be inferred from the fact that in the original *waqfiyya* the founder stipulated that he would be the first beneficiary – a stipulation which only the Ḥanafī school allows.[12] The severance of the juridical connection between the founder and the endowed property was also in accordance with the Ḥanafī doctrine; the document reads that "the founder excluded the *waqf* from his ownership, removed it from his possession and endowed it as *waqf* for the sake of Allāh" (*akhraja mā waqafahu ʿan milkihi wa-abānahu ʿan iyāzatihi wa-jaʿalahu waqfan li-llāhi*).[13]

In the conversion of private property to *waqf*, the ultimate severance of the juridical connection takes place when the founder appoints a proxy and conveys the property to that person (*sallama taslīman*). This makes the act of endowment complete and irrevocable (*tamma al-waqf wa-lazima*).[14] The fourth *waqfiyya* says that after having removed the property from his ownership and possession, the founder conveyed the property to the *nāẓir* (administrator). Since the founder stipulated that he himself would be the first *nāẓir*, the administrator mentioned in the fourth *waqfiyya* was probably the *nāẓir li-taslīm*, a temporary administrator who symbolized the severance of the juridical connection prior to the conveyance of the endowed property to the permanent *nāẓir*, in this case the founder himself.[15]

---

12 According to the Ḥanbalī school, such a stipulation is not valid but the founder may use the proceeds of the *waqf*. Peters, "Waḳf": 61i; cf. Miriam Hoexter, "*Ḥuqūq Allāh* and *Ḥuqūq al-ʿIbād* as Reflected in the *Waqf* Institution." *Jerusalem Studies in Arabic and Islam* 19 (1995): 138; Rapoport, "Legal Diversity in the Age of *Taqlīd*": 220. On the doctrine of the Mālikī school, see A. Layish, "The Mālikī Family *Waqf* according to Wills and *Waqfiyyāt*." *Bulletin of the School of Oriental and African Studies* 46.1 (1983): 29; cf. Winter, "Inter-*Madhhab* Competition in Mamlūk Damascus": 203.

13 *Sijill* I, Waqf 1, p. 14, line 4; cf. Heffening, "Waḳf": 1097i.

14 *Sijill* I, Waqf 1, p. 14, line 6; Waqf 2, p. 24, lines 6–8; Waqf 3, p. 28, lines 1–2; *Sijill* II, Waqf 4, p. 115, lines 4–5; cf. Omar Hilmi, *A Gift to Posterity on the Laws of Evqaf*. trans. C. R. Tyser and D. G. Demetriades. 2nd edition (Nicosia, 1922): 1, art. 4 (*lāzim*); Heffening, "Waḳf": 1097i.

15 *Sijill* II, Waqf 4, p. 115, line 4; cf. Heffening, "Waḳf": 1097i; Johansen, *The Islamic Law on Land Tax and Rent*: 31. On administration of the *Waqf*, see Peters, "Waḳf": 63i. On the competition among the schools on a judicial level, see Rapoport, "Legal Diversity in the Age of *Taqlīd*": 227; cf. A. N. Poliak, *Tōledōt haj-jeḥāsīm haq-qarqaʿijjīm be-Miṣrajim, Sūrijā we-Ereṣ-Jiśrāʾēl be-sōf jemē hab-bēnajim ū-baz-zemān he-ḥādāš* [*History of Agrarian Relations in Egypt, Syria and Palestine in Medieval and Modern Times*] (Jerusalem, 1940): 12; I.M. Lapidus, "Muslim Urban Society in Mamlūk Syria." In *The Islamic City*, eds.

Although the *waqf*s under examination were drawn up in accordance with the Ḥanafī doctrine, judges and other functionaries belonging to other schools testified to their validity. For example, the *qāḍī*s of all three other schools testified in the *sharīʿa* courts of Aleppo and Ḥamā regarding the first *waqfiyya*.[16] For the second *waqfiyya* both the *qāḍī al-quḍāt*s, and the Shaykh al-Islāms of all three other schools were mobilized.[17] The Shāfiʿī *qāḍī al-quḍāt* registered the third *waqfiyya* and had his Ḥanbalī and Mālikī colleagues testify to its validity.[18]

The jurists were probably assembled from all schools in order to secure their support in the event that someone would contest the validity of the *waqfiyya*.[19] Beyond the judicial level there is no indication in these documents that school affiliation played any role in forming the class identity of the Mamlūk elite in Syria.[20] Practical and pragmatic considerations appear to have been stronger than theological or social loyalties.

## 4 The Founders of the *Waqf*s

Until the Ottoman occupation of al-Shām the genealogy of the Ughulbak family consists of six successive generations, four of which are relevant for the present essay.[21] The genealogy starts with Ughulbak b. ʿAbdallāh b. Sulaymān al-Jāshankīr (d. 761/1359). Ughulbak is referred to as "al-Sayfī, the son of [ʿAbdallāh b.] Sulaymān al-Malikī al-Ṭāhirī,[22] one of the clients (*mawālin*) of

A.H. Hourani and S.M. Stern (Oxford, 1970): 204–5; and Rafeq, "The Application of Islamic Law in the Ottoman Courts in Damascus": 411.

16 *Sijill* 1, Waqf 1, p. 6, line 16 – p. 7, line 19.

17 *Sijill* 1, Waqf 2, p. 20, lines 2ff.

18 *Sijill* 1, Waqf 3, p. 24, line 13 – p. 25, line 2.

19 Cf. Saghbini, *Mamlukische Urkunden aus Aleppo*: 31–3.

20 Cf. Daniella Talmon-Heller, "The Shaykh and the Community: Popular Hanbalite Islam in 12th–13th Century Jabal Nablus and Jabal Qasyūn." *Studia Islamica* 79 (1994): 117–9; Daniella Talmon-Heller, "Fidelity, Cohesion, and Conformity within Madhhabs in Zangid and Ayyubid Syria." In *The Islamic School of Law: Evolution, Devolution, and Progress*, eds. P. Bearman, R. Peters and F.E. Vogel (Cambridge, MA., 2005); Dafna Ephrat, "Religious Leadership and Associations in the Public Sphere of Seljuk Baghdad." In *The Public Sphere in Muslim Societies*, eds. Miriam Hoexter, Sh. N. Eisenstadt, and N. Levtzion (Albany, 2002): 37–41.

21 For the pedigree, see Saghbini, *Mamlukische Urkunden aus Aleppo*: 29.

22 "Ẓāhirī" refers to a sultan with the royal *laqab* "al-Ẓāhirī," i.e., a Mamlūk of *al-Malik al-Ẓahīr*; cf. Amalia Levanoni, "The Sultan's *Laqab*: A Sign of New Order in Mamluk Factionalism?" In *The Mamluks in Egyptian and Syrian Politics and Society*, eds. M. Winter and Amalia Levanoni (Leiden, 2004): 95; D.P. Little, "The Governance of Jerusalem under

the *ṭablkhānāh* in Aleppo, and its second chamberlain (*ḥājib*)."[23] From this we may infer that Sulaymān and Ughulbak played a role in the Mamlūk military hierarchy. The title "al-Jāshankīr" suggests that Sulaymān had served in the Sultan's court.[24] The title "al-Sayfī" points to Ughulbak's affiliation with the Sayfiyya, i.e., Mamlūks who passed from the service of the amīrs to that of the sultan after their master's death or dismissal. However, the status of the Sayfiyya was far inferior to that of other units of royal Mamlūks, especially in political terms.[25] With regard to seniority, the rank of *amīr ṭablkhānāh* was second to the *amīr mi'a wa-muqaddam alf*, i.e. the commander of a household force of 100 horsemen and head of a company of 1,000 warriors of the *ḥalqa*. The *amīr ṭablkhānāh* was entitled to purchase and maintain 40 Mamlūks in addition to maintaining a military band.[26] The Second Chamberlain (*ḥājib*) of Aleppo had jurisdiction in disputes between the amīrs and the soldiers. This senior post in the Mamlūk hierarchy was usually held by amīrs of 40 and occasionally by amīrs of 100.[27]

The founder of the first *waqf* is referred to as the noble (*karīm*); the honorable (*maqarr*); the sublime (*ʿālī*); the client, i.e. Mamlūk (*mawlawī*), the Grand Amīr (*al-amīrī al-kabīrī*);[28] the *makhdūmī*, i.e. the master into whose service

Qāytbāy." In *The Mamluks in Egyptian and Syrian Politics and Society*, eds. M. Winter and Amalia Levanoni (Leiden, 2004): 148.

23 *Sijill* I, Waqf 1, p. 9, line 4.

24 Saghbini, *Mamlukische Urkunden aus Aleppo*: 15–7; for Sulaymān's mausoleum, see Ibid: 24.

25 D. Ayalon, "Studies on the Structure of the Mamlūk Army – I."*Bulletin of the School of Oriental and African Studies* 15.2 (1953): 204, 220, 222. Al-Sayfī is an abbreviation of Sayf al-Dīn, a title conferred on almost every amīr during the latter part of the Mamlūk sultanate, and hence without any significance. See D. Ayalon, "Names, Titles and 'Nisbas' of the Mamlūks."*Israel Oriental Studies* 5 (1975): 213.

26 D. Ayalon, "Studies on the Structure of the Mamlūk Army – II." *Bulletin of the School of Oriental and African Studies* 15.3 (1953): 467 ff.; P.M. Holt, "Mamlūks." *Encyclopaedia of Islam*, 2nd edition: VI: 326i; F. Bauden, "The Recovery of Mamluk Chancery Documents in an Unsuspected Place." In *The Mamluks in Egyptian and Syrian Politics and Society*, eds. M. Winter and Amalia Levanoni (Leiden, 2004): 70.

27 Holt, "Mamlūks": 326ii; cf. P.M. Holt, "Ḳansạwh al-Ghawrī." *Encyclopaedia of Islam*, 2nd edition: IV: 552i; D. Ayalon, "Studies on the Structure of the Mamlūk Army – III." *Bulletin of the School of Oriental and African Studies* 16.1 (1954): 60; Drory, "Founding a new Mamlaka": 176–7; C.F. Petry, *Twilight of Majesty: The Reigns of the Mamlūk Sultans al-Ashraf Qāytbāy and Qānṣūh al-Ghawrī in Egypt* (Seattle, 1993): 42. For details on the family's genealogy and property of Ughulbak in Aleppo, see Saghbini, *Mamlukische Urkunden aus Aleppo*: 11–28.

28 On the titles of *amīrs*, see. M.A. Hiyari, "The Origins and Development of the Amīrate of the Arabs during the Seventh/Thirteenth and Eighth/Fourteenth Centuries." *Bulletin of the School of Oriental and African Studies* 38 (1975): 523, fn. 89.

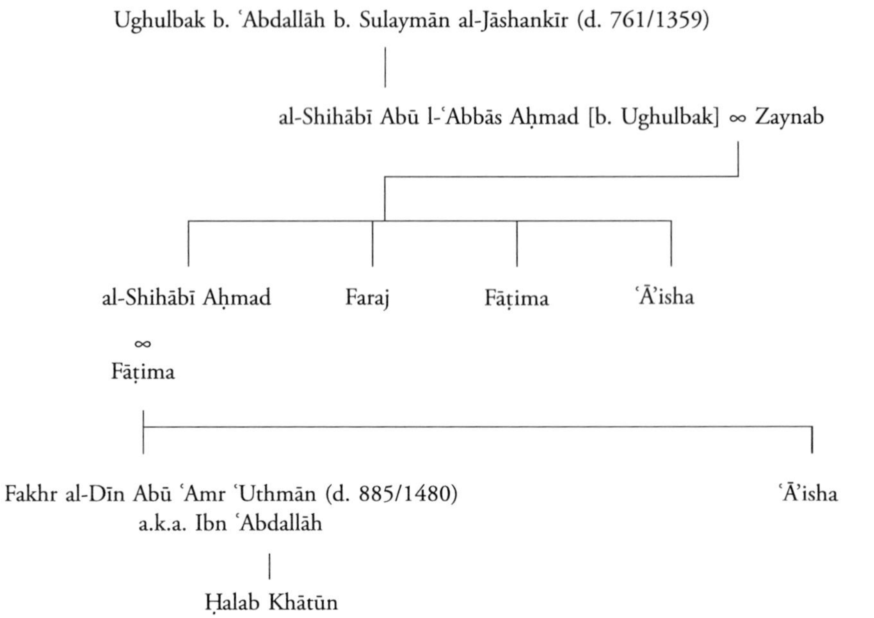


FIGURE 13.1 The members of the Ughulbak family mentioned in this article

the Mamlūk enters after having received his manumission from his *ustādh*, the purchasing master;[29] al-Shihabī[30] Abū l-ʿAbbās Aḥmad, the son of Ughulbak *ẓahīr al-mulūk wa'l-salāṭīn* (the supporter of the kings and sultans).[31]

The Arabic name of the founder suggests that he belonged to "the sons of people" (*awlād al-nās*), a special unit consisting of free-born Muslims, the sons of the amīrs and of Mamlūks who had integrated within the troops (*ajnād*) of the *ḥalqa*, a corps of free, non-Mamlūk, cavalry whose rank in the hierarchy was generally second to the Mamlūks.[32] Although the *awlād al-nās* were a rela-

29 Ayalon, "Studies on the Structure of the Mamlūk Army – I": 216.

30 Abbreviation of Shihāb al-Dīn; it does not, however, suggest affiliation to any particular family; rather, it is conferred on the sons of the Mamlūks. The title corresponds to Aḥmad, the private name of the founder. See Ayalon, "Names, Titles and 'Nisbas' of the Mamlūks": 230.

31 *Sijill* 1, Waqf 1, p. 9, line 4. The same son of Ughulbak also founded the second *Waqf*. He is referred to in its deed of foundation as al-Shihābī Aḥmad or Shihāb al-Dīn Aḥmad, the son of al-Zaynī Ughulbak. *Sijill* 1, Waqf 2, p, 20, line 2; and p. 21, lines 12–3, 18.

32 Ayalon, "Studies on the Structure of the Mamlūk Army – I": 204; D. Ayalon, "Awlād al-Nās." *Encyclopaedia of Islam*, 2nd edition, I: 765; T. Sato, *State and Rural Society in Medieval Islam: Sultans, Muqtaʿs and Fallahun* (Leiden, 1997): 121, 241; Amalia Levanoni, *A Turning Point in the Mamluk History: The Third Reign of al-Nāṣir Muḥammad Ibn Qalāwūn (1310–1341)* (Leiden, 1995): 42–51; Y. Rapoport, *Marriage, Money and Divorce in Medieval*

tively privileged social group, they did not tend to be part of the military and ruling establishment. They were entitled to the allocation of lands as charity pensions without being committed to military service (*rizaq jayshiyya*), just as other categories belonging to the *ḥalqa*.[33] Mamlūk society – to use D. Ayalon's phrase – was "a non-hereditary one-generation nobility." The permanent recruitment of new slaves and their integration into the military establishment culminated in the exclusion of the descendants of the Mamlūks and their absorption into the local Arabic-speaking Muslim population.[34]

By the time of al-Ashraf Qā'it Bāy and Qānṣawh al-Ghawrī, the role of the *awlād al-nās* as reserve forces had become marginal; the sultans frequently neglected their training altogether and froze their stipends. Their position in the military hierarchy was therefore insecure. If the *awlād al-nās* succeeded in retaining their forefathers' *iqṭāʿāt* (agricultural lands leased in return for a contractual payment) they might have acquired a significant portion of the state's lands, which thus would not have been available for redistribution to future generations of troops. Due to the price inflation of the fifteenth century, the *awlād al-nās* seem to have enjoyed more social prestige than material advantage. Yet they persisted as a distinct, self-conscious interest group, clinging to their peripheral status at the lowest fringes of the ruling elite.[35] Since the founder of the *waqf* under review here belonged to the *awlād al-nās*, the title *al-amīr al-kabīr* should be considered as an embellished honorific one without any institutional significance.[36]

The founder of the third *waqfiyya* is referred to as "al-Shihābī Aḥmad, the son of the late honorable al-Shihābī Aḥmad b. al-Zaynī Ughulbak b. ʿAlam

*Islamic Society* (Cambridge, 2005): 21. Cf. John Meloy, "Awlād al-Nās." *The Encyclopaedia of Islam – Three*, Part 2 (2007): 184–5.

33 A.N. Poliak, *Feudalism in Egypt, Syria, Palestine, and the Lebanon 1250–1900* (London, 1939): 29, 32–3.

34 Holt, "Mamlūks": 323ii, 325ii; Ayalon, "Names, Titles and 'Nisbas' of the Mamlūks": 193; Winter, "Mamluks and their Households in Late Mamluk Damascus": 298, 306–8; Drory, "Founding a new Mamlaka": 170. On the promotion of *awlād al-nās* within the army, see Amalia Levanoni, "*Awlād al-Nās* in the Mamluk Army during the Baḥrī Period." In *Mamlūks and Ottomans: Studies in Honor of Michael Winter*, eds. A.J. Ayalon and D. Wasserstein (London and New York, 2006).

35 Petry, *Protectors or Praetorians?*: 86–7.

36 During the first century of the Mamlūk sultanate the title meant simply and literally a senior *amīr*. Since the end of fourteenth century the title was annexed to the office of *atābak al-ʿasākir*, the Commander in Chief. Holt, "Mamlūks": 327i; Ayalon, "Studies on the Structure of the Mamlūk Army – III": 58–9; cf. D. S. Richards, "Glimpses of Provincial Mamluk Society from the Documents of the Ḥaram al-Sharīf in Jerusalem." In *The Mamluks in Egyptian and Syrian Politics and Society*, eds. M. Winter and Amalia Levanoni (Leiden, 2004): 47.

al-Dīn Sulaymān."[37] This indicates that both the son and the paternal grandson of Ughulbak bore the name of Shihāb al-Dīn Aḥmad.[38] The third *waqfiyya* provides more details on the founder's genealogy and titles, as well as other information. The document describes him as

> our *mawlā*, his honor, the sublime, [he] of noble origin (*aṣilī*), al-Shihābī Aḥmad, the son of the late honorable, the sublime Mamlūk (*mawlawī*) the *makhdūmī* al-Shihābī Aḥmad, son of the late al-Sayfī Ughulbak al-Ẓāhirī who is well-known (*shahīr*) because of his [paternal] grandfather (*jadd*), [Ughulbak] al-Malikī al-Ẓāhirī, one of the clients (*mawālin*) of Ṭablkhānāh in Aleppo and its second Chamberlain (*ḥājib*)] from among the notables (*aʿyān*), overlords (*sāda*),[39] and the amīrs (*umarāʾ*) of Aleppo, the Protected (*Ḥalab al-shahbāʾ*).[40]

These titles are a clear indication that we are dealing with the *awlād al-nās* as a civil, rather than a military elite. Shihāb al-Dīn Aḥmad, the paternal grandson of Ughulbak, was also well-known for his religious education and integrity, for which he was awarded the control of the al-Ṭunbughā Mosque in Aleppo.[41]

The founder of the fourth *waqf*, the paternal great-grandson of Ughulbak, is presented in the deed as

> the honorable, the sublime *al-amīrī al-kābīrī*, the eminent (*al-fāḍilī*), the worldly (*al-ʿallāmī*), *al-ʿālimī*,[42] the skilled (*bāriʿ*), the eloquent (*balīgh, mufawwah*), the supportive (*al-sanadī*), *al-sayyidī*, the unique (*al-awḥadī*), *al-malikī*, *al-makhdūmī*, the glory (*al-fakhrī*), Abū ʿAmr ʿUthmān, son of the honorable, the sublime, *al-amīrī al-kabīrī*, ... the son of al-Shihābī Abū l-ʿAbbās Aḥmad, son of the honorable al-Zaynī Ughulbak al-Ḥanafī.[43]

It seems that ʿUthmān did not inherit most of the titles attributed to his ancestors, for there is no mention of ʿUthmān as the *mawlā* of *al-amīr al-kabīr*. He

37 *Sijill* I, Waqf 3, p. 21, lines 17–8.

38 Cf. Saghbini, *Mamlukische Urkunden aus Aleppo*: 12–4, 17–9.

39 The sons of the sultans, who were also included in the *awlād al-nās* as an elite unit, were called *al-asyād*, or *awlād al-mulūk*." Ayalon, "Studies on the Structure of the Mamlūk Army – II": 458.

40 *Sijill* I, Waqf 3, p. 25, lines 13–4.

41 Saghbini, *Mamlukische Urkunden aus Aleppo*: 18.

42 Many of the *awlād al-nās* left the military service and became *fuqahāʾ*. Ayalon, "Awlād al-Nās": 765; Ayalon, "Studies on the Structure of the Mamlūk Army – II": 456. Cf. Poliak, *The History of Agrarian Relations*: 49.

43 *Sijill* II, Waqf, 4. p. 95, lines 7–9.

thus probably only inherited their shares in the estate and portions in the entitlement to the proceeds of the *waqfs*. His Arabic name also suggests that he was not a Mamlūk. For example, in one of the deeds of sale which are part of the same family archives he is referred to simply as Ibn ʿAbdallāh.[44] In general, the adoption of such an anonymous genealogy signifies the conversion to Islam and in this case it signals a disengagement from the obscure infidel past of the Mamlūks. However, the adoption of a Muslim name also entailed a distancing from the military aristocracy.[45]

Fakhr al-Dīn Abū ʿAmr ʿUthmān (d. 885/1480) is the most famous member of Ughulbak family. He started his career in Aleppo where he was appointed as the commander of the Karkar Citadel. When the Ottoman sultan Meḥmed II approached Aleppo, Qāʾit Bāy could not count on ʿUthmān's loyalty. In order to strengthen his own political position in the region, ʿUthmān married off his daughter to Badr al-Dīn Ḥasan, the son of the treasurer (*wakīl*) of Aleppo's *bayt al-māl*. In 875/1475 he was appointed Chief Secretary (*kātib al-sirr*) and Controller of the Army (*nāẓir al-jaysh*) at Aleppo.[46] Later he retired from all his positions in the city and went to Cairo in order to obtain an authorization (*ijāza*) in religious studies. Eventually he returned to Aleppo, where he was appointed Executive Adjutant (*dawādār*).[47] In 884/1479 he reached the peak of his career when Qāʾit Bāy appointed him commander of Qalʿat al-Rūm.[48]

ʿUthmān had three daughters, the most famous of whom was Ḥalab Khātūn, who inherited a fortune from her father.[49] She was married to Muḥibb al-Dīn Abū al-Ṭanāʾ Maḥmūd b. Āghā, the Chief Secretary in Cairo. After the Ottomans had defeated Qānṣawh al-Ghawrī at the battle of Marj Dābiq in 1516, Ḥalab Khātūn returned to Aleppo. In 926/1650, shortly after her husband had died, she married the *qāḍī* of Aleppo and later moved to Damascus.[50] In Aleppo Ḥalab Khātūn endowed buildings for public welfare, such as the al-Zaytūn Mosque and a public fountain (*sabīl*), which still exists in the present ʿAntar quarter of the town, where her mausoleum is also located.[51]

44 *Sijill* I, Transaction 2, Sale, p. 2, line 12 – p. 6, line 16.

45 D. Ayalon, "Mamlūks." *Encyclopaedia of Islam*, 2nd edition, VI: 318i, 319i; Winter, "Mamluks and their Households in Late Mamluk Damascus": 304.

46 Cf. Drory, "Founding a new Mamlaka": 182.

47 Cf. Petry, "The Estate of al-Khuwand Fāṭima al-Khaṣṣbakiyya": 279.

48 Saghbini, *Mamlukische Urkunden aus Aleppo*: 19–22; for Fakh al-Dīn ʿUthmān's mausoleum, mosque, Jāmiʿ Bāb al-Aḥmar, and baths (*ḥamāms*), see Ibid: 24–7.

49 Saghbini, *Mamlukische Urkunden aus Aleppo*: 29.

50 Ibid: 22–3.

51 Ibid: 27–8.

"Sitt Ḥalab," the daughter of ʿUthmān and the agnatic great-great-granddaughter of Ughulbak, was also the founder of the fifth *waqf*.[52] In 910/1504, she endowed half of the village of Takhārīn in the district of Aleppo, a transaction which seems to reflect the status of women in the ruling class of the civil elite into which the Mamlūks' descendants had become integrated.[53] An earlier example of the transfer of property by women is the transfer by Fāṭima, the wife of al-Shihābī Aḥmad (the agnatic grandson of Ughulbak) and her daughter, ʿĀʾisha, of their shares in Aḥmad's estate, which was jointly owned (*mushāʿ*) by the legal heirs, to their individual ownership (*tamlīk*).[54]

## 5 The Endowed Properties

All schools of law except the Mālikīs prescribe that only a tangible asset (*ʿayn*) that is clearly defined and exists at the moment of endowment can validly be transformed into *waqf*. The Ḥanafī school adheres to the principle that only immovable property (both *ʿushr* and *kharāj* land) can be endowed as *waqf*, but it allows exceptions in the case of movable goods that follow immovable property, such as slaves, animals, and agricultural tools belonging to a rural estate. Mālikī jurists permit the endowment of the *manfaʿa*, the revenue of landed property and the rent of leased property.[55] Ḥanafī jurists exclude gardens, plantations, and pastures from tenancy because they belong to the category of *ijāra istihlāk*, "tenancy of consumption."[56]

The endowments in our documents include several types of property. The rural properties consist of entire villages in the region of Aleppo, including the lands and everything connected to them, and agricultural land of various

52 Gaube and Wirth state that "Sitt Ḥalab" was the founder of the al-Zaytūn Mosque, which confirms our identification of her with Ḥalab Khātūn; Heinz Gaube and Eugen Wirth, *Tübinger Atlas des Vorderen Orients, Beihefte Bd. 58: Aleppo: Historische und geographische Beiträge zur baulichen Gestaltung, zur sozialen Organisation und zur wirtschaftlichen Dynamik einer vorderasiatischen Fernhandelsmetropole* (Wiesbaden 1984): 397–8.

53 Recorded in the *sijill* of Ḥamā. The *Waqfiyya* was copied in the margins of the fourth *Waqfiyya*; see *Sijill* 11, Waqf 4, p. 98, line 6 – p. 100, line 16.

54 Saghbini, *Mamlukische Urkunden aus Aleppo*: Arabic documents, 70–4. Cf. Richards, "Glimpses of Provincial Mamluk Society": 50. Petry has observed this phenomenon in Mamlūk society in later medieval Egypt as well. C.F. Petry, "Class Solidarity versus Gender Gain: Women as Custodians of Property in Later Medieval Egypt." In *Women in Middle Eastern History: Shifting Boundaries in Sex and Gender*, eds. Nikki Keddie and Beth Baron (New Haven, 1991): esp. 330–3; cf. Rapoport, *Marriage, Money and Divorce*: 29; J.A. Reilly, "Women in the Economic Life of Late-Ottoman Damascus." *Arabica* 42 (1995).

55 Peters, "Waqf": 60; Heffening, "Waḳf": 1096ii; Poliak, *Feudalism*: 33.

56 Johansen, *The Islamic Law on Land Tax and Rent*: 26.

kinds: cultivated land, plantations of a variety of fruit trees, as well as roads, irrigation canals, pools and cisterns, irrigation rights, water rights in the River Qūt ("a permanent right so long as the water flows in the river"),[57] and oil presses (*miʿṣara*; pl. *maʿāṣir*).[58] The urban properties include roofed buildings and stories of buildings (*ṭibāq*) in prestigious neighborhoods of the old city of Aleppo and in the vicinity of the citadel, well-known mosques, shops, *khān*s,[59] warehouses (*makhāzin*), public baths (*ḥamām*s), and the rights of use of material appurtenances that were sold with the property (*manāfiʿ*, *marāfiq*).[60] The urban real estate fell into the category of "property reserved for profitable use," *milk muʿadd lil-istighlāl*, that is, all kinds of property that are acquired or built for the purpose of being put to profitable use, or which are leased for periods of more than three successive years.[61] All schools of law only permit the endowment of property of which the full ownership and the right of disposition are vested in the founder of the *waqf*.[62]

The *waqfiyya*s under examination confirm that the founder was the owner of the property prior to its endowment, that the property was in his possession and that he disposed of it freely (*lam yazal mālikan ḥāʾizan bi-jamīʿ mā huwa lahu wa-bi-milkihi wa-bi-yadihi wa-ḥawzihi wa-taṣarrufihi*),[63] "until the very moment of this endowment,"[64] without opposition by anyone, and that there was no legal objection to the endowment of the property.[65] The *sharīʿa* court had to establish that these conditions had been strictly and fully adhered to before confirming the validity of the *waqf*.[66]

---

57 *Sijill* II, Waqf 4, p. 104, line 4; cf. Poliak, *The History of Agrarian Relations*: 33 (water rights, wells, mills, irrigation dams, canals), 49 (flowing water), 51 (water supply); Petry, "The Estate of al-Khuwand Fāṭima al-Khaṣṣbakiyya": 283.

58 Cf. Winter, "Mamluks and their Households in Late Mamluk Damascus": 298–9.

59 Cf. N. Luz, "Urban Residential Houses in Mamluk Syria: Forms, Characteristics and the Impact of Socio-cultural Forces." In *The Mamluks in Egyptian and Syrian Politics and Society*, eds. M. Winter and Amalia Levanoni (Leiden, 2004): 347; J.A. Reilly, "Properties around Damascus in the Nineteenth Century." *Arabica* 37 (1990): 110.

60 To be distinguished from abstract rights (*ḥuqūq*); Jeanette A. Wakin, *The Function of Documents in Islamic Law: The Chapters on Sales from Ṭaḥāwī's Kitāb al-Shurūṭ al-kabīr* (Albany, 1972): 51; cf. Saghbini, *Mamlukische Urkunden aus Aleppo*: 39; Johansen, *The Islamic Law on Land Tax and Rent*: 27; Luz, "Urban Residential Houses in Mamluk Syria": 345; Petry, "The Estate of al-Khuwand Fāṭima al-Khaṣṣbakiyya": 283; Reilly, "Properties around Damascus in the Nineteenth Century": 93.

61 Johansen, *The Islamic Law on Land Tax and Rent*: 67, 107.

62 Cf. Peters, "Waḳf": 60ii; Heffening, "Waḳf": 1096ii.

63 *Sijill* I, Waqf 1, p. 8, line 15; p. 9, line 8.

64 *Sijill* I, Waqf 2, p. 21, line 14; Waqf 3, p. 25 lines 3, 15.

65 *Sijill* II, Waqf 4, p. 95, line 13.

66 *Sijill* I, Waqf 1, p. 14, line 9 – p. 15, line 6; cf. Saghbini, *Mamlukische Urkunden aus Aleppo*: 47; see above.

A.N. Poliak notes that the majority of the *waqf*s during the Mamlūk period were established on former *iqṭāʿāt* and sultan's lands, i.e. *kharāj* lands. However, prior to their endowment, the *kharāj* lands were converted into *milk* lands first.[67] Otherwise, it was prohibited to sell *iqṭāʿāt* of *dīwān al-jaysh* as well as *waqf* property because they were deemed as "public property" (*amlāk āmma*).[68]

## 6 State Ownership, Private Property, and *Waqf*

Now that we have established that the *awlād al-nās* in Aleppo possessed property in full ownership, the question arises of how they obtained it. It is clear that Aḥmad, the paternal grandson of Ughulbak, and especially his son, ʿUthmān, bought property in private transactions. Twenty-two documents in the family archive deal with the purchase of property. Two of the transactions were by Aḥmad, the rest by ʿUthmān, both of whom purchased property from private owners. In some cases it is possible to identify among the sellers Mamlūks or their heirs,[69] and in one case the seller was a woman, probably the daughter of a Mamlūk.[70]

Some of the endowed properties belonged to the founder in their entirety, but in most cases portions held in *mushāʿ*, jointly-owned property measured by *qīrāṭ*, are specified.[71] This suggests that the properties were purchased by voluntary transactions rather than through confiscation. As we shall see below, the possibility that part of this private property was transmitted to the founders by means of inheritance cannot be ruled out.

In four cases, the founders bought private property from the *bayt al-māl*, the Public Treasury.[72] Since the Representation of the Public Treasury (*wakālat bayt al-māl*) was defined as one of the "religious functions" (*waẓāʾif dīniyya*), the representatives of the *bayt al-māl* obtained religious education and enjoyed

---

67 Poliak, *The History of Agrarian Relations*: 49–50; see below.

68 Saghbini, *Mamlukische Urkunden aus Aleppo*: 40.

69 *Sijill* 1, Sale, p. 40, line 9 – p. 43, line 9 (the heirs of al-Sayfī Yastabak [?] al-Khamrāwī); Sale, p. 34, line 15 – p. 37, line 5 (ʿUmar b. Aḥmad b. al-Saffāḥ al-Mardāshī).

70 *Sijill* 1, Sale, p. 46, line 14 – p. 49, line 7 (al-Ṭuruntāy bint ʿAbdallāh, the owner of a storehouse).

71 Cf. Petry, "The Estate of al-Khuwand Fāṭima al-Khaṣṣbakiyya": 283.

72 *Sijill* 1, Sale, p. 2, line 12 – p. 6, line 16; Sale. p. 52, line 10 – p. 55, line 4; Sale, p. 55, line 4 – p. 57, line 12; Sale, p. 58, line 15 – p. 64, line 14; cf. Johansen, *The Islamic Law on Land Tax and Rent*: 81 (investment of capital in purchase of lands from the Public Treasury either as tax assignment or as proprietary rights with regard to state lands).

the status of *qāḍīs*.[73] The *bayt al-māl* was instrumental in providing the amīrs and the *awlād al-nās* with properties in full ownership. The Public Treasury accumulated private property from various sources. As a residuary heir, it inherited the estates of those who died without heirs, e.g. after outbreaks of the plague.[74] The *bayt al-māl* in Safed was in charge of the administration of heirless estates, the supervision of the validity of transactions in which the state was involved (for example in cases of public estates), and of supervising orphans' rights of entitlement in *waqf* property.[75] The Mālikī school did not acknowledge the doctrine of *radd*; in the absence of agnates, the residue of the estate after its apportionment among the Qurʾānic heirs therefore devolved to the *bayt al-māl*.[76] This practice provided an additional incentive to convert estates into *waqf*. Another source for the accumulation of property by the *bayt al-māl* was the confiscation of private property and *waqfs*.[77]

It was common practice for Mamlūk sultans to grant amīrs *iqṭāʿāt* for the upkeep of military households in return for service.[78] *Iqṭāʿ* does not only denote an administrative grant of land, but also a source of revenue, such as annual allowances from tax revenue, or customs or excise taxes levied by the central government temporarily allocated by the state to the amīr. This consisted of an average annual income that corresponded to the amīr's military rank.[79] Property accumulated by individual Mamlūks was regarded as part of a vast fiscal reservoir held collectively by the entire military oligarchy, and upon their death, the property had to be restored to the *dīwān al-jaysh* for redistribution as *iqṭāʿ*.[80]

There is no evidence in our documents that amīrs and the *awlād al-nās* endowed property that had been granted to them as military *iqṭāʿ*.[81] Under the first Mamlūk sultans, *iqṭāʿāt* were hereditary subject to the loyal behavior of their holders and their descendants' ability to perform the military duties of the amīrs. The amīrs' minor sons received allowances of money, meat, bread,

73 Saghbini, *Mamlukische Urkunden aus Aleppo*: 37.

74 Johansen, *The Islamic Law on Land Tax and Rent*: 15, 83.

75 Drory, "Founding a new Mamlaka": 185.

76 N.J. Coulson, *Succession in the Muslim Family* (Cambridge, 1971): 49–51.

77 Little, "The Governance of Jerusalem under Qā'itbāy": 151, 152, 159; Richards, "Glimpses of Provincial Mamluk Society": 46, 49; Petry, *Protectors or Praetorians?*: 172.

78 C.I. Cahen, "Iḳṭāʿ" *Encyclopaedia of Islam*, 2nd edition, III: 1090i; Holt, "Mamlūks": 326i; A. Meier, "Waḳf. II.2. In Syria" *Encyclopaedia of Islam*, Supplement, XII, Fasc. 11–2: 826i.

79 Poliak, *Feudalism*: 18; Poliak, *The History of Agrarian Relations*: 36.

80 Petry, "The Estate of al-Khuwand Fāṭima al-Khaṣṣbakiyya": 279–81, 284; cf. Poliak, *The History of Agrarian Relations*, 40; Bauden," The Recovery of Mamluk Chancery Documents": 70–2.

81 Cf. Winter, "Mamluks and their Households in Late Mamluk Damascus": 298.

and forage, and on becoming adults they were affiliated with the *ḥalqa*.[82] When the *iqṭāʿāt* ceased to be hereditary, the amīrs were anxious to transfer their estates to their descendants without being bound by the duty of military service. The pension estates were granted to the amīrs' sons "as charity" (*ʿalā sabīl al-birr wa'l-ṣadaqa*) without the obligation to perform military service, that is, as compensation for being deprived of the amīrs' *iqṭāʿāt*.[83]

The *sharīʿa* makes a clear distinction between *kharāj* land on the one hand, the bare ownership of which is vested in the state while the individual only has the right to usufruct; and *milk*, on the other, in which both ownership and usufruct are vested in the individual. According to the classical literature, Muslims have to pay *ʿushr*, tithe, on conquered lands assigned to them by the ruler. *Kharāj* was established as a land tax that was incumbent on Muslims and non-Muslims alike. The payment of *kharāj* tax was proof of property rights. The *sharīʿa* does not permit the conversion of *kharāj* land into *ʿushr* land and vice-versa. *Kharāj* and *ʿushr* taxes are also due from *waqf*.[84] During the Ayyūbid and Mamlūk periods, *zakāt*, in addition to *ʿushr* and *kharāj*, was levied on Egyptian and Syrian peasants, contrary to Islamic law.[85] Unlike the *ʿushr*, the *kharāj* tax was levied collectively upon the villages (but not in urban areas) according to the amount of produce obtained from the land.[86] In fact, the Mamlūk sultanate only collected fees from *kharāj* lands and gave up those from *iqṭāʿāt* lands, pension lands, and *aḥbās* (a special category of *waqf* property under the supervision of *dawādār al-sulṭān*), as well as the tithe from the owners of *milk* lands. The peasants paid tenancy fees to their direct lord, regardless of whether the land was *kharāj* or *milk*.[87]

Poliak has demonstrated the role of the *bayt al-māl* in converting *kharāj* land into *milk*. Apart from arbitrary confiscation by the sultan, this was the easiest way of transforming military estates granted as charity pensions into lifelong hereditary possessions. The Mamlūk jurists circumvented the *sharʿī* prohibition of such a conversion by basing the caliph's discretion to grant conquered lands and ownerless lands to Muslims on the theory that such property becomes the *milk* of the entire Muslim community.[88] In fact, the *bayt al-māl*,

82 Poliak, *Feudalism*: 28.

83 Poliak, *Feudalism*: 32; Poliak, *The History of Agrarian Relations*: 41.

84 Johansen, *The Islamic Law on Land Tax and Rent*: 9–12; C. Orhonlu, "Kharāj, III. In Ottoman Turkey." *Encyclopaedia of Islam*, 2nd edition, IV: 1054i.

85 T. Sato, "ʿUshr", *Encyclopaedia of Islam*, 2nd edition, X: 918ii.

86 Cahen, "Kharādj." *Encyclopaedia of Islam*, 2nd edition, IV: 1030ii–31i; Orhonlu, "Kharādj": 1054i; Levanoni, *A Turning Point*: 46.

87 Poliak, *The History of Agrarian Relations*: 11–2; cf. Heffening, "Waḳf": 1096ii.

88 Poliak, *Feudalism*: 36.

in its capacity as the caliph's representative, sold numerous ownerless *kharāj* lands as *milk* properties. Moreover, holders of *iqṭāʿāt* transmitted them to the *bayt al-māl* out of their own free will in order to redeem them as *milk* (*tamlīk*).[89] The fact that transactions between the founders and the *bayt al-māl* were confirmed by the *sharīʿa* court implies that the properties were *milk*, since only *milk* and *waqf* properties were under the jurisdiction of the *sharīʿa* court; cases pertaining to *iqṭāʿāt* and estates granted as pensions came under the jurisdiction of military judges.[90]

## 7 *Waqf*s and Agriculture

Our documents provide some information on agrarian relations between the founders of the *waqf*s and the tenants. Thus in one case the endowed rural properties included peasants' dwellings (*dūr bi-aydī* [or *li-suknā*] *al-fallāḥīn*) with specified names,[91] which may mean that the peasants were attached to the households. Poliak notes that the servile tenants paid the rents levied on *milk* and *kharāj* lands to the landlord. In Syria these rents constituted a fixed share (*muqāsama*) of the produce: between one-third and one-quarter, but one-sixth for irrigated lands. Most of the landlords lived in the cities, their only concern being the collection of the usufruct fees and state taxes from their tenants; the *ʿushr* due from the residue of the crops left to the peasants after the *muqāsama*, was levied as well. The cultivation of agricultural lands was structured on the basis of the *mushāʿ* system, the land being re-divided every year by lottery (*queʿa*) among the members of the clan in accordance with the number of work animals.[92]

One of our *waqfiyya*s stipulates that "the *nāẓir* will collect the proceeds (*yastaghill*) from the property with the exception of two flour mills which must be rented to someone capable of securing their functioning."[93] This seems to indicate a long-term lease, or "double-lease" (T. *icarateyn*), as it came to be known in the Ottoman period. The purpose of this practice, which evades the principle of the inalienability of *waqf* property under the *sharīʿa*, is to stimulate

89 Ibid: 36–7; Poliak, *The History of Agrarian Relations*: 50; Heffening, "Waḳf": 1099i.

90 Poliak, *The History of Agrarian Relations*: 12.

91 *Sijill* I, Waqf 1, p. 10, lines 11–3; *Sijill* II, Waqf 4, p. 98, lines 15–6 – p. 99, lines 1–3; cf. Luz, "Urban Residential Houses in Mamluk Syria": 349; see below.

92 Poliak, *The History of Agrarian Relations*: 57–8, 60, 65; Poliak, *Feudalism*: 67; Levanoni, *A Turning Point*: 46.

93 *Sijill* II, Waqf 4, p. 113, line 13.

the renovation of dilapidated *waqf* property.[94] During the Mamlūk period, the difference between tax and rent on small agricultural holdings ceased to exist.[95] The jurists regarded the land tax paid by the owner of the landed property or the *waqf* administrator as a *virtual* share of the rent collected from the peasants.[96] The judicial basis of this transformation was the doctrine of *istiḥsān*.[97]

## 8 Motives for Creating Endowments

In the *waqfiyya*s in our possession, the technical terms *waqf dhurrī* (or *ahlī*) and *waqf khayrī* do not occur. The distinction between the two terms is not relevant in *sharʿī waqf* law because the creation of an endowment in favor of descendants and other relatives is regarded as a charitable act.[98] These technical terms only became current in modern codifications of *waqf* law,[99] and more so in reformist legislation of the institution of the *waqf*, which abolished the family *waqf* altogether and accommodated the *khayrī waqf* to modern economic and social requirements.[100] Nevertheless, the distinction between the two kinds of *waqf* can be traced in our family archive.[101]

---

94 E. Tyan, "Idjār, Idjāra." *Encyclopaedia of Islam*, 2nd edition, III: 1017ii; G. Bear, "Ḥikr." *Encyclopaedia of Islam*, Supplement, XII, Fasc. 5: 368ii; H. Gerber, *Economy and Society in an Ottoman City: Bursa, 1600–1700* (Jerusalem, 1988): 171–5; H. Gerber, *State, Society and Law in Islam: Ottoman Law in Comparative Perspective* (New York, 1994): 108–9; A. Marcus, *The Middle East on the Eve of Modernity: Aleppo in the Eighteenth Century* (New York, 1989): 310–1; Miriam Hoexter, "Adaptation to Changing Circumstances: Perpetual Leases and Exchanged Transactions in *Waqf* Property in Ottoman Algiers." *Islamic Law and Society* 4.3 (1997): 319 ff.; cf. J.A. Reilly, "Urban Hegemony in the Hinterland of Ottoman Damascus: Villages, Estates and Farms in the Nineteenth Century." In *Histoire économique et sociale de l'Empire ottoman et de la Turquie (1326–1960)*, ed. D. Panzac (Paris, 1995). Also in *Collection Turcica* 8 (1995): 458.

95 Johansen, *The Islamic Law on Land Tax and Rent*: 69, 81–3.

96 Ibid: 101–2, 104.

97 Ibid: 30–1, 54, 110–1.

98 For a general discussion of these terms both on the theoretical and practical level, see Hoexter, "*Ḥuqūq Allāh* and *Ḥuqūq al-ʿIbād*"; cf. T. Ito, "Aufsicht und Verwaltung der Stiftungen im mamlukischen Ägypten." *Der Islam* 80 (2003); Heffening, "Waḳf": 1096ii; Levanoni, *A Turning Point*: 6.

99 See, e.g., Qadrī, *Kitāb Qānūn al-ʿadl wa-l-inṣāf*: art. 17 (*al-birr ʿalā al-dhuriyya … wujūh al-khayrāt*); Hilmi, *A Gift to Posterity on the Laws of Evqaf*: arts. 16 (*muessesati khairiye*), 24 (*zurriyet*).

100 A. Layish, "Waḳf, II. 5. In the Modern Middle East and North Africa." *Encyclopaedia of Islam*, 2nd edition, XI.

101 Cf. Winter, "Mamluks and their Households in Late Mamluk Damascus": 299.

The *waqfiyyas* contain many expressions of piety, including religious formulas at the beginning and the end of the documents, invocations and prayers for the soul of the Prophet, his family and Companions, Qurʾānic verses, invocations of the sanction of Allāh and the angels against anyone trying to encroach on the *waqf*, and statements characterizing the endowment as an act pleasing to Allāh (*qurba*).[102] We also find references to charity, such as the welfare of orphans and the poor; allocations of cloth, bread, and meat; allocations of allowances to readers of the Qurʾān for the commemoration of the founder, his parents, and the rest of the Muslims;[103] the manumission of Muslim female slaves as part of the procedure of *kaffāra* (religious expiation); allocations of allowances to the mosques in Mecca and Medina, as well as the mosques of al-Aqṣā and al-Khalīl;[104] allocations to the *madrasa* constructed by the founder in Aleppo, etc.[105] C. F. Petry reports that Qāʾit Bāy and al-Ghawrī made large investments in endowments to promote piety, scholarship, and welfare. Together, the two sultans initiated a third of all the *waqf* documents that have survived from the Mamlūk period.[106] Undoubtedly, the above-mentioned evidence reflects a strong Islamic consciousness and profound religious piety.[107] At the same time, we should not rule out the possibility that the founder's allocations to charity and public purposes were inspired by practical considerations.[108] The desire to project an image of a devoted, pious Muslim taking care of public welfare out of concern and responsibility toward society and God may have been instrumental in obtaining political ends.

Within the context of practical considerations the founder's desire to preserve the integrity of the patrimony seems to have provided a very strong motive for the creation of *waqfs*.[109] The *sharʿī* law of inheritance does not allow

102 Heffening, "Waḳf": 1096ii; Saghbini, *Mamlukische Urkunden aus Aleppo*: 46.

103 *Cf. Marcus, The Middle East on the Eve of Modernity*: 274–5, 305.

104 Cf. Ibid.: 305.

105 *Sijill* I, Waqf 1, p. 12, line 3; p. 13, lines 3–4; Waqf 2, p. 21, line 18 – p. 23, line 4; Waqf 3, p. 26, line 10; p. 27, lines 11–2; *Sijill* II, Waqf 4, p. 109, line 11 – p. 110, line 13; Waqf 5, p. 100, lines 10–6; cf. Winter, "Mamluks and their Households in Late Mamluk Damascus": 299; Poliak, *Feudalism*: 37–8 (maintenance of mosques, *madrasas*, mausoleums, and monasteries of dervishes in the Ḥijāz); Hoexter, "*Ḥuqūq Allāh* and *Ḥuqūq al-ʿIbād*": 146; Marcus, *The Middle East on the Eve of Modernity*: 304–5).

106 Petry, *Protectors or Praetorians?*: 196.

107 Cf. Ayalon, "Mamlūks": 319ii.

108 Such as the defense of coasts against European corsairs, the payment of ransom for Muslims captured by them, the provision of water supply, and hospitals. Poliak, *Feudalism*: 37–8; on liberation of prisoners, see Qadrī, *Kitāb Qānūn al-ʿadl wa-l-inṣāf*: 57, art. 194.

109 In most *Waqfiyyas*, the founder assigns entitlement to charitable purposes after the extinction of his immediate children (*ṣulb*) and their descendants; cf. Marcus, *The Middle*

the owner of property the freedom to determine the devolution of his estate after his death. Severe limits are placed on testamentary disposition and under the *ultra vires* doctrine (in Sunnī law) it is prohibited to make a bequest in favor of a legal heir. Even with respect to a stranger or a relative who is excluded from inheritance in the presence of a specific relative, a bequest may not exceed one-third of the estate.[110] These prohibitions were cumbersome in daily life and were hence circumvented by various devices. The institution of the *waqf* enabled a Muslim to maintain control of his estate both in his lifetime and after his death. Although the act of endowment becomes complete (*munjaz*) and operative (*nāfidh*) immediately, the founder may, in accordance with Abū Yūsuf's doctrine, stipulate in the *waqfiyya* that he will be the first beneficiary and the first administrator of the *waqf*.[111] The founder may also name specific beneficiaries and the consecutive order of unborn beneficiaries after his death, their portions in the entitlement, and the mode of its transmission from one generation to the next, without being bound by the *sharʿī* law of inheritance.

## 9 Entitlement and Inheritance

In theory the physical integrity of the property in perpetuity is secured by the mere act of endowment, but it is also necessary to secure the cohesion of entitlement within the circle of agnates. This can be achieved by the founder's stipulations pertaining to the order of the beneficiaries, the inter-generational transmission of entitlement, and its mode of division between the sexes. These conditions are a matter of practice rather than of law, and – within the maneuvering space allowed by the *sharīʿa* – they may therefore differ from one founder to another.

In all the *waqfiyyas* studied for this paper, the founder designated himself as the first beneficiary, either exclusively or in combination with charities.[112] Next come the founder's immediate children and their descendants, until the line comes to an end. In only one *waqfiyya* did the founder (Sitt Ḥalab Khātūn) leave the entire entitlement to charity after her death.[113] The division of entitlement between the sexes occurred "in accordance with the *sharʿī* fractional

*East on the Eve of Modernity*: 210; Gerber, *State, Society and Law*: 152 (Aleppo between 1770–1830).

110 Coulson, *Succession in the Muslim Family*: 213–4, 235–6.

111 Heffening, "Waḳf": 1096i–ii.

112 Cf. Layish, "The Family *Waqf* and and the *Sharʿī* Law of Succession in Modern Times": 357–8.

113 *Sijill* 11, Waqf 5, p. 100, lines 10–6; see below.

shares of the estate" (*ḥasab al-farīḍa al-sharʿiyya*), i.e. male heirs took twice the portion of the females within the same degree (*daraja*) of relationship to the founder.[114]

Entitlement is transmitted from one generation of beneficiaries to the next within each of the branches (*per stirpes*) independently, regardless of whether or not there are other relatives in the same degree. Thus the descendants enter into the position of the parent, in accordance with the principle of representation, and divide between them the parent's share in the entitlement to the proceeds of the *waqf*. According to the *sharʿī* rules of inheritance, those who are nearer in degree to the *praepositus* totally exclude those who are more distant from the estate.[115] However, contrary to the agnatic patterns of intergenerational transmission, in some instances females in successive generations did not only benefit from their shares in the entitlement, but also transmitted them to their own descendants, thus infringing upon the male agnates' dominance in this hereditary system.[116] However, the evidence of the transmission of entitlement to cognatic descendants is equivocal, and should hence be treated with some caution. For example, one *waqfiyya* stipulates that entitlement should be transmitted to the descendants "*ʿalā naslihim wa-ʿaqibihim.*" "*Nasl*" denotes "descendants" or "progeny" of both sexes, agnatic, and cognatic. The same *waqfiyya* stipulates that if no agnatic or cognatic descendants remained (*wa-lam yabqa* … [someone related to the founder] *bi-āb min al-ābāʾ wa-lā bi-umm min al-ummahāt*), the entitlement should be transmitted to other beneficiaries.[117] It is not clear whether the founder meant that the transmission should be in the agnatic and cognatic lines simultaneously, or successively.

Naturally, preference in entitlement is given to the immediate issue (*ṣulb*) of the founder. In one case, the founder stipulated that entitlement should be transmitted, after him, to his son and daughter and apportioned in accordance

114 See, e.g., *Sijill* I, Waqf 1, p. 12, line 6; cf. Rapoport, *Marriage, Money and Divorce*: 27; Marcus, *The Middle East on the Eve of Modernity*: 211; Layish, "The Family *Waqf* and and the *Sharʿī* Law of Succession in Modern Times": 375–7.

115 Cf. Layish, op. cit., 366 ff.; D. Powers, "The Maliki Family Endowment: Legal Norms and Social Practices." *International Journal of Middle Eastern Studies* 25 (1993): 383.

116 Layish, "The Family *Waqf* and the *Sharʿī* Law of Succession in Modern Times": 369 ff; Rapoport, *Marriage, Money and Divorce*: 28.

117 *Sijill* I, Waqf 1, p. 12, lines 7–9, 13; It should be noted that some jurists claim that "*ʿaqib*" should be interpreted restrictively as referring only to agnatic descendants of both sexes. A. Layish, "The Mālikī Family *Waqf* according to Wills and *Waqfiyyāt*." *Bulletin of the School of Oriental and African Studies* 46.1 (1983): 16; Layish, "The Family *Waqf* and the *Sharʿī* Law of Succession in Modern Times": 370–1; Powers, "The Mālikī Family Endowment": 383, 399–400; cf. E. D. Lane, *Arabic-English Lexicon*. Revised format, 2 vols. (Cambridge, 1984): 2101ii.

with the *sharʿī* inheritance rules. After the daughter's death, her share was to be transmitted to her brother and his descendants, regardless of whether she had any children of her own. Only if the son died without leaving descendants would his share be transmitted to his sister, the founder's daughter.[118] In another case the founder, who had no sons at the time of the foundation of the *waqf*, stipulated that entitlement should be transmitted, after him, to his daughter and to any sons who might be born to him in the future. He also assigned entitlement to his two wives in accordance with *sharʿī* inheritance rules, one-eighth to be apportioned equally between them if there were children, and one-quarter if there were none. The founder further stipulated that in case of the death of either wife her share was to be transmitted to any children that might be born to the founder, and that if either of his wives remarried after his death, she would forfeit her entitlement.[119]

Upon the extinction of the founder's line (i.e. his children and their agnatic and cognatic descendants), entitlement was to be transmitted to the founder's relatives from other classes or *parentelas* (*ṭabaqāt*). In the first *waqfiyya*, these were the founder's full sister (Ḥalab Khātūn) and his three paternal first cousins (*awlād ʿamm*), along with freed slaves (i.e. Mamlūks), each group receiving one-third of the entitlement. Upon the extinction of these beneficiaries, entitlement was to pass to agnatic and cognatic descendants within each group, and upon their extinction to those of the other two groups, until all the descendants of all three groups had become extinct. It is interesting to note that the entitlement to the *waqf* proceeds was to be divided among the freed slaves on the basis of full equality between the sexes, and that both sexes were allowed to transmit their shares to their descendants, that is, agnates and cognates.[120] Hence it seems that the Mamlūks were not focused on maintaining entitlement within the circles of agnatic descendants.

ʿUthmān, the paternal great-grandson of the Mamlūk amīr Ughulbak, stipulated that if he died without offspring, entitlement should be apportioned as follows: one-third to his mother and full sister, whereby, after the sister's death, her rights would pass to her descendants on the basis of equality between the sexes; one-third to his freed slaves and their descendants; and one-third to the *madrasa* that had been built by the founder.[121] None of the documents appear to contain bequests in favor of freed slaves, but we cannot rule out the

118 *Sijill* 1, Waqf 3, p. 29, lines 9–15.

119 *Sijill* 1, Waqf 2, p. 23, lines 6–7; cf. Waqf 3, p. 26, lines 11–3; Layish, "The Family *Waqf* and the *Sharʿī* Law of Succession in Modern Times": 382–4.

120 *Sijill* 1, Waqf 1, p. 12, line 13 – p. 13, line 2; cf. G. Baer, "The *Waqf* as a Prop for the Social System (Sixteen–Twentieth Centuries)." *Islamic Law and Society* 4.3 (1997): 275–57.

121 Cf. Richards, "Glimpses of Provincial Mamluk Society": 50, 52.

possibility that the allocation of one-third of the entitlement to freed slaves was inspired by *sharʿī* doctrine, which allows a testamentary disposition in favor of a stranger, i.e., someone who is not a legal heir, within one-third of the estate.[122] D. S. Richards notes that women treated their freedmen and freedwomen as heirs within the circle of the "extended family," or as legatees in a testamentary disposition.[123]

Upon the extinction of all the descendants, entitlement passed to charitable purposes in Mecca and Medina.[124] If it was impossible to convey the revenues to their destination due to lack of security on the roads, the revenues had to be distributed among the *fuqarāʾ* and *masākīn* of *ummat Muḥammad* (i.e. poor and needy Muslims) in accordance with the *nāẓir*'s discretion.[125] In other words, the revenues passed to groups that would never cease to exist, in accordance with the *sharʿī waqf* law. According to Abū Yūsuf, for the entitlement to be valid, the founder had to specify at the end of the order of beneficiaries an eternal charitable purpose, such as "the poor" or "mosques," i.e. something that in the nature of things will never cease to exist.[126] In some cases the founder stipulated that upon extinction of all descendants, entitlement was to be transmitted to the poor among his relatives (*dhawū raḥim*) along with other beneficiaries.[127] This is relevant to one document in the archive under examination. I have noted earlier that Sitt Ḥalab endowed half of the village of Takhārīn in the district of Aleppo. She stipulated in her *waqfiyya* that she would be the first beneficiary and, after her, the entire entitlement would pass to charitable purposes (*jihāt birr*), which she specified (*ʿayyanat*) and arranged according to the successive order of the beneficiaries (*rattabat*).[128]

An order of succession (*ḥaṣr irth*) provides some information about the transmission of estates and rights of entitlement to *waqf* within the Ughulbak family. Abū al-ʿAbbās Shihāb al-Dīn Aḥmad, the son of Ughulbak left behind his wife, Zaynab, and their four children: al-Shihābī Aḥmad, Faraj, Fāṭima, and ʿĀʾisha. Zaynab, Faraj, Fāṭima, and ʿĀʾisha predeceased al-Shihābī Aḥmad, whereupon their *sharʿī* shares in the estate, as well as their rights of entitlement

122 Testamentary *Waqf*, i.e. an endowment that takes effect upon the founder's decease, is common practice in the Mālikī school. Layish, "The Mālikī Family *Waqf* and the *Sharʿī* Law of Succession in Modern Times": 3–5; Powers, "The Maliki Family Endowment": 387.

123 Richards, "Glimpses of Provincial Mamluk Society": 50–1.

124 Cf. transmission of entitlement to the *Nāẓir al-Ḥaramayn bil-Quds wa-l-Khalil*; Little, "The Governance of Jerusalem under Qāʾitbāy": 144–5.

125 *Sijill* II, Waqf 4, p. 111, line 8 – p. 112, line 8.

126 Cf. Qadrī, *Kitāb Qānūn al-ʿadl wa-l-inṣāf*: art. 6; Heffening, "Waḳf": 1097i.

127 *Sijill* I, Waqf 2, p. 23, lines 13–4; cf. Layish, "The Family *Waqf* and the *Sharʿī* Law of Succession in Modern Times": 364–5.

128 *Sijill* II, Waqf 5, p. 98, line 14 – p. 100, line 16.

in the *waqf* founded by Abū al-ʿAbbās Aḥmad (the son of Ughulbak), were transmitted to al-Shihābī Aḥmad. When the latter died his estate was transmitted to his wife, Fāṭima, his son, Abū ʿAmr ʿUthmān, and his daughter, ʿĀʾisha. Aḥmad's rights to the entitlement in the *waqf* founded by him were transmitted to his children in accordance with the terms of the *waqfiyya*.[129]

## 10 Administration of the *Waqf*

The administrator (*nāẓir*) of the *waqf was* in charge of the daily management of property and the transactions of property under the supervision of the *sharīʿa* court. The Mamlūk amīrs used the *waqf* institution as an instrument to transmit property (or the usufruct thereof) as well as a marker of social status and influence on their descendants. There is a clear correlation between the beneficiary and the administrator. Thus, the founder, who is first in the order of beneficiaries, appoints himself or his proxy as the first administrator.[130] Next in order comes the most capable of his sons, in terms of administration (*al-arshad fa-l-arshad*).[131] Poliak justly argues that the appointment of descendants as hereditary administrators is inspired by the desire to enable them to control the *waqf* as the family's patrimony, and to use the proceeds to their own advantage, even against the founder's stipulations.[132] Ayalon notes that in order to secure the economic position of their descendants, who were prohibited from joining the ruling military elite, the Mamlūks appointed them as administrators and supervisors of *waqf*s established in favor of religious institutions.[133]

The founders invariably regarded men as more capable administrators than women, probably because the males were committed to the preservation of the agnatic patrimony. This explains the stipulation that the most capable of the male agnates (*awlād al-ẓahr*) among the descendants be nominated as administrator. In one case, the founder stipulated that the supervision should pass to his son ʿUthmān and after him *lil-arshad fa-l-arshad* of ʿUthmān's descendants. Only after their extinction should the administration pass to the most capable of his daughter ʿĀʾisha's descendants. Occasionally the founder

129 Saghbini, *Mamlukische Urkunden aus Aleppo*, Arabic documents: 67.

130 Heffening, "Waḳf": 1097ii.

131 Cf. Qadrī, *Kitāb Qānūn al-ʿadl wa-l-inṣāf*: 46, art. 154ff.

132 Poliak, *Feudalism*: 38; Poliak, *The History of Agrarian Relations*: 50; cf. Petry, *Protectors or Praetorians?*: 196–7; U. Haarmann, "The Sons of Mamluks as Fief-holders in Late Medieval Egypt." In *Land Tenure and Social Transformation in the Middle East*, ed. Tarif Khalidi (Beirut, 1984): 144–5.

133 Ayalon, "Mamlūks": 319ii.

stipulates that the *nāẓir* should be "both a member of the founder's family and a beneficiary" (*min ahl al-wāqif wamustaḥiqqihi*), or he explicitly stipulates that a "stranger" (*ajnabī*), i.e. someone who is not a blood relative, must not be appointed as *nāẓir*. In one case, the founder stipulated that if women "proved themselves dedicated exclusively" (*fa-in tamaḥḥadū*) to administration, then the most capable among them could be appointed as *nāẓir* – which suggests that women could dispose of property, perform transactions, and be relied upon to preserve the integrity of the patrimony.[134]

In one instance the founder, Aḥmad b. al-Sayfī b. Ughulbak, appointed as joint *nāẓirs* for the management of the *waqf* property (after himself and in the absence of his proxy) his father's freed slave (*ʿatīq*, i.e. Mamlūk) who had been promoted to the rank of *amīr kabīr*, Ṭurunṭāy b. ʿAbdallāh, and his own freed slave and *amīr kabīr*, Jamāl al-Dīn ʿAbdallāh b. ʿAbdallāh. When either of them died, the survivor should continue as *nāẓir* on his own.[135] The employment of slaves in large estates of *iqṭāʿāt* and *waqfs* has been discussed in the literature.[136] As we have seen, the title "*amīr kabīr*" may have had little or no significance. However, if one of the founder's children or descendants, either agnates or cognates (*nasluhu wa-ʿaqibuhu*), proved himself more capable to run the *waqf* property, one of the two Mamlūks would function as a trained (*shādin*) supervisor (*mushārif*) based on their good reputation as administrators of *waqf* in the villages.[137] It seems that the Mamlūks distinguished themselves in running the family patrimony during the lifetimes of the founder and his father. When Mamlūks are designated as beneficiaries they are nominated as administrators of their portions of the *waqf* property.[138]

Ayalon has described the relationship between the patron and his manumitted slaves in terms of family.[139] It is therefore not surprising that, as we have seen, poor manumitted slaves belonged to the category of the founder's poor relatives for the purpose of apportionment of entitlement. Freed slaves played a central role in the administration of the patrimony during the patron's lifetime, and since they could not inherit from him according to the *sharʿī* rules of inheritance, the patron rewarded them for their good services by assigning them a share in the entitlement as beneficiaries and by appointing them as

134 Cf. Winter, "Mamluks and their Households in Late Mamluk Damascus": 310; Levanoni, *A Turning Point*: 184; Rapoport, *Marriage, Money and Divorce*: 27–8; Marcus, *The Middle East on the Eve of Modernity*: 313.

135 *Sijill* II, Waqf 4, p. 113, line 2.

136 Johansen, *The Islamic Law on Land Tax and Rent*: 12, 17.

137 *Sijill* I, Waqf 1, p. 13, lines 13–5; cf. Baer, "The *Waqf* as a Prop": 277–9.

138 *Sijill* II, Waqf 4, p. 113, line 2.

139 Ayalon, "Mamlūks": 318ii.

administrators with high wages.[140] D. Crecelius, who has studied Mamlūk society in eighteenth-century Egypt, reports that Mamlūk amīrs would stipulate in their *waqfiyyas* that manumitted slaves be appointed as supervisors alongside the founder's children as beneficiaries. Moreover, some amīrs would marry freed slaves to women from the master's harem in order to secure the continuity of the household and its protection. This was done in view of the patron's estimation that his own sons were not capable of defending the family patrimony against intruders who often seized the estates of deceased amīrs. They were also expected to secure the rights of women and children in the estates.[141]

In a *waqf* in favor of the Umawī Mosque in Aleppo, the founder appointed the *khaṭīb* and *imām* and their respective successors as *nāẓir*s of the *waqf*.[142] If the appointment of a specific person as *nāẓir* proved impossible, the function would be transferred to the *qāḍī* (*ḥākim*) of Aleppo. When the line of beneficiaries ended, entitlement was awarded to charitable purposes – a mosque, *madrasa*, or *turba*, for example – and the administration of the *waqf* should then be transferred to the respective *nāẓir*s of these institutions. When entitlement was awarded to the *fuqarā*ʾ and *masākīn*, the administration was to be transferred to the "most learned and pious among the Ḥanafī *ʿulamā*ʾ in Aleppo."[143] In one case the founder stipulated that the administration of the *waqf* should pass to the most capable among the "poor and needy [Muslims]." The phrase "*fuqarā*ʾ *wa-masākīn*" should not be taken literally, however, as it more probably refers to pious people submissive to God.[144]

The *nāẓir* was entitled to a wage in return for his work. The wages mentioned in our documents range from one-third to one-half of the *ʿushr* levied on the yields (*mutaḥaṣṣil*) or revenues (*rayʿ*) of the *waqf*. The two aforementioned *amīr kabīr*s who were jointly nominated as *nāẓir*s were assigned two-thirds of the *ʿushr* tax to be divided between them equally.[145] These rates are very

140 *Sijill* II, Waqf 4, p. 111, lines 8–15; cf. Marcus, *The Middle East on the Eve of Modernity*: 53.

141 D. Crecelius, "Problems of ʿAbd al-Raḥmān Katkhuda's Leadership of the Qazdughli Faction." In *The Mamluks in Egyptian and Syrian Politics and Society*, eds. M. Winter and Amalia Levanoni (Leiden, 2004): 379; cf. Poliak, *Feudalism*: 37.

142 *Sijill* I, Waqf 2, p. 24, line 4.

143 *Sijill* I, Waqf 3, p. 27, line 15; *Sijill* II, Waqf 4, p. 113, line 6.

144 *Sijill* I, Waqf 1, p. 13, line 18; cf. Hans Wehr, *Arabic-English Dictionary: The Hans Wehr Dictionary of Modern Written Arabic* (Wiesbaden, 1979): *miskīn*, 909ii; Lane, *Lexicon*: *faqīr*, 2426iii; Miriam Hoexter, "Charity, the Poor, and Distribution of Alms in Ottoman Algiers." In *Poverty and Charity in Middle Eastern Contexts*, eds. M. Bonner, M. Ener, A. Singer (Albany, 2003): esp. 148–51; Miriam Hoexter, *Endowments, Rulers and Community. Waqf al-Ḥaramayn in Ottoman Algiers* (Leiden, 1998): 31–2; Hoexter, "*Ḥuqūq Allāh* and *Ḥuqūq al-ʿIbād*": 145 ff.

145 *Sijill* I, Waqf 1, p. 13, line 16 – p. 14, line 2; and Waqf 3, p. 27, line 16, respectively; cf. Baer, "The *Waqf* as a Prop": 270 (the normal rate of wage was 10–5 percent).

high given that the *nāẓir*s were also entitled to their shares of the revenues as beneficiaries.

## 11 Expropriation

By definition *waqf*s were meant to be perpetual.[146] In reality, however, many pious endowments ceased to exist after their unlawful seizure by neighboring holders of *iqṭāʿāt*. Occasionally amīrs requested the court's permission to sell *waqf*s. Since this is prohibited by law, the transaction was formally defined as *istibdāl*, and the *qāḍī* received the *waqf*'s value in money, so as to replace the original *waqf* with a new one.[147] Moreover, occasionally *waqf* property was expropriated without any compensation.[148]

As noted above, Sitt Ḥalab, the great-great-granddaughter of the Mamlūk amīr Ughulbak, endowed half of the village of Takhārīn in the vicinity of Aleppo as a *waqf*. Previously this part of the village had been purchased by the *bayt al-māl* from Sitt Ḥalab's father, ʿUthmān, after the latter had endowed it as *waqf*. The transaction was carried out by means of *istibdāl*, the exchange of the endowed property for another property that becomes *waqf* in its stead. This was done with judicial permission (*idhn ḥukmī*) from the secretary of the state (*amīn al-sirr*) and the mufti of the representative of the sultanate in Cairo. Following the transaction, the endowed rural property became "unconfined private property" (*milk ṭalq*) and was transferred to the administrator of the Inheritance Department (*nāẓir dawāwīn al-irth*) in the Public Treasury. No mention is made of the property offered in exchange for the *waqf*. The *waqfiyya* mentions that the property "passed into the hands (*āl … ilā*)" of Sitt Ḥalab, either through inheritance from her father, who had reinstated the village as private property or by virtue of a direct purchase from the *bayt al-māl*, before she once again endowed it as *waqf*.[149]

The proliferation of *waqf* property in the Mamlūk state seems to be due to the fact that private property was not immune from expropriation. Petry estimates that all holders of property, civilian and military alike, were exposed to threats to the integrity of their estates.[150] There is, however, evidence in our

146 Peters, "Waḳf": 60ii.

147 See the chapter on *istibdāl* in Qadrī, *Kitāb Qānūn al-ʿadl wa-l-inṣāf*: 39, art. 129ff.; cf. Levanoni, *A Turning Point*: 168; Hoexter, "Adaptation to Changing Circumstances": 322; Marcus, *The Middle East on the Eve of Modernity*: 311.

148 Poliak, *The History of Agrarian Relations*: 52; cf. Hoexter, "*Ḥuqūq Allāh* and *Ḥuqūq al-ʿIbād*": 153.

149 *Sijill* 11, Waqf 5, p. 99, line 5 – p. 100, line 16.

150 Petry, *Protectors or Praetorians?*: 197.

documents that the founders of *waqf*s bought landed properties from the *bayt al-māl* shortly before they endowed them, which suggests that the endowment was intended to secure the properties against confiscation.[151] For instance, the purchase of the lands of the village of al-Manṣūriyya from the *bayt al-māl* and their endowment as *waqf* appear in the family register successively, one after another.[152] In another case the founder constructed a public bath (*ḥamām*) on his private-owned plot, and shortly afterward endowed it as a *waqf*.[153]

Indeed, the creation of an endowment proved to be the safest security against expropriation, provided, of course, that the sultan was restrained by the religious sanction inherent in the *waqf* institution. This sanction seems to have been stronger with respect to *waqf* for charitable purposes due to the nature of the beneficiaries – religious institutions such as mosques and *madrasas*. On the other hand, there was less incentive for and public interest in protecting endowments against expropriation which were in favor of the founder's family, the more so because of the bad reputation associated with the administrators of family *waqf*s.[154] Moreover, according to Petry, endowments were in principle tax-free; revenues could be subject to taxation but the property itself was exempt from taxes to assure the *waqf*'s perpetuity. Hence, the *waqf* was instrumental in the protection of the integrity of the patrimony. In addition, the *waqf* could secure a reliable source of revenue for the founder's descendants.[155] Petry's assessment that endowments were in principle tax-free is not corroborated by our documents. In one case, the founder stipulated in the *waqfiyya* that the division of the entitlement among the beneficiaries would take place only after "the rent fees and the *kharāj* tax have been paid" (*wa-ṣarf mā ʿalayhi min al-ḥikr wa-l-kharāj*).[156] In other words, the *kharāj* tax is treated as if it were a debt that was payable before apportionment of the entitlement.

However, the sultans were not always deterred from confiscation of *waqf* property or their revenues, especially in times of crisis. Thus Qānṣawh al-Ghawrī manipulated *waqf*s to subsidize new military units outside the Mamlūk ranks.[157] He did not hesitate to confiscate royal estates, as in the case of al-Ashraf Qāʾit Bāy, who had died without heirs. Moreover, Qānṣawh

151 Cf. Rapoport, *Marriage, Money and Divorce*: 27.

152 *Sijill* 1, Sale, p. 2, line 12 – p. 6, line 16 and p. 6, line 16 – p. 16, line 3; cf. Hoexter, *Endowments, Rulers and Community*: 15–6.

153 *Sijill* 1, p. 16, line 3 – p. 20, line 1 and p. 20, line 1 – p. 24, line 13. Cf. Reilly, "Properties around Damascus in the Nineteenth Century": 107–8.

154 Poliak, *Feudalism*: 37; Poliak, *The History of Agrarian Relations*: 50.

155 Petry, *Protectors or Praetorians?*: 196–7.

156 *Sijill* 1, Waqf 2, p. 2, line 2.

157 Petry, *Twilight of Majesty*: 235; Petry, *Protectors or Praetorians?*: 166.

al-Ghawrī imposed new taxes on *waqf* property. The sultans enlisted the support of *qāḍīs* to sanction the validity of such acts.[158] On the whole, however, confiscation of *waqf* properties was rare because of the public criticism aired by the *ʿulamāʾ* and the Mamlūk elite.[159]

## 12 The Founder's Stipulations

Founders tended to stipulate that the apportionment of proceeds (*rayʿ*) among the beneficiaries took place only after payment of his debts (*duyūn thābita fī dhimmatihi*), that the proceeds should be spent first and foremost on the current upkeep of the *waqf* property, and on its development, construction, renovation, and restoration (*tarmīm*), as well as on the promotion of its usefulness (*ʿimārat al-waqf wa-iṣlāḥuhu wa-ṣalāḥuhu*), and that only the surplus should be apportioned to the beneficiaries.[160] The maintenance of the *waqf* property included: the acquisition of riding animals like horses, mules, donkeys (*duwābb*), and young camels (*abkur*); the purchase of seeds (*bidhār*) and tools (*ālāt*),[161] as well as the recruitment of salaried workers (*ʿawāmil*).[162] Jurists seem to think of *iqṭāʿ* and *waqf* as typical examples of big estates cultivated through the employment of slaves and salaried laborers.[163] This would refer to cases where the founder of the *waqf* preferred to cultivate the land on his own, that is, by means of hired laborers, rather than by a contract of share-cropping (*muzāraʿa*).[164] Poliak notes that the owners of the *iqṭāʿāt* were reluctant to invest money and energy in enterprises such as digging irrigation canals, on account of the uncertainty regarding their ability to retain the *iqṭāʿāt* in their possession and transmit them to their descendants by means of inheritance. They were further deterred by the possibility that the increase in productivity as a result of the investment in agricultural households would encourage state expropriation of that part of the property which exceeded the permissible quota of revenues allowed to the military rank of amīr.[165] No such

158 Petry, *Twilight of Majesty*: 81, 146–7, 165, 206–8, 235; E. Ashtor, "Ḳāʾit Bāy." *Encyclopaedia of Islam*, 2nd edition, IV: 463ii.

159 Heffening, "Waḳf": 1099i; Petry, *Protectors or Praetorians?*: 197, 209.

160 Cf. Heffening, "Waḳf": 1097ii.

161 Jurists consider land, seed, work, and cattle as the four most important elements in the process of agricultural production. Johansen, *The Islamic Law on Land Tax and Rent*: 55.

162 *Sijill* I, Waqf 1, p. 13, lines 5–7; Waqf 3, p. 28, line 1; *Sijill* II, Waqf 4, p. 113, lines 7–13; cf. Reilly, "Urban Hegemony": 461.

163 Johansen, *The Islamic Law on Land Tax and Rent*: 12.

164 Cf. Ibid.: 15, 17, 25, 50; Marcus, *The Middle East on the Eve of Modernity*: 312.

165 Poliak, *The History of Agrarian Relations*: 55.

considerations, however, seem to have existed with respect to the investment in *waqf* property, due to its relative security.

Our documents contain further stipulations for defending the *waqf* property against encroachment by trespassers and usurpers. Thus it is not permitted to rent properties to beneficiaries or violent lessees, lest they dominate the leased properties. Likewise, it is not permitted to rent roofed buildings (*musaqqafāt*), mills (*ṭawāḥīn*) for a period exceeding three years, or to conclude a new rent contract before the expiration of the old one and the return of the property to the *nāẓir*.[166] Finally, the founder avails himself of the option to introduce the following conditions: *istibdāl* (exchange of *waqf* property), *taghyīr* (changing the existing conditions), *ziyāda* (an increase of allocations to beneficiaries), *nuqṣān* (decrease of allocations), *ʿaṭāʾ* (grant entitlement, i.e., the inclusion of new beneficiaries), and *ḥirmān* (deprivation, i.e., the exclusion of beneficiaries at his discretion).[167]

## 13 Conclusion

The documents from this family archive from Aleppo which dates back to the late Mamlūk period reveal some significant aspects of the social and economic role of the *waqf* in this era, which formed a transitional stage in the transformation of the *awlād al-nās* from a military to a civil elite.

Over centuries the so-called *waqf khayrī* played an important role in fostering charitable purposes, social welfare, religious services, and education in sovereign Muslim societies. Broadly speaking, in view of the limited involvement of the Islamic state in providing social services,[168] these functions were performed by the institution of *waqf*s by rulers, governors, and senior officials as individuals rather than in their capacities as servants of the state.[169] The descendants of Mamlūk amīrs were part of this social stratum and they too seem to have been conscious of their responsibilities toward society and of their public image.

166 *Sijill* I, Waqf 1, p. 13, lines 9–12; Waqf 3, p. 28, line 1; *Sijill* II, p. 113, lines 13–4. Cf. Johansen, *The Islamic Law on Land Tax and Rent*: 34; Rafeq, "The Application of Islamic Law in the Ottoman Courts in Damascus": 412, 418.

167 *Sijill* I, Waqf 4, p. 114, lines 9–10. On the "Ten Conditions," see Qadrī, *Kitāb Qānūn al-ʿadl wa-l-inṣāf*: 34, arts. 119–23.

168 Cf. J. Schacht, *An Introduction to Islamic Law* (Oxford, 1964): 76–7, 206–7.

169 Miriam Hoexter, "*Waqf* Studies in the Twentieth Century: The State of the Art." *Journal of the Economic and Social History of the Orient* 41.4 (1998): 476–7.

The family *waqf* was instrumental in circumventing the Islamic law of inheritance and preserving the agnatic patrimony. Although the *waqf* was generally used as a device to deprive women from their rights in estates, we find significant deviations from the "traditional" patterns of intergenerational transmission; females of various degrees of relationship to the founder did not only qualify as beneficiaries alongside agnates, but also transmitted their shares to their descendants. Moreover, the founders occasionally allowed the appointment of women as administrators of the *waqf*, provided they had proven their capability.[170] It is also clear that women owned and disposed of property independently.[171] For example, Sitt Ḥalab, who had no interest in preserving the agnatic patrimony, endowed half a village for charitable purposes, a trend which is also discernible in other times and places.[172]

These findings seem to be in harmony with the status of women in the civil elite into which the descendants of the Mamlūk amīrs were integrated. Ayalon has observed that while the Mamlūk amīrs married female slaves from countries of their origin or daughters of Mamlūks, the *awlād al-nās* married local women, mainly daughters of senior officials, rich merchants, or distinguished *ʿulamāʾ*, thus accelerating their integration into the local population.[173]

Manumitted slaves played a decisive role in running the households of their patrons during their lifetime and after their death; they were treated as members of the patron's family: they were allocated significant portions of the endowments' revenues and served as administrators of the *waqf*s.

Beyond these social and economic findings, this study provides essential information relating to legal history. We have circumstantial evidence that the tension between doctrine and practice was mitigated by the ability of the *waqf* legal system to accommodate everyday requirements. The introduction of four *sharīʿa* courts created legal pluralism, which served as the juristic basis for adapting the institution of the *waqf* to social and economic pressures. By resorting to the Ḥanafī court in Aleppo, the founder was able to secure his nomination as the first beneficiary in addition to his nomination as the first administrator of the *waqf*. Clearly, the combination of these two functions

170 Cf. Rapoport, *Marriage, Money and Divorce*: 27–9.

171 Cf. Ibid.: 13–4, 24–7.

172 Cf. Petry, "The Estate of al-Khuwand Fāṭima al-Khaṣṣbakiyya": 277–94 (Qāʾitbāy's wife owns property and endows *Waqf*s). Marcus, *The Middle East on the Eve of Modernity*: 210–1, 304; Hoexter, "*Waqf* Studies in the Twentieth Century": 481–2; Powers, "The Maliki Family Waqf": 386; Reilly, "Women in the Economic Life": 89–90.

173 Ayalon, "Mamlūks": 319ii. On frustrations of the *awlād al-nās* desiring to integrate into the Mamlūk elite, see Haarmann, "The Sons of Mamluks": 144; cf. Lapidus, "Muslim Urban Society in Mamlūk Syria": 205.

accorded the founder complete control of the *waqf* during his lifetime. Similarly, by resorting to the Mālikī court, the founder remained the owner (with some restrictions) of the endowed property and could hence revoke the *waqf* at his will.[174] Moreover, the fact that the Mālikī doctrine facilitated the *bayt al-māl*'s domination of estates by virtue of its status as a residuary heir, provided additional incentive to establish *waqf*s.[175] By resorting to a Ḥanbalī *qāḍī*, the administrator extended the scope of maneuver in alienating *waqf* property by means of *istibdāl*, regardless of whether or not the founder stipulated such an option for the administrator.

It could be argued that the simultaneous resort to the courts of the four schools did not change the substantive law of each of the schools, and yet if one regards the four institutions as one (Sunnī) legal body, the combination of elements of all schools brought about a new, useful legal entity.[176] The option one has to resort to the courts of four schools, guided by practical considerations, resembles the eclectic method (*takhayyur, talfīq*) adopted in modern legislation in Islamic states.[177]

In this connection it is worth noting in passing that legal devices (*ḥiyal*) in the Ḥanafī school were instrumental in bringing customary commercial law in harmony with the *sharīʿa*. Thus, a sale including the right of redemption (*bayʿ al-wafāʾ*) made usury possible without changing the substantive *sharʿī* rule prohibiting it.[178] The Mālikī "judicial practice" (*ʿamal*) in North Africa is an example of a realistic law bridging the gap between strict doctrine and the customary legal system, although its impact on theory is disputed.[179] And finally, confiscation of *waqf* property by sultans may be regarded as an attempt to bend the *waqf* institution, rather than *waqf* law, to *raison d'état*. This policy, which has been adopted by contemporary states, has diminished the motivation to establish *waqf*s.[180] In all these cases, the changes in the legal practice were caused by procedural and administrative, rather than substantive, measures.

174 Peters, "Waqf": 62.

175 Layish, "The Mālikī Family *Waqf*": 1–5.

176 Cf. Marcus, *The Middle East on the Eve of Modernity*: 103, 106.

177 A. Layish, "The Transformation of the *Sharīʿa* from Jurists' Law to Statutory Law in the Contemporary Muslim World." *Die Welt des Islams* 44.1 (2004): 89ff.

178 Schacht, *An Introduction to Islamic Law*: 78–82.

179 L. Milliot, *Introduction à l'étude du droit musulman* (Paris, 1953): 167–78; Schacht, *An Introduction to Islamic Law*: 61–2; J. Berque, "ʿAmal." *Encyclopaedia of Islam*, 2nd edition; N.J. Coulson, *A History of Islamic Law* (Edinburgh, 1964): 143ff.

180 Cf. Layish, "Waḳf, II. 5. In the Modern Middle East and North Africa."

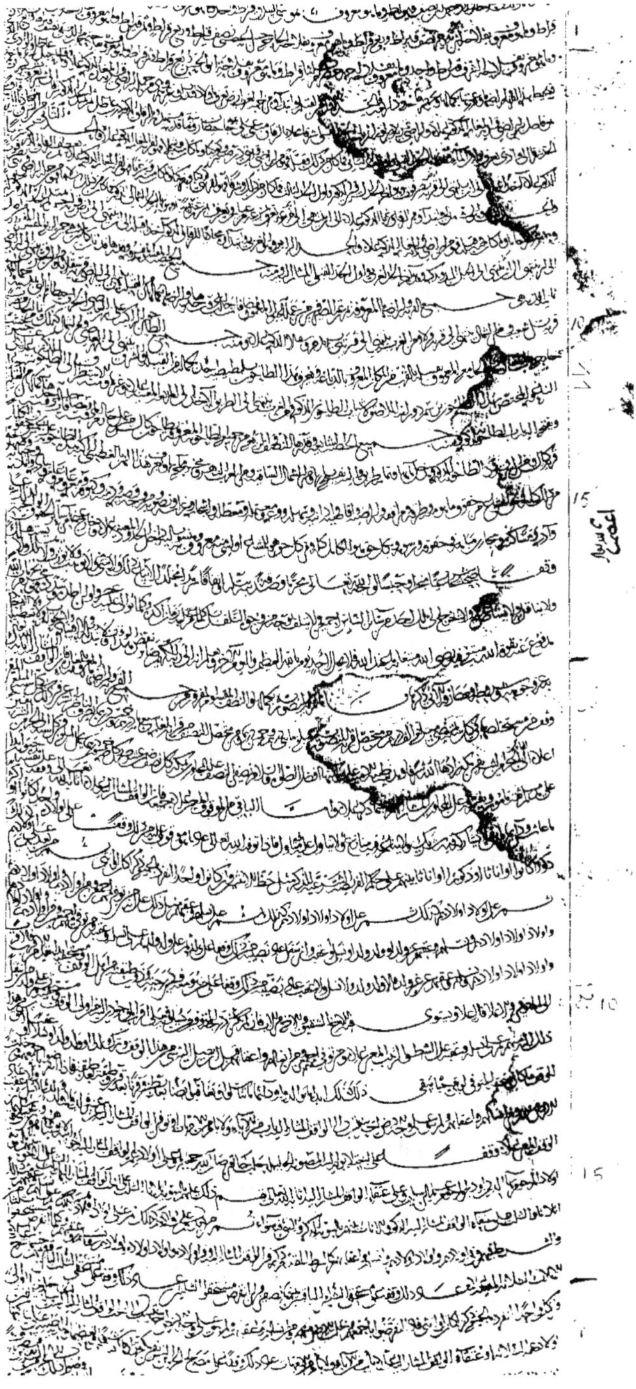

FIGURE 13.2

## Bibliography

### Archival Sources

The Ughulbak family archive from Aleppo consists of 32 facsimile reproductions of the original documents in Arabic. *Staatsbibliothek Preussischer Kulturbesitz. 25 Jahre in Berlin, Sammeln – Forschen – Bilden. Aus der Arbeit der Stiftung Preussischer Kulturbesitz 1961–1986*, Berlin: 208, No. 196, Sign. Hs. Or. 6948.

*Jāmi al-mustanadāt al-ʿāʾid li-ʿāʾilat Ughulbak al-ḥalabiyya al-mamlūkiyya.* Annotated edition of 24 documents in Arabic. In Saghbini, *Mamlukische Urkunden aus Aleppo* (see below).

### Secondary Sources

Ashtor, E. Ḳāʾit Bāy. *Encyclopaedia of Islam*, 2nd edition, IV: 462–3.

Ayalon, D. Awlād al-Nās. *Encyclopaedia of Islam*, 2nd edition, I: 765.

Ayalon, D. Mamlūks. *Encyclopaedia of Islam*, 2nd edition, VI: 314–21.

Ayalon, D. 1953. Studies on the Structure of the Mamlūk Army – I. *Bulletin of the School of Oriental and African Studies* 15.2: 203–28.

Ayalon, D. 1953. Studies on the Structure of the Mamlūk Army – II. *Bulletin of the School of Oriental and African Studies* 15.3: 448–76.

Ayalon, D. 1954. Studies on the Structure of the Mamlūk Army – III. *Bulletin of the School of Oriental and African Studies* 16.1: 57–90.

Ayalon, D. 1975. Names, Titles and "Nisbas" of the Mamlūks. *Israel Oriental Studies* 5: 189–232.

Baer, G. Ḥikr. *Encyclopaedia of Islam*, Supplement, XII, Fasc. 5: 368–70.

Baer, G. 1997. The *Waqf* as a Prop for the Social System (Sixteen–Twentieth Centuries). *Islamic Law and Society* 4.3: 264–97.

Bauden, F. 2004. The Recovery of Mamluk Chancery Documents in an Unsuspected Place. In *The Mamluks in Egyptian and Syrian Politics and Society*, eds. M. Winter and Amalia Levanoni. Leiden: 59–76.

Berque, J. ʿAmal. *Encyclopaedia of Islam*, 2nd edition: 1427–9.

Cahen, C.I. Iḳṭāʿ. *Encyclopaedia of Islam*, 2nd edition, III: 1088–91.

Cahen, C.I. Kharādj. *Encyclopaedia of Islam*, 2nd edition, IV: 1030–4.

Coulson, N.J. 1964. *A History of Islamic Law*. Edinburgh.

Coulson, N.J. 1971. *Succession in the Muslim Family*. Cambridge.

Crecelius, D. 2004. Problems of ʿAbd al-Raḥmān Katkhuda's Leadership of the Qazdughli Faction. In *The Mamluks in Egyptian and Syrian Politics and Society*, eds. M. Winter and Amalia Levanoni. Leiden: 373–86.

Drory, J. 2004. Founding a New Mamlaka: Some Remarks Concerning Safed and the Organization of the Region in the Mamluk Period. In *The Mamluks in Egyptian and Syrian Politics and Society*, eds. M. Winter and Amalia Levanoni. Leiden: 163–87.

Ephrat, Dafna. 2002. Religious Leadership and Associations in the Public Sphere of Seljuk Baghdad. In *The Public Sphere in Muslim Societies*, eds. Miriam Hoexter, Sh.N. Eisenstadt, and N. Levtzion. Albany: 31–48.

Gaube, Heinz and Eugen Wirth. 1984. *Tübinger Atlas des Vorderen Orients, Beihefte Bd. 58: Aleppo: Historische und geographische Beiträge zur baulichen Gestaltung, zur sozialen Organisation und zur wirtschaftlichen Dynamik einer vorderasiatischen Fernhandelsmetropole*. Wiesbaden.

Gerber, H. 1988. *Economy and Society in an Ottoman City: Bursa, 1600–1700*. Jerusalem.

Gerber, H. 1994. *State, Society and Law in Islam: Ottoman Law in Comparative Perspective*. New York.

Haarmann, U. 1984. The Sons of Mamluks as Fief-holders in Late Medieval Egypt. In *Land Tenure and Social Transformation in the Middle East*, ed. Tarif Khalidi. Beirut: 141–68.

Heffening, W. Waḳf. *Encyclopaedia of Islam*, 1st edition: 1096–113.

Hilmi, Omar. 1922. *A Gift to Posterity on the Laws of Evqaf*. trans. C.R. Tyser and D.G. Demetriades. 2nd edition. Nicosia.

Hiyari, M.A. 1975. The Origins and Development of the Amīrate of the Arabs during the Seventh/Thirteenth and Eighth/Fourteenth Centuries. *Bulletin of the School of Oriental and African Studies* 38: 509–24.

Hoexter, Miriam. 1995. *Huqūq Allāh* and *Ḥuqūq al-ʿIbād* as Reflected in the *Waqf* Institution. *Jerusalem Studies in Arabic and Islam* 19: 133–56.

Hoexter, Miriam. 1997. Adaptation to Changing Circumstances: Perpetual Leases and Exchanged Transactions in *Waqf* Property in Ottoman Algiers. *Islamic Law and Society* 4.3: 319–33.

Hoexter, Miriam. 1998. *Endowments, Rulers and Community: Waqf al-Ḥaramayn in Ottoman Algiers*. Leiden.

Hoexter, Miriam. 1998. *Waqf* Studies in the Twentieth Century: The State of the Art. *Journal of the Economic and Social History of the Orient* 41.4: 474–95.

Hoexter, Miriam. 2003. Charity, the Poor, and Distribution of Alms in Ottoman Algiers. In *Poverty and Charity in Middle Eastern Contexts*, eds. M. Bonner, M. Ener, A. Singer. Albany: 145–62.

Holt, P.M. Ḳanṣawh al-Ghawrī. *Encyclopaedia of Islam*, 2nd edition, IV: 552–53.

Holt, P.M. Mamlūks. *Encyclopaedia of lslam*, 2nd edition, VI: 321–31.

Ito, T. 2003. Aufsicht und Verwaltung der Stiftungen im mamlukischen Ägypten. *Der Islam* 80: 46–66.

Johansen, B. 1988. *The Islamic Law on Land Tax and Rent: The Peasants' Loss of Property Rights as Interpreted in the Hanafite Legal Literature of the Mamluk and Ottoman Periods*. London.

Lane, E.D. 1984. *Arabic-English Lexicon*. Revised format, 2 vols. Cambridge.

Lapidus, I.M. 1970. Muslim Urban Society in Mamlūk Syria. In *The Islamic City*, eds. A.H. Hourani and S.M. Stern. Oxford: 195–205.

Layish, A. 1983. The Mālikī Family *Waqf* according to Wills and *Waqfiyyāt*. *Bulletin of the School of Oriental and African Studies* 46.1: 1–32.

Layish, A. 1997. The Family *Waqf* and the *Sharʿī* Law of Succession in Modern Times. *Islamic Law and Society* 4.3: 352–88.

Layish, A. 2004. The Transformation of the *Sharīʿa* from Jurists' Law to Statutory Law in the Contemporary Muslim World. *Die Welt des Islams* 44.1: 85–112.

Layish, A. Waḳf, II. 5. In the Modern Middle East and North Africa. *Encyclopaedia of Islam*, 2nd edition, XI: 78–81.

Levanoni, Amalia. 1995. *A Turning Point in the Mamluk History: The Third Reign of al-Nāṣir Muḥammad Ibn Qalāwūn (1310–1341)*. Leiden.

Levanoni, Amalia. 2004. The Sultan's *Laqab*: A Sign of New Order in Mamluk Factionalism? In *The Mamluks in Egyptian and Syrian Politics and Society*, eds. M. Winter and Amalia Levanoni. Leiden: 79–115.

Levanoni, Amalia. 2006. *Awlād al-Nās* in the Mamluk Army during the Baḥrī Period. In *Mamlūks and Ottomans:* Studies in Honor of Michael Winter, eds. A.J. Ayalon and D. Wasserstein. London and New York: 96–105.

Little, D.P. 1984. *A Catalogue of the Islamic Documents from al-Ḥaram al-Sharīf in Jerusalem*. Beirut.

Little, D.P. 2004. The Governance of Jerusalem under Qāytbāy. In *The Mamluks in Egyptian and Syrian Politics and Society*, eds. M. Winter and Amalia Levanoni. Leiden: 143–61.

Luz, N. 2004. Urban Residential Houses in Mamluk Syria: Forms, Characteristics and the Impact of Socio-cultural Forces. In *The Mamluks in Egyptian and Syrian Politics and Society*, eds. M. Winter and Amalia Levanoni. Leiden: 339–55.

Marcus, A. 1989. *The Middle East on the Eve of Modernity: Aleppo in the Eighteenth Century*. New York.

Meier, A. Waḳf. II.2. In Syria. *Encyclopaedia of Islam*, Supplement, XII, Fasc. 11–12: 823–8.

Meloy, John. 2007. Awlād al-Nās. *The Encyclopaedia of Islam – Three*, Part 2: 184–5.

Milliot, L. 1953. *Introduction à l'étude du droit musulman*. Paris.

Orhonlu, C. Kharāj, III. In Ottoman Turkey. *Encyclopaedia of Islam*, 2nd edition, IV: 1053–5.

Peters, R. Waḳf. I. In the Classical Islamic Law. *Encyclopaedia of Islam*, 2nd edition, XI: 59–63.

Petry, C.F. 1991. Class Solidarity versus Gender Gain: Women as Custodians of Property in Later Medieval Egypt. In *Women in Middle Eastern History: Shifting Boundaries in Sex and Gender*, eds. Nikki Keddie and Beth Baron. New Haven: 122–42.

Petry, C.F. 1993. *Twilight of Majesty: The Reigns of the Mamlūk Sultans al-Ashraf Qāytbāy and Qānṣūh al-Ghawrī in Egypt*. Seattle.

Petry, C.F. 1994. *Protectors or Praetorians? The Last Mamlūk Sultans and Egypt's Waning as a Great Power*. Albany.

Petry, C.F. 2004. The Estate of al-Khuwand Fāṭima al-Khaṣṣbakiyya: Royal Spouse, Autonomous Investor. In *The Mamluks in Egyptian and Syrian Politics and Society*, eds. M. Winter and Amalia Levanoni. Leiden: 277–94.

Poliak, A.N. 1939. *Feudalism in Egypt, Syria, Palestine, and the Lebanon 1250–1900*. London.

Poliak, A.N. 1940. *Tōledōt haj-jeḥāsīm haq-qarqa'ijjīm be-Miṣrajim, Sūrijā we-Ereṣ-Jiśrā'ēl be-sōf jemē hab-bēnajim ū-baz-zemān he-ḥādāš* [*History of Agrarian Relations in Egypt, Syria and Palestine in Medieval and Modern Times*]. Jerusalem.

Powers, D. 1993. The Maliki Family Endowment: Legal Norms and Social Practices. *International Journal of Middle Eastern Studies* 25: 379–406.

Qadrī, Muḥammad. 1320/1902. *Kitāb Qānūn al-ʿadl wa-l-inṣāf lil-qaḍāʾ ʿalā mushkilāt al-awqāf*. 3rd edition. Cairo.

Rapoport, Y. 2003. Legal Diversity in the Age of *Taqlīd*: The Four Chief *Qāḍīs* under the Mamluks. *Islamic Law and Society* 10.2: 210–28.

Rapoport, Y. 2005. *Marriage, Money and Divorce in Medieval Islamic Society*. Cambridge.

Rafeq, Abdul-Karim. 2006. The Application of Islamic Law in the Ottoman Courts in Damascus: The Case of the Rental of *Waqf* Land. In *Dispensing Justice in Islam: Qadis and their Judgments*, eds. Muhammad Kh. Masud, R. Peters and D.S. Powers. Leiden: 411–25.

Reilly, J.A. 1990. Properties around Damascus in the Nineteenth Century. *Arabica* 37: 91–114.

Reilly, J.A. 1995. Urban Hegemony in the Hinterland of Ottoman Damascus: Villages, Estates and Farms in the Nineteenth Century. In *Histoire économique et sociale de l'Empire ottoman et de la Turquie (1326–1960)*, ed. D. Panzac. Paris: 455–70. Also in *Collection Turcica* 8 (1995): 455–70.

Reilly, J.A. 1995. Women in the Economic Life of Late-Ottoman Damascus. *Arabica* 42: 79–106.

Richards, D.S. 2004. Glimpses of Provincial Mamluk Society from the Documents of the Ḥaram al-Sharīf in Jerusalem. In *The Mamluks in Egyptian and Syrian Politics and Society*, eds. M. Winter and Amalia Levanoni. Leiden: 45–57.

Saghbini, Souad. 2005. *Mamlukische Urkunden aus Aleppo: Die urkundensammlung* (ǧāmiʿal-mustanadāt) *der mamlukisch-aleppinischen Familie Uġulbak*. Hildesheim: Zürich & New York.

Sato, T. 1997. *State and Rural Society in Medieval Islam: Sultans, Muqtaʿs and Fallahun*. Leiden.

Schacht, J. 1964. *An Introduction to Islamic Law*. Oxford.

Schacht, J. ʿUshr. *Encyclopaedia of Islam*, 2nd edition, x: 917–9.

Talmon-Heller, Daniella. 1994. The Shaykh and the Community: Popular Hanbalite Islam in 12th–13th Century Jabal Nablus and Jabal Qasyūn. *Studia Islamica* 79: 103–20.

Talmon-Heller, Daniella. 2005. Fidelity, Cohesion, and Conformity within Madhhabs in Zangid and Ayyubid Syria. In *The Islamic School of Law: Evolution, Devolution, and Progress*, eds. P. Bearman, R. Peters and F.E. Vogel. Cambridge, MA: 94–116.

Tyan, E. Īdjār, Īdjāra. *Encyclopaedia of Islam*, 2nd edition, III: 1017.

Wakin, Jeanette A. 1972. *The Function of Documents in Islamic Law: The Chapters on Sales from Ṭaḥāwī's Kitāb al-Shurūṭ al-kabīr*. Albany.

Wehr, Hans. 1979. *Arabic-English Dictionary: The Hans Wehr Dictionary of Modern Written Arabic*. Wiesbaden.

Winter, M. 2001. Inter-*Madhhab* Competition in Mamlūk Damascus: al-Ṭarsūsī's Counsel for the Turkish Sultans. David Ayalon Memorial Volume, *Jerusalem Studies in Arabic and Islam* 25: 195–211.

Winter, M. 2004. Mamluks and their Households in Late Mamluk Damascus: A *Waqf* Study. In *The Mamluks in Egyptian and Syrian Politics and Society*, eds. M. Winter and Amalia Levanoni. Leiden: 297–316.

CHAPTER 14

# *Waqf*s and *Ṣūfī* Monasteries in the Ottoman Policy of Colonization: Sulṭān Selīm I's *Waqf* of 1516 in Favour of Dayr al-Asad

> '… to the Shaykh, the *imām*, the lion, the hero … at the report of whose exploits the ears rejoice … and whose miraculous deeds deserve to be recorded in golden ink by day and by night …' Selīm the First '… the descendants of the lion are all lion cubs …'
>
> AL-BŪRĪNĪ

∴

## Introduction[1]

A folktale[2] current among the inhabitants of Dayr al-Asad, a little village in Western Galilee on the Acre – Safad road, reports that in the early sixteenth century a Ṣufī shaykh named al-Asad was once travelling towards Safad when he came upon some inhabitants of the Christian village of al-Biʿna, which then contained a monastery (*dayr*) and a Crusader church, and was insulted by them; moreover, while he was praying by the village spring, a lion (*asad*) appeared and devoured his donkey. Nothing daunted, the shaykh put his saddle on the lion's back, mounted and galloped eastward until he suddenly found himself face to face with the Sulṭān Selīm I (or according to others, Süleymān 'Qānūnī'). The *sulṭān*, to indemnify him for the insults of the Christians and in

1 This article is based on a lecture given at the Van Leer Institute, Jerusalem, on 13 November 1983, on a study day marking the first anniversary of the death of Professor Gabriel Baer. [Originally published in the *Bulletin of the School of Oriental and African Studies*, L/1 (1987), pp. 61–89.]

2 The story which prompted this research was told to my colleague, Dr. Amihoud Israely, by an inhabitant of the village; it is reproduced in his book, *Biqʿat Beit Ha-Kerem ve-Yishuveha – Gisha Ḥevlit*, Haifa, 1979, 23. It also figures, with slight variations, in notes taken by my colleague, Professor Hava Lazarus-Yafeh; I thank her for placing them at my disposal and for the help she gave me subsequently. My colleagues, Professors Amnon Cohen and Michael Winter, read the manuscript and made valuable comments, for which I am very grateful. Needless to say that I alone am responsible for any mistakes that may have remained.

 | DOI:10.1163/9789004680920_016

recognition of his courage and resourcefulness, permitted him to settle at Dayr al-Biʿna. Some say that the shaykh returned to the village on the lion's back after the *sulṭān* had expelled the Christians. Thereupon, so the story continues, Christian Dayr al-Biʿna became Muslim Dayr al-Asad. The Christian population established a new settlement, called al-Biʿna, about half a kilometre south of Dayr al-Asad. There is today at al-Biʿna a small Christian minority, which in the opinion of the people of Dayr al-Asad originates from Dayr al-Biʿna.

The taming of lions is a motif known from other times and places – also in this region – and there is thus a natural inclination to treat the whole story as just a charming folktale without historical significance. However, the circumstances of the Islamization of Dayr al-Biʿna receive confirmation from an unexpected source.

When the Sulṭān Selīm had consolidated his rule at home and was enjoying a short respite from his troubles in the east, he turned his attention to the Sunnī Arab world in the south. On 24 August 1516, he defeated the Mamlūk Sulṭān Qānṣūh al-Ghūrī at Marj Dābiq, north of Aleppo. Aleppo and Damascus opened their gates to him without a fight (late September 1516). This great Ottoman victory marked the beginning of a religious and political re-orientation.[3] Selīm stayed in Damascus for about two months (until December 1516) before moving on to Egypt for the decisive battle with the Mamlūks at Rīdāniyya near Cairo (22 January 1517).[4] While still in Damascus, grappling with logistic problems, he took time off to establish, before the Qāḍī of Damascus, a *waqf* in favour of an obscure Ṣūfī shaykh in an out-of-the-way place.

## 1 The *waqfiyya* – Its Contents and the Question of Its Authenticity

The *waqfiyya* is a document of considerable length (about 3,000 words). Its main content is as follows: The Sulṭān Selīm, immediately after taking the coastal cities from the Mamlūks and after Allāh had saved him from the faction of Satan and the infidels – this seems to refer to the expulsion of the Christians from Dayr al-Biʿna[5] – dedicated the whole of the monastery of Dayr al-Biʿna (including a courtyard, residential buildings, places of retreat and cisterns), as

3 J.H. Kramers, art. 'Selīm I', *Encyclopaedia of Islam*, Leiden and London, 1913 ff., 217; Muḥammad Kurd ʿAlī, *Khiṭaṭ al-shām*, part II, Damascus, 1925, 317–19.

4 Kramers, 'Selīm I', 215; Shams al-Dīn Muḥammad Ibn Ṭūlūn, *Mufākahat al-khullān fī ḥawādith al-zamān*, ed. Muḥammad Muṣṭafā, part II: *922–926* [H.], Cairo, 1964, 24.

5 The infidels referred to may be the Mamlūks, in which case political antagonism would have been expressed in religious terms. I thank my teacher and colleague, Professor David Ayalon, for confirming the possibility of this interpretation.

well as some land, olive groves and vineyards, to the mosque of the monastery and to the Ṣūfī shaykh Ibn ʿAbd Allāh al-Asadī, a man of many parts. After the latter's death, the entitlement was to pass to his male agnatic descendants, to the exclusion of females, until the end of all generations and, when there were no more of them, to the monastery and the mosque. The administration of the *waqf* and the office of *imām* were likewise to go to the shaykh, and after his death to the most qualified of his male descendants. Selīm stipulated that the shaykh and those of his male descendants who would be living at the monastery should read chapters of the Qurʾān for the exaltation of the souls of the dedicator and his parents. The *waqfiyya* was authenticated by the *qāḍī*.

Certain peculiar facts may raise doubts as to the authenticity of the document. The appellation 'Selīm Khān,' commonly used by the biographers of the period,[6] is here enlarged by the interposition of the word 'al-Awwal', 'the First', which, indeed, has been crossed out (l. 5). This is, of course, an anachronism. As far as is known, the appellation 'Selīm I' only came into use after the eleventh Ottoman *sulṭān* had been proclaimed Selīm II in 1566, i.e. 46 years after the death of Selīm I (1520).[7] Moreover, the names of all the signatories of the *waqfiyya* – the Qāḍī of Damascus, the Ottoman Qāḍī, the scribe and the witnesses – seem to have been written with the same ink, the same pen and by the same person.

I possess two texts of that *waqfiyya*, probably copied from the same original, one in 1949 or in early 1950, the other in 1957. There are differences between the two texts that are slight and may be due to difficulties in deciphering certain words of the original document. But there are also substantial differences: the first text omits a part of the definition of the boundaries of the *waqf* that appears in the second text. It is difficult to estimate the degree of good faith in that omission. The doubt increases in view of the fact that this *waqfiyya* was not produced in land settlement proceedings. And lastly, according to the first text, the *waqfiyya* was drawn up before the Qāḍī of Damascus, and according to the second text, before the Qāḍī of Aleppo. Such a discrepancy obviously calls for an explanation.

In spite of all these question marks, the *waqfiyya* is not a forgery. To be sure, it is not the original *waqfiyya* of 1516 but a copy of it with certain additions and alterations. The document in my possession is written in Arabic and authenticated by the local Qāḍī of Damascus. This authentication was in turn authenticated by a judge appointed by the Ottoman government. The local *qāḍī* notes that the endowment deed has been produced to him, whence it may be

---

6 See, e.g., Ibn Ṭūlūn, part II, 23, 25.

7 J.H. Kramers, art. 'Selīm II', *Encyclopaedia of Islam*, Leiden and London, 1913 ff., 277.

inferred that the *waqfiyya* was prepared out of court, apparently in Arabic.[8] The text in my possession was probably first copied upon the instructions of the *qāḍī* of the Sharīʿa Court of Acre; a copy of a judgement by him relating to the *waqf*, of 1254/1838, is likewise in my hands. This judgement, which was lost for some time, was recently found in the knitting box of the wife of a *mutawallī* of the *waqf* of Dayr al-Asad.[9] The text of the *waqfiyya* in my possession begins with the words 'The contents of this *waqfiyya* are …,' which may indicate that this *waqfiyya* is a copy of the original.[10]

The subject of the proceeding in 1838 was a dispute between beneficiaries of the *waqf*, descendants of the Shaykh al-Asad. Shaykh ʿUmar al-Asadī and others contended in court that some of their cousins were trespassing on the land and olive grove of the *waqf* that had been dedicated to the descendants of Shaykh Muḥammad al-Asad, thus violating the stipulations of the dedicator; they asked the court to enable all the legal beneficiaries to receive their share. The *qāḍī* asked to see the endowment deed so that he might study its provisions. The judgement says that the *waqfiyya* was produced to him. In my opinion, the document produced to him was a copy, authenticated by the *qāḍī* who had issued it, of the original *waqfiyya*, and a copy of that copy is the one in my possession.

A summary of the *waqfiyya* in the judgement of the Qāḍī of Acre indeed indicates that he was in possession of the full text. He notes that according to the terms of the *waqfiyya*, the *nāẓir* is responsible for the collection of the income of the land and the olive trees of the *waqf* and that it is primarily to be spent on the maintenance of the mosque at Dayr al-Biʿna; the surplus is to be appropriated, as a charity, to Shaykh Muḥammad al-Asad and subsequently to his descendants in equal shares on a *per capita* basis – since the dedicator did not say [in the *waqfiyya*]: 'The higher degree excludes the lower' (*al-ṭabaqa al-ʿulyā taḥjub al-suflā*). In other words, descendants of a lower degree (grandchildren and great-grandchildren) are to enter the cycle of beneficiaries on the principle of representation – contrary to the Muslim system of succession – and be thereupon entitled to shares equal to those of descendants of the first degree (children). It should be noted that the *imām* of the mosque and *zāwiya* of Dayr al-Asad and the *mutawallī* of the *waqf* have maintained and certified in a communication to the Ministry of Religious Affairs that according to the

8 Cf. Kurd ʿAlī, part II, 229, 231.

9 Ḥ. Kenaʿan, 'Ha-Waqf mi-Yemei ha-Sulṭan Selīm ha-Qoder', *Ha-Aretz*, 24 November, 1960. See Judgement of the Sharīʿa Court of Acre of 1838 (Appendix B).

10 Cf. R. Veselý, 'Trois certificats délivrés pour les fondations pieuses en Égypte au XVI^e^ siècle', *Oriens*, 21–2, 1971, 286 [8], 293. But see ibid., 296 [2].

dispositions of the dedicator the income of the *waqf* is to be distributed as stated above.[11] The sharing of entitlement *per capita* is rather unusual in the Ḥanafī school but very common in the Mālikī.[12] The Qāḍī of Acre decided that the 'age-old' practice with regard to the sharing of the entitlement of the *waqf* of Dayr al-Asad was contrary to the dedicator's stipulation, which was tantamount to 'a text of the *sharʿī* legislator,' and he ordered that that stipulation be complied with. He also ordered the defendants who had trespassed on the *waqf* to pay rent on the planted land and appointed a son of one of the *nāẓir*s to serve by the side of his father – this too in accordance with the terms of the *waqfiyya*.

It seems that the Sharīʿa Court of Acre has recently accepted the validity of the *waqfiyya* when appointing several inhabitants of Dayr al-Asad as *mutawallīs* of the Dayr al-Asad *waqf*. The District Court of Haifa likewise held, in reliance on the judgement of the Sharīʿa Court of Acre of 1838, that the existence of the *waqf* had been proved. The Land Settlement Officer had dismissed an application by the *mutawallīs* for registration in the name of the *waqf* of a plot of land of approximately 62 dunams on which quarries had been operated since 1949, and had ordered its registration in the name of the State as land of the *mīrī* category. The *mutawallīs* had petitioned the Supreme Court, which permitted the submission of a copy of the judgement of the Sharīʿa Court of Acre of 1838 as evidence of the existence of the *waqfiyya* of 1516. It held that there was no reason to doubt the authenticity of that ancient document and that, together with the testimony of inhabitants of Dayr al-Asad, it was sufficient to prove the establishment of the *waqf* centuries before. At the same time, the court was unable to determine with certainty the identity of the dedicator: whether it was the Sulṭān Selīm, as the *mutawallīs* asserted, or perhaps Shaykh Muḥammad al-Asad himself, as the Land Settlement Officer assumed. The court expressed astonishment at the fact that the *waqfiyya* had not been produced to it and rejected the allegation of the *mutawallīs* that the document was not in their possession because their representative had quoted passages from it purporting to confirm his assertion that the quarries were in the area of the *waqf*.[13] The court surmised that the document had not been produced

11 Muslim Division of the Ministry of Religious Affairs, File HM/4/3 No. 437 of 11 March, 1949; No. 596 of 27 June, 1957.

12 A. Layish, 'The Mālikī family *waqf* according to wills and *waqfiyyāt*', *BSOAS*, XLVI, 1, 1983, 23–5 and the reference in n. 126; cf. K.L. Brown, 'Notes on the significance of waqf in a Tunisian *Zāwiya*', in G. Baer and G. Gilbar (ed.), *Social and economic aspects of the Muslim waqf* (forthcoming?).

13 In 1957, the *mutawallī* of the *waqf* wrote to the Minister of Religious Affairs that he had in his possession a *waqfiyya* proving that a certain quarry site, the subject of a dispute with

to any authority because it apparently did not support the *mutawallīs*' claim to the quarries, and it decided that even though the existence of the *waqf* had been properly proved, this was not evidence that the quarries belonged to the *waqf*.[14]

Circumstantial evidence of its genuineness can be found also in the *waqfiyya* itself. The date of its registration, 20 Dhū al-Qaʿda 922/17 December 1516, tallies with the time of Sulṭān Selīm's short stay in Damascus. The anachronism in the *waqfiyya* may be due to the fact that it was copied in the middle of the twentieth century, when the founder of the *waqf* was known as Selīm I. The copyist noticed his slip and hastened to cross out the expression 'the First'.

Among Selīm's epithets in the preamble to the *waqfiyya* appears the title *Khādim al-Ḥaramayn al-Sharīfayn*, servant of the holy cities Mecca and Medina. Some say that this title was only conferred on him about a year after the conquest of Egypt; after consolidating his rule there, he received the oath of allegiance of the Sharīf of Mecca and sent a *ḥajj* caravan from Damascus. However, there is express evidence that Selīm assumed that title from the Mamlūk Sulṭān Qānṣūh al-Ghūrī – for he, and not the ʿAbbāsid Caliph, bore it – upon Qānṣūh's death after the battle of Marj Dābiq; he is described by that title in January 1517, before the conquest of Egypt on the 22nd of that month, in the Friday *khuṭba*. Ibn Ṭūlūn likewise reports that on Friday, 7 Ramaḍān/3 October 1516, i.e. shortly after the surrender of Damascus and before the campaign for the conquest of Egypt, when Selīm attended prayers at the Umayyad Mosque, the *khaṭīb* addressed him – along with his other honorific titles – as *Sulṭān [al-Ḥaramayn al-Sharī]fayn*.[15]

Circumstantial evidence that the *waqfiyya* refers to Selīm I rather than, as the biographer al-Būrīnī and, in his wake, al-Muḥibbī wrongly assumed, to Süleymān the Magnificent, is the closeness in time of the founding of the *waqf* to events connected with Selīm. The *waqf* is said to have been founded

---

the Land Settlement Officer, was part of the *waqf*. Muslim Division File HM/4/3 No. 596 of 27 June 1957 (letter from *mutawallī* to Minister of 26 June 1957); No. 607 of 28 June 1957 (letter from Qāḍī of Acre, of 21 May 1957); No. 609 of 28 June 1957 (letter from Būlus Būlus, of 22 May 1957). Cf. U. Heyd, *Ottoman documents on Palestine 1552–1615*, Oxford, 1960, 177–9.

14 Civil Appeal No. 102/60. Jābir Muḥammad Ḥusayn al-Asadī and two others, as *mutawallīs* of the *waqf* of Shaykh Muḥammad al-Asadī, v. State of Israel, *Piskei Din* (Judgements of the Supreme Court), XVI (5721/22–1961), 123–32.

15 Kramers, 'Selīm I', 215; Th. W. Arnold, *The Caliphate*, London, 1965, 144–5 and the source indicated in n. 12; Kurd ʿAlī, part II, 222; Ibn Ṭūlūn, part II, 32–3. Cf. Butrus Abu-Manneh, 'A note on the keys of the Kaʿba', *Islamic Quarterly*, XVIII, 3–4, 1974, p. 73, n. 1.

immediately after the conquest of the coastal cities.[16] These cities were taken from the Mamlūks by Selīm and not by Süleymān. The fact that the locality mentioned in the *waqfiyya* is called there Dayr al-Biʿna although the place has for centuries been known as Dayr al-Asad further corroborates the authenticity of the document. Additional support for the assumption that the document before us is a copy of the original *waqfiyya* may perhaps be found in the certifications of the three *qāḍīs* of Damascus. The first *qāḍī* certifies, in the first person, the validity of the *waqfiyya*. Then there is a switch to the third person: '[This was] written by ... the *qāḍī* at the House of Worship [mosque][17] of Damascus, *may Allah forgive him every offence*.'[18] If the words emphasized [by me] are to indicate that the *qāḍī* has meanwhile died,[19] then they are an addition made by the first copyist of the *waqfiyya* in Damascus to distinguish that *qāḍī* from the third *qāḍī*. The certification of the local Qāḍī of Damascus is certified *simultaneously* by the *qāḍī* appointed by the Turkish authorities. The third *qāḍī*, who was asked for a certified copy of the *waqfiyya*, certifies the validity of the *waqfiyya* and adds after his name the words 'the then (*yawmaʾidhin*) Qāḍī of Damascus.'[20] The word 'then' is meant to distinguish that *qāḍī* from the first *qāḍī*. As the signature of the third *qāḍī* is also not the real one, the inescapable conclusion is that the document in my possession is a copy of a certified copy of the original document.[21] The identity of the copyist of the *waqfiyya* became known to me during a visit to Dayr al-Asad. Following a request by the *imām* for assistance in financing religious services, the Director of the Muslim Division of the Ministry of Religious Affairs asked for and received a copy of the *waqfiyya*.[22] That copy bears the date stamp of the ministry of the 3 Tishri 5710/1950. The attribution of the certification of the *waqfiyya* to the

16 Al-Ḥasan b. Muḥammad al-Būrīnī, *Trājim al-aʿyān min abnāʾ al-zamān*, part 1, ed. Ṣalāḥ al-Dīn al-Munajjid, Damascus, 1959, 179; Muḥammad al-Muḥibbī, *Taʾrīkh khulāṣat al-athar fī aʿyān al-qarn al-ḥādī ʿashar*, [Cairo], al-Maṭbaʿa al-Wahhābiyya, 1284/1867, 177.

17 See Selīm I's *waqfiyya* of 1516 (Appendix A), n. 148.

18 *ʿufiya ʿanhu* 'he has been forgiven', a usual expression of modesty; see, e.g., the judgement of 1838 (Appendix B), l. 4, and the judgement of 1856 (pls. II, III).

19 This is not certain. *Ghafara allāh lahu* is a usual expression of modesty and humility also in relation to living persons. Cf. R.Y. Ebied and M.J.L. Young (ed. and tr.), *Some legal documents of the Ottoman period*, Leiden, 1976, 6, 34; the *waqfiyya* of Ḥājj Adīb Saʿīd Muḥammad Jabr, of 1371/1952, *sijill* of the Sharīʿa Court of Jaffa. The *waqfiyya* was published in G. Baer and A. Layish, *Waqf ba-Ḥevra ha-ʿAravit ha-Modernit*, Akademon, Jerusalem, 1971, 27.

20 Cf. '*ḥālan*' in Judgement of the *Sharīʿa* Court of Acre of 1838 (Appendix B), l. 3.

21 At my visit to Dayr al-Asad on 20 March 1984, Ibrāhīm al-Asadī hinted that the original of the *waqfiyya* – in dilapidated condition – was in the village.

22 Muslim Division, File HM 4/3 No. 437 of 11 March 1949; File HM 21/787 of 9 September 1949.

Qāḍī of Aleppo – in accordance with the 1957 version – is apparently erroneous, for afterwards it is said that the *waqfiyya* was certified by the *qāḍī* appointed by the state authorities in Damascus.[23]

The judgement of the Qāḍī of Acre of 1838, which is in my possession, adds to his title the expression 'the present' (*ḥālan*),[24] i.e. the *qāḍī* officiating at the date of the judgement. Then comes the formula 'he has been forgiven' (*ʿufiya ʿanhu*), but this time there can be no doubt that we have to do with an expression of humility.[25] At any rate, this document too is not the original but a copy, as attested by the fact that the signatures of the *qāḍī*, the scribe and the witnesses are written with the same pen and ink and by the same person.

## 2 The Reasons for the Establishment of the *waqf*

In what context must we view the establishment of the *waqf* and why did Selīm make the dedication precisely at Dayr al-Biʿna? He seems to have been prompted by the wish to enlist the religious sanction for political ends.

The establishment of a *waqf* is in itself an act of piety for its own sake, an act of righteousness (*birr*) and a work pleasing to God (*qurba*), especially as the proceeds of the *waqf* are intended for the welfare of the people in a Muslim country, where state-operated welfare institutions are lacking.[26] Selīm undoubtedly had sincere religious feelings. In his youth, he had received religious instruction from a well-known *mawlā* whom he rewarded later, after ascending the throne, by making him Qāḍī of Aleppo. He built a *medrese* near Hagia Sophia in Istanbul and showed great sympathy for the Ṣūfīs. There is evidence that he befriended Ṣūfīs in Istanbul and appointed some to important religious and governmental posts. A well-known *ʿālim* who had adopted the Ṣūfī *ṭarīqa* was appointed as his *imām* even before his accession; when he had become *sulṭān*, he appointed him as his teacher, paid him 100 dirhams a day and assigned many villages to him, apparently for tax-farming purposes (*iltizām*).[27] Selīm's

---

23 See Selīm I's *waqfiyya* of 1516 (Appendix A), n. 149.

24 Cf. A. Saarisalo, 'A waqf-document from Sinai', *Studia Orientalia* (Helsingforsiae), VI, 1933, Arabic, pp. 1, 41; English, pp. 6, 11.

25 See, e.g., Judgement of the Sharīʿa Court of Acre of 1838 (Appendix B), l. 4 and Judgement of the Sharīʿa Court of Ṣafad of 1293/1876 (pls. II, III).

26 J.N.D. Anderson, 'The religious element in waqf endowments', *Journal of the Royal Central Asian Society*, 38, 1951, 292–9; G. Baer, 'The waqf as a prop for the social system (sixteenth–twentieth centuries)', in Baer and Gilbar; S.D. Goitein and A. Ben Shemesh, *Ha-Mishpaṭ ha-Muslimi bi-Medinat Yisraʾel*, Jerusalem, 1957, 156–7.

27 Aḥmad b. Muṣṭafā Ṭāşköprüzāde, *Al-Shaqāʾiq al-nuʿmāniyya fī ʿulamāʾ al-dawla al-ʿuthmāniyya*, in the margin of *Kitāb wafayāt al-aʿyān wa-anbāʾ abnāʾ al-zamān lil-Qāḍī Ibn*

lively concern for Ṣūfism is attested also by his profound regard for the tomb of its most outstanding representative, Ibn al-ʿArabī of Spain, who had died in Damascus in 638/1240. During his short stay in Damascus in 1516, while still busy with preparations for war, he gave orders to refurbish Ibn al-ʿArabī's tomb and build a sumptuous Ṣūfī mosque-cum-monastery in the al-Ṣāliḥiyya quarter, and established a well-endowed *waqf* for the maintenance of services at the mosque. After the Ottoman conquest, Ibn al-ʿArabī became a kind of official saint. There is also evidence that Selīm befriended Ṣūfīs in Aleppo and Damascus, visited the tombs of other Ṣūfī holy men and lavished charity upon the poor.[28] The Ṣūfīs enjoyed considerable prestige in that period also at the courts of the Mamlūks and of al-Mutawakkil, the ʿAbbāsid caliph in Cairo.[29]

En route to Gaza, on the heels of the retreating Mamlūk forces, Selīm took time to make a pilgrimage to the holy places in Jerusalem and Hebron, and before going to war against the Mamlūk *sulṭān* he obtained a *fatwā* from a well-known *muftī*, authorizing a war against Sunnī Muslims, just as he had previously obtained a *fatwā* for a war against the Ṣafavids. A Venetian historian says that he was a cruel, bellicose ruler, who feared no one but the Şeyḫ ül-Islām. Even before the conquest of Egypt, Selīm showed extreme concern for the holy places in Mecca; this helped him to secure the allegiance of the Sharīf of Mecca after that conquest. His name was mentioned in the Friday *khuṭba* at the great mosques of the holy cities, with all the religious-political implications involved, as it has been at the mosques of Cairo after the battle of Rīdāniyya. The *ḥajj* caravan which set out from Damascus in December 1517 was the first that brought a cover for the Kaʿba as a gift from an Ottoman *sulṭān*. As a result of all this, the title *Khādim al-Ḥaramayn al-Sharīfayn* took on real significance, which greatly enhanced Selīm's prestige throughout the Muslim world at a time when the institution of the caliphate was declining. He also tried – without much success – to win the Caliph al-Mutawakkil over to his side and use him for political purposes, apparently because of what little religious-symbolical authority he still possessed.[30]

---

*Khaliqān*, part I, Cairo, 1299 A.H., 598–600, 614, 635–6, 640–1, 649–50, 654–5. For *iltizām* cf. Heyd, 141.

28 Ibn Ṭūlūn, part II, 36, 68, 70, 72, 79, 85, 97, 124; Kurd ʿAlī, part II, 225–6; ibid., part VI, Damascus, 1347/1838, p. 138, no. 381, and p. 143; Saʿd al-Dīn b. Ḥasanjān, *Tāj al-tawārīkh*, II [Istanbul, 1279 A.H.], 342–3, 379–80; M. Winter, 'Sheikh ʿAli Ibn Maymūn and Syrian Sufism in the sixteenth century', *Israel Oriental Studies*, VII, 1977, 295, 307.

29 J.S. Trimingham, *The Sufi orders in Islam*, Oxford, paperback, 1973, 76, 240 and the source indicated there; Ibn Ṭūlūn, part II, 14–15; Kurd ʿAlī, part II, 222.

30 Saʿd al-Dīn, II, 349–51; Kramers, 'Selīm I', 215–17; Arnold, 139–41 (and Ibn Iyās, as cited in n. 2), 148–9, 152–3; Kurd ʿAlī, part II, 231, 319.

Why did Dayr al-Biʿna, a small and apparently quite unimportant locality, attract the *sulṭān*'s attention? In the Crusader period, it was called Dayr al-Biʿna by the Arabs and Saint Georges Lebeyne by the Crusaders. According to Prawer, 'Lebeyne' is a corruption of 'al-Biʿna' and 'Saint Georges' a corruption of *sajara* 'groves', in which the region in fact abounds. The *waqfiyya* refers to the monastery of the village of al-Biʿna, which is situated in al-Sāghūr, a subdivision of the Safad district. In the centre of the village, remnants of a fortified church, with towers and loopholed corner turrets, have been uncovered. In the Crusader period, this locality was of prime strategic importance since it dominated the route from the seaport of Acre to the fortress of Safad. There is evidence from that period that this position was a target of military raids. The Beyt Ha-Kerem valley was of importance also because of its fertility.[31]

Baybars made Safad, the largest town in Galilee, the centre of the administration of the region because of its Crusader citadel. It provided administrative and religious services to the entire rural area surrounding it. Its remoteness from the sea lent importance to the road connecting it with Acre. The Safad district was a sub-division of al-Shām, and the Damascus – Safad axis was thus important for obvious reasons. Baybars encouraged Muslims from Damascus to settle in Safad.[32] Safad's strategic importance may perhaps be gathered from the fact that, according to Ibn Ṭūlūn, 'the inhabitants of the citadel sent its keys to Hünkār [Selīm]' a short time after the surrender of Damascus. Selīm placed the Safad district under the Governor of Damascus. A further indication of Safad's importance may be that when Selīm was busy with the conquest of Egypt and rumours spread that the Ottoman army had been defeated and Selīm captured, a revolt broke out in the city and the Ottoman governor had to entrench himself in the citadel until the storm blew over.[33]

It should also be noted that Selīm's conquests in the East made a deep impression on the Christian world. There is evidence that Pope Leo X tried to enlist France and England against the Ottomans, and though Selīm contrived

---

31 Y. Prawer, *Toledot Mamlekhet ha-Tzalbanim be-Eretz Yisra'el*, II: *Mas'ey ha-Tzlav veha-Mamlakha ha-Sheniya*, Jerusalem, 1971, p. 35, p. 489, n. 25, p. 491; Israely, 21–2, 31–2 and the sources indicated there. For details of the remnants of the Crusader castle and church see G. Foerster, 'Zihuy shel Seridim Tzalbaniyim Nishkaḥim be-Dayr al-Asad sheba-Galil ha-Merkazi', *Teva va-Aretz*, XI, 1969, 230–1; *The survey of Western Palestine*, I, Sheets I–VI, London, 1881, 168. For a sketch of the Crusader castle see Rockefeller Museum, File 45, Deir al-Asad, Report No. 3837, by N. Makhouly of 10 December, 1946. I wish to thank Mr. Ronnie Reich, of the Antiquities Department, Rockefeller Museum, for the valuable help extended to me.

32 Y. Drori, 'Penei ha-Tequfa: Eretz Yisra'el ba-Medina ha-Mamlukit', in A. Cohen (ed.), *Shilṭon ha-Mamlukim veha-ʿOthmanim (1260–1804)*, VII, Jerusalem, 1981, 51.

33 Ibn Ṭūlūn, part II, 33, 41; Kurd ʿAlī, part II, 227.

to neutralize his adversaries by political and economic means,[34] he must have been aware of their anxieties. Against this background, we may have to understand Selīm's remark in the *waqfiyya* that he is establishing the *waqf* 'immediately after the conquest of the coastal cities'. He seems to have wished to note that he was concerned about the renewal of European aggressiveness; this concern is illustrated by the fact that while Jerusalem, Gaza, Safad and al-Kerak were under the command of the Governor of Damascus, Jānberdī al-Ghazzālī, who had defected from the Mamlūk to the Ottoman camp, Homs, Tripoli and other coastal cities were under Turkish command, apparently because this, by the nature of things, seemed safer in the event of a European attack on the coastal cities. In fact, such an attack was not long in coming. In 926/1519, Venetians (or Portuguese) carried out a raid on Beirut, where they stayed for three days until they were ejected by the Ottomans.[35]

It seems that the settling of the Ṣūfī shaykh at Dayr al-Biʿna on the initiative or with the assistance of the *sulṭān* must be understood as part of a drive for the colonization and Islamization of recently conquered areas sensitive in regard to security (the inhabitants of Dayr al-Asad believe that the reason for the establishment of the Ṣūfī settlement and the *waqf* was that the population of the area had a reputation for rebelliousness). Express evidence of such a drive with respect to Dayr al-Biʿna is provided by the biographer al-Būrīnī (d. 1615); his account was copied, with some additions, by al-Muḥibbī. Here are its main points: Shaykh Asad al-Biqāʿī studied Ṣūfism in Damascus; from there he moved to the Safad district to settle in a monastery at the foot of a mountain near the village of al-Biʿna; the place had formerly been known as Dayr al-Khiḍr,[36] and Christians had been living there; the Sulṭān Süleymān had removed them from there and commanded al-Asad to settle there with his children and Ṣūfī devotees, and indeed he 'obeyed the sublime command', living at the said monastery until his death in 977/1569.[37] In other words: instead of the Christian settlement at Dayr al-Biʿna, the *sulṭān* wished to establish a Muslim settlement based on Shaykh Asad, his family and, more important, a nucleus of Ṣūfī followers of the shaykh, apparently in the expectation that his great fame would attract further settlers. It is significant in this context that under the terms of the *waqfiyya* Shaykh Asad was to serve as *imām* of the mosque which, in the circumstances of the case, might be regarded as a Ṣūfī

34 Kramers, 'Selīm I', 216; Arnold, 149.

35 Kurd ʿAlī, part II, 227, 228; Winter, *ʿAlī Ibn Maymūn*, 290 and the sources indicated in n. 50.

36 Al-Khiḍr is the Arabic name of Saint George (I am obliged to my colleague, Dr. Butrus Abu-Manneh, for pointing this out to me).

37 Al-Būrīnī, part I, 178–9; al-Muḥibbī, 177.

*zāwiya* (the *zāwiya* established in Safad by his son Aḥmad was likewise called *jāmiʿ*); he was, moreover, to serve as *mutawallī* and *nāẓir* of the *waqf*, that is to say, that in addition to his function as a spiritual leader he was also in charge of the economic administration of the settlement. In difference to biographical literature, the *waqfiyya* has Selīm rather than Süleymān initiate the settlement. The foregoing shows beyond doubt that the *waqf* was established by Selīm. The question arises why the biographers and, in their wake, the inhabitants of Dayr al-Asad, substitute Süleymān for him. Both biographers focus on Asad's son, Aḥmad. They give full details of the dates of his life and death, his education and his movements, while treating the story of his father's settling at Dayr al-Biʿna like a matter of the distant past. This may be the reason for the mistake as to the identity of the *sulṭān*.

Moreover, al-Būrīnī was a contemporary of the Sulṭān Süleymān, who too used the Ṣūfī *zāwiya* and the *waqf* for political purposes. There is evidence that Süleymān, not long after the establishment of the *waqf* in favour of Shaykh al-Asad, expelled Christians from a monastery, confiscated their property and dedicated it to a Ṣūfī shaykh and his descendants and followers. The similarity of the two cases leaves no room for doubt. The *sijill* of the Sharīʿa Court of Jerusalem of the sixteenth century clearly reflects a systematic policy of Islamization of holy places populated by Christians. The ill-treatment of the Franciscans on Mt. Zion was indeed accepted practice in the late fifteenth century under Mamlūk rule, but it intensified immediately after the Ottoman conquest. In 1524, the church near 'David's Tomb' was confiscated and converted into a mosque. A few years later, the Christians were made to help in building the walls of Jerusalem. Their expulsion from Mt. Zion proceeded gradually and systematically. At first, parts of the monastery buildings were annexed to 'David's Tomb' and handed over to dervishes for residential purposes, and finally, in 956/1549, Süleymān issued a *firman* ordering all monks and other 'Franks' to move away from the vicinity of the tomb and inviting Ṣūfīs to occupy the dwellings of the monks; the property of the Christians was confiscated by the *sulṭān* and dedicated, as a *waqf*, to the Ṣūfī Aḥmad al-Dajānī and his descendants and followers. That shaykh, like Shaykh Muḥammad al-Asad in his time, was regarded as 'the head of the gnostics' (*quṭb al-ʿārifīn*) in his generation and 'the paragon of mystics' (*qidwa al-sālikīn*). The dedicator stipulated that the *mashyakha* should be conferred on the Ṣūfī shaykh, that is to say that he should be in charge of the *zāwiya*. It seems that in this case too Ottoman policy was guided by considerations of security and Islamization. Fear of an attack by Christian pirates prompted the decision to repair the citadel; and the wish to strengthen the Muslim character of Jerusalem, while diminishing the Christian element, impelled the authorities to assist in the establishment of a Ṣūfī *zāwiya* headed by a shaykh whose fame would induce dervishes to settle there. It is interesting to note in this connexion that the Palestinian *taḥrir* registers of the sixteenth century reflect a significant rate of emigration of Christians from the area south of Jerusalem (Bethlehem, Bayt Jala and Hebron). This process, whether it began towards the end of the Mamlūk period or resulted from the Ottoman conquest, undoubtedly gathered momentum at the beginning of the Ottoman period, apparently because of the presence of Muslim holy places in the region.[38]

The circumstances of the Islamization of Mt. Zion may perhaps allow conclusions as to the technique adopted in the Islamization of Dayr al-Biʿna. True, according to al-Būrīnī, the *sulṭān* at first expelled the Christians and afterwards ordered al-Asad to move into the place with his Ṣūfī followers, but the *waqfiyya* indicates that the sequence of events was somewhat different, more like the technique of creeping annexation used in the case of Mt. Zion. According to the *waqfiyya*, Selīm dedicated the monastery to the mosque and the Ṣūfī shaykh, and the mosque had been built within the monastery to enable the name of Allāh to be incessantly uttered (in the context of Ṣūfī worship) (ll. 21, 22); this means that the mosque-cum-*zāwiya* at Dayr al-Biʿna already existed at the time the *waqf* was established or, more precisely, the mosque was built within the church-fortress (as the inhabitants of the village have it), and the detailed description in the *waqfiyya* of the residential buildings of the monastery(-fortress), the retreats (*khalāwī*) (originally used by the Christians) etc. (ll. 9 ff.) must be understood against this background. Thus, the Ṣūfī settlement at Dayr al-Biʿna came into being *before* the expulsion of the Christians and the establishment of the *waqf.*

Some unexpected evidence of the correctness of this assumption is contained in a recently discovered document which was probably used in preparing Shaykh Muḥammad al-Asad's pedigree from the Prophet Muḥammad onwards. The author and date of that document are not stated in it, but since it mentions descendants of the shaykh it was clearly not composed in his time. In this document we read: '… the *imām*, the *ʿālim*, the outstanding wise man, the Ṣūfī … who is a model [for those going the Ṣūfī way] … our *sayyid* and *mawlā* … the Shaykh Muḥammad al-Asad, who lived at Dayr al-Biʿna in 916 [1510]' (ll. 32–6).[39] It thus appears that Muḥammad al-Asad was already

38 A. Cohen, '"Lo Yarashta ve-Lo Gerashta" – Yehudei Yerushalayim ve-Gerush ha-Frantzisqanim me "Har Zion"', *Cathedra*, 22 (January 1982), 62–3, 69–71; Heyd, 149; M. Winter, 'Reforma Ḥevratit ve-Datit ba-Ṣufiyut ha-Me'ukheret', *ha-Mizraḥ he-Ḥadash*, XXXI, 1986 (in press); A. Cohen and B. Lewis, *Population and revenue in towns of Palestine in the sixteenth century*, Princeton, 1978, 32–3.

39 See the Genealogical Document (pl. IV).

in Dayr al-Biʿna six years before the Ottoman conquest. Of course, Selīm's intervention – the expulsion of the Christians ('the faction of Satan, the polytheists and unbelievers') and the conversion of their property into a *waqf* – was intended to consolidate the Ṣūfī settlement and complete the ousting of the Christians from the site, similarly to what happened on Mt. Zion. It should also be remembered that the Safad region was a famous centre of the activity of the Ṣūfī orders. There is evidence in Ibn Ṭūlūn's chronicle (late fifteenth and early sixteenth century) of well-known Ṣūfīs living in Safad who were followers of Ibn al-ʿArabī, including some who made pilgrimages to his tomb in Damascus.[40] Selīm stipulated in the *waqfiyya* that if, when there were no more descendants, it should prove impossible to spend the proceeds of the *waqf* on the monastery and the mosque, they should go to the Safad poor, by which he may have meant the Ṣūfīs, who led austere, ascetic lives.

Great importance attaches in this connection to the fact that Shaykh Asad received his Ṣūfī training from Shaykh Muḥammad Ibn ʿArrāq of Damascus, who belonged to the school of Ibn al-ʿArabī. Ibn ʿArrāq was the son of a Circassian emir. After meeting in Beirut a follower of Ibn al-ʿArabī, viz. the Moroccan Shaykh Sīdī ʿAlī Ibn Maymūn, who propagated Ṣūfism in Syria and Turkey in the sixteenth century, he developed a keen interest in mysticism and became an ascetic. He served as a *qāḍī* in the al-Ṣāliḥiyya quarter of Damascus, travelled a great deal about the Muslim world and met with well-known Ṣūfīs in Safad and Egypt. After Ibn Maymūn's death, Ibn ʿArrāq succeeded him as the head of a Ṣūfī order. That order, known as al-ʿArrāqiyya or Khawāṭiriyya, was part of the Madyaniyya order. Ibn Maymūn's Ṣūfism belonged to the Shādhilī stream, which in Syria was tolerant of pluralistic streams in Ṣūfism. Ibn Maymūn and Ibn ʿArrāq were associated with the Ḥanbalī school of law in Damascus. Both had a military record. Ibn Maymūn fought the Portuguese and volunteered to strengthen the fortifications of the Lebanese coastal town of Batrūn, which in the late Middle Ages was frequently attacked by the 'Franks'. Ibn ʿArrāq, originally an army officer, defended Beirut against Christian pirates.[41]

Ibn ʿArrāq's qualities probably did not escape Selīm's notice. There is evidence that the shaykh had great influence on him. In 1517, the *qāḍīs*, *ʿulamāʾ* and 'righteous men' assembled at the Umayyad Mosque in Damascus by order of the Nāʾib and the Ottoman Qāḍī because the public was alarmed by the threat of some harsh measure. Three of those assembled reported that the Prophet Muḥammad had appeared to them in a dream and instructed them to

40 Ibn Ṭūlūn, part I, *884–921* [*H.*], Cairo, 1381/1962, 57–8, 328, 335.

41 Ibid., 320; Winter, *ʿAlī Ibn Maymūn*, 281, 287–97, 307; Trimingham, 89–90, 278.

summon the people through the *wāʾiz* of the mosque 'to pray and to implore the victorious Sulṭān Selīm Khān' [to waive the intended measure]; afterwards they were to go to the Shaykh Muḥammad Ibn ʿArrāq in the Ṣāliḥiyya quarter and ask him to intercede with the *sulṭān* on their behalf.[42] It seems indeed that Selīm became friendly with some religious functionaries in Damascus who, as a result, enjoyed certain immunities. Thus, when he was once in the city, he was the guest of Shaykh Muḥammad Badakhshī at the Umayyad Mosque. He kept silent a long time out of respect for the shaykh and, at the end of the meeting, asked the shaykh to pray for him; on another occasion, he submitted a religious-legal question to him. Selīm was said to have been one of those who 'believe in asking assistance from the pure spirits of the prophets and noble entombed.'[43]

Some of the witnesses who signed the *waqfiyya* bear the title *sayyid*, which may have been an honorific bestowed upon Ṣūfī shaykhs. One witness is described as *fakhr al-sāda*, perhaps because of his position in the hierarchy of shaykhs.

## 3 The Question of Shaykh al-Asad's Identity

It is quite possible that Shaykh Muḥammad al-Asad followed in the footsteps of his master Ibn ʿArrāq, i.e. that he won fame as a man of both the book and the sword. Selīm may have known him through Ibn ʿArrāq; at any rate, the detailed description of his qualities in the *waqfiyya* suggests that Selīm knew him well. The *waqfiyya* contains elements tending to support the folkloric conception of al-Asad's identity. It mentions a Ṣūfī of unusual prominence: a saintly man close to the deity, an outstanding expert on religion, the supreme authority among Ṣūfī shaykhs, a teacher and educator of Ṣūfī novices and of devout and godfearing persons wishing to join the Ṣūfī *ṭarīqa*, a preacher attracting masses of listeners; the dedicator admiringly calls him 'the light of religion'. The *waqfiyya* also contains possible references to miracles worked by al-Asad, though no express mention of the taming of the lion. There are numerous expressions denoting great courage and strength, such as 'lion', 'hero' and '*sayyid* envied by the generations and the span of the outstretched arm [scil. powerful persons]'. Tongues are said to honour themselves by describing Asad and ears to delight in hearing about his exploits; his miraculous deed (*karāma*) 'deserves to be recorded in golden ink by day and by night'.

42 Ibn Ṭūlūn, part II, 62–3.

43 Saʿd al-Dīn, II, 343. Cf. Winter, ʿAlī *Ibn Maymūn*, 297, 305.

Who was Shaykh al-Asad? We have reliable testimony on his descendants, who left their traces in chronicles and legal documents. The biographer al-Būrīnī reports that the shaykh's son, Aḥmad b. Asad (944/1537–1010/1601) 'grew up in the service of the Creator', moved from Dayr al-Biʿna to Safad and there propagated the *ṭarīqa*; he established a *zāwiya* which was formerly known as Jāmiʿ al-Ṣadr. The other sons continued to live at Dayr al-Asad. They had a special *wird* (Ṣūfī version of prayers), which they had learnt from their father. Shaykh Aḥmad transmitted his saintliness and reputation as a miracle man to his descendants: 'The descendants of the lion are all lion cubs and the ecstatic (*ṣāḥib ḥāl*) breeds only ecstatics.' Allāh blessed their progeny; they spread and multiplied and were famous for their outstanding qualities. Evidence of Asad's descendants is supplied by the *sijill* of the Sharīʿa Court of Acre of 1838 in connexion with disputes between them over the distribution of the proceeds of the *waqf* of Dayr al-Asad. We also find an entry in the *sijill* of Safad of the second half of the nineteenth century concerning the transfer of the posts of *imām* and *mu'adhdhin* of the *zāwiya* of the saintly Sīdī Walī Allāh Muḥammad al-Asad from Shaykh Aḥmad al-Asadī to his two sons.[44]

Tracing Asad's origin is, by the nature of things, more difficult. The *waqfiyya* refers to him as Ibn ʿAbd Allāh al-Asadī (l. 30), and the judgement of the Qāḍī of Acre of 1838 calls him Muḥammad al-Asad (l. 16). Al-Būrīnī provides the earliest reference to his origin: he hails from the village of Ḥammārā. Al-Muḥibbī adds that this village is in the al-Biqāʿ district, whence the name of his son: Aḥmad b. Asad al-Biqāʿī. Muḥammad al-Asad moved from his village to Damascus, where he studied Ṣūfism under Ibn ʿArrāq. From there he went to the Safad region and settled in Dayr al-Biʿna, as stated above. There is supporting evidence as to his geographical origin: one of the informants concerning Aḥmad al-Asadī is 'the Imām al-Darwishiyya bi'l-Shām',[45] and one of the

44 Al-Būrīnī, Part I, 179; al-Muḥibbī, 177. According to a family tree of Shaykh Muḥammad al-Asad, he had four sons, none of whom was called Aḥmad, but a grandson by his son Maḥfūẓ bore that name. This family tree is a copy, made by Muḥammad Abū Saʿūd Asadī and Yāsīn Qāsim Ḥusayn on 19 April 1960, of 'the old family tree (*sajara*)'. See Fig. 14.1; judgement of the Sharīʿa Court of Acre of 1838 (Appendix B); l. 5, judgement of the Sharīʿa Court of Safad of 1273/1856. Later, in 1291/1874, the son who had been appointed *imām* asked to be paid for his services at the *zāwiya*, and the Nā'ib permitted him to collect his remuneration out of the *zāwiya waqf*. He again asked for and obtained pay in 1293/1876. The three judgements are written on the same sheet (see Figs. 14.2, 14.3). I am indebted to Engineer B. Dichter for placing that sheet at my disposal. For evidence on the descendants of Shaykh Muḥammad al-Asad in the *sijill* of Safad of the late seventeenth century see Ebied and Young, 36, 38 and 41.

45 Al-Būrīnī, part I, 178; al-Muḥibbī, 177.

FIGURE 14.1 The family tree of Shaykh Muḥammad al-Asad

FIGURE 14.2 Judgements of the Sharīʿa Court of Safad of 1273/1856, 1291/1874 and 1293/1876

FIGURE 14.3 Judgements of the Sharīʿa Court of Safad of 1273/1856, 1291/1874 and 1293/1876

من فاطمة الزهرة بنت محمد صلى الله عل
وسلم وفاطمة الزهرة اعقب الحسن والحسن
والحسن اعقب محمد الباقر رضي الله عنه و
الباقر اعقب زين العابدين رضي الله عنه
وزين العابدين اعقب عبد الله المحض
رضي الله عنه وعبد الله المحض اعقب
موسي الجون وموسي الجون اعقب عبد الله
رضي الله عنه وعبد الله اعقب موسي
رضي الله عنه وموسي اعقب داود رضي
الله عنه اعقب محمد رضي الله ومحمد اعقب
يحي الزاهد رضي الله عنه ويحي الزاهد اعقب
عبد الله رضي الله عنه وعبد الله اعقب
موسي رضي الله عنه وموسي اعقب العالم
العلامه الكامل العارف بالله تعالي
الباز الاشهب والطراز المذهب سيدنا وا
ومولانا الشيخ محيي الدين عبد القادر
الجيلاني قدس الله سره العزيز ونفعنا الله

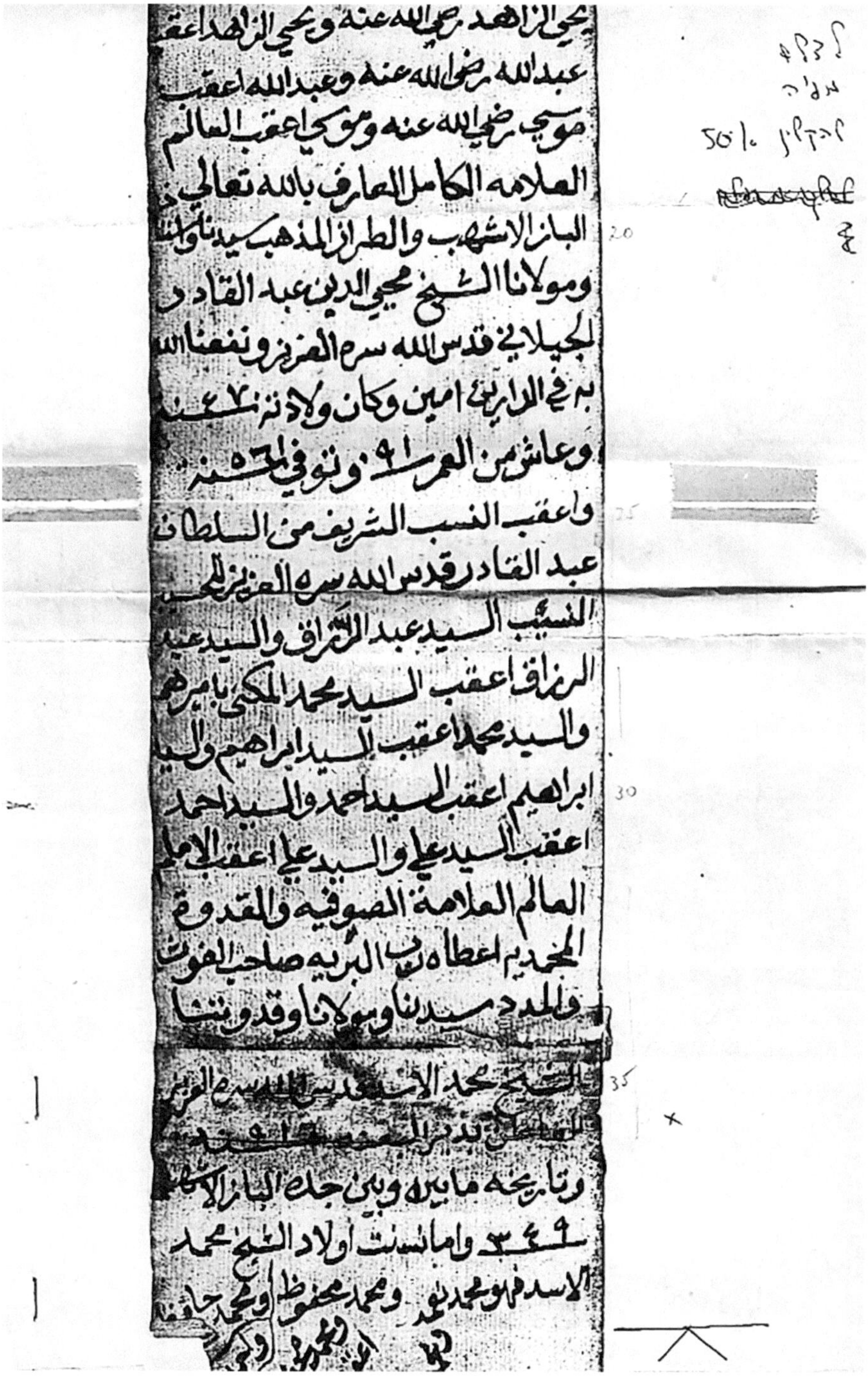
يحيى الزاهد رضي الله عنه ويحيى الزاهد اعقب
عبد الله رضي الله عنه وعبد الله اعقب
موسى رضي الله عنه وموسى اعقب العالم
العلامه الكامل العارف بالله تعالى
الباز الاشهب والطراز المذهب سيدنا وا
ومولانا الشيخ محيي الدين عبد القادر
الجيلاني قدس الله سره العزيز ونفعنا الله
به في الدارين امين وكان ولادته سنة ٤٧١
وعاش من العمر ٩١ وتوفي في سنة ٥٦٠
واعقب النسب الشريف من السلطان
عبد القادر قدس الله سره العزيز المحسن
النسيب السيد عبد الرزاق والسيد عبد
الرزاق اعقب السيد محمد المكي بابراهيم
والسيد محمد اعقب السيد ابراهيم والسيد
ابراهيم اعقب السيد احمد والسيد احمد
اعقب السيد علي والسيد علي اعقب الامام
العالم العلامه الصوفيه والمقدوم
المخدوم اعطاه رب البريه صاحب الفوث
والمدد سيدنا ومولانا وقدوتنا
الشيخ محمد الاسعد قدس الله سره العزيز
وتاريخه ما بينه وبين جده الباز الاشهب
سنة ٩٤٣ واما نسبت اولاد الشيخ محمد
الاسعد فهو محمد نور ومحمد محفوظ ومحمد حافظ

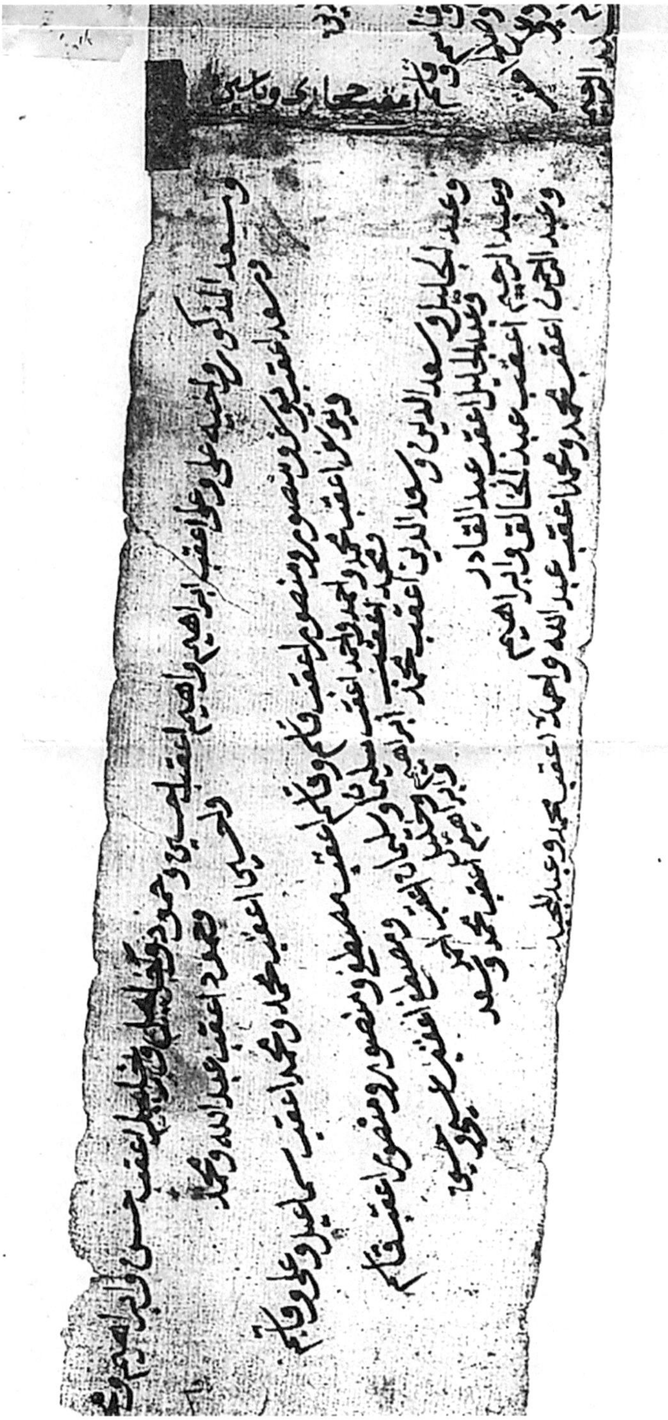

FIGURE 14.4A–C A genealogical document

witnesses who signed the judgement of the Qāḍī of Acre of 1838 is the Shaykh Ḥasan al-Biqāʿī.

Was Shaykh Ibn ʿAbd Allāh al-Asadī the founder of a family order bearing his name, a name given him for taming a lion (as reported in the folktale), or did he merely establish at Dayr al-Biʿna an extension to an existing Damascene order, just as his son Aḥmad established an extension at Safad? Certain facts speak for the latter possibility. The Damascene biographer and historiographer Ibn Kathīr (d. 744/1377) mentions an eminent shaykh, ʿAbd Allāh al-Yūnīnī, surnamed Asad al-Shām, of the village of Yūnīn, near Baʿlbek, who died in 617/1220, i.e. some three hundred years before Selīm I appeared in the region. He had a *zāwiya* at Yūnīn to which Ṣūfīs made pilgrimages as he was known for his piety and asceticism. That shaykh was both a mystic and a warrior. He is said to have left his *zāwiya* to join Ṣalāḥ al-Dīn in his wars against the Crusaders, 'missed not a single foray' and shot stones weighing 80 rotls each from his bow. He was surnamed Asad al-Shām because of ecstatic states of mind and visionary experiences (*aḥwāl wa-mukāshafāt*) indicating an ability to work miracles (*karāmāt*). It is reported that while he was once purifying himself in the waters of the Thawr[ā] river near Damascus a Christian passed over the 'White Bridge' with a mule carrying a load of wine. The animal suddenly stumbled and the load fell down. The shaykh interrupted his ablutions and helped the Christian to put the wine back onto the mule. Moreover, he asked the Qāḍī of Kerak, who was an eyewitness of the incident, to lend a hand, much to the latter's bewilderment. When the Christian finally arrived with his merchandise at the wine merchant's house in ʿAqaba, with the *qāḍī* in his wake, it appeared to everybody's surprise that the wine had turned into vinegar. The Christian hurried back to the shaykh and, of course, at once converted to Islam through him.[46] Both miracles, that of 'Asad al-Shām' and that of Muḥammad al-Asad, are accompanied by portents relating to Islamization. Since, moreover, the two shaykhs hail from the same region, it is not inconceivable that we have to do here with one Ṣūfī family order with extensions at Dayr al-Biʿna and Safad. If this is so, the miracle ascribed to Muḥammad al-Asad may in reality be a metamorphosis of the one ascribed to Shaykh ʿAbd Allāh al-Yūnīnī. This surmise is supported by the assignment of Muḥammad al-Asad, in the folktale, to the Qādirī order. This assignment is corroborated by his pedigree, according to which his great-grandfather in the seventh degree was the founder of the Qādirī order, ʿAbd al-Qādir al-Jīlānī (d. 561/1166). Moreover, there are those who identify the person buried in the *maqām* in Dayr al-Asad with ʿAbd al-Qādir al-Jīlānī. The latter was a saint recognized in the Muslim world; he has numerous *maqāms*

46 Abū 'l-Fidā' al-Ḥāfiẓ Ibn Kathīr, *Al-Bidāya wa'l-nihāya*, XIII (2nd ed.), Beirut, 1977, 93–4; Trimingham, 240. As for the name of the river, see Ibn Ṭūlūn, part I, 64, 358.

in various places.[47] The Qādirī order had footholds in Syria as early as 1300 but was not firmly established there until the fifteenth century, when the first Qādirī *zāwiya* – the Dāʿūdiyya – was founded in Damascus.[48] There is no indication in the sources that Muḥammad al-Asad regarded himself as belonging to the al-ʿArrāqiyya or al-Madyaniyya order although he studied Ṣūfism under Ibn ʿArrāq. One of the subdivisions of the Qādirī order was called al-Asadiyya. Some sources of the late fifteenth century contain information on 'al-Madrasa al-Asadiyya' and a *khānaqāh* called al-Asadiyya, both in Damascus; the latter was built by Asad al-Dīn b. Shīr Kūh, the *walī* of its *mashyakha*, Najm al-Dīn b. al-Qurashiyya al-ʿAbbāsī and others; Asad al-Dīn also built a *ribāṭ* in Damascus. The locations of the *khānaqāh* and the *ribāṭ* are not known,[49] nor is the degree of relevance of either to our subject. It should perhaps be noted, though, that the river Thawrā, mentioned in connection with the miracle of 'Asad al-Shām', flows through the al-Ṣāliḥiyya quarter of Damascus. Near the 'White Bridge' (over which Selīm marched) is al-Khānaqah al-Ghazziyya. One of the spokesmen on its behalf in 926/1519 was Ibrāhīm al-Biqāʿī, who may have been related to our Shaykh Asad al-Biqāʿī.[50]

There is still one unresolved problem. Selīm's *waqfiyya* calls Ibn ʿAbd Allāh al-Asadī 'the famous lion whose noble descent is through [or: consists in his being] a son of their emir (*amīruhum*)' (l. 30). Who is this emir? Al-Muḥibbī distinguishes between 'al-Biqāʿ al-ʿAzīzī' and 'al-Biqāʿ al-Baʿlbakī'. The former, according to him, 'was descended from the King al-ʿAzīz, who was a son of the Sulṭān Ṣalāḥ al-Dīn Yūsuf b. Ayyūb and the staff of whose *wilāya* had its seat at Kerak'. Does the biographer mean to say that the Ṣūfī shaykh's noble descent consisted in blood-relationship to Ṣalāḥ al-Dīn al-Ayyūbī, who is buried in Damascus?[51] It is interesting to note that Ṣalāḥ al-Dīn and Kerak also figure in the story of the deeds of 'Asad al-Shām'. It should further be noted that one of the witnesses who signed Selīm's *waqfiyya* was Jamāl al-Dīn Yūsuf b. Ayyūb, entitled 'Fakhr al-Aʿyān'. This too would seem to confirm the connexion with Ṣalāḥ al-Dīn. In this case as well, the solution of the problem is aided by a datum from an unexpected source. Muḥammad al-Asad's pedigree indicates that his great-grandfather in the fourth degree was 'the Shaykh Amīruhum' and that 'Amīruhum' is an epithet of one Sayyid Muḥammad (*al-mukannā*

47 See the Family Tree of Shaykh Muḥammad al-Asad (pl. 1); Lazarus-Yafeh, *Notes*; Trimingham, 41, 43; Winter, ʿAlī *Ibn Maymūn*, 305.

48 Trimingham, p. 21, n. 5, and p. 43.

49 Ibid., Index, *s.v.* 'Asadiyya', 271; Ibn Ṭūlūn, part I, 32; Kurd ʿAlī, part VI, p. 134, no. 351, p. 139, no. 395.

50 Ibn Ṭūlūn, part II, 35, 75, 112–13.

51 Al-Muḥibbī, 177; Kurd ʿAlī, part VI, 157.

*bi-Amīruhum*); this epithet may be an indication of exalted status and perhaps of relationship to Ṣalāḥ al-Dīn al-Ayyūbī.[52]

## 4 The Ṣūfi Monastery and the *waqf* as Instruments of the Ottoman Policy of Colonization and Islamization

Selīm I's *waqf* in Dayr al-Bi'na in favour of a miracle-working Ṣūfī shaykh can only be understood in the light of the role played by roving Ṣūfī dervishes and their monasteries in the colonization and Islamization of conquered areas, especially border areas, in the Ottoman period and even earlier, from the eleventh century, upon the westward drive of the Seljūqs. Ṣūfī activity was closely linked with the spread of Islam and its culture in Anatolia and did not weaken after the collapse of the Seljūq state of Rūm. The consolidation of the Ṣūfī order in the fifteenth century went hand in hand with the growth and consolidation of the Ottoman Empire. The dervish mystics contributed to the shaping and consolidation of militant Islam. They provided religious inspiration and sanction to the *ghāzīs* and even took part in the fighting themselves.[53] In this respect, the Ottomans continued the policy of the Ayyūbids and Mamlūks. There is evidence of dervishes playing an active role in the defence of Islam in the period of the Crusades.[54] The failure of the Crusades and the displacement of the Crusaders from their last positions in Palestine encouraged the aspirations of the Ṣūfīs to establish *zāwiyas* in Jerusalem and elsewhere. These aspirations fell in with the policy of Ṣalāḥ al-Dīn, who in 585/1189 established the Khānaqāh Ṣalāḥiyya in Jerusalem and for that purpose had the palace of the Latin Patriarch there evacuated.[55] Instead of a cold, legalistic Islam, the Ṣūfī mystics offered religious enthusiasm accompanied by ramified social activities, providing security to the individual, and in this way won support among the Christians of Anatolia and even among the non-Arab populations of Central Asia and North Africa. Although the *'ulamā'* were the backbone of the Ottoman administration, the Ṣūfī orders rather than the *medreses* ministered to the religious needs of the people. The Ṣūfī organizations, unlike the state-operated *khānaqāhs*, were linked with popular movements and so showed greater powers of survival. In

52 See the Family Tree (pl. I). Muḥammad Abū 'l-Sa'ūd Asadī confirms that we have to do here with a personal name (*Amīrahum*). I wish to thank my colleague, Professor G. Goldenberg, for clarifying the linguistic structure of the name; Genealogical Document (pl. IV).

53 Trimingham, 9, 23–4, 67–8.

54 One of them, 'Asad al-Shām', was discussed above. For more evidence see Trimingham, 240.

55 Drori, 53; Trimingham, 17 and the sources indicated there.

fact, the orders played an important part in religious, political and social life throughout the history of the Ottoman Empire.[56]

Barkan's pioneer study, based on a fifteenth-century land and population census, reveals the decisive role played by the dervishes and their monasteries in the Ottoman colonization of Anatolia and Rumelia. The dervishes provided settlement nuclei combining diligent, sophisticated agricultural manpower with religious zeal. These nuclei were set up in places essential from a security point of view: on strategic traffic arteries, passes and trade and caravan routes, along extended frontiers and in the midst of Christian populations. The monasteries, with all the economic and religious-cultural facilities they comprised, ensured a solid Ottoman presence in the places of settlement. The Ottoman regime induced dervishes to establish monasteries in conquered territories, already at the invasion stage, by various incentives: allocations of land, defrayal of the cost of settlement and cultivation; exemption from taxes and from the duty to supply grain to the army at low prices; immunity from interference by Ottoman officials in the affairs of the monastery. It is interesting to note that, according to a local tradition, Selīm granted the lands of Christian Dayr al-Biʿna to Shaykh Muḥammad al-Asad and exempted him from government taxes. He also granted the people of the new Muslim settlement exemption from service in the Ottoman army. Moreover, the settlement enjoyed the status of a place of refuge (*ma'man*): criminals found shelter there from pursuit by the authorities. It seems that the Sulṭān granted all these privileges to encourage Muslim settlement in a locality whose Christian population had recently been evacuated.

The monasteries, besides being places of settlement, served as hostels or inns for travellers and wayfarers and were in charge of day-to-day security in the region, including the safety of travellers on the roads. Some monastery shaykhs had garrison troops at their disposal and even participated themselves in military and police operations. The monasteries were a kind of vantage points, defence posts or gendarmerie stations.[57]

---

56 Trimingham, 23–4, 67–70, 232.

57 Ömer Lutfi Barkan, 'Les fondations pieuses comme méthode de peuplement et de colonisation. Les derviches colonisateurs de l'époque des invasions et les couvents (saviyé),' *Vakiflar Dergisi*, II, 1942 (partie française), 59–65; Suraiya Faroqhi, 'The Tekke of Haci Bektaş: social position and economic activities', *International Journal of Middle East Studies*, VII, 2, 1976, 183, 195–6; V. Mutafčieva, 'Problèmes fondamentaux de l'étude du vakf en tant que partie de la structure sociale et économique des Balkans sous la domination ottomane (XV$^{e}$–XIX$^{e}$ s', in Baer and Gilbar; İ. Metin Kunt, 'The *vakif* as instrument of public policy: notes on the Köprülü family vakifs', in Baer and Gilbar; Barkan's above-mentioned research was a very important source of inspiration for the socio-historical analysis of the *waqfiyya*. I am indebted to my colleague, Dr. Miriam Hoexter, for drawing my attention

Similarly, the settlements of *fuqarāʾ* (saints) in the Sudan were instruments of a policy of colonization (settling of uninhabited areas), Islamization and cultural integration. The *fuqarāʾ* too were induced by various benefits to settle in border areas. The Sanūsī *zāwiya* played a prominent part in the social, religious and political integration of Cyrenaica. The Bedouin integrated into the Sanūsī order, out of which the Libyan state grew, by means of *zāwiyas* adapted to the tribal system. The Sanūsī *zāwiyas* were positioned in accordance with security, political and economic considerations: at oases, on trade routes, at tribal centres, near wells, at crossroads, on coastal highways and on Greco-Roman sites.[58]

The *waqf* was instrumental in carrying out the policy of colonization and Islamization of the Ottoman Empire. The Ottoman authorities used it extensively to induce dervishes to settle. They were granted the entitlement of wealthy *waqfs*. The *waqf* financed not only religious institutions but also public buildings, highways, bridges and the like. It was, moreover, an important factor in economic life. There is evidence of Christians converting to Islam to enjoy the economic and cultural advantages of the *waqf*. One of these advantages was the immunity, conferred by the religious sanction of the *waqf*, from expropriation by the authorities. The religious functionaries performing ritual functions at institutions maintained by a *waqf* – there were thousands of such *waqfs* in the Balkans – were not only colonizers but zealous missionaries of Islam. Striking examples of the enlistment of *waqfs* in the service of government policy are the *waqfs* of the members of the Köprülü family who were grand viziers in the second half of the seventeenth century. The Ottoman officials who established *waqfs* throughout the empire identified themselves with the state.[59]

In the Ottoman period, many *waqfs* were established in favour of Ṣūfī monasteries. Only a minority belonged to specific *ṭarīqas*. In this matter too the Ottomans continued the tradition of the Ayyūbids and the Mamlūks.[60] Some monasteries owned much real estate and derived very high incomes from it. Similarly, the *waqfs* of orders in Cyrenaica and Tunisia comprised tens of thousands of hectares of land, as well as other property.[61] There is evidence from the early sixteenth century of Ottoman *sulṭāns* being aware of the importance of *waqfs*, monasteries and dervishes as instruments of government. The Sulṭān

---

to that article. Interview with Muḥammad Abū 'l-Saʿūd al-Asadī on 1st January, 1984, and with Ibrāhīm al-Asadī on 20 March, 1984.

58 R.S. O'Fahey, 'Endowment, privilege and estate in the central and eastern Sudan', in Baer and Gilbar; E.E. Evans-Pritchard, *The Sanusi of Cyrenaica*, Oxford, 1949, 70–1, 78, 84; Nicola A. Ziadeh, *Sanūsiyah: a study of a Revivalist movement in Islam*, Leiden, 1968, 114–15.

59 Barkan, 63–4; Mutafčieva; Kunt; Faroqhi, 193, 206.

60 Baer; Trimingham, 7, 18, 169; W. Heffening, art. 'Waḳf', *Encyclopaedia of Islam*, IV, 1932, 1098–9.

61 Faroqhi, 194, 206–7; Evans-Pritchard, 74–8; Ziadeh, 115, 117; Brown.

Bāyezīd II, the father of Selīm I, honoured Haci Bektaş and added him to the list of the beneficiaries of his *waqfs*. He also visited the saint's *türbe* and spread a precious cover over its cupola.[62] In 923/1517, a decree was issued by the Nā'ib, the Ottoman Qāḍī and the Defterdār of Damascus requiring the submission of financial reports on the activities of *waqfs* in favour of *medreses*, *türbe*s and *khānaqāh*s for the previous year; this decree caused alarm among the administrators of the *waqfs*. We thus see that the establishment of *waqfs* in favour of monasteries was a common phenomenon in Damascus in the days of Selīm.[63]

There is evidence of *waqfs* being created for the express purpose of building fortresses, as well as khāns and intermediate stations, to ensure the safety of Mecca pilgrims. In the second half of the seventeenth century, one of the grand viziers of the house of Köprülü established by means of a *waqf* an impressive array of institutions, including fortresses designed to protect caravans of traders and pilgrims against Bedouin raids. The *waqf* was supposed to finance the maintenance of the fortresses and their garrison out of its income.

Because of the importance of the security services rendered by the monasteries to the Ottoman regime, the status of the shaykh of the monastery, who had originally been autonomous, gradually changed into that of a government official. The Ottoman *sulṭāns* also sought to strengthen the authority of local leaders active in the colonization of Rumelia by granting them the entitlement of *waqfs*.[64] Ṣūfī settlements protected by *waqfs*, of which Shaykh al-Asadī's settlement at Dayr al-Biʿna was an instance, were thus part of a systematic policy of the Ottoman regime, intended to achieve political and security aims.

## 5 Ṣūfī Settlement Nuclei and Descendants of the Founders

Ottoman colonization policy was aimed at the establishment, in monasteries, of dervish settlements whose nucleus was a Ṣūfī shaykh and his family. The income of the *waqfs* set up in favour of the monasteries was earmarked for the shaykh and his male agnatic descendants until the end of all generations. It is with good reason, therefore, that the founders of the monasteries are regarded as the founders of the new settlements.[65] The nucleus of Dayr

62 Faroqhi, 184. See also ibid., 185, 206.

63 Ibn Ṭūlūn, part II, 65, 73. The establishment of *waqfs* in favour of *zāwiyas* is a tradition continuing well into the twentieth century. See Sharīʿa Court of Jaffa, *Sijillāt al-Ḥujuj*, vol. 223, p. 14, no. 435 of 23 June 1942 (a Naqshabandī *zāwiya* in Jerusalem); Sharīʿa Court of Acre, *Waqfiyyat* al-Shādhilī, Acre, of 1312/1894, Judgement of 12 December 1936, and Tarshīḥā, File no. 12/1280, Judgement of 28 July 1930.

64 Barkan, 63, 65; Kunt. Cf. Evans-Pritchard, 77.

65 Barkan, 60, 62, 63.

al-Asad is Shaykh Muḥammad al-Asad and his family. The shaykh's pedigree shows graphically how four fertile branches of male agnatic descendants issued from his four sons. In 1957, there were 800 'Asadī souls'. At the time of my visit to the village, in 1984, they numbered about three times as many; they were about half the population of the village, with offshoots in other localities from Acre to Safad. The other clans in the village are descended from strangers who found refuge there at various times, enjoying the protection of the Ṣūfī shaykh's family. Shaykh Muḥammad al-Asad's descendants enjoy the proceeds of, and administer the *waqf* to this day. This is attested by entries in the *sijills* of the Sharīʿa Courts. When the Muslim Division of the Ministry of Religious Affairs wished to collect the income of the *waqf* property in the village, the *mutawallīs* maintained that it was a family *waqf* and that its proceeds must be distributed among the male descendants in accordance with the terms of the *waqfiyya*.[66]

The inhabitants of the village of Haci Bektaş, which is named after its founder, are descended from a common ancestor. They administer the *tekké* and are in control of its property. A survey of the *waqfs* of Istanbul of the middle of the sixteenth century mentions a *waqf* in favour of the descendants of Haci Bektaş. In the sixteenth century and later, that family was allotted contributions and other income not connected with the *tekké* on condition that it open a *zāwiya* and serve wayfarers. The Mevlevi *dergāh* in Konya and some smaller *tekkés* were likewise administered, and their property controlled, by the family of the founder.[67] 'Family' orders formed by a Ṣūfī shaykh and his descendants are a recognized feature in the Muslim world. A notable instance is the Qādirī order, to which Shaykh Muḥammad al-Asad probably belonged. Those orders were an important stage in the development of organized, institutionalized Ṣūfism.[68] A typical case is that of the Sanūsī order. In a Tunisian town established on the basis of a family *zāwiya*, the male descendants of the founder of the *zāwiya* made up about 90 per cent of the population in 1916 and about 60 per cent in 1976.[69]

In the Ottoman Empire, the important functions at the institutions of the monasteries, viz. the *mashyakha*, the *imāma*, and the *wikāla* (administration) of the *waqf* property, passed by inheritance within the families of the founders, and so did the privileges, exemptions and immunities. This was a universal

---

66 Judgement of the Sharīʿa Court of Acre of 1838 (Appendix B); Muslim Division, File HM/4/3, 2 August 1949, no. 596 of 27 June 1957 (the *mutawallī*'s letter to the Minister of Religious Affairs of 26 June 1957); interview with Muḥammad Abū 'l-Saʿūd Asadī of 6 January 1984; Kenaʿan.

67 Faroqhi, 191–2, 198, 207.

68 Trimingham, 15–16, 168.

69 Ibid., 118 f.; Brown.

phenomenon, of which evidence is available from all over the Muslim world. The *mashyakha* of the *zāwiya* of Haci Bektaş passed by inheritance among his descendants for centuries.[70] In the *zāwiya* of Shaykh Muḥammad al-Asad, the *mashyakha, imāma* and *wikāla* – in addition to the entitlement of the proceeds of the *waqf* – were transmitted within the family of the founder in accordance with the terms of the *waqfiyya*; there is evidence that the stipulations of the dedicator were usually complied with. The transmission of the functions of *imām* and *mu'adhdhin* from father to son is also attested in the case of the *zāwiya* in Safad, which is an extension of the aforementioned.[71] In the Sanūsī order, the *mashyakha* likewise passed from father to son. The rights and immunities of the *fuqarā'* in the Sudan similarly passed by inheritance within their families.[72]

According to popular tradition in Dayr al-Asad, its founder, Shaykh Muḥammad al-Asad, is buried in the centre of the village. The tomb is in a room adjacent to the hall serving as a *zāwiya* and mosque. Owing to the shaykh's reputation as a miracle worker and redoubtable fighter, people make pilgrimages to his tomb and tend it in order that they may be blessed (*lil-tabarruk*). The *maqām* is believed to have supernatural qualities, such as the power to cure various diseases and infertility and to produce rain. By the tomb, votive ceremonies are held (attended also by Christians), as well as circumambulations (*ṭawāf*) with green flags inscribed with the *shahādatān*, to the accompaniment of drums and cymbals – all according to the Ṣūfī rite. Women also take part in these events.[73] At the time of my visit, the *imām*, Shaykh Muṣṭafā Khālid ʿArnūs al-Asad, summoned the people to afternoon prayers by means of electronic devices. In the mosque, the walls of which were adorned with numerous inscriptions, an old man was engaged in religious studies. The tomb was decorated with coloured carpets and surrounded by banners. The place looked well preserved and well tended.

Legends and tombs of saints also played an important part in the colonizing ventures of the Ottoman Empire. The founding fathers, emigrants who settled in foreign lands, were invested with an aura of heroism. It was customary for the family of the first settler, who had the reputation of a saint, to build a monastery on the site of his grave. The family soon developed into a settlement bearing the name of the founding father. The *türbe* of the saint was sometimes situated at a strategically or commercially important crossroads, which, of

70 Barkan, 65; Trimingham, e.g., 15, 20, 71, 73, 83, 173–4; Faroqui, 192.

71 Judgement of the Sharīʿa Court of Acre of 1838 (Appendix B); Judgements of the Sharīʿa Court of Safad of 1856, 1874 and 1876 (pls. II, III); Kenaʿan.

72 Evans-Pritchard, 65, 85; O'Fahey.

73 Lazarus-Yafeh, *Notes*.

course, facilitated the regime's colonization policy.[74] Similarly, in Cyrenaica, the worship of saints greatly helped to strengthen the position of the Sanūsī order among the Bedouin; the practice was transferred to the person of the Grand Sanūsī, whom the Bedouin came to regard as a saint, a miracle man with a *baraka* that he transmitted to his descendants. His tomb was the largest and most sumptuous in Cyrenaica. In the Sudan, too, the saints (*fuqarā'*) were agents of Islamization employed by the local rulers.[75]

Shaykh Muḥammad al-Asad, who settled in Dayr al-Biʿna, was a newcomer from the vicinity of Damascus. Being a stranger is virtually a prerequisite for success as a mystic, for 'no prophet is accepted in his own country'. A stranger is not identified with any local grouping and therefore more likely to enjoy the confidence of all sides. Almost all the shaykhs of Sanūsī *zāwiyas*, including the Grand Sanūsī, as well as the marabouts in Cyrenaica, were strangers from the west. The saint of the *zāwiya* of the Tunisian town explored by Brown was from Morocco, and the *fuqarā'* in the Sudan were generally strangers roaming border regions.[76]

## 6 Summary

Legal documents may be first-rate sources for the purposes of historical research. The document before us sheds light on an impressive instrument of the policy of colonization and Islamization of conquered areas in the Ottoman Empire. That policy seems to have been applied not only in Anatolia and Rumelia but also in the Arab provinces, at least in Palestine. The sources, including *waqfs* of the *sulṭāns* and senior Ottoman officials in favour of Ṣūfī *zāwiyas* and shaykhs, should be re-examined in this connexion.[77] Against the background of that policy, it is not surprising that Sulṭān Selīm took time out to establish a *waqf* at Dayr al-Biʿna: he did so in order to turn Dayr al-Biʿna into Dayr al-Asad. Such acts were not trifles but important affairs of state. It seems that some folk traditions should be taken more seriously as historical sources, provided, of course, that they can be substantiated by documents.

---

74 Barkan, 61, 63, 65; Faroqhi, 183.

75 Evans-Pritchard, 65, 66, 69, 82–3; Ziadeh, 115, 121–2; Brown; O'Fahey.

76 Trimingham, 168; Evans-Pritchard, 82–3; Brown; O'Fahey.

77 A tendency to reinforce the Muslim presence – weakened by the Crusader regime – at Islamic holy places in Palestine through *waqfs* in favour of Ṣūfī *zāwiyas* existed even before the Ottoman conquest. A case in point is the *waqf* of Abū Madyan, of 720/1320, in favour of a *zāwiya* in the Maghribī Quarter of Jerusalem. See L. Massignon, *Documents sur certains waqfs des lieux saints de l'Islam*, Paris, 1952, 82 ff.; A.L. Tibawi, *The Islamic pious foundations in Jerusalem*, London, 1978, 9 ff.

## Appendix A. Transcript of Selīm I's waqfiyya of 922/1516 in Favour of Muḥammad al-Asad[78]

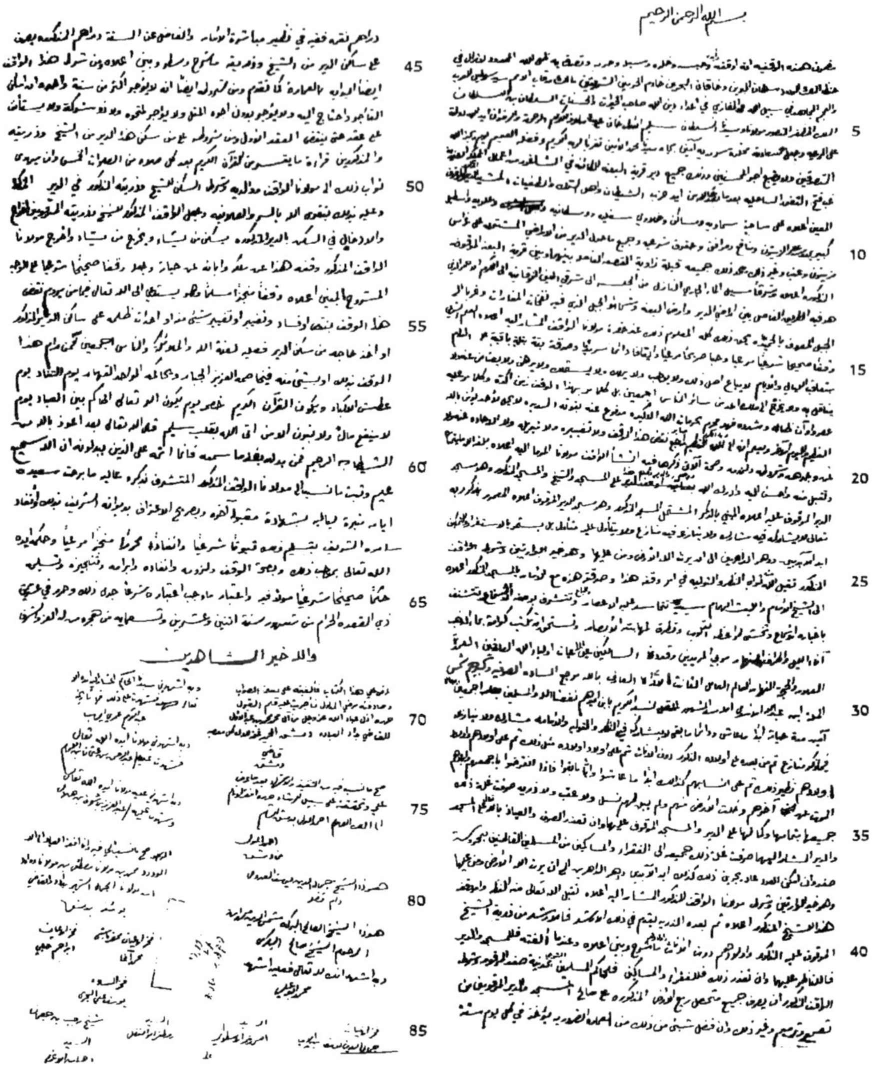

FIGURE 14.5 Selīm I's *waqfiyya* of 922/1516 in favour of Muḥammad al-Asad

78 The copyist of the *waqfiyya*, except the certifications by the *qāḍīs* and witnesses at the end, is Muḥammad Abū 'l-Saʿūd al-Asadī of Dayr al-Asad. At a meeting with him in the village on 6 January 1984, I produced the document to him. He identified his handwriting by comparisons with documents in his possession and said he had made the copy over thirty years before. I have in my possession a further copy, written by an as yet unidentified person on 26 June 1957 (hereinafter: 'the 1957 version'). There are slight differences between the two versions. The first version seems to be truer to the original than the second.

*Translation*

1. In the name of Allāh the Merciful and Compassionate[79]
2. The contents of this *waqfiyya* are [as follows:] It [i.e. the *waqf*] is dedicated, perpetuated, tied up inalienably,[80] eternalized, set aside for public purposes, consecrated[81] and bestowed as a charitable gift[82] by God's shadow[83] which is spread out [on earth], may he never cease to be under the protection of
3. the beloved king,[84] the *sulṭān* of the two continents, the ruler of the seas,[85] the servant of the two holy cities [Mecca and Medina], the subduer of the necks of peoples,[86] the overlord of the Arab and non-Arab *sulṭāns*,
4. the warrior of the holy wars for Allāh,[87] the fighter of the sacred fight against the enemies of Allāh's religion, the doer of good and charitable deeds, the *sulṭān* and son of a *sulṭān*,
5. the victorious king, our lord, the Sulṭān Selīm Khān,[88] may He [God] have mercy upon his noble fathers and be well-pleased with them, may Allāh strengthen his dynasty's rule
6. over his flock and establish his happiness for ever, amen. [Selīm establishes the *waqf*] in honour of our lord Muḥammad because he wishes to be close to his noble master and his all-embracing kindness on the day when Allāh rewards[89]
7. those who practise charity and does not withhold recompense from the doers of good deeds.

---

Both documents were placed at my disposal by the Muslim Division of the Ministry of Religious Affairs, to which I am grateful for this and for the considerable help I was given by it in various ways while conducting the research.

79 Underneath this line, the 1957 version has the words 'Praise be to God the Praiseworthy'.

80 'Tied up inalienably' means precluded from any transaction; it is synonymous with 'dedicated'.

81 Cf. Saarisalo, English, p. 12: (9); Arabic, p. 5: (9).

82 Literally: 'given without recompense in this world', the requital being of a religious nature. Cf. Saarisalo, Arabic, p. 5: (9), English, p. 12: (9). On the connexion between charity and *waqf* see N.A. Stillman, 'Waqf and ideology of charity in medieval Islam', in Baer and Gilbar.

83 One of the titles of Sulṭān Selīm I and other *sulṭāns*. See Arnold, 128, 130, 135, *138*, *154*, 161, 203.

84 *Al-Wadūd* – one of the attributes of Allāh.

85 Titles of the Ottoman *sulṭāns*. See Arnold, 147, 161, 203.

86 Titles of the Ottoman *sulṭāns*. Cf. Arnold, 156; A. Cohen (ed.), *Shilṭon ha-Mamlukim veha-'Othmanim (1260–1804)*, VII, Jerusalem, 1981, 99.

87 Titles of the Ottoman *sulṭāns*. Cf. Arnold, 155–6.

88 A common title of Selīm I. See Arnold, 153; Cohen, *Shilṭon ha-Mamlukim veha-'Othmanim*, 99. See the article, p. 62.

89 The 1957 version has *yajzī*.

It is [i.e. The dedicated property includes] the whole[90] of the monastery of the village of al-Biʿna,[91] which is situated in al-Sāghūr,[92] [one] of the subdivisions of the Safad district.[93]

8. [The *waqf* was established] immediately after the conquest of the coastal cities, after Allāh had saved him [Selīm] from the faction of Satan, the polytheists and unbelievers.[94] The reference is to the monastery dedicated
9. as aforesaid,[95] with its roofless inner courtyard, residential buildings, lower, middle and upper retreats,[96] a large stable,
10. an oil-press where olives are pressed,[97] cisterns,[98] natural resources,[99] *sharʿī* [81] rights[100] and all the land around the monastery containing olive trees,
11. vines etc. The following demarcate the monastery[101] on all sides: in the south – the *zāwiya* of al-Qaṣʿa,[102] which separates the two [i.e. the monastery and al-Qaṣʿa?] from the above-mentioned al-Biʿna village that has been dedicated as a *waqf*;
12. in the east – the watercourse which runs down from al-Jalsa to[103] the area east of the al-Fūqāniyya spring and to the Red Vineyard
13. through which[104] the road passes that separates the lands of the monastery from the lands of al-Biʿna; in the north – the mountain on

---

90 The 1957 version has the words 'Khirbat Ḥawtal' after 'the whole of'.

91 This was the name of the Christian village before it became Muslim Dayr al-Asad. See the article, p. 61.

92 See the article, p. 67.

93 On the administrative division of the Safad district in the sixteenth century see Cohen, *Shilṭon ha-Mamlukim veha-ʿOthmanim*, 101.

94 The derogatory expressions are taken from the Qurʾān. See, e.g., 58: 19 (*ḥizb al-shayṭān*); 31: 13, 34: 22, 40: 35 (*shirk*); 5: 64, 65, 60: 17, 18 (*tughyān*).

95 Thus (*al-mubayyan*) in the 1957 version. The earlier version has *al-muʿayyan*.

96 *Khalāwī*. Cf. 'retreat' in Trimingham, 75; Cohen, *Gerush ha-Frantzisqanim*, 68; Heyd, p. 178 n. 6. We have to do here with a Christian monastery converted into a Ṣūfī *zāwiya*.

97 The place is today called 'Maʿāṣir Ḥaṣriyya'. See Muslim Division, File HM/4/3 no. 596 of 27 June 1967.

98 These cisterns exist to this day. See Israely, 23, and the sources indicated there.

99 Cf. *marfiq* (something that has some benefit or advantage) in E.W. Lane, *Arabic-English lexicon*, London, 1863. In land settlement proceedings at Dayr al-Asad, the *mutawallīs* of the *waqf* requested that the nearby quarries be considered part of the *waqf* property. See the article, p. 64.

100 Such as rights of passage. Cf. Ṣalāḥ al-Dīn al-Munajjid, *Kitāb waqf ʿUthmān b. Asʿad b. al-Munajjā*, Damascus, 1949, p. 27, ll. 10–12; Veselý, 297 [11].

101 The word *al-dayr* appears only in the 1957 version.

102 Al-Qaṣʿa is a place near the village which has been identified by Muḥammad Abū 'l-Saʿūd al-Asadī.

103 In the 1957 version, the word *allatī* replaces *ilā*, producing the reading '… from al-Jalsa, which is east of the spring.'

104 *Fīhi* is a scribal error; the 1957 version has *fī*.

which gusts of wind blow into the caves;[105] and in the west – the area facing

14. the mountain known as al-Ḥamīda [which borders on the aforementioned [?] Khirbat Ḥawtal; in the east, there is also the watercourse [that runs] from al-Khashab; in the west, there is also the road which separates the lands of the monastery from the lands of al-Biʿna; in the north, there is also the road on which traffic is heavy [a public road], which separates the lands of Khirbat Ḥawtal from the lands of al-Biʿna and Naḥf].[106]

All this, of which our lord, the dedicator, has *sharʿī* cognizance, is lawfully regarded

15. as a valid [without any technical or substantive flaw] *sharʿī waqf* which must be respected,[107] as an explicit endowment[108] in binding form and as a permanent, eternal *waqf* and an absolute charity,[109] which last forever and ever, through alternating nights and days [until the end of time].
16. The *waqf* property must not be sold, given away, held in or taken into private ownership, mortgaged or exchanged,
17. or pass or be transmitted into anyone's ownership. Moreover, the more time passes since [the creation of this] *waqf*, the more valid it becomes; the more days go by,
18. the more lasting and mighty [is its effect]; Allāh's strict prohibitions apply to it, and it is protected by His firmly established power; no one who believes in mighty Allāh
19. and in Judgement Day and who knows that he will return to his noble master[110] may oppose or alter it or exchange it for something else or detract from it[s terms],
20. objects, conditions,[111] irrevocability[112] or legal force.

The dedicator, our above-mentioned lord – may Allāh grant him whatever he hopes for,

21. accede to his requests and be gracious to him, and may he come to Allāh and find mercy – has dedicated the monastery constituting this *waqf* to the mosque and the shaykh. The above-mentioned mosque

---

105 The caves are on the hillside overlooking the village. It seems that strong winds produce 'blowing' sounds at the entrances to the caves, whence the latter's name. See *nafkha* in Lane.

106 The passage in square brackets has been omitted in this version. It appears in the 1957 version.

107 In execution proceedings. Cf. Saarisalo, Arabic, p. 1, 3: (22), 4: (1); English, p. 7, 10: (22), 11: (1).

108 The letter *sīn* was apparently omitted owing to a scribal error.

109 Charity in the *waqf* sense. See Stillman.

110 I.e. who believes in the hereafter.

111 Cf. al-Munajjid, p. 27, ll. 1–3.

112 Cf. Ömer Hilmi, *A gift to posterity on the laws of Evqaf*, tr. C.R. Tyser and D.G. Demetriades (2nd ed.), Nicosia, 1922, art. 4.

22. belongs to and is contained in the monastery dedicated to it – it was built for the incessant repetition (*dhikr*[113]) of the name of God
23. the Most High; no partner shall share [the proceeds of the *waqf*] with him [scil. with the shaykh], contest [his rights] or distort [the meaning of this *waqfiyya*]; moreover, [the *waqf*] shall endure in its stability and utter firmness
24. forever and ever, until Allāh inherits the earth and what is on it, He being the best of heirs.[114]

The said dedicator –

25. may Allāh deign to reward him – has stipulated that the supervision and administration of this *waqf* and charity [*waqf*], together with the office of *imām* of the said mosque, be entrusted
26. to the shaykh, the *imām*, the lion, the hero and *sayyid*[115] envied by the generations and by the span of the outstretched arms [scil. by the powerful people],[116] by the description of whose person the tongues honour themselves, at the report of whose exploits the ears rejoice,
27. whose sermons fill the hearts with fear, whose awesomeness causes looks to be downcast, whose miraculous deeds[117] deserve to be recorded in golden ink
28. by day and by night, a mentor of Ṣūfī novices, a model for those who go [the Ṣūfī way];[118] he is the most honoured of those near to Allāh,[119] those who know [Him],[120] a learned guide,
29. an authority, a man of understanding, an *ʿālim* who practises what he preaches, a person who humbles himself [before God], who pronounces words of reverence (*awwāh*[121]), who knows Allāh;[122] the supreme authority of the Ṣūfī shaykhs[123] and the greatest of them, the luminary of religion (*shams*

---

113 *Dhikr* in the Ṣūfī sense. See Trimingham's Glossary, 302, s.v. *dhikr*.

114 The expression is taken from the Qurʾān. See, e.g., 21: 89, 28: 57. See also Tibawi, p. 12 n. 12.

115 *Sayyid* is an equivalent of *sharīf* or an honorific title bestowed on Ṣūfī shaykhs. Cf. *sīdī* in Heyd, p. 149, n. 1.

116 The length of the arm is a measure of physical strength.

117 Cf. Trimingham, 26, 104, 141, 145.

118 Cf. Heyd, 149; Veselý, 290[3].

119 Should read *ʿayn aʿyān* [without *al-*] *awliyāʾ*, and so has the 1957 version. Cf. Trimingham's Glossary, 313, s.v. *walī*.

120 The knowledge of God in the mystic sense. See in Trimingham's Glossary, 300, s.v. *ʿārif*.

121 In a Ṣūfī sense (*dhikr*); or: who finds shelter with the Creator, also in a Ṣūfī sense. See also Lane ('… addresses himself with earnest supplication [to God]').

122 Gnostic, mystical knowledge, as opposed to intellectual knowledge (*ʿilm*). This epithet is given also to the Ṣūfī Ibn al-ʿArabī. See Kurd ʿAlī, Part II, 225. Cf. *quṭbu 'l-ʿārifīn* in Heyd, 128.

123 *Sāda*, pl. of *sīdī*. See above, n. 115.

30. *al-milla*[124]), Ibn ʿAbd Allāh al-Asadī, the famous lion (*asad*), whose noble descent (*nasab*) is via [or: consists in his being] a son of Amīruhum;[125] may Allāh's blessing come to us and to all Muslims through his prayer.[126]
31. Amen.

[The proceeds of the *waqf* shall be enjoyed by the shaykh] throughout his lifetime and forever as long as he survives on earth; no one shall share the supervision, administration or *imāma* with him or dispute his rights,

32. as stated above. Afterwards, after his death, [the entitlement] shall pass to his male children, to the exclusion of the females; afterwards, to his children's children in the same way; afterwards to their children and the latters'
33. children in the same way; afterwards, to the [agnatic] descendants (*ansāb*) of the last mentioned so long (*dāʾiman*[127]) as any of them are alive and survive. When none of them are left, when death has removed all of them
34. and the earth has become empty of them, when no agnatic descendants (*nasl, ʿaqb, dhuriyya*)[128] remain, the proceeds [of the *waqf*]
35. shall all be spent on the mosque and the monastery to which the *waqf* was dedicated. If, God forbid, it should not be possible to spend [the proceeds] on the above-mentioned mosque
36. and the monastery, they shall all be spent on the Muslim poor and wretched of the besieged and fortified[129] town
37. of Safad. If it is again possible [to spend the proceeds of the *waqf* for the original purposes], this shall be done. The foregoing arrangement shall prevail[130] forever, until Allāh inherits the earth and what is on it,
38. He being the best of heirs.

Our lord, the above-mentioned dedicator – may Allāh accede to his requests – has stipulated that the supervision and affairs of the *waqf*

39. shall be entrusted to the above-mentioned shaykh and afterwards, [after his death,] to his descendants: precedence in this matter shall be given

---

124 The expression *shams al-milla* is very common in al-Fārābī. I wish to thank my colleague, Professor M. Swartz, for drawing my attention to this fact.

125 On the significance of this genealogical relationship see the article, p. 73.

126 Cf. *Nafaʿa Allāh bi-barakatihi* – 'may God grant benefits in answer to the benedictions pronounced by Him' in the *waqfiyya* of Abū Madyan. See Massignon, 98–9; Ibn Ṭūlūn, part II, 23–4 (... *al-sulṭān ... yasʾal al-duʿāʾ min ahl dimashq*), 33 (*ʿinda al-duʿāʾ lahu*).

127 Thus in the 1957 version. The earlier version has *wa-ayyan*.

128 *Nasl* and *dhuriyya* are synonymous terms for the descendants of sons and daughters until the end of all generations; *ʿaqb* means the descendants of the sons (to the exclusion of the daughters), i.e. agnatic descendants only. See Abū Bakr Aḥmad b. ʿAmr al-Shaybānī al-maʿrūf bi'l-Khaṣṣāf, *Kitāb aḥkām al-awqāf*, [Cairo], 1904, 93, 94 and 97. The document before us seems to refer to agnatic descendants only.

129 *Maḥrūsa* became an epithet of a large town. Cf. Saarisalo, Arabic, p. 1; English, pp. 6 and 7.

130 Cf. Saarisalo, Arabic, p. 6: (28); English, pp. 14–15: (28).

to the best qualified (*al-arshad fa'l-arshad*[131]) among the descendants of Shaykh

40. [Muḥammad al-Asad[132]], to whom the *waqf* is dedicated: the males and their children, to the exclusion of the females and their children, as explained above. If this is not possible [because no beneficiaries survive] (*wa-ʿindamā alfathu*[133]), then [the proceeds of the *waqf* shall be spent] on the mosque and the monastery
41. [at the discretion of] the supervisor[134] thereof; and if this too is impossible, then [they shall be spent] on the poor and wretched [at the discretion of] the *sharʿī qāḍī* (*ḥākim*) of the town of Safad.
42. The above-mentioned dedicator has stipulated that the income from the produce of the land (*arḍ*[135]) shall be expended on the above-mentioned mosque and the monastery for
43. repairs, refurbishments and the like; if anything is left after the necessary building work, six
44. silver dirhams are to be paid every day to the *imām* for the maintenance of the *imāma*; the balance remaining after those six dirhams is to be expended
45. on the inhabitants of the monastery: the shaykh and his descendants, as explained above. The dedicator has also stipulated
46. [that the income of the *waqf* shall be expended] first and foremost, on construction [repairs], as stated above. He has further stipulated that [land] may only be leased out for a period of up to one year and provided that the leasing is practicable
47. and necessary; no [land] is to be leased unless the rent is adequate; [land] is not to be leased to an idle (*mutaḥawwij*[136]) or violent person; a new lease contract is not to be signed
48. before the previous contract has expired. [The dedicator] has also stipulated which of those living in the monastery
49. – the shaykh and his descendants – is to read as much as he can, after each of the five prayers, from the noble Qurʾān and to devote
50. the reward for this to our master, the dedicator, and his parents.[137] [The dedicator] has stipulated that the right of residence in the monastery shall belong to the shaykh and his descendants

131 Cf. Hilmi, art. 298.

132 The Shaykh's name appears the in 1957 version.

133 The 1957 version has *alghathu* which here has the same meaning.

134 Should read *falil-nāẓir*.

135 The 1957 version has *al-waqf*.

136 An 'idle lessee' (see *kharaja yataḥawwaj* in Lane) is not sufficiently serious and trustworthy. Thus in the 1957 version; the version before us has *mutaḥḥawih*, apparently due to a copyist's error.

137 Cf. Layish, 6.

51. and that he shall therefore fear Allāh in private and publicly. The dedicator has left to the shaykh and his descendants the right to deny or permit
52. residence in the monastery: they may admit or evict whomsoever they wish.[138]

Our master,

53. the dedicator, has given up the ownership of this *waqf* and severed himself from it. He has established it, in the manner
54. explained above, as a valid, lawful and complete (*munjazan*[139]) *waqf* in respect of which delivery has been effected; he asks Allāh, the Most High, that whoever interferes
55. with this *waqf* by violation, cancellation (*fasād*[140]), alteration or partial alteration or by maltreating an inhabitant of the above-mentioned monastery
56. or taking anything from the living quarters therein shall be cursed by Allāh, the angels and all creatures; a person who wishes to do any
57. of these things to the *waqf* or to part of it is to be judged by Allāh and sentenced by the Creator on the Day of Judgement, the Day
58. of the Thirsty Liver; the noble Qurʾān is to be his adversary on the day when Allāh, the Most High, is the judge of mankind, when
59. neither wealth nor sons[141] are of any avail and only [he is acceptable] who comes to Allāh saying wholeheartedly: 'May Allāh be extolled' after 'May God save me from
60. Satan the accursed;' 'If someone changes it [a person's will] after hearing it, his sin [will rest] upon him. Allāh hears
61. and knows.'[142]

There has been verified what is attributed to our lord,[143] the above-mentioned dedicator, who enjoys great fame, whose days do not cease being happy

62. and whose nights are luminous (*munīra*[144]); it has been verified by final acceptable testimony and by express admission therein in his honourable chambers, and the implementation (*infād*[*h*][145])

---

138 For details of the 'Ten stipulations' see Muḥammad Qadrī Pashā, *Kitāb qānūn al-ʿadl lil-qaḍāʾ ʿalā mushkilāt al-awqāf*, Cairo, 1902, p. 35, arts. 120 f.

139 'Complete' in the legal sense. Cf. *nājiz* in Saarisalo, Arabic, p. 2: (13); English, p. 9: (13).

140 Cf. Saarisalo, Arabic, p. 8: (50), (51); English, p. 17: (50), (51).

141 Cf. Qur'ān, 26: 88; al-Munajjid, p. 33, ll. 2 f.

142 Quoted from the Qur'ān, 2: 181. The Qur'ānic prohibition of altering a will is here extended to a *waqf*. In the 1957 version, the quotation appears in brackets.

143 Cf. *Ṣaḥḥa ʿindī* in Saarisalo, Arabic, p. 4; Engish, p. 11.

144 Thus according to the 1957 version; the earlier version has *muʿtabara* [?] 'respected'.

145 Cf. *nufūdh* in Saarisalo, Arabic, p. 7: (46); English, p. 16: (46).

63. of the honourable order was by delivery [of the property to the *mutawallī*]. [The *waqfiyya*] has been drawn up validly and lawfully and executed, registered and completed in binding form. May it be approved
64. by Allāh the Most High, on the strength of the present [proceedings], as regards its validity, irrevocability, implementation, verification, completion and delivery.
65. Given as a valid and lawful award meeting all requirements, with due regard to what has to be taken into account and in proper legal form.

Written on the 20th
66. of the holy month of Dhū al-Qaʿda in the year nine hundred and twenty-two of the Hijra[146] of him who has the power and the honour.[147]
67. Allāh is the best of witnesses.

*Right-hand column*
68. There has been produced to me this deed and I have found it conforming to legally established practice,
69. its meaning being satisfactory, and I have signed it in confirmation.
70. Written by the humblest servant of Allāh the Sublime and Most High, of the family of Muḥammad, Muḥammad b. ʿAbd al-Awwal,
71. Qāḍī at the House of Worship (*dār al-ʿibāda*[148]) of Damascus[149] the Protected (*maḥmiyya*),[150] may Allāh forgive him every offence.
72. Qāḍī of Damascus[151]
74. Everything stated here in respect of implementation and the testimony of witnesses appears valid and faultless after this document has been produced
75. to me and I have established its authenticity in a rational manner. I, Aḥmad, poorest (*afqar*[152]) of creatures
76. before the Omniscient King [Allāh], judge appointed (*muwallā*)[153] [by the Ottoman authorities] in Damascus al-Shām [Syria], have written this.
77. Aḥmad, judge appointed in Damascus
79. Shaykh Jamāl al-Dīn Yūsuf al-ʿAdawī, may his honour last forever.

---

146 I.e. 17 December, 1516.

147 I.e. the Prophet Muḥammad. Cf. Ebied and Young, 6, 32.

148 What is meant is probably the mosque. It is usual for a court of law to sit in a mosque. Cf. 'House of God' (in Mecca) in Arnold, 161. *Bayt al-ʿibāda* has a wider meaning; it includes also a Ṣūfī monastery (*dayr*), a synagogue and a church. See Kurd ʿAlī, part VI, 3.

149 The 1957 version mentions Aleppo instead of Damascus, probably due to a scribal error since the *waqfiyya* is later said to have been confirmed by a judge appointed in Damascus.

150 Cf. al-Būrīnī, part I, 179; Veselý, 257[5], 286[6].

151 The 1957 version mentions Aleppo instead of Damascus. See above, n. 149.

152 The 1957 version has *afḍal* ('the most distinguished') instead of *afqar*.

153 Cf. Ebied and Young, 34–8, 70 (Deputy Judge).

81. The shaykh whose blessing is good, Shams al-Dīn Muḥammad, son of the late Shaykh Ṣāliḥ al-Bakrī.
83. I hereby attest that you [by means of the *waqf*, have done a merciful deed] for Allāh, which I attest.

Muḥammad Abū ʿAlī

85. Fakhr al-Aʿyān[154] Sayyid[155] Jamāl al-Dīn Yūsuf b. Ayyūb Aḥmad ʿUmar al-Istwānī

*Left-hand column*

68. Our master, the above-mentioned Qāḍī (*ḥākim*), may Allāh the Most High strengthen him, had me testify on it [on the *waqf*], and I testified on the date [of this document].

ʿAbd al-Karīm ʿUmarī Ayyūb

72. The judge appointed [by the Ottoman authorities], may Allāh the Most High strengthen him, had me testify on it [on the *waqf*], and I testified.

ʿAbd al-Raḥmān b. ʿUthmān b. al-Laḥḥām

74. The judge appointed [by the Ottoman authorities], may Allāh the Most High strengthen him, had me testify, and I testified.

ʿAbd al-ʿAzīz b. Dasūq b. Hilāl[156]

78. What is attributed to me with regard to it [the *waqf*] is valid and faultless. I, poorest (*afqar*[157]) of creatures before Allāh, a lover of mankind,[158] Muḥammad b. Mawlānā Muṣṭafā b. Mawlānā Dāʾūd [Dāwud] b. Mawlānā al-Jamāl, known as Dāwud, who was then[159] Qāḍī of Damascus.
82. Fakhr al-Aʿyān, the Court Usher[160] Fakhr al-Aʿyān Muḥammad Āghā Ibrāhīm Ḥalabī
84. Fakhr al-Sāda[161] Yūsuf ʿAlī al-Baḥrī
85. Sayyid Muṣṭafā Abū ʾl-Fāḍil Shaykh Rajab b. Jaʿmān
87. Sayyid Ḥasan b. ʿAbd al-ʿAzīz Sayyid Aḥmad b. Abū ʿAzm

[This is a transcript of the *waqfiyya* of Shaykh Muḥammad al-Asad, an inhabitant of Dayr al-Asad in the Acre District[162]]

---

154 Literally: 'Pride of the Notables', an honorific. Cf. Ebied and Young, 32 and 33.

155 Cf. Heyd, p. 149, n. 1.

156 In the 1957 version, the name of the witness is ʿAbd al-ʿAzīz b. Ṭalāl.

157 The 1957 version has *afkhar* ('the most excellent') instead of *afqar*.

158 One of the attributes of Allāh.

159 *Yawmaʾidhin* here means 'at present'. See the article p. 65 and n. 20 there.

160 Cf. Ebied and Young, pp. 33, 34, 36, and p. 69, n. 16, and the source indicated there.

161 Literally: 'the Glory of the Ṣūfī Shaykhs' (see above, n. 115) – an honorific title. Cf. Ebied and Young, 32, 41.

162 The sentence in square brackets appears only in the 1957 version; it seems to have been added by the copyist. Beside it is the date of the copy: 26 June, 1957.

## Appendix B. Judgement of the Sharīʿa Court of Acre of 1254/1838

FIGURE 14.6 Judgement of the Sharīʿa Court of Acre of 1254/1838

*Translation*

1. The case is as stated herein.[163]
2. Praise be to God, the One Deserving of Thanks Before him who is insignificant before the Most High, al-Sayyid Qāsim ʿUrābī,
3. Qāḍī of the fortified,[164] well-protected[165] city of Acre,
4. who has been forgiven.[166]
5. The following appeared at the *sharʿī* session devoted to Allāh the Glorious: Shaykh ʿUmar al-Asadī, Shaykh Aḥmad ʿAssāf, Shaykh ʿAbd Allāh al-Jiddiyya [?], Shaykh Muḥammad al-Ṭah and Shaykh Muḥammad Ibrāhīm. They pleaded in their own names
6. and as legal representatives of their agnatic cousins, of their own free will. They pleaded against some of their cousins, viz. Shaykh Ḥusayn al-Yāsīn, Shaykh Aḥmad Ḥidāya, Shaykh ʿAlī al-Ṣafiyy, Ḥasan al-Khalīl, Ibrāhīm al-Khalīl and Qāsim Asad,
7. who were present with them at the *sharʿī* session. The former told the latter, in their statement of claim and orally, pointing at them: 'You are trespassing on the lands and olive-trees of the *waqf*. The olive-trees were dedicated
8. to the descendants of Shaykh Muḥammad al-Asad, may Allāh sanctify his precious secret, and to us and your other cousins. You are thus infringing the stipulations of the dedicator, and we demand that the dedicator's express written directions be followed,
9. since this is what is legally required in order that every holder of a right [of entitlement in the *waqf*] may receive what is due to him.' In consequence of this demand, [the production of] the *waqf* deed was requested [by the *qāḍī*] in order that it might be seen what its contents were and what stipulations had been made by the dedicator.
10. The *waqf* deed was produced, and so was the evidence in their possession, and after the inspection of the evidence and the deed and the hearing of the admissions, all with regard to the *waqf* and its terms and their confirmation,

163 Cf. Saarisalo, English, p. 6; Arabic, p. 1.

164 Cf. the *waqfiyya* of 1516 (Appendix A), right-hand column, l. 71 and the source indicated in n. 150.

165 Cf. ibid., l. 36 and n. 129.

166 Cf. ibid., right-hand column, l. 71.

11. the evidence was found[167] to be useless with regard to the dedicator's stipulations because it was based on non-*sharʿī* foundations. The terms of the *waqf*, after mentioning its boundaries,

12. provide that the proceeds of the land and olive-trees collected by the administrator shall first and foremost be expended on repairs to the mosque at Dayr al-Biʿna and that the remainder shall be earmarked as a charity for the benefit of Shaykh

13. Muḥammad al-Asad throughout his lifetime; after his death, it is to go to his male descendants, to the exclusion of the females. According to the dedicator's stipulation, the proceeds of the *waqf* are to be divided among the descendants *per capita* (*ʿalā ʿadad ruʾūs*), in equal shares, since he does not say:

14. 'The higher degree excludes the lower.'[168] The practice followed since olden times is thus contrary to the dedicator's stipulation, which, by their [the defendants'] own admission, is tantamount to a text of the *sharʿī* legislator [i.e. of the Qurʾān or the *sunna*].

15. Under these circumstances, our lord the Sharʿī Judge declares that the practice shall be in accordance with the dedicator's stipulation, that is to say, the administrator shall register all the lands of the *waqf* in a book and shall let them

16. to whoever wishes to rent them at their value, and the proceeds shall be expended, first and foremost, on repairs to the mosque; the remainder shall be divided, *per capita* among the descendants of Shaykh Muḥammad al-Asad in accordance with

17. the dedicator's stipulations.

Given by way of a binding, faultless, valid declaration and reduced to writing.

As for the olive-trees in the possession of the defendants, the latter do not admit them to be *waqf* and have, in fact, taken physical possession of them. They have long since

18. insisted, without anybody challenging them, that the olive-trees shall remain in their possession on the ground that physical possession is the best proof of ownership. In view of all the foregoing, he [the *qāḍī*] orders them to pay the rent of the land planted with olive-trees since they have admitted

---

167 Should read *wujidat*.

168 On the *per capita* division of entitlement see above.

19. that it is *waqf*. One of the administrators of the *waqf*, Shaykh Aḥmad Ḥidāya, did not comply with the *sharʿī* award and wished to continue the practice of infringing the stipulations
20. of the dedicator. It was proved, by *sharʿī* proof, that he wished to detach a parcel of land from the lands of the dedicator on the ground that it was his; his betrayal[169] and failure to act
21. in accordance with the stipulation made by the dedicator in the *waqf* deed [brought about his dismissal].

As the requirement of being the most suitable of the descendants[170] is met by Shaykh Aḥmad ʿAssāf, a son of one

22. of the administrators, Shaykh Ṣāliḥ ʿAssāf, and in view of [the latter's] inability to look after the interests of the *waqf*, and since his son, Shaykh Aḥmad ʿAssāf, has legally proved that he is the most suitable, our lord the Sharʿī Judge has appointed him
23. administrator of the said *waqf* by the side of his father and told him that he must faithfully discharge his duties in accordance with the stipulations of the dedicator and in the manner most useful to the *waqf*.

Given by way of a valid, binding *sharʿī* declaration

24. conforming to *sharʿī* requirements.

Written at the beginning of the glorious month of Shaʿbān in the year one thousand two hundred and fifty-four of the Hijra.

25. Shaykh Ḥasan al-Biqāʿī Shaykh Sayyid Aḥmad The Scribe: ʿAbd al-Nabiyy
ʿAlī Sulaymān
Sayyid ʿAbd Allāh
Efendi Abū ʾl-Hudā
Ḥājj Ibrāhīm al-Nimr Nūr [?]
Muṣṭafā Efendi Nūr Allāh
Sayyid Yaḥyā al-Safiyy Ḥasan Efendī Abū ʾl-Hudā

---

169 'Treason' (*khiyāna*) in the sense of dereliction of duty as administrator of the *waqf*.

170 Cf. the *waqfiyya* of 1516 (Appendix A), ll. 38–40 and the source indicated in n. 131.

CHAPTER 15

# The Mālikī Family *Waqf* according to Wills and *Waqfiyyāt*

*In memoriam Professor Gabriel Baer*

## Introduction*

The complex of relations between the family *waqf* and the law of succession is particularly noteworthy in the Mālikī school because of the special character of both the system of succession and the *waqf* in that school as compared with other schools. This study is based on about a hundred legal documents out of a collection of *waqf* documents from Tangier of the period from the middle of the eighteenth to the early twentieth century[1] and on *waqfiyyāt* from other North African sources. Only fifteen items of this material deal with a family *waqf* established according to the Mālikī doctrine. This is of course a very small, random sample which can only serve for illustration; nor is there any certainty that all patterns of the family *waqf* are represented. The quantitative analysis should therefore be treated with caution; it points, at the most, to general tendencies.

The purpose of this article is to indicate some characteristics of the Mālikī *waqf* and to analyse them in the context of the succession law of that school. The conclusions drawn are tentative, awaiting confirmation by further research.[2] This study is complementary to an earlier one by the author on the

---

* Originally published in the *Bulletin of the School of Oriental and African Studies*, XLVI/1 (1983), pp. 1–32.

1 *Les habous de Tanger. Registre officiel d'actes et de documents.* Texte arabe. *Archives Marocaines*, XXII, Paris, 1914. A short French summary of these documents (hereinafter referred to as F.) appeared in Vol. XXIII of the same year.

2 I wish to thank the late Professor Baer for encouraging me to examine the family *waqf* in the context of the law of succession according to the Ḥanafī and Mālikī schools and aiding me in various ways. Professor Baer and Professor David Powers read the manuscript and made valuable comments. Dr. Miriam Hoexter placed at my disposal legal documents and other

 DOI:10.1163/9789004680920_017

family *waqf* and the law of succession mainly according to the Ḥanafī doctrine, and it is also designed in its structure to emphasize the differences between the two schools as to the family *waqf*. To determine the position of the early Mālikī school on the *waqf*, I used material culled by the late orientalist Joseph Schacht from early Mālikī literature.[3] The discussion of the legal aspects of the *waqf* and of succession is not an end in itself but is solely intended as an aid to social analysis.

What distinguishes the Mālikī system of succession from those of other schools – and this is a very fundamental point – is the status of *bayt al-māl* as a residuary heir. The other Sunnī schools (and the Shīʿa) hold that *bayt al-māl* has no standing in intestate succession except in the absence of relatives of the deceased. The Mālikī school does not recognize the principle of the *radd*, the reversion of the residue to the Qurʾānic heirs (*dhawū al-farāʾiḍ*) when their prescribed portions do not exhaust the estate and there are no male agnates (*ʿaṣaba*) – a rather infrequent occurrence – and holds that the residue belongs to *bayt al-māl*. According to all the other Sunnī schools, only the spouses do not enjoy the *radd*. Moreover, in the absence of Qurʾānic and agnatic heirs – an even less likely contingency than the aforementioned one – those schools assign the estate to cognatic heirs (*dhawū al-arḥām*), while the Mālikī school holds that cognates never inherit and that the estate passes to *bayt al-māl*.[4]

Another expression of the status of *bayt al-māl* as a residuary heir in the Mālikī doctrine is the ban on disposing of more than one-third of an heirless estate by will. According to the other schools, the testator is not subject to the *ultra vires* doctrine and may thus dispose of the whole heirless estate; where the sole heir is the testator's spouse, the whole residue may be disposed of by will after deducting the portion of that heir, for, as stated, the spouse does not enjoy the *radd*.[5]

The status of *bayt al-māl* in succession is indeed reflected in nineteenth-century Mālikī legal documents from Tangier. Thus, in one case, the deceased

---

material, collected by her, on the family *waqf* in Algeria and rendered me useful help, for all of which I am greatly indebted to her. I also thank Dr. Aviva Schussman for her assistance in the early stages of the work. It goes without saying that I alone am responsible for any errors which may have remained. The article is based on a paper submitted to the Workshop on Economic and Social Aspects of the Muslim Waqf, held under the auspices of the Institute for Advanced Studies, The Hebrew University of Jerusalem, Mount Scopus, Jerusalem, on 1–20 February 1981.

3 I am indebted to Professor Albert Hourani of St. Antony's College, Oxford, for kindly inviting me to inspect Joseph Schacht's Papers (now at the Bodleian Library, Oxford) and extending warm hospitality to me.

4 N.J. Coulson, *Succession in the Muslim family*, Cambridge, 1971, 49, 91.

5 Ibid., p. 243; *idem*, 'Bayt al-Māl' *EI* (second ed.), 1142.

left a mother, who took one-sixth of the estate as a Qur'ānic heir, and uterine brothers and sisters, who together took their Qur'ānic portion, i.e. one-third, while the remaining half of the estate went to *bayt al-māl* as the residuary heir. As stated, according to the Mālikī school, the Qur'ānic heirs do not enjoy the *radd*. According to the other Sunnī schools, the residue would have been divided among the heirs in the same proportion. *Bayt al-māl* appointed a representative to claim its share in court and indeed realized its right.[6] In another case, the deceased left a wife and a daughter, who took one-eighth and one-half, respectively, as Qur'ānic heirs. *Bayt al-māl* took the residue: three-fifths.[7] According to the other schools, the daughter would have taken the whole residue because, as stated, a spouse does not enjoy the *radd*.

In a case of a different kind, it was noted that a person had died 'without leaving an heir ... other than *bayt māl al-muslimīn*'. He had, by will, dedicated his dwelling to the Great Mosque, but someone objected on the ground that the will was valid only in respect of one-third of the dwelling, and indeed only one-third was eventually taken over by the *waqf*;[8] the remaining two-thirds passed to *bayt al-māl*. As stated, under these circumstances, the testator is subject to the *ultra vires* doctrine. In another case, a man bought two-thirds of a room from *bayt al-māl* and dedicated them to the Great Mosque. Previously, the first third of that room had been dedicated to the same mosque by a manumitted slave (*ma'tūq*). We seem to have to do here with property of which one-third was willed to the manumitted slave, who could not inherit from his master even in the absence of legal heirs, while the remaining two-thirds fell to *bayt al-māl* as the residuary heir.[9] In yet another case, a man dedicated 'the whole of the house known as *bayt al-māl* to the Great Mosque', directing the *nāẓir* to take possession of it on behalf of the *waqf* and to ensure that a certain person living in the house was not ejected. We seem to be dealing here with property supposed to belong to *bayt al-māl*, probably in the absence of heirs, and with an attempt to deprive *bayt al-māl* of its status as a residuary heir by dedicating the whole property to a *khayrī* purpose.[10]

The above instances show the strong position of *bayt al-māl* with regard to heirless estates or estates with only Qur'ānic heirs; this position provides a very powerful motive in the Mālikī school to oust *bayt al-māl* as a residuary heir by means of a *waqf* or a will. It should be noted that in thousands of

6 Tanger, 428–9 (F., 201–2).
7 Ibid., 409 (F., 189).
8 Ibid., 252 (F., 103–4).
9 Ibid., 258 (F., 106); R. Brunschvig, "Abd', *EI* (second ed.), 31.
10 Tanger, 165 (F., 85). See also ibid., 166 (F., 85).

succession orders issued over a period of about twenty years the *sijill* of the *sharīʿa* courts in Israel, which decide according to the Ḥanafī doctrine, record only one case in which the court decided that the estate should pass to *bayt al-māl* in the absence of heirs.[11] In North Africa, *bayt al-māl* has a status also with regard to *waqf* property dedicated to *khayrī* purposes. The *nāẓir* transfers the part of the entitlement intended for the poor to *bayt al-māl* for distribution among them.[12]

The Mālikī *waqf*, too, has several unique features which distinguish it from its counterpart in other schools. Mālikī jurists define the *waqf* as the gift of the usufruct of a thing, binding on the giver so long as the thing exists; the ownership of the thing remains with the giver, though as bare ownership only (*al-maḥbas iʿṭāʾ manfaʿat shayʾ muddat wujūdihi lāziman baqāʾuhu fī mulk muʿṭihi wa-law taqdīran*). The owner remains the *nu propriétaire* without the right to use the substance of the property. If for any reason the usufruct of the *waqf* can no longer be applied to the purpose for which the *waqf* was established, the property reverts to the founder and after him to his legal heirs.[13] The usufruct (*manfaʿa*) of the property can also be dedicated.[14] In the Ḥanafī school, on the other hand, it is a moot question to whom the ownership of the property passes after dedication. According to al-Shaybānī, Abū Yūsuf and others, the ownership passes to Allāh, while Abū Ḥanīfa, like Mālik and al-Shāfiʿī, holds that the founder and his heirs retain the right of ownership but are prevented from exercising it; in other words, the property is ownerless (*ghayr mamlūk*). According to some Shāfiʿī jurists and Aḥmad Ibn Ḥanbal, the ownership passes to the beneficiaries.[15]

The dominant type of *waqf* in the Tangier documents is the testamentary *waqf*. i.e. a *waqf* established by will (*ʿalā sabīl al-waṣiyya*), subject to the *ultra vires* doctrine: it is valid within the limits of one-third of the estate and no disposition may be made in favour of a legal heir. The Mālikī jurist Sīdī Khalīl declares that if entitlement to the *waqf* is intended only for the descendants of the founder successively, it is effected out of that third and regarded as

---

11 A. Layish, *Women and Islamic Law in a non-Muslim state*, Jerusalem and New York, 1975, 311.

12 E. Mercier, *Le code du hobous ou ouakf selon la législation musulmane*, Constantine, 1899, 81. On a modem substitute for *bayt al-māl* see J.N.D. Anderson, *Islamic Law in Africa*, new impression. London. 1970, 95. See also Coulson. 'Bayt al-māl', *EI* (second ed.), 1141 ff.

13 Mercier, 9–11; L. Milliot, *Introduction à l'étude du droit musulman*. Paris, 1953, p. 555 § 652 50.

14 W. Heffening, 'Waḳf'. *Shorter encyclopaedia of Islam*, Leiden and London, 1953, 1096 and the reference to Sīdī Khalīl indicated there. Cf. J.-P. Charnay. *La rie musulmane en Algérie d'après la jurisprudence de la première moitié du XX^e siècle*, Paris, 1965, 106 f.

15 Heffening, 'Waḳf', 1097; J. Schacht, *An introduction to Islamic Law*, Oxford, 1964, 125–6, 134–5.

an inheritance transmitted to an heir (*illā muʿaqqaban kharaja min thulthihi faka-mirāth lil-wārith*).[16] The testator-founder must not, even within the limits of the third of the estate permitted to be willed, give preference to one heir over other heirs because no disposition may be made in favour of a legal heir.[17] But we shall see below that the personal limitation, and sometimes also the quantitative one. is not applied in practice. The testator sometimes stipulates expressly that the *waqf* shall only become effective after his death, as usual in the case of wills.[18] Most of the references in Tangier documents to testamentary *waqfs* within the limits of one-third of the estate concern *waqfs* for *khayrī* purposes.[19]

The testamentary *waqf* probably originates with the early Mālikī school in Medina. References to such *waqfs* can be found in *al-Mudawwana al-kubrā* (edited by Saḥnūn), which reflects the views of Mālik, and in other early Mālikī sources. Mālik's doctrine on this matter is basically identical with that of Abū Ḥanīfa, who declares that a *waqf* not made in the manner of a will is invalid. This means that the *waqf* only takes effect after the death of the testator and that he may revoke it in his lifetime.[20]

There are many instances of the will applying to one-third of the estate while the other two-thirds are divided among the legal heirs.[21] In some isolated cases, a testamentary *waqf* was established in respect of the whole estate and the legal heirs consented after the testator's death, i.e. were excluded from entitlement to the *waqf* with their consent.[22] On the other hand, there are more instances of legal heirs opposing a testamentary *waqf* on the ground that it exceeded one-third of the estate; the will was eventually reduced to one-third, and two-thirds were divided among the legal heirs.[23]

16 Mercier, 43.

17 Tanger, F., 12.

18 See, e.g., ibid., 350 (F., 154), 454–5 (F., 211); O. Pesle, *La théorie et la pratique des habous dans le rite malékite*, Casablanca, n.d., 66.

19 See, e.g., Tanger, 2 (F., 33–4), 32 (F., 43), 33 (F., 43), 288 (F., 118), 294 (F., 123), 290 (F., 121), 294 (F., 122–3), 295 (F.. 123), 319 (F., 137), 320 (F., 138), 363 (F., 160), 418 (F., 194–5). In all these cases, the reference is to a *khayrī waqf*. It is not always stated that the testamentary *waqf* was within the limits of one-third of the estate.

20 J. Schacht, 'Early doctrines on waqf', *Mélanges Fuad Köprülü*, Istanbul, 1953, 445, 450 and the sources indicated there. Cf. A.A.A. Fyzee, *Outlines of Muhammadan Law* (third ed.), Oxford, 1964, 277 and the source indicated in note (u).

21 See, e.g., Tanger, 60 (F., 57), 167 (F., 86).

22 See, e.g., ibid., 292 (F., 121–2), 312 (F., 132).

23 See, e.g., ibid., 426–9 (F., 199–202), 426 (F., 198); Mercier, 118–19. Cf. A. Layish, 'The Druze testamentary waqf', *Studia Islamica*, 71 (1990), pp. 127–154.

On the other hand, a *waqf* established by dedication is not subject to any quantitative limitation. It comes into force there and then (*munajjaẓ*) and the founder cannot revoke it.[24] There are indeed instances of *waqfs* established in the ordinary way. Thus, in one case, a woman dedicated the room in which she lived, declaring that the *waqf* was to come into force immediately.[25]

In many cases, the *waqf* is described as eternal (*mu'abbad, mukhallad, ʿalā al-ta'bīd*), 'until Allāh inherits the earth and those upon it, He being the best of heirs' (*ilā an yarith Allāh al-arḍ wa-man ʿalayhā wa-huwa khayr al-wārithīn*).[26] In fact, the founder generally stipulates that when there are no more beneficiaries from his family, entitlement shall pass to some eternal *khayrī* purpose, such as relief of the poor or the upkeep of a mosque.[27] An eternal *khayrī* purpose at the end of the line of beneficiaries is a condition of the validity of the *waqf* according to the Ḥanafī (and Ibāḍī) but not the Shāfiʿī school.[28] But sometimes the founder directs that when there are no more beneficiaries from among his descendants, the property shall revert to his nearest agnatic relative.[29]

The North African Mālikī school in fact knows a temporary *waqf*. Under its doctrine, which, too, originates in the ancient Medinese doctrine, the property, when there are no more beneficiaries, reverts to its original owner or, if he has died, to his heirs, among whom it is divided by the ordinary rules of succession.[30] Mālikī jurists disagree as to the nature of the property which reverts to the founder or his heirs. According to some, they acquire full ownership of the property (*yarjiʿ mulkan lil-muḥbis aw li-warathatihi*). Others hold that the reverting property retains its *waqf* character (*ʿalā sunnat marājiʿ al-aḥbās*) with all the attendant restrictions (prohibition of sale and any other disposition) imposed on the beneficiaries. A *waqf* is not inherited according to

24 Schacht, *Early doctrines*, 445, 450 and the sources indicated there; Schacht's Papers, Waqf File, extracts from *al-Mudawwana al-kubrā* (ed. Saḥnūn), xv, 98, 99; *Kitāb aḥkām al-waqf* (ed. Hilāl). 8, 106, 171; Heffening, 1097; Abū Bakr Aḥmad ʿAmr al-Shaybānī al-maʿrūf bi'l-Khaṣṣāf, *Kitāb aḥkām al-waqf* [Cairo], 1904, 259.

25 Tanger, 368 (F., 161).

26 See, e.g., ibid., 505 (F., 234); Pesle, 74, 77, 78; Mercier, 21; E. Zeys et Mohammed Ould Sidi Saïd, *Recueil d'actes et de jugements arabes avec la traduction française et des notes juridiques*, 2e ed., Alger, 1946, 23; Milliot, p. 556 § 654.

27 See, e.g., Tanger, 48 (F., 49), 398 (F., 183); Pesle, 76.

28 Anderson, *Africa*, 77, 164.

29 Pesle, 73–4.

30 Schacht, *Early doctrines*, 446–7, 449 and the reference to *al-Mudawwana* indicated there; J.N.D. Anderson, 'The religious element in waqf endowments', *Journal of the Royal Central Asian Society*, XXXVIII, 1951, 293; *idem*, *Africa*, 379.

the *sharʿī* rules; the heirs are agnatic relatives in a certain order and the wife does not inherit.[31]

Pesle notes that the founder often stipulates that immovables dedicated as *waqf* shall revert to the nearest inheriting descendants. In one case, a man dedicated a house to his children and their descendants, directing that when there were no more of them it should revert to the nearest agnatic heir (*ʿaṣaba*); this probably meant that the house was to revert as a *waqf*; at any rate, it is not stated that the full ownership (*mulk*) should revert to the heirs.[32] In another case, a man who willed a *waqf* to his daughter and her descendants stipulated in the will that if he became economically distressed (*iḥtāja*) he should be entitled to revoke (*rajaʿa*) the will and sell the property.[33] Moreover, some Mālikī jurists hold that not only the founder is entitled to revoke the *waqf* but also his heirs. Where the purpose for which it was established has lapsed, the *waqf* reverts to the legal heirs of the founder (according to the Mālikī school: if they are poor) or is used for the public good.[34]

Contrary to the Ḥanafī and other schools, which forbid the sale of a *waqf* by the beneficiaries, some Mālikī jurists permit them to sell it provided they are economically distressed. This permission is effective only if the founder has stipulated for it and the beneficiaries are his immediate heirs (his children).[35]

## 1 The Beneficiaries

### 1.1 The Founder

In the case of *waqfs* established according to the Ḥanafī doctrine, the founder usually makes dedication 'in favour of himself during his lifetime' (*ʿalā nafsihi muddat ḥayātihi*) even if the purpose of the *waqf* is a *khayrī* one. This practice finds support in the Ḥanafī doctrine, more exactly in the teachings of Abū Yūsuf. If the founder also appoints himself *mutawallī*, he has possession of the property and enjoys its fruits as if nothing had happened (except, of course,

31 For more detail see Pesle, 61–4; Tanger, F., 12–13.

32 Pesle, 73–4.

33 Ibid., 16–17.

34 Heffening, 1097; A. Sabatery, *Eléments de droit musulman*, Alger, 1867, p. 59, 28 octobre 1865 – Ben Haddon c. Kheroufa.

35 Mercier, 39; Schacht's Papers, Waqf File, extract from *al-Mudawwana*, xv, 102. Cf. Anderson, *Africa*, 77; P. Lienhart, 'Family waqf in Zanzibar', a paper submitted to the Conference held at the East African Institute of Social Research, Makerere College, June 1958, p. 17.

that he must not affect any transactions in respect of it).[36] The Mālikī school, on the other hand, does not permit a person to dedicate property in favour of himself; a *waqf* of this kind is invalid. In fact, even the French courts in Algeria, which applied Islamic law as appellate courts, decided, in the nineteenth and the early twentieth century, that according to the Mālikī school the founder might not assign entitlement to the *waqf* to himself as the first beneficiary and that, if he did so, the *waqf* was of no effect. In Tangier documentary material, the author has not come across a single case in which the founder stipulates that he shall be the first beneficiary and that only after his death shall entitlement pass to others. Mercier confirms that this practice is not common.[37]

At the same time, it was rather usual in Tangier for a person to stipulate in a testamentary *waqf* that one-third of his estate should, after realization, serve to cover various expenses incurred in relation to him after his death, such as burial expenses, besides other *khayrī* purposes.[38] In one case, a man established a *waqf* by will in favour of his grave – for the upkeep of students (*ṭalaba*) who were to say prayers there. It is not stated whether the will related to one-third of the estate. The *qāḍī*, after consulting the Mālikī jurist Sīdī Khalīl's *Mukhtaṣar*, decided that the will contained nothing contrary to the *sharīʿa*. In another case, a woman dedicated two-thirds of her property to the Great Mosque and the remaining third was to cover the expenses of her funeral.[39] Sometimes people provide for the expenses of their funeral by an ordinary will not connected with a *waqf*. Thus, in one case, a woman directed in her will that a shop owned by her should be sold and the proceeds used to purchase the shrouds and pay for the burial and the funeral repast.[40]

The Mālikī school not only forbids a person to make dedication in favour of himself but also to appoint himself administrator (*nāẓir*, *mutawallī*) of the *waqf* established by him – this, too, in contrast to the Ḥanafī school; if he does so, the *waqf* is null and void.[41] But it seems that this prohibition was not always upheld. Thus, in one case, a man established a *waqf* in favour of some students

---

36 A. Layish, 'The family *waqf* and the Sharʿī Law of Succession according to *Waqfiyyāt* in the *Sijill* of *Sharīʿa* Courts', in G. Baer (ed.), *Social and economic aspects of the Muslim waqf*, § 1A; Anderson, 'Religious element', 292; al-Khaṣṣāf, 21.

37 Heffening, 1096; Sabatery, p. 55, 4 novembre 1863 – Ben Ha mod c. Ben Mohammed; Charnay, 106; Schacht, *Introduction*, 98. For the attitude of the Shāfiʿī and other schools on this question see Anderson. *Africa*, 54, 77; Lienhart, 4; Mercier, 159.

38 See, e.g., Tanger, 408 (F., 189).

39 Ibid., 176 (F., 89) and 376 (F., 166), respectively.

40 Ibid., 317 (F., 136).

41 Heffening, 1097; Schacht, *Early doctrines*, 451.

(*ṭalaba*) on condition that they recited *al-Ḥizb* at the Great Mosque. The founder stipulated that he should be the *nāẓir* of the *waqf* during his lifetime and that after his death the office should pass to the most deserving of his sons.[42] As the founder did not stipulate that entitlement to the *waqf* should remain with him during his lifetime, it seems that the reference is to a Mālikī *waqf*. The administrative function enables the founder to exercise supervision over the property but he lacks entitlement.

The founder can mitigate or even circumvent the prohibitions of the Mālikī school in various ways. Sometimes he dedicates property to his minor or as-yet-unborn children and holds possession of it on their behalf; it seems that they receive it when they reach the age of competence for dealing with property. Sometimes the founder stipulates that when there are no more beneficiaries or descendants of beneficiaries the property shall revert to him; we have already seen that this is permitted according to the Mālikī school although there is disagreement as to the nature (full ownership or *waqf*) of the reverting property.[43] Of course, dedication by will is the best, and also the most frequent, way of ensuring full control – possession and usufruct – of the testator-founder over the property during his lifetime, for, as stated, the testamentary *waqf* becomes effective only upon the death of the testator; until then he enjoys full ownership and may even revoke the *waqf*. The Mālikī population, which is the majority of the population of Algeria, establishes *waqfs* according to the Ḥanafī doctrine, and the French courts decided that if the founder, contrary to the Mālikī prohibition, reserved entitlement to himself the *waqf* was to be regarded as valid as if it had been established according to the Ḥanafī doctrine, even if that doctrine was not expressly referred to in the *waqfiyya*.[44]

### 1.2 *Beneficiaries of the First Series*

#### 1.2.1 The Spouse Relict

The widow is a Qur'ānic heir who is not excluded from the succession under any circumstances. She takes one-eighth of the succession along with a child or an agnatic grandchild how low soever and one-quarter where there is neither. There was only one case in which a man-made dedication in favour of his spouse, and not even as the sole beneficiary but along with his orphaned grandchildren. If she had been the sole beneficiary, the *waqf* might have been

42 Tanger, 397 (F., 182–3). *Al-ḥizb* is either special prayers composed by the founders of orders or a sixtieth part of the Qur'ān. I am obliged to Professor Gabriel Baer for pointing this out to me. See also H. Wehr, *A dictionary of modern written Arabic*, Beirut, 1974, 173.

43 Pesle, 65, 74, 78.

44 Sabatery, p. 62, 9 mai 1866 – Mestoul c. Ben Malek.

regarded as an attempt to circumvent the *radd* doctrine, according to which – in the view of all schools – the spouse does not participate in the residue when the Qurʾānic heirs have taken their portions and the estate is not exhausted. In the case under reference, the intention was to give preference to this spouse over another, who indeed, together with other heirs, challenged the validity of the testamentary *waqf*.[45]

As against this Charnay notes that, especially after World War I, a tendency was discerned in Algeria to favour the wife and women of other degrees of relationship to the founder in regard to entitlement so that they might not be dependent on the benevolence of his descendants. There is, in fact, evidence of descendants of founders contesting the validity of *waqfs* in favour of women. In one case, which occurred in Kabylia, the Chambre de révision musulmane, the supreme court of appeal in the period of French rule, helped a destitute elderly woman in deviation from the *sharīʿa* by regarding her expulsion from her husband's house, tantamount to divorce according to custom, as a regular divorce in order to secure her entitlement, which according to a stipulation of the founder was denied her as a married woman. The founder's descendants sought to exclude her from entitlement on the formal ground that under religious law she was married.[46]

On the other hand, there are several instances of the spouse being excluded from entitlement to the *waqf*. Thus, in one case, the testator dedicated one-third of the estate to orphaned grandchildren while the spouse and other heirs took their *sharʿī* portions of the two remaining thirds. In another case, the spouse challenged the validity of a testamentary *waqf* in favour of a stranger which comprised one-half of the estate, and the stranger indeed received only the legal third permitted to be willed. In Algeria, too, there were instances of women being excluded from the succession, by means of a *waqf*, on the initiative of the descendants of the founder, and on the other hand, numerous actions brought by women against their exclusion. Since many such *waqfs* were created shortly before the founder's death, we find instances of their being invalidated on the strength of the women's contention that he had been incapacitated by mortal illness. The principal motive for the exclusion of women is fear that the property might pass out of the family.[47]

There was no instance of a woman dedicating her property to her husband either as the sole beneficiary or along with other beneficiaries. In other words, the husband, who is a Qurʾānic heir, was, if alive at the time the *waqf* came into

45 Tanger, 426 ff. (F., 199 ff.); Coulson *Succession*, 41.
46 Charnay, 103–4, 108.
47 Tanger, 95 (F., 68) and 424 (F., 198), respectively; Charnay, 99–101.

effect, deprived of his *sharʿī* portion of the estate as regards the dedicated part. Mercier and Pesle confirm that spouses are usually excluded from entitlement to the *waqf*.[48]

### 1.2.2 The Children of the Founder

As expected, the first series of beneficiaries of the *waqf* consists preponderantly of descendants of the founder. Of fifteen family *waqfs* established according to the Mālikī doctrine, nine, i.e. 60 percent, were in favour of children of the founder – sons and daughters, including as-yet-unborn ones.[49] If to these we add three *waqfs* in favour of grandchildren whose father died in the founder's lifetime, we may say that 80 percent of all family *waqfs* were in favour of children of the founder or their descendants. In two cases (13 percent), there were other beneficiaries along with the children. Mercier found that 95 percent of all *waqfs* (the reference seems to be to family *waqfs*) were in favour of sons and their agnatic descendants and, when there were no more of them, daughters or their descendants. From statistics based on family *waqfs* established according to the Ḥanafī doctrine, we find that 70 percent were in favour of the founder's sons and daughters. In 80 percent of these cases, the founder's children enjoyed entitlement by themselves, in 20 percent along with others.[50]

These data reflect the founder's wish to emphasize the immediate connection between the sequence of generations and entitlement to the *waqf*. It is true that even under the Islamic law of succession the deceased's children take the lion's share of the estate, but they inherit along with the Qurʾānic heirs, who take their fixed portions before the residue is divided among the children. It seems that the allocation of entitlement to orphaned grandchildren and to agnatic relatives took place where none of the founder's own children were living.

### 1.2.3 Daughters

Where a man simply dedicates his property to his 'children', he means both sons and daughters.[51] In the absence of a son, the daughter takes one-half of the estate as a Qurʾānic heir, and two or more daughters take two-thirds. Along with a son, the daughter, by virtue of the *taʿṣīb* principle, becomes an agnatic heir who takes half as much as he.[52]

---

48 Mercier, 131; Pesle, 62. Cf. Layish, 'Family *waqf* and succession', § IB (The spouse relict).

49 Mercier, 159; Pesle, 77; Zeys, 22. Cf. Lavish, 'Family *waqf* and succession', § IB (Children).

50 Mercier, 131.

51 Mercier, 55–6; Tanger, 398 (F., 183), 400 (F., 184).

52 Coulson, *Succession*, 41–2.

The Mālikī jurist Sīdī Khalīl holds that Mālik Ibn Anas, in contrast to the Ḥanafī school, forebade the deprivation of a daughter of entitlement and that 'a waqf in favour of males to the exclusion of daughters is void (*baṭala*)', and the French courts in Algeria in fact decided accordingly.[53] One may in fact gain the impression that the accepted norm is dedication to sons and daughters without discrimination (as to the apportionment of entitlement between them and the right of daughters to transmit their shares in the entitlement to their descendants; see below). Some founders simply use the word 'children' (*awlād*) and others refer expressly to sons and daughters.[54] In one exceptional case, a man gave preference to one of his daughters over her brothers and sisters. He established a *waqf* in her favour and that of her descendants after her; only when there were no more of them was entitlement to pass to her brothers and sisters, the direct descendants of the founder. There is no indication of the reason for the preferential treatment of the daughter. In Kabylia, it might happen that a woman assigned entitlement to the *waqf* to her daughters in preference to her husband's heirs and that only when there were no more daughters was entitlement to pass to the latter. In order to give preference in entitlement to daughters, Algerian Muslims use various devices; e.g. the founder may acknowledge a debt to his daughter of a certain amount and in discharge of that debt assign to her the usufruct of certain *waqf* property.[55] *Waqfs* established under the Ḥanafī doctrine included cases in which the founder directed that his daughter or daughters should be the sole beneficiaries of the first series after him, but he seems to have done so for the simple reason that he had no sons, and he may have wished in this way to prevent the daughters being supplanted by distant agnates.[56]

On the other hand, there are instances of express exclusion of daughters from entitlement to the *waqf*, and Pesle holds that this is the accepted norm. Thus it happens that a man 'makes dedication in favour of the sons, not the daughters' (*ḥabasa ʿalā al-banīn lā al-banāt*). As stated, Mercier says that the commonest pattern is for the founder to stipulate that only when there are no more sons or agnatic descendants of sons shall entitlement pass to the daughters of the founder or, if they are no longer alive, to their descendants.[57]

---

53 Mercier, 28, 56, 64. The Ḥanbalī school extends this prohibition to any heir. See Anderson, 'Religious element', 298; Sabatery, p. 53, 23 mars 1863 – Naaman Bey c. Housse; Charnay, 106.

54 See, e.g., Tanger, 48 (F., 49), 398 (F., 183), 400 (F., 184); Pesle, 73, 74, 77.

55 Mercier, 141 ff.; Charnay, 102, 105.

56 Layish, 'Family *waqf* and succession', § 1B (Children) and the sources indicated in notes 34–6.

57 Pesle, 75; Mercier, 131. Cf. Milliot, p. 550 § 645.

In one exceptional case, the founder directed that his son and his as-yet-unborn sons, and after them their male descendants, to the exclusion of the females (*al-dhukūr dūn al-ināth*), until the end of all generations, should be the beneficiaries of the *waqf*. This of course is express discrimination against daughters, contrary to the prohibition by the Mālikī school. Only when there were no more of these agnatic descendants (*ʿaqb al-dhukūr*) – a not very likely contingency – was the *ḥabs* to pass to the founder's own daughters and after them to the daughters of his male descendants (*banāt dhukūr dhuriyyatihi*), that is to say, to the agnatic females in each generation. When no one was left of these two groups – an even less likely contingency – the *ḥabs* was to pass to the descendants of the founder's daughters (*dhuriyyat banāt al-wāqif*) and those of the daughters of his sons (*banāt banīhi*), how low soever (*wa-in asfalna*), without discrimination between males and females (*al-dhakar wa'l-unthā fī dhālik sawā*). In other words, equality of the sexes – as required by the Mālikī school – is practised in this case with regard only to the cognatic descendants.[58]

In Algeria, it was customary not to disadvantage unmarried and impecunious daughters with regard to entitlement, but it seems that they had entitlement, though on a basis of full equality with sons, for their lifetime only and were not able to transmit it to their heirs. As we shall see below, the imposition by means of a stipulation of such a restriction by the founder on females was very frequent.

The Ḥanafī school sets no bars to the exclusion of daughters from entitlement, and the French courts in Algeria in fact decided that the wish and conditions of the founder should as a rule be respected even if they entailed deprivation of unmarried, helpless and impecunious daughters and even if it had not been stated expressly that the *waqf* had been established in accordance with the Ḥanafī doctrine.[59] In one case, in which a *waqf* had been established in favour of the founder's sons only, the excluded daughter appointed her husband to claim her share of her father's estate in court as her agent (*tawkīl*), but the *qāḍī* dismissed her claim. At the same time, the French court occasionally made an exception, deciding that a *waqf*, even if established according to the

58 Mercier, 159–61.

59 Milliot, p. 550 § 645; Sabatery, pp. 55–6, 24 décembre 1863 – Ben Bouzekri c. Ben Youssef; pp. 60–1, 9 Janvier – Ben Brahim c. El Arabi; pp. 61–2, 12 février 1866 – Zeleikha c. Mohammed Cherif; pp. 62, 9 mai 1866 – El Mestoul c. Ben Malek.

Ḥanafī doctrine, was invalid if it involved deprivation of orphaned, poor, and unmarried daughters.[60]

### 1.2.4 Mother and Father

The mother is a Qur'ānic heir who is never excluded from the succession. She takes one-sixth of the estate along with a child or an agnatic grandchild or with brothers and sisters of the deceased and one-third in their absence. The author has come across no case in which the founder let his mother share in the entitlement in any manner whatsoever. On the contrary, there is at least one express instance of her being excluded from it. A man established a *waqf* in favour of his spouse and his orphaned agnatic and cognatic grandchildren whereas several legal heirs, including the founder's mother, contested the validity of the *waqf*. In the *sijill* of Jaffa the author came across only one case of dedication in favour of the mother as the sole beneficiary of the first series, and this cannot alter the assessment that there is a clear tendency to deprive the mother of her *sharʿī* right in the estate. Nor was there among the Mālikī *waqfs*, any more than among the Ḥanafī, one in favour of the founder's father, who inherits in two capacities: as a Qur'ānic heir and as an agnatic heir.[61]

### 1.2.5 Grandson and Granddaughter

As is known, the principle of representation is not recognized in the Sunnī law of succession, and an orphaned agnatic grandson does not take the share of his father who pre-deceased his grandfather. An agnatic granddaughter takes one-sixth of the estate as a supplement to the two-thirds allotted to daughters as a collective portion. Two or more daughters exclude the granddaughter *de facto* from the succession. In the absence of daughters, the grand-daughters take two-thirds of the estate, and by the side of an agnatic grandson of the same degree, the granddaughter becomes a residuary heir.[62]

The testamentary *waqf* makes it possible to circumvent the law of succession by establishing a *waqf* in favour of an orphaned grandson to the extent of up to one-third of the estate. Thus, in one case, a woman willed one-third of her estate to her grandsons, the children of her deceased son.[63] In another

---

60 Zeys, p. 43; Sabatery, p. 63, 28 juin 1866 – Ben Heussein c. Boukhalem.

61 Tanger, 426 (F., 199); Coulson, *Succession*, 43 f.; Layish, 'Family *waqf* and succession', § 1B (Parents).

62 Coulson, *Succession*, 52 ff., 144.

63 Tanger, 100 (F., p. 70, n. 6). It is not certain that the reference is to a testamentary *waqf*. On the 'obligatory will' as a remedy to the exclusion of orphaned grandsons from the succession see Coulson, *Succession*, 143 f. On the Egyptian *Waqf* Law of 1946 which adopts the

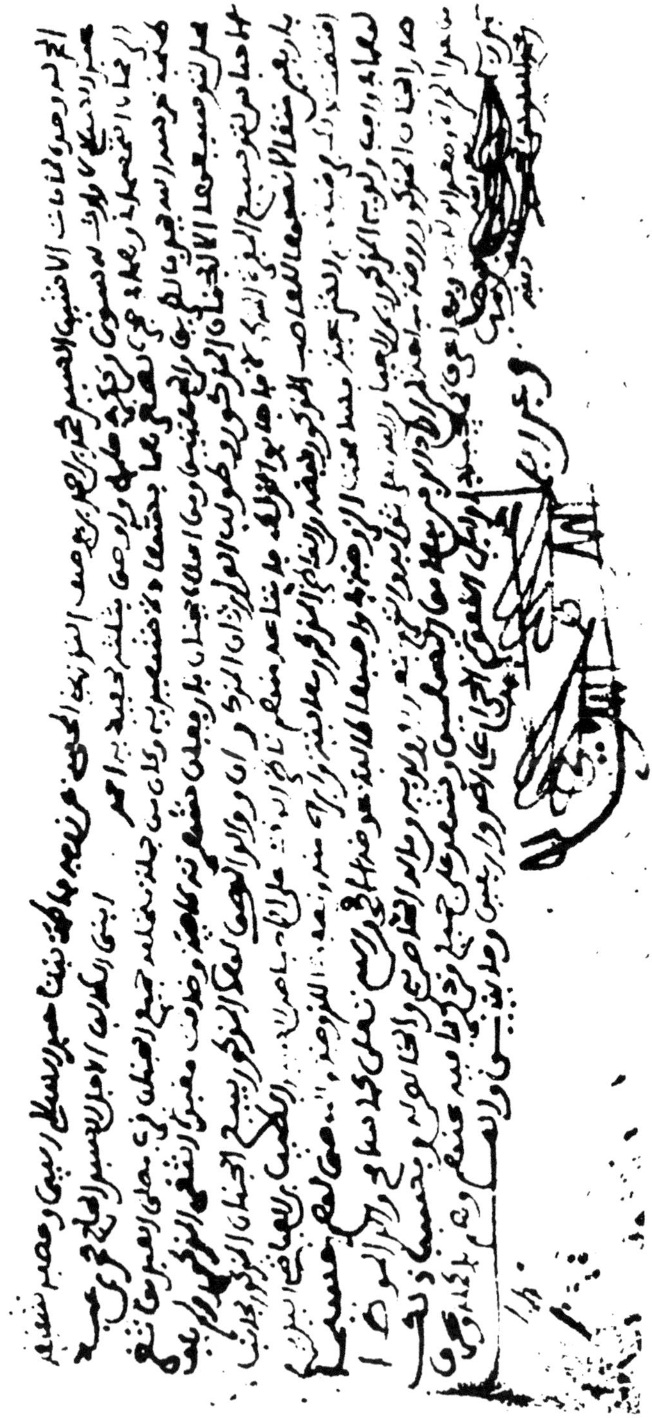

FIGURE 15.1 Will within the limits of one-third of the estate, in favour of orphaned grandsons
*ARCHIVES MAROCAINES*, XXII, PARIS, 1914, 95

case, a man willed one-third of his property (*awṣā bi-thulthihi*) to his minor cognatic (?) grandsons, depriving his spouse and his brother of this third (but not of their right to inherit two-thirds of his estate). In a further case, a man-made dedication to orphaned agnatic and cognatic grandsons by the side of his spouse.[64] Such equality of agnatic and cognatic grandsons is revolutionary from the point of view of the law of succession. In no case was a *waqf* established in favour of a granddaughter, either agnatic or cognatic, in the first series of beneficiaries.

### 1.2.6 Siblings and Other Relatives

A uterine brother or sister takes one-sixth of the estate as a Qurʾānic heir, and two or more brothers or sisters take one-third, males and females sharing equally. They are excluded from the succession by the deceased's child, agnatic grandson, father and agnatic ascendant how high soever. An agnatic brother is excluded by the son, agnatic grandson and father. The principle of strength of the blood tie operates between brothers.[65] There was no case of a *waqf* in favour of a brother or brothers of the founder of any strength of the blood tie. On the contrary, there is one instance of exclusion of uterine brothers from entitlement. A man willed half of his house to the *waqf* of Tangier. Several heirs of the founder, apparently including uterine brothers, claimed one-quarter of the house both as legal heirs and on the strength of abutter's preemption rights (*shufʿa*). Mercier found that in 95 percent of cases the founder's brothers became beneficiaries of the *waqf* only when there were no more sons or descendants of sons or daughters or descendants of daughters, a contingency which is obviously unreal.[66]

In one case, the founder assigned entitlement to the *waqf* to his brother's children (but not to their descendants) and after them to the *ḥazzābīn* (reciters of *al-Ḥizb*).[67] In another case, a woman directed in her will that her dwelling should be given to her sister for life and after the sister's death should become a *waqf* in favour of the mosque of Tangier. In yet another case, a woman willed one-third of her estate to two agnatic relatives, brothers – between them – of the whole blood, and the two other thirds to a *khayrī* purpose. Whether this was an ordinary will or a testamentary *waqf*, she was not entitled to will more

principle of representation in entitlement see J.N.D. Anderson, 'Recent developments in *Sharīʿa* law IX. The *waqf* system', *The Muslim World*, XLII, 1952, 269.

64 Tanger, 95 (F., 68) and 426 (F., 199), respectively. See also Tanger, F., 12.

65 Coulson, *Succession*, 39, 67 ff.

66 Tanger, 71 (F., 62–3). Cf. Sabatery, p. 58, 20 mars 1865 – Ben Mohammed c. Bent Mohammed.

67 Tanger, 408 (F., 488–9). See also ibid., 59 (F., p. 57, n. 4) – a will in favour of nieces and a sister.

than one-third of her estate, especially as she had legal heirs (according to the *ʿudūl*, one legal heir).[68]

### 1.2.7 Poor Relatives

Sometimes a *waqf* is established in favour of poor relatives as beneficiaries already of the first series. Thus, in one case, a man dedicated one-third of his property as a *waqf* to the shrine of an ancestor. Half of the income of this *waqf* was destined for the distribution of bread among poor descendants of the ancestor and the other half for distribution among the reciters of *al-Ḥizb* at the shrine of that *quṭb* (*ṣufī* saint). In another case, a man dedicated some property to financing the Qurʾānic studies of his and other Muslims' children.[69]

### 1.2.8 Strangers

There was only one instance of a *waqf* in favour of a stranger, as distinct from a relative. The founder dedicated one-half of his house to him and his descendants. Upon contestation of the legality of this testamentary *waqf* by the spouse, the bequest was reduced to the third permitted to be willed, and this was assigned to the stranger. The motive for the dedication is not known.[70]

## 2 Transmission of Entitlement from Beneficiaries of the First Series to Their Descendants in Successive Generations

### 2.1 *Degrees and Branches*

The pattern known from Ḥanafī *waqfs* of the transmission of entitlement from the beneficiaries of the first series to successive generations of their descendants[71] emerges also from the *waqfs* established according to the Mālikī doctrine, with the fundamental difference that in the former the founder is the first beneficiary while in the latter his immediate descendants form the first series of beneficiaries. This pattern does not agree with the Islamic law of succession, which does not recognize the principle of representation.[72] The

68 Ibid., 371 (F., 163–4) and 168 (F., p. 87, n. 1), respectively. Cf. Layish, 'Family *waqf* and succession', § 1B (Siblings).

69 Tanger, 503 (F., 232) and 494 (F., 228), respectively. Cf. Layish, 'Family *waqf* and succession', § 1B (Poor family members).

70 Tanger, 424 (F., 198). Cf. Layish, 'Family *waqf* and succession', § 1B (Dedication to others than legal heirs).

71 Layish, 'Family *waqf* and succession', § 2A.

72 For exceptions within the outer family circle see Coulson, *Succession*, 92–8; Milliot, p. 481 § 548.

right of succession passes on within the whole parentela, according to the degree (*daraja*) system, and not in the branches (*farʿ*). Those nearer in degree to the deceased exclude the more distant ones from the succession, and only when there are no more heirs of the nearer degree do those of the more distant degree inherit. In other words, an orphaned grandson – i.e. one whose father died in the grandfather's lifetime – of any degree does not take his father's share in the estate. He is excluded from the succession by his uncles, who are nearer in degree to the deceased.

According to Khalīl and other Mālikī jurists, if the founder designates the beneficiaries *collectively* (e.g. 'my children'), then, when one of them dies, his share passes to the remaining beneficiaries of the same degree; but if the beneficiaries are designated *by name*, the share of the deceased passes to the beneficiaries of the next degree. Where the beneficiaries are the founder's children and their descendants until the end of all generations, the matter of representation depends on the wish of the founder: if the descendants of the children are mentioned 'along with' (*wa*) the children in the same formula, the principle of representation is to be applied; but if it is said that the descendants come 'after' (*thumma*) the children, the principle of representation is not to be applied and the descendants' turn comes only when the last of the children are dead,[73] that is to say, transmission is according to degrees. It seems, however, that practice, as far as reflected in the documents before us, does not agree with the position of the Mālikī jurists.

As in the *waqfs* established according to the Ḥanafī doctrine, so in the Mālikī *waqfs* the stipulations of the founder as to the mode of transmission of entitlement from the beneficiaries to their descendants are substantially contradictory. On the one hand, he directs that entitlement shall pass from generation to generation in such a way that 'the higher degree excludes the lower degree' (*wa-taḥjub al-ṭabaqa al-ʿulyā al-ṭabaqa al-suflā*).[74] Some say expressly that 'the sons shall not share in this [the entitlement to the *waqf*] by the side of the fathers [or: their fathers]' (*lā yadkhul fī dhālik al-abnāʾ maʿa wujūd al-abāʾ* [or *abāʾihim*]. An Algerian Mālikī *waqfiyya* says similarly: 'A child has no right to enjoy the usufruct of the *waqf* along with his father' (*wa'l-walad lā yastaḥiqq istighlāl al-ḥabs maʿa abīhi*).[75] This means that those nearer in degree to the deceased debar from entitlement not only those who inherit through them but also those who inherit through those of the same degree who have died. In other words: the orphaned grandson is deprived of father's share in the

73 Milliot, pp. 551–2 §§ 646–7.

74 Mercier, 64–5. *Ṭabaqa* here means degree. See Mercier, 160.

75 See, e.g., ibid., 159; Tanger, 426 (F., 199); Pesle, 77; Zeys, 22.

entitlement by his uncle. As stated, this stipulation agrees with the *sharʿī* norm in the law of succession.

On the other hand, the founder adds a stipulation which reverses the position. After stipulating that sons shall not benefit so long as fathers exist he adds: 'and if a father dies, his son shall take his place' (*wa-idhā māta ab qāma maqāmahu waladuhu*) or 'if a son dies, his son shall take his place' (*fa-idhā māta ibn qāma ibnuhu maqāmahu*), or, similarly, in Algeria: 'and if a person dies leaving descendants, the descendants shall take his place, whether they are many or one' (*wa-man māta ʿan ʿaqb qāma ʿaqbuhu maqāmahu taʿaddada aw ittaḥada yaqtasimuhu al-mutaʿaddid wa-yanfaridu bihi al-muttaḥid*).[76] This is, of course, a simple and clear case of transmission of entitlement in branches, based on the principle of representation. To remove any doubt, some add expressly: 'He whose father died before exercising his right to entitlement [because the grandfather was still alive then] is entitled to become a beneficiary to the extent that his father would have become one had he died after doing so' (*wa-man māta abūhu qabla istiḥqāqihi al-waqf istaḥaqqa tanāwul al-waqf mithl mā talaqqā aṣluhu thumma māta*). In other words, an orphaned grandson of any degree takes his parent's share in the entitlement. Where two mutually contradictory stipulations appear together, the second is deemed to invalidate the first.[77]

In the absence of descendants of the beneficiaries, the question of representation is irrelevant and transmission proceeds according to degrees. The founder stipulates routinely: 'The share of him who dies without issue passes to him who is left over in his degree' (*wa-man māta minhum min ghayr ʿaqb rajaʿa naṣībuhu li-man baqiya fī ṭabaqatihi*), or he says: '… his right in the *waqf* shall pass to him who is in his degree or, if there is none [such], to the nearest to him' (*… rajaʿa mā kāna yastaḥiqquhu min al-ḥabs li-man huwa fī darajatihi wa-in lam yakun li-aqrab qarīb ilayhi*), that is to say, to his nearest relative, or, similarly, in Algeria: 'and if a person dies without issue, his share shall pass to a partner who is in his degree if there is one, and if there is none, to the partner nearest to him [as to blood-relationship]' (*wa-man māta min ghayr ʿaqb rajaʿa naṣibuhu li-mushārkihi fī ṭabaqatihi in wujida wa-illā fali-aqrab mushārikihi*).[78] As already noted by the author on another occasion, the transmission of entitlement to the descendants of the beneficiaries-of-the-first-series in branches, in application of the principle of representation and in circumvention of the *sharʿī* criterion of degrees, is an expression of an institutional change in the

76 Mercier, 142; Tanger, 400 (F., 184); and Zeys, 22, respectively.

77 Mercier, 160. See also ibid., 55. Cf. Layish, 'Family *waqf* and succession', § 2A (representation).

78 Tanger, 398 (F., 183), 426 (F., 199); Mercier, 142, 160; Pesle, 77; Zeys, 22. Cf. Lienhart, 4.

structure of the family: the transition from the extended family, in which the orphaned grandchild is deprived of every right of succession, to the nuclear family, in which the orphaned grandchild takes precedence over his uncle. This trend finds expression also in modern legislation. The Egyptian *Waqf* Law of 1946 provides that in a *waqf* in favour of one's descendants in successive generations (*murattab al-ṭabaqāt*) no ascendant (*aṣl*) shall debar (*yaḥjub*) the descendants (*farʿ*) of another and that a deceased ascendant's share in the entitlement shall pass only to his descendants. This reform finds support in the Mālikī doctrine.[79]

But it seems that in practice the principle of representation is not always strictly adhered to and that the two systems – the branch and the degree system – sometimes intermingle. Thus, in one case, a man established a *waqf* in favour of his daughter and her descendants, to be succeeded, when there were no more of them, by her two brothers and four sisters and their descendants after them. He so made two mutually contradictory stipulations successively, viz. sons shall not benefit from the *waqf* along with any ascendants, and when an ascendant dies, his child shall step into his shoes. The daughter died, transmitting the whole entitlement to her son, as required. Then the son died without issue, transmitting entitlement to his mother's four sisters, again in accordance with the stipulation of the founder; his mother's two brothers had died before her, but their descendants, by virtue of the degree criterion embodied in the first stipulation, did not receive their share of the entitlement. Then one of the sisters died without issue, and her share of the entitlement was divided equally between the remaining three sisters, i.e. relatives of the same degree as the deceased sister. Then another sister died, and her third of the entitlement passed to her daughter, by virtue of the principle of representation embodied in the second stipulation, and not to the remaining two sisters, as required by the first stipulation. Then another sister died without issue and her third passed to the last surviving sister, i.e. a relative of the same degree as she. At this stage, the division of entitlement was as follows: two-thirds were in the possession of the surviving sister and one-third was in the possession of the daughter of a deceased sister. In other words, the beneficiaries belonged to different degrees. Most of them had reached their position according to the degree system and a minority according to the branch system based on the principle of representation. In a case of another kind, which occurred in Constantine, two brothers, in dedicating their property, stipulated that entitlement should pass to the one of them who survived the other, and after him, to the children of both and their descendants, half to each branch.

79 Anderson, '*Waqf* system', 273; Layish, 'Family *waqf* and succession', § 2A.

In other words, the first stipulation reflects the degrees principle (the brothers inherited from a common source – their father) and the second stipulation the representation principle (by branches).[80]

### 2.2 *Entitlement and Transmission thereof to Descendants*

A distinction must be made between the entitlement (*istiḥqāq*) of beneficiaries of every degree and the right of the beneficiary to transmit his share of the entitlement to his descendants. As regards that right, the founder is guided by two considerations: the sex of the beneficiary and the line of descent (paternal or maternal)[81] by which the beneficiary is related to him. As stated, the beneficiaries of the first series are usually sons and daughters, without discrimination between them. When there are no more of them, entitlement passes to their children and after these to their children's children (*ʿalā aʿqābihim wa-ʿaqāb aʿqābihim mā tanāsalū wa-imtaddat furūʿuhum*).[82] The founder is sometimes careful to note that by 'descendants' he means males and females (*dhukūran wa-ināthan*).[83] As we have seen above, the founder makes stipulations as to the transmission of entitlement from generation to generation. However, in most of the *waqfs* of Tangier and in other sources it is not said in what line of descent or in what order entitlement is to be transmitted. All that is said is that when there are no more descendants of children (sons or daughters) of the deceased entitlement shall pass to some *khayrī* purpose.[84]

It may safely be stated that females participate in entitlement in every series of beneficiaries. There is express evidence to this effect: the *waqfiyya* or the will contain instructions as to how entitlement shall be apportioned between males and females. On the other hand, both express and indirect evidence permits us to affirm with a high degree of certainty that only male agnates, in every series, have the right to transmit their share to their descendants – males and females without discrimination; the process repeats itself in every subsequent generation. Even where the founder simply says 'in favour of my children' (*ʿalā awlādī*), most Mālikī jurists hold that what is meant is that entitlement shall pass to agnatic descendants (of both sexes) but transmit only through male agnates, in all generations down to the last. The founder sometimes states that he makes dedication 'in favour of his children and children's children through the males (*dhukūr*)', which means his agnatic descendants of both sexes.[85]

80 Mercier, 141–9; Charnay, 105.
81 Layish, 'Family *waqf* and succession', § 2B.
82 See, e.g., Tanger, 398 (F., 183); Zeys, 22.
83 See, e.g., Tanger, 48 (F., 49), 424 (F., 198); Mercier, 58–9.
84 See, e.g., Tanger, 48 (F., 49), 398 (F., 183), 400 (F., 184); Pesle, 77.
85 Mercier, 58–9.

According to the same sources, the term *ʿaqb*, extremely frequent in the *waqfs* of Tangier, means the founder's own children, male and female, and after them the children of his male children (*walad al-ṣulb dhakaran aw ināthan thumma awlād al-dhukūr*). In the context of our discussion, this means that only the founder's own children, of both sexes, and after them the children, of both sexes, of the males of every degree in all subsequent generations are entitled to the *waqf* while the daughters of every degree terminate their branches: they benefit but do not transmit their right to their descendants. Milliot explains that since, in the Muslim family, blood-relationship (parenté) is determined by way of the males, the term *ʿaqb* should be interpreted restrictively as referring only to agnatic descendants (of both sexes). Khalīl and other Mālikī jurists hold that the term *walad* in relation to the transmission of entitlement, e.g. 'my children's children' (and also expressions like 'origin' (race, lignée) or 'my sons'), should generally be understood as meaning only agnatic descendants, unless the founder stated expressly that also the descendants of a daughter should be entitled.[86]

Confirmation for the assumption that the founder's children of both sexes, in every generation or degree, are entitled to the *waqf* but that only male agnates may transmit their share of the entitlement to their descendants may be obtained from the *waqfiyyāt* established according to the Ḥanafī doctrine. The set formula reflecting the status of woman in this matter is 'the children of males, to the exclusion of the children of females' (*awlād al-ẓuhūr* (or *dhukūr*) *dūn awlād al-buṭūn*). That is to say: entitlement in every generation passes only to the agnatic descendants (of both sexes), the cognatic descendants being excluded.[87] Similarly, we find the following in Pesle, in a glossary of technical terms relating to the beneficiaries of *waqfs* : '… et les fils des fils à l'exclusion des fils des filles' (*wa-awlād dhukūrihim dūn walad al-banāt*), that is to say: entitlement passes to the agnatic children, the cognatic children being excluded, and 'male agnates take, to the exclusion of female ones' (*yatanāwa'l al-rijāl min al-ʿaṣaba dūn al-nisāʾ*), which latter utterance must be interpreted in the same way.[88] In Algeria, too, it has been observed that entitlement is transmitted only to agnatic descendants (of both sexes), the children of daughters being excluded: their mother's share passes to agnatic cousins in the same branch. To avoid the exclusion of the descendants of daughters, various devices are sometimes resorted to, e.g., the father of such descendants persuades their grandmother to sell her share of the entitlement fictitiously to their mother. Such a

86 Ibid., 59–62, and the Mālikī sources indicated there; Milliot, p. 553 § 649. Cf. Lienhart, 4.

87 Layish, 'Family *waqf* and succession', § 2B (*awlād al-ẓuhūr*).

88 Pesle, 78–9 and 81, respectively. Cf. Lienhart, 17.

sale is valid according to French legislation provided that the purchaser is not a beneficiary. A French court decided that according to the Ḥanafī doctrine the founder of a *waqf* was permitted to assign entitlement to the descendants of one of his children to the exclusion of the descendants of the other children.[89]

Having ascertained how entitlement passes from generation to generation or from degree to degree within the parentela of the founder's descendants, we still have to determine who are the beneficiaries when there are no more descendants. The *waqfs* of Tangier give the impression that the founder did not go beyond his children and their descendants in all successive generations but directed that when there were no more of them entitlement should pass to some *khayrī* purpose in Tangier, such as the Great Mosque, Qurʾān reciters or religious functionaries.[90] Where the *waqf* is in favour of relatives other than children, such as grandchildren, or of strangers, the founder also does not go beyond the descendants, in all successive generations, of the beneficiaries of the first series but directs that when there are no more of them entitlement shall pass to some local *khayrī* purpose. Similarly, in *waqfiyyāt* established according to the Ḥanafī doctrine, in Palestine or other countries, it has been observed that the founder does not provide for his relatives beyond the descendants of the beneficiaries of the first parentela but directs that when there are no more of them entitlement shall pass to some *khayrī* purpose.[91]

In some cases in the Ottoman Empire and in Egypt, when there were no more descendants of the founder, entitlement passed to his manumitted slaves and their descendants and sometimes to those of his father and their descendants. This is a clear indication that the founder preferred them to relatives of other parentelas and was using the mechanism of the *waqf* to circumvent the law of succession, under which a manumitted slave has no part nor lot in his master's estate.[92]

Where the *waqf* is in favour of the founder's own children, he is guided by considerations of their welfare, which accounts for his wish that when there are no more of them entitlement shall pass to their descendants until there are no more of these. But there is no family motive where the beneficiary is not the founder's own child. The motive here is personal – the wish to benefit a particular person dear to him, and he therefore directs that upon the beneficiary's death entitlement shall not pass to the latter's descendants but to some *khayrī*

89 Charnav, 105, and Sabatery, p. 59, 15 septembre 1865 – Bourkaïb c. Roure, respectively.

90 See, e.g., Tanger, 48 (F., 49), 398 (F., 183), 400 (F., 184). Cf. Pesle, 77.

91 See, e.g., Tanger, 426 (F., 199), 424 (F., 198); Layish, 'Family *waqf* and succession', § 2B.

92 G. Baer, 'The Waqf as a prop for the social system (16th–20th centuries)', in his (ed.), *Social and economic aspects of the Muslim waqf* (free slaves).

purpose. One founder did so in respect of his brother's children. In another case, a woman dedicated one-third of her property to two agnatic relatives and two-thirds to some Qur'ān reciters who were to benefit simultaneously with the former, and she seems to have intended that after the death of those two their shares should pass to the Qur'ān reciters.[93]

In other cases, persons dedicated property to orphaned grandsons, probably with the intention of righting the wrong of the Muslim succession law, which does not recognize the principle of representation. Although the founders did not prescribe to whom entitlement should pass after the death of the grandsons we may assume that they intended them to transmit it to their descendants and not to their uncles. But the founders allotted them only one-third of the estate, and in one case it was stated that the founder had legal heirs (a spouse and an agnatic brother) who took two-thirds.[94]

Pesle notes that in his day (the late nineteenth and early twentieth centuries) it was rare for the founder not to prescribe who should be the beneficiaries when there were no more descendants; the most frequent practice was to stipulate that entitlement should pass to the nearest agnatic relatives.[95] If he did not say who were to be the beneficiaries when there were no more descendants, there were, according to the Mālikī school, two possibilities: either the property remained a *waqf* and entitlement passed to the nearest agnatic heirs or the full ownership of the property reverted to the nearest heirs (according to the *sharʿī* order of heirs).[96]

Mercier presents a totally different pattern of family *waqf* – apparently the one most frequent in Algeria – in which the entitlement of the family members does not end with the last of the descendants of the first parentela but continues into other parentelas of relatives of the founder. On the face of it, there is some resemblance here to the agnatic-parentelas method of the Muslim system of succession, but there are material differences, as we shall see below. As stated, Mercier found that 95 percent of family *waqfs* were established 'in favour of agnatic descendants. When there are no more of them, entitlement passes to the daughters and their descendants and then to the brothers etc.'.[97] As regards the agnatic descendants, he seems to have meant that both sexes, in every generation, were entitled but that only male agnates could transmit their right to their descendants, as set out above. According to this system, the

93 Tanger, 408 (F., 188–9) and 168 (F., p. 87, n. 1), respectively.

94 Ibid., 95 (F., 68) and 100 (F., p. 70, n. 6), respectively.

95 Such a *waqfiyya* see in Pesle, 74.

96 Pesle, 73.

97 Mercier, 131.

Qur'ānic heirs are deprived; they are hardly ever included in the first series of beneficiaries, even by the side of the agnatic descendants. The daughters, too, are deprived because they may not transmit their share to their descendants, whereas according to the law of succession they are Qur'ānic heirs and, by the side of some of the same degree, become agnatic heirs. According to Mercier's pattern, daughters and their descendants become entitled only when there are no more male agnates of the first parentela, while according to the *sharʿī* law of succession this is where the second parentela – the father of the founder and his descendants, i.e. the brothers and sisters of the founder and their descendants – comes in.

A distinction between entitlement and the right to transmit it to one's descendants is made also in the category of cognatic descendants of the founder. As in the category of agnatic descendants, daughters in every generation share in the entitlement along with sons, but only males may transmit their share to their descendants. Mercier finds that this rule is expressed by a special technical term – *ʿaqb*: the children of the founder's own daughters or of the first daughter of his male descendants and [after them] the descendants of males in this new line, how low soever. And again, as in the category of agnatic descendants, entitlement stops in every generation with the daughter who excludes subsequent descendants of her branch. Pesle's dictionary notes that, in the opinion of some jurists, the terms *dhuriyya* and *nasl* designate the children of the daughters, and in an even narrower interpretation, only the males among them,[98] who, as stated, are alone capable of transmitting their share of the entitlement.

The practice of preferring males in the transmission of entitlement – in every generation – even in the maternal line has been observed with certainty in *waqfs* established in Palestine according to the Ḥanafī doctrine. There it was explained by fear of the number of beneficiaries increasing excessively through the inclusion of descendants of both the paternal and the maternal line[99] and of entitlement passing out of the agnatic family through the transfer of parts thereof to cognatic branches. As stated, in a cognatic group of beneficiaries, every male opens a new agnatic line, of which he is the head.[100] Females are thus deprived not only in the category of agnatic descendants but also 'on their own ground' – in the category of cognatic descendants. Mālikī jurists, such as

98 Ibid., 62–4; Pesle, 79.

99 According to Mercier, the term *dhuriyya* includes all the descendants of both the agnatic and cognatic branches and all of them participate in entitlement on a *per capita* basis; see Mercier, 64.

100 Layish, 'Family *waqf* and succession', § 2B (Cognatic relatives). See also Mercier, 57.

Sīdī Khalīl, sharply reject the deprivation of women of their rights by the use of collective terms (such as *dhuriyya*),[101] but it seems that reality is stronger.

In Zanzibar, a tendency has been observed to prefer cognatic over agnatic relatives in *waqfs*, and some apportion entitlement among the descendants without distinction of sex or line of descent. This phenomenon has already been observed in the first parentela; moreover, cognatic females have the right to transmit their share of the entitlement to their descendants, which constitutes a fundamental difference from Mercier's pattern. The origin of this phenomenon must apparently be sought in the customary law of a matriarchate which has survived in certain regions.[102]

According to Mercier's pattern, when there are no more cognatic descendants, entitlement passes to the siblings of the founder and to their descendants 'on the same conditions'; it seems that Mercier is referring to the conditions applicable to the members of the first parentela. That is to say: the sons and daughters in every generation are entitled to the *waqf*, but only the sons transmit their right – to the agnatic branches. Mercier does not say in what order brothers of different degrees of strength of the blood-tie succeed to entitlement, but it seems that, on the analogy of agnatic and cognatic descendants, agnatic brothers and their descendants precede cognatic brothers and their descendants and that, among the agnates, germane brothers precede consanguine brothers.[103]

When there are no more brothers or descendants of brothers, it is the turn of the uncles and their descendants, in Mercier's terminology 'agnates or near relatives, etc.',[104] probably in the order of parentelas of the Islamic law of succession. The author has come across only one case in which the founder, a woman, assigned entitlement to her brothers and sisters, but not as beneficiaries of the first series. Entitlement was at first assigned to a daughter and her descendants of both sexes, and only when they were all dead was it to pass to her two brothers and four sisters. It seems that they were all germane brothers and sisters.[105] According to Mercier, numerous jurists of the Mālikī (and the Ḥanafī) school surmise that many persons prefer to make dedication in favour of their wives and of poor people of both sexes (other than relatives) rather than of wealthy siblings.[106] The existence of this tendency is, in a certain sense, confirmed by the Tangier documents. True, dedication is not often made

101 Mercier, 64.
102 Lienhart, 15, 17.
103 Mercier, 64. Cf. Lienhart, 5; Coulson, *Succession*, 34–5.
104 Mercier, 64.
105 Ibid., 141 ff.
106 Ibid., 28, 64.

there in favour of the wife or the local poor but, as we have seen, the founder may stipulate that when there are no more descendants of the first parentela entitlement shall pass to a *khayrī* purpose and not to agnatic blood-relations in other parentelas.

Mercier brings one exceptional *waqfiyya* which shows some interesting deviations from the basic pattern indicated above. A man dedicated his property to his living son and to 'every male that will be born to him in his lifetime', and when they were dead, 'to their male children and children's children, to the exclusion of females, so long as they are fruitful and multiply and extend their branches in Islam' (*'alā awlādihim wa-awlād awlādihim al-dhukūr dūn al-ināth mā tanāsalū wa-imtaddat furū'uhum fī 'l-Islām*). When there were no more male agnates (*'aqb al-dhukūr*), entitlement was to pass from the *ḥabs* to whoever of the founder's own daughters (*banāt ṣulb al-wāqif*) might still be alive and to the daughters of his male descendants (*banāt dhukūr dhuriyyatihi*), i.e. to the agnatic daughters in every generation. When this category of beneficiaries was also exhausted, entitlement was to pass from the *ḥabs* to the descendants of the daughters (*dhuriyyat al-banāt*), 'i.e. both to the daughters of the founder and to the daughters of his sons how low soever' (*a'nī banāt al-wāqif wa-banāt banīhī wa-in asfalna*). When all the beneficiaries of these categories were dead, entitlement was to pass from the *ḥabs* to the Ḥaramayn al-Sharīfayn.

In sum, there are three categories of relatives of the founder who are entitled to the *waqf* successively: (1) The founder's own sons and their male descendants. The daughters, in every generation, are not entitled even during their lifetime. This appears from the founder's stipulation that entitlement shall be apportioned '*per capita*' among males (*dhukūr*) only. (2) The founder's own daughters and the daughters of his male descendants in every generation. In other words, this is an exclusive group of agnatic females, in which there is no room for males. This appears from the founder's stipulation that entitlement shall be apportioned '*per capita*', without discrimination, among descendants of two degrees: living daughters and daughters of males. (3) Descendants, of both sexes, of living daughters, and after them, descendants of daughters of sons how low soever, that is to say, a group of cognatic beneficiaries of both sexes. This appears from the founder's stipulation that males and females shall be equal for the purposes of the allocation of entitlement, which shall be apportioned '*per capita*' among beneficiaries of all degrees.

The first category deprives women not only in that they have no right to transmit entitlement – this is no deviation from Mercier's ordinary pattern – but also in that, in every generation, they are not entitled during their lifetime. As stated, the exclusion of women from entitlement is contrary to the

Mālikī doctrine. On the other hand, the exclusive group of agnatic females is an innovation in favour of women in the sense that only women benefit in every generation although they still have no right to transmit their share in the entitlement to their branches; this right is reserved to males even though they realize it only through their daughters. Mercier observes that this category of beneficiaries is peculiar and has no parallel. It should, of course, be noted that the beneficiaries of this category only get their turn when the first category is exhausted, and this in itself constitutes deprivation.

Lastly, the cognatic beneficiaries do not get their turn until the first two categories are exhausted, which may take quite a long time. The innovation in this category as against the group of cognatic descendants in Mercier's pattern is that the daughter in every generation not only shares in the entitlement but also transmits her share to her descendants. The absence, perhaps inspired by the Mālikī doctrine, of discrimination between the sexes is confined to the category of cognatic relatives.[107]

The pattern represented by this *waqfiyya* is exceptional, confirming the rule that in a patrilineal society, for the purposes of entitlement to the *waqf* as well as of succession and other matters, agnatic relatives take clear precedence over cognatic relatives within every parentela and in the order of the parentelas. This precedence is prompted, first and foremost, by the wish to preserve the integrity of the family property and to prevent entitlement to it passing out of the agnatic family. The *waqf* is an essential instrument for circumventing the law of succession.[108]

## 3 Mode of Apportioning Entitlement

Having ascertained the beneficiaries of the first series and the mode of transmission of their rights to their descendants, we proceed to note three basic ways in which entitlement to a Mālikī family *waqf* is apportioned.

### 3.1 *Apportionment According to the* 'sharʿī' *Norm*

In comparison with the *waqfs* established in Palestine according to the Ḥanafī doctrine,[109] it seems that apportionment pursuant to the '*sharʿī*' norm of the

107 Ibid., 159–62. See there for the full text of the *waqfiyya,* its translation into French and the author's notes.

108 For more detail see below, § III.3. Cf. Layish, 'Family *waqf* and succession', § 2B (compromise between patrilineal and matrilineal system).

109 Ibid., § 3A.

law of succession, i.e. sons taking twice as much as daughters, is not very frequent. The author has only come across it in a few isolated cases. Thus, a man dedicated some property to his daughter and her descendants of both sexes and directed that 'a male shall have the equivalent of the portion of two females' (*lil-dhakar mithl ḥaẓẓ al-unthayayn*). When there were no more descendants of the daughter, entitlement was to pass to the founder's brothers and sisters on the same principle of apportionment. In this particular case, the daughter had only a son, who took the whole entitlement, and the founder's brothers died before the daughter so that, when the turn of the founder's sisters came, they took the whole entitlement in equal shares.[110] This case shows that the '*sharʿī*' apportionment applies not only to the founder's descendants but also to his brothers and sisters. In fact, in the presence of a germane brother, a sister of the same strength of the blood-tie turns from a Qurʾānic into an agnatic heir, who takes half as much as the brother, just as the daughter turns from a Qurʾānic into an agnatic heir in the presence of a son.

On the face of it, it would seem that the founder wished to determine the shares of the legal heirs in the entitlement in accordance with the *sharʿī* norm. It is interesting to note that in one case, the French court in Algeria voided a *waqf* created in favour of the founder's daughter to the exclusion of his son by the same woman, on the strength of verse 12 (verse 11 in the Egyptian edition) of the Sūra of Women which grants sons double the portion of daughters. The judge held that the Qurʾānic provision did not permit him to deprive the son of the inheritance either directly or indirectly, that the establishment of a *waqf* contrary to that provision must be regarded as a disguised donation contrary to Islamic law and that, therefore, the *waqf* must be voided and the estate divided between the son and the daughter in accordance with the *sharʿī* law of succession.[111] But even if 'there is a motive to secure the *sharʿī* apportionment between the sexes in entitlement, it should be noted that, in glaring contradiction to the *sharʿī* norm, the daughter enjoys the fruits of the *waqf* during her lifetime only and cannot transmit it to her descendants. In Palestinian *waqfiyyāt*, such an apportionment is often described as being 'in accordance with the *sharʿī* law of succession' (*ḥash al-farīḍa al-sharʿiyya*), which, in the author's opinion, is a pious phrase intended to provide legitimation for the founder's wish to exclude or disadvantage Qurʾānic heirs, for the whole purpose of the *waqf* is to bypass the *sharʿī* law of succession. Milliot, too, denies the connection between the *sharʿī* norm of succession and entitlement, and in any case, Muslim jurists supply no grounds for the claim that the

110 Mercier, 141 ff. Cf. Zeys, 22–3; Charnay, 102, 105.

111 Sabatery, pp. 57–8, 8 mars 1865 – Ben Aïssa c. Ben Aïssa. Cf. Lienhart, 3.

preferential treatment of sons in succession should extend also to *waqf*. The author has already suggested on a previous occasion that this apportionment is an independent norm conforming to customary law.[112] Pesle, too, says that he has come across *waqfs* in which entitlement was apportioned on the basis of males taking twice as much as females. The same phenomenon has also been observed among the Ibāḍīs in Zanzibar.[113]

The paucity of cases in which entitlement was apportioned between the sexes in the *sharʿī* manner may be due to the ban imposed by the Mālikī school – it is attributed to Mālik Ibn Anas – on discrimination between males and females as regards entitlement; such a ban does not exist in the doctrine of Abū Yūsuf of the Ḥanafī school (which is followed in *sharīʿa* courts in Palestine). Moreover, the Mālikī school does not recognize the founder's right to stipulate that entitlement shall be apportioned among the beneficiaries 'in accordance with their shares as legal heirs' because *waqf* and succession are mutually exclusive systems, and if the founder has so stipulated and has not revoked the *waqf*, the judge will take no account of the stipulation and will apportion entitlement equally '*per capita*' – among the beneficiaries.[114] But this assumption, too, must be treated with caution, for the prevention – which, as stated, is an accepted norm – of daughters from transmitting entitlement to their descendants expressly contradicts the Mālikī ban.

### 3.2 *Equal Apportionment*

A different apportionment of entitlement to a Mālikī family *waqf* is based on equality between the sexes. It is accepted practice for a man who makes dedication in favour of his children and their descendants to stipulate that 'males and females are equal' (*al-dhakar wa'l-unthā sawāʾ*) [as to entitlement] or that there shall be no discrimination between sons and daughters.[115] This refers not only to the first series of beneficiaries but to the beneficiaries of all generations. The equal apportionment of entitlement between the sexes may be inspired by the Mālikī norm, which, as stated, prohibits discrimination against females.

The Mālikī jurist, Sīdī Khalīl, holds that in the event of the founder not stipulating expressly that entitlement shall be divided equally between the sexes such equality shall be regarded as self-understood.[116] At the same time,

112 Milliot, p. 553 § 650; Layish, 'Family *waqf* and succession', § 3A. Cf. Zeys, 23.

113 Pesle, 75; Anderson, *Africa*, 77; Lienhart, 4.

114 Mercier, 28 (and the Mālikī source indicated there), 43–4.

115 See, e.g., Tanger, 398 (F., 183), 505 (F., 234); Pesle, 74.

116 Mercier, 56; Milliot, p. 553, § 650.

it seems that a good deal is left to the personal whim of the founder. He sometimes uses both kinds of apportionment, the '*sharʿī*' and the equal, simultaneously. Thus, in one case, the founder prescribed that 'in the first series [of beneficiaries – orphaned grandsons and granddaughters] the dwelling shall be divided equally between males and females' (*wa'l-dhakar wa'l-unthā min al-ṭabaqa al-ūlā sawā' fī al-suknā*) but immediately added that 'as regards the income, a male shall have the equivalent of the portion of two females' (*wa-fī al-ghalla lil-dhakar mithl ḥaẓẓ al-unthayayn*).[117]

### 3.3 *Apportionment 'per capita'*

The norm accepted by Mālikī jurists is that, in the absence of another direction by the founder, entitlement shall be apportioned '*per capita*', without distinction of sex, among beneficiaries of the same class and degree. When entitlement passes from ascendants to descendants according to the principle of representation (without separation between them – see above), the children of each male ascendant apportion his share of the entitlement among themselves unless the founder has directed '*per capita*' apportionment, in which case the children of all branches take equal shares. This latter is a more sophisticated method of apportionment, which is likewise based on equality, 'according to the number of heads', of all the beneficiaries existing in a particular situation. But this equality does not necessarily prevail between the sexes within the same degree of relationship to the founder; it prevails, first and foremost, between beneficiaries of different degrees. This method partly adopts the principle of representation in the sense that it recognizes the transmission of entitlement from generation to generation by way of the branches. Descendants in every branch enter the group of beneficiaries by way of the parent they represent. But once they have entered it, the degree to which they belong or the share of the parent they represent is no longer relevant. The beneficiaries of all degrees and of all branches take equal shares of the entitlement. Sometimes, indeed, the founder at first stipulates that sons shall not share in the entitlement along with ascendants, i.e. relatives nearer in degree to him, but later he directs that sons and ascendants shall share in the entitlement together '*per capita*'.[118]

This method does not necessarily correct inequities towards women or cognatic relatives due to the mode of transmission of entitlement from generation to generation. Thus, in the exceptional *waqf* referred to above,[119] a man dedicated his property to three categories of beneficiaries successively. The

117 Tanger, 426 (F., 199). Cf. Layish, 'Family *waqf* and succession', § 3B.

118 Milliot, pp. 652–3 §§ 648 and 650; Mercier, 65, 159–61.

119 See above, pp. 20–21.

first category included his sons and their male descendants; he stipulated that 'if one of the male beneficiaries dies, leaving a son or sons, the son or each son shall be entitled to a portion together with the other living beneficiaries since it [entitlement] shall be apportioned among the living [beneficiaries] according to the number of heads, whether they are of the same or of a different degree' (*wa-man māta min al-dhukūr yatruk waladan dhakaran aw awlādan dhukūran istaḥaqqa kull minhum ḥaẓẓan maʿa baqiyyat al-mawjūdīn min ahl al-ḥabs bi-ḥaythu yuqsam bayn al-mawjūdīn ʿalā ʿadad al-ruʾūs ittaḥadū fī 'l-ṭabaqa aw ikhtalafū*). The founder further stipulated that if one of these beneficiaries died without issue 'his share shall pass to the other beneficiaries [of his degree] on a basis of equality, without discriminating between any of them and any others' (*rajaʿa naṣībuhu lil-bāqīn baʿdahu ʿalā al-sawāʾ wa'l-iʿtidāl min ghayr tafḍīl li-baʿḍ dūn al-baʿḍ*).[120] In this case, equality is confined to the degree, whereas agnatic daughters in every generation, as well as cognatic relatives, are completely excluded.

On the other hand, equality between different degrees is sometimes confined to women. Thus, in the *waqf* discussed above, the founder dedicated entitlement in the second category of beneficiaries to his daughters and to the daughters of males in every generation, i.e. to an exclusive category of agnatic females, stipulating that entitlement 'shall be apportioned among them according to the number of their heads without any group being preferred over any other' (*yuqsam baynahunna ʿalā ʿadad ruʾūsihinna min ghayr tafḍīl al-farīq ʿalā al-ākhar*), which means that the daughters and the daughters of males were to share entitlement equally, without a degree nearer to the founder taking precedence over a more distant one.[121]

Sometimes *per capita* apportionment relates to cognates of different degrees whilst maintaining equality between the sexes. Thus it is said in the same *waqf* that when the first two categories are exhausted, entitlement shall pass to a third category of cognatic descendants of both sexes, 'males and females being equal in that entitlement is apportioned among them according to the number of heads, whether they are of the same degree or of different degrees' (*al-dhakar wa'l-unthā fī dhālik sawāʾ bi-ḥaythu yūzaʿ al-ḥabs baynahum ʿalā ʿadad al-ruʾūs ittafaqū ṭabaqatan aw ikhtalafū*).[122]

Lastly, there is a further variant of *per capita* apportionment, in which full equality is maintained both between lines of descent and sexes. In such cases, it is said in the *waqfiyya*: 'Males and females of every side [paternal and maternal] take [a share in the entitlement]' (*yatanāwal al-dhukūr wa'l-ināth min ayy*

120 Mercier, 65, 159–60.
121 Ibid., 160.
122 Ibid.

*jiha kānū*).[123] This corresponds to Mercier's definition of *dhuriyya*, according to which all the founder's descendants of the male and female branches, i.e. agnates and cognates, of both sexes, share in entitlement *per capita*.[124] The phenomenon under reference has also been observed in Zanzibar, where it has been noted that it causes a geometrical increase in the number of beneficiaries. Thus, in one case, the number of beneficiaries of a hundred-year-old *waqf* was 1,000, and each of them was supposed to receive 10 shillings once in ten years. Sometimes *per capita* apportionment is combined with other forms of apportionment. Thus, e.g., in a case relating to Kabylia (where the principle of representation does not apply), the Chambre de révision musulmane decided that entitlement should be apportioned *per capita* in the first degree and by branches, i.e. according to the principle of representation, in the following degrees.[125]

It should be noted that in *waqfs* established in Palestine under the Ḥanafī doctrine *per capita* apportionment is not usual while apportionment on the basis of equality between the sexes is usual to some extent.[126] On the other hand, the Tangier documents contain no instances of apportionment based on economic considerations, i.e. in units as complete as possible and according to types of property.[127] At the same time, the founder sometimes uses the mechanism of the testamentary *waqf* to allocate one-third of the estate to one or some of the beneficiaries. He occasionally concentrates that third in some particular property, probably from economic considerations. The Druzes, who enjoy absolute freedom of testation under their religious law, use the mechanism of the will to apportion the estate among the heirs in units as complete and economic as possible with a view to preventing excessive fragmentation of the family property and disputes among the heirs.[128]

## 4 Founder's Stipulations Concerning Beneficiaries

As we have seen, the founder's stipulation that a female agnate may enjoy the proceeds of the *waqf* during her lifetime only but may not transmit her share to her descendants is very common in Mālikī as well as in Ḥanafī *waqfs*. Its

123 Pesle, 81.
124 Mercier, 64.
125 Lienhart, 16; Charnay, 102.
126 Layish, 'Family *waqf* and succession', § 3B.
127 Cf. ibid., § 3C.
128 See, e.g., Tanger, 33 (F., 43); A. Layish, *Marriage, divorce and succession in the Druze family*, Leiden, 1982, 320–2.

main reason is the founder's wish to prevent parts of the entitlement to the family property passing out of the agnatic family in consequence of a daughter's marriage.

On the other hand, stipulations imposing restrictions on the conduct of the beneficiaries seem to be rather infrequent. In the Tangier documents, the author has not come across a single instance of the founder making a daughter's entitlement conditional on her being unmarried, divorced or widowed or of her losing her right upon her marriage, stipulations very frequent in Ḥanafī *waqfs* and likewise prompted by the founder's fear that the daughter might transfer her entitlement to her descendants by an exogamous marriage. At the same time, it should be noted that Pesle describes 'the exclusion of daughters from it [entitlement] in the event of marriage' (*ikhrāj al-banāt minhu idhā tazawwajna*) as a known phenomenon. Charnay, too, noticed this phenomenon in Algeria; he explained the exclusion of women by a desire to avoid jealousy after the founder's death. He seems to mean tensions between the sons of the founder and the family to which the woman belongs after her marriage. The French court in Algeria would confirm the validity of *waqfs* excluding daughters from entitlement upon their marriage. But in these cases there are clear indications that the *waqfs* were established according to the Ḥanafī doctrine.[129]

The Tangier documents give one instance of a man dedicating his property to his children and their descendants on condition they live in his dwelling.[130] The dedication of the founder's dwelling is expressly referred to by Mālik Ibn Anas, and according to Schacht this proves that 'the *ḥabs* of houses as envisaged by Mālik is concerned mainly not with securing revenue but living accommodation in the old "family home" for succeeding generations'.[131] This assumption is confirmed by a tendency observed in Zanzibar to dedicate dwellings to one's descendants in the expectation that some of them will continue to live therein and thus preserve a tangible link with the founder after his death. Against this background we must understand his strict prohibition of letting the house.[132]

Conspicuous by its absence is a stipulation assuring the wife, because of her total or partial exclusion from entitlement, of the right of residence in the founder's house and a fixed subsistence allowance which is a kind of 'maintenance out of the estate'. Such a stipulation is fairly frequent in Ḥanafī *waqfs*. Assuring a woman of entitlement during her lifetime (without the right of

---

129 Charnay, 103; Sabatery, p. 54, 27 juillet 1863 – Bent Sliman c. Ben el Serir. Cf. Layish, 'Family *waqf* and succession', § 4B(2); Pesle, 75.

130 Tanger, 48 f., 49.

131 Schacht's Papers, Waqf File; Schacht comments on an extract from *al-Mudawwana*, xv, 107.

132 Lienhart, 11. See there on devices to circumvent this prohibition of the founder.

transmitting it to her descendants) is no effective solution to the problem of maintenance of the widow or unmarried daughter since without an express stipulation she has no right to live in the founder's house. In Algeria, according to Milliot, even if a man-made dedication in favour of his male descendants only, without stating his intentions as to his daughters, and the exclusion of the latter has been declared valid, it is usual to assume that he wished to preserve needy unmarried daughters from distress, and they have the right to claim maintenance from the beneficiaries; in fact, the French courts used to decide that an excluded female was also entitled to maintenance and clothing if she was poor. In other words, here is an instance of 'maintenance out of the estate' not anchored in religious law but in custom, in the practice of the courts.[133]

In a case of a different kind, a man established a *waqf* in favour of the *ḥazzābīn* (reciters of *al-Ḥizb*) of a certain *zāwiya* but stipulated that the *waqf* should only pass to the *ḥazzābīn* when his brother's children were no longer alive and that the latter should only be entitled if they were *ṭalaba*, students of religion, and recited *al-Ḥizb* at that *zāwiya*. This last stipulation may be an expression of the founder's wish to 'encourage' the beneficiaries to study religion assiduously and thus to enhance the prestige of his family.[134]

The paucity of stipulations in Mālikī *waqfs* may be due to that school's ban on stipulations imposing restrictions on the conduct of beneficiaries and, especially, depriving a woman of her share because of her marriage and restoring it to her only when she becomes a widow.[135] The Ḥanafī school, on the other hand, holds that such stipulations are valid both in respect of the founder's daughter and his wife. In fact, as stated, they are quite common in Ḥanafī family *waqfs*.[136] It should be noted that the prohibition of restrictions on the conduct of beneficiaries is consonant with the trend of modern legislation.[137]

## 5 Summary and Conclusions

The Islamic system of succession is destructive of family property in that it causes its division among a great number of heirs and into uneconomic units.

---

133 Milliot, p. 550 § 645; Charnay, 101; Layish, 'Family *waqf* and succession', § 4A. Cf. Ömer Hilmi Effendi, *The laws of Evqaf*, trans. C. R. Tyser and D. G. Demetriades (second ed.), Nicosia, 1922, p. 43, art. 176.

134 Tanger, 408 (F., 188–9). Cf. Layish, 'Family *waqf* and succession', § 1B (Poor family members) and the source indicated in n. 57.

135 Mercier, 56 and the source indicated there.

136 Al-Khaṣṣāf, 65; Hilmi, p. 37, art. 158; Layish, 'Family *waqf* and succession', § 4B(2).

137 Anderson, '*Waqf* system', 268.

Succession involves a great number of participants; Qur'ānic and agnatic heirs participate simultaneously (not successively) – subject, of course, to the rules of priorities and exclusions – and this increases the fragmentation of the property and the shrinking of the shares of the participants *ad infinitum*.[138] Islamic law does not know the principle of primogeniture.[139] Succession is not limited to direct descendants but includes relatives of different parentelas and different degrees of kinship to the deceased.

Outside elements penetrate into the family through the Qur'ānic group of heirs : spouses, who may belong to different blood groups (exogamous marriages), inherit from each other and transmit parts of their estate to their heirs and so property passes out of the family; Islamic law does not know the institution of community property; there is absolute separation of property between the spouses, and each of them has full legal capacity to dispose of his or her property, including the right to transfer it, in any manner whatsoever (sale, gift and, of course, transmission by way of inheritance), out of the family. Other female heirs – the daughter, mother, aunt, cousin, etc., of the deceased – may likewise, by marriage to a stranger or otherwise, take property out of the family on intestate succession. The structural means to prevent property passing out of the family is the marriage of paternal first cousins. In such a marriage, the husband inherits from the wife in two capacities: as a husband he is a Qur'ānic heir, who, in the absence of children, takes one-half of her estate (by the side of children he takes only one-quarter but there is no danger then of the property passing out of the family), and as an agnatic relative he takes the residue.[140]

The family property is divided after the death of every holder of a right in any of it. The estate is not divided economically and according to types of property; all the heirs, including also strangers, share in all types of property according to their proportionate shares in the estate and thus establish a joint ownership, a kind of family *mushā'*, which leads to constant quarrels among them. The dissolution of joint ownership is also not effected in an economic manner.[141] The strong position of *bayt al-māl* as a residuary heir in the Mālikī system of succession likewise contributes to the fragmentation of the family property. The Qur'ānic heirs are not entitled to the *radd*, *dhawū al-arḥām* do not inherit at all, and the shares of both in the estate pass to *bayt al-māl*.

---

138 Layish, *Women and Islamic law*, p. 302, n. 159.

139 Coulson, *Succession*, 35.

140 Ibid., 97. Cf. G. Baer, *Population and society in the Arab East*, London, 1964, 65 ff. vol. XLVI. part 1.

141 Coulson, *Succession*, 2.

The Muslim will is not an effective means of circumventing the law of succession because the testator is bound by the *ultra vires* doctrine: nothing may be willed to a legal heir and not more than one-third of the estate to a stranger. To obviate bypassing *bayt al-māl*, the Mālikī school prohibits willing more than one-third of an heirless estate. Under these circumstances, it is not surprising that in Mercier's view the Prophet Muhammad did not realize that the law of succession laid down in the Qurʾān by him, though perhaps adapted to natural equality – the reference is probably to the institutionalization of the Qurʾānic group of heirs – was entirely contrary to the interest of the family as an economic unit and did not further the consolidation of the family on its ancestral domain.[142]

Observers all agree that the main purpose of the family *waqf* is circumvention of the Islamic law of succession.[143] On another occasion, the author has dealt extensively with the advantages of the *waqf* as an instrument for circumventing the law of succession, especially in the sense that it involves no quantitative or personal restriction, that is to say, the estate may be altogether withdrawn from the application of the law of succession and dedication may also be made in favour of legal heirs.[144] The Mālikī *waqf* has several advantages, from the point of view of the founder and the beneficiaries, over the Ḥanafī *waqf*. It may be of a temporary character, enabling the owner of the property to revoke it, and the dedicated property may be returned to the heirs, although the nature of the returned property is controversial. Moreover, the testamentary *waqf*, very frequent in the Mālikī school in North Africa, is governed by the law of wills with all the resulting advantages, especially that it only becomes effective upon the death of the founder while during his lifetime he has the actual enjoyment of his property and may even revoke the dedication.

Though most of the population of Algeria belongs to the Mālikī school most of the *waqfs* there were established according to the Ḥanafī doctrine.[145] The same position seems to have prevailed in regions of North Africa under an effective Ottoman administration, which enforced the Ḥanafī doctrine by means of a *sharʿī* judicial system manned by Turkish (Ḥanafī) *qāḍīs*, as was the case in the Mid-Eastern Arab provinces of the Ottoman Empire.[146]

---

142 Mercier, 129–31.

143 Heffening, 1100; Mercier, 25–7, 44; Schacht, *Introduction*, 19; Anderson, '*Waqf* system', 257; Lienhart, 3; Baer, 'The Waqf as a prop'.

144 For more detail see Layish, 'Family *waqf* and succession', Introduction.

145 Sabatery, p. 61, 12 février 1866 – Zeleikha c. Mohammed Cherif; M. Morand, *Études de droit musulman algérien*, Alger, 1910, 258; Milliot, p. 550 § 645.

146 J. Schacht and A. Layish, 'Maḥkama 4. The Arab Lands and Israel in the Modern Period', *EI* (second ed.) vol. 6 (Leiden, 1991), 22–25.

However, aware of the advantages of the Mālikī over the Ḥanafī doctrine from the point of view of women (prohibition of their exclusion from entitlement) or of the founder or the beneficiaries (possibility of revocation or annulment of the *waqf*), persons who belonged to the Ḥanafī school or had established *waqfs* under the Ḥanafī doctrine sought to make use of the differences between the two schools in order to solve various legal problems that could not be solved on the basis of the Ḥanafī doctrine.[147] The reference is especially to women seeking to obtain the annulment of *waqfs* that excluded them from entitlement. Thus, in one case, a woman sued for annulment of the *waqf* on the ground that the *waqfiyya* did not say expressly that the dedication was made in accordance with the Ḥanafī doctrine. In another case, a Mālikī *qāḍī* annulled a *waqf* excluding the founder's wife because the former, contrary to the position of the Mālikī school, had designated himself as the first beneficiary (and because the *ḥiyāza*, the taking possession of the dedicated property, had not taken place). In yet another case, a Mālikī *qāḍī* dismissed an action for annulment of a *waqf* established according to the Ḥanafī doctrine on the formal ground only that a Ḥanafī *qāḍī* who had previously given a decision in the same matter had declared the *waqf* valid.[148]

It should be noted that the French courts in Algeria also took account of the position of the Mālikī school, especially as regards the ban on the exclusion of women and of heirs generally, although they translated their prohibitory directions into terms of French legal principles (such as *droit naturel*).[149] At the same time, they saw to it that a *waqf* was designed clearly in accordance with one of the two doctrines, the Mālikī or the Ḥanafī, they being distinct and opposite legal systems; if a *waqf* did not meet this requirement, the courts would annul it.[150]

On the other hand, there were those who relied on the Ḥanafī school when no relief could be obtained from the Mālikī. Thus, in one case, a Ḥanafī *qāḍī* was asked to authorize the exchange (*muʿāwaḍa*, which is the equivalent of *istibdāl*) of some *waqf* property on the ground that it was in ruins (*inhadama*) and brought no benefit (*manfaʿa*). The Mālikī school does not permit such transactions.[151]

The *waqf* is indeed an efficient means of circumventing the law of succession. The legal documents show that the Qurʾānic heirs, and especially the

147 Sabatery, p. 61, 12 février 1866 – Zeleikha c. Mohammed Cherif; Charnay, 106 ff.

148 Charnay, 101; Zeys, 28–30 and 30–1, respectively.

149 Sabatery, p. 58, 31 mars 1865 – Ben Abd el Ouahed c. Ben Mohammed; p. 61, 12 février 1866 – Zeleikha c. Mohammed Cherif; Schacht, *Introduction*, 98–9.

150 Sabatery, p. 56, 2 mai 1864 – Bent ben Chohra c. ben Chohra.

151 Zeys, 35.

spouse and the ascendants, how high soever, of the founder are, as a rule, excluded from entitlement. Collaterals participate rarely, and not in the first series along with the children, but only when the sons and daughters and their descendants are no longer alive. The daughter shares in the entitlement, sometimes on the basis of equality with the son, in contrast to the *sharʿī* norm, but – and this is the principal deprivation – she may not transmit her share to her descendants; this right is reserved to the son, who transmits it to his sons and daughters; agnatic female descendants in every generation are entitled but do not transmit their entitlement. Some hold that the founder's own daughters and his agnatic female descendants in every generation are excluded also from entitlement during their lifetime, although some Mālikī jurists, such as Sīdī Khalīl, think that a stipulation to this effect invalidates the *waqf*. Schacht has found that the wish to exclude daughters, and especially their descendants, exists particularly in the middle classes.[152]

A *waqf* in favour of an orphaned grandson is likewise a means of circumventing the *sharʿī* law of succession, which, as stated, does not recognize the principle of representation and deprives a grandson of the share his father would have received had he not predeceased the grandfather. The main object of the *waqfs* is concentration of entitlement in agnatic descendants, who are the direct link between the generations. Only the males among them may transmit entitlement to their descendants. Cognatic descendants are relegated to the end of the queue and are often completely excluded, in which case entitlement passes to a *khayrī* purpose immediately after the agnatic beneficiaries are exhausted. In such circumstances, the intention is not so much to exclude cognates as to bypass *bayt al-māl*, which, according to the Mālikī school only, is the residuary heir when no more Qurʾānic or agnatic heirs are alive.

Mercier says:

> les musulmans ont trouvé dans le hobous le moyen d'en atténuer les effets [i.e. the effects of the law of succession]. Le succès général de cette institution n'a pas d'autre cause, son emploi, pas d'autre but. Quiconque a eu entre ses mains un certain nombre de chartes constitutives a pu s'en convaincre. [153]

Indeed, he who has studied *waqfiyyāt* and other documents dealing with *waqfs* requires no further proof of the correctness of Mercier's remarks. Perhaps the

152 Mercier, 56, 64, 131; Pesle, 62, 74–5; J. Schacht, 'Law and justice', in P.M. Holt, A.K.S. Lambton and B. Lewis (ed.), *The Cambridge history of Islam, II*, Cambridge, 1970, 561.

153 Mercier, 131. Cf. Heffening, 1100.

best proof are *waqfs* in favour of part of the legal heirs while other heirs were excluded; claims by Qurʾānic heirs excluded from entitlement for part of the dedicated property by virtue of their status as legal heirs; disputes between the *nāẓir* of a *waqf* and the legal heirs;[154] a claim by legal heirs for the substance of the *waqf* on the ground that the *waqf* was void, that it was defective or illegal; a claim by heirs of the founder for the bare ownership when the intermediate beneficiaries had died and the *waqf* was to go to the poor; and opposition of the heirs to the sale of the *waqf* property by the beneficiaries (this sale was valid under French legislation).[155]

The founder is undoubtedly guided by regard for the welfare of his children and their descendants but, contrary to the law of succession, which is adapted to the structure of the extended family, he wishes to concentrate entitlement within the nuclear family. This is strikingly expressed by the recognition of the principle of representation, foreign to the law of succession, as the basis of the transmission of entitlement from generation to generation. In other words, entitlement passes to descendants according to the branch system and not according to the degree system. Schacht surmised that the exclusion of daughters and especially their descendants, i.e. cognatic relatives of the category of Qurʾānic heirs, 'strengthen[s] the old Arab patriarchal family system';[156] he seems to have been thinking of entitlement based on the pre-Islamic group of agnatic relatives, which does not recognize *dhawū al-farāʾiḍ* and in which cognatic relatives are also fairly strongly represented. But Schacht's assumption should be qualified by noting that the original agnatic system, underlying the 'old Arab patriarchal family', has not been adopted in its entirety and that the application of the principle of representation to the apportionment of entitlement is a material deviation from it. With this reservation, we may indeed say that the *waqf* as a means to circumvent the law of succession, though likewise anchored in the *sharīʿa*, in fact reflects the victory of custom over the *sharīʿa*.[157]

It seems that the founder is more interested in preserving the integrity of the property than of the extended family.[158] We may say that the *waqf* is designed to achieve the twin objects of preserving the integrity of the property and of providing for a selected group of agnatic descendants. The first object is achieved by 'blocking' or freezing ownership and prohibiting any transaction in respect of the property.[159] While the removal of the property from the

---

154 See, e.g., Tanger, 168 (F., p. 87, n. 1); 71 (F., 62–3); and 303 (F., 126), respectively.
155 Mercier, 121, 134–5.
156 Schacht, 'Law and justice', 561. For more detail see Layish, 'Family *waqf* and succession', § 5.
157 Layish, 'Family *waqf* and succession', § 5; Mercier, 27.
158 On this question see Layish, 'Family *waqf* and succession', § 5.
159 Pesle, 73. Cf. Charnay, 109.

economic cycle has many drawbacks in terms of property relationships, its main advantage is that by keeping the property out of reach of creditors it prevents its dissipation by the founder and his heirs, for a *waqf* cannot be pledged or charged. Moreover, the religious sanction attached to the *waqf* provides a certain immunity from highhanded practices of covetous rulers.[160] The second object of the *waqf* is achieved by creating a kind of 'patrimoine familial intangible'[161] for descendants in male line.

In sum, what distinguishes the Mālikī family *waqf* from the Ḥanafī? Substantive features, and especially its temporary character, which enable the founder to revoke it and restore the property to himself or his heirs (although there is disagreement as to the nature of the returned property); frequency of the testamentary *waqf*, which, at least in theory, is subject to the *ultra vires* doctrine of the law of wills; and inability of the founder to stipulate that he shall be the first beneficiary or to appoint himself the first *mutawallī*, although he can circumvent these prohibitions by dedication by means of a will, which only comes into force upon his death.

Both the Mālikī and the Ḥanafī school tend to exclude Qurʾānic heirs from the succession, but a testamentary *waqf* permits doing this legally in respect of only one-third of the estate; both schools tend to concentrate entitlement in children and their descendants; the Mālikī school prohibits the exclusion of the daughters from entitlement and this seems to carry some weight in practice, although there is no unanimity in the matter: some hold that the disinheritance of daughters is the accepted norm.[162]

In both schools, entitlement is transmitted according to the branch system, based on the principle of representation, and not according to the degree system adopted by the law of succession, and in this framework precedence is given to agnates over cognates from considerations of integrity of the family property: only when there are no more of the former do the latter get their turn; in both lines of descent, the paternal and the maternal, the daughter in every generation benefits but may not transmit her share in the entitlement to her descendants lest any rights pass out of the agnatic family. But whereas in North African Mālikī *waqfs* – though not in the documents on which this paper is based – we find that when there are no more descendants of the founder entitlement passes to other parentelas (siblings and their descendants, uncles and their descendants) according to the pattern of the law of succession and that only when there are no more of these, either, does it pass to some

160 Mercier, 44. 131; Heffening, 1100; Schacht, 'Law and justice', 561.
161 Mercier, 131. Cf. Charnay, 99, 105, 109.
162 Cf. Charnay, 109.

permanent *khayrī* purpose, in Palestinian Ḥanafī *waqfs*, when there are no more first-parentela descendants of the founder, entitlement passes direct to a *khayrī* purpose, omitting the agnatic parentelas. In Mālikī *waqfs*, radical deviations from the above pattern have been observed which have no parallel in Ḥanafī *waqfs*.

It seems that a material difference exists between the two schools in the mode of apportionment of entitlement between the sexes and between degrees. Whereas in the Ḥanafī school, apportionment is mainly determined by the '*sharʿī*' norm in the sense that males receive twice as great a share as females, it seems that in the Mālikī school the dominant pattern is equal apportionment between the sexes and *per capita* apportionment, which latter expresses equality between degrees and also between lines of descent; both are contrary to the *sharʿī* law of succession.

Lastly, it seems that stipulations imposing restrictions on the conduct of beneficiaries, especially females, such as a clause making entitlement dependent on a woman's marital status, are less frequent in the Mālikī school. Although this generally operates in favour of the women, it also involves disadvantages, the most striking of which is failure to assure living accommodation and subsistence to spouses and unmarried daughters, contrary to a practice so thoroughly institutionalized in the Ḥanafī *waqf* that it may be regarded as a customary version of 'maintenance out of the estate'.

The Mālikī religious-legal norm, as far as it has a practical effect, operates in diametrically opposed directions. On the one hand, the unique status of *bayt al-māl* as a residuary heir in the Mālikī doctrine increases the inducement to establish a *waqf* in order to circumvent the law of succession; on the other hand, the Mālikī doctrine has a moderating and restraining effect with regard to Qur'ānic heirs and daughters of the founder, for the testamentary *waqf* excludes Qur'ānic heirs to the extent of only one-third of the estate dedicated as a *waqf* while the remaining two-thirds are reserved to the legal heirs. The religious-legal ban on the exclusion of daughters from entitlement finds expression in the assignment of a place to them in the first series of beneficiaries (this is disputed by some) and especially in the equal apportionment of entitlement between the sexes and in the absence of stipulations imposing restrictions on the daughters' conduct.

CHAPTER 16

# The Family *Waqf* and the *Sharʿī* Law of Succession in Modern Times

## 1 Introduction*

This essay aims to clarify who the principal beneficiaries of the waqf are, how entitlement is transmitted to their descendants and apportioned among the beneficiaries, and how the stipulations of the founder affect this process. In this context an attempt will be made to evaluate the principles and motives that guide the founder in determining the order of the beneficiaries and the apportionment of entitlement among them, the ways in which the waqf is used as a means of circumventing the Islamic rules of inheritance, and the social implications of such use as regards the structure of the family and the relative status of its members.

The findings of this study are based on about 60 *waqfiyya*s culled from various sources; most of them are from the *sijill* of the Sharīʿa Court of Jaffa of the Mandatory and Israeli periods, while others date from the end of the Ottoman era. A few *waqfiyya*s were obtained from the Sharīʿa Courts of Jerusalem and Acre, from the *Encyclopedia* of ʿAlī Pasha Mubārak,[1] and from literature on the Maghrib and Africa. Most of the *waqfiyya*s were established in accordance with the rules of the Ḥanafī school. A few conform to the doctrines of the Mālikī, the Shāfiʿī and the Ḥanbalī schools, or to Ibāḍī doctrine. This is, of course, a small and random sample, and the conclusions are therefore tentative. No attempt will be made to evaluate the findings in quantitative terms although they may provide some notion of tendencies. So as to facilitate comparison, this article

* I would like to thank the honorable *qāḍī*s of the *sharīʿa* courts in Israel and the President of the Sharīʿa Court of Appeal, Shaykh Aḥmad Nāṭūr, for providing access to the *sijills* (court records) and for their warm hospitality and help in carrying out this study. This article is part of a comprehensive research project on "Muslim Waqf in Palestine and Israel from the late Ottoman Period until the 1980s," which is supported by a grant from the Israel Science Foundation. My teacher and colleague, the late Professor Gabriel Baer, and my colleague Professor David Powers read an earlier draft of this article and made valuable comments for which I am most grateful.

[Originally published in *Islamic Law and Society*, 4/3 (1997), pp. 352–388.]

1 ʿAlī Pasha Mubārak, *al-Khiṭaṭ al-Tawfīqiyya al-Jadīda* (Cairo, A.H. 1304–05).

 | DOI:10.1163/9789004680920_018

is organized along the same pattern as my studies of the Mālikī family waqf and of bequests as intruments for circumventing the *sharʿī* inheritance rules.[2]

The Islamic inheritance system was formulated during the first century of Islam. It combined two components: male agnatic heirs (*ʿaṣaba*) originating in customary law (although the order of transmission of the estate to them is not totally clear), and heirs nominated by the Qurʿān (*dhawū ʾl-farāʾiḍ* and *dhawū ʾl-arḥām*). In its classical form the Islamic inheritance system was adapted to the extended family consisting of three generations (the doctrine of representation was not recognized), with a clear tendency to improve the status of females and certain cognates.[3]

The "golden rule" of Islamic inheritance law is that first the Qurʾānic heirs take their fixed portions, whereupon the residue goes to the male agnates. The system of priorities is determined by three criteria: class,[4] degree of relationship[5] and strength of blood-tie.[6] Alongside agnatic heirs, a female turns from a Qurʾānic heir taking a fixed portion into an agnatic heir (*taʿṣīb*) taking half the share of a male agnate of the same degree.[7] Only in the absence of heirs within the inner family (Qurʾānic heirs and *ʿaṣaba*) does the right of succession, according to all Sunni schools except the Mālikī, pass to the outer

2 See Layish, "The Mālikī Family *Waqf* according to Wills and *Waqfiyyāt*," *Bulletin of the School of Oriental and African Studies*, vol. 46, no. 1–2 (1983): 1–32; idem, "Bequests as an Instrument for Accommodating Inheritance Rules: Israel as a Case Study," *Islamic Law and Society*, vol. 2. no. 3 (1995): 282–319.

3 The formation of the Islamic inheritance rules is disputed among scholars. Coulson argued, on the basis of a socio-historical approach, that the tribal customary law of the Ḥijāz prior to the emergence of Islam provided the infrastructure of Islamic inheritance law. Powers argues, on the basis of a literary-historical analysis of key Qurʾānic verses and certain prophetic *ḥadīth*s, that classical Islamic inheritance law emerged out of what he refers to as "the proto-Islamic law of inheritance," to wit, an Arabian variety of Near Eastern provincial law. For more details see N.J. Coulson, *Succession in the Muslim Family* (Cambridge, 1971); idem, *A History of Islamic Law* (Edinburgh, 1964); idem, *Conflicts and Tensions in Islamic Jurisprudence* (Chicago, 1969); David S. Powers, *Studies in Qurʾan and* Ḥadīth: *The Formation of the Islamic Law of Inheritance* (Berkeley and Los Angeles, 1986); idem, "The Islamic Inheritance System: A Socio-Historical Approach," in Chibli Mallat and Jane Connors (eds.), *Islamic Family Law* (London, 1990), 11–29 (see there the references to Coulson's works). See also J. Schacht, "Mīrāth," *Encyclopaedia of Islam*, 2nd ed. (Leiden, 1993), VII, 106–11.

4 Parentela signifies all those who trace their descent from one ancestor: the son and his descendants, the father and his descendants, etc.

5 A relative nearer in degree to the deceased excludes a more distant one: a son excludes a grandson, etc.

6 Germane brothers (same father and mother) exclude consanguine brothers (same father but different mothers), and the latter exclude uterine brothers (same mother but different fathers).

7 Coulson, *Succession in the Muslim Family*, 31–34, 41–42, 243.

family (all other relatives). The Mālikī school holds that such relatives never inherit and that in the absence of Qur'ānic and male agnatic heirs the estate passes to the public treasury (*bayt al-māl*) as a residuary heir; it is also not allowed in such a case to make a will that exceeds one-third of the estate. Moreover, the Mālikī school does not recognize the doctrine of *radd* according to which – according to all other schools – the residue of the estate, when the Qur'ānic heirs' prescribed portions do not exhaust the estate and there are no male agnates, is to be returned to all the qualifying Qur'ānic heirs, except the spouse relict, in proportion to their respective rights; the Mālikī school holds that the residue belongs to the public treasury.[8]

The law of bequest (*waṣiyya*) in Sunnī Islam supplements the compulsory inheritance rules. The individual is not free to determine the future of his property after his death by favoring or depriving legal heirs. Under the *ultra vires* doctrine, two restrictions exist with regard to wills, one quantitative and the other personal: no more than one-third (net) of the estate may be bequeathed, and nothing may be bequeathed to a legal heir (the Shīʿī doctrine does not include the personal restriction). A will disregarding these restrictions is valid only with the consent of the legal heirs.[9] Thus, the Muslim will, although various uses have been made of it, is not an effective means of circumventing the rules of inheritance.[10] It is certainly possible to make a testamentary disposition in favor of an orphaned agnatic grandson, who is not considered a legal heir, but in no case may the bequest exceed one-third of the estate. I have encountered in the *sijill* of the *Sharīʿa* courts dispositions for orphaned agnatic grandsons.[11] Moreover, bequests may not be made to a person not yet born at the time the will is drawn up,[12] whereas the main purpose of succession is a continuous connection between generations.

Another way of circumventing the rules of inheritance is by making a gift *inter vivos* (*hiba*). Persons sometimes give all or part of their property to their

---

8 Ibid., 49, 91; Layish, "The Mālikī Family *Waqf*," 1–2.

9 Coulson, *Succession in the Muslim Family*, 1–2; chaps. 13–14.

10 For recent developments in this regard see Layish, "Bequests."

11 Layish, "Bequests," 291–92. Cf. Powers, "The Islamic Inheritance System," 23, 26–27; Baer, "The Waqf as a Prop for the Social System," in this issue, see above, 273; P. Lienhart, "Family Waqf in Zanzibar," a paper submitted to the Conference held at the East African Institute of Social Research, Makerere College, June 1958, 15; Sharīʿa Court of Jaffa, Sijill Qarārāt, vol. 2, p. 391, no. 548, file 32/59 (28 May 1959); ibid., p. 558, no. 564, file 106/62 (18 November 1962); Sharīʿa Court of Bethlehem, Sijill Ḥujaj ʿĀmma, vol. 5, p. 176, no. 36/2 (10 April 1967); ibid., vol. 15, p. 75, no. 30/2 (2 April 1974). See also Sharīʿa Court of Jaffa, Sijill, vol. 27, p. 317, no. 317 (27 Dhū al-Qaʿda 1305).

12 Abū Bakr Aḥmad b. ʿAmr al-Shaybānī al-maʿrūf bi'l-Khaṣṣāf, *Kitāb aḥkām al-awqāf* (n.p. [Cairo], 1904), 40.

children in exchange for a promise that the children will provide for their upkeep until their death.[13] This entails a risk: the donor has no guarantee of appropriate recompense, nor is he protected in the event of breach of promise. At any rate, it seems that this practice is not very widespread in Palestine and Israel; people seem naturally loath to part with their property during their lifetime. Yet another way around the law is to have the heirs renounce (*tanāzul*) their rights upon or after the issue of the succession order by the court, sometimes even after the property has been registered in their name in the Land Register. Renunciation at this stage is made by way of "sale without consideration" to another heir.[14] Renunciation is, however, voluntary (taking into account, of course, pressure from agnates) and, above all, the owner of the estate obviously has no control over the proceedings.

All the remedies referred to above are palliatives. The waqf, on the other hand, has many advantages as a means of circumventing the inheritance rules. The apportionment of entitlement among the beneficiaries is not subject to the *ultra vires* doctrine, and, moreover, the use of the property (such a as residence) may be apportioned economically and in complete units. Entitlement may be vested in persons yet unborn,[15] and, according to the Ḥanafī school, there is nothing to prevent the founder from stipulating that he or she shall enjoy the income of his or her property for life. The corpus of the property remains intact and may not be the subject of any transaction save under circumstances specified by law and in accordance with procedures (i.e., *istibdāl*) requiring the approval of the court; the *waqfiyya* may allocate monies for day-to-day maintenance and for refurbishing and construction; it may also stipulate the form of management (designation of the *mutawallī* etc.). The "ten conditions" allow the founder a great measure of flexibility as to the particulars of entitlement and management; they also enable him to replace one property with another.[16] The waqf thus enables the founder to determine the

13 A. Layish, *Women and Islamic Law in a Non-Muslim State* (Jerusalem New York, 1975), 295–96; idem, "Bequests," 283 and the references to sources indicated in fn. 2; Powers, "The Islamic Inheritance System," 19–22, 24–26; Jaffa, Sijill Qarārāt, vol. 1, p. 38, no. 68, file 29/52 (13 May 1952). Cf. A. Layish, *Marriage, Divorce and Succession in the Druze Family* (Leiden, 1982), 348.

14 Layish, *Women and Islamic Law*, 290–92; Powers, "The Islamic Inheritance System," 25. Cf Layish, *Marriage, Divorce and Succession*, 347–48.

15 al-Khaṣṣāf, 40.

16 The "ten conditions" enable a founder to avail himself of the option of inserting in the *waqfiyya* in the future stipulations such as including or excluding beneficiaries and preferring some of the beneficiaries to others. For details see Muḥammad Qadrī, *Kitāb qānūn al-ʿadl wa'l-inṣāf li'l-qaḍāʾ ʿalā mushkilāt al-awqāf*, 3rd ed. (Cairo, 1320/1902), p. 35, arts. 120ff.; J.N.D. Anderson, "Recent Developments in Sharīʿa Law IX. The Waqf System," *The*

fate of his or her property during his or her lifetime and after his or her death and, especially, to prevent its fragmentation among subsequent generations of beneficiaries.[17]

We must not, however, overlook the shortcomings of the institution. The founder does in fact deprive his or her heirs of full ownership of the property. According to the dominant view in the Ḥanafī school, ownership becomes bare ownership; at any rate, it is given up by the founder and does not pass to the beneficiaries. The property is taken out of the economic cycle, with all the material disadvantages that this implies.[18] Lastly, the severance of the juridical tie between the beneficiaries and the property may lead to neglect of property and to corruption among the *mutawallīs*, who become the principal beneficiaries of the waqf and who may seek to exploit it for personal enrichment before they are replaced.[19] Public criticism of waqf in recent times has led to a series of reforms in Arab countries, culminating in its complete abolition in Egypt. The Egyptian Waqf Law of 1946 (and in its wake the Lebanese Waqf Law of 1947) eliminated some of the advantages of the waqf as a means of circumventing the inheritance rules, seeking to coordinate the two systems. Thus, for example, entitlement was limited to two generations, after which the waqf was again to become ordinary property in all respects. In addition, the *ultra vires* doctrine with respect to one-third of the estate was extended to the waqf.[20] Nevertheless, the prevailing view is – or was until the mid-twentieth century reforms – that the waqf provides an excellent means of circumventing the Muslim rules of inheritance.[21]

---

*Muslim World*, vol. 42 (1952): 264; idem, "The Religious Element in Waqf Endowments," *Journal of the Royal Central Asian Society*, vol. 38 (1951): 292 and the source indicated there.

17 E. Mercier, *Le code du hobous ou ouakf selon la législation musulmane* (Constantine, 1899), 44; Layish, "Bequests," 283 and the references to sources indicated in fn. 1; Powers, "The Islamic Inheritance System," 22, 26; Lienhart, 4.

18 Cf. Lienhart, 3, 17; A. Layish, "Druze Testamentary Waqf," *Studia Islamica*, 71 (1990), 127–54.

19 Cf. Y. Reiter, "The Administration and Supervision of *waqf* Properties in 20th Century Jerusalem," in Faruk Bilici (ed.), *Le waqf dans le monde musulman contemporain* (*xix*e–*xx*e *siècles*). *Fonctions sociales, économiques et politiques*, Institut Français d'Etudes Anatoliennes (Istanbul, 1994), 169–82; E. Ginio, "Violations of Founder's Stipulations in the Sharīʿa Court of Jaffa during the British Mandate," in this issue, see below, 389–415.

20 Anderson, "Waqf System," 268–71.

21 Baer, "The Waqf as a Prop," [pp. 264–97]; Ömer Lūtfi Barkan, "Awqāf in the Ottoman Empire: Fifteenth and Sixteenth Centuries," a paper submitted to International Seminar on Social and Economic Aspects of the Muslim Waqf, Jerusalem, 24–28 June 1979; A. Marcus, "Piety and Profit: The waqf in Eighteenth-Century Aleppo," a paper submitted to the above-mentioned seminar; Ömer Barkan, "Şerʿī Miras Hukuku ve Evlāthk Vakiflar," *Istanbul Universitesi Hukuk Fakültesi Mecmuasi*, vol. 7, no. 1 (Istanbul, 1940), 161–62; Anderson, "Wakf System," 257; Lienhart, 14.

## 2 Beneficiaries

### 2.1 *Founder*[22]

All *waqfiyyas* confirmed by courts of Ḥanafī *qāḍīs* state that the founder makes the dedication "for his own benefit for the duration of his life" (*ʿalā nafsihi muddat ḥayātihi*).[23] Even where the dedication is made for public (*khayrī*) purposes, it is sometimes stipulated that the founder alone shall enjoy the income of the waqf as long as he lives.[24] The juridical basis for this practice is provided by the Ḥanafī jurist Abū Yūsuf.[25] On the other hand, in all waqfs confirmed by *qāḍīs* of other schools (Mālikī, Shāfiʿī, Ḥanbalī and Ibāḍī) the founder, apparently for doctrinal reasons, does not designate himself as the initial beneficiary.[26]

The lenience of the Ḥanafī school allows the founder to enjoy the whole of the income until his or her death as if it were still his or hers. He or she usually appoints himself or herself as *mutawallī* for life and only afterward do entitlement and management pass to others in accordance with the terms of the *waqfiyya*.[27] The only change as result of the dedication is that the founder cannot effect transactions with respect to the property (he is no longer the owner) and is subject to all the restrictions attaching to the management of a waqf.

### 2.2 *The Spouse Relict*[28]

In the cases covered by this study, dedication to a wife[29] as sole beneficiary after the founder, although they have children, is extremely rare, although it

---

22 Cf. Layish, "The Māliki Family *Waqf*," 5–7.

23 Jaffa, Sijill, vol. 64, p. 87 (6 Shaʿbān 1313). Cf. Barkan, "Awqāf in the Ottoman Empire"; N. Caspi, "The Waqf in Jaffa in the Early Nineteenth Century (1800–1840)," unpublished seminar paper, The Hebrew University of Jerusalem, 1972 (Hebrew), 25.

24 Jaffa, Sijill Qarārāt, file 600/78 (5 October 1978).

25 al-Khaṣṣāf, 21; Qadrī, arts. 103–04; Muḥammad Amīn Ibn ʿĀbidīn, *Ḥāshiyat Radd al-muḥtār ʿalā durr al-mukhtār* (2nd impression, Ḥalabī ed. Cairo, 1966), vol. 4, 384.

26 Mercier, 159 (the Mālikī school of law); J.N.D. Anderson, *Islamic Law in Africa*, new impression (London, 1970), 77 (the Shāfiʿī and Ibāḍī schools of law); idem, "Waqfs in East Africa," *Journal of African Law*, vol. 3, no. 3 (1959), 155; Lienhart, 4ff., Uff. (the Shāfiʿī and Ibāḍī schools of law); Ṣalāḥ al-Dīn al-Munajjid, *Kitāb waqf al-Qāḍī ʿUthmān ibn Asʿad ibn al-Munajjā* (Damascus, 1949), 31.

27 A. Layish, "The Muslim *Waqf* in Jerusalem after 1967: Beneficiaries and Management," in Bilici (ed.), *Le waqf dans le monde musulman contemporain*, 158ff.

28 Cf. Layish, "The Mālikī Family *Waqf*," 7–8; idem, "Bequests," 286–88.

29 The wife and husband, as Qurʾānic heirs, take one-eighth and one-quarter, respectively, of the estate along with a child, agnatic grandchild, agnatic great-grandchild, etc., and one-quarter and one-half, respectively, in the absence of such. Neither spouse enjoys the *radd*. See Coulson, *Succession in the Muslim Family*, 41.

is not unusual to make a dedication to a wife and children concurrently.[30] A waqf in favor of the wife as sole beneficiary may be due to the founder's wish to circumvent the *radd* doctrine. In all cases covered by this study the spouses had children, and the waqf therefore seems to have been intended to assure the wife of her *sharʿī* portion of the income, against her deprivation by male agnates.[31] In only one case did a wife dedicate her property to her husband as sole beneficiary after her. In another case a woman dedicated the rent of two houses to her husband and to another woman (her co-wife?) in equal shares. It should be noted that the Egyptian Waqf Law of 1946 (section 27) provides that a woman may deprive her husband of his entitlement if he repudiates her or takes an additional wife.[32]

### 2.3 *Children*[33]

The most characteristic feature of the first series of beneficiaries after the founder is that in 70 percent of the *waqfiyya*s it consists of the children (sons and daughters of the founder or, as they are sometimes called, *ṣulb*, i.e., his or her immediate offspring as distinct from grandchildren[34] It seems that the other *waqfiyya*s do not mention children of the founder because there were none. This preponderance of children as beneficiaries reflects the founder's wish to emphasize the direct link between generations. The children enjoy the income exclusively in 80 percent of the cases and concurrently with other heirs (spouse, grandchildren and other agnates) in 20 percent of the cases.[35] The *waqfiyya* sometimes indicates that the beneficiaries in the first series are not only the existing children of the founder but also those who may be born in the future.[36] According to the Ḥanafī school, it is not necessary to indicate

30 See e.g., Jaffa, Sijill Ḥujaj, vol. 238, p. 36, no. 528 (27 July 1946); ibid., Sijill Qarārāt, file 195/71 (25 April 1971); ibid., file 80/74 (17 April 1975).

31 Jaffa, Sijill Ḥujaj, vol. 238, p. 36, no. 578 (27 July 1946); Jerusalem, Sijill, Muḥammad ʿAbd al-Raḥmān al-ʿAlamī (2 April 1932).

32 Jaffa, Sijill Ḥujaj, vol. 197, p. 17, no. 41 (14 February 1932); ibid., vol. 206, p. 78, no. 257 (10 June 1935); Anderson, "Waqf System," 269. Cf. Barkan, "Awqāf in the Ottoman Empire."

33 Cf. Layish,"The Mālikī Family *Waqf*," 8–10; David S. Powers, "The Maliki Family Endowment: Legal Norms and Social Practices," *International Journal of Middle East Studies*, 25 (1993), 386–87; Layish, "Bequests," 288–90.

34 Omer Hilmi Effendi, *The Laws of Evqaf*, trans. C.R. Tyser and D.G. Demetriades, 2nd ed. (Nicosia, 1922), p. 3, art. 23; Anderson, *Islamic Law in Africa*, 77; Mercier, 100.

35 See, e.g., Jaffa, Sijill Ḥujaj, vol. 208, p. 33, no. 53 (5 February 1936); ibid., Sijill Qarārāt, file 80/74 (17 April 1975); Lienhart, 4; Jerusalem, Sijill, Muḥammad ʿAbd al-Raḥmān al-ʿAlamī (2 April 1932); ibid., file 35/3092–3 ([?] Jumādā II 1265/1848).

36 See, e.g., Jaffa, Sijill Ḥujaj, vol. 206, p. 78, no. 257 (10 June 1935); ibid., Sijill Qarārāt, file 80/74 (17 April 1975). Cf. Caspi, 27.

this expressly but sufficient to say simply "children;" if, however, as is rather frequent, express reference is made to "existing children" or their names are mentioned, children who may be born in the future will have no rights.[37] Mention of the unborn children occurs also in *waqfiyya*s established under the rules of other schools.[38]

The founder usually states expressly that his sons and daughters shall be the beneficiaries. He sometimes uses the term "child" (*walad*) or "children" (*awlād*). *Walad* means both male and female child, but Sunnī legal theory, to reconcile any apparent conflict between the Qurʾān and the *sunna*, interprets it as meaning a male child for the purpose of succession,[39] and this interpretation may possibly have been borrowed in drafting *waqfiyya*s. In some cases the founder states expressly that the waqf is in favor of male children (*awlād dhukūr*),[40] and not daughters.

In only isolated instances are the rights of sons curtailed or completely denied. In one such case a man dedicated his property to three of his sons, stipulating that only when they and their male descendants were extinct would entitlement pass to his other three sons (probably by another woman).[41] In another case a man directed that the beneficiaries of the first series should be his grandsons by his first-born son, who had died, and after them their descendants, and that only when the latter were extinct should entitlement pass to his second son and his descendants. At the same time he appointed the latter as *mutawallī* of the waqf. The reason for the exclusion in this case seems to have been the founder's wish to provide for his orphaned agnatic grandsons, who were probably minors, and perhaps to help them establish a household of their own when they reached adulthood. The practice under discussion has been observed in Israeli Druze community, with the difference that there provision for orphaned minor grandsons is made by means of a will and the estate is distributed among all the sons only after the younger sons have "married out of [funds of] the estate," that is to say, collected their dowers out of the patrimony and established their households with family money.[42] It should also be noted that what seems to be exclusion of a son from entitlement is not

37 Jaffa, Sijill Qarārāt, file 195/71 (25 April 1971); Hilmi, pp. 14–15, art. 151.

38 al-Munajjid, 30; Mercier, 159.

39 Coulson, *Succession in the Muslim Family*, 66 (no reference to Arabic legal sources is provided to support this assertion). See also Mercier, 56.

40 See, e.g., Jaffa, Sijill Ḥujaj, vol. 210, p. 4, no. 152 (14 April 1937); ibid., vol. 222, p. 87, no. 321 (2 June 1942); ibid., vol. 243, p. 22, no. 642 (2 October 1947).

41 Jaffa, Sijill Ḥujaj, vol. 191, p. 57, no. 142 (4 April 1929).

42 Ibid., vol. 173, p. 177, no. 278 (26 September 1921); Layish, *Marriage, Divorce and Succession*, 322–23. See also, Jaffa, Sijill, vol. 77, p. 70 (17 Shawwāl 1317).

necessarily so. The son may have received his share on an earlier occasion, by way of a gift or otherwise, and the *waqfiyya* may be intended to achieve equitable treatment of the other sons.[43]

In some cases the founder directed that his daughter or daughters[44] should be the sole beneficiaries of the first series after him and should transmit their rights to their children, apparently because there were no sons – at any rate, there is no reference to sons in connection with designation of the position of *mutawallī*.[45] In one such case we are told that the property accrued to the founder "by way of inheritance" from his son,[46] that is to say, the son's death paved the way for the daughter as a sole beneficiary. Moreover, in some cases the daughter was appointed *mutawallī* after the founder's death,[47] and this too may be an indication of the absence of sons. Sometimes the founder apportions the income in equal shares between his daughter and a public purpose.[48] In such cases, the daughter would have taken the whole of the estate under the rules of inheritance: half as her Qur'ānic portion and half by virtue of the *radd* doctrine.

### 2.4 *Parents*[49]

We have encountered only one case of dedication to a mother[50] as sole beneficiary of the first series: Two germane sisters dedicated their contiguous properties to their mother, giving her precedence over the children of the founders (and the founders themselves). One of the *waqfiyyas* mentions that

43 Cf. Layish, *Marriage, Divorce and Succession*, 320.

44 Under *sharʿī* rules of inheritance, in the absence of sons a daughter takes half, and two or more daughters take two-thirds of the estate as Qur'ānic heirs. A daughter alongside a son, by virtue of the *taʿṣīb* doctrine, becomes an agnatic heir entitled to half the share of the son. See Coulson, *Succession in the Muslim Family*, 41–42.

45 See, e.g., Jaffa, Sijill, vol. 64, p. 87 (6 Shaʿbān 1313); ibid., Sijill Ḥujaj, vol. 218, p. 87, no. 31 (26 January 1941); ibid., Sijill Qarārāt, file 474/71 (16 September 1971); Caspi, 32; Anderson, *Islamic Law in Africa*, 96.

46 Jaffa, Sijill Qarārāt, vol. 1, p. 38, no. 68, file 29/52 (13 May 1952).

47 Jaffa, Sijill Ḥujaj, vol. 218, p. 87, no. 31 (26 January 1941); ibid., Sijill Qarārāt, file 26/72 (22 January 1972).

48 Jaffa, Sijill Qarārāt, vol. 1, p. 38, no. 68, file 29/52 (13 May 1952).

49 Cf. Layish, "The Mālikī Family *Waqf*," 10; Layish, "Bequests," 290.

50 The mother of the deceased, as a Qur'ānic heir, takes one-sixth of the estate along with a child or agnatic grandchild or with brothers and sisters of the deceased, and one-third in the absence of all these. The father is an heir in a dual capacity: as a Qur'ānic heir he takes one sixth of the estate along with a child, agnatic grandson, agnatic great grandson, etc., and as an agnatic heir he takes the residue in the absence of such heirs; along with a daughter or agnatic granddaughter he may inherit both capacities at the same time. See Coulson, *Succession in the Muslim Family*, 43ff.

the property in question had passed to the founder from her mother, under a contract of sale made four years earlier. We may be dealing here with a gift in return for a promise by the daughters to provide for the mother out of the estate. The other *waqfiyya* states that the mother is entitled to reside in the dedicated building.[51] The sources mention no instance of a waqf in favor of the founder's father. The conclusion arising from these findings is that parents, who are never excluded from succession, are excluded from entitlement to the waqf. Of course, one cannot rule out the possibility that the parents were already dead at the time the waqf was established.

### 2.5 *Grandchildren*[52]

There are instances of a founder wishing to circumvent the inheritance rules so as to apply the principle of representation to the waqf already in the first series of beneficiaries, that is to say, to enable the orphaned grandson to step into his father's shoes.[53] The founder thus assigns the income concurrently to his children and to a grandson through one of his sons who has died. In a case from Zanzibar the validity of an Ibāḍī *waqfiyya* was challenged in court because it put grandsons on a par with sons.[54] It should be noted that first in Egypt and subsequently in other Muslim countries, an attempt has been made to solve the problem of the participation of the orphaned grandson in the succession through the device of the "obligatory bequest," which, however, must not exceed one-third of the estate.[55] In 1996, the "obligatory bequest" was introduced in Israel by means of a "legal circular" (*marsūm qaḍāʾī*) issued by the members of the Sharīʿa Court of Appeal.[56]

There are several instances of agnatic granddaughters[57] enjoying the income of the waqf in the first series concurrently with the children – sons and daughters – of the founder. They were all orphans. In one such case the

51 Jaffa, Sijill Qarārāt, file 598/74 (21 October 1974); ibid., file 724/76 (26 October 1976).

52 Cf. Layish, "The Mālikī Family *Waqf*," 11–12; Layish, "Bequests," 291–92.

53 An agnatic grandson is excluded from succession *de jure* not only by his father, but also by his paternal uncle (a son of the deceased), for the principle of representation is not recognized. In the absence of sons of the deceased, the grandson is a residuary heir of high priority. See Coulson, *Succession in the Muslim Family*, 52–53.

54 Jerusalem, Sijill, file 35/3092–3 ([?] Jumādā II 1265/1848), and Lienhart, 4, respectively. See also Jaffa, Sijill Ḥujaj, vol. 173, p. 177, no. 278 (26 September 1921).

55 Coulson, *Succession in the Muslim Family*, 143ff.

56 *Marsūm qaḍāʾī*, no. 3 of 4 February 1996. This will be discussed in a separate essay.

57 The agnatic granddaughter takes one-sixth of the estate not as a separate portion but as a supplement to the two-thirds allotted to the daughters as a collective portion. Two or more daughters exclude de facto the granddaughter from the succession. In the absence of daughters, two or more granddaughters take two-thirds of the estate. Alongside an

granddaughters took precedence over the son of the deceased.[58] Owing to the existence of a son of the deceased in each of these instances, the granddaughters were not entitled to a share according to the compulsory inheritance rules. In one instance, cognatic granddaughters were included among the beneficiaries of the first series concurrently with a son of the founder. Needless to say, under the Sunnī rules of inheritance a cognatic granddaughter is not considered a legal heir in the presence of male agnates and Qurʾānic heirs.[59]

### 2.6 *Siblings*[60]

There is only one instance in our corpus of a waqf in favor of a brother[61] and two instances of a waqf in favor of a brother's sons as beneficiaries of the first series. In all these cases the reference is to an agnatic brother, and in one case the founder took care to state expressly that the term *akh* meant *ʿaṣabī*, agnatic, i.e., germane or consanguine and not uterine, brother. Significantly, the dedications in favor of brothers were made by women, no doubt in an effort to keep entitlement to revenues and the management of the waqf within the family. In all these cases the founders appear to have had no children.[62]

In a very instructive case from Zanzibar a woman made a dedication to a half-brother and half-sister (the *waqfiyya* does not stipulate agnatic or cognatic), completely excluding a germane brother. The *sharʿī qāḍī*s held that the *waqfiyya* was contrary to the provisions of the *sharīʿa*, that the germane brother must share in the entitlement, that the germane brother excluded the half-brother and half-sister because of his stronger blood-tie with the founder, and that entitlement would pass to them only if the germane brother died without issue. Predictably, the (non-*sharʿī*) Supreme Court decided that the

---

agnatic grandson of the same degree, the granddaughter, by virtue of the *taʿṣīb* doctrine, becomes a residuary heir. See Coulson, *Succession in the Muslim Family*, 54ff.

58 Jerusalem, Sijill, file 35/3092–3 ([?] Jumādā II 1265); Jaffa, Sijill Ḥujaj, vol. 173, p. 177, no. 278 (26 September 1921).

59 Jaffa, Sijill Ḥujaj, vol. 208, p. 33, no. 53 (5 February 1936); Coulson, *Succession in the Muslim Family*, 31ff., 144.

60 Cf. Layish, "The Mālikī Family *Waqf*," 12; idem, "Bequests," 292–94.

61 A uterine brother or sister takes a fixed portion – one-sixth – of the estate as a Qurʾānic heir, and two or more take one-third in equal shares (without distinction of gender). They are excluded by the child, agnatic grandchild, father, agnatic grandfather, agnatic great-grandfather, etc. of the deceased. An agnatic brother is excluded by the son, agnatic grandson and father. A germane brother excludes a consanguine or uterine brother because of the greater strength of the blood-tie. See Coulson, *Succession in the Muslim Family*, 36, 67ff.

62 Jaffa, Sijill Ḥujaj, vol. 224, p. 111, no. 61 (8 February 1943); ibid., vol. 186, p. 9, no. 34 (13 January 1927); Jerusalem, Sijill, Muḥammad ʿAbd al-Rahmān al-ʿAlamī (2 April 1932).

terms of the *waqfiyya* were valid.[63] While the opinion of the *qāḍīs* was in accordance with the strength-of-blood-tie doctrine of the *sharʿī* rules of inheritance, it seems that the institution of waqf was resorted to because it is not bound by this doctrine.

There are three instances of dedication to a germane sister,[64] in one of which the founder was a woman. In each case the sister shared with other beneficiaries of the first series. In one case the founder's intention to assist his needy sister is manifest, and in another the founder stipulated that after the sister's death the entitlement should pass to the sons of the founder's paternal uncle, who were also to act as *mutawallīs*.[65] There is also an instance of a dedication to the daughter of a sister (probably uterine) of the founder as sole beneficiary of the first series.[66] Here, too, the founders appear to have been childless.

### 2.7 *Other Relatives*[67]

In some cases persons dedicated their property to relatives (*aqārib*) as beneficiaries of the first series. In all but one the relatives shared entitlement with others: agnatic relatives of a specified degree of relationship to the founder, liberated slaves (*ʿutaqāʾ*), and the poor of a particular locality. Where the dedication is to indeterminate "relatives," these do not include children or parents.[68] It seems that in all the cases in question the reference is to male agnates of distant parentelas or classes whose chances of inheritance under the compulsory rules are extremely small. Among these relatives, precedence is given to the one nearest to the founder in terms consanguinity and degree, and not in order of succession.[69] In all the cases the founder seems to have had no children; at any rate, none are mentioned in the *waqfiyyas*. The position of

---

63 Lienhart, 13–14.

64 A uterine sister is excluded by a male agnatic descendant or ascendant. A germane or consanguine sister takes a fixed portion as a Qurʾānic heir – one-half of the estate – and two or more such sisters take two-thirds. A sister becomes a residuary heir alongside an agnatic brother of the deceased having the same strength of blood-tie. In the absence of such a brother and in the presence of a daughter or agnatic granddaughter, the sister inherits as "residuary along with another" (*aṣaba maʿa ghayrihā*). Agnatic sisters, like agnatic brothers are excluded by the son, agnatic grandson or father of the deceased. An agnatic (germane or consanguine) sister excludes a uterine sister because of the stronger blood-tie. See Coulson, *Succession in the Muslim Family*, 39, 67ff.

65 Jaffa, Sijill Ḥujaj, vol. 216, p. 57, no. 131 (20 March 1940); ibid., vol. 243, p. 22, no. 642 (2 October 1947); Jerusalem, Sijill, Muḥammad ʿAbd al-Raḥmān al-ʿAlamī (2 April 1932).

66 Jaffa, Sijill Ḥujaj, vol. 229, p. 12, no. 536 (27 August 1944).

67 Cf. Layish, "Bequests," 294.

68 Hilmi, p. 35, art. 153.

69 Ibid., 36, art. 156.

*mutawallī* was conferred on the most competent relative and not, as one might have expected, on a son.[70]

### 2.8 *Poor Family Members*[71]

In some cases property was dedicated to poor family members of different classes and degrees of relation to the founder, as beneficiaries of the first series. A waqf in favor of specific beneficiaries according to specified criteria – in this case, poverty – is considered valid.[72] Some founders make a dedication in favor of poor family members without mentioning their names or degrees of relationship to him or her. In such cases descendants of the founder take precedence over other relatives.[73]

A different criterion for entitlement is higher religious education. Thus, in one case a founder directed that the beneficiaries in the first series after his death should be the male members of his family who study theology at al-Azhar or some other religious school.[74] This case, like dedications to poor family members, involves exclusion of heirs who do not fulfill the special requirements. This last case also involves an attempt to make use of a waqf to enhance the prestige of the family. In an exceptional case from Zanzibar, a Shāfiʿī *qāḍī* dedicated his religious library to his children and their agnatic descendants and appointed the most devout of his sons as *mutawallī* after him. The founder no doubt sought to keep the library intact and to ensure that it would be used by those of his descendants who might wish to continue in his occupation, thereby maintaining the social status of the family.[75]

### 2.9 *Other-Than-Legal Heirs*[76]

In one exceptional case a woman dedicated her property to her *maʿnawī* son, the person who meant as much to her as a son whom "I have brought up myself and have regarded as my child all my life."[77] Since formal adoption is not recognized in Islam, such a "child" receives nothing under the Islamic inheritance

---

70 Jaffa, Sijill Ḥujaj, vol. 205, p. 29, no. 623 (19 November 1934); ibid., vol. 216. p. 57, no. 131 (20 March 1940); Jerusalem, Sijill, Muḥammad ʿAbd al-Raḥmān al-ʿAlamī (2 April 1932); Mubārak, vol. 4, pp. 77–79; ibid., vol. 6, pp. 54–55.

71 Cf. Layish, "The Mālikī Family *Waqf*," 13.

72 Hilmi, p. 33, art. 143; Qadrī, art. 113; Ibn ʿĀbidīn, 451; Jaffa, Sijill Ḥujaj, vol. 216, p. 57. no. 131 (20 March 1940); ibid., vol. 234, p. 57, no. 751 (21 October 1945). Cf. G. Baer, *A History of Landowner ship in Modern Egypt 1800–1950* (London, 1962), 157.

73 See, e.g., Jaffa, Sijill Ḥujaj, vol. 202, p. 23, no. 518 (23 November 1933); Hilmi, p. 44, art. 180.

74 Jaffa, Sijill Qarārāt, file 474/71 (16 September 1971).

75 Lienhart, 11. Cf. Baer, "The Waqf as a Prop," in this issue. See above, 264–97.

76 Cf. Layish, "The Mālikī Family *Waqf*," 13; idem, "Bequests," 294–95.

77 Jaffa, Sijill Ḥujaj, vol. 197, p. 17, no. 41 (14 August 1932).

rules. Similarly, while these rules do not permit a liberated slave (*ʿatīq*, pl. *ʿutaqāʾ*) to inherit from his master, there is no legal bar to his nomination as beneficiary of a waqf.[78] ʿAlī Mubārak mentions many instances of persons dedicating a waqf to liberated slaves, as sole beneficiaries or along with others, in the first series after the founder or in other series.[79]

There are several instances in our corpus of dedications to non-relatives, who, of course, receive nothing under the inheritance rules. In one case ʿAbdallāh Pasha, the *wālī* of Sidon, dedicated his property to his *nāẓir*; in another a woman dedicated her property to a non-relative and appointed him *mutawallī* after her. In both cases the non-relative was permitted to transmit the entitlement to his descendants.[80] In yet another case a woman concurrently nominated a non-relative woman and her own germane sister as beneficiaries of the first series. The non-relative's entitlement was for her lifetime only; after her death it was to pass to the sons of the founder's paternal uncle. The dedication may have been a reward for faithful service.[81]

## 3 Transmission of Entitlement from Beneficiaries to Their Descendants

### 3.1 *Degrees and Branches*[82]

The dominant feature reflected in the *waqfiyyas* in our corpus is the transmission of entitlement from the beneficiaries of the first series to their descendants, generation after generation, in a manner that differs from the *sharʿī* rules of inheritance. According to the inheritance rules, a relative nearer in degree to the deceased excludes a more distant one of the same class,[83] even if the latter does not inherit through him. When all the relatives of a nearer

78 R. Brunschvig, "ʿAbd," *Encyclopaedia of Islam*, 2nd ed. (Leiden, 1960), I, 31; Qadrī, art. 107; Hilmi, p. 38, art. 160. Cf. Barkan, "Awqāf in the Ottoman Empire."

79 See, e.g., Mubārak, vol. 4, pp. 77–79; vol. 5, pp. 18–19, 125–28; vol. 6, p. 65. Cf. Baer, "The Waqf as a Prop," above, 264–97; J. Michael Rogers, "Central Asian *Waqfiyyas* of the Fifteenth and Sixteenth Centuries: The Endowments of Khwāja Aḥrār," a paper submitted to International Seminar on Social and Economic Aspects of the Muslim Waqf, Jerusalem 24–28 June 1979.

80 Acre, Sijill, ʿAbdallāh Pasha, 1267/1850; Jaffa, Sijill Ḥujaj, vol. 218, p. 11, no. 516 (13 November 1940).

81 Jaffa, Sijill Ḥujaj, vol. 243, p. 22, no. 642 (2 October 1947). Cf. Layish, *Women and Islamic Law*, 294.

82 Cf. Layish, "The Mālikī Family *Waqf*," 13–15.

83 Coulson, *Succession in the Muslim Family*, 33–34.

degree to the deceased are extinct, the estate is redistributed among the relatives of the more distant degree, and so on.

I have not encountered a clear, unambiguous instance of entitlement passing from the beneficiaries to their descendants according to the criterion of degree.[84] More precisely, all *waqfiyyas*, without exception, stipulate that entitlement shall pass from beneficiaries to descendants, "degree after degree and generation after generation" (*ṭabaqatan baʿd ṭabaqa wa-naslan baʿd nasl* or *wa-jīlan baʿd jīl*),[85] in such a manner that "the higher generation excludes the lower generation" (*al-ṭabaqa al-ʿulyā taḥjub al-ṭabaqa al-suflā*). Some *waqfiyyas* add that "descendants (*farʿ*) are not entitled so long as their ascendant (*aṣl*) lives."[86] In one case the *waqfiyya* says: "When one of these *ṭabaqāt* becomes extinct the distribution [of the income of the waqf among its members] shall cease and the income shall be distributed among [the members of] the *ṭabaqa* which comes after it."[87] Immediately afterward, however, the founder changes the order of the stipulations: "The descendants take the place of the ascendant, and the ascendant excludes only his own descendants and not the descendants of another" (*wa-yaqūm al-farʿ maqām aṣlihi wa-yaḥjub al-aṣl farʿahu lā farʿ ghayrihi*).[88] Other *waqfiyyas* emphasize that the descendants take only the share of their father and do not share in the portion of others.[89] In other words, the lower generation steps into the shoes of the higher generation; this is the simplest and clearest expression of the doctrine of representation (*tanzīl*) which is, of course, not recognized by the *Sharʿī* rules of inheritance.[90] It should be noted that under the Egyptian Waqf Law of 1946, in a waqf in favor of descendants in successive generations, no ascendant excludes the descendants of another person, and a deceased person's share in

84 The term for "degree" in the *waqfiyyas* is *ṭabaqa*, but *daraja* is also found. See Jaffa, Sijill Ḥujaj, vol. 197, p. 17, no. 41 (14 February 1932); ibid., Sijill Qarārāt, file 80/74 (17 April 1975); Mercier, 160.

85 See, g.g., Sijill Ḥujaj, vol. 191, p. 15, no. 77 (17 February 1929); ibid., vol. 129, p. 145, no. 209 (5 June 1932).

86 Jaffa, Sijill Qarārāt, file 724/76 (26 October 1976); ibid., Sijill Ḥujaj, vol. 226, p. 144, no. 582 (12 October 1943). Cf. Mercier, 64–65.

87 Jerusalem, Sijill, Muḥammad ʿAbd al-Raḥmān al-ʿAlamī (2 April 1932).

88 Ibid.; Jaffa, Sijill Ḥujaj, vol. 191, p. 92, no. 148 (6 April 1929); ibid., vol. 205, p. 71, no. 688 (29 December 1934); ibid., vol. 220, p. 5, no. 394 (21 July 1941); ibid., vol. 231, p. 93, no. 252 (2 April 1945); Acre, Sijill, ʿAli Pasha (22 April 1925). Cf. Caspi, 26; Qadrī, arts. 109–10; Ibn ʿĀbidīn, 471.

89 Jaffa, Sijill Ḥujaj, vol. 224, p. 111 no. 61 (8 February 1943). See also ibid., vol. 210, p. 4, no. 152 (14 April 1937).

90 Coulson, *Succession in the Muslim Family*, 91ff. Cf. Mercier, 55.

the entitlement passes exclusively to his descendants (section 32). This legal reform is contrary to the Ḥanafī doctrine.[91]

Moreover, the founder stipulates that only in the absence of a child of a deceased beneficiary does his entitlement pass to brothers in his *ṭabaqa* and in the absence of brothers to persons not further specified of his degree (*daraja*) and *ṭabaqa* (the terms seem to be synonymous here).[92] Other stipulations are more specific: "To the relative nearest to him [viz., the deceased beneficiary] in degree" (*aqrab ilayhi darajatan*), or "to the nearest" (*al-aqrab fa'l-aqrab*), the reference being to the nearest as regards consanguinity and degree (not order of succession).[93] Some founders stipulate that in the absence of a child or brother of a deceased beneficiary, his portion shall pass "to the ascendant from which the entitlement came" (*aṣl al-ghalla*) to be redistributed among the existing beneficiaries.[94]

The most striking application of the doctrine of representation to the waqf is the orphaned grandson's right to his father's entitlement. The founders regularly stipulate that where a beneficiary who predeceases his ascendant leaves a son, i.e., an orphaned grandson, great-grandson, etc., the latter steps into his shoes: he becomes entitled to that which his ascendant would have been entitled to were he still alive, i.e., if he had survived the grandfather and realized his entitlement. Some founders are careful to specify in the *waqfiyya* that beneficiaries of a higher degree, i.e., uncles of the grandson, who are still alive "have no right or entitlement in the portion of the ascendant" who has died. Thus, the criterion of degree has been superseded by representation.[95] In one case a man dedicated property to his orphaned grandsons as beneficiaries of the first series after him, generation after generation, stipulating that upon the extinction of one *ṭabaqa* of beneficiaries "the [income of the] waqf should be distributed among the living and the dead" and that the share of the deceased beneficiaries should be transferred to their descendants. This is a complete realization of representation.[96]

---

91 Anderson, "Waqf System," 273.

92 Jaffa, Sijill Ḥujaj, vol. 218, p. 24, no. 548 (5 December 1940); ibid., Qarārāt, file 195/71 (25 April 1971); ibid., file 80/74 (17 April 1975); Lienhart, 4. Cf. Qadrī, arts. 111–12.

93 Jaffa, Sijill Ḥujaj, vol. 199, p. 131, no. 65 (20 February 1933); ibid., vol. 231, p. 93, no. 252 (2 April 1945); Hilmi, p. 36, art. 156; Ibn ʿĀbidīn, 474.

94 See, e.g., Jaffa, Sijill Ḥujaj, vol. 202, p. 23, no. 518 (23 November 1933); ibid., vol. 224, p. 111, no. 61 (8 February 1943); ibid., p. 144, no. 582 (12 October 1943). Cf. Anderson, "Waqf System," 274.

95 See, e.g., Jaffa, Sijill Qarārāt, file 195/71 (25 April 1971), file 80/74 (17 April 1975); Acre, Sijill, Muḥammad Khalīl al-Shaʿbī ([?] Rajab 1116/1704); Mercier, 65, 160.

96 Jaffa, Sijill Ḥujaj, vol. 173, p. 177, no. 278 (26 September 1921). Cf. Hilmi, pp. 33–34, art. 145. Cf. Ginio, "Violations of Founder's Stipulations" below, 389–415.

Concern for the orphaned grandson is one of the most salient features of the Muslim waqf, which makes it possible to correct what some may regard as a wrong in the inheritance rules, which, as stated, do not recognize representation. We have noted above that Egypt and other countries sought to correct that "wrong" by means of the "obligatory bequest." But redress of this type was not complete because a will is limited to one-third of the estate, which may be less than the share of the deceased beneficiary. On the other hand, the Egyptian Waqf Law of 1946 provides that the founder, unconstrained by the one-third limit, may transfer to his orphaned grandsons such part of the entitlement as is equal to the part they would have inherited through their parent had he been alive at the time of the founder's death (section 29).[97]

The stipulations of the founder concerning the transfer of entitlement from beneficiaries to descendants in future generations seem to contradict one another materially. On the one hand, the founder stipulates, that entitlement shall pass from generation to generation in such manner that the higher generation shall exclude the lower, meaning that the order of beneficiaries is binding and that so long as a member of a higher generation is alive no member of a lower generation may become a beneficiary; this system conforms with the *sharʿī* inheritance rules. On the other hand, the founder stipulates that entitlement shall pass linearly from the ascendant to his own descendants only, according to the doctrine of representation. In other cases the order of stipulations is reversed: it is first stipulated that entitlement should pass from the ascendant to the descendants, and second that the higher *ṭabaqa* should exclude the lower.[98] Qadrī maintains that the second stipulation is considered to cancel the first.[99] Reiter, however, has found that in Jerusalem during the British Mandate, the *qāḍīs* regarded the two stipulations as complementary rather than contradictory: the doctrine of representation was applied until the grandchild's father's generation expired, whereupon entitlement was redistributed among the beneficiaries of the subsequent generation, including orphans from a lower generation who represented their deceased father. This quasi-representation of orphans was, however, limited to one generation.[100]

97 Anderson, "Waqf System," 269–70.

98 See, e.g., Jaffa, Sijill Ḥujaj, vol. 202, p. 23, no. 518 (23 November 1933); ibid., vol. 218, p. 11, no. 516 (13 November 1940); ibid., p. 54, no. 574, (24 December 1940); ibid., vol. 229, p. 12, no. 563 (27 August 1944).

99 Qadrī, art. 102.

100 Y. Reiter, "Family *Waqf* Entitlements in British Palestine (1917–1948)," *Islamic Law and Society*, vol. 2, no. 2 (1995), 182ff. and the references there to Islamic legal literature.

### 3.2 *Entitlement and Transmission Thereof to Descendants*[101]

The *waqfiyyas* distinguish clearly between entitlement (*istiḥqāq*) in the different *ṭabaqāt* and the right to transmit it to descendants. The two main criteria guiding the founder in this matter are the gender and line of descent (patrilineal or matrilineal) of the beneficiary. These criteria are of great importance with respect to keeping entitlement within the family of the founder.

As noted above, the founder is free to determine already in the first series of beneficiaries which of his descendants and relatives of different degrees shall be entitled to the income of the waqf. These are usually sons and daughters (or males and females of whatever degree of relationship to the founder), without any discrimination as to the right to entitlement itself (though not necessarily regarding its apportionment, as will be seen below). But the beneficiaries of the first series sometimes consist entirely of sons or, rarely – probably because the founder had no sons – only of daughters. As to the second and subsequent series of beneficiaries, which usually consist of descendants of beneficiaries of the first series and their descendants to the last generations, the rule is that both males and females are entitled to the income of the waqf in any particular series but that only males may transmit entitlement to their descendants (males and females). Thus, *waqfiyyas* often stipulate that, after the founder, entitlement shall pass to his sons and daughters, but the entitlement of daughters lasts for life only, and that when a daughter dies "with or without progeny (*ʿaqb*), her portion shall pass to *aṣl al-ghalla*" to be redistributed among the existing beneficiaries; or it is stipulated that "her portion shall not pass to her children and children's children but to her brothers who are actual beneficiaries."[102]

The *waqfiyya* of Muḥammad ʿAbd al-Raḥmān al-ʿAlamī of Jerusalem is clear on this point. It says, *inter alia:*

> When any daughter of the [first] *ṭabaqa* dies, her portion shall revert to *aṣl al-ṭabaqa* – the beneficiaries – and nothing shall pass from her to her children ... and when a daughter of the son dies, her entitlement shall pass to her agnatic (*ʿaṣabī*) brother or to the son of her agnatic brother, and nothing of her entitlement shall pass to her children or children's children, if she has any, nor to her sisters or the children of her sisters,

101 Cf. Layish, "The Mālikī Family *Waqf*," 16–21; Reiter, "Family *Waqf* Entitlements," 177–79.

102 See, e.g., Jaffa, Sijill Qarārāt, file 195/71 (25 April 1971); Acre, Sijill, Fāṭima Nūr al-Dīn al-Yashrūṭī al-Shādhilī (12 December 1936). Cf. Powers, "The Maliki Family Endowment," 400; idem, "A Court Case from Fourteenth-Century North Africa," *Journal of the American Oriental Society*, vol. 110, no. 2 (1990), 235.

> if she has any such relatives; and if she has no nephew, the entitlement shall pass to *aṣl al-ghalla* … and in order to avoid a [mistaken] interpretation (*ta'wīl*), the founder declares that the children of females have no right [to transmit entitlement] in the waqf … since the children of the females are denied (*maḥrūmūn*) [this right] and take nothing of the waqf [in order to transmit it].[103]

Where the *waqfiyya* says that entitlement passes from *ṭabaqa* to *ṭabaqa* "to the children of the males, not to the children of the females" (*awlād al-ẓuhūr dūn awlād al-buṭūn*) or "not to the children of daughters of sons,"[104] this should be interpreted in a restricted sense: females have no right to transmit entitlement to their descendants, but they have the right, in each *ṭabaqa*, to enjoy the income of the waqf for life. This interpretation is borne out by stipulations of the founder regarding the apportionment of entitlement between the sexes in each *ṭabaqa*.[105]

Sometimes, however, a female of a second series is deprived not only of the right to transmit entitlement but of entitlement itself. Thus, in one case the original version of the *waqfiyya* stipulates that entitlement shall pass "only to the children of the males, not to the children of the females, in any *ṭabaqa* …"; when one of the male children dies leaving a child, male or female, "his portion shall pass to his male and *female* children in equal shares" (emphasis added). In an amended version of this *waqfiyya*, drawn up a year later, the word "female" at the end of the stipulation has been deleted, suggesting that the founder intended to deprive the females of the second series of entitlement as well.[106]

The inability of the female to transmit entitlement is not limited to the children of the founder but extends also to other relatives, of varying degrees and classes, such as grandchildren, great-grandchildren, and siblings.[107] As a rule, an agnatic female in all *ṭabaqāt* is entitled to the income of the waqf but debarred from transmitting entitlement. Entitlement passes from generation to generation, lineally within branches, through agnatic descendants only or,

---

103 Jerusalem, Sijill, Muḥammad ʿAbd al-Raḥmān al-ʿAlamī (2 April 1932).

104 Jaffa, Sijill Ḥujaj, vol. 191, p. 15, no. 77 (17 February 1929); A. Layish, "*Waqf*s and Ṣūfī Monasteries in the Ottoman Policy of Colonization: Sulṭān Selīm I's *waqf* of 1516 in favour of Dayr al-Asad," *Bulletin of the School of Oriental and African Studies*, vol. 50, pt. 1 (1987), p. 83, lines 32–33. Cf. Ibn ʿĀbidīn, 467.

105 See, e.g., Jaffa, Sijill Ḥujaj, vol. 231, p. 93, no. 252 (2 April 1945); Sijill Qarārāt, file 474/71 (16 September 1971); ibid., file 80/74 (17 April 1975).

106 Jaffa, Sijill Ḥujaj, vol. 220, p. 5, no. 394 (21 July 1941); ibid., vol. 222, p. 87, no. 321 (2 June 1942). See also ibid., vol. 210, p. 4, no. 152 (14 April 1937).

107 Jaffa, Sijill Ḥujaj, vol. 173, p. 177, no. 278 (2 September 1921); ibid., vol. 216, p. 57, no. 131 (20 March 1940); ibid., vol. 224, p. 111, no. 61 (8 February 1943).

in a stereotyped formula, "their descendants (*dhuriyyatuhum wa-nasluhum wa-ʿaqbuhum*), the children of the males to the exclusion of the children of the females (*awlād al-dhukūr dūn awlād al-ināth*)."[108]

Support for denying entitlement to females where there are male beneficiaries may be found in the Ḥanafī doctrine in views attributed to Abū Ḥanīfa and Abū Yūsuf, although al-Khaṣṣāf does not admit it.[109] In any event, the exclusion of females is a matter of custom rather than law. The phenomenon has also been observed in places where the Ḥanafī school does not prevail, such as Zanzibar where the Shāfiʿī and Ibāḍī schools prevail, and North Africa, a stronghold of the Mālikī school, which – according to Mercier – prohibits the exclusion of cognatic descendants.[110]

As a rule the founders expressly stipulate in the *waqfiyya* that "the children of the females are absolutely excluded from entitlement so long as one of the children of the sons is alive." Only when there are no agnatic descendants does entitlement pass to the cognatic descendants.[111] The founder usually stipulates that when his sons and their descendants are all dead entitlement shall pass to his daughters (*banāt ṣulb al-wāqif*) and their descendants.[112] In one case a man dedicated the income of his property to three of his sons and their descendants, after them to three other sons and their descendants, and only after these to his daughters and their descendants.[113] Some founders stipulate that when the descendants of the son are all dead entitlement shall pass to granddaughters and their descendants, "generation after generation [of descendants of the daughters]" (*baṭnan baʿd baṭn*).[114]

The exclusion of cognatic descendants manifests itself in various ways. In one case a germane brother and sister established a waqf stipulating that they would be entitled to the income of their respective properties for life and that after their death entitlement should pass to needy descendants of the

108 See, e.g., Jaffa, Sijill Ḥujaj, vol. 197, p. 145, no. 209 (5 June 1932); ibid., vol. 205, p. 71, no. 688 (29 December 1934); ibid., vol. 237, p. 109, no. 479 (1 July 1946); ibid., Sijill Qarārāt, file 80/74 (April 1975).

109 al-Khaṣṣāf maintains that agnatic and cognatic descendants, without distinction, are entitled to the proceeds of the waqf. See al-Khaṣṣāf, 28.

110 Mercier, 159, 161. It should be mentioned, however, that *walad* is defined by Mālik as a man's sons and daughters and the son's male children, and *ʿaqib* is defined by Mālikī jurists as agnatic descendants. See Powers, "The Maliki Family Endowment," 399–400.

111 See, e.g., Jaffa, Sijill Ḥujaj, vol. 191, p. 15, no. 77 (17 February 1929); ibid., vol. 197, p. 145, no. 209 (5 June 1932); ibid., vol. 218, p. 54, no. 574 (24 December 1940); ibid., p. 87, no. 31 (26 January 1941); Mercier, 64.

112 Mercier, 160.

113 Jaffa, Sijill Ḥujaj, vol. 191, p. 57, no. 142 (4 April 1929).

114 See, e.g., ibid., vol. 208, p. 33, no. 53 (5 February 1936).

brother. Only when there were no such descendants would entitlement pass "to the nearest of the needy relatives of the two founders." The position of the *mutawallī* was likewise assigned to the brother and his descendants. Similarly, a man established a waqf in favor of his needy sons and their descendants who were continuing their studies at al-Azhar; only in the absence of such descendants was entitlement to pass to daughters' children who continued their religious studies.[115]

The founder usually specifies that the mode of transmission of entitlement to the following generation shall be "according to the stipulations and order" (*ḥasb al-shurūṭ wa'l-tartīb*) laid down in respect of agnatic descendants, i.e., from the ascendant to his descendants, whilst applying the doctrine of representation: the children of a daughter or other female relative take their share in the entitlement, and orphaned cognatic grandchildren take the share to which their mother would have been entitled had she been alive at the time of the founder's death.[116] But there are exceptional modes of transmitting entitlement, viz., the system of the *ṭabaqāt*. A *waqfiyya* in favor of al-Zāwiya al-Shādhiliyya al-Yashruṭiyya in Tarshīḥā (in western Galilee), for example, stipulates that upon extinction of the males and their descendants the residue of the entitlement shall, after satisfaction of the requirements of the *zāwiya*, pass to the children of the founder's daughters and their descendants, "*ṭabaqa* after *ṭabaqa*, the nearer *ṭabaqa* [i.e., nearer to the founder] taking precedence."[117]

The distinction between entitlement and the right to transmit it to descendants exists in the case of cognatic relatives as well. Entitlement is shared by males and females in each generation,[118] but, the right of transmission is granted only to males. In other words, the cognatic female, like the agnatic, benefits but does not transmit her entitlement to her children.[119] There may be two reasons for this: (1) an economic one – if females were allowed to transmit entitlement to their children, the number of beneficiaries would double from

115 Ibid., vol. 234, p. 57, no. 751 (21 October 1945), and Jaffa, Sijill Qarārāt, file 474/71 (16 September 1971), respectively.

116 See, e.g., Jaffa, Sijill Ḥujaj, vol. 210, p. 4, no. 152 (14 April 1937); ibid., vol. 218, p. 24, no. 548 (5 December 1940); ibid., p. 87, no. 31 (26 January 1941); Jaffa, Sijill Qarārāt, vol. 1, p. 38, file 29/52 (13 May 1952).

117 Acre, Sijill, file 1280/30 (28 July 1930).

118 See, e.g., Jaffa, Sijill Ḥujaj, vol. 197, p. 145, no. 209 (5 June 1932); ibid., vol. 218, p. 87, no. 31 (26 January 1941); ibid., Sijill Qarārāt, file 474/71 (16 September 1971).

119 See, e.g., Jaffa, Sijill Ḥujaj, vol. 191, p. 57, no. 142 (4 April 1929); ibid., vol. 202, p. 23, no. 518 (23 November 1933); ibid., vol. 226, p. 144, no. 582 (12 October 1943); ibid., vol. 229, p. 12, no. 563 (27 August 1944).

generation to generation; (2) every male, even a cognatic one, may be regarded as the head of a new agnatic family.

Daughters are also excluded from the position of *mutawallī* but unlike the case of the transmission of entitlement, a fixed order is not always strictly adhered to in all the *ṭabaqāt*. Thus, ʿAlī Pasha, on establishing a waqf in Acre, stipulated that the position of *mutawallī* after him should be entrusted to the most capable (*li'l-arshad fa'l-arshad*) of his sons, and after his sons to the most capable of his daughters, and after the death of all his sons and daughters to the most capable of the descendants of his sons and daughters in each generation.[120]

In rare cases, persons dedicated their property to their daughters as beneficiaries of the first series and to their daughters' descendants,[121] no doubt because, as noted, the founder had no sons; this assumption is corroborated by the fact that no sons or agnatic descendants are mentioned as beneficiaries or *mutawallīs*. In Zanzibar, on the other hand, we find instances of precedence being given to cognatic over agnatic relatives; a founder sometimes stipulates that entitlement shall pass to "cognatic descendants only." The special status of cognates also finds expression in an inclination of founders to apportion entitlement among all their descendants – without distinguishing between cognates and agnates – which leads to the doubling of the number of beneficiaries in each generation.[122]

Another variant is represented by a case that also occurred in Zanzibar. A man dedicated his property to his sons and daughters and to the descendants of his sons, stipulating that upon their extinction entitlement should pass concurrently to his siblings, to their descendants of both sexes, and to his cognatic descendants ("the children of the females"), and, upon the extinction of all these, to other cognatic relatives.[123] Placing the agnatic siblings of the founder on a par with his cognatic descendants is a compromise between the patrilineal and the matrilineal system. It is interesting to note that such compromises also exist in the application of the compulsory inheritance rules. In one of the tribes of the Gold Coast the court allots two-thirds of the estate to the cognatic heirs under customary law and one-third to the sons. Similarly, cognates are the principal heirs in several places in Kenya and Tanganyika.[124]

120 Acre, Sijill, ʿAlī Pasha (22 April 1925). Cf. Caspi, 41.

121 See, e.g., Jaffa, Sijill, vol. 64, p. 87 (6 Shaʿbān 1313).

122 Lienhart, 15–17.

123 Ibid., 5. Cf. Layish, "The Mālikī Family Waqf," 19–21.

124 Anderson, *Islamic Law in Africa*, 112, 145, 276.

## 4 Mode of Apportionment of Entitlement

After the founder has determined the beneficiaries of the first series and the mode of transmission of entitlement from generation to generation, it remains for him to determine the mode of apportionment of entitlement in each series.

### 4.1 *Apportionment "according to the* Sharʿī *Fractional Shares of the Estate"*[125]

The commonest method of apportionment is the one often described as "according to the *sharʿī* fractional shares" (*ḥasb al-farīḍa al-sharʿiyya*), which means that a male receives twice the portion of a female (*al-dhakar mithl ḥaẓẓ al-unthayayn*).[126] This apportionment between the sexes reflects the *sharʿī taʿṣīb* doctrine, which is applied in its original meaning to the founder's children and agnatic descendants, the principal beneficiaries of the income of the waqf.[127] The founder also stipulates that if one of his male children dies without issue his portion shall pass to *aṣl al-ghalla* and be apportioned among the existing beneficiaries "according to the *sharʿī* fractional shares."[128]

Sometimes the founder specifies that entitlement shall be apportioned among his immediate offspring in the "*sharʿī*" manner and after them pass to their agnatic descendants, without indicating how it is to be apportioned among the latter;[129] the intention here seems to be that it shall be apportioned on the same basis in all generations. Uncertainty as to the mode of apportionment exists where the founder makes no stipulation in this regard. Among the Ibāḍīs in Zanzibar, the vague statement that the waqf is in favor of the beneficiaries and their descendants means that a male takes twice the portion of a female, whereas among the Shāfiʿīs it is customary for entitlement to be apportioned equally between the sexes.[130]

There are also instances of the founder insisting on "*sharʿī*" apportionment of entitlement in the case of orphaned agnatic granddaughters, where there are grandsons of the same degree of relationship to him, apparently in

---

125 Cf. Layish, "The Mālikī Family *Waqf*," 21–23; idem, "Bequests," 296.

126 See, e.g., Jaffa, Sijill, vol. 77, p. 70 (17 Shawwāl 1317); ibid., Sijill Qarārāt, file 80/74 (17 April 1975). Cf. Caspi, 25.

127 See, e.g., Jaffa, Sijill Ḥujaj, vol. 231, p. 93, no. 252 (2 April 1945); ibid., Sijill Qarārāt, file 80/74 (17 April 1975); Acre, Sijill, ʿAlī Pasha (22 April 1925).

128 Jaffa, Sijill Ḥujaj, vol. 237, p. 109, no. 479 (1 July 1946); ibid., vol. 238, p. 36. no. 578 (27 July 1946).

129 Ibid., vol. 226, p. 144, no. 582 (12 October 1943).

130 Anderson, *Islamic Law in Africa*, 77.

accordance with the accepted *taʿṣīb* doctrine.[131] In all such cases, however, the founder had a son or sons, and, as we know, an orphaned agnatic grandson does not inherit along with sons of the deceased because of non-recognition of the doctrine of representation. In other words, the substantial deviation from the *sharʿī* inheritance rules in the fundamental matter of participation in entitlement did not prevent the adoption of the *sharʿī* norm in regard to the apportionment of entitlement among the beneficiaries.

There are isolated instances of the application of the *sharʿī* norm in relation to the founder's wife. In one case the founder apportioned entitlement as follows: one-eighth to his wife (her Qurʾānic portion in the presence of children), and the remainder to the children "in accordance with the *sharʿī* fractional shares."[132] Where the wife is the sole beneficiary of the first series – which, as stated, is very uncommon[133] – she takes the entire estate, not only her *sharʿī* share. Since the wife (like the husband) does not enjoy the *radd*, the waqf mechanism makes it possible to circumvent that doctrine.

There are indications that the *sharʿī* norm inspires the apportionment of entitlement in cases in which the daughter is the sole beneficiary after the founder. In several such cases, the founder assigned to his daughter half of the property, which is her *sharʿī* portion as a Qurʾānic heir, assigning the other half to public purposes.[134] Apportionment between males and females of the same degree in accordance with the *sharʿī* norm (i.e., the *taʿṣīb* doctrine) is practiced with regard to other agnatic relatives as well. This practice has also been encountered in Zanzibar.[135]

The "*sharʿī*" apportionment is also fairly common among members of the outer family (i.e., relatives other than the Qurʾānic heirs and male agnates).[136] In one case a woman established a waqf in favor of her son and his descendants, stipulating that if he died leaving children of both sexes these should be entitled to half the income of the waqf and that the other half should go to granddaughters through her deceased daughter, provided that the apportionment between her son and her orphaned cognatic granddaughters or between the heirs of the three is "in accordance with the *sharʿī* fractional shares: a male

---

131 See, e.g., Jaffa, Sijill Ḥujaj, vol. 173, p. 177, no. 278 (26 September 1921); ibid., vol. 218, p. 24, no. 548 (5 December 1940); Jerusalem, Sijill, file 35/3092–3 ([?] Jumādā II 1265/1848).

132 Jaffa, Sijill Ḥujaj, vol. 238, p. 36, no. 578 (27 July 1946). See also ibid., Sijill Qarārāt, file 80/74 (17 April 1975).

133 See, e.g., Jaffa, Sijill Qarārāt, file 195/71 (25 April 1971).

134 Jaffa, Sijill, vol. 64, p. 87 (6 Shaʿbān 1313); Jaffa, Sijill Qarārāt, vol. 1, p. 38, no. 68, file 29/52 (13 March 1952).

135 Jerusalem, Sijill, Muḥammad ʿAbd al-Raḥmān al-ʿAlamī (2 April 1932); Lienhart, 4.

136 See, e.g., Jaffa, Sijill, vol. 64, p. 87 (6 Shaʿbān 1313); ibid., vol. 218, p. 87, no. 31 (26 January 1941).

receives twice as much as a female."[137] In the presence of a son those granddaughters would have taken nothing according to the *sharʿī* inheritance rules; it therefore seems that the *sharʿī* norm referred to is the proportion between the share of the male and that of the female. The founder probably intended to give her granddaughters their deceased mother's share by virtue of the doctrine of representation. The son's portion was indeed twice that of each of the granddaughters, but since they were not of the same degree of relationship to the founder, the apportionment was not *sharʿī* in the strict sense. Lastly, similar to the apportionment among agnatic descendants according to the "*sharʿī*" norm, the founder directed that when entitlement passed to the cognatic descendants it would be apportioned in the same manner.[138]

The *sharʿī* apportionment of entitlement between the sexes within the outer family has to some extent a basis in the *sharʿī* inheritance rules,[139] but it is doubtful whether the founders were aware of this. They apportioned entitlement according to the "*sharʿī*" norm even where the beneficiaries were children of a non-relative having no connection whatsoever with the founder.[140] In cases in which apportionment "according to the *sharʿī* fractional shares" conforms with those rules the founder's intention seems to have been to reinforce the *sharʿī* rights of "weak" heirs, such as the wife, and in this way to ensure their non-exclusion from the income of the estate during their lifetime, before entitlement passes to the agnatic descendants.[141] Where there is no such conformity, however, the assignment of a double portion to the male seems to have become an independent norm accepted in day-to-day practice. In fact, it is not alien to customary law.

### 4.2 *Per Capita Apportionment*[142]

Another method of apportioning entitlement is based on the equality of all existing beneficiaries "according to the number of heads" (*ʿalā ʿadad al-ruʾūs*), occasionally with no distinction between the sexes. This method is especially widespread in North Africa. The beneficiaries may be of the same *ṭabaqa*, such

137 Jaffa, Sijill Ḥujaj, vol. 208, p. 33, no. 53 (5 February 1936).

138 See, e.g., Jaffa, Sijill Ḥujaj, vol. 218, p. 54, no. 574 (24 December 1940); ibid., vol. 229, p. 12, no. 563 (27 August 1944).

139 Coulson, *Succession in the Muslim Family*, 94, 100ff.

140 Jaffa, Sijill Ḥujaj, vol. 218, p. 11, no. 516 (13 November 1940); Coulson, *Succession in the Muslim Family*, 93, 100–01.

141 Cf. Lienhart, 3.

142 Cf. Layish, "The Mālikī Family *Waqf*," 23–25; Powers, "The Maliki Family Endowment," 399; Reiter, "Family *Waqf* Entitlements," 179–81; Layish, "Bequests," 296–300.

as children of the founder, including those yet to be born.[143] Equality under these circumstances means that, contrary to the usual *sharʿī* norm, males and females of the same degree of relationship to the founder participate in entitlement in equal shares.

Beneficiaries also may be of different degrees of relationship to the founder. The commonest pattern is that of children and grandchildren. In such cases, a person establishing a waqf in favor of his children stipulates that if one of them dies leaving male children "each of them shall be entitled to a portion together with the other existing male beneficiaries according to the number of heads, whether they belong to the same or to different *ṭabaqāt*." Transmission of entitlement from generation to generation is by branches, the descendants in each branch joining the group of beneficiaries through the ascendant whom they represent. Once they have joined, the *ṭabaqa* to which they belong and the share of the ascendant are immaterial; beneficiaries of all degrees and all branches take equal shares.[144]

The founder may stipulate that if one of his children dies without issue his portion shall go in equal shares to all his immediate offspring, male and female, who are beneficiaries.[145] There are instances of equal apportionment between women of different degrees of relationship to the founder, though not between females and males of the same degree.[146]

Per capita apportionment is recognized by the Ḥanafī and Ḥanbalī schools as part of the *sharʿī* system of succession in the outer family. Moreover, the egalitarian apportionment between the sexes has a basis in prophetic *ḥadīth*.[147] When the founder does not expressly direct apportionment "according to the *sharʿī* fractional shares," he is presumed to intend apportionment between his sons and daughters in equal shares.[148] A female founder tends to adopt an egalitarian attitude toward the sexes.[149]

Two methods, "*sharʿī*" and per capita apportionment, may apply in the *waqfiyya* simultaneously, each one designed for a particular group of beneficiaries.

143 See, e.g., Jaffa, Sijill Ḥujaj, vol. 206, p. 78, no. 257 (10 June 1935); ibid., Sijill Qarārāt, file 598/74 (21 October 1974).

144 Mercier, 65, 159–61. Cf. Kenneth L. Brown, "Notes on the Significance of Waqf in a Tunisian *Zāwiya*" a paper submitted to International Seminar on Social and Economic Aspects of the Muslim Waqf, Jerusalem, 24–28 June 1979.

145 Jaffa, Sijill Ḥujaj, vol. 205, p. 71, no. 688 (29 December 1934); ibid., vol. 220, p. 5, no. 394 (21 July 1941); Mercier, 160.

146 Jaffa, Sijill Qarārāt, file 26/72 (22 January 1972); Jerusalem, Sijill, Muḥammad ʿAbd al-Raḥmān al-ʿAlamī (2 April 1932).

147 Coulson, *Succession in the Muslim Family*, 93–94, 100–01; Qadrī, art. 108; Ibn ʿĀbidīn, 444.

148 Hilmi, pp. 34–35, art. 149; al-Khaṣṣāf, 27.

149 Qadrī, art. 108; Ibn ʿĀbidīn, 471. Cf. Marcus, "Piety and Profit."

In one case, for example, the founder stipulated that his children and their descendants and, when these became extinct, his brothers and their descendants, should be entitled on the basis of males taking twice the share of females, while more distant relatives should participate on the basis of complete equality between the sexes. In another case, the founder directed that entitlement should be apportioned between her daughters and their descendants "according to the *sharʿī* fractional shares" and, upon their extinction, should pass to her germane brothers and their descendants on the basis of equality between males and females.[150] There seems to have been no consistent method of apportionment between the different groups of beneficiaries; everything seems to have depended on the wishes of the founder.

### 4.3 *Economic Apportionment*[151]

In several *waqfiyyas* the economic considerations which guided the founder in apportioning entitlement are apparent. Apportionment was, as far as possible, in complete units and by types of property. The founder seems to have intended thereby to prevent disputes among beneficiaries. Had he not done so, entitlement to all the different types of property would have been shared by all the beneficiaries according to a certain proportion. A kind of "*mushāʿ*" of entitlement would have been created, a system which is a constant source of disputes among heirs. The thirteenth-century Ḥanbalī *qāḍī*, ʿUthmān b. Asʿad al-Munajjā, who was by all reports a sensible man and an experienced householder, assigned to each of his three sons and three daughters the enjoyment of certain property, including a residential building, a bathhouse (*ḥammām*), land, a *ḥākūra*, a garden, a *bustān*, plantations and trees, in complete units as far as possible, sometimes to some of them jointly; to the children to be born in the future he left five-sixths of the income of other immovable property.[152] A wealthy Jerusalemite apportioned his seven houses and other property as follows: the family residence to his children and their agnatic descendants; one house to the children of needy male family members who would study at al-Azhar or some other religious school; a new block of flats to his six sons, each receiving a particular flat to live in or let; a dwelling unit consisting of two rooms and facilities to three of his daughters; a unit of similar size to a fourth daughter; a smaller dwelling unit to his two wives; and a cave with a right of passage to a fifth daughter. Each of these family members had a separate order

150 al-Munajjid, 30–31; Jaffa, Sijill Ḥujaj, vol. 199, p. 131, no. 65 (20 February 1933). See also Jerusalem, Sijill, Muḥammad ʿAbd al-Raḥmān al-ʿAlamī (2 April 1932).

151 Cf. Layish, "Bequests," 298–99.

152 al-Munajjid, 27–30.

of subsequent beneficiaries fixed for him or her and, no less important, was appointed as the *mutawallī* for the property the entitlement of which was transmitted to him or to her. The appointment of the beneficiary as *mutawallī* of the property whose income he enjoys creates a personal bond between him and the property, which may contribute to a more economic and orderly management of the waqf property. The independent management certainly also tends to reduce friction between the beneficiaries. Apportionment of the estate by types of property and in units as complete as possible – out of economic considerations and with the intent to reduce friction among family members to a minimum – is common in the Druze community, where this mode of apportionment is made by means of a free will not subject to the *ultra vires* doctrine.[153]

## 5 Stipulations of The Founder[154]

### 5.1 *Ensuring Maintenance of Females*[155]

Alongside the exclusion of females from entitlement, there exists a tendency to ensure them a right of residence and a subsistence allowance. In one case, for example, the founder directed that only "male, not female, descendants" should be entitled, but made this conditional upon the daughters of the males having a right of residence in the house.[156] In another case, in which the founder excluded his two wives from entitlement, he assigned the right to live in the family residence to them and their children, and only after their death, to the beneficiaries. Moreover, he stipulated that if the place proved too small, an additional dwelling should be rented for them, and the beneficiaries should pay the rent out of the income of the waqf.[157] In yet another case, in which the founder dedicated a certain house to his daughters for them to live in, he stipulated that any *mutawallī* who charged them rent should be dismissed.[158]

The dedication of a house or some living quarters with utilities to the wife and daughters, as their share in the entitlement, is fairly common. At the same time, it should be noted that women have a right of residence only if the founder has expressly so stipulated in the *waqfiyya*; if he has not, they

153 Jaffa, Sijill Qarārāt, file 474/71 (16 September 1971); Layish, *Marriage, Divorce and Succession*, 321.

154 Cf. Layish, "The Māliki Family *Waqf*," 25–27; idem, "The Muslim *Waqf* in Jerusalem," 157–58.

155 Cf. Layish, "Bequests," 300–01.

156 Jaffa, Sijill Ḥujaj, vol. 186, p. 9, no. 34 (13 January 1927). Cf. Caspi, 38.

157 Jaffa, Sijill Ḥujaj, vol. 191, p. 57, no. 142 (4 April 1929).

158 Ibid., vol. 218, p. 24, no. 548 (5 December 1940).

are entitled only to the income of the waqf, provided, of course, that they are beneficiaries.[159]

Besides the right of residence, a woman totally excluded from entitlement is sometimes granted a fixed monetary allocation of varying amounts, which may be larger than her share in the entitlement would have been were she a beneficiary. In one case, for example, the founder allotted his wife 40 Palestinian Pounds (£P) per year for life; after her death the sum was to be apportioned among the beneficiaries. Moreover, he appointed her *mutawallī* of the waqf immediately after himself.[160] In another case, in which the daughters of the founder and the females in all generations in both the patrilineal and the matrilineal line of descent were excluded, the founder stipulated that the *mutawallī* should allot each of the daughters 3 £P per year as long as she lived. Similarly, an agnatic (probably orphaned) granddaughter was allotted 500 piasters a year in addition to her share in the entitlement, along with the son and daughters of the founder. In another case the founder directed that his son's widow be paid an allowance "so long as she has no husband."[161]

The assurance of housing and a subsistence allowance is not only compensation for exclusion from entitlement, but also a customary form of "maintenance out of the estate," which is not known in Islamic law. According to the latter, a widow is entitled to maintenance only during the waiting period (*ʿidda*), which is four months and ten days. Theoretically, she has a share in the estate of her husband (or her father) from which she may derive maintenance, but since she is often deprived of this right[162] the waqf mechanism makes it possible to ensure her maintenance on a voluntary personal basis until her death. The same phenomenon has been observed among the Druze, except that the mechanism there is not the waqf but a will not bound by the *ultra vires* doctrine. It is customary to bequeath a right of residence and the enjoyment of certain property to one's wife and daughter while limiting these rights to their lifetime; after the wife's or daughter's death the property passes to the testator's children.[163]

---

159 Hilmi, p. 43, art. 176.

160 Jaffa, Sijill Ḥujaj, vol. 226, p. 144, no. 582 (12 October 1943). See also ibid., vol. 191, p. 15, no. 77 (17 February 1929); ibid., vol. 231, p. 93, no. 252 (2 April 1945). Cf. Caspi, 38.

161 Jaffa, Sijill Ḥujaj, vol. 173, p. 177, no. 278 (26 September 1921). See also ibid., vol. 229, p. 12, no. 563 (27 August 1944).

162 Layish, *Women and Islamic Law*, 290ff.

163 Layish, *Marriage, Divorce and Succession*, 338ff.

### 5.2 *Restrictions on Females' Freedom of Marriage*[164]

As noted, a founder frequently stipulates that a female may enjoy income from the waqf during her lifetime but may not transmit this right to her heirs – at least not so long as agnatic descendants of the founder exist; she "enjoys but does not transmit."[165] After her death her right passes to the agnatic descendants and, only when none are left, to the cognatic ones.[166]

It is common to make the entitlement to housing and income of females of different degrees of relationship to the founder conditional on their being unmarried. The stereotypical formula is: "A female has a right of residence so long as she is single (*ʿāziba*), unmarried or husbandless (*khāliya min al-azwāj*); if she marries, her right lapses and reverts to the beneficiaries, but if she is repudiated or her husband dies, her portion is restored to her," and so on.[167] Some make the daughter's right to housing conditional upon her being needy (*muḥtāja*) or upon her existing accommodation being too small, adding that if she is no longer needy (*istaghnat*) or marries, "her portion shall pass to *ghallat al-waqf*" for reapportionment among the existing beneficiaries; if she becomes needy again or is repudiated, her portion shall be restored to her, and so on, "until Allāh inherits the earth and its inhabitants. …"[168]

In the case of the founder's wife, entitlement is likewise conditional upon her not remarrying when she becomes a widow. In one case, a founder assigned one-quarter of the income of the waqf to his two wives on condition that they were "husbandless … and if one of them remarries, her portion shall lapse and pass to the other, and if she [the other] also remarries, or dies, her portion shall pass to *aṣl al-ghalla* [for reapportionment]." In another case the founder assigned one-quarter of the entitlement to the wife of an agnate, stipulating that if she married someone else (after the death of that relative) her right in the waqf would terminate and pass to her children by her present husband, and, in any case, if she has children by her second husband, they shall have no

164 Cf. Layish, "Bequests," 301–02.

165 See, e.g., Jaffa, Sijill Ḥujaj, vol. 218, p. 154, no. 574 (24 December 1940); ibid., vol. 229, p. 12, no. 563 (27 August 1944); ibid., vol. 237, p. 109, no. 479 (1 July 1946).

166 For more details see above, [380f.]. Cf. Caspi, 38.

167 Jaffa, Sijill Ḥujaj, vol. 197, p. 17, no. 41 (14 February 1932); ibid., vol. 231, p. 93, no. 252 (2 April 1945); Acre, Sijill, file 1280/30 (28 July 1930). Cf. Barkan, "Awqāf in Ottoman Empire"; Caspi, 26.

168 Jerusalem, Sijill, file 35/3092–3 (Jumādā II 1265/1848); Jaffa, Sijill Ḥujaj, vol. 197, p. 17 no. 41 (14 February 1932); ibid., vol. 202, p. 23, no. 518 (23 November 1933). Regarding the quotation cf. Qurʾān, 19:40.

right in this waqf and her share in the entitlement shall pass to her children by her present husband.[169]

This last case illustrates why the entitlement of a female is made conditional upon her being unmarried. It is feared that she might transfer her right to her descendants by another husband, i.e., outside the circle of the founder's agnates.[170] This fear of fragmentation of entitlement by marriage is also the reason for the frequent stipulation in *waqfiyya*s that entitlement shall pass from generation to generation "to agnatic and not to cognatic descendants," although agnatic females in each generation are granted entitlement for life. Sometimes the founder appoints his wife *mutawallī* after him, stipulating, for the same reason, that the appointment shall be valid "so long as she is husbandless." In one case the founder allotted the *nāẓir* of the waqf a fixed monthly salary, "which shall pass to his descendants" probably with the office of *nāẓir*, provided that these descendants are by the *nāẓir*'s (present) wife who is an agnatic granddaughter of the founder. In other words, if he repudiates his present wife and takes another, he will not be able to transmit the office of *nāẓir* to his descendants by the second wife.[171] Since the *mutawallī* plays a central role as manager of the waqf property and distributor of the income in accordance with the stipulations of the founder, it is regarded as highly important that the office should not pass out of the family by marriage.

The schools of law are divided on the question of making the entitlement of a female dependent upon her marital status. The Ḥanafī school permits dedicating a dwelling to a daughter, granddaughter, great-granddaughter, etc., and to a wife, on the condition that she does not marry or remarry and does not leave the house; if she does, she loses her right in the dwelling and cannot regain it without the express consent of the founder.[172] The Mālikī school, on the other hand, forbids stipulating that a daughter loses her right in the waqf upon her marriage.[173] The Egyptian Waqf Law of 1946 and, in its wake, the Lebanese Waqf Law of 1947, provide that stipulations of the founder which impair the freedom of marriage or residence of the beneficiaries or disqualify them for entitlement because of monetary debts are invalid. This innovation is based on the views of neo-Ḥanbalī reformers.[174]

---

169 Jerusalem, Sijill, Muḥammad ʿAbd al-Raḥhmān al-ʿAlamī (2 April 1932). Cf. Baer, *History of Landownership*, 166.

170 Cf. Ginio, "Violations of Founders' Stipulations" below, 394ff.

171 Mubārak, vol. 6, pp. 54–55.

172 al-Khaṣṣāf, 65; Hilmi, p. 37, art. 158; Qadrī, art. 106; Ibn ʿĀbidīn, 452.

173 Mercier, 56 and the source indiated there.

174 Anderson, "Waqf System," 268.

## 6 Summary and Conclusions[175]

The mechanism of the waqf makes it possible to circumvent the inheritance rules, tailored to the extended family (the higher generation excludes the lower generation; non-recognition of representation), and to concentrate entitlement on descendants of the founder as beneficiaries of the first series.[176] This is especially manifested by a weakening of the position – sometimes even the complete exclusion – of the Qurʾānic heirs, such as parents, grandparents, cognatic sisters and brothers of the founder, none of whom belong to the nuclear family (the spouses and their unmarried children).[177] According to the inheritance rules, the Qurʾānic heirs take their prescribed portions concurrently with the agnatic heirs, subject, of course, to the rules of priorities and exclusion. Unlike the system of succession, waqf entitlement – with only a few exceptions – is not apportioned concurrently among beneficiaries of different degrees of relationship to the founder but passes from one generation or series to the next successively, and this too furthers the concentration of entitlement on beneficiaries belonging to the nuclear family.

The transmission of entitlement from beneficiaries of the first series to their descendants proceeds by branches, i.e., while applying the doctrine of representation, which also fits the nuclear family, in contrast to the *sharʿī* system of degrees, which is adapted to the extended family. The most striking phenomenon in this context is the right of an orphaned grandson, great-grandson, etc., to take the share that his ascendant would have taken if he had been alive at the time of the grandfather's death. The waqf mechanism makes it possible to bypass what the reformers regard as a social wrong anchored in the *sharīʿa* which modern legislation has tried to amend by means of the "obligatory bequest."

The conversion of property into a waqf makes it possible to keep it intact and prevents its division among heirs, which is indeed the founder's principal aim.[178] On the other hand, this mechanism does not further the preservation and cohesion of the extended family. On the contrary, it contributes substantially to its fragmentation, not only because of the exclusion of some Qurʾānic

175 Cf. Layish, "The Mālikī Family *Waqf*," 27–32; idem, "The Muslim *Waqf* in Jerusalem," 150–55; idem, "Bequests," 310–19.

176 Cf. Powers, "The Maliki Family Endowment," 386.

177 Cf. Marcus, "Piety and Profit"; Qadrī, art. 17.

178 Cf. Barkan, "Şerʿī Miras Hukuku ve Evlāthk Vakiflar," 167–68; Baer, *History of Landowner ship*, 164ff.; Barkan, "Awqāf in the Ottoman Empire"; Marcus, "Piety and Profit"; Powers, "The Maliki Family Endowment," 384, 394, 401; Rogers; Brown; Layish, "The Mālikī Family Waqf," 30ff.; idem, "Bequests," 312–13.

heirs and the application of the principle of representation, but also and mainly because of the severance of the juridical connection between the beneficiaries and the property of the founder (they are not its owners) and because of their exclusion from actual possession of the property (they do not even have the right of residence unless the founder has expressly so stipulated)[179] and from the use thereof (the *mutawallī* leases out residential buildings and land for short periods [*ījāra wāḥida*] or long periods [*ījāratayn*] in accordance with economic considerations). The connection between the beneficiaries and the estate of the founder is limited to seasonal monetary enjoyment of waqf income, which diminishes from generation to generation as the number of beneficiaries increases (the number of beneficiaries may of course decrease, but this is less likely in modern times); there is of course nothing here to encourage the cohesion of the family. It has already been observed that in the absence of property the extended family tends to disintegrate into its nuclear units.[180] From the point of view of the beneficiaries, endowed property is almost tantamount to absence of property. The fact that the founder appoints as *mutawallī* the most capable of his sons or male agnatic descendants is no effective remedy since the rest of the family members – the beneficiaries – are deprived of direct contact with the endowed property.

Although the inheritance rules cause fragmentation of the family property, it contributes less to the disintegration of the extended family than the waqf because the legal heirs are not deprived of ownership and use of the property and there is a tendency, at least in the first generation after the deceased, to preserve the estate as collective property ("joint family"); the land registers contain many instances of family *mushāʿ* in accordance with succession rights. In the long run, of course, structural pressures and inconsistencies between the distribution of ownership rights and the contribution of the different family members to the joint labor force do lead to disintegration of the extended family.[181] Rosenfeld's observation is based on rural society, but there is no reason to dispute the importance of property for the cohesion of family also in urban society.

Regarding entitlement to the income of waqf, as in many other domains, a patrilineal society accords definite precedence to agnates over cognates in all series of beneficiaries after the founder. The cognates are disadvantaged

179 Qadrī, arts. 79–81; Ibn ʿĀbidīn, 374–75.

180 G. Baer, *Population and Society in the Arab East* (London, 1964), 58ff. and the sources indicated there; H. Rosenfeld, "Change, Barriers to Change, and Contradictions in the Arab Village Family," *American Anthropologist*, vol. 70, no. 4(1968): 734ff.

181 Rosenfeld, 737ff., 742ff.

not only as to the order of beneficiaries in the first series but also as to the transmission of entitlement to descendants. This right is reserved for male agnatic descendants; cognates only get their turn when no agnates are left.[182] This marks a victory of custom over the *sharīʿa*, which sought to improve the position of some cognatic heirs. It seems paradoxical that this victory is made possible by the waqf institution, which is firmly anchored in the *sharīʿa*. Only in places where the matrilineal system prevails do cognates take precedence, likewise by virtue of custom.

As a rule females in both the patrilineal and the matrilineal line of descent enjoy the income of the waqf but do not transmit their right to their descendants so long as there are sons or agnatic male descendants of the founder. The principal reason for this is fear lest the family property or the enjoyment of its income be fragmented as a result of exogamous marriages. For the same reason the conduct and activities of females are subject to restrictions, especially as regards marriage. At the same time, females deprived of entitlement are often assured the right of residence and maintenance until death or marriage. This is a non-institutionalized customary manifestation of the doctrine of "maintenance out of the estate," which is not known in the *sharʿī* system of inheritance.

The *sharʿī* norm is invoked routinely in *waqfiyyas*. The stipulation for the transmission of entitlement to the next generation according to degrees is mitigated by a subsequent stipulation for transmission by branches. The apportionment of entitlement "in accordance with the *sharʿī* fractional shares" completely ignores the *sharʿī* priorities in and exclusion of inheritance, which are the very core of the inheritance rules. While granting the male double the portion of the female indeed reflects a *sharʿī* norm, it also validates a customary conception with respect to females. Paradoxically, what would seem by modern reformers to be a progressive norm, viz., the apportionment of entitlement on a per capita basis regardless of degree and gender, in fact stems from the *sharīʿa*.

Extensive use of the waqf mechanism to circumvent the inheritance rules so as to deprive Qurʾānic heirs has prompted modern legislatures to restrict the founder's freedom of action by coordinating the law of waqf and the rules of inheritance and wills, as is evident from reforms in the two systems. Thus, for example, the freedom of establishing waqf in favor of a legal heir or a stranger has been limited to one-third of the property, similar to the quantitative limitation on the Muslim will. Every dedication beyond that limit necessitates the assignment, to the descendants, parents and spouse of the founder, of

182 Cf. Powers, "The Maliki Family Endowment," 385.

entitlements proportional to their share in the compulsory inheritance rules, similar to the device of the "obligatory bequest" in modern legislation.

The patterns of family waqf as an instrument for circumventing the Islamic inheritance rules, with minor variations, reflect differences in school of law and local social conditions. These patterns prevail all over the Muslim world: from North Africa in the west, through the Middle East, to India in the east.[183] The same patterns have also been observed in family waqfs established by Christians and Jews in *sharīʿa* courts, and they seem to have been inspired by the same motivation.[184] Moreover, the founder's stipulations are phrased in almost identical terms, although these stipulations are not a matter of Islamic law but rather of social practice. There is good reason to believe that most of the founders have no solid legal training. Hence, one may conclude that the *qāḍī*, or the scribe, or notary, or some other religious functionary[185] well acquainted with legal formularies (*shurūṭ* literature), shaped the founder's stipulations reflecting his specific requirements in uniform terms. It is likely that the beneficiaries of the first series after the founder are named by the founder himself. However, the possibility that the rest of the ingredients, such as the transmission and mode of entitlement, reflect the social philosophy of the *qāḍī*s and scribes who formulated the *waqfiyya*, rather than that of the founder, cannot be ruled out.[186]

---

183 See, e.g., Gregory C. Kozlowski, *Muslim Endowments and Society in British India* (Cambridge U.P., 1985), 40, 53–60.

184 R. Shaham, "Christian and Jewish *Waqf* in Palestine during the Late Ottoman Period," *Bulletin of the School of Oriental and African Studies*, vol. 54, pt. 3 (1991), 460–72.

185 Cf. Powers, "The Maliki Family Endowment," 396.

186 Shaykh Aḥmad Nāṭūr, President of the Israeli Sharīʿa Court of Appeal, explains that the study of legal formularies is part of the curriculum of legal studies at al-Azhar. Although most Israeli *qāḍī*s are graduates of Israeli universities, they nevertheless are acquainted with these formularies. Nāṭūr maintains that the *qāḍī*s do not interfere with the substance of the *waqfiyya*s, their only task being to formulate the founder's stipulations in the required legal formularies. He further maintains that founders are fully aware of the practical consequences of these formularies, namely, the preservation of the endowed property and the entitlement under the control of the founder's male agnatic descendants (personal communication, October 9, 1996). A former *qāḍī* in East Jerusalem who serves as a notary confirmed to Reiter that before formulating the *waqfiyya* he is concerned to elicit the founder's stipulations regarding vital issues such as the identity of the initial series of beneficiaries after the founder and the ultimate beneficiary of the waqf, that is, a charitable institution. This *qāḍī* adds that he does not explain to a lay founder all the subtleties pertaining to the transmission and mode of entitlement of waqf revenues. The founder who is familiar with these details has a greater measure of control over the substantial stipulations of the *waqfiyya* (personal communication from Reiter, 10 October 1996).

CHAPTER 17

# Bequests as an Instrument for Accommodating Inheritance Rules: Israel as a Case Study

*In memoriam Shaykh Muḥammad Ḥubayshī*

## 1 Introduction: The Family Waqf and the Bequest as Alternative Instruments for Circumventing the Inheritance Rules*

Although religious motives, such as charity, are important for the founding of family *waqf*s (pious endowments), it seems that the founder (*wāqif*) of a *waqf* is guided primarily by practical considerations – most prominently his desire to maintain the patrimony intact within the control of his male agnates.[11]

* I would like to thank the honorable Qāḍī of the Sharīʿa Court of Jaffa (recently promoted to President of the Sharīʿa Court of Appeal), Shaykh Aḥmad Nāṭūr; the late Qāḍī of the Sharīʿa Courts of Acre and Haifa, Shaykh Muḥammad Ḥubayshī; the former Qāḍīs of the Sharīʿa Court in West Jerusalem, Shaykh Zakī Amīn Mudlij and Shaykh Fārūq al-Zuʿbī (both of whom were recently promoted to the Sharīʿa Court of Appeal); and the Director of the Sharīʿa Courts in Israel, Dr. Ṣubḥī Abū Ghūsh, all of whom made it possible for me to examine the *sijill*s of the Sharīʿa Courts. Thanks are due also to the Ministry of Justice for allowing free access to the land registers, and to my students, Hillel Cohen and Eliyahu Stern, for their technical assistance. This article is part of a comprehensive research project on "The Muslim *Waqf* in Palestine and Israel from the Late Ottoman Period until the 1980s," which is supported by the Israel Science Foundation, which is administered by the Israel Academy of Sciences and Humanities. My colleague, David Powers, read an earlier draft of this article and made valuable comments for which I am most grateful. Any remaining shortcomings are my own.

[Originally published in *Islamic Law and Society*, 2/3 (1995), pp. 282–319.]

1 *Islamic Law and Society* 4/3 (1997), pp. 352–388; idem, "The Mālikī Family Waqf according to Wills and Waqfiyyāt," *Bulletin of the School of Oriental and African Studies*, XLVI, pt. 1 (1983), 27ff.; David S. Powers, "The Islamic Inheritance System: A Socio-Historical Approach," in *Islamic Family Law*, ed. Chibli Mallat and Jane Connors (London: Graham and Trotman, 1990), 22, 26, 28; idem, "A Court Case from Fourteenth-Century North Africa," *Journal of the American Oriental Society*, 110.2 (1990), 241–42; idem, "*Fatwā*s as Sources for Legal and Social History: A Dispute over Endowment Revenues from Fourteenth-Century Fez," *Al-Qanṭara*, xi, 2 (1990), 333; idem, "The Mālikī Family Endowment: Legal Norms and Social Practices," *International Journal of Middle Eastern Studies*, 25 (1993), 379, 384ff., 394, 401; Yitzhak Reiter,

 | DOI:10.1163/9789004680920_019

The family *waqf* serves as the instrument *par exellence* for circumventing the inheritance rules (*ʿilm al-farāʾiḍ*). It is not the only means to this end, however. Other means are wills, renunciation of succession rights, gifts *inter vivos*, and sale without consideration.[2] Invoking a distinction made by social scientists between inheritance laws and inheritance systems, Powers regards all these tools as components of a larger and flexible Islamic inheritance system. Most of these tools were created by the *fuqahāʾ* as practical solutions for circumventing the inheritance rules and adapting them to social and economic pressures.[3] Renunciation and gifts are less common – the former because the required consent of the legal heirs cannot always be obtained, the latter because people tend not to relinquish their estates while alive.[4] By contrast, in its Ḥanafī version, the *waqf* institution enables the founder to be the sole beneficiary during his lifetime and to appoint himself first administrator of the *waqf*.[5]

The *ultra vires* doctrine pertaining to bequests in Sunnī Islam, that is, the prohibition of bequeathing more than one-third of the estate and/or in favor of a legal heir (unless the consent of the legal heirs thereto is obtained after

"Family *Waqf* Entitlements in British Palestine (1917–1948)," *Islamic Law and Society*, 2:2 (1995), 192–93; Abraham Marcus, "Real Property and Society in the Premodern Middle East," in *Property, Social Structure and Law in the Modern Middle East*, ed. Ann Elizabeth Mayer (Albany: SUNY Press, 1985), 122.

2 See Layish, "The Family *Waqf* and Succession," 19–30; Powers, "The Islamic Inheritance System," 20–26; idem, "Orientalism and Legal History: The Attack on Muslim Family Endowments in Algeria and India," *Comparative Studies in Society and History*, vol. 31, no. 3 (1989), 567–68; Abraham Marcus, *The Middle East on the Eve of Modernity. Aleppo in the Eighteenth Century* (New York: Columbia University Press, 1989), 210; Ron Shaham, "The Muslim Family in Egypt 1900–1955: Continuity and Change. A Study based on the *Sijill* (Records) of the *Sharīʿa* Courts" [in Hebrew], Ph.D. thesis, The Hebrew University (Jerusalem, 1991), 261ff., 276, 283; Brinkley Morris Messick, III, "Transactions in Ibb: Economy and Society in a Yemeni Highland Town," Ph.D. thesis, Princeton University (Princeton, 1978), 377–79; Maya Shatzmiller, "Women and Property Rights in al-Andalus and the Maghrib: Social Patterns and Legal Discourse," *Islamic Law and Society*, 2:3, (1995), 243–44, 249–50. For *nadhr*, see J.N.D. [Norman] Anderson, *Islamic Law in Africa* (London: Frank Cass, new impression, 1970), 17 nt. 2, 30, 370; Isaac Hollander, "Parashat '*ʿarṣa*' mi-Ḥujaryriyya," in *Le-Rosh Yosef, Meḥqarim be-ḥokhmat Yisrael* (Texts and Studies in Judaism), ed. Yosef Tobi (Jerusalem: Afikim, 1995), 535 and fn. 69.

3 Powers, "The Islamic Inheritance System," 19–20, 23, 27 nt. 66; idem, "The Mālikī Family Endowment," 379, 402; idem, "A Court Case from Fourteenth-Century North Africa," 243; idem, "Orientalism and Legal History," 571.

4 Aharon Layish, *Women and Islamic Law in a Non-Muslim State* (Jerusalem and New York: Israel Universities Press and John Wiley, 1975), 290–92, 295–96.

5 Layish, "The Family *Waqf* and Succession," 22.

the testator's death),[6] is probably the main reason the family *waqf* has flourished. Had full freedom of testation existed in Islam, there would have been no incentive to develop the family *waqf*. This notion is supported by the fact that the Druze, who enjoy complete freedom of testation under both religious and statutory law, do not resort to the family *waqf* to circumvent the law of inheritance in either its Ḥanafī or Israeli version.[7]

The foundation of family *waqf*s has almost ceased in Israel, as reflected in data on new *waqf*s established during the British Mandate and since the emergence of the State of Israel. The *sijill* of the Sharīʿa Court of Jaffa mentions thirty-eight new *waqf*s – all but two of them family *waqf*s – created during the British Mandate period. The *sijill* of the same court during the years 1950–1981, when its jurisdiction extended also to Lod and Ramla, mentions only two new *waqf*s. Even taking the different population sizes into account, one must conclude that new *waqf*s are rarely founded nowadays. The same applies to most other courts: The Israeli *sijill* of Acre (until 1991) mentions only six new *waqf*s – all of them for charitable purposes. The Israeli *sijill*s of Haifa (1977–1983), Nazareth (until 1970), and Ṭayyiba (until 1968) do not mention a single new *waqf* of any kind. Although it is true that since 1967 the *waqf* institution has revived in Jerusalem, this is an anomaly explainable in political and social terms.[8]

The decline of *waqf* in the modern period stems from a variety of causes, chief among them reforms introduced beginning in the nineteenth century which led to the complete abolition of *waqf* in several Arab countries in the twentieth century; the rise of the "welfare state" in which the well-being of the individual and the community has become the responsibility of the state; the decline of religion as a personal philosophy and binding way of life, together with the adoption of a rational and economic philosophy; and, finally, the increased safety of property in the modern state. To these and other reasons must be added a cause peculiar to Israel: most Muslim *waqf*s became

---

6 Noel J. Coulson, *Succession in the Muslim Family* (Cambridge: Cambridge University Press, 1971), 235ff.

7 Aharon Layish, "The Druze Testamentary *Waqf*", *Studia Islamica*, LXXI (1990), 143.

8 Aharon Layish, "The Muslim *Waqf* in Jerusalem after 1967: Beneficiaries and Management," *Le waqf dans le monde musulman contemporain (XIXe–XXe siècles). Fonctions sociales, économiques et politiques*, ed. Faruk Bilici, *Varia Turcica*, xxvi (Istanbul: Institut Français d'Etudes Anatoliennes, 1994), 148–49, 163–67; Yitzhak Reiter, *Ha-Waqf bi-[Ye]rushalayim, 1948–1990* (Jerusalem: The Jerusalem Institute for Israel Studies, 1991), Research Series No. 42, 16–17, 38–43, 126ff. Cf. Faruk Bilici, "Sociabilité et expression politique islamistes en Turquie: Les nouveaux *vakıfs*," *Revue Française de Science Politique*, vol. 43, no. 3 (1993), 412–34.

absentees' properties in the circumstances obtaining when the State was established, although no legal bar against founding new *waqf*s exists.[9]

Reforms in the law of inheritance in the contemporary Muslim world have profoundly reduced the incentive to establish family *waqf*s. These reforms have made the *sharʿī* law of inheritance increasingly flexible, strengthening the rights of succession of heirs within the nuclear family and allowing more freedom to determine the disposition of one's estate after one's death.[10] In Israel freedom of testation with regard to Muslims has been extended to the point that the family *waqf* has almost completely lost its *raison d'être*. Until 1965 it was legally permitted to make a will only of *mulk* property and movables while *mīrī* property was regulated under the Ottoman Succession Law of 1913, which was absorbed in the Succession Ordinance of 1923. This Ordinance allowed the making of a civil will of *mulk* property and movables. However, this option was not available to Muslims (Section 20). The Women's Equal Rights Law of 1951 extended the Ottoman Succession Law to *mulk* property and movables, provided all parties were over eighteen and had, of their own free will, consented before the religious court to litigate in accordance with the law of their religious community. The Succession Law of 1965 abrogated the special provisions of the *mīrī* category in matters of succession, thus lifting the restriction placed on the disposal of *mīrī* property by will. Along with absolute freedom of testation, the law introduced maintenance out of the estate – alien to Islamic law – to serve as a remedy against a will depriving an heir of the estate and to give expression to the principle that the needs of the dependent relatives must be satisfied before the residue of the estate is apportioned among the heirs.[11]

Wills, unlike family *waqf*s, are an established practice (although not as widespread as succession orders issued on intestacy) in Israeli Muslim society. Since the emergence of the State, there is evidence in the *sijill*s of the *sharīʿa* courts of selected years (see below) of ninety-four new wills in favor of family members and non-relatives, in addition to wills in favor of charitable purposes such as the Waqf of Al-Istiqlāl and the World Bahai Organization, both of which are located in Haifa.[12] Fifty-two percent of all the wills were drawn up or registered in the Sharīʿa Court of Jaffa (1950–1980), whose

9 Layish, "The Muslim *Waqf* in Jerusalem," 146–47, and the sources indicated there.

10 Coulson, *Succession in the Muslim Family*, 135ff.; Aharon Layish, "Mīrāth. 2. In Modern Islamic Countries," *The Encyclopaedia of Islam*, new ed. (Leiden: E. J. Brill, 1990), vol. 7, pp. 111–13.

11 For more details see Layish, *Women and Islamic Law*, 280–82. See also 305 below.

12 Sharīʿa Court of Haifa, Sijill Daʿāwā, vol. 12, p. 9 file [?]/83, no. 29/83 (25 April 1983); and Acre, file 487/87 (10 December 1987), respectively. Cf. Marcus, *Aleppo in the Eighteenth Century*, 302; Messick, "Transactions in Ibb," 380.

jurisdiction also comprises Lod, Ramla, Beersheba (until 1978) and Jerusalem (until 1987). Thirty-nine percent were in Acre (1948–1991), and the rest in Haifa (1977–1983) and Nazareth (1947–1970). Not a single will was registered in Ṭayyiba (1950–1968). It is very likely that the number of wills created is even larger since the oral declaration of a bequest out of court (in the presence of witnesses) is valid.[13] In fact, the probate proceedings occasionally take place several years after the testator's death.[14]

## 2 Legatees

### 2.1 *The Spouse Relict*[15]

One-fifth of the wills were made in favor of the spouse relict, either as a sole legatee or along with others, usually children. In seven cases the wife was the sole legatee. This is a high rate, considering the rarity of endowments created in favor of a wife as a sole beneficiary, after the founder, when the latter has children.[16] In several cases there were no heirs besides the wife, and it seems that the main reason for the will was the testator's wish to circumvent the doctrine of *radd*[17] which does not apply to the spouse relict. The wife is entitled only to her Qur'ānic share (1/4 or 1/8) of the estate. Since the Public Treasury (*bayt al-māl*) does not exist in Israel, the residue of the estate would be transmitted to the General Custodian in the Ministry of Justice, a contingency that helps to explain why Muslims make a will.[18] In the rest of the cases, wills favored the wife and deprived other heirs of the estate. Occasionally, the testator justified the will by his wish to recompense his wife for having assisted

13 Coulson, *Succession in the Muslim Family*, 215ff.

14 See, for example, Jaffa, Sijll Qarārāt, vol. 17, pp. 72–73, file 835/76, no. 84 (13 December 1976) (forty years passed between the making of the will and its probate, and thirteen years since the testator's death); Acre, file 33/86 (15 February 1986) (eighteen and thirteen years, respectively); Acre, Sijill, vol. 23, p. 28, file 69/88 (6 March 1988) (twenty-six and twenty-five years, respectively).

15 Cf. Coulson, *Succession in the Muslim Family*, 41.

16 Layish, "The Family *Waqf* and Succession," 22.

17 According to the *radd* doctrine, when the prescribed portions of the Qur'ānic heirs, in the absence of male agnates, do not exhaust the estate, the residue is returned to all the entitled Qur'ānic heirs. See Coulson, *Succession in the Muslim Family*, 49–51.

18 Jaffa, Sijill Qarārāt, vol. 1, p. 385, file 23/59, no. 539 (31 March 1959); Acre, file 51/87 (26 February 1987); Acre, Sijill, vol. 24, p. 9, file 3/89 no. 9/89 (17 January 1989); Coulson, *Succession in the Muslim Family*, 50. Cf. Shaham, "The Muslim Family in Egypt," 264ff.; Layish, "The Family *Waqf* and Succession," 23. See 313–14 below.

him in collecting the property and for "serving him in the best manner."[19] In one case, the will seems to have been prompted by doubt as to whether the spouses were legally married (the validity of the marriage is a precondition to the mutual right of inheritance between spouses).[20] In only one instance did a will favor the husband as a sole legatee. This may be due to the fact that the husband predeceased the testatrix. In this particular case, both spouses bequeathed their respective properties to each other. The mutual bequest between spouses corresponds with the Succession Law of 1965, the principle innovation of which is the primacy of the spouse in succession.[21]

In twelve cases the testator bequeathed his property to his wife along with children or others, a pattern familiar from family *waqf*s created in Jaffa during the Mandate period. It has been suggested that the founder intended to secure the wife's *sharʿī* inheritance portion in the event of an attempt by male agnates to deprive her of it.[22] In several instances, the will favored the wife and sons while depriving the daughters. This pattern reflects a tendency to prevent fragmentation of the patrimony while securing maintenance for the wife.[23] In one instance, the testator bequeathed all of his immovable property to his five sons while reserving his cash money, gold jewelry and diamonds for his wife (and minor sons).[24] Occasionally a will favors the wife only. In one case, a man bequeathed immovable property to his wife while totally depriving his son and other heirs. In another case, a man bequeathed his estate to his wife and daughter to be shared by them equally, so that the wife's share of the bequest was four times larger than her Qurʾānic share (1/8).[25] In other cases, the estate was to be shared equally (that is, per capita) by the wife, sons and daughters.[26] In a case in which it seems that the spouses did not have children of their own, the estate was to be shared equally by the wife and two

19 Jaffa, Sijill Qarārāt, vol. 10, p. 199, file 1/73, no. 357 (1 January 1973); Acre, file 519/85 (22 November 1985).

20 Jaffa, Sijill Qarārāt, vol. 1, p. 311, file 29/58, no. 481 (17 May 1958). See further Layish, *Women and Islamic Law*, 293ff.

21 Jaffa, Sijill Qarārāt, vol. 10, p. 34, file 255/72, no. 56 (22 June 1972). Cf. Layish, "The Family *Waqf* and Succession," 23; idem, *Women and Islamic Law*, 281.

22 Layish, "The Family *Waqf* and Succession," 23.

23 Acre, file 33/86 (30 September 1968 and 15 February 1986); Nazareth, Sijill Ḥujaj, vol. 24, p. 110. file 174/67, no. 110 (18 December 1967); Haifa, Sijill Daʿāwā, vol. 6, p. [110], no.[28/80] (16 June 1980).

24 Haifa, file 55/83 (16 May 1983).

25 Acre, file 98/85 (5 March 1985); and Acre, Sijill, vol. 25, p. 65, file 185/90 (7 April 1990), respectively.

26 Haifa, Sijill Daʿāwā, vol. 9, p. 51, file 125/82, no. 37/82 (7 October 1982); Acre, Sijill, vol. 23, file 69/88, no. 28/88 (6 March 1988).

nephews. This pattern demonstrates a compromise between the testator's concern for the wife's welfare and his concern for keeping the patrimony within the control of the agnates.[27] Even in cases in which the testator bequeaths the estate to agnates such as sons and nephews, he often reserves the right of residence – an important component of maintenance – for the wife for her lifetime.[28] Conversely, there is explicit evidence of the wife being completely disinherited. In one case in which the children were the sole legatees, the wife's consent to her deprivation was obtained out of court. In another case, a man bequeathed the residence that he shared with his wife to his young son "with no coproprietor (*sharīk*) or opposer [to the will]".[29]

### 2.2 *Children*

Half of the wills favored the testator's children – born and unborn (for the bequest to be valid, the legatee must be in existence at the time of the testator's death).[30] Children were the sole legatees in 80 percent of the cases, and in the rest they shared the estate with others, usually the testator's wife. In the family *waqf* in Mandatory Jaffa, the corresponding figures with regard to children were 70 percent and 80 percent, respectively.[31] This pattern reflects a wish to emphasize the direct link between generations at the expense of other relatives of whatever degree. More significant in this context is the fact that in twenty-three wills (almost half of the wills favoring children) sons were the sole legatees. In such wills the testator may be guided by a variety of considerations: (1) When there are no Qur'ānic heirs, a will insures that sons, especially minor sons, are not deprived of the estate by agnates of lower parentelas, such as the testator's brothers (the legatees' uncles);[32] alternatively, the testator may wish to divide the estate between the sons in units as complete and economically sound as possible.[33] (2) Explicit or implicit deprivation of other heirs, especially the wife and married daughters, probably in order to prevent the fragmentation of the patrimony through out-married females.[34] (3) Concern

27 Acre, Sijill, vol. 24, p. 14, file 51/89, no. 14/89 (3 January 1989).

28 Haifa, file 57/80 (29 May 980); Acre, file 58[?]/88 (18 December 1988).

29 Acre, file 673/90 (4 February 1991); and Haifa, file 164/80 (6 November 1980), respectively. Cf. Shaham, "The Muslim Family in Egypt," 267–68.

30 Coulson, *Succession in the Muslim Family*, 227–28.

31 Layish, "The Family *Waqf* and Succession," 23.

32 For example, Jaffa, Sijill Qarārāt, vol. 3, p. 124, file 89/64, no. 197 (8 July 1964); Acre, file 166/86 (8 May 1986); Sijill, vol. 23, p.115, file 307/88, no. 115/88 (22 February 1988).

33 Acre, file 249/87 (22 June 1987); file 399/87 (1 November 1987); Sijill, vol. 23, p. 28, file 69/88 (6 March 1988); Sijill, vol. 24, p. 17, no. 17/89 (31 January 1989). See 298 below.

34 Jaffa, Sijill Qarārāt, vol. 2, p. 506, file 101/61, no. 566 (12 December 1961); Acre, file 251/85 (21 July 1985); file 406/87 (30 September 1987); Haifa, file 164/80 (6 November 1980).

for minor or unmarried sons. It is quite common to allocate the family residence or even an entire house to minor or unmarried sons to provide them with an opportunity to marry and "establish their own house" at the expense of the patrimony, an opportunity that adult sons had already availed themselves of. This phenomenon has been observed in Druze wills.[35] (4) The desire to recompense (*iḥsān*) one particular son for handling the testator's affairs faithfully and especially for providing him with maintenance (while depriving other heirs).[36] I came across only one instance of explicit deprivation of a testator's son: "a final and absolute deprivation (*ḥirmān nihāʾī qaṭʿī*) which cannot be revoked." Although no reason was given for the deprivation, the testator published an advertisement in a newspaper that read, "I wash my hands of him" (*wa-qad bariʾtu minhu*).[37]

Five wills, all by women, favored daughters as sole legatees. Under the inheritance rules, a daughter, in the absence of Qurʾānic heirs and male agnates, takes the entire estate by virtue of the *radd* doctrine. In such cases, the purpose of the will might be to secure her right and prevent her being deprived by distant relatives.[38] In one case in which the will was in favor of three daughters, its purpose was to allocate the residence to one of the daughters, who was probably unmarried.[39] In several cases, wills made by women favored daughters, even married daughters, to the exclusion of other legal heirs.[40] It seems that women are less concerned than men about fragmentation of the patrimony through out-married daughters. Indeed, I have not found a single instance of a man making a will in favor of daughters as sole legatees. In seven instances, the will favored sons and daughters as sole legatees. A daughter becomes an agnatic heir alongside a son, entitled to half the share of a son by virtue of the *taʿṣīb* doctrine.[41] Some evidence indicates that this *sharʿī* norm is applied

35 Acre, file 138/85 (26 March 1985); file 406/87 (30 September 1987); Haifa, file 164/80 (6 November 1980); Jaffa, Sijill Qarārāt, vol. 22, p. 136, file 716/79, no. 134 (7 October 1979); Aharon Layish, *Marriage, Divorce and Succession in the Druze Family* (Leiden: E.J. Brill, 1982), 318ff.

36 Jaffa, Sijill Qarārāt, vol. 10, p. 32, file 244/72, no. 53 (19 June 1972); vol. 10, p. 353, file 396/73, no. 604 (2 September 1973).

37 Haifa, Sijill Daʿāwā, vol. 9, p. 51, file 125/82, no. 37/82 (7 October 1982).

38 Acre, Sijill, vol. 24, p. 133, file 440/89, no. 133/89 (27 September 1989); file 207/90 (6 May 1990). Cf. Layish, "The Family *Waqf* and Succession," 24ff.; Shaham, "The Muslim Family in Egypt," 269; Shatzmiller, "Women and Property Rights," p. 231ff., 254ff.

39 Jaffa, Sijill Qarārāt, vol. 3, p. 62, file 202/63, no. 96 (25 November 1963).

40 Acre, file 144/86 (24 March 1986); file 285/82 (19 September 1982). Cf. Shaham, "The Muslim Family in Egypt," 264.

41 Coulson, *Succession in the Muslim Family*, 41–42.

in wills made by men.[42] In only one instance did a man bequeath his estate to his children without awarding males twice the share of females, creating a will for his as yet unborn children, "males and females in equal shares."[43] By contrast, female testatrixes appear not to discriminate between daughters and sons, manifesting a clear tendency to treat sons and daughters equally and, occasionally, to prefer daughters over sons.[44]

### 2.3 *Parents*[45]

No wills favoring parents were found. Most likely no question of deprivation arises as the parents of the testator (who generally makes the will at an advanced age) are already deceased. Similarly, I did not come across a single instance of a *waqf* in favor of parents in Jaffa during the Mandate period.[46]

### 2.4 *Grandchildren*[47]

Some evidence points to the exclusion of orphaned grandchildren from the estate by means of wills, in a manner corresponding to the *sharʿī* norm. In one case, a woman bequeathed her estate to her children, stipulating that if one of them predeceased her the estate should be divided among the surviving children.[48] Eleven wills, however, favored grandchildren, mostly orphaned grandsons. Wills favoring orphaned grandchildren are intended to correct what the reformers regard as a distortion originating in the *sharʿī* law of inheritance. In several Middle Eastern countries, this problem has been corrected through the "obligatory bequest," which enables orphaned agnatic and cognatic grandchildren to take their parent's share or up to one-third of the estate.[49] Several testators created bequests in favor of orphaned agnatic

---

42 Jaffa, Sijill Qarārāt, vol. 2, p. 475, file 34/61, no. 498 (11 July 1961); vol. 3, p. 16, file 55/63, no. 24 (17 July 1963); vol. 24, pp. 177–78, file 380/80, no. 155 (3 July 1980).

43 Acre, Sijill Qarārāt, vol. 5, file 80/63 (6 June 1963).

44 Jaffa, Sijill Qarārāt, vol. 10, p. 64, file 1307/72, no. 107 (19 July 1972); vol. 2, p. 540, file 29/62, no. 532 (23 July 1962); Acre, vol. 23, p. 93, file 290/88, no. 93/88 (26 June 1988).

45 Cf. Coulson, *Succession in the Muslim Family*, 43ff.

46 Layish, "The Family *Waqf* and Succession," 25–26.

47 Cf. Coulson, *Succession in the Muslim Family*, 31, 52ff., 143–44.

48 Jaffa, Sijill Qarārāt, vol. 10, p. 64, file 1307/72, no. 107 (19 July 1972). See also Haifa, Sijill Daʿāwā, vol. 9, p. 51, file 125/82, no. 37/82 (8 October 1982).

49 Coulson, *Succession in the Muslim Family*, 143ff.; Layish, "Mīrāth," 112; Shaham, "The Muslim Family in Egypt," 260. Cf. Layish, "The Family *Waqf* and Succession," 26; Yitzhak Reiter, "The Muslim *Waqf* in Jerusalem under the British Mandate as Reflected in the Records (*sijill*) of the Sharīʿa Court" [in Hebrew], Ph.D. thesis, The Hebrew University (Jerusalem, 1990), 159–60; idem, "Family *Waqf* Entitlements in British Palestine," 181ff.; Shaham, "The Muslim Family in Egypt," 273ff.

grandsons "within the rate of their father's portion (*naṣīb*) in the estate had he survived me." In other words, the principle of representation, not recognized under the *sharīʿa*, is applied here: the grandsons step into their father's shoes.[50] In one case, a woman bequeathed her *sharʿī* portion (one-sixth) of the estate of her predeceased son to her thirteen grandsons and granddaughters. In return she expected them to look after her affairs and provide her with maintenance in the same way her son had during his lifetime.[51] In another case, a woman bequeathed her house to her three agnatic grandsons and a granddaughter who were in her custody (*ḥaḍāna*). Her son, whose first wife had died, had married another woman who was fully occupied with her own children. The testatrix wished to recompense her grandchildren "who respect and esteem her" by providing them with maintenance (*siyāna*). Moreover, any grandchild who marries and has no residence of his own may join her in the house that she shares with the other grandchildren.[52] Elsewhere, it has been observed that a will favoring a minor grandchild while his father (that is, the testator's son) is alive may serve as a means for circumventing the inheritance rules to the advantage of the grandchild's father. Since the grandchild is not a legal heir there is no bar to making a will in his favor. The testator expects the minor legatee's property to be administered by his father, the favored son, in effect increasing that son's share in the estate at the expense of other heirs.[53] Although this practice was not observed in Israeli *sijill*s, the possibility of using the will for this purpose cannot be excluded.

Several instances of wills, all by women, favored cognatic grandchildren. In one case, the grandson's mother (the daughter of the testatrix) was still alive and consented to being deprived.[54] The preference of males over females even among cognates has been observed in the family *waqf*. The founder stipulates that when there are no more agnatic descendants, entitlement should pass to cognatic descendants, to be shared by males and females in each generation,

50 Jaffa, Sijill Qarārāt, vol. 1, p. 391, file 32/59, no. 548 (28 May 1959); vol. 2, p. 558, file 106/62, no. 564 (18 November 1962). See also Acre, file 229/90 (22 May 1990); Nazareth, Sijill 26 (1911–18), p. 242, no. 24 (the grandson was in his mother's custody). Cf. Aharon Layish, "The Islamization of the Bedouin Family in the Judean Desert, as Reflected in the *Sijill* of the *Sharīʿa* Court," in *The Changing Bedouin*, ed. Emanuel Marx and Avshalom Shmueli (New Brunswick, New Jersey: Transaction Books, 1984), 50; Shaham, "The Muslim Family in Egypt," 263.

51 Jaffa, Sijill Qarārāt, vol. 8, p. 146, file 304/71, no. 207 (28 June 1971).

52 Jaffa, Sijill Qarārāt, vol. 8, p. 125, file 267/71, no. 172 (8 June 1971).

53 Powers, "The Islamic Inheritance System," 23, 26; Tomas Gerholm, "Aspects of Inheritance and Marriage Payments in Yemen," in *Property, Social Structure, and Law in the Modern Middle East*, ed. Ann E. Mayer (Albany: SUNY Press, 1985), 131.

54 Jaffa, Sijill Qarārāt, vol. 2, p. 601, no. 646 (16 June 1963). See also vol. 3, p. 20, file 109/63 (26 July 1963). Cf. Layish, "The Family *Waqf* and Succession," 26–27, 33ff.

although the right of transmitting entitlement to subsequent generations is granted only to males.[55]

### 2.5 *Siblings*[56]

Eight wills favored brothers and sisters (most of them agnates) or their children. In several cases, the absence of other heirs was mentioned explicitly. Maintaining the integrity of the estate within the control of the extended agnatic family, in the absence of sons, seems to have been the primary motivation behind such wills. In one case, two germane brothers bequeathed their immovable properties to each other, stipulating that "no one has the right to oppose him [the legatee] with regard to anything [pertaining to the bequeathed property]." This may indicate that there were other heirs. It seems that the patrimony was transmitted to the brothers through inheritance and was kept in joint ownership (*mushāʿ*) with a view to preventing, for economic or other reasons, its fragmentation among other heirs. Upon the death of one of the brothers, the other becomes the head of the extended family and in full control of the patrimony.[57] Support for this assumption is found in several wills made by women in which the bequest is used as an instrument to reintegrate the patrimony following its fragmentation through inheritance by women. In one case, two germane sisters bequeathed to their germane brother, "with our complete consent and with no compulsion or coercion," all of their properties, including "our rights in the estate [of their deceased father]." They requested the court to instruct the Land Registry (*ṭābū*) and the Department of Land Settlement to effect the transaction and register their rights, after their death, in their brother's name. A year previously, the two sisters had given this brother a general power of attorney (*wakālā ʿāmma*) "to protect (*muḥāfaẓa*) our inheritance rights and to register them as our properties [in the Land Registers]." They also authorized him to sell (*bayʿ*) their properties, to mortgage (*rahn*) them, to exchange them [for other properties] (*istibdāl*), to take possession (*qabḍ*) of their price (*thaman*), to hire and lease them for rent (*ījār*) and to represent them in all necessary contacts with the official authorities.[58] In one instance, however, a woman deprived her agnatic brother of the estate.[59]

55 Layish, "The Family *Waqf* and Succession," 33ff.

56 Cf. Coulson, *Succession in the Muslim Family*, 39, 67ff., 71.

57 Jaffa, Sijill Qarārāt, vol. 3, p. 142, file 119/64, no. 224 (23 September 1964). Cf. Henry Rosenfeld, *Hem hayu fallaḥim* ([Tel Aviv]: Hakibbutz Hameuchad, 1964), 86.

58 Jaffa, Sijill Qarārāt, vol. 1, p. 252, file 47/56, no. 392 (20 December 1956). See also vol. 1, p. 474, file 49/61, no. 497 (11 July 1961). Cf. Powers, "*Fatwā*s as Sources for Legal and Social History," 336ff.; idem, "The Islamic Inheritance System," 25; Layish, "The Family *Waqf* and Succession," 29.

59 Jaffa, Sijill Qarārāt, vol. 2, p. 524 [573?], file 34/62, no. 503 (22 April 1962).

The act of depriving sisters of the estate should also be assessed within the context of efforts to prevent the fragmentation of the patrimony. There is one explicit piece of evidence to this effect pertaining to a uterine sister.[60] Only two bequests in favor of sisters or their children (nieces) were found (there was no indication of the existence of other heirs besides the legatees). In the first case, it seems that the testator intended to prevent the exclusion of the cognatic sister by her agnatic sister.[61] A bequest in favor of needy minor nephews may compensate for their being deprived of the patrimony since their father predeceased their paternal grandfather.[62]

### 2.6 *Other Relatives*

In seven cases, bequests were made in favor of relatives, most of them male agnates, whose relationship to the testator is not indicated.[63] In some of the cases, the testator stipulated that "no one has the right to oppose [this bequest] under any circumstances" and it may well be that the testator intended to deprive non-agnatic heirs.[64] In two cases, women bequeathed their properties to their agnates. When the estate was probated, the testators claimed that the bequests were made in return for service (*khidma*) and maintenance rendered to them. The true motive for the bequests, however, may have been different. In the first case, the testatrix stated that the object of bequest included "what had been transmitted to her by way of inheritance" (*mā āl ilayhā bi-ṭarīq al-irth*) from her husband (by exogamous marriage). It may well be that the true motive behind this bequest was to enable the agnatic relative take control of her share in the estate.[65] In one case, a woman bequeathed her property in favor of a cognatic niece of her husband, that is, the testatrix was the widow of the legatee's maternal uncle (*khāl*). The combination of cognatic blood relationship within the outer family and relationship by marriage does not produce a real chance for inheritance. On the face of it, it seems that the testatrix was motivated by humanitarian considerations. In any case, the bequest subsequently was declared null and void by the court because of insufficient witnesses to its validity.[66]

---

60 Jaffa, Sijill Qarārāt, vol. 2, p. 521, file 21/61, no. 497 (5 April 1962).

61 Acre, file 149/85 (14 May 1985); Jaffa, Sijill Qarārāt, vol. 5, pp. 96–97, file 279/69, no. 162 (23 October 1969). Cf. Layish, "The Family *Waqf* and Succession," 28.

62 Acre, file 194/85 (26 May 1985). Cf. Shaham, "The Muslim Family in Egypt," 264ff.

63 Cf. Layish, "The Family *Waqf* and Succession," 28.

64 Jaffa, Sijill Qarārāt, vol. 2, p. 540, file 59/62, no. 531 (23 July 1962); vol. 3, p. 149, file 130/64, no. 238 (27 October 1964).

65 Jaffa, Sijill Qarārāt, vol. 1, p. 392, file 20/59, no. 550 (4 June 1959); vol. 3, p. 194, file 99/65, 321 (19 December 1965).

66 Jaffa, Sijill Qarārāt, vol. 3, p. 76, file 1/64, no. 116 (13 January 1964); and p. 90, file 5/65, no. 139 (10 February 1964).

### 2.7 *Non-Relatives*

Sixteen bequests (17 percent, half by women) were made in favor of non-relatives. This is a significant percentage. In only one instance there is evidence to the effect that there was no heir.[67] In most cases, however, there is no indication as to the existence of heirs. The main reason given for making a will in favor of a non-relative is the testator's wish to recompense the legatee for prolonged and devoted service.[68] Women usually make wills in favor of unrelated women in return for service.[69] There are, however, instances of wills in favor of unrelated men as well.[70] In one case, a woman bequeathed all of her property to a non-relative while totally depriving her agnatic brother.[71] Making a will in favor of non-relatives while depriving agnates testifies to the woman's full capacity to dispose of her property. According to Ḥanafī doctrine, when a man dies without surviving blood relatives and without having made a valid will, his estate passes to the Public Treasury by way of escheat.[72] In Israel, an estate with no legal heir passes to the General Custodian in the Ministry of Justice. The testator, however, is not bound by the *ultra vires* doctrine and may dispose of the entire estate by will. A bequest in favor of a non-relative is, thus, a very simple and efficient means – compared to *waqf* and gift *inter vivos* – of preventing the estate from falling into the hands of a non-Muslim state. Although no evidence in the *sijill* points explicitly to such a motivation, the possibility cannot be ruled out.

## 3 Mode of Apportionment of the Bequeathed Property

Whereas a testator is free to name the legatees, unlike the founder of a *waqf*, he may not stipulate the mode by which the legatee's rights are to pass from one generation to another.[73] By virtue of the will the legatee acquires full ownership of the bequeathed property and is free to dispose of it as he wishes.

67 Jaffa, Sijill Qarārāt, vol. 1, p. 329, file 60/58, no. 516 (11 November 1958).

68 Jaffa, Sijill Qarārāt, vol. 18, p. 78, file 414/77, no. 78 (9 June 1977); Acre, file 365/86 (27 July 1986); Acre, Sijill Qarārāt, vol. 5, p. 45, file 82/63, no. 45 (6 June 1963). See also Jaffa, Sijill Qarārāt, vol. 2, p. 543, file 77/62, no. 538 (9 September 1962); p. 546, file 91/62, no. 546 (3 October 1962); vol. 10, p. 288, file 70/73, no. 409 (15 February 1973). Cf. Layish, "The Family *Waqf* and Succession," 28.

69 Jaffa, Sijill Qarārāt, vol. 2, p. 571, file 4/63, no. 587 (15 January 1963); vol. 3, p. 96, file 38/64, no. 151 (1 March 1964); vol. 12, p. 75, file 579/74, no. 117 (9 January 1975).

70 Jaffa, Sijill Qarārāt, vol. 1, p. 329, file 60/58, no. 516 (11 November 1958); vol. 2, p. 570, file 130/62, no. 584 (15 January 1963).

71 Jaffa, Sijill Qarārāt, vol. 2, p. 524 [573?], file 34/62, no. 503 (22 April 1962).

72 Coulson, *Succession in the Muslim Family*, 243.

73 Cf. Layish, "The Family *Waqf* and Succession," 30ff.

### 3.1 *Apportionment "According to the* Sharʿī *Rules of Inheritance"*

This mode of apportionment, the most common in family *waqf*s established according to Ḥanafī doctrine,[74] is rare in wills. In one case, a man bequeathed his entire property to his two sons, excluding only his daughter's "*sharʿī* entitlement (*istiḥqāq*) in the estate had he died intestate," which he bequeathed to her.[75] In another case, a man willed his property to his daughter and her husband, to be shared equally between them. In the absence of a son the daughter's portion as a Qurʾānic heir is one-half, and it may well be that the testator was inspired by the *sharʿī* norm, although in the absence of Qurʾānic heirs and male agnates she could take the entire estate by the *radd* doctrine.[76]

### 3.2 *Equal Apportionment*

By contrast, equal apportionment of the estate among legatees is quite common. Equal apportionment may be confined to the testator's children. In one case, a woman bequeathed her property equally to her sons and daughters by her present and former husbands.[77] In some cases, the testator stipulated that the estate be apportioned equally between his wife and children. When the number of the legatees is below eight – and there is at least one such case – this is for the benefit of the wife.[78] Instances of equal apportionment to grandsons and granddaughters of the same degree have been noted. In such cases, the *taʿṣīb* doctrine, according to which a grandson takes twice the portion of a granddaughter, otherwise would have applied upon intestacy. In one case, a woman bequeathed her *sharʿī* portion (1/6) in her son's estate to her thirteen orphaned grandsons and granddaughters, to be apportioned equally among them.[79] No instance of equal apportionment of the estate among relatives of different blood relationships has been noted. One will did favor children and grandchildren concurrently, but, contrary to what has been observed in family *waqf*, the mode of per capita apportionment, that is, equality of all the existing legatees regardless of degree, was not applied. Instead, the estate was apportioned according to the criterion of gender, combined with the doctrine of representation. The estate was apportioned equally between the testator's

74 Ibid., 37ff.

75 Jaffa, Sijill Qarārāt, vol. 2, p. 475, file 34/61, no. 498 (11 July 1961); vol. 3, p. 16, file 55/63, no. 24 (17 July 1963); vol. 24, pp. 177–78, file 380/80, no. 155 (5 July 1980).

76 Jaffa, Sijill Qarārāt, vol. 3, p. 8, file 97/63, no. 14 (8 July 1963).

77 Jaffa, Sijill Qarārāt, vol. 10, p. 64, file 1307/72, no. 107 (19 July 1972).

78 Acre, Sijill, vol. 23, p. 28, file 69/88, no. 28/88 (6 March 1988). See also Haifa, Sijill Daʿāwā, vol. 9, p. 51, file 125/82, no. 37/82 (7 October 1982).

79 Jaffa, Sijill Qarārāt, vol. 8, p. 146, file 304/71, no. 207 (28 June 1971). See also vol. 8, p. 125, file 267/71, no. 172 (8 June 1971).

son (1/4) and his orphaned agnatic grandsons, who took their deceased father's portion (1/4), on the one hand, and his three daughters, who took one-half, on the other.[80]

Although one may find legal support for equal apportionment between the sexes (and for per capita apportionment) in the *ḥadīth* and in Ḥanafī doctrine,[81] it is doubtful that the testator, in stipulating such an apportionment, was inspired by these sources, since the compulsory inheritance rules tend to favor males over females (according to the *taʿṣīb* doctrine) and male agnates (*ʿaṣaba*) over cognates (*dhawū al-arḥām*)). There seems to be a causal connection between the testator's gender and equal apportionment. In most cases, a female bequeaths her estate to her children or grandchildren, regardless of gender, on the basis of equality. It is only natural that women are sensitive to the status of females as heirs. Most likely they are less concerned than men with preserving the patrimony and preventing its fragmentation through out-marrying daughters.[82]

As far as the status of women and cognates is concerned, equality between the sexes, between relatives of different blood relationship, and between the testator's wife and children with respect to their rights in the estate, might reflect a change of values – in the liberal direction – in the social philosophy of men. Quite possibly the Ottoman Succession Law of 1913 (in its modified versions in the Succession Ordinance of 1923 and the Women's Equal Rights Law of 1951) and the Israeli Succession Law of 1965, superimposed from above on the indigenous Muslim society, brought about a normative change in this philosophy. These laws do not distinguish between males and females or between agnates and cognates, and the 1965 law immensely increases the wife's portion in the estate as compared to her portion under the *sharīʿa*. The application of the (modified) Ottoman law in the *sharīʿa* courts and the resort of Muslims to civil courts in matters pertaining to succession, and the making of wills in conformity with the provisions of the Israeli law and their being probated even in *sharīʿa* courts,[83] seem to have facilitated the introversion of the equality norm with respect to the apportionment of the estate. These are, of course, tentative conclusions that require confirmation from further research on the practice of wills in the pre-modern period.[84]

80 Acre, file 222/90 (22 May 1990). Cf. Layish, "The Mālikī Family *Waqf*," 23ff.

81 See Layish, "The Family *Waqf* and Succession," 41, and the reference in fn. 124. Cf. Reiter, "Family *Waqf* Entitlements in British Palestine," 179–81.

82 Cf. Layish, "The Muslim *Waqf* in Jerusalem," 154.

83 See 305ff. below.

84 Cf. Layish, "The Mālikī Family *waqf*," 23ff.; idem, "The Family *Waqf* and Succession," 40ff.

### 3.3 *Economic Apportionment*

Economic apportionment of the estate, that is, apportionment by type of property and in units that are as economically sound as possible, is the most common mode of testamentary apportionment. The economic rationale of this mode of apportionment is obvious: its purpose is to prevent a "family *mushāʿ*" created by intestate succession. Joint ownership of all the heirs based on their portions in each type of property may cause severe damage to the patrimony, especially to immovable property, since it is impossible to effect any transaction relating to the estate without the prior consent of all the heirs. Joint administration of the estate by all heirs is also a source of disputes. Economic apportionment is very common among the Druze who enjoy complete freedom of testation, and is common to some extent in Muslim family *waqf*.[85]

Muslim wills display great variation with respect to economic apportionment. When the legatees are sons only, the tendency is to apportion the land, households and residential apartments in complete units, while cash resources are apportioned equally. Sometimes a young son who has not established a house of his own is preferred with respect to allocation of the residence, while the other sons receive other properties as compensation.[86] In one case, a testator clearly distinguished between property designated for sons and that designated for daughters, bequeathing to his five sons four parcels of land (approximately forty dunams altogether) to be apportioned equally between them, and bequeathing to his five daughters one parcel of land (the size of which was not mentioned) to be apportioned equally between them. The testator may have wished to prevent the fragmentation of the main patrimony through his out-married daughters. The concentration of the daughters' rights in one parcel probably was intended to minimize the possible damage to the patrimony.[87] Women, too, apportion their estates among their children by will in sound economic units.[88]

When the legatees are the wife and children, the tendency is to bequeath the immovables to the sons only, while depriving the wife and daughters thereof, lest through exogamous marriage the agnatic family lose the wife's and daughters' portions in the estate. Instead, the testator allocates to the women money, jewelry, and the right to reside in a house or apartment for their lifetime, that

85 Layish, *Marriage, Divorce and Succession in the Druze Family*, 321, 348; idem, "The Family *Waqf* and Succession," 42. Cf. Marcus, "Real Property and Society," 113, 116.

86 Acre, file 249/87 (22 June 1987); Sijill, vol. 24, p. 17, no. 17/89 (31 January 1989); Haifa, Sijill Daʿāwā, vol. 6, file 164/80 (6 November 1980).

87 Jaffa, Sijill Qarārāt, vol. 10, p. 32, file 244/72, no. 53 (16 June 1972).

88 See, for example, Jaffa, Sijill Qarārāt, vol. 3, p. 62, file 202/63, no. 96 (25 November 1963); vol. 22, p. 136, file 716/79, no. 136 (7 October 1979).

is, the testator provides economic security and maintenance in compensation for depriving the women of immovable property. Assets such as cars and tractors, which traditionally serve as means of livelihood for men, are allocated exclusively to sons.[89] Even in the absence of a son, the testator prefers distant agnates over his wife with respect to immovables, apparently guided by the wish to maintain the patrimony intact.[90]

Only on rare occasions does the testator bequeath full ownership of his residence or land to his wife, presumably on the assumption that upon his wife's death the property will pass to his sons.[91] In one case, a testator bequeathed landed property to his three sons and wife to be apportioned among them in complete units, though probably not on an equal basis. In his original will, created eighteen years earlier, he had stipulated that the sons should compensate the daughters with money in return for their deprivation from the estate.[92]

### 3.4 *Mixed Apportionment*

Occasionally the testator apportions the estate in a manner that combines concurrently several modes of apportionment according to the type of the estate and the legatee. In one case, a testator allocated to his two sons a "taxi's number [license]" to be shared equally by them; allocated his wife and two of his [unmarried] daughters the residential house, and stipulated that upon the daughters' marriage the house will pass in full ownership to the wife; the rest of the estate – immovable and movable property as well as money kept in banks – was allocated to his eight children (including the above-mentioned sons and daughters) "to be shared between them equally without distinction between male and female or between bachelor and married."[93] In another case, the testatrix combined the "*sharʿī*" and the equal apportionment modes as follows: immovable and movable property, as well as the contents of the residential house and the residue of the money – left after the allocation of specified amounts to someone's children – is to be shared by her two sons and daughter, the first son taking one-half, the second son and the daughter one-quarter each. The double portion of the first son, compared to the daughter's portion, corresponds to the *sharʿī taʿṣīb* doctrine, although there is no indication in the *sijill* that the testatrix was inspired by this doctrine.[94]

---

89 See, for example, Haifa, file 55/83 (16 May 1983); file 57/80 (29 May 1980).

90 See, for example, Acre, file 58[?]/88 (18 December 1988); Acre, Sijill, vol. 24, p. 14, file 51/89, no. 14/89 (3 January 1989).

91 See, for example, Haifa, Sijill Daʿāwā, vol. 5, p. [110], no. [28/60] (19 June 1980).

92 Acre, file 33/86 (15 February 1986 and 30 September 1968).

93 Acre, file 98/85 (5 March 1985).

94 Acre, Sijill, vol. 23, p. 55, file 191/88, no. 55/88 (19 April 1988).

## 4 Stipulations of the Testator

### 4.1 *Ensuring Maintenance of Females*

Alongside the exclusion of females from the estate, the testator usually inserts in the bequest stipulations that are intended to ensure their maintenance and a subsistence allowance. In one case, a man bequeathed a plot of land and a house to two of his sons, on the condition that the son who received the house provide the testator's wife and two daughters the "right of residence" (*ḥaqq al-suknā*) on the ground floor for their lifetimes. He further stipulated that the son provide one-half of the merchandise of a shop to these daughters. In another case, a man bequeathed his entire property to his three sons and wife, totally excluding his three daughters; however, he stipulated (*ishṭarata*) that each of the three sons pay 500 NIS (new Israeli shekels) to be allocated equally between their three sisters. He further stipulated that if this amount were not paid, "none of them [the sons] will have the right of taking possession (*ḥaqq al-istimlāk*) of the bequeathed land nor the right of disposition (*taṣarruf*) thereof."[95] In another case, a man bequeathed his entire estate to one of his sons while instructing him "to proceed with providing [maintenance] (*takāful*) to his sisters and brothers [the testator's daughters and sons] as he [the son] has been doing while I am alive." In a similar case, a man bequeathed his entire property to two of his sons while instructing them "to maintain (*muḥāfaẓa*) their mother and sisters [the testator's wife and daughters] and their [the married daughters'?] families."[96]

Assuring weak heirs of housing and a subsistence allowance while totally excluding them from the estate is tantamount to "maintenance out of the estate," a concept that is alien to Islamic law but exists in Jewish law, where a daughter does not inherit in the presence of a son.[97] However, in Israeli Muslim society this is a matter of practice rather than law since we are dealing here with legal heirs, mainly Qurʾānic heirs. The phenomenon of customary "maintenance out of the estate" is common in Israeli Druze wills. Similarly, this practice has been widely observed in family *waqf*.[98]

95 Haifa, Sijill Ḥujaj, vol. 7, file 57/80 (29 May 1980); and Acre, file 33/86 (30 September 1968), respectively.

96 Acre, file 251/85 (21 July 1985); and Haifa District Court, inheritance file, 1177/85 (3 October 1985) (unpublished), respectively.

97 Menachem Elon, *Hamishpaṭ Haʿivri*, vol. 1, (2nd ed., Jerusalem: The Magnes Press, 1978), 336, 371ff.

98 Layish, *Marriage, Divorce and Succession in the Druze Family*, 338ff., 343, 369–70; idem, "The Family *Waqf* and Succession," 43–44; idem, "The Mālikī Family *Waqf*," 26.

### 4.2 *Restrictions on Females' Freedom of Marriage and Right to Own or Dispose of Property*

Quite often the testator stipulates that a female's right to the estate is dependent on her marital status: a bachelor or a widow is entitled, whereas a married woman is debarred. The testator is guided by the fear that parts of the patrimony will be removed from the agnatic family's control through the marriage of females to non-agnates. Such stipulations interfere with females' freedom of marriage. Occasionally the testator stipulates explicitly that a female's right of residence will lapse on her marriage. In one case, it was argued in court that a man had bequeathed his estate to his brother on the condition that the testator's widow would be entitled to reside in a specified apartment so long as she did not marry.[99] Moreover, even in cases in which the testator bequeaths full ownership in the residential house to a daughter or a wife, he commonly stipulates that this right persists so long as she does not marry and that upon her marriage the right lapses and her portion in the estate reverts in full ownership to other legatees.[100] In one case, discussed above, a man bequeathed the ground floor of his house to his wife and agnatic nephew to be shared by them equally in full ownership. He stipulated, however, that upon his wife's death her share would pass to the nephew as the sole owner of the house.[101] In other words, although the wife had full ownership of her portion in the estate during her lifetime, she effectively was debarred from transmitting it to her heirs either through intestate succession or testamentary disposition.

Ḥanafī doctrine recognizes the validity of usufructuary bequests which impose restraints and time limits upon the legatee. In such bequests it is permissible to bequeath the right of residence in a house and to restrict it in terms of time (for example, until the legatee's marriage). However, in bequests of property in which full ownership is vested in the legatee, any condition contrary to this legal effect is null and void. Thus, any condition stipulating that upon the legatee's marriage or death his rights in the estate revert to other legal heirs or legatees is void, and the legatee is entitled to take the estate as absolute owner and dispose of it as he wishes, including transmitting it to his own heirs. In several Arab countries, modern legislation has adopted a more liberal attitude toward conditional bequests. A testator's condition that restricts freedom of marriage (and residence) is valid only if there is some legal

99 Haifa District Court, inheritance[?] files 730/85, 970/85 (Ḥijāzī et al. vs. Abū Shanab et al.), *Pesaqim*, 1986, vol. III, 521–24. See also Acre, Sijill, vol. 25, p. 65, file 185/90 (7 April 1990). Cf. Shaham, "The Muslim Family in Egypt," 270.

100 Acre, file 122/85 (20 March 1985).

101 Acre, file 58[?]/88 (18 December 1988).

benefit to the testator, to the legatee, or to some other person and provided that the condition is neither forbidden nor contrary to the purposes of the *sharīʿa*.[102] Stipulations to the effect that a female's right is dependent on her marital status are common also in family *waqf*. Here, too, modern legislation in several Arab countries has invalidated a founder's stipulation restricting a beneficiary's freedom of marriage (or residence, or disqualifying him or her from entitlement because of monetary debts).[103]

### 4.3 *Control on the Religious and Moral Conduct of the Legatees*

In one case, a man bequeathed his entire estate to his sons while instructing them to" fear God" (*taqwā Allāh*), to allocate to the poor as charity an amount equivalent to 140 dinars as well as 25 kg of almonds of the estate's produce during the season of the pilgrimage to Mecca (*al-mawsim*), and to maintain good relations with people.[104] This may be considered an attempt to direct the religious and moral behavior of the legatees.

## 5 Consent of the Heirs to the Bequest

The validity of the *ultra vires* dispositions depends upon the consent of the legal heirs subsequent to the testator's death. The heirs should be of full legal capacity, not subject to interdiction, and they must give their consent freely. In default of consent, a bequest in favor of a legal heir fails completely, while a bequest that exceeds the bequeathable third is valid only to the extent of the bequeathable third. If there are no legal heirs, the testator is not subject to the *ultra vires* doctrine and may dispose of the entire estate by will. If the sole surviving heir is the spouse relict, the testator has complete freedom to bequeath her or him the residue of the estate after the deduction of the spouse relict's portion, since the latter is not entitled to any surplus by way of *radd*.[105]

It is common for the testator, while making and registering the bequest in court, to instruct the legal heirs not to object to it after his death even though they may be deprived of the estate. In one case, a man bequeathed his entire estate to one of his sons, instructing his other sons and daughters not to oppose the will. He then informed the court that the children "had consented to my wish with no objection." In another case, discussed above, a

102 Coulson, *Succession in the Muslim Family*, 222–23.

103 Layish, "The Family *Waqf* and Succession," 44–46; idem, "The Mālikī Family *Waqf*," 25–27.

104 Haifa District Court, inheritance file 1177/85 (3 October 1985) (unpublished).

105 Coulson, *Succession in the Muslim Family*, 243ff.

woman bequeathed her entire estate to one of her sons in return for a sum of money she had borrowed from him. She then instructed all the heirs to consent to the will after her death and warned that whoever withheld his consent would be obliged to reimburse her son, the sole legatee, for her debt out of his pocket.[106] Debts on the estate should be paid before its distribution among the legal heirs.[107]

There is considerable evidence bearing upon the consent of heirs in bequests submitted to the court for probate. Usually, all the legal heirs appear in court, testify to the validity of the bequest, acknowledge that they have no objection to its content, and ask the court to endorse it.[108] In one case in which a woman bequeathed her entire estate to her cognatic grandson, her daughter, who was the sole heir, "allowed [that is, consented to] (*ajāzat*) her mother's will in favor of her son." In a similar case, the testator's agnatic cousin, as the sole heir, "allowed" the bequest in favor of his, the cousin's son, while "renouncing (*yatanāzal*) his own *sharʿī* and *qānūnī* right" in the estate.[109] In several cases the heirs' consent was obtained out of court. In one case, a man bequeathed his estate to his sons and daughters, depriving his wife. The son, who initiated the probate, informed the court that the legatees (*muntafiʿūn*) who were the testator's heirs, as well as his wife, had consented to the bequest and "allowed" it. He introduced the written consent of all the heirs except for the wife and subsequently undertook to obtain her consent, which was obtained and submitted to the court. In the meantime, the content of the bequest was advertised in a newspaper and no objection to the bequest was raised during a period of fifteen days. In another case, the sole legatee of an estate claimed in court after the testator's death that all the legal heirs had consented to the bequest. Two of these heirs, an agnatic aunt and a cousin, confirmed in court that they had consented to the bequest; a uterine sister (a Qurʾānic heir), who was not present in court, did not confirm her consent.[110] When females give consent in favor of male agnates it is likely that pressure has been exerted on them to refrain from seeking their *sharʿī* rights of intestate succession. Females

106 Acre, file 251/85 (21 July 1985); and Nazareth, Sijill Ḥujaj, vol. 15, pp. 34–35, no. 5/58 (6 April 1950), respectively. See also Haifa, Sijill Daʿāwā, vol. 6, p. [110], no. [28/60] (19 June 1980).

107 Coulson, *Succession in the Muslim Family*, 235.

108 See, for example, Jaffa, Sijill Qarārāt, vol. 17, pp.72–73, file 835/76, no. 84 (13 December 1976); vol. 3, p. 62, file 202/63, no. 96 (25 November 1963).

109 Jaffa, Sijill Qarārāt, vol. 2, p. 601, no. 646 (16 June 1963); and Acre, Sijill Daʿāwā, vol. 6, p. 1, file 1/64, no. 1/64 (5 January 1964), respectively. It seems that the "*qānūnī*" right refers to his share according to the Ottoman Succession Law of 1913 since the testator died before the promulgation of the Succession Law of 1965.

110 Acre, file 673/90 (4 February 1991); and Jaffa, Sijill Qarārāt, vol. 2, p. 521, file 21/61, no. 497 (5 April 1962), respectively. Cf. Messick, "Transactions in Ibb," 377.

tend to submit to such pressure since, in society based on agnation, they prefer security anchored in blood relationship over property rights. Therefore, a female's consent to a bequest, even if given in court, cannot be taken at face value. It is even more difficult for the qāḍī to control the process of obtaining consent out of court.[111]

Prior to the promulgation of the Succession Law of 1965, qāḍīs were usually aware of the necessity of obtaining consent to bequests that deviate from the *ultra vires* doctrine. In one case, a woman bequeathed her entire estate to a non-relative while depriving her agnatic brother. The brother consented to the bequest and "allowed it willingly and out of his free choice" in return for monetary compensation. The qāḍī, Shaykh Ṭāhir Ḥamād, endorsed the bequest after having established: "It is well-known that a bequest is not operative (*nāfidha*) except with the consent of the heirs."[112] In another case, however, the same qāḍī endorsed a bequest, relying on the consent of the testator's female agnates while ignoring the absence from court of the testator's uterine sister, whose consent had not been obtained.[113] Usually, the consent of the heirs is requested for bequests in favor of legal heirs and of the *entire* estate, with no explicit reference, however, to the issue of bequests that exceed the bequeathable third.

## 6 "Civil" Bequests according to the Israeli Law of Succession

The Succession Law of 1965 has downgraded the jurisdiction of the *sharīʿa* courts in matters of succession and wills from exclusive to concurrent, that is, jurisdiction in these matters has been transferred to the district court unless all the parties concerned have consented in writing to the jurisdiction of the religious court (Sections 151(a) and 155(a)). The provisions of the law apply if the matter is heard before a district court. If, however, the parties have consented to its jurisdiction, the *sharīʿa* court *may* "follow its religious law" provided that, if the parties include a minor (under eighteen) or a person declared legally incompetent, his rights of succession, either upon intestacy or under will, are not to be less than they would have been under the Succession Law (Section 155(c)). Since the *mīrī* category has been abolished for the purposes of succession (Section 149), consent to the jurisdiction of the religious court

111 Cf. Layish, *Women and Islamic Law*, 290–91.

112 Jaffa, Sijill Qarārāt, vol. 2, p. 524[573?], file 34/62, no. 503 (22 April 1962). See also vol. 3, p. 16, file 55/63, no. 24 (17 July 1963); Layish, *Women and Islamic Law*, 312.

113 Jaffa, Sijill Qarārāt, vol. 2, p. 521, file 21/61, no. 497 (5 April 1962).

is sufficient to allow for the application of the *sharʿī* will not only to *mulk* and movables but also to *mīrī*.[114]

The probating of a number of Muslim bequests took place in district courts. The exact scope of this phenomenon can be assessed only on the basis of systematic study of probates issued by civil courts. A good notion of Muslims' resort to district courts may be obtained from cases dealing with intestacy, the most common way of transmitting an estate.[115] Additional evidence on succession orders and probates of bequests that took place in civil courts may be obtained from land registers. In the early 1970s, I concluded that Israeli Muslims preferred the more intimate atmosphere of the *sharīʿa* court to the alien, impersonal civil court which was identified with the government authority.[116] Since then several Muslim judges have been appointed to district courts and it seems that Muslim inhibitions about resorting to these courts have diminished.[117] Other causes for this attitudinal change are Muslims' integration into Israeli society, the spread of knowledge of the Hebrew language among Arabs raised in Israel, and the emancipation of women. Muḥammad Fāʿūr, a clerk of the Haifa Land Registry, reports that in urban areas such as Acre, the tendency of resorting to district courts for initiating probate is much stronger than in rural areas, and that young lawyers trained in Israeli law prefer the civil court to the *sharīʿa* court.[118] However, the patterns of entitlement that emerge from bequests probated by civil courts are essentially the same as in bequests confirmed by *sharīʿa* courts. What is perhaps unique about the civil courts is the attempts by females to oppose their being deprived of the estate.[119] The preference of sons has also been observed in a sample of bequests made by inhabitants of Umm al-Faḥm recorded in Haifa land registers.[120]

Qāḍīs are generally unaware of the requirement of obtaining the parties' consent to the jurisdiction of the *sharīʿa* court in matters pertaining to probate, and their attention to this requirement generally has been drawn by heirs. In

---

114 Layish, *Women and Islamic Law*, 281–82, 309. Section 155(c) – according to the amended version of 1981.

115 See, for example, *Pesaqim (District)*, vol. 30, p. 72ff.; 1979, pt. 2, p. 89ff. See also *Pisqei Din* (Supreme Court sitting as Court of Appeal on civil matters), vol. 33, pt. 2, 1979, p. 34ff.; vol. 46, pt.1, 1992, p. 749ff.

116 Layish, *Women and Islamic Law*, 331–32.

117 In 1993 there were four Muslim judges in the district courts of Nazareth (two), Haifa and Tel Aviv. Aṭallāh Manṣūr, *Ishim ʿAravim be-Yisraʾel* (Jerusalem: Sikkuy, 1993), 9.

118 Interview conducted by Eliyahu Stern (May 1992).

119 Haifa District Court, inheritance files 730/85 and 970/85 (Ḥijāzī et al. vs. Abū Shanab et al., *Pesaqim*, 1986, 3, pp. 512ff.; Inheritance files 457/86, 698/86, 699/86 (Abū Ḥusayn et al. vs. Jabbārīn Ḥafīẓa), p. 520ff.; Inheritance file 1177/85 (3 October 1985)(unpublished).

120 See, for example, deed files 11563, 10321, 16409.

one case, a legatee protested the probate on the ground that jurisdiction was vested in the district court by virtue of Section 151(a) of the Succession Law of 1965 and that consent of the heirs to the jurisdiction of the *sharīʿa* court had not been obtained as required under Section 155(a). Consequently, Shaykh Muḥammad Ḥubayshī refrained from dealing with the matter. In another case, Shaykh Tawfīq ʿAsaliyya issued a probate in reliance on Section 155. He did not indicate explicitly that he was referring to Section 155(a), and in any case the parties were not requested to consent to his jurisdiction. The qāḍī may have been referring to the application of the *sharīʿa* under Section 155(c).[121] In orders of succession issued by *sharīʿa* courts until the mid-1970s it has been observed that only a few qāḍīs were fully aware of the requirement of obtaining the parties' consent to the jurisdiction of the *sharīʿa* court. Most of them dealt with the issue of consent in the context of the application of the *sharʿī* inheritance rules rather than in the context of the jurisdiction of the *sharīʿa* court, as required under Section 155(a). As already mentioned, the parties' consent to the jurisdiction of the *sharīʿa* court implies the application of the *sharīʿa*.[122]

Several bequests confirmed in the Sharīʿa Courts of Acre and Haifa during the period of the late Shaykh Muḥammad Ḥubayshī create the impression that they were drawn up in conformity with the provisions of the Succession Law of 1965 rather than the *sharīʿa*. In one case, the testatrix stated that she was registering her bequest "in accordance with the Israeli laws and regulations applicable, including the Succession Law of 1965." While this bequest starts with a religious formula common in religious bequests, otherwise it has no substantial elements that may be related unequivocally to the *sharīʿa*. Her statement that she was fully qualified, mentally and physically, and that she had signed the bequest willingly and of her free choice with no coercion or compulsion may be rooted in the provisions of the Israeli succession law (Sections 26, 30). A few years later the court issued probate in accordance with the Succession Law of 1965.[123] In other cases, testators requested confirmation of their bequests "by virtue (*bi-mūjib*) of the Israeli Succession Law of 1965." The bequests involved the whole estate and were made in favor of legal heirs, and there was no indication whatsoever concerning the parties' consent to

---

121 Acre, file 25/86 (5 March 1986); and Jaffa, Sijill Qarārāt, vol. 5, pp. 96–97, file 279/69 (23 October 1969), respectively.

122 For example, Jaffa, Sijill Qarārāt, vol. 9, p. 106, file 583/71, no. 195 (5 January 1972); vol. 10, p. 297, file 234/73, no. 538 (7 July 1973); vol. 13, p. 191, file 112/75, no. 191 (11 March 1975); p. 288, file 261/75, no. 288 (13 May 1975); vol. 14, p. 277, file 707/75, no. 277 (19 November 1975); Layish, *Women and Islamic Law*, 308–09.

123 Acre, file 133/81 (5 April 1981); and file 166/86 (8 May 1986), respectively.

these bequests. Nor was there any indication that "the Israeli Succession Law" implied the parties' consent either to the jurisdiction of the *sharīʿa* court or to the application of the *sharīʿa* as required under Section 155(a) and (c), respectively. Again, religious formulas and legal elements that can be identified in the *sharīʿa* (such as the testator's mental and physical competence, the making of the bequest willingly and of free choice, etc.) are incorporated in the bequest, but the possibility that these bequests were made and probated in accordance with the provisions of the Succession Law of 1965 cannot be ruled out.[124] Shaykh Muḥammad Ḥubayshī occasionally would add, while issuing a probate, that the testator "transmitted his statutory estate" (*inḥaṣara irthuhu al-qānūnī*), or "this distribution is valid by virtue of the bequest and the Law of Succession of 1965."[125]

The above-mentioned evidence from the Sharīʿa Courts of Acre and Haifa suggests that what we have here is not just the technical confirmation of wills by virtue of the competence vested in the *sharīʿa* court under Section 155(a), but rather vital substantive and procedural elements based in Israeli succession law, which distinguish a civil bequest from a religious one. According to Ḥanafī doctrine, a purely oral declaration of a bequest is valid. Moreover, an oral bequest may be validated exclusively by the testimony of witnesses who were present at its declaration.[126] Yet most if not all the bequests were made in writing, many of them in the *sharīʿa* court in the presence of the qāḍī.[127] The bequests were made contrary to the *ultra vires* doctrine, that is, they were made in favor of legal heirs and concerned the entire estate. Considerable evidence shows that the qāḍī confirmed such bequests, paying little attention to these restrictions or to the requirement of obtaining the heirs' consent to bequests deviating from the *ultra vires* doctrine.[128] One wonders whether the lack of objection on the part of the legal heirs to the content of a bequest, as advertised in a newspaper by the *sharīʿa* court prior to the issuance of a probate, was conceived by the late qāḍī – albeit with no apparent justification – as consent to both deviation from the *ultra vires* doctrine and the jurisdiction of

---

124 Haifa, Sijill Daʿāwā, vol. 6, file 164/80 (6 November 1980); vol. 9, p. 51, file 125/82, no. 37/82 (7 October 1982). See also vol. 6, p. 6, file [?]/83, no. 29/83 (25 April 1983).

125 Acre, file 166/86 (8 May 1986); file 399/87 (1 November 1987); Sijill, vol. 23, p. 115, file 307/88, no. 115/88 (22 February 1988); p. 28, file 69/88, no. 28/88 (6 March 1988).

126 Coulson, *Succession in the Muslim Family*, 215–16.

127 For example, Haifa, Sijill Daʿāwā, vol. 6, p. [110], no. [28/80] (19 June 1980); file 164/80 (6 November 1980); vol. 9, p. 51, file 125/82, no. 37/82 (7 October 1982); Acre, file 133/81 (5 April 1981); file 285/82 (13 September 1982); file 47/85 (27 January 1985).

128 For example, Acre, file 33/86 (30 September 1968 and 15 February 1986); file 51/87 (26 February 1987). Cf. Shaham, "The Muslim Family in Egypt," 265.

the *sharīʿa* court.[129] Moreover, in one case the qāḍī issued a probate resting on Sections 25, 39 and 66(a) of the Succesion Law of 1965.[130] Section 25 provides that the court may issue probate regardless of technical defects in the bequest, including defects in the lawfulness of the witnesses (a very sensitive issue under the *sharīʿa*), provided the court is convinced of the bequest's authenticity. Section 39 provides that no rights in the estate by virtue of a bequest may be claimed unless probate has been issued in accordance with the provisions of Chapter 5 of the statute. Section 66(a) provides that the court may declare the heirs' rights under both intestacy and testamentary disposition by virtue of probate. It goes without saying that these sections are meant to be applied only in district courts.

Making a bequest in conformity with an Israeli statute in the *sharīʿa* court is hardly surprising. Such a phenomenon – with regard to intestacy – was already observed in the 1970s. Some of the qāḍīs used to distribute estates according to dual systems: *mulk* property and movables according to *sharīʿa* law, and *mīrī* property according to Israeli succession law. In one instance, a qāḍī distributed the entire estate, regardless of its legal categories, in accordance with the Israeli statute although the religious court may "follow its religious law," that is, distribute the entire estate, including the *mīrī* category, according to the *sharʿī* law of inheritance.[131] Remnants of this dual distribution also may be found in bequests. Occasionally, Shaykh Muḥammad Ḥubayshī would state, while issuing probate, that the testator "transmitted his *sharʿī* and statutory (*qānūnī, niẓāmī, intiqālī*) estate in accordance with the written bequest."[132] It seems that this formula relates to the *mulk* and *mīrī* categories, respectively. This dual distribution has been relevant since the application of the Ottoman Succession Law of 1913 to *mīrī* property. The distinction between the two categories ceased to be relevant with the promulgation of the Succession Law of 1965, which abrogated the category of *mīrī* for the purposes of succession, and, in any case, this category was totally abolished by the Land Law of 1969. It goes without saying that the distinction between the two categories is meaningless in the context of bequests since it was not legally permitted to make a will with regard to *mīrī* property. It thus seems that the resort to this formula

129 I owe this observation to my colleague, Advocate Ori Stendel.

130 Haifa, Sijill Daʿāwā, vol. 5, file 37/77 (19 May 1977).

131 Layish, *Women and Islamic Law*, 309–10. Cf. idem, "The Islamization of the Bedouin Family," 49.

132 Acre, file 149/85 (14 May 1985); file 251/85 (21 July 1985); file 51/87 (26 February 1987); file 58[?]/88 (18 December 1988); vol. 24, p. 9, file 3/89, no. 9/89 (17 January 1989); p. 78, file 229/89, no. 78/89 (27 June 1989); p. 133, file 440/89, no. 133/89 (27 September 1989).

by the qāḍī is a rhetorical routine devoid of any substantive significance.[133] To sum up, what has been observed in the Sharīʿa Courts of Acre and Haifa is tantamount, in almost every respect, to civil bequests which are expected to be probated by a civil court.[134] The religious formulas inserted in the bequests may be regarded as an embellishment that serves to legitimize, in *sharʿī* terms, the "civil" character of the bequests.

## 7 Summary and Conclusions

The bequest has become a useful instrument for settling property relations in Israeli Muslim society. Its motives are essentially the same as those pertaining to family *waqf*. Some of the motives are traditional and some reflect new conditions that are unique to Israeli Muslims. The testator's religious outlook is doubtless an important source of inspiration in making a bequest, as it is with founding a family *waqf*. In most bequests the testator incorporates religious formulas to demonstrate that he desires to perform an act that may "satisfy God – may He be exalted – and afford Him gratification" (*iḥtisāban li-wajhi allāh taʿālā wa-'btighāʾan li-marḍātihi*).[135] The bequest verses in the Qurʾān (2:180, 240) instruct the believer anticipating death to bequeath his or her property to parents, wives, and near relatives. These verses were abrogated, in part, by subsequent Qurʾānic verses that established rules of inheritance (4:11–12, 176), and by prophetic *ḥadīths* and the infallible consensus of the community that imposed personal and quantitative restrictions on testamentary disposition (the *ultra vires* doctrine).[136] However, the basic attitude toward testamentary dispositions as an act of charity entailing reward in the Hereafter seems to have remained intact. The uniform style of the religious formulas inserted in wills drawn up in *sharīʿa* courts points to the qāḍīs' active role in drafting these formulas.

The main purpose of testamentary dispositions in Israeli Muslim society is, however, to serve as a means of circumventing the compulsory inheritance rules (*ʿilm al-farāʾiḍ*). Until the promulgation of the Succession Law of 1965, this mechanism was not an efficient means to this end, being bound to the

133 Cf. Jaffa, Sijill Qarārāt, vol. 17, pp. 72–73, file 835/76, no. 84 (13 December 1976).

134 Cf. Edoardo Vitta, *The Conflict of Laws in Matters of Personal Status in Palestine* (Tel Aviv: S. Bursi, 1947), 169.

135 Jaffa, Sijill Qarārāt, vol. 20, p. 89, file 459/78, no. 89 (12 July 1978).

136 Coulson, *Succession in the Muslim Family*, 213ff.; David S. Powers, *Studies in Qur'an and Ḥadīth* (Berkeley and Los Angeles: University of California Press, 1986), 21ff., 51–52, 143ff., 184ff.

*ultra vires* doctrine, although to some extent Muslims managed to circumvent the *ultra vires* doctrine by exerting pressure on legal heirs to consent to their disinheritance in favor of male agnates. One wonders whether the qāḍīs made every effort to ascertain that such consent was given willingly. Since 1965 the testamentary disposition has become the chief instrument in this respect, due to a combination of factors:

a. The Succession Law of 1965 removed the bar – dating back to the Ottoman period – against making a will with respect to *mīrī* property, the prevailing type of property in rural areas. Two-thirds of all wills in my corpus were established subsequent to the promulgation of this law.
b. The downgrading of the *sharīʿa* courts' jurisdiction from exclusive to concurrent in matters of succession and wills makes complete freedom of testation according to the Israeli succession law available to Muslims in district courts, and, as mentioned, the reluctance of Muslims to resort to these courts appears to have diminished since the late 1960s.
c. It seems that Israeli succession law, intended to be applied only in civil courts, has had a substantial impact on molding the normative attitudes and social practices of segments of the Muslim population exposed to Israeli-Jewish society.[137] This applies also to qāḍīs: Most of the present qāḍīs, including members of the Sharīʿa Court of Appeal, are graduates of Israeli faculties of law, humanities, and social sciences.[138] The recently retired President of the Sharīʿa Court of Appeal, Shaykh Tawfīq ʿAsaliyya, was the last qāḍī to graduate from al-Azhar. Shaykh Aḥmad Nāṭūr, President of the Sharīʿa Court of Appeal, concedes that qāḍīs apply Israeli statutory provisions even in circumstances in which they are fully authorized by the Knesset to apply the *sharīʿa*. He has recently reminded the qāḍīs that the *ultra vires* doctrine should be strictly observed in the *sharīʿa* courts.[139] In the early 1950s, when most of the qāḍīs were trained in traditional *sharīʿa*, they vehemently opposed the original Succession Bill of 1952 according to which exclusive jurisdiction in matters of succession was to be transferred from the *sharīʿa* to the district court and the *sharʿī* law of inheritance was to be superseded entirely by secular law. Protest meetings were held in mosques with a view to preventing the enactment of the statute.[140] Usually, social and economic change

137 Cf. Layish, *Women and Islamic Law*, 329ff.
138 Three of seven qāḍīs are graduates of faculties of law and three are graduates of faculties of humanities and social sciences (Yitzhak Reiter, personal communication, 26 June, 1995).
139 Personal communication, 23 August, 1994.
140 See further Layish, *Women and Islamic Law*, 310–11.

stimulates legal change, not the other way around. In Israel, however, this applies only to Jewish society. Knesset legislation, introduced in conformity with internal pressures within Jewish society, is being superimposed on Muslim society from above.

Resort to bequests as an instrument for circumventing the inheritance rules is shaped by several factors, chief among them the testator's wish to maintain the patrimony intact under the control of the agnatic (and, if possible, the nuclear) family. This cannot be achieved by means of the compulsory rules of inheritance which are adapted to the extended, rather than nuclear, family, and which tend to divide the patrimony among a large number of heirs and into economically unsound units: Qurʾānic and agnatic heirs participate in the inheritance simultaneously rather than successively. The Qurʾānic heirs may transmit their shares, in turn, to their respective heirs through exogamous marriages and otherwise. All the heirs in a given case are entitled to their *sharʿī* shares in the estate in all types of property, thus establishing joint ownership (*mushāʿ*) which often leads to disputes among the heirs and other problems that may have a negative impact.[141] Against this, the complete freedom of testation available to Israeli Muslims enables the testator to fully determine the disposition of his estate after his death.

The main tendency of the testamentary patterns is the testator's effort to prevent the fragmentation of the patrimony by preserving it in the hands of his immediate male issue, that is, his sons, or – in their absence – other male agnates. Wives and daughters, in most cases, are allotted residential rights and subsistence allowances rather than full ownership in the estate. The main reason for the exclusion of Qurʾānic heirs seems to be the testator's fear that their shares in the estate might be lost to the family through exogamous marriage. Concentrating the estate in units as complete and as economically sound as possible, within the exclusive ownership of the testator's sons or agnates, without other heirs participating along with them concurrently in the estate, is another manifestation of the testator's effort to maintain the integrity of the patrimony. The bequest in favor of orphaned grandchildren is also motivated by the desire to circumvent the inheritance rules. The notion of representation is alien to inheritance law; a grandchild whose parent predeceases his grandfather is excluded from the latter's estate by his paternal uncle, who is closer in degree to the praepositus. Since an orphaned grandchild is not a legal

141 Layish, "The Family *Waqf* and Succession," 46–48; idem, "The Mālikī Family *Waqf*," 27–28. Cf. Powers, "The Mālikī Family Endowment," 379, 394; idem, "Orientalism and Legal History," 566; Marcus, "Real Property and Society," 113, and the sources indicated in nt. 5; Messick, "Transactions in Ibb," 376.

heir, there is no *sharʿī* bar against making a bequest in his favor within the bequeathable third. Thus, the bequest makes it possible to correct, by means of the "obligatory bequest," what the modern legislator regards as a social wrong based on the *sharīʿa*.[142]

Another reason for circumventing the inheritance rules by means of a bequest relates to the problem of absentees' property which emerged when the State of Israel was established. There is much evidence to this effect in land registers.[143] One way to prevent absentees' property or shares in such estates from falling under the control of the Custodian is to bequeath the entire estate to legal heirs who are present. Such a motive is indicated implicitly on various occasions. For example, in one case the testator declared that he had property "at his complete disposal (*taṣarruf*), though part of it is [legally] under the control of the Custodian of Absentees' Property." He bequeathed his entire estate to his son "as a reward in return for maintenance provided by the latter," and instructed that "the heirs or non-heirs must not oppose him [the testator]." This seems to be an attempt to prevent the Custodian from taking control of the shares of the absentee heirs after the testator's death.[144] In this connection mention should be made of bequests in favor of non-relatives, apparently intended to prevent the devolution of heirless estates into the hands of the General Custodian in a non-Muslim state. I have come across only one instance in which the *sharīʿa* court decided that an heirless estate, upon intestacy, should pass to *bayt al-māl*.[145]

Another factor (not very frequent) for making a bequest is the testator's wish to reimburse the legatee for money borrowed from him. In one case,

142 Cf. Layish, "The Family *Waqf* and Succession," 46; idem, "The Mālikī Family *Waqf*," 29.

143 E. g., Haifa Land Registry, block 20302, file/deed 3993, parcel 1 (6 March 1988); file/deed 10684/1–2, parcel 28 (19 August 1983). Aharon Liskovski [Layish], "'Hanifqadim hanochaḥim' bi-Israel," *Hamizrah Hehadash*, vol. 10, no. 3 (1960), 186–92.

144 Jaffa, Sijill Qarārāt, vol. 10, p. 32, file 244/72, no. 53 (19 June 1972). See also Jaffa, Sijill Qarārāt, vol. 3, p. 194, file 99/65, no. 321 (19 December 1965); Acre, Sijill Daʿāwā, vol. 6, p. 1, file 1/64, no. 1/64 (5 January 1964); Jaffa, Sijill Qarārāt, vol. 3, p. 194, file 99/65, no. 321 (19 December 1965); Acre, Sijill Daʿāwā, vol. 6, p. 1, file 1/64, no. 1/64 (5 January 1964); Jaffa, Sijill Qarārāt, vol. 3, p. 194, file 99/65, no. 321 (19 December 1965). See also Acre, Sijill Daʿāwā, vol. 6, p. 1, file 1/64, no. 1/64 (5 January 1964); Jaffa, Sijill Qarārāt, vol. 2, p. 475, file 34/61, no. 498 (11 July 1961); vol. 3, p. 16, file 55/63, no. 24 (17 July 1963); and vol. 24, pp. 177–78, file 380/80, no. 155 (3 July 1980). Cf. Layish, *Women and Islamic Law*, 304. The use of the bequest as a means for depriving the Custodian of his shares in absentees' property was confirmed by the Custodian, Mr. Yehezkiel Shamash, who has considerable evidence to this effect (personal communication, 2 February, 1995).

145 Layish, *Women and Islamic Law*, 311. Cf. Shaham, "The Muslim Family in Egypt," 265; Reiter, "The Muslim *Waqf* in Jerusalem under the British Mandate," 99; Layish, "The Mālikī Family *Waqf*," 1–3, 28.

discussed above, a woman bequeathed her property to one of her sons. She explained that she had borrowed a sum of money from him but had been unable to repay the debt during her lifetime. She instructed the other heirs to consent to the bequest after her death and warned that whoever withheld his consent would be obliged to pay her debt out of his own pocket. In another case a man bequeathed his property to a non-relative to cover expenses the latter had incurred while the testator was hospitalized. He stipulated, however, that the legatee should pay his (the testator's) debts.[146]

The *sharʿī* law of inheritance is designed to protect the Qur'ānic heirs, a group consisting mainly of females and cognates within the inner family circle. These relatives are considered weak heirs in a society based on agnation. Traditional *sharʿī* testamentary disposition, bound by the *ultra vires* doctrine, cannot seriously disturb the inheritance rules without the consent of the Qur'ānic heirs. However, the extent to which freedom of bequest (by virtue of either the Israeli succession law or day-to-day practice) affects the position of the Qur'ānic heirs deserves consideration, inasmuch as, since 1965, Israeli Muslims have been able legally to bequeath not only *mulk* and moveable property but also *mīrī* property.

Generally speaking, it seems that the position of the Qur'ānic heirs has been negatively affected, although a clear distinction should be made between the various heirs. A testator's effort to concentrate the patrimony in the hands of sons and male agnates naturally affects the position of females in the estate. There are instances of bequests in which full ownership of property is bequeathed to a wife, occasionally even shares larger than her *sharʿī* portion on intestacy. Likewise, there are instances of equal apportionment of the estate between sons and daughters or between grandsons and granddaughters. However, depriving wives and daughters of the estate still seems to be the dominant pattern. Even when bequests are made in their favor, the testator often stipulates that their entitlement is dependant on their marital status, which implies that a married woman is deprived of her rights in the estate. Some testators bequeath females lifetime usufruct, rather than the full ownership of property, which means that they cannot transmit their rights in the property to their issue or effect any transaction thereof. In this respect the testator seems to be using the bequest to control the marital behavior of his wife and daughters. While excluding his wife and daughters from the estate, the testator is usually anxious to secure their economic well-being by allocating them subsistence allowances and residential rights in a house or a flat for the

146 Nazareth, Sijill Ḥujaj, vol. 15, pp. 34–35, no. 5/58 (6 April 1950); and Jaffa, Sijill Qarārāt, vol. 3, p. 140, file 110/64, no. 219 (2 September 1964), respectively.

duration of their lifetimes. This is tantamount to maintenance out of the estate which, in Muslim society, is a matter of practice rather than law.

Forty-one percent of the bequests were made by women,[147] decisive proof – if proof is still needed – that Muslim women enjoy the freedom to own and dispose of property.[148] The wills occasionally contain data pertaining to the source of the bequeathed property, indicating that a woman inherited the property from her father,[149] her husband[150] or her son.[151] Isolated evidence indicates that women earn money and accumulate property independently.[152] The bequests demonstrate a woman's capacity to dispose of property, especially in circumstances in which the legatees are females, cognates, and non-relatives. In such circumstances, there is no doubt that women enjoy the freedom of testation uninhibited by pressures exerted by agnates. Indeed, without exception, bequests to daughters as sole legatees and to cognatic grandchildren were made by women. In bequests by women in favor of their children, no tendency to deprive daughters has been observed. On the contrary, there is a clear tendency to apportion the estate equally between sons and daughters, and, occasionally, even to prefer the latter over the former. It seems that women are less concerned than men about the impact of out-marrying daughters upon the unity of the patrimony. This assumption finds support in bequests by women in favor of non-relatives of both sexes in return for devoted treatment and other services rendered by the legatees, occasionally even while depriving an agnatic relative. When a woman makes a bequest in favor of an agnatic relative, we cannot rule out the possibility that she has done so under pressure exerted by that agnate, or another, rather than of her own free will, as required by both *sharʿī* and statutory law. It may well be that the bequest is being used by the agnates as an instrument for reconcentrating the patrimony following its fragmentation upon intestacy.[153]

147 Cf. Layish, *Women and Islamic Law*, 294.

148 Cf. Marcus, "Real Property and Society," 113, 117ff., 119, 120; Martha Mundy, "Women's Inheritance in Highland Yemen," *Arabian Studies*, 5 (1979), 161–87; Messick, "Transactions in Ibb," 389, 399–400; Annelies Moors, "Women and Dower Property in Twentieth-Century Palestine: The Case of Jabal Nablus," *Islamic Law and Society*, 1:3 (1994), 301–31; Shatzmiller, "Women and Property Rights", 253ff.

149 Jaffa, Sijill Qarārāt, vol. 1, p. 392, file 20/59, no. 550 (4 May 1959); vol. 2, p. 506, file 101/61, no. 566 (12 December 1961); vol. 10, p. 64, file 1307/72, no. 107 (19 July 1972).

150 For example, Jaffa, Sijill Qarārāt, vol. 2, p. 601, no. 646 (16 June 1963); vol. 7, p. 168, file 27/71, no. 198 (10 January 1971).

151 For example, Jaffa, Sijill Qarārāt, vol. 8, p. 146, file 304/71, no. 207 (28 June 1971). Cf. Layish, *Women and Islamic Law*, 303.

152 For example, Jaffa, Sijill Qarārāt, vol. 12, p. 75, file 579/74, no. 117 (9 January 1975).

153 For example, Jaffa, Sijill Qarārāt, vol. 1, p. 252, file 47/56, no. 392 (20 December 1956). See above, 293; Layish, *Women and Islamic Law*, 294.

The abolition of the *mīrī* category with regard to succession, provided for in the Succession Law of 1965, has exposed weak heirs to the danger of being deprived of their rights with respect to the entire estate, including the former *mīrī* category, which constitutes the bulk of the land in the State. Until 1965 the vast majority of wills were made in urban environments. Thus, for example, of thirty wills registered in the Sharīʿa Court of Jaffa, whose jurisdiction includes Jaffa, Lod, Ramla, West Jerusalem, and its countryside (until 1987) and the Negev (until 1978), 90 percent were made by urban residents. Against this, not a single will was registered in the Sharīʿa Court of Ṭayyiba, whose jurisdiction includes the villages of the Little Triangle. Since the promulgation of the Succession Law of 1965, a dramatic change has been observed in the division of wills. Out of thirty-six wills registered in the Sharīʿa Court of Acre, whose jurisdiction includes Acre, Haifa (until 1971), and the villages of Western Galilee, 53 percent were made by villagers and 44 percent by residents of Acre. In the Sharīʿa Court of Haifa, whose jurisdiction includes Haifa and its countryside, seven wills were registered between 1977–83, five of them by villagers and only two by residents of Haifa. Prior to the Succession Law of 1965 I came across only isolated instances of bequests with respect to *mīrī* property.[154] The qāḍīs are usually cognizant of the distinction between *mulk* and *mīrī* categories. Such a distinction is made by them also with respect to probates. For example, in one case the qāḍī ruled that *mulk* and movable property should be transmitted to the son of the testatrix in accordance with her bequest, while *mīrī* property should be transmitted to him in accordance with the law of inheritance, by virtue of his being the sole heir. By contrast, the Druze, who reside mainly in rural environments, bequeath property irrespective of its legal category and with no distinction between *mulk* and *mīrī*, even prior to the promulgation of the Succession Law of 1965.[155] It seems reasonable to assume that most of the wills made by Muslims in rural areas after 1965 were made with respect to the former *mīrī* category.

Wills made by Bedouin also should be mentioned. On the face of it, this phenomenon is surprising since the Bedouin do not as a rule resort to *sharīʿa* courts in matters of succession, but rather divide the estate in accordance with tribal custom.[156] Bedouin resort to *sharīʿa* courts in this matter, as in other matters of personal status, has increased with their sedentarization.[157] Among the

154 Jaffa, Sijill Qarārāt, vol. 2, p. 601, no. 646 (16 June 1963); and Acre, Sijill Daʿāwā, vol. 6, p. 1, file 1/64, no. 1/64 (5 January 1964). Cf. Shaham, "The Muslim Family in Egypt," 263.

155 Jaffa, Sijill Qarārāt, vol. 3, p. 59, file 142/63, no. 48 (2 September 1963) and p. 124, file 89/64, no. 197 (8 July 1964); Layish, "The Druze Testamentary *Waqf*," 139.

156 Aḥmad Nāṭūr, "Shariʿa u-minhag ba-mishpaḥa ha-bedewit ba-Negev ʿal pi ha-pesiqa shel beit ha-din ha-sharʿi bi-Beʾer Sheva," *Hamizrah Hehadash*, vol. xxxiii (1991), 110–11.

157 Layish, "The Islamization of the Bedouin Family," 39–40, 49.

Bedouin of the Negev, whose traditional social framework is to some extent still preserved, the will is used unequivocally to preserve the patrimony's integrity.[158] Among the Bedouin of Galilee, who are in an advanced stage of transition to rural society, no tendency toward depriving women of the estate has been observed. Moreover, a tendency toward equal treatment of men and women, or at least a concern for their welfare, has been observed.[159] Wills deviating from the *ultra vires* doctrine have been observed also among the Bedouin of the Judaean Desert and it seems that they were inspired by tribal custom ("*Jāhilī*" wills) rather than normative *sharīʿa*.[160]

In sum, the bequest, like the family *waqf*,[161] has become an efficient instrument for the circumvention of the inheritance rules. According to one researcher, the original import of the Qurʾānic inheritance legislation was to allow a large measure of testamentary freedom.[162] With the patterns discerned among the Muslims of Israel, we now seem to have come full circle.[163] Efforts to consolidate the patrimony's integrity under the control of male agnates, while depriving Qurʾānic heirs and females, mark in many respects a victory of custom over the *sharīʿa*. However, while the family *waqf* developed outside the law of inheritance in order to accommodate that law to social and economic pressures, traditional *sharʿī* testamentary disposition, bound by the *ultra vires* doctrine, does not replace the compulsory rules of inheritance, but rather complements it from within. The freedom of testation that prevails among Israeli Muslims makes it possible to replace the inheritance rules altogether, and in this respect it is similar to the *waqf* mechanism. Once the testamentary disposition managed to release itself from the bonds of the *ultra vires* doctrine – to the extent that this is manifested in the *sharīʿa* courts presided over by Shaykh Muḥammad Ḥubayshī – the family *waqf* lost its *raison d'être* as a means of circumventing the inheritance rules.[164] Testamentary disposition free of any restriction has many advantages compared to the family *waqf*:

158 Jaffa, Sijill Qarārāt, vol. 17, pp. 72–73, file 835/76, no. 84 (13 December 1976); and vol. 2, p. 521, file 21/61, no. 497 (5 April 1962), respectively.

159 Acre, file 33/86 (30 September 1968 and 15 February 1986); file 98/85 (5 March 1985); Nazareth, Sijill Ḥujaj, vol. 24. p. 110, file 174/67, no. 5/82 (18 December 1967).

160 Aharon Layish and Avshalom Shmueli, "Custom and *Sharīʿa* in the Bedouin Family according to Legal Documents from the Judaean Desert," *Bulletin of the School of Oriental and African Studies*, xlii, pt. 1 (1979), 40–41.

161 Layish, "The Family *Waqf* and Succession," 47; idem, "The Mālikī Family *Waqf*," 30.

162 See Powers, *Studies in Qurʾan and Ḥadīth*, 21ff., 145ff.

163 I owe this observation to David Powers.

164 On the causes of the revival of Muslim *waqf* in East Jerusalem after 1967, see Layish, "The Muslim *Waqf* in Jerusalem," 148–49, 163ff.; Reiter, "The Muslim *Waqf* in Jerusalem under the British Mandate," 99; cf. idem, "Family *Waqf* Entitlements in British Palestine," 192–93.

It becomes operative only upon the testator's death; until then he or she is the full and exclusive owner of his or her property in every respect; he or she may revise the will and even revoke it if desired, as indeed happens occasionally.[165] Moreover, the will makes it possible to distribute the estate in an economically sound manner, thus avoiding the negative consequences associated with the compulsory rules of inheritance. Unlike the founder of a family *waqf*, the testator is not allowed to determine the mode of transmission of the estate from one generation to the next and the mode of its distribution among the heirs in every generation. Instead, the testator leaves the legatees full discretion concerning all issues pertaining to the devolution of the estate to their heirs. As a full owner of his share in the estate, the legatee is entitled to administer it independently, thus avoiding conflicts of interest that arise in family *waqf* between the beneficiaries and the *mutawallī*. Whereas the juridical link between the beneficiary and the endowed property is severed by the act of dedication, the juridical link between the legatee and the bequeathed property does not cease, and this, in turn, provides a strong incentive to adequate management of the estate. Since full ownership of the bequeathed property is vested in the legatee, bequests (unlike, with some qualifications, *waqf* property) are not removed from economic circulation.

165 For example, Jaffa, Sijill Qarārāt, vol. 2, p. 591, file 49/63, no. 627 (16 April 1963); vol. 3, p. 90, file 5/65, no. 139 (10 February 1964); vol. 17, p. 214, file 384/77, no. 215 (15 June 1977); Nazareth, Sijill Ḥujaj, vol. 24, p. 110, file 174/67, no. 5/82 (18 December 1967).

CHAPTER 18

# The Muslim *Waqf* in Israel

On 2 February 1965, the Knesset passed the 'Absentees' Property Law' Amendment No. 3 (Release and Use of Endowment Property, 5725/1965).[*,1] This law effected a substantial change in the *waqf*, an institution so deeply rooted in Muslim society since earliest times that it has assumed a religious, sacred character. The *waqf* developed and consolidated in the course of time on a gigantic scale, and its negative effects are felt to this day in the society, economy and, especially, agrarian regime of several countries.

It is customary to regard the management of the *waqf* as one of the constituent elements of communal organization in Middle Eastern society for centuries past. We might mention many factors – religious, social and economic – which contributed to the development of the *waqf* in Muslim society.[2] The act of endowing contains an element of charity with a religious connotation; the *waqf* preserves the family property, enables circumvention of Muslim succession rules which make for fragmentation of the estate, prevents expropriation by the government, etc. Paradoxically, one of the reasons for the spread and strengthening of that institution may have been precisely a lack of communal organization in Muslim society. Communal organization is characteristic especially of the recognized religious communities which were tolerated in the Muslim state and which, therefore, were granted a certain measure of autonomy in regard to religious jurisdiction, the management of communal property, religious services, educational, welfare and health institutions and the like. The origin and background of the *millet* system show clearly that communal organization is alien to orthodox Islam. The lack of a tradition of communal organization in Muslim society, together with inactivity of the central and local authorities of the Muslim state in the field of social services, created conditions for the development of the *waqf*, which somehow made up for the absence of governmental and communal initiative. This aspect is worthy of notice in appraising the reforms introduced in the *waqf* in modern times.

---

* Originally published in *Asian and African Studies*, 2 (1966), pp. 41–76.

1 *Sefer ha-Ḥuqqim* No. 445 of 5 February 1965. For full text see Appendix.

2 On the factors of the development of the *waqf* see in greater detail S.D. Goitein and A. Ben Shemesh, *Muslim law in Israel* (Hebrew), Jerusalem, 1957, pp. 154–8; G. Baer, *Population and society in the Arab East*, London, 1964, p. 143.

 | DOI:10.1163/9789004680920_020

What little experience Israel Muslims have in the management of *waqf* property (and in other facets of communal administration) was gained during the Mandatory era, when Palestine ceased to be part of a Muslim state and became a separate administrative unit. The status of Muslims was equalized with that of the other recognized religious communities. The British administration set up an official communal agency for them, viz. the Supreme Muslim Council, and to this secular body it entrusted the care of all aspects of communal organization.

This organization collapsed totally upon the termination of the Mandate and the outbreak of the War of Independence. The members of the Supreme Muslim Council went abroad. The religious functionaries – *muftīs*, *qāḍīs*, *ʿulamāʾ* and senior personnel of the mosques – likewise left for Arab countries.[3] The religious legal system disintegrated, Muslim endowments were abandoned, communal educational, welfare and health institutions ceased to exist.

The Israel Government set about rehabilitating the organization of the Muslim community: the *Sharīʿa* Courts system was reconstituted with the same measure of jurisdiction as it had in Mandatory days;[4] marriage registrars were appointed, who act in coordination with the *Sharīʿa* Courts; regular monetary grants are given to about 200 Muslim religious functionaries (*imāms*, *khaṭībs*, *wāʿiẓs*, *muʾadhdhins* and caretakers, who serve at about 120 mosques throughout the country). Attention is paid to holy sites, i.e. mosques and cemeteries; existing ones are repaired and renovated, and new ones established. Muslim Committees have been set up in several towns where Muslim communities exist; they are concerned with religious services, welfare and religious instruction. A large Muslim orphanage has been opened in Acre, looked after by a board consisting of religious functionaries and public figures. Though the Muslims have no communal school system of their own, Muslim children are given religious instruction within the framework of the State schools. A special course has been held at the al-Jazzār Mosque in Acre for the training of religious functionaries in Muslim and general law as a reserve of future *qāḍīs*.

One of the problems of communal organization which until recently had not found a solution was the management of the Muslim *waqf* property. That property had passed to the Custodian of Absentees' property owing to circumstances connected with the establishment of the State, and its management had been withheld from the Muslim community. The Absentees'

3 Of all the *muftīs* and *qāḍīs* who served in official capacities during the Mandate, only one – Shaykh Ṭāhir al-Ṭabarī, the former Muftī and Qāḍī of Tiberias – has remained in Israel.

4 See A. Layish, 'Muslim religious jurisdiction in Israel', *Asian and African Studies* (AAS), vol. 1, 1965, pp. 49–79.

Property (Amendment No. 3) (Release and Use of Endowment Property) Law is designed to solve that problem. It will enable the Custodian to release *waqf khayrī* property (whose income is destined for public purposes, such as welfare, education and religious services) to Muslim boards of trustees to be set up in towns and villages, and *waqf dhurrī* property (whose income is intended for the family and descendants of the dedicator) to the beneficiaries. The release of the property will be accompanied by certain adjustments in the institution of the *waqf*. Before discussing the details of the law, let us review the factual situation as it has evolved until now.

## 1 The Powers of Shariʿa Courts in Regard to *waqf*

The wide powers wielded by *Sharīʿa* Courts in regard to *waqf* at the end of the Ottoman era were considerably reduced under the Mandate. The following is a review of the main changes which then occurred as regards material and personal jurisdiction and material law.

### 1.1 *Material Jurisdiction*

The Order in Council of 1922, from which almost all the religious courts in Israel derive their powers in matters of *waqf*,[5] restricted the jurisdiction of *Sharīʿa* Courts to *waqf*s of the *mulḥaq* category, i.e. *waqf*s whose administrators (*mutawallīs*) are private persons (these *waqf*s are mostly family endowments). Under article 52, *Sharīʿa* Courts shall have 'subject to the provisions of any Ordinance or of the Order of 20th December 1921 establishing a Supreme Council for Moslem Religious Affairs, or of any Orders amending the same, exclusive jurisdiction in cases of the constitution or internal administration of a Wakf constituted for the benefit of Moslems before a Moslem Religious Court'. Other matters relating to *waqf* came within the jurisdiction of the civil courts.[6]

Under the 1921 order, the Supreme Muslim Council was given unlimited control of the *waqf*s of the *maḍbūṭ* category, i.e. those whose management and the use of whose revenue were seen to by the *maʾmūr al-awqāf* independently

5 This is true of the Rabbinical Courts until 1953 (see below). The Druzes were recognized as a religious community only in 1957 – see A. Layish (Liskovski), 'Druze communal jurisdiction in Israel', *Hamizrah Hehadash*, vol. 11, No. 4 (44), 1961, pp. 258–62. The Druze courts derive their powers in matters of *waqf* (and personal status) from the Druze Religious Courts Law, 5723/1962, which was passed by the Knesset on 25 December 1962. See also below.

6 Frederic M. Goadby, *International and inter-religious private law in Palestine*, Jerusalem, 1926, p. 129.

of the *Sharīʿa* Court (they were generally *awqāf khayriyya*);[7] it was also given the right to supervise the administration of the *waqf*s of the *mulḥaq* category, whose establishment and internal management were, as stated, under the exclusive jurisdiction of the *Sharīʿa* Courts.[8] In 1937, these powers of the Supreme Muslim Council passed to a Government committee appointed by order of the High Commissioner (Defence [Moslem Waqf] Regulations, 1937). The Qāḍīs Law, 5721/1961, revoked the 1921 order establishing the Supreme Muslim Council. The revocation of this order raised the question of the continuance of the 1937 Regulations. The Supreme Court inclines to the view that these Regulations subsist independently of the 1921 order.[9] There are those, however, who hold that the revocation of the order implicitly voided also the 1937 Regulations. If this view is correct, the powers of the *Sharīʿa* Courts may have automatically regained their original extent, the extent they had prior to the promulgation of the 1921 order. In other words: since 1961, the *Sharīʿa* Courts in Israel may have had exclusive jurisdiction in matters relating to the establishment and internal management of Muslim endowments of both the *mulḥaq* and the *maḍbūṭ* categories.

Another notable change in the status of the *Sharīʿa* Courts under the Mandate was the negation of their power to deal with matters relating to the ownership and possession of land incidentally to dealing with matters of *waqf*. Until World War I, the *Sharīʿa* Courts had sole jurisdiction in matters of land of the different categories. In matters relating to *mulk*, they proceeded in accordance with the *Mecelle*, and in matters relating to other land in accordance with the Ottoman Land Code of 1858.[10] In 1914, the material jurisdiction of the *Sharīʿa* Courts became restricted to matrimonial and *waqf* matters, other matters being referred to the State courts.[11] But the *Sharīʿa* Courts continued to deal with land matters to the extent that the clarification of questions relating to *waqf* was involved. In 1918, the Military Administration issued an order prohibiting civil courts of first instance and *Sharīʿa* Courts 'until further notice' from adjudicating matters relating to the ownership or possession of land.[12]

7 Moreover, the *Sharīʿa* Courts were dependent on the Supreme Muslim Council in that the latter was competent to appoint and dismiss *qāḍīs* (Order of 21 December 1921, clause 8).

8 Order of 1921, clause 15. On the management of the *waqf* by the Supreme Muslim Council see in greater detail below.

9 See High Court of Justice (HCJ) No. 282/61, Muḥammad al-Surūjī, Dr. Jamīl al-Quṭb and Zuhayr Zakariyyā *v.* Minister of Religious Affairs and Acre Muslim Committee, *Pisqey Din*, vol. 17, p. 188.

10 See A. Ben Shemesh, *Land laws in the State of Israel* (Hebrew), Tel Aviv, 1953, pp. 11–12. See also Ottoman Land Code of 1858, art. 4A.

11 In greater detail, see Layish, *AAS*, vol. 1, 1965, pp. 52–3.

12 Military Proclamation of 24 June 1918, art. 23.

Jurisdiction in these matters was transferred to special Land Courts in 1921,[13] from these to District Courts in 1948[14] and has not been restored to the *Sharīʿa* Courts to this day. Moreover, an Ordinance of 1925 provided expressly that any matter relating to a right of ownership or possession of land was to be heard before a civil court even if one of the parties alleged that the land was *waqf*.[15] Questions as to the existence of a *waqf* or as to its being *ṣaḥīḥ* (genuine, i.e. established on *mulk* land) or *ghayr ṣaḥīḥ* (non-genuine, i.e. established on *mīrī* land)[16] have, since 1948, been under the jurisdiction of the District Court.[17]

All the above, of course, does not relate to lands which are *waqf **ghayr ṣaḥīḥ***, since *Sharīʿa* Courts had no jurisdiction as to these even during the final period of the Ottoman Empire; it was not possible to dedicate *mīrī* land as a genuine *waqf* without first converting it into *mulk* in one of the ways provided therefor by law.[18] In the legal respect, there is almost no difference between *mīrī* and *waqf ghayr ṣaḥīḥ*: the latter, too, is subject to all the Ottoman laws dealing with *mīrī*, especially the Land Code of 1858.[19] In actual fact, the application of these laws was not very strict in Ottoman days. *Mīrī* would be dedicated without the competent authority's consent being asked, and even without notifying it; and if afterwards the question of the validity of the *waqf* arose, resort would be had to a religious court, which dealt with the matter without regard for the secular laws.

The Mandatory legislator perceived the close connection between land matters and matters of personal status, and especially succession, and realized that special training was required in order to sort out cases involving endowments of religious communities. An Ordinance of the year 1928 provided, therefore, that upon the application of the Director of Lands the Supreme Muslim Council should appoint a *qāḍī* of the *Sharīʿa* Court, or a person approved for service as *qāḍī* by the Government, to issue succession certificates to Muslims, to decide succession disputes and to deal with other matters of personal status

13 Cf. Ben Shemesh, p. 321; F.M. Goadby and M.J. Doukhan, *The land law of Palestine*, Tel Aviv, 1935, p. 373.

14 Courts (Transitional Provisions) Ordinance, 5708/1948, sect. 8.

15 Civil and Religious Courts (Jurisdiction) Ordinance, 1925, sect. 5.

16 More exactly, whereas *waqf ṣaḥīḥ* involves the dedication of the ownership, in the case of *waqf ghayr ṣaḥīḥ* it is not the ownership that is dedicated (since it belongs to the State), but the tithe, or the right of use or possession, of *mīrī*. This kind of endowment is known also as *mīrī mawqūfa* – see Y. Shimoni, *The Arabs of Eretz Israel* (Hebrew), Tel Aviv, 5707 (1946–7), pp. 87–8.

17 See Ben Shemesh, p. 35.

18 Ottoman Land Code of 1858, art. 121.

19 Ibid., art. 4B. Cf. Ben Shemesh, p. 33; M. Doukhan, *Land laws in the State of Israel* (Hebrew), Jerusalem, 5713 (1962–3), p. 66.

of Muslims.[20] The Ordinance provided further that a land settlement officer, called upon to deal with any *waqf* property, might (and the Court interpreted this as 'must') invite a *qāḍī* (or, in the case of another community, a religious judge of the latter) to sit in as an advisory judge and brief him on the *waqf* law involved.[21]

### 1.2 *Personal Jurisdiction*

Under Ottoman rule and during the first years of the British administration – until 1922 – the *Sharīʿa* Courts had jurisdiction also in *waqf* matters of members of other communities. A non-Muslim could establish an endowment only before the *Sharīʿa* Court and, of course, in accordance with Muslim *waqf* law. This method was frequently resorted to in Palestine by both Christians and Jews.[22]

The new political situation created in the country after World War I put an end to the special status of the Muslims in relation to the other recognized religious communities. This found its expression in article 52 of the Order in Council in the restriction of the jurisdiction of the *Sharīʿa* Courts to *waqf*s established for the benefit of Muslims. In other words: their jurisdiction became confined to Muslim parties because a non-Muslim cannot make an endowment for a Muslim purpose.[23] As to non-Muslim endowments established before *Sharīʿa* Courts prior to the Order in Council and not converted into charitable trusts, within the meaning of the Charitable Trusts Ordinance, 1924, the *Sharīʿa* Courts retained only concurrent jurisdiction (i.e. by consent of the parties) in matters relating to the establishment or validity of those endowments. All other matters were assigned to the respective religious courts or to the civil court.[24]

### 1.3 *Material Law*

The law applicable to this day to *waqf* matters in *Sharīʿa* Courts is Muslim *waqf* law. Unlike matters of personal status, this area hardly knew interference by secular legislation.[25] The Mandatory legislator, even when trying to introduce

---

20 Land (Settlement of Title) Ordinance, 1928, sect. 11(a). The same applies, *mutatis mutandis*, to other religious communities. Ibid., sect. 11(b).

21 Ibid., sect. 11(d). For a judgment relating to this issue see Ben Shemesh, p. 284.

22 Instances are known of such *waqf*s being created even after 1922 (Goitein and Ben Shemesh, pp. 161–2).

23 Ibid., p. 161.

24 See below, p. 49.

25 On interference of the Israeli legislator in matters of matrimonial law see Layish, *AAS*, vol. 1, 1965, pp. 60–79.

amendments he thought essential, was careful not to impinge directly on laws based on the *Sharīʿa* and therefore chose an indirect route: the validation of certain acts done by the *Sharīʿa* Court after approval had been obtained from a body acting under secular law.[26]

The Land Transfer Ordinance of 1920[27] provides that any disposition, which includes also the establishment of a *waqf* of whatever kind (sects. 2 and 3), is valid only if the Director of Land Registration has consented to it (sect. 4); without this consent, the disposition is null and void (sect. 11[1]). In other words: the completion of the act of dedication by the *Sharīʿa* Court in accordance with the relevant religious law is not sufficient; the act is valid only if a government official has given his consent.[28] However, attempts to ensure, through that Ordinance, that land transactions be effected only at the Land Registry Office, and that every disposition of land not registered in the Land Register be voided, were not completely successful. Many people continued to make dispositions without resort to the Registry Office.[29]

Further interference in the activity of the *Sharīʿa* Courts constituted the order establishing the Supreme Muslim Council, which, too, was a secular body. The *Sharīʿa* Courts were no longer permitted to do any act in respect of endowments of the *ḥikr, ijāratayn* or *istibdāl* category without the unanimous consent of the Council. This restriction was designed to hinder attempts to gain control of *waqf* property by circumventing Muslim *waqf* law.[30]

The Mandatory authorities were not pleased with the subjection of the *waqf* to the religious courts and sought a way to reform that institution radically – again, without directly impinging on the religious laws of the communities. The procedure adopted consisted of two stages intended to complement each other: (a) creating legal machinery for establishing endowments before a civil court under secular law; (b) creating machinery for converting an endowment established before a religious court into a secular endowment.

The Charitable Trusts Ordinance of 1924 (*Laws of Palestine*, ch. xiv) enabled the dedication of property for charitable, educational and religious purposes: assistance to the poor; the encouragement of education and intellectual improvement; the encouragement of religion and religious observance, and

26 Cf. J.N.D. Anderson, *Islamic law in the modern world*, London, 1959, p. 91.

27 See Ben Shemesh, p. 254ff.

28 An unregistered judgment of a religious court in a matter of *waqf* is considered *ultra vires* (see E. Vitta, *The conflict of laws in matters of personal status in Palestine*, Tel Aviv, 1947, p. 173). See also Goitein and Ben Shemesh, pp. 159–60, 197–9; Ben Shemesh, p. 256.

29 See the remarks of the Minister of Justice in the Knesset, *Divrey ha-Knesset* (Knesset Proceedings), Third Session of the Fifth Knesset, No. 32, p. 2128.

30 Order of 1921 establishing the Supreme Muslim Council, clause 8(2); cf. Shimoni, p. 89.

the like.[31] Exclusive jurisdiction in all matters of charitable trusts was vested in the District Court.[32] The Charities (Public Trustee) Ordinance of 1925 (*Laws of Palestine*, ch. xv) enabled the conversion of an existing *waqf* established before a religious court into a charitable trust. After the person charged with the management of the *waqf* or a person entitled to enjoy its proceeds had applied to a religious court to discharge the incumbent trustees and to appoint a public trustee for the property, that court could convert the *waqf* into a charitable trust within the meaning of the Charitable Trusts Ordinance.[33] Non-Muslim endowments created before *Sharīʿa* Courts could likewise be converted into charitable trusts within a short time.[34]

However, those two Ordinances did not achieve their purpose as far as the Muslims were concerned. The dedicators preferred a known institution connected with the *Sharīʿa* legal system and Muslim *waqf* law to an alien secular institution connected with a civil legal system and secular law. We may assume that the *qāḍī*s of the *Sharīʿa* Courts – and, under the Mandate, the Supreme Muslim Council, which controlled the religious legal system – likewise did not favour the conversion of a *waqf* into a charitable trust.

The Land (Acquisition for Public Purposes) Ordinance, 1943, may, in a sense, be likewise regarded as interfering in the material law applicable to *waqf*. Endowment property acquired under that Ordinance is exempt from all limitations and restrictions applying to *waqf*, and the *mutawallī* or (in the absence of a *mutawallī*) the *waqf* administration are given all the powers and rights conferred by the Ordinance upon the owner or occupier of land, including the right to compensation.[35]

The powers of Christian and Jewish religious courts were equalized by the Order in Council with those of the *Sharīʿa* Courts. But this equality is merely theoretical: they were given exclusive jurisdiction as to any matter relating to the creation and internal management of a *waqf* or religious endowment created before the religious court in accordance with the religious law of the community. In the case of the Christian courts, this has practical effect only

31 Charitable Trusts Ordinance, sect. 2. These purposes may be comprised in a *waqf khayrī*, but no family endowments can be made within the framework of this secular institution. In England (the Charitable Trusts Ordinance is based on the English trust), endowments may be made also in favour of families, but these endowments are not eternal (Goadby, p. 131), Cf. Vitta, p. 173.

32 Charitable Trusts Ordinance, sect. 42. See also sect. 30 (special powers of the Court), sect. 22 (appointment of trustee) and sect. 27 (termination of trust).

33 Charities (Public Trustee) Ordinance, sect. 24.

34 Within 18 months from the promulgation of the Civil and Religious Court (Jurisdiction) Ordinance, 1925 (sect. 2 of the Ordinance). Cf. Vitta, p. 173.

35 Land (Acquisition for Public Purposes) Ordinance, sect. 24.

in so far as the community has a religious law dealing with *waqf*.[36] In respect of Christian and Jewish endowments established before *Sharīʿa* Courts prior to the promulgation of the Order in Council in 1922 and which had not for any reason become charitable trusts (these are the greater part of the religious endowments at present existing), Christian and Jewish religious courts were given exclusive jurisdiction only in matters relating to internal management.[37] They have no jurisdiction whatever in matters relating to the establishment or validity of such endowments. Jurisdiction in these matters was transferred to the civil courts whilst leaving concurrent jurisdiction to the *Sharīʿa* Courts; that is to say, the *Sharīʿa* Courts are competent to deal with matters of this kind with the consent of the parties.[38]

The powers of the Christian courts have remained unchanged to this day. In contrast, the jurisdiction of the Rabbinical Courts in matters of *waqf* (and personal status) was reduced in 1953 from exclusive to concurrent.[39]

In this connection, we should also mention the powers of the Druze religious courts first set up in 1963. The original (1960) draft of the Druze Religious Courts Law contained no provisions as to jurisdiction in *waqf* matters. This would have meant that that jurisdiction remained with the civil courts. In view of the demand of the heads of the community that their courts be granted the same powers as other religious courts,[40] a new draft (of 1962) contained certain amendments: the Druze religious courts were to have exclusive jurisdiction in all matters relating to the creation or internal management of Druze endowments established in future before a Druze religious court under Druze religious law, while they were to have only concurrent jurisdiction as to matters relating to the creation or internal management of a Druze endowment established in the past before another religious court or established in the past according to Druze custom, but not before any religious or civil court.[41]

However, this amendment, too, was unsatisfactory to the heads of the Druze community, so that the Knesset eventually granted the Druze courts exclusive jurisdiction not only as to matters relating to the creation or internal

36 Order in Council, art. 53(3), 54(3).

37 If the dedicator does not belong to a religious community or if his community has no religious court, matters relating to the internal management of the endowment are under the jurisdiction of the civil court (Civil and Religious Courts [Jurisdiction] Ordinance, 1925, sect. 3[b]).

38 Ibid., sect. 2–3. Matters relating to the ownership or possession of such endowments are under the sole jurisdiction of the civil courts (sect. 5 of the Ordinance). Cf. Goadby, p. 130; Vitta, pp. 149–50, 171, 174.

39 Rabbinical Courts Jurisdiction (Marriage and Divorce) Law, 5713/1953, sect. 1, 9.

40 See Layish, *Hamizrah Hehadash*, vol. 11, No. 4, pp. 258–9.

41 Druze Religious Courts Bill, 5722/1962, sect. 6 (see *al-Yawm*, *ha-Tzofeh* and *ʿAl ha-Mishmar* of 10 April 1962).

management of religious endowments that would be created before Druze courts, but also as to endowments created in the past according to Druze custom, but not before any judicial authority.[42]

## 2 *Waqf* Management under the Mandate

During most of the Mandatory period, the Supreme Muslim Council had unlimited control over Muslim *waqf* property (except, as stated, property of the *mulḥaq* category). *Waqf* committees existed in the towns of Jerusalem, Jaffa, Acre, Nablus, Hebron and Gaza. Each committee consisted of a *muftī* (or, in his absence, a senior *ʿālim*), the *maʾmūr al-awqāf* and two Muslim notables. The committee was competent to dismiss *waqf* management officials (with the approval of the Muslim Council) and to supervise the *mutawallīs* managing *waqf* property of the *mulḥaq* category.[43] These committees were subordinate to a General Waqf Committee headed by the Mufti of Jerusalem, who was at the same time President of the Supreme Muslim Council.[44] The members of the General Committee were all the *maʾmūrs* and one member of each local endowments management. The General Committee was charged with preparing the annual budget and submitting it to the Council for approval.[45] The Supreme Muslim Council had power[46]

a. to appoint the General Manager and the *maʾmūrs* and to supervise their committees;
b. to approve the annual budget of the Waqf Management, bringing it to the-knowledge of the Government;

42 Druze Religious Courts Law, 5723/1962, sect. 4. In view of the contention of Shaykh Amīn Ṭarīf, the spiritual leader of the Druze Community, that Druze *waqfs* had never been established before a *Sharīʿa* Court or any other judicial authority, the whole paragraph dealing with Druze *waqfs* created prior to the coming into force of the Law before a religious or civil court was deleted. In matters of personal status, the competence of the Druze Courts was equated to that of the Rabbinical (not the Christian) Courts, i.e. they were given exclusive jurisdiction only in matters of marriage and divorce and merely concurrent jurisdiction in other matters of personal status (ibid., sect. 4 and 5). The law published was in *Sefer ha-Ḥuqqim* No. 383 of 3 January 1963; its text appeared also in the 'Documents' section of *Hamizrah Hehadash*, vol. 15, No. 1–2 (57–8), 1965, pp. 97–101.

43 Order of 1921, clauses 13–15. The Council had no control over the income of *waqf mulḥaq*, but it had the supervision of the management of that property by the *mutawallīs* and of the use of its proceeds.

44 Although this was not required by the 1921 Order.

45 Order of 1921, clauses 10–12.

46 Ibid., clause 8.

c. to dismiss any endowment official or official employed by Muslim institutions maintained with *waqf* funds, notifying the Government of the dismissal and the reasons for it;
d. to publish a report on its activities and a financial report;
e. to investigate every Muslim *waqf* and produce evidence as to its rights in respect thereof, with a view to transferring it to the Muslim *waqf* administration;[47]
f. subject to certain procedure – vary, amend or supplement any directives relating to the management of endowments and promulgate new directives, giving notice to the Government.

The Government took upon itself to collect the *waqf* tithes (from *waqf ghayr ṣaḥīḥ* property) and to transfer them to the *waqf* administration[48] and did so until the early thirties.

Reliable data on the extent of Muslim *waqf* property in Palestine under the Mandate do not exist.[49] Estimates of *waqf ghayr ṣaḥīḥ* lands vary between 600,000 and one million dunams. From the thirties onwards, the annual revenue from tithes on that property was fixed, totalling LP 30,000, which, during the last years, was about 45–50 percent of the overall revenue.

The estimates of *waqf ṣaḥīḥ* lands range from approximately 80,000 to approximately 100,000 dunams, half thereof family *waqf* of the *mulḥaq* category from which the Waqf Management of the Supreme Muslim Council, as stated, has no income, and the remainder *waqf khayrī* with a total annual income of LP 10,000–20,000. During the last twenty years of the Mandate, the total annual income of the Waqf Management from all sources averaged LP 50,000–75,000. In 1946, the total income was LP 134,000.

The General Endowments Committee of the Supreme Muslim Council strove to increase its income from *waqf ṣaḥīḥ* by converting *waqf mulḥaq* into *waqf maḍbūṭ*. To achieve that purpose, it exploited the dependence of the *Sharīʿa* legal system on the Council. Although the question whether a *waqf* was *ṣaḥīḥ* or *ghayr ṣaḥīḥ* and similar questions were under the jurisdiction of the civil courts, the determination of the purpose of an endowment, and especially questions relating to the internal management of *waqf mulḥaq* (including the appointment and dismissal of *mutawallīs*) were (and still are) under the sole jurisdiction of the *Sharīʿa* Courts. *Qāḍīs* were frequently pressured to

47 The Mandatory authorities hastened to return to the Muslim Waqf Management various property the income of which had in the past gone to the Ottoman Treasury (Ben Shemesh, p. 33; Shimoni, p. 78).

48 Order of 1921, clause 16.

49 For data on the extent and income of the *waqf* property see Shimoni, pp. 81, 88, 90; A. Granovsky, *Land system of Palestine* (Hebrew), Tel Aviv, 5709 (1948–9), pp. 136, 137, 143.

order the removal of *waqf* property from the control of private *mutawallīs* and their delivery to the *waqf* committees of the *ma'mūrs*. This led to several applications to the High Court of Justice and the High Commissioner for intervention in the activities of the *Sharīʿa* Courts.

In 1937, at the height of the disturbances, Ḥājj Amīn al-Ḥusaynī was dismissed from all his posts, including the chairmanship of the General Waqf Committee which he held in his capacity as Mufti of Jerusalem. In the same year, the Supreme Muslim Council and the General Waqf Committee were deprived of all their powers in regard to *waqf* matters and of all their property, as well as of the control of the *waqf* property managed by them; all these were transferred to an appointed Government committee. These measures were taken by the High Commissioner by a special enactment, the Defence (Muslim Waqf) Regulations, 1937.[50] Until 1948, the Muslim endowments were managed by variously composed appointed committees of British and Muslim officials. The last committee was appointed by the High Commissioner in 1946 and consisted of three Muslims.[51]

## 3 The Legal Status of *waqf* Property

The events following the 1947 United Nations resolution on the partition of Palestine, viz. the flight of large sections of the Arab population from Israel to Arab countries or to areas of Palestine then held by enemy forces, created the problem of absentees' property, of which Muslim *waqf* property is a part. The managers of *waqf* property of the various categories – *mutawallīs* and members of the governmental endowments committee – and many persons having rights of enjoyment in endowments left the country or became absentees. The status of this property, like that of absentees' property generally, was defined by the Emergency (Absentees' Property) Regulations, 5709/1948, later superseded by the Absentees' Property Law, 5710/1950.[52] The term 'absentees' property' includes also *waqf*, although this is not expressly stated.[53] According to the

50 Defence (Muslim Waqf) Regulations, 1937, *Palestine Gazette*, 1937, Suppl. II, pp. 913, 973 (English edition).

51 The members of the committee were Rūḥī ʿAbd al-Hādī, Muḥammad Tawfīq al-Ṭībī and Waṣfī ʿAnabtāwī.

52 On the problem of absentees' property in general see A. Liskovski, 'Absentees who are in Israel', *Hamizrah Hehadash* vol. 10, No. 3(39), 1960, pp. 186–7.

53 The term 'endowment' occurs in section 9(d) of the Absentees' Property Law: 'vested property, being an endowment …'.

definition contained in the Law,[54] it means 'immovable and movable property, money, any vested or contingent right in property, goodwill and any right in a body of persons or in the management thereof, of which an absentee was the legal owner or which an absentee enjoyed or held, himself or through another.' This definition comprises the different categories of Muslim *waqf*, both as to its legal nature (*ṣaḥīḥ* and *ghayr ṣaḥīḥ*) and as to the form of its management (*mulḥaq* and *maḍbūṭ*).

However, the relevant part of that definition gave rise in recent years to doubts as to the content of the right in *waqf* conferred on the Custodian. The original intention of the formulator of the Law was that full ownership should be vested in the Custodian.[55] One of the objects of the Absentees' Property Law (but not of the earlier Absentees' Property Regulations) was to enable the Custodian to transfer absentees' property to agencies concerned with development (the Development Authority) so that it might be used in accordance with the needs of the national economy.[56] The Custodian maintains that he is not merely the trustee but the owner of the *waqf* property, just as he is the owner of the other absentees' property.

The question of the status of the Custodian in respect of *waqf mulḥaq* property was dealt with by the Supreme Court sitting as a High Court of Justice.[57] The Court held that what had been vested in the Custodian was not the ownership of the *waqf* property, but only the right of management of the absent *mutawallī* (and the rights of the absent beneficiaries). This approach is based on the concept 'right in a body of persons or in the management thereof' occurring in the definition of 'property' in the Absentees' Property Law. 'Body of persons' means, *inter alia*, an institution owning property, a definition applicable to an endowment. Hence it was concluded that if the manager of a *waqf*, the *mutawallī*, was an absentee, the right of management was vested in the Custodian.

As a result of this conception of the status of the Custodian in respect of *waqf* property, the question arose as to the power of the *Sharīʿa* Court to remove the Custodian from his position with regard to such property and to appoint another *mutawallī* instead, seeing that the 'internal management' assigned to the *Sharīʿa* Court by article 52 of the Order in Council includes also the

---

54 Ibid., sect. 1.

55 See the Explanatory Note to the Absentees' Property (Release and Use of Endowment Property) Bill, 5724/1964, *Hatzaʿot Ḥoq*, No. 629 of 15 October 1964.

56 See Liskovski, *Hamizrah Hehadash*, vol. 10, No. 3, p. 189.

57 See HCJ No. 332/52, Yaʿqūb Ḥasūna *v.* Custodian *et al.* (*Pisqey Din*, vol. 6, p. 1198); HCJ No. 69/55, Būlus Ḥannā Būlus *v.* Minister of Development *et al.* (*Pesaqim ʿElyon*, vol. 23, 1956, pp. 151–5).

appointment of *mutawallīs*. In its first judgment relating to this question (HCJ No. 332/52), the High Court of Justice held that the *Sharīʿa* Court could not, by appointing a *mutawallī*, convert absentees' property into non-absentees' property and remove the Custodian from office. According to this judgment, absentees' property which is an endowment may pass to the new *mutawallī* only after the Custodian has released it through the mechanism provided in the Absentees' Property Law.

By contrast, in the other judgment relating to this question (HCJ No. 69/55), the High Court of Justice found that the 'right of management' vested in the Custodian became void upon the appointment of a new *mutawallī*; it was not immune from voidance by the *Sharīʿa* Court, just as the property might have been removed from the absentee *mutawallī* himself for reasons of *Sharīʿa* law. According to this view, the Custodian steps into the shoes of the absentee *mutawallī* and is thus subject to the *Sharīʿa* legal system and the material law applicable in it as to all matters relating to the management of *waqf* property.[58]

As stated, these two judgments deal with *waqf mulḥaq*. As for *waqf maḍbūṭ* property, it was managed by the committee appointed under the Defence (Muslim Wakf) Regulations, 1937. When the members of that committee had become absentees, the property was vested in the Custodian. As the committee had been subordinate to the High Commissioner (and not to the *Sharīʿa* Court), the Custodian is subordinate to the Government, which has taken the place of the High Commissioner, and has nothing to do with the *Sharīʿa* Court in this matter.

The Qāḍīs Law, 5721/1961, designed to regulate permanently the appointment of *qāḍīs*, emptied the 1921 order constituting the Supreme Muslim Council of its main content. The powers of the Council and its Endowments Committee in regard to *waqf* had, as stated, been taken from them as early as 1937 and been transferred to an appointed Government committee. The 1921 order was accordingly rescinded.[59] As we have already noted, it has been contended that the rescission of the order implied the rescission of the Defence (Muslim Waqf) Regulations, 1937, and the extension of *Sharīʿa* Court jurisdiction to *waqf maḍbūṭ* property, which is why the question of the Custodian's dependence on the *Sharīʿa* Court also in matters relating to the management of *waqf maḍbūṭ* property was now apt to arise. This question has not yet been

58 On the circumstances under which the *Sharīʿa* Court may remove a *mutawallī* from office, see Ömer Hilmi, *The laws of Evqaf*, translated by C.R. Tyser and D.G. Demetriades, second edition, Nicosia, 1922, sects. 308, 313, 314, 316, 317, 321, 330, 340–42.

59 Qāḍīs Law, 5721/1961, sect. 25.

fully clarified.[60] The Custodian, at any rate, holds that even if the jurisdiction of the *Sharīʿa* Courts has theoretically been extended to include all categories of *waqf*, the rights vested in him with regard to *waqf maḍbūṭ* property no longer depend on the absentee, so that he can rely on the immunity granted him from interference of the *Sharīʿa* Court in his affairs.

## 4 Muslim *waqf* Management in Israel

The management of the Muslim *waqf* property vested in the Custodian of Absentees' Property is based on a fundamental differentiation between property which is a holy place (such as a mosque or a cemetery) and secular property. This differentiation, which is unknown in Muslim law, was made in view of the requirements of the Muslim community. Endowments which are holy places, and their secular appurtenances,[61] are managed by the Director of the Muslim and Druze Department of the Ministry of Religious Affairs as the agent of the Custodian for this purpose.

Out of the income of the secular *waqf* property managed by him, the Custodian makes allocations for Muslim religious purposes, in addition to the income derived by his agent at the Ministry of Religious Affairs from the property managed by him. In the budget year 1964/5, the Custodian allocated IL 120,000, while the income of his agent totalled approximately IL 50,000. The total *waqf* income expended to date on the religious requirements of the Muslim community (in addition to the amounts allocated by the Ministry of Religious Affairs out of its ordinary budget) is approximately IL 1,500,000, i.e. IL 900,000 out of the income of the Custodian and the remainder out of the direct income of his agent at the Ministry of Religious Affairs. The income from *waqf* property was mainly expended for the following purposes: the activities of the Muslim committees appointed by the Minister of Religious Affairs in the towns of Jaffa, Acre, Haifa, Lod and Ramla; repairs to mosques and cemeteries; holiday grants to religious functionaries; sermons and other religious ministrations in prisons; religious instruction and grants to Muslim students; and the training of religious functionaries in religious and general law.

The consideration (*amwāl al-badal*) received for *waqf* property acquired by the Development Authority under the Land Acquisition (Validation of Acts

60 As stated, the Supreme Court inclines towards the view that the 1937 Regulations have independent existence and hence that the Custodian is subordinate to the Government, and not to the *Sharīʿa* Court.

61 Such as the parade of shops attached to the al-Jazzār Mosque in Acre.

and Compensation) Law, 5713/1953, has been spent on the establishment of institutions and enterprises in the fields of education, health, social welfare, religious services and the like for the benefit of the Muslim community. Some three million pounds have so far been allocated, mainly for the following purposes: the establishment of regional health centres as well as clinics; an orphanage (at Acre); buildings for kindergartens; buildings for elementary, secondary and comprehensive schools in urban and rural areas and for Beduin in the Negev and in Galilee; loan funds for students at the teachers' college and for indigent persons; playgrounds, clubs and the like.

The assignment of absentees' property to the Custodian in 1948 was a provisional measure. Its management by him was originally intended as an interim solution pending a permanent peace agreement with the Arab countries. According to the Emergency Regulations (Absentees' Property), 5709/1948, the Custodians' task was to take care of the property on behalf of the absentee owners, beneficiaries and possessors and to restore it to them once the emergency was over. He was debarred from relinquishing or transferring it, from leasing it out on long-term lease, etc. Only when it became apparent that the hopes of an early peace agreement were illusory was the need felt to replace the temporary tenure of absentees' property with a permanent one. This was done by the Absentees' Property Law, 5710/1950, which enabled the Custodian to transfer the property to the Development Authority.

The problem of property which is technically absentees' property though its owner is really resident in Israel is about to be solved because the Custodian almost invariably releases it (or consideration received for it) to the owner.[62] By contrast, the question of the Muslim *waqf* has not yet found a solution satisfactory to the members of the Muslim community. In Muslim and general Arab circles, claims are often made whose main purpose is to restore the *waqf* property to the community. The legality of the vesting of the Muslim *waqf* in the Custodian is challenged on the grounds that the bare property of that institution belongs to God,[63] while the usufruct and management thereof belonged

62 See Liskovski, *Hamizrah Hehadash*, vol. 10, No. 3, pp. 190–2. By October 1965, the cases of over 10,750 claimants, i.e. about two thirds of all potential claimants, had been settled. They received as compensation over 41,500 dunams of land and about 17 million pounds in cash. About 2,700 further claimants are at present negotiating for the settlement of their claims. It is estimated that the problem will have been fully solved in two or three years' time.

63 For that reason, *waqf* may not be transferred or otherwise made the subject of any transaction. See Goitein and Ben Shemesh, pp. 159, 196; S. Yifraḥ. *The law of the Custodian* (Hebrew), publ. by the Bar Association, Tel Aviv, 1953, p. 41; Ḥ. Kena'an, 'Allah is not an absentee …', *ha-Aretz*, 21 April 1952; Rāshid Ḥusayn, 'God is a refugee', *al-Mirṣād*, 7 January 1960.

to the Muslim community generally, and not to any particular committee or other body. Someone even defined the Muslim *waqf* in this context as *mulk mushāʿ* of the Muslim community.[64] Another claim is that only a Muslim body may manage Muslim *waqf* property.

Most of these contentions are aimed at restoring the management of the endowments to those who had it under the Mandate, i.e. to the Supreme Muslim Council. The fact that from 1937 onwards these endowments had been managed by an appointed Government committee is consciously or unconsciously ignored. Some demand the establishment of bodies to which the management of the *waqf* would be handed over, but in many cases these proposed bodies are very similar to the committees of the former *maʾmūr*s.[65]

The fact that the Custodian has released to several Christian communities ecclesiastical *waqf* and other ecclesiastical assets which were likewise absentees' property has, of course, increased dissatisfaction among the Muslim community. The internal organization of the recognized Christian communities enabled them to make use of this advantage. The property of the Greek Orthodox community in Israel is registered in the name of the Patriarchate of Jerusalem.[66] The location of the latter in the Old City of Jerusalem originally made that property absentees' property. At the same time, there was no legal bar to the Custodian's releasing it to the Patriarchate. The property of the Greek Catholic (Melkite) community is registered in the name of the archdiocese comprising Acre, Haifa, Nazareth and the rest of Galilee. The Muṭrān (Archbishop) Ḥakīm, the head of the community, left the country during the War of Liberation, but returned shortly afterwards. Here, too, there was no obstacle to the Custodian's releasing the property to the body concerned, although that body was technically an absentee.

The Muslim community in Israel, on the other hand, has no official governing bodies,[67] and Muslim *waqf* property is registered in the name of the *maʾmūr*s who have left the country. In the absence of a competent juristic person, the Custodian has no one to release property to. An essentially similar

64 Ṭāhir Fāhūm in *Daʿwat al-Jabha*, a one-time publication issued by ʿIṣām al-ʿAbbāsī, Haifa, 15 February 1960.

65 See, e.g., a detailed proposal sent by the secretaries of the Muslim Advisory Committees in Acre, Haifa and Jaffa to the Home Affairs Committee of the Knesset on 7 July 1958.

66 This does not apply to property registered in the name of the community councils (*al-majlis al-millī*) in several towns and villages. These councils are juristic persons and enjoy a certain autonomy in the management of the property.

67 There are those who hold that the Muslims are not a recognized religious community within the meaning of the Order in Council and the Succession Ordinance. See M. Silberg, *Personal status in Israel* (Hebrew), Jerusalem, 1957, pp. 32–3.

situation prevails with regard to the Arab Evangelic Episcopal Church in Israel. This Church is not recognized as a 'religious community'[68] and has no official governing bodies in Israel. Its property is registered in the name of various communal institutions (societies under Ottoman law), clergymen and private persons. It was vested in the Custodian by reason of the absentee status of all these persons.

Besides demands for the release of *waqf khayrī* property to the Muslim community as a whole, there are personal claims with regard to family endowments. They emanate from people asserting rights in the proceeds, or in the management, of the endowments. As to the former, there is no bar to satisfying them under the existing law because the Custodian may surrender the income of endowments for purposes indicated in the endowment deed.[69] As to the claimants to rights of management, they may be original *mutawallī*s who are technically absentees or new *mutawallī*s appointed by *Sharīʿa* Courts after the vesting of the property in the Custodian.

## 5 The Release of *waqf* Property to Muslims

Since under the existing law the Custodian cannot release *waqf maḍbūṭ* property to the Muslim community, it was suggested to the Muslim Committees in the towns that they manage that property as the agents of the Custodian. Such an arrangement exists with regard to the property of the Evangelic Episcopal community in Israel.[70] As, however, this arrangement did not satisfy the Committees, the Government, on 28 July 1958, decided to amend the existing law in a manner enabling the Custodian to release the property to Muslim committees to be established for that purpose. According to the Absentees' Property (Muslim Religious Endowments) Bill, 5719/1959,[71] the Custodian was to be authorized to release *waqf khayrī* property[72] in the towns of Tel Aviv-Jaffa, Ramla, Lod, Haifa, Acre, Nazareth and Shafā ʿAmr. The released property was

68 The part of this community which is in Jordan was recognized as a 'religious community' a few years ago.

69 Absentees' Property Law, 5710/1950, sect. 9(d).

70 The Chairman of the Evangelic Episcopal Council in Israel manages the property as the agent of the Custodian.

71 *Hatzaʿot Ḥoq*, No. 381 of 24 February 1959.

72 Section 1 of the Bill defines *waqf khayrī* as 'property of Muslim religious endowments: *waqf* property which, or the proceeds of which, is or are used exclusively for purposes of religious worship, education, charity or burial, and which has not been dedicated for the benefit of the dedicator or the members of his family or the members of another family while still alive'.

to be entrusted to local boards of trustees, which were to take the place of the absentee *waqf* managers (i.e. the *maʾmūrs*). The committees were to be appointed by the Government and be subject to its directives, and their budget was to require its approval.[73] Every board was to manage the released property as a body corporate, competent to acquire rights and enter into obligations and be subject to inspection by the State Comptroller.[74]

In that it was to enable the Custodian to release *waqf khayrī* property[75] in towns in which Muslim communities exist, the Bill envisaged a reform in the internal management of *waqf maḍbūṭ*. If we accept the view that upon the rescission of the 1921 Order the 1937 Regulations became void, too, and the jurisdiction of the *Sharīʿa* Courts was extended to include also *waqf maḍbūṭ*, that jurisdiction was to lapse in respect of the *waqf* property released to the boards of trustees; for, notwithstanding the provisions of any other law, those boards were to be subject in respect of all matters concerning the management of the property solely to the instructions of the Government or a person appointed by it in that behalf.[76]

On the other hand, if we adopt the view (favoured by the Supreme Court) that the 1937 Regulations exist independently of the 1921 Order, jurisdiction of the Government in *waqf maḍbūṭ* matters was to be maintained.

At the same time, the Bill did not go so far as to envisage reforms in the essential character of the *waqf*. The board of trustees was to have the same authority with regard to *waqf* property as the *maʾmūr* had had immediately before the Custodian was vested with it,[77] i.e. the right of management only; this implies that all the restrictions applying to the *waqf* (and first and foremost the prohibition of the transfer of right of ownership thereof) were to apply also to property managed by the boards of trustees. In other words: the dependence of the boards of trustees on the Government as to everything connected with the internal management of the property released to them was not to change the basic status of that property as *waqf*, with all the implications of this term. Moreover, there would have been a great resemblance between these boards of trustees and the *waqf* committees headed by *maʾmūrs* of the Mandatory period.

---

73 Sects. 2–5 of the Bill.

74 Sects. 6 and 7 of the Bill.

75 Family *waqf* property can be released by the Custodian to its *mutawallīs* under the existing law, even if they are technically absentees, and he has in fact done so in several cases.

76 Sect. 4 of the Bill.

77 Sect. 3 of the Bill.

The Third Knesset did not get round to passing the Absentees' Property (Muslim Religious Endowments) Bill, 5719/1959, before its dissolution.[78] In April 1964, the Government decided to present to the Knesset a new Bill, based on the 1959 Bill, but containing certain changes which amounted to a radical reform of the Muslim *waqf*. The Bill was finally passed by the Knesset on 2 February 1965. The new law – the Absentees' Property (Release and Use of Endowment Property) Law, 5725/1965[79] – differs substantially from the original Bill in that the *ownership* of the *waqf* was freed from all the restrictions hitherto applying to it. The Custodian may now transfer to the boards of trustees not only the right of management of *waqf khayrī* property[80] (as proposed in the 1959 Bill), but the ownership of that property free from 'any restriction, qualification or other similar limitation imposed by or under any law or any document relating to an endowment'.[81]

Another innovation in the law, as against the 1959 Bill, is the release of family endowment property to the beneficiaries, which had hitherto been impossible for the Custodian. Indeed, under the old law, too, the Custodian was able to release family *waqf* property, but only, as already mentioned, in respect of the right of management, and to the *mutawallīs*, not to the beneficiaries. As to the latter, the Custodian was able to allot them amounts out of the income of the endowment, but they had no connection whatever with the property itself. The new law permits the Custodian to transfer the full ownership of family endowment property to the beneficiaries,[82] in accordance, of course, with their proportionate share in the benefit.

The removal of all restrictions from the right of ownership of *waqf* enables the beneficiaries and the boards of trustees to treat property released to them as their own. Family *waqf* property becomes upon its release ordinary property in all respects and may then be transferred, and used for any purpose, without restraint.

The boards of trustees, too, may treat property released to them as their own, but with certain restrictions. They may not in any manner transfer property

---

78 The Bill was passed in the first reading and referred to the Finance Committee but the latter did not manage to consider it and submit it for the second and third readings before the elections to the Fourth Knesset.

79 *Sefer ha-Ḥuqqim*, No. 445 of 5 February 1965. For full text see Appendix.

80 The new law defines the term '*waqf khayrī*' not positively, as the 1959 Bill did, but negatively: an endowment which is not a family *waqf* (sect. 3 of the law: addition of section 29A[a]).

81 Ibid.

82 Ibid.

which includes a mosque.[83] A further restriction relates to the use of the income of and consideration received for the endowments managed by them. They are not, indeed, restricted anymore to the purposes for which the endowment was established[84] or to the Muslim *waqf* laws containing clear provisions in the matter. However, the law states specifically to what purposes they may apply *waqf* income: relief of the poor, scholarships to pupils at schools, vocational training, health, religious instruction, religious worship or custom, and any other purpose approved by the Government, all for the requirements of the Muslim residents in the area of operation of the board.

The consideration (*amwāl al-badal*), on the other hand, is to be expended on the founding of orphanages, schools, including vocational schools, clinics, mosques and any other similar establishment approved as aforesaid for the purposes of the Muslim inhabitants.[85] This distinction between the use of the income and the use of the consideration was not made in the 1964 Bill;[86] by laying down that the consideration should be used only for the founding of establishments and not for day-to-day expenses, the Knesset intended to preserve a time-hallowed Muslim institution in a manner appropriate to modern society. To enable a rational, economic use of these monies, the law does not restrict the boards of trustees to using the consideration for the purposes of residents of their own area of operation.

The law was intended also to remove doubts that had arisen following the judgments in HCJ 332/52 (Ḥasūna *v.* Custodian) and HCJ 65/55 (Būlus *v.* Minister of Development) and to assert the original intention of the legislator that the Custodian should have not only the right of management but the full ownership of absentees' endowment property.[87] The vesting of the ownership in the Custodian free from the restrictions applying to *waqf* property is, of course, a necessary prerequisite to achieving the aforesaid objects concerning

83 Ibid., sect. 3: addition of sect. 29C. The prohibition of transfers involving mosques (although the ownership is vested in the board of trustees) did not appear in the Absentees' Property (Amendment No. 3) (Release and Use of Endowment Property) Bill, 5725/1964. In the original 1959 Bill, the board of trustees was of course debarred from making any transfer whatsoever, even of secular *waqf* property, since it had not the ownership of the property.

84 In many cases, the purpose for which the endowment was established is non-existent or unknown.

85 Sect. 3 of the 1965 law: addition of sect. 29E.

86 The consideration was permitted to be used for the same purposes as the income.

87 Sect. 1 of the 1965 law: addition of sect. 1A(1) after sect. 4(a) of the original law of 1950. See Explanatory Note to the Absentees' Property (Release and Use of Endowment Property) Bill, 5724/1964.

the transfer of the full ownership of *waqf khayrī* property to the boards of trustees and of family *waqf* property to the beneficiaries.

In response to the demands of Muslim Knesset members that *waqf khayrī* property be released not only in urban but also in rural areas, the law provides that the Government shall designate, as may be necessary, additional localities where boards of trustees shall be established.[88] The law thus aims at establishing boards of trustees wherever in Israel *waqf* property and a Muslim community are to be found. These committees, which, as stated, are to be appointed by the Government, will manage the endowment property released to them. Every committee will be a body corporate, competent to acquire and transfer any right; the board is to prepare an annual budget of its income and expenditure, which will require the approval of the Government and, on certain conditions, be subject to inspection by the State Comptroller.[89]

In those places where no Muslim community exists and where there is thus no one to whom to release endowment property, the Custodian is to use such property, its income and the consideration received for it for the same purposes as are prescribed for the boards of trustees.[90]

The release of Muslim endowment property by the Custodian is thus coupled in the new law with basic reforms in the institution of *waqf*. The law differs from the 1959 Bill in that it enables the Custodian to release *waqf khayrī* property not only in urban but also in rural areas and in that it deals with the release of family endowment property to the beneficiaries. But the main peculiarity of this law is, as stated, the freeing of *waqf* from all restrictions hitherto applying to it and its integration into the economic cycle of the country. This aim is achieved by permitting the transfer of the ownership of *waqf* and the use of its income and of the consideration received for it for worthy causes not necessarily specified in the endowment deed, all at the discretion of the new owners of the endowments and without resort to the institutional machinery provided by Muslim *waqf* law.

---

88 Sect. 3 of the 1965 law: addition of sect. 29H. This section did not appear in the original Bill of 1959. The area of the boards of trustees to be established in towns is coextensive with the area of the local authority (ibid., sect. 3: addition of sect. 29B). A similar provision was not enacted for boards of trustees in villages because most villages have as yet no local government.

89 Sect. 3 of the 1965 law: addition of sect. 29B–29F.

90 Ibid., sect. 3: addition of sect. 29G. The addition of this section obviates the need for sect. 9(d) of the original law of 1950, which provided that the Custodian may release, for the purposes for which the endowment was established, all or part of the income of the endowment property vested in him. That subsection was in fact repealed (sect. 2 of the 1965 law).

However, the Knesset was cautious in introducing reforms in the Muslim *waqf*. Although there is no hint of this institution in the Qur'ān and its link with ancient Muslim tradition is tenuous,[91] it became established in Muslim society and was invested by it with a religious aura, so that it has remained one of the principal characteristics of that society until modern times. As it does when handling personal status matters closely bound up with religion,[92] so here too, the Knesset took care, as far as possible, not to impair the powers of the *Sharīʿa* Courts. The provisions of the law apply only to endowment property which had been vested in the Custodian and not in any way to other endowment property, so that the *Sharīʿa* Courts will continue to have exclusive jurisdiction in matters relating to family endowment property which was not vested in the Custodian or which was created after the promulgation of the Absentees' Property Law.[93] As for matters relating to the internal management of *waqf khayrī* property, which was mostly of the *maḍbūṭ* category, they were, as stated, not under the jurisdiction of the *Sharīʿa* Courts during the Mandate, either.[94] The new law applies to all *waqf maḍbūṭ* property by reason of the absentee status of the *maʾmūr*s.

The new law corresponds to the modern trend in the legislation of Arab countries in matters of *waqf*. Those countries realize that the *waqf* does not suit conditions in a society in process of Westernization, striving to modernize its economy. The freezing of the ownership of the *waqf* has kept large tracts of land out of the economic cycle, prevented their development and produced adverse side effects in the social sphere.[95] Several Arab countries do not now content themselves with tightening the supervision of *waqf* property and its management or with the transfer of that property to direct government management, but aim at introducing reforms in the actual institution of *waqf*.

---

91 This facilitated the introduction of reforms in the *waqf*, unlike other Muslim institutions. See Goitein and Ben Shemesh, pp. 154–5, 171. Although art. 52 of the Order in Council deals at one and the same time with matters of personal status, which are closely bound up with religion, and matters of *waqf*, there is no connection between the two. The Order in Council did not concern itself with the *waqf* as a matter pertaining to personal status, but because the *waqf* is under the jurisdiction of the *Sharīʿa* Courts by virtue of the Muḥammadan Code of Procedure of 8 Muḥarram 1336 (25 October 1918), which came into force in Palestine on 6 July 1919 (Goadby, p. 128).

92 See Layish, *AAS*, vol. 1, 1965, pp. 75–7.

93 Absentees' Property (Amendment) Law, 5711/1951: addition of sect. 28A. For details see Liskovski, *Hamizrah Hehadash*, vol. 10, No. 3, p. 188.

94 The question of the dependence of this kind of *waqf* upon the *Sharīʿa* Courts arose only after the rescission in 1961 of the 1921 Order establishing the Supreme Muslim Council (see above).

95 For more details see Goitein and Ben Shemesh, pp. 169–71.

The Israeli legislator adopted, *mutatis mutandis*, several rules and principles laid down by the Arab states in introducing reforms in the *waqf*. The distinction between *waqf ahlī* and *waqf khayrī*, though irrelevant from a religious point of view and having no foundation in law,[96] is a salient feature of those reforms. This distinction according to the purpose of the endowment guided the Israeli legislator as well.

In empowering the Custodian to transfer the full ownership of family *waqf* property to the beneficiaries, lifting all the restrictions hitherto applying to it, the Knesset followed the example of several Arab states, especially Syria and Egypt, although it did not go so far as they.[97] Those two states abolished the family *waqf* completely and forbade the establishment of *waqf* of this kind in future. The 1965 law, as stated, abolished only the family *waqf* vested in the Custodian and does not apply to other family endowments. Nor is there any provision in the law prohibiting the establishment of a family *waqf* in the future. Like the legislatures of those two states, the Knesset gave preference to the beneficiary over the *mutawallī* and prescribed that the ownership of family endowments should pass to the former.[98]

The revolutionary regime in Egypt introduced far-reaching changes in the *waqf khayrī*. In that country it was at first attempted to reform that institution, as far as possible, without basic changes in its legal status. The achievement of this purpose depended largely on the willingness of the *Sharīʿa* Courts to aid in the implementation of the Government's policy, and they did indeed cooperate. Thus, for instance, the *Sharīʿa* Court acceded to the request of the Ministry of Waqfs a short time after the 1952 revolution, to appoint it *nāẓir* of approximately 100,000 feddans of *waqf khayrī* property in place of the exiled King Fārūq. However, the main factor likely to hinder the introduction of reforms by this method was the private manager of *awqāf khayriyya*, who is certainly the strongest element in the *waqf* system.[99] Egyptian (and Syrian) legislation was

96 Ibid., p. 162.

97 For a general survey of the reforms in the *waqf khayrī* and *waqf ahlī* in Syria and Egypt see Baer, pp. 154–5; on the reform of the *waqf* in Egypt see G. Baer, 'Waqf reform in Egypt', *St Anthony's Papers, Middle Eastern Affairs*, No. 1, London, 1958, pp. 71–6. See also G. Baer, 'Agrarian reform in Egypt – summary and appreciation' (Hebrew), *Hamizrah Hehadash*, vol. 9, No. 1–2, (33–4), 1958, pp. 13–19. The following survey is based on these articles. On the reform of the family *waqf* in Lebanon see J.N.D. Anderson, 'Recent developments in Sharīʿa law: IX, The waqf system', *Muslim World*, vol. 42, 1952, pp. 257–76.

98 The Egyptian law of 1952 abolishing family *waqfs* indeed gives preference to the founder of the *waqf* over the beneficiaries in the event that he is still alive and had the right to revoke the founding of the *waqf*. But in every other case the property is registered in the name of the beneficiaries, who, in any event, supplant the *nāẓir*.

99 Cf. Goitein and Ben Shemesh, pp. 165–6.

thus aimed, first and foremost, at abolishing the institution of *waqf* manager (*mutawallī, nāẓir*) and transferring the *waqf khayrī* property to the management of the State. The nationalization of the management of that property did not, in effect, change its legal status as *waqf* property: the severest restriction applying to *waqf*, viz. the prohibition of the transfer of ownership, remained in force. But the abolition of the private manager was likely to facilitate the implementation of the Government's reform policy. A further change introduced in Egypt – also within the limits of the *waqf* system – was the enablement of the Minister of Waqfs to expend the income of *waqf khayrī* property (with the approval of the Supreme Waqf Council and the *Sharīʿa* Court) for purposes not specified in the endowment deed, and it has probably not been difficult to give a very wide interpretation to this right when making use of it.

But Egypt went even further, introducing reforms that affected the essential content of the *waqf*. A law of 1957 provided that all agricultural lands belonging to the *waqf khayrī* category (the *waqf* problem in Egypt is mainly agricultural) should be transferred to the Land Reform Committee for distribution to agriculturists and that the consideration received for those lands should be invested by the Waqf Ministry in development enterprises. Upon the transfer of the full ownership thereof to the Land Reform Committee, that property was freed from all restrictions applying to *waqf*.

The Knesset followed the same course, though not by the same stages. In Israel it was not necessary to concentrate the management of the *waqf khayrī* property in the hands of the Government because it generally belonged to the *maḍbūṭ* category and thus had become absentees' property. But besides lifting the ban on the transfer of the ownership of the *waqf*, the Israeli legislator laid down that *waqf khayrī* property, its income and the consideration received for it, should be used exclusively for the purposes of the Muslim population. The board of trustees should be allowed to treat the property released to them as their own, subject to the restrictions indicated above. The Knesset did not prohibit the establishment of *waqf khayrī* in the future any more than it imposed such a prohibition in the case of family endowments.

On 7 November 1965, the Government appointed boards of trustees in the towns of Haifa, Acre, Lod, and Ramla. Each board consists of 5–7 Muslim members resident in the town.[100] The boards of trustees in the other towns mentioned in the law – Nazareth, Shafā ʿAmr and Tel Aviv-Jaffa – will be appointed at a later date. It is to be expected that the Custodian will soon transfer to the boards of trustees Muslim endowments which are holy places (mosques and cemeteries) and their secular appurtenances, with the income of which the

100 See *ʿAl ha-Mishmar, ha-Tzofeh, ha-Aretz and al-Yawm* of 8 November 1965.

boards will be able to finance the requirements of the Muslim inhabitants in the sphere of their communal organization.

It is too early to assess the practical results of the new law. Much depends on the manner of its implementation, the functioning of the boards of trustees and the readiness of the beneficiaries of the family endowments to register their rights of benefit in the Land Register as ownership rights. At any rate, there can be no doubt that the law will have far-reaching repercussions on the economic plane, although in Israel the *waqf* problem is not a serious agrarian problem, as it is in Egypt. The law is significant on the social plane as well. True, some of the causes of the expansion of the *waqf* in the past no longer exist in present-day Muslim society, in which the traditional frameworks are weakening, and the tendency to dedicate property seems, on the whole to have declined.[101] Yet, the problem does not concern endowments to be created in the future, but those created in the past and which have evolved a solid institutional structure. This survey does not deal with the social aspects of the *waqf*, which are a subject for separate research.

The Absentees' Property (Release and Use of Endowment Property) Law, 5725/1965, relates, as stated, only to endowment property vested in the Custodian. It thus aims mainly at reforms in the Muslim *waqf* insofar as it is absentees' property. The law does not apply to endowments of other communities. To complete the picture of Knesset legislation in matters of *waqf*, we should review, at least briefly, those principles of the Immovable Property Bill, 5724/1964, which relate to *waqf*.[102] This Bill is to bring about a radical reform in the entire system of land laws existing in Israel. *Inter alia*, all the Ottoman land laws are to be abolished (sect. 237). The Bill also deals with religious

101 In 1963, Israel *Sharīʿa* Courts dealt with 13 cases relating to *waqf* matters, out of a total of 2,921 cases relating in their vast majority to matters of personal status. In 1964, the respective figures were 10 and 3,126. See Ministry of Religious Affairs, *Bulletin of the Muslim and Druze Division*, Jerusalem, vol. 9, No. 1–2, 1964, p. 48; ibid., No. 3–4, 1964, p. 26. Most of the cases concerned the appointment of *mutawallīs* for endowment property held by the Custodian of Absentees' Property. A new motive for the establishment of *waqfs* originates in the special circumstances prevailing in Israel. It happens that people dedicate their property when there is a danger that the shares of potential heirs who are absentees and are not in Israel may be vested in the Custodian of Absentees' Property. It is well known that dedicating one's property is a common method of circumventing the Muslim law of inheritance (see Layish, *AAS*, vol. 1, 1965, p. 75.).

102 *Hatzaʿot Ḥoq*, No. 612 of 15 June 1964. See also the opening remarks of the Minister of Justice at the first reading in the Knesset on 22 June 1964, *Divrey ha-Knesset*, Third Session of the Fifth Knesset, No. 32, pp. 2126–34; *ha-Aretz*, 23 June 1964. It is too early to analyse that Bill in detail since it may undergo changes in the course of the Knesset proceedings.

endowments of religious communities which were dedicated under Muslim law.[103] The *waqf* as a category of land, and all the categories of land at present existing under the Ottoman Land Code of 1858, are to be abolished and-a uniform category of land, based on full ownership, is to be introduced (sect. 3).

Concerning the *waqf* as a religious endowment, the Bill distinguishes between *waqf dhurrī* on the one hand and *waqf khayrī* and *waqf mundaras* on the other.[104] The family *waqf* is to be abolished altogether and is to be registered in the name of the beneficiaries as owners (sect. 231[5]), and the establishment of family *waqfs* is to be prohibited in future (sect.232[1]). *Waqf khayrī* and *waqf mundaras*, on the other hand, are not to be abolished. The ban on the transfer of the ownership of endowments of this category is to be retained with a certain qualification.[105] Also, no changes are to be made in the persons of the managers and they are to adhere to the purposes of the endowment.[106]

The Bill distinguishes fundamentally between endowments designed for religious purposes, which are to remain within a religious framework and under religious jurisdiction, and charitable trusts, which are in future to be managed according to secular law and under civil jurisdiction. Endowments intended for religious instruction, houses of worship or cemeteries are to be registered in the name of those entitled to manage them according to religious law and are to be subject to religious law (sect. 231[4]), and this is to apply also to endowments of this kind which may be established in the future (sect 232[2]). Endowments of the *mundaras* or *khayrī* category are indeed to be registered in the name of those entitled to manage them according to the law applicable to the endowment concerned (i.e., first and foremost, religious law) as trustees, but are to be governed by the provisions of the Charitable Trusts Ordinance; if persons entitled as aforesaid cannot be found, the endowments are to be vested in the Public Trustee of Charities (sect. 231[3]); and this is to apply also to endowments of this kind which may be established in the future (sect. 232[3]).

For the implementation of the above principles, the Minister of Justice is to appoint a 'Waqf Property Regulation Board' headed by a District Judge, which is to examine the validity of every *waqf* from the point of view of the law

103 Until 1922, dedications could only be made before the *Sharīʿa* Court (see above).

104 *Waqf mundaras* is *waqf dhurrī* which has become *waqf khayrī* upon the passing away of all the descendants of those entitled to benefit from the income of the endowment.

105 The trustee may only sell, exchange or mortgage the endowment property with the consent of the Court (Charitable Trusts Ordinance of 1924, sect. 12[1]). At the same time, the status of the trustee with regard to the charitable trust is not the same as that of the *mutawallī* with regard to the *waqf* (see Goadby, pp. 132–3).

106 Unless the Court lays down other purposes within the scope of those specified in the law (ibid., sects. 5 and 30).

applicable to it and the eligibility of those claiming the right of management thereof (sect. 231[1] and [2]).

The Bill supplements in various respects the 1965 law. As to family *waqf*, the approach is the same: complete abolition. The only difference is that the Immovable Property Bill also prohibits the establishment of family endowments in the future. As against this, there are differences in approach with regard to *waqf kharyī* (and *mundaras*). The Immovable Property Bill would not, on the one hand, alter the status and form of management of *waqf*s intended for religious purposes, but on the other, would restrict the power of the *Sharīʿa* Courts by excluding charitable trusts from their jurisdiction, although this act is not to alter the legal status of that property or the identity of its managers. The 1965 law does not, indeed, impair the powers of the *Sharīʿa* Courts, but it frees endowments from all restrictions applying to them, while transferring them to boards of trustees.

## Appendix. Absentees' Property (Amendment No. 3) (Release and Use of Endowment Property) Law 5725–1965[107] (Official Translation)

*Amendment of section 4.*

1. (a) In section 4 of the Absentees' Property Law 5710–1950[108] (hereinafter referred to as "the principal Law"), the following subsection shall be inserted after subsection (a):

> (1A)(1) Where any property is an endowment under any law, the ownership thereof shall vest in the Custodian free from any restriction, qualification or other similar limitation prescribed, whether before or after the vesting, by or under any law or document relating to the endowment if the owner of the property, or the person having possession or the right of management of the property, or the beneficiary of the endowment, is an absentee. The vesting shall be as from the 10th Kislev, 5709 (12th December, 1948) or from the day on which one of the aforementioned becomes an absentee, whichever is the later date.

---

107 Passed by the Knesset on 30 Shevat, 5725 (2 February 1965) and published in *Sefer ha-Ḥuqqim* No. 445 of 3 Adar Alef, 5725 (5 February 1965), p. 58; the Bill and an Explanatory Note were published in *Hatzaʿot Ḥoq* No. 629 of 5725, p. 48.

108 *Sefer ha-Ḥuqqim* of 5710, p. 86 – LSI vol. 4, p. 68; *Sefer ha-Ḥuqqim* of 5711, p. 70 – LSI vol. 5, p. 63; *Sefer ha-Ḥuqqim* of 5716, p. 34 – LSI vol. 10, p. 31.

(2) The provisions of this subsection shall not void any restriction, qualification or other similar limitation prescribed by or under this Law or imposed by the Custodian and shall not void any transactions effected by him.

(b) This section shall have effect retroactively as from the date of the coming into force of the principal Law.

*Amendment of section 9.*[109]

2. Subsection (d) of section 9 of the principal Law shall be repealed.

*Addition of sections 29 A–H.*

3. The following sections shall be inserted after section 29 of the principal Law:

"*Release of endowment property.*

29A. (a) Where the Custodian releases any endowment property vested in him and which was dedicated for the benefit of the members of the family of the dedicator or of the members of another family, and the beneficiaries are still alive, he may transfer the ownership of the property to them. Where he releases any endowment property vested in him which was not dedicated as aforesaid, he may transfer the ownership thereof to a board of trustees appointed under section 29B or 29H.

(b) Property transferred as aforesaid shall be free from any restriction, qualification or other similar limitation prescribed by or under any law or any document relating to the endowment.

(c) For the purposes of this section and of sections 29B to 29H, "endowment property" means Muslim *waqf* property being immovable property validly dedicated.

*Boards of trustees.*

29B. The Government shall, by notice in *Reshumot*, appoint boards of trustees for the area of each of the following local authorities:

| | |
|---|---|
| Tel Aviv – Jaffa | Acre |
| Ramla | Nazareth |
| Lod | Shefar'am (Shafā 'Amr) |
| Haifa | |

109 Editor's note: Section 9 (d) reads as follows: 'Where the vested property is an endowment, the Custodian may expend all or part of its income for the purposes for which the endowment was created.'

The boards of trustees shall manage the endowment property situated in the area of the authority and which had been released and been transferred to them under section 29A.

*The board of trustees – a body corporate.*
29C. A board of trustees shall be a body corporate competent to acquire and transfer any right, enter into any obligation and be a party to any legal proceeding and to any contract. But a board of trustees shall not in any manner transfer immovable property which includes a mosque.

*Budget.*
29D. A board of trustees shall prepare an annual budget of income and expenditure in connection with the property under its control. The budget shall require the approval of the Government and upon such approval being given shall bind the Board of Trustees.

*Management of property by board of trustees.*
29E. The board of trustees –

(1) shall manage the property under its control and shall use the income thereof for the following purposes: relief of the poor, scholarships to pupils at schools, vocational training, health, religious instruction and religious worship or custom, and any other purpose approved by the Government, all for the requirements of the Muslim inhabitants within the area of operations of the board;
(2) shall use the consideration received for property which ceases to be under its control for the establishment of institutions of the following kinds: orphanages, schools, including schools for vocational training, clinics, mosques and any other similar institution approved by the Government, all for the requirements of the Muslim inhabitants;
and all notwithstanding any provision contained in or made under any law or any document relating to an endowment, and subject to the directions of the Government or a person appointed by it in that behalf.

*Inspection by State Comptroller.*
29F. A board of trustees shall be subject to inspection by the State Comptroller after and in so far as the Finance Committee of the Knesset or the State Comptroller has decided that the inspection shall become operative.

*Use of endowment property by Custodian.*
29G. The endowment property vested in the Custodian and not released, and the income of and consideration received for such property, shall be used by the Custodian for the same purposes for which a board of trustees may use income of and consideration received for property under section 29F.

*Additional boards of trustees.*
29H. The Government shall, as may be necessary, by declarations in *Reshumot*, designate further localities in the areas of which boards of trustees shall be established.".

LEVI ESHKOL
Prime Minister

PINCHAS SAPIR
Minister of Finance

SHNEUR ZALMAN SHAZAR
President of the State

# PART 5

## *Islamic Law in a Non-Muslim State*

CHAPTER 19

# The Heritage of Ottoman Rule in the Israeli Legal System: The Concept of *Umma* and *Millet*

## 1 Introduction

This essay[1] presents an anomaly in the Israeli legal system created by changing political circumstances. At the core of the anomaly are the concepts *umma*, the Muslim political entity, and *millet*, a communal framework regulating the status and organization of the tolerated religious communities (Christians and Jews) in the Ottoman Empire. Being a residue of the reality of a sovereign Islamic state, these concepts, once dissociated by historical circumstances from the legal and cultural framework in which they arose, required adjustment to the alien juridical environment of a non-Muslim country with its Western political and socio-cultural orientation. Oddly, the substance (though not the terminology) of these concepts, with some indispensable changes, have survived into the present during a period of almost ninety years after the collapse of the Ottoman Empire. The issue under study represents a highly instructive example of what sociologists and anthropologists designate as "legal pluralism"[2] – in this specific case – transmitted from the multi-religious and communal structure characterizing the Ottoman Empire.

In the Qurʾan, the term *umma* signifies a religious community corresponding to that of *milla*. Beginning with the chapters, or suras, of the Medinan period, the term acquired the narrower connotation of an autonomous Muslim

---

1 This essay is based on a lecture held at Yad Izhak Ben-Zvi, Jerusalem, during a conference on "The Ottomans in Palestine and the Middle East" organized under the auspices of the Hebrew University, Ben-Gurion University, Haifa University, and Tel Aviv University on June 8–9, 2005 on the occasion of Prof. Amnon Cohen's retirement from the Hebrew University. Prof. Ruth Lapidoth (Faculty of Law, Hebrew University), Prof. Assaf Likhovski (Faculty of Law, Tel Aviv University), and Dr. Ido Shahar (Department of Sociology and Anthropology, Tel Aviv University) read an earlier draft of this essay and offered useful comments for which I am most grateful.

Originally published in Peri Bearman, Wolfhart Heinrichs, and Bernard G. Weiss (eds.), *The Law Applied: Contextualizing the Islamic Sharīʿa. A Volume in Honor of Frank E. Vogel* (London, 2008), pp. 128–149.

2 Dupret, Berger and al-Zwaini, *Legal Pluralism in the Arab World.*

 | DOI:10.1163/9789004680920_021

entity coupled with political authority and religious and social components.[3] The term *milla* had a variety of denotations throughout Muslim history; thus, for instance, in sixteenth-century Jerusalem, it designated the Muslims rather than the tolerated religious communities.[4] Towards the end of the Ottoman Empire, as *millet* it signified both "a religious community" and a national entity.[5]

The *millet* system is based on the concept of protection (*dhimma*) granted by means of a contract between the Muslim sovereign and the protected subjects: the first party undertakes to ensure the rights of the second party to manage its own communal and religious affairs, and to provide safety and immunity against arbitrary acts; the second party responds by professing loyalty to the first party. The protection reflects a tolerated status, second-degree citizenship. A series of signs were designated to identify the protected subjects (*dhimmīs*) from the Muslims.[6]

In a Muslim state, the *umma*, the Muslim political entity, is the sovereign; hence there is no need to define its legal status. Islamic law (Shariʿa) regulates also the status of the non-Muslims in the state. Broadly speaking, the Shariʿa courts were state courts and their jurisdiction comprised also non-Muslims. In the second half of the nineteenth century, civil courts designated to apply the new codes, including the Mejelle, the Ottoman civil code, were constituted beside the Shariʿa courts.

Benjamin Braude has found that, contrary to conceptions firmly rooted in Western literature on the Ottoman Empire, the *millet* system was not a unified, organized, and institutionalized system, but rather "a set of arrangements, largely local, with considerable variation over time and place" obtained with each of the older communities – the Greeks (embracing all the orthodox Christian subjects of the sultan), the Armenians, and the Jews – and within which framework a measure of legal autonomy was granted to each community.[7]

The first cracks in the *millet* system, with signs of a reshuffling of the relations between the Muslim *umma* and the *millets*, appeared in the nineteenth century. On the theoretical level (though not necessarily in practice) the *Hatt-i*

3 Bosworth, "The Concept of *Dhimma* in Early Islam;" Lewis, *The Jews of Islam*, 20–40; Braude and Lewis, "Introduction," 5–10; Friedmann, *Tolerance and Coercion in Islam*, General Index, *dhimma, dhimmīs*.

4 Cohen, "On the Realities of the *Millet* System," 8; cf. Braude and Lewis, "Introduction," 30.

5 Karpat, "*Millets* and Nationality;" Lewis, *The Emergence of Modern Turkey*, 329; Ursinus, "Millet," 62b.

6 Cahen, "D̲h̲imma," 227a.

7 Braude, "Foundation Myths of the *Millet* System," 69–70, 73–4 (the citation is from p. 74); Lewis, *The Jews of Islam*, 125–26.

*Hümayun* decree of 1856 proclaiming equality between Muslims and non-Muslim subjects of the Empire[8] was in glaring contradiction to the very nature of the *millet* concept. Moreover, the protection that European powers granted to members of various *millets* by means of extra rights (*berāt*), anchored in the Capitulations agreements (whose scope increased progressively from the sixteenth century onwards), transformed them from the status of dhimmis under the protection of Islam to something approaching the status of resident foreigners or foreign nationals, that is, subjects of the Domain of War (*dār al-ḥarb*), whose duties and rights were defined by the West rather than by Islam.[9] Broadly speaking, in spite of these events, the *millet* system as an organizational framework survived until the collapse of the Ottoman Empire.

## 2 The Ottoman Heritage in Palestine under British Mandate

The point of departure in this essay is the accumulative legal and administrative heritage of the *millet* system as consolidated since the nineteenth century and transferred to Palestine under the British Mandate. Practically speaking, the main components of this heritage are: judicial autonomy in matters of personal status in accordance with the community's religious law, administration of the communal property (*waqf*, church property), observance of religious worship, and a recognized status of the heads of the communities as their representatives towards the state.[10]

Following World War I, Palestine ceased to be part of a Muslim territory, which status had legal and political repercussions. At first blush, one would expect a complete redefinition of the status of the Muslims and the tolerated religious communities within the new political framework. With the collapse of the Ottoman Empire, however, its heritage of legal pluralism as anchored in the *millet* system did not change overnight. The policy of the British government – in line with its colonial legal policy at the time[11] – was to preserve the status quo[12] in matters pertaining to religion and law, subject to obligations undertaken under the Mandate and also subject to changes resulting from the turnover of the political rule. Britain's obligations under the Mandate entailed, inter alia, the safeguarding of the civil and religious rights, including

8 Braude and Lewis, "Introduction," 30–1.

9 Ibid., 28–9, 32.

10 Cf. Englard, *Religious Law in the Israeli Legal System*, 13.

11 Likhovski, *Law and Identity in Mandate Palestine*, 55–8.

12 On status quo in different contexts, see Lapidoth, *The Basic Law*, 16 n. 6.

the holy shrines, of all the inhabitants of Palestine, irrespective of race and religion; the guarantee to respect the personal status of all the people and communities and their religious interests; and the management of the administration of the religious endowments (*waqf*), in accordance with the religious law and the stipulations of their founders. Broadly speaking, the capitulary privileges, including the benefits of Consular jurisdiction and protection as formerly enjoyed by foreigners in the Ottoman Empire, were suspended.[13] The preservation of the status quo was required also to secure the continuity of the law in the transition period from the Ottoman period to Mandate rule. This policy is clearly reflected in the Palestine Order-in-Council, 1922–1947 (hereinafter POC), Article 46, which provides that the civil courts should exercise jurisdiction "in accordance with the Ottoman law in force in Palestine on November 1st, 1914, or otherwise declared to be in force by public notice."

The British policy of preserving the status quo regarding the autonomy of the recognized communities[14] is manifested in various domains. Formally, the Muslims were not included in the category of the recognized religious communities that had been granted judicial autonomy in matters of personal status,[15] though in actual fact they enjoyed judicial autonomy. The Muslims declined to be defined as a religious community (*ṭāʾifa*) within the same category as Jews and Christians. The British government was fully aware of this sensitivity, and the establishment in December 1921 of the Supreme Muslim Council (hereinafter SMC) seems to have been prompted by the desire to compensate the Muslims for the lack of a Muslim sovereign. At a Muslim conference held late in 1920, on the eve of the constitution of the SMC, the High Commissioner expressed the Government's desire

> to establish a body representing the country's Muslims in order both to assure them complete control over their religious endowments and that the Muslim community might feel that the *sharīʿa* courts were being supervised by people of its choice. The Government does not want to take the place of the *sheikh ül-Islām*.[16]

After his election as president of the SMC, Ḥājj Amīn al-Ḥusaynī invested much energy in promoting the status of Jerusalem in the eyes of the Muslim world

13 Vitta, *The Conflict of Laws*, 6–7.

14 For details, see Englard, *Religious Law in the Israeli Legal System*, 13; Cohen, *Personal Introduction*, 230.

15 See Annex to the Palestine-Order-in-Council, 1939 and First Schedule to Succession Ordinance, 1923, in Vitta, *The Conflict of Laws*, 284.

16 Cited from Porath, *The Emergence of the Palestinian Arab National Movement*, 195–96.

and enhancing the importance of the Temple Mount (*al-Ḥaram al-Sharīf*) with its mosques.[17] The president of the Council was empowered to nominate the *qadis* – a function traditionally vested in the Muslim ruler; the *muftis* – traditionally independent but nevertheless institutionalized in the Ottoman Empire; and the religious functionaries of the mosques, to manage the *waqf* properties, both *maḍbūṭ* and *mulḥaq*. Under the late Ottoman rule, the former were administered directly by the Ministry of Waqf while the latter were administered by the Shariʿa Courts subject to the Ministry's supervision.[18] The SMC was also in charge of the educational system. Indeed, well-informed observers defined the Muslim Council as "a state within a state."[19]

Various domains of the Shariʿa that had been codified, such as the Ottoman civil code of 1876, known as the Mejelle, the Family Rights Law of 1917, as well as the Land Law of 1858 and the Procedure of the Shariʿa Court Law of 1917 (both of which rely heavily on the Shariʿa), survived in Palestine. Moreover, the Mejelle, which is based almost exclusively on Hanafi doctrine, was applied in the civil courts with respect to all the residents of the country regardless of religion or community, as it was during the Ottoman period. Needless to say, domains of the Shariʿa that had not been codified, such as criminal law entailing fixed Qurʾanic punishments (*ḥudūd*), and homicide and bodily injury entailing retaliation (*qiṣāṣ*), which are within the area of private law, though remaining intact, were not applied in practice; this is due to the fact that the Shariʿa as a jurists' law is a personal rather than territorial law. Naturally, these sanctions could not be applied in a non-Muslim state.

Article 52 of the POC, the principal enactment defining the powers of the Shariʿa courts, granted them exclusive jurisdiction in all matters of personal status of Muslims, both nationals and foreigners (the latter on condition that under their own national law they were amenable to the jurisdiction of Muslim religious courts), as well as in cases of *waqf* constitution or internal administration (subject to the provisions of the 1921 Order establishing the SMC pertaining to the *waqf*). The Shariʿa courts were bound to apply the Ottoman Sharʿi Law of Procedure of 1917.

The Rabbinical and Christian religious courts, on the other hand, had exclusive jurisdiction only in matters of marriage and divorce, alimony, and confirmation of wills (but concurrent jurisdiction, i.e., with the consent of the parties, in other matters of personal status) of nationals belonging to the Jewish

17 Ibid., 205–7. On other considerations that may have prompted the establishment the SMC, see ibid., 199–200; Kupferschmidt, *The Supreme Muslim Council*, 24–8.

18 Reiter, *Islamic Endowments in Jerusalem under British Mandate*, 6–16.

19 Porath, *The Emergence of the Palestinian Arab National Movement*, 197.

and Christian communities, as well as the constitution or internal administration of *waqfs* founded before the Rabbinical and Christian courts, respectively, according to the respective religious law (Arts. 53 and 54). The difference regarding the scope of jurisdiction between the Muslim and non-Muslim judiciary is a clear heritage from the Ottoman *millet* system. Moreover, although the Shariʿa courts ceased to be state courts with residuary jurisdiction with respect to non-Muslims, they nevertheless retained remnants of this jurisdiction. Thus they had concurrent jurisdiction in matters pertaining to the establishment or validity of *waqfs* founded by Jews and Christians before a Shariʿa court prior to the promulgation of the Palestine Order-in-Council.[20] Such endowments were common practice during the Ottoman period and had continued to some extent into the Mandate period. In cases of blood money (*diya*), i.e., compensation or damages for homicide or bodily injury, the Shariʿa courts had exclusive jurisdiction where all parties were Muslims, and where the parties were non-Muslims, concurrent jurisdiction, that is, conditional on the parties' consent to litigate before the Shariʿa court.[21] This, too, is a heritage from the Ottoman period. According to the Shariʿa, blood money is part of the victim's estate and hence should be divided among the victim's relatives in accordance with Islamic rules of inheritance.

The autonomy pertaining to the legal system (the constitution of religious courts and nomination of judges), the administration of *waqf* and church property, and the appointment of clergy and other positions in Christian churches remained intact during the Mandate because the Patriarchs were located outside the territory of Palestine. Thus the Patriarchs could function regardless of political changes in the region. Out of ten recognized religious communities, nine were Christian: Orthodox and Catholics of various denominations as well as Latins. Each of these communities had an internal constitution. The constitution of the Greek Orthodox (the largest Christian community in Palestine) served, in its broad outlines, as a model for other communities. Each of these communities was headed by a Patriarch or Archbishop assisted by a synod or other central body.[22] The organization of the Jewish community, headed by the Sephardi Ḥakham-bashi, was based on Ottoman regulations of 1864. The Jewish Community Rules of 1928 resolved some uncertainties regarding membership in the community.[23] Other religious communities, such as the Druze,

20 Layish, "The Muslim *Waqf* in Israel," 47.

21 Art. 6 of the Civil and Religious Courts (Jurisdiction) Ordinance, 1925; Vitta, *The Conflict of Laws*, 146 n. 1.

22 Vitta, *The Conflict of Laws*, 65, 113–14.

23 Ibid., 65–7, 105, 125.

the Evangelical-Episcopal, and other Protestant groups, were not recognized during the Mandate in the best Ottoman tradition, notwithstanding pressures exerted on the British Government to the contrary.

The Mandate's sporadic intervention in matters of personal status was carried out by means of criminal legislation intended to deter potential violators of the law without infringing upon the validity of the religious law. This was the case, for instance, with respect to the restrictions imposed on the age required for contracting marriage. Moreover, Muslims *qua* Muslims were exempted from the criminal sanction imposed on polygamy; since polygamy is permitted under the Shariʿa, they had a "good defense" against this charge.[24]

Occasionally, even the declared policy of non-discrimination between inhabitants on grounds of religion, as anchored in the Mandate and statutory legislation with a view to adapting the legal norm to international obligations, failed to stand the test of implementation. Thus Article 15 of the Mandate, which guarantees complete freedom of conscience and free exercise of all forms of worship "subject only to the maintenance of public order and morals," could secure against execution on the charge of apostasy from Islam (*ridda*), but not the deprivation of a Protestant widow of a Muslim from his estate on grounds of difference in religion (*ikhtilāf fī l-dīn*). Nor did the Succession Ordinance of 1923, which prohibits the deprivation of a legal heir from the estate on grounds of difference in nationality or religion (with respect to the deceased), provide the widow with a remedy. The Supreme Court ruled that the decision handed down by the Shariʿa court was unassailable because Article 24(2) of the Succession Ordinance contradicted Article 52 of POC which grants the Shariʿa court exclusive jurisdiction in all matters of personal status pertaining to Muslims.[25]

Naturally, the subordination of the Muslims in Palestine to the British Mandate put them in a serious dilemma, to wit, the Shariʿa is not properly equipped to be applied in non-Muslim territory.[26] In Muslim medieval legal discourse, to the extent that the jurists were ready to address this issue, they debated whether Muslims might reside in the Domain of War (*dār al-ḥarb*) and whether the observance of religious prescriptions outside the Domain of Islam (*dār al-islām*) was a valid fulfillment of religious duties from the point of view of the religious law.[27]

24 Ibid., 54–5.

25 Ibid., 9.

26 Layish, "Adaptation of a Jurists' Law to Modern Times," 169–70.

27 Abou El Fadl, "Islamic Law and Muslim Minorities."

Another problem faced by Muslims in Palestine devolves upon the structure of authority in the state. Islam does not recognize the concept of separation of powers. In accordance with the Sharīʿa, the executive and judicial powers (theoretically there is no legislative authority in Islam) are vested in the Muslim sovereign, who may delegate to his representatives any of these powers or the combination of both at one and the same time. In the late Ottoman period, qadis quite often were engaged in administrative functions in the provinces alongside their judicial function. Thus the qadi of Jerusalem served as the chief administrative officer in his district.[28] In spite of the introduction of the concept of separation of powers in Palestine, remnants of the traditional conception of authority still survived. The President of the SMC had the power to nominate the qadis, which is one of the symbols of sovereignty in a Muslim state. Moreover, as president of the Council and Mufti of Jerusalem, Ḥājj Amīn al-Ḥusaynī combined both temporal and religious-legal authorities in the best tradition of the Righteous Caliphs. Earlier, the British Military Governor designated the Mufti of Jerusalem as the Grand Mufti (*al-muftī al-akbar*), a title that did not exist previously in Palestine, and in fact treated him as the "Representative of Islam in Palestine." The Muslims regarded the function of the Mufti of Jerusalem as equivalent to that of the "Shaykh al-Islām," i.e., "Mufti of Palestine." Broadly speaking, the British administration, too, considered the Mufti of Jerusalem as the "head of the Muslim community in Palestine.[29] Needless to say, both the SMC and the Sharīʿa courts operated by virtue of secular statutes.

Article 51 of POC defines "matters of personal status" (marriage, divorce, etc.) in accordance with Western rather than Islamic legal conceptions. This in turn restricted the Sharīʿa courts' jurisdiction. Thus, for instance, "legal capacity" is not defined as a matter of personal status, and hence it is not included in Article 51,[30] though in judicial practice it was presumed to "accompany" matters that were within the jurisdiction of the religious courts. Article 52 curtailed the personal jurisdiction of the Sharīʿa courts with respect to non-Muslims. In the event that the parties to a dispute belonged to different religions or communities, the Chief Justice (in Israel, the President of the Supreme Court) would decide the competent tribunal to deal with the dispute.[31] In 1919 the British government adopted the Ottoman Family Rights Law of 1917, but excluded

28 Porath, *The Emergence of the Palestinian Arab National Movement*, 186.

29 Ibid., 188, 190, 194.

30 Legal capacity is included in "matters of personal status" within the meaning of Art. 7 of the Ottoman Procedure of the Sharīʿa Court Law of 1917.

31 Vitta, *The Conflict of Laws*, 14–6.

from its applicability non-Muslims. The original version of the law regulated the matters of personal status of all Ottoman subjects regardless of religion or community.

The British Mandate integrated the religious laws of all the communities in the general legal system and all the religious courts were brought under the control of the High Court of Justice. The jurisdiction vested in civil courts (alongside concurrent jurisdiction of the religious courts, i.e., with the consent of the parties, and incidental jurisdiction) in matters of personal status indirectly curtailed the scope of application of the religious law of the respective communities.

Under the Shariʿa, renouncing Islam (*ridda*) publicly is punishable by death for Muslims. According to the Hanafi doctrine, apostasy is not a crime entailing Qurʾanic punishment (*ḥadd*), but nevertheless male apostates are liable to the death penalty on the grounds that they have become potential enemies to Islam. It is recommended (not obligatory) to grant the apostate a delay of three days to repent, failing which he is put to death. Female apostates, on the other hand, must be imprisoned and beaten until they repent.[32] Clearly, the British government in Palestine could not reconcile the Islamic doctrine pertaining to conversion with its international obligations under the Mandate. It therefore circumvented the harsh sanctions under the Shariʿa by channeling the procedure of conversion from one religion to another to the technical secular procedure of transferring from one religious community to another. The Religious Community (Change) Ordinance of 1927 enables a Muslim or a member of any other religious community to abandon his religious community and to join another; the change of community according to specified procedure was valid and effective under the general law without bearing any consequences on the validity of the religious law.[33]

The government made it possible to endow property for charitable purposes, education, and religion other than by means of the religious court and religious law and to convert religious endowments into secular endowments for charitable purposes. In the second half of the 1930s, in the midst of the Palestinian national revolt, the British government transferred the administration of Muslim *waqf* from the SMC to an appointed state committee in accordance with Defense (Muslim *Waqf*) Regulations of 1937.[34]

---

32 Peters, *Crime and Punishment in Islamic Law*, 64–5.

33 For further detail on application of the Ordinance, see Vitta, *The Conflict of Laws*, 68–76.

34 Layish, "The Muslim *Waqf* in Israel," 45–6, 57.

## 3 The Ottoman Legal Heritage in Israel

The Ottoman legal heritage as anchored and consolidated in Mandatory legislation passed into Israel by virtue of Section 11 of the Law and the Administration Ordinance of 1948, which provides that the law in force in Palestine on the day of the declaration of the establishment of the State of Israel shall remain in force so long as it is not repugnant to this Ordinance or to other laws which may be enacted in future legislation by the State.[35]

With the end of the British Mandate and the outbreak of war in 1948, the communal organization of the Muslims in Israel collapsed completely. The members of the SMC and the religious-legal elite (muftis, qadis, and ulama) left the country; the religious judicial system, the *waqf* administration, and communal educational and welfare institutions crumbled and ceased to exist. The government of Israel set about rehabilitating the organization of the Muslim community. The undefined status of the Muslims remained, however, intact: they were not recognized as a "religious community" within the meaning of the POC.

The Muslim judicial system was reconstituted within the general legal system. Until 2001, the Shariʿa courts enjoyed the widest jurisdiction in matters of personal status compared to any other religious community. Moreover, they still deal with conversion to Islam of Jewish and Christian women (mainly for marriage purposes) in much the same way they did during the Ottoman period. Occasionally, the Shariʿa courts conclude marriages of mixed parties, that is, a Muslim male with a non-Muslim female, and deal with disputes of such couples, although, as already noted, in the event that the spouses belong to different communities, it is up to the President of the Supreme Court to determine the court competent to deal with the matter. Some of the qadis have not internalized the fact that specified domains of the Shariʿa that had been codified, as in the case of the family law pertaining to marriage and divorce, ceased to be jurists' law applicable everywhere and became territorial law that bears no validity outside the boundaries of Israel.[36]

At the same time there is ample evidence to the effect that Israeli Muslims are losing their unique status dating back to the Ottoman Empire. The government has rejected all their attempts to run their communal affairs in total independence from the state, in contrast with the practice of some Christian

35 Friedmann, "The Effects of Foreign Law on the Law of Israel," 194ff.

36 Layish, "Adaptation of a Jurists' Law to Modern Times," 170–1. On the repercussions of the codification of Jewish law by Western-oriented scholars, see Likhovski, "The Invention of 'Hebrew Law' in Mandatory Palestine," 351, 353.

communities. Muslim attempts to establish a religious or secular-temporal authority in charge of the Shariʿa judiciary outside of the general legal system, of the *waqf* administration, and of the religious services were frustrated by the government.[37] Moreover, while promulgating the Qāḍīs Law of 1961, the Knesset, under the impact of the political events that transpired during the Mandate under the leadership of Ḥājj Amīn al-Ḥusaynī, the president of the SMC, abrogated the 1921 Ordinance pertaining to the constitution of the Council (Art. 25).

Until 2002 the Shariʿa courts were subject administratively to the Ministry for Religious Affairs and since then to the Ministry of Justice. The decisions of the Shariʿa courts are subject to judicial review by the Supreme Court in its capacity as a High Court of Justice (hereinafter HCJ) rather than an instance of appeals; in practice, however, the HCJ is seldom resorted to. Qadis are elected by an appointment committee (the majority of whose members are Muslims) chaired by the Minister of Justice, and appointed by the president of the State; and they are required to pledge allegiance to the State. Article 7 of the Qāḍīs Law, however, does not require qadis to dispense justice in accordance with Israeli statutes. In daily practice, the Shariʿa Court of Appeal ignores Israeli laws pertaining to personal status unless these have been explicitly addressed to religious courts.

With the establishment of the State of Israel, the Jews ceased to be a "religious community";[38] in some respects their status approximated that of Muslims in a Muslim state. Jewish law, however, does not apply in matters other than personal status. Christian communities enjoy the widest autonomy as far as the status of the heads of church, organization of the judiciary, and church property are concerned. The Catholic churches have a hierarchical structure with supreme authority and their institutions engage in legislating, adjudicating, executing penalties, and imposing social sanctions. They do not need the support of the state to run their internal affairs.[39]

In 1957, the government recognized the Druze as a religious community on the basis of the Religious Communities (Organisation) Ordinance of 1926, which regulates the establishment of communal institutions. In 1963 the Druze were

---

37 Peled, *Debating Islam in the Jewish State*, 53–7, 141–48, 158; Dumper, *Islam and Israel*, 38; Abou Ramadan, "Judicial Activism," 292–96.

38 The voluntary registration in the Register of "Knesset Israel," the Jewish community in Palestine organized by statute under the Jewish Community Rules of 1928, was replaced, in 1949, by the obligatory registration of all the inhabitants of the State. Hence, the statutory "Jewish community" ceased to exist. Cohen, *Personal Introduction*, 230; Englard, *Religious Law in the Israeli Legal System*, 13; Vitta, *The Conflict of Laws*, 65–7, 105.

39 Englard, *Religious Law in the Israeli Legal System*, 13.

again recognized as a religious community, this time within the meaning of the POC, for the purpose of establishing religious courts with jurisdiction similar to those of the Rabbinical courts. Earlier, in 1961, the Spiritual Leadership of the Druze community in its statutory capacity as "Religious Council," adopted the law of personal status of the Druze community in Lebanon of 1948 in order for it to be applied, with some important modifications, by the Druze religious courts in Israel.[40] Needless to say, the Druze, who had seceded completely from Islam, could not be tolerated and hence recognized as a religious community under any kind of Muslim rule. The Evangelical Episcopal Church in Israel and the members of the Bahai Faith were subsequently recognized in 1970 and 1971, respectively, as religious communities within the meaning of POC.

The Mejelle, the Ottoman civil law, was abolished in 1984 as far as the civil courts are concerned, but it is still valid and applicable in the Shariʿa courts. The Ottoman Land Law of 1858 was replaced by the Land Law of 1969.[41]

The Knesset intervened intensively in matters of personal status and succession with a view to improving the legal status of women. Section 1 of the Women's Equal Rights Law of 1951, the keystone of legislation in these matters, provides: "A man and a woman shall have equal status with regard to any legal act; any provision of law discriminating, with regard to any legal act, against women as women shall be of no effect." The Knesset, for obvious reasons, could hardly adopt the legislative techniques, such as a ruler's administrative regulations (*siyāsa sharʿiyya*), public interest (*maṣlaḥa*), the eclectic expedient (*takhayyur, talfīq*), and reinterpretation of textual sources (neo-*ijtihād*), that were customary in Arab countries to give the reforms the character of an internal refurbishing of the Shariʿa.[42] However, out of regard for the legal systems of the various religious communities anchored in the Ottoman *millet* system, the Knesset abstained from interfering with any religious prohibition or permission as to marriage and divorce; in this sensitive domain procedural provisions and penal sanctions were adopted as deterrents in preference to substantive provisions which would have invalidated the relevant religious law. Another self-enforced restriction was in matters for which provisions superseding religious law were enacted, whereby the parties were usually given the option of litigating in accordance with religious law.

The following are the main reforms introduced by the Knesset, from the perspective of Islamic law:[43]

---

40 Layish, *Marriage, Divorce and Succession in the Druze Family*, 1–15.
41 Layish, *Women and Islamic Law in a Non-Muslim State*, 280–82.
42 Layish, "The Transformation of the *Sharīʿa* from Jurists' Law to Statutory Law," 92–5.
43 Layish, "The Status of the *Sharīʿa* in a Non-Muslim State," 174–76.

1. The minimal age of marriage for women (which is not recognized in Islamic law) was raised from 15 years, as under Mandatory law, to 17 years, as under the Ottoman Family Rights Law of 1917, but at the same time the "good defenses" based on the Shariʿa (such as the guardian's consent to the marriage of a minor girl) against a charge of contravention of age-of-marriage legislation were abrogated, and the penal sanction was increased. A district court (but not a religious court) was empowered to permit the marriage of a girl of sixteen.
2. Polygamy (which is permitted under Islam) was prohibited. The defense granted to Muslims qua Muslims by the Mandatory government against a charge of polygamy was abolished. Instead, Muslims have been granted two defenses against such a charge: prolonged absence or mental illness of the spouse.
3. Divorcing one's wife against her will (which is permitted in Islam) – unless permission to do so has been given by the qadi – was forbidden by criminal legislation.
4. The woman was acknowledged as a natural guardian of her children along with their father, but the Shariʿa court may decide otherwise if it deems it in the best interest of the child. Under the Shariʿa, only the father and after him agnates in a specified order are natural guardians. The terminal age of guardianship was raised to 18 for both sexes.
5. The Ottoman Law of Succession of 1913, a replica of a German law which does not differentiate between males and females and between agnates and cognates, applied originally only to the category of *mīrī* property, the full ownership of which is vested in the state while possession and usufruct are vested in the individual. The British government adopted the law in 1923. Since 1951, the law was applied also to property in full private ownership (*mülk*) and movable unless all the parties, being adults, agreed to litigate in accordance with the religious law of inheritance. The Succession Law of 1965 provides for perfect equality between the sexes in all categories of property, either *mīrī* or *mülk*, and secures complete freedom of testamentary disposition. Unlike the religious *ultra vires* doctrine, Israeli law permits the disposition of the entire estate by will and in favor of a legal heir. However, the law applies only in the civil court; in cases where the Shariʿa court is empowered by the parties to deal with the matter, it may apply the Shariʿa rules of inheritance to all categories of property.
6. The Maintenance (Securing Payment) Law of 1972 transferred the burden of securing maintenance to the wife after being fixed by a Shariʿa court judgment, to the National Insurance Institute, and the latter is required to collect the debt from the husband.

7. The Law of Property Relations between the Spouses of 1973 provides that upon the dissolution of a marriage, the value of the spouses' combined property, in the absence of agreement, should be equally divided between husband and wife. This is a far-reaching innovation from the point of view of the religious law, which does not recognize community property between the spouses; a divorced wife is entitled only to waiting-period maintenance and deferred dower (if stipulated in the marriage contract).

Needless to say, the Knesset's reforms undermine the patrilineal and patriarchal infrastructure of the traditional Muslim family.[44] The Ottomans started this process with the codification of the family law dealing with marriage and divorce, followed by some of the Arab countries which even expanded the domains of codification within the family law. Although these reforms were inspired to a very large extent by European norms and ideas regarding the status of women, the reforms were presented as an internal development within the Shariʿa. In Israel the reforms in the family law are the result of social and political pressures for the liberation of women initiated by Jewish feminist organizations. The reforms have been imposed from above on Muslim society although significant parts of it are not yet ready to absorb them.

In 2001, following pressures exerted by Arab feminist organizations, the exclusive jurisdiction of the Shariʿa courts was downgraded significantly concurrently with the extension of the jurisdiction of the civil Family Courts to matters of personal status, other than marriage and divorce, pertaining to Muslims (and Christians).[45] In other words, the Family Courts now share jurisdiction on equal terms with the Shariʿa courts. Thus, in a matrimonial dispute between spouses in matters of personal status (to the exclusion of marriage and divorce), either of the spouses who precedes the other in filing a suit before any of the two tribunals, the Shariʿa court or the Family Court, determines the court before which the matter is to be heard. One would expect the spouses to choose the tribunal according to the nature of the issue being disputed, e.g., the wife would prefer the Family Court in a case of maintenance while the husband would prefer the Shariʿa court in a case of obedience.[46] Undoubtedly, the

44 Cf. Layish, "Reformist Matrimonial Legislation and the Collapse of the Muslim Patrilineal Family."

45 Family Court Law (Amendment No. 5), 2001. *Sefer Haḥuqim*, 1810, 14.11.01; Abou Ramadan, "Judicial Activism," 293–94.

46 Shortly after the establishment of the state, the government considered the possibility of abolishing the religious judiciary of all communities and transferring their jurisdiction in matters of personal status to the civil courts. The Jewish religious parties in the coalition vehemently rejected the initiative. They joined forces to this end with the spokesmen of the Shariʿa courts. Cohen, *A Personal Introduction*, 227.

jurisdiction shared by the two tribunals will bring about far-reaching changes in the status of the Shariʿa in Israel since whenever an issue is brought before the Family Court, the Shariʿa will be applied in the light of the principles of Israeli law and in accordance with the civil rules of evidence and procedure.[47] In a meeting on June 14 2006 with civil judges of the Family Court in Jerusalem, intended to brief them regarding the application of the Shariʿa in matters pertaining to maintenance, custody, and guardianship, the judges expressed concern about subject matters that have not undergone codification within the Ottoman Family Rights Law. Since most of the judges lack free access to Arabic legal literature, the present writer forwarded the suggestion to have the second legal circular (*marsūm qaḍāʾī*) issued by the Shariʿa Court of Appeal in 1995 translated into Hebrew. This circular provides criteria for assessing the rates of maintenance due to the wife in accordance with current requirements and transfers the discretion for fixing these rates from the informants (*mukhbirūn*) to the qadi.[48] A further suggestion was made for the compilation of a concise comparative manual of Islamic legal rules of the subject matter according to the different schools of law (*madhhab*s) in order to enable the civil judges to adopt the doctrine that yields the desirable judicial result according to the judge's discretion. In other words, the Family Court will not be bound by the Hanafi school, which since Ottoman rule in this region has been the officially recognized one in the Shariʿa courts, regardless of the school affiliation of the parties involved. This suggestion is inspired by the judicial practice of the Shariʿa Court of Appeal presided over by Qadi Ahmad Nāṭūr. Nāṭūr views the legal literature of the schools as a global reservoir out of which it is possible to derive elements in harmony with the conditions of modern times.[49] This technique is calculated to spare the civil judges the need to resort to English literature on Anglo-Muhammadan Law. Clearly, where the Knesset has intervened in matters of personal status or where the Supreme Court has handed down decisions pertaining to these matters that are deemed binding precedents, the civil judges are bound by the Israeli civil legal norms and are exempted from applying the Shariʿa.

In matters pertaining to succession, since 1965 the Shariʿa courts have concurrent jurisdiction, that is, depending on the consent of all the parties concerned, failing which the jurisdiction remains with the civil court.

In circumstances where the Shariʿa cannot offer solutions appropriate for a modern society, Muslims have recourse to civil courts. The Supreme Court

47 Layish, "Adaptation of a Jurists' Law to Modern Times," 173–74.

48 Ibid., 184–88.

49 Ibid., 192–94.

does not hesitate to intervene in such circumstances by creating civil legal norms complementary to the Shariʿa as in the case of civil paternity based on biological relationship regardless of whether or not the child's parents are married to each other. The Supreme Court's decision is based on the Israeli legislation and the courts' judicial practice, on norms of the State of Israel as a Jewish democratic state, on Jewish law, and on American and English judicial practice. To clarify the position of Islamic law on the relevant issues, the Supreme Court, due to lack of access to Islamic legal literature, resorts to the Anglo-Muhammadan law.[50]

The Shariʿa Court is the main arena in which Muslims in Israel can exercise some measure of autonomy, especially with respect to application of those parts of the Shariʿa that have not been codified. Most of the qadis nominated in the first years after the emergence of the state were graduates of al-Azhar, and, broadly speaking, their judicial decisions reflect a traditional approach. Thus they rejected provisions in the Ottoman Family Rights Law that are not in harmony with Hanafi doctrine, but this did not deter them from applying without inhibition the Knesset's legislation in matters of personal status explicitly addressed to religious courts. The present generation of qadis comprises no graduates of al-Azhar (although there was a graduate of the University of Hebron, which in terms of its attitude to Islamic law is as traditional). Most of the qadis have degrees from faculties of humanities, social sciences, education, and law conferred by Israeli universities. They regard themselves as avant-garde in the movement for legal and social reform. However, they insist on carrying out reforms their own way without the intervention of the Knesset. Thus President Nāṭūr of the Shariʿa Court of Appeal recently turned down a suggestion to replace the Ottoman Family Rights Law by a new law of personal status which would absorb the reforms introduced in Middle Eastern and North African countries. A committee consisting of religious functionaries and experts on Islamic law was to prepare a bill of family law to be endorsed by the Knesset *en bloc*, i.e., without interference in its substance. The reason for the rejection of the legislative initiative was Qadi Nāṭūr's reluctance to allow the Knesset's involvement in the process of preparing such a law. In his view, statutory codification is appropriate for independent Muslim countries; in the absence of a Muslim sovereignty or Muslim legislative authority in Israel, the only option left is to introduce reforms by means of legal circulars and judicial practice of the Shariʿa Court of Appeal.[51]

---

50 Ibid., 180–82.

51 Ibid., 213–14.

Apparently for the same reason, the qadis of the Shariʿa Court of Appeal – under the strong effect of the Israeli Supreme Court – absorb and Islamize Israeli legal principles and institutions, such as the welfare of the child, natural justice, legal precedent, and the right of standing, by means of traditional Islamic legal mechanisms such as *maṣlaḥa* and *siyāsa sharʿiyya*.[52] Islamization of legal institutions from foreign cultures was characteristic of the Shariʿa in its formative period when it displayed an impressive assimilative power upon reaching close contact with the conquered cultures in the West and East.[53] Needless to say, the situation of Israeli Muslims as a tolerated community puts them on the defensive. Due to the disconnection of Israeli Muslims from high Islamic legal educational institutions in the Muslim world (Egypt is disinclined to admit Israeli Muslim students to al-Azhar), it is unlikely that Israeli qadis will come up with a new legal methodology, within the framework of orthodox Shariʿa, capable of carrying the burden of legal reform in family law. On the contrary, the impression is that the Shariʿa in Israel is being discomfited by Israeli principles of law on its own soil, that is, in the Shariʿa courts.[54]

The Supreme Court, on its part, imposes on the Islamic judiciary legal norms, which are occasionally not in harmony with the Shariʿa, in matters of personal status pertaining to basic civil rights in the light of the principles of the Basic Law: Human Dignity and Liberty (1992) and other basic laws promulgated in the early 1990s. Some observers do not rule out the possibility of the development of a dual legal system in matters of personal status according to the division of the judiciary: the Shariʿa courts will apply the Shariʿa (either in its codified or non-codified version), subject only to the changes introduced by the Knesset's legislation, and the civil courts will apply a pure civil law (though not in matters pertaining to marriage and divorce).[55]

The events following the 1947 United Nations resolution on the partition of Palestine and the war of 1948 and, in its wake, the migration of large sections of the Arab population from Israel to Arab countries or to areas in Palestine then held by Arab forces, created the problem of absentee property of which Muslim *waqf* is a part. The members of the *waqf* committee appointed by the British government to replace the *waqf* committee of the SMC in accordance with Defense (Muslim *Waqf*) Regulations of 1937, also left the country and hence the *waqf maḍbūṭ* property administered by that committee was

52 Ibid., 198–207; cf. Likhovski, "The Invention of 'Hebrew Law' in Mandatory Palestine," 365.

53 Schacht, *An Introduction to Islamic Law*, 15–22.

54 Cf. Abou Ramadan, "The Transition from Tradition to Reform, " 635.

55 Layish, "Adaptation of a Jurists' Law to Modern Times," 219–20 and the reference to I. Naveh's Ph.D. dissertation.

declared absentee property. The *waqf mulḥaq* property was declared absentee property only to the extent that their private administrators (*mutawalli*), subject to the Shariʿa court supervision, were deemed absentee. Although Israeli law, jurisdiction, and administration were applied to East Jerusalem in 1967,[56] the Israeli government decided, out of political considerations, to exclude *waqf* property in East Jerusalem from the status of absentee property within the meaning of the law of 1950.[57]

In view of the requirements of the Muslim community, the Custodian of Absentees' Property transferred the management of holy places, such as mosques and cemeteries, and their non-religious appurtenances to the Director of the Division of Muslim and Druze Affairs of the Ministry of Religious Affairs as the Custodian's agent. Out of the income of the non-religious *waqf* property, the Custodian made allocations for Muslim religious purposes through Muslim advisory committees appointed by the Minister of Religious Affairs in towns in which Muslim communities existed. The Custodian spent the consideration (*amwāl al-badal*) received for *waqf* property acquired by the statutory Development Authority on the establishment of institutions in the fields of education, health, social welfare, religious services, and the like for the benefit of the Muslim community throughout the country.

This state of affairs did not satisfy the Muslims, who demanded a revival of the SMC and the transfer to it of the *waqf* property. The fact that the Custodian had released to the Greek Orthodox and Greek Catholic (Melkite) communities their *waqf* and other ecclesiastical assets that were likewise absentee property (these properties were registered in the names of the Patriarchate of Jerusalem and the Archbishop of Acre, Haifa, Nazareth, and the rest of Galilee, respectively), of course, aggravated the dissatisfaction among the Muslim community. The legality of the vesting of the Muslim *waqf* in the Custodian was challenged on the grounds that according to the dominant view in the Hanafi school, the bare ownership (*raqaba*) of the *waqf* property belongs to God, the entitlement (*istiḥqāq*) to the beneficiaries, and the management of the *waqf* to the administrator (*mutawalli*). Broadly speaking, the HCJ adopted this view and held that what had been vested in the Custodian was not the ownership of the *waqf* but rather the right of management for the absent *mutawalli*. On one occasion the HCJ decided that this right became void upon the appointment of a new *mutawalli* by the Shariʿa court. These decisions applied to *waqf mulḥaq*, and did not affect the status of *waqf maḍbūt*, this being outside the supervision of the Shariʿa court.

56 Lapidoth, *The Basic Law*, 22, 53.

57 Reiter, *Islamic Institutions in Jerusalem*, 42; Dumper, *Islam and Israel*, 101, 108–9.

In 1965, far-reaching reforms – modeled on the Egyptian reforms in the *waqf* institution in the 1950s–were introduced in the Muslim *waqf* to the extent that it fell within the category of absentee property:

1. The *waqf* property "free from any restriction, qualification or other similar limitation prescribed [...] by or under any law [i.e., the Shariʿa] or document relating to the endowment [i.e., the *waqfiyya*]" was vested in the Custodian retroactively since 1950. In other words, full ownership in the *waqf* property, in addition to the right of management and the right of entitlement, was vested in the Custodian provided the person having either possession or the right of management, or the beneficiary was absent. This reform was intended to remove doubts that had arisen following the aforementioned decisions of the HCJ regarding the substance of the right vested in the Custodian and to assert the original intention of the legislator.
2. The Custodian is empowered to transfer the family *waqf* property to the beneficiaries in full ownership, free from any restrictions hitherto applying to the *waqf*, in accordance with their shares in the entitlement. In other words, the beneficiaries become owners of their shares in the released property and can dispose of it at will without any limitation.
3. The Custodian is authorized to release public *waqf* property (*khayrī*) in full ownership in six towns in which Muslim communities exist. The released property is to be entrusted to Muslim boards of trustees to be appointed by the Government. The boards may dispose of the property (provided it does not include a mosque), use the income thereof for social and cultural purposes without being bound by the founder's stipulations, and invest the consideration of property sold in institutions established for the aforementioned purposes. The boards are subject to inspection by the State Comptroller.
4. In places where no Muslim community exists and hence no board of trustees is to be appointed, the Custodian is instructed to allocate the proceeds of and consideration received for the *waqf* property for the same purposes as are prescribed for the boards of trustees.[58]

In the past the *waqf khayrī* institution played an important role in fostering charity, social welfare, religious services, and education in sovereign Muslim societies. Generally, in view of the limited involvement of the Islamic state

58 Layish, "The Muslim *Waqf* in Israel." For analysis of the 1965 law and its implementation, see Dumper, *Islam and Israel*, 43–62, 126–27; Reiter, "An Assessment of the Reform in the Muslim *Waqf*;" Peled, *Debating Islam in the Jewish State*, 137–39.

in providing social services,[59] these functions were performed by the *waqf* institution – in the Ottoman Empire, rulers, governors, and senior officials assumed this function as individuals rather than in their capacities as servants of the state. Clearly, the importance of the role of the *waqf khayrī* increases in the absence of Muslim sovereignty.[60] During the Mandate period in Palestine, the administration and control of the *waqf* property by the SMC provided the funds for the maintenance and promotion of Muslim communal affairs.

In the past, the founder's desire to preserve the integrity of the agnatic patrimony seems to have been the main motive for establishing family *waqf* (*dhurrī, ahlī*). Since there is no full freedom of testamentary disposition in Islam, it being bound by the *ultra vires* doctrine of the Shariʿa, the family *waqf* was one of the main devices used to circumvent the Shariʿa rules of inheritance. The Ottoman Succession Law of 1913 prohibited the drawing up of a will on *mīrī*, or state-owned, property. The Israeli Succession Law of 1965, which does not distinguish between *mülk* and *mīrī* estates, permits full freedom of testamentary disposition and hence there is no longer any need to resort to the *waqf* mechanism in order to preserve the patrimony within the agnatic family. Indeed, the motive to establish family *waqf* in Israel has almost completely disappeared.

## 4 Conclusion

The Ottoman-Muslim concepts of *umma* and *millet* can be said to have virtually lost their original raison d'être in Israel. The transition from the Mandate to the State of Israel promoted the Jewish nature of the State at the expense of the Muslim legacy. The Knesset persistently strives to disconnect itself from the Ottoman-Muslim (and British) legal heritage[61] and to replace it with genuine Israeli legislation deriving its inspiration from Jewish law ("religious legislation")[62] and the so-called "Israeli heritage." The jurisprudence of the civil courts, which in recent years have enjoyed wide jurisdiction in matters of Muslim personal status (to the extent that they are not inhibited from resorting to these courts) and a fortiori the jurisprudence of the Supreme Court, which creates new civil legal norms (as in the case of civil paternity) alongside the Shariʿa or in its place, have left their mark on the judicial practice of the Shariʿa courts.

---

59 Cf. Schacht, *An Introduction to Islamic Law*, 76–7, 206–7.

60 Cf. Dumper, *Islam and Israel*, 126 (the *waqf* system as a "mediating institution" in a non-Muslim state).

61 Friedmann, "The Effects of Foreign Law on the Law of Israel," 201–6.

62 Elon, *Religious Legislation*.

Nevertheless, parts of the Ottoman legacy based on the concept of the *umma* and *millet* system still survive. Although Muslims in Israel have ceased to be an *umma* in the original sense of the term and for all practical purposes have actually become a religious community, no formal positive expression of their new status is to be found in Israeli law: they are not recognized as a religious community within the meaning of POC or any Israeli statute (although the Shariʿa courts are recognized and integrated within the state legal system). The traditional concept of the *millet*, i.e., "religious community," as a functional and organizational framework ostensibly survived with respect to all religious communities (to the exclusion of the Jews) subject to one very significant difference: the communities are no longer connected to a Muslim state; rather they are connected to a Jewish state.

Legal pluralism is, in essence, another residual element of the Ottoman legal heritage in Israel: the division between religious and secular law or between religious and secular courts has survived in the country, although with some variations. Thus the individual has some leeway to maneuver between one judiciary or another, in accordance with court jurisdiction. Moreover, secular law and religious law coexist even within the same court – be it religious or secular. This represents the outcome of a situation whereby secular legislation is administered in religious courts and religious law in the civil courts with respect to specific matters in the realm of personal status. This coexistence of two profoundly different legal systems is historically based on the tolerance bestowed by the Muslim sovereign upon the tolerated religions within the framework of the *millet* system. In Israel, the survival of this spirit of tolerance towards religious communities will depend on several factors, such as the strength of the Jewish religious parties within the government, the international protection extended by European powers to various Christian communities since the eighteenth and nineteenth centuries,[63] and the forces of inertia, or status quo, dating back to the Ottoman Empire.[64] We are not dealing here with two independent legal systems, civil and religious, that coexist side by side; rather, we are dealing with autonomy exercised by the Shariʿa within the space reserved for it by Israeli law. With due reservations, the roles of *umma* and *millet* can be said to have been reversed: The Jews have replaced the Muslims as *umma*, and the Muslims the Jews as a *millet*.[65]

---

63 Lapidoth, *The Basic Law*, 15–6.

64 The issue of status quo is still relevant today. See the Fundamental Agreement between the Holy See and the State of Israel of 1993; Lapidoth, *The Basic Law*, 36, 101.

65 Hooker's distinction between a "dominant legal system" and a "servient legal system" (Hooker, *Legal Pluralism*, 7–8), though borrowed from a colonial situation, may be relevant in the Israeli context. I owe this observation to Ido Shahar.

Of course, in domains outside the jurisdiction of religious courts, such as worship and religious prescriptions, the Shariʿa is still sovereign and unassailable, allowing for the circumstance that in a non-Muslim state it is impossible to impose their application on Muslims by means of the executive authority; at most, social sanctions may be used to this end.

Finally, due to the Israeli-Palestinian conflict, the concepts of *umma* and *millet* have acquired a national dimension par excellence. Both Muslims and Jews in Israel define themselves in religious and political terms. The loyalty to the religious framework, regardless of whether the religious community is the majority or the minority, has been translated into national political terms. This is, not surprisingly, not new; in the nineteenth century, the Greek and Armenian *millet*s in the Ottoman Empire emerged as national entities.[66]

## References

Abou El Fadl, Khaled, "Islamic Law and Muslim Minorities: The Juristic Discourse on Muslim Minorities from the Second/Eighth to the Eleventh/Seventeenth Centuries," *Islamic Law and Society* 1 (1994), 141–87.

Abou Ramadan, Moussa, "Judicial Activism of the Shariʿah Appeals Court in Israel (1994–2001): Rise and Crisis," *Fordham International Journal* 27 (2003), 254–98.

Abou Ramadan, Moussa, "The Transition from Tradition to Reform: The Shariʿa Appeals Court Rulings on Child Custody (1992–2001)," *Fordham International Journal* 26 (2003), 594–655.

Bosworth, C.E., "The Concept of *Dhimma* in Early Islam," in B. Braude and B. Lewis (eds.), *Christians and Jews in the Ottoman Empire. The Functioning of a Plural Society*, vol. 1. *The Central Lands* (New York 1982), 37–51.

Braude, B., "Foundation Myths of the *Millet* System," In B. Braude and B. Lewis (eds.), *Christians and Jews in the Ottoman Empire. The Functioning of a Plural Society*, vol. 1. *The Central Lands* (New York 1982), 69–88.

Braude, B. and B. Lewis, "Introduction," in B. Braude and B. Lewis (eds.), *Christians and Jews in the Ottoman Empire. The Functioning of a Plural Society*, vol. 1. *The Central Lands* (New York 1982), 1–34.

Cahen, Cl., "D̲himma," *The Encyclopaedia of Islam*, New ed. (1991), 2:227–31.

Cohen, A., "On the Realities of the *Millet* System: Jerusalem in the Sixteenth Century," in B. Braude and B. Lewis (eds.), *Christians and Jews in the Ottoman Empire. The Functioning of a Plural Society*, vol. 2, *The Arabic-Speaking Lands* (New York 1982), 7–18.

66 Karpat, "*Millets* and Nationality;" Lewis, *The Emergence of Modern Turkey*, 329.

Cohen, H., *Mavo' Ishi; Autobiographia* ["Personal Introduction. Autobiography"] (Or Yehuda 2005).

Dumper, M., *Islam and Israel. Muslim Religious Endowments and the Jewish State* (Washington, D.C. 1994).

Dupret, B., M. Berger, and Laila al-Zwaini (eds.), *Legal Pluralism in the Arab World* (The Hague 1999).

Elon, M., *Haqiqa datit be-huqei medinat Yisra'el uba-shephita shel batei mishpat u-batei din rabaniyim* ["Religious Legislation in the Laws of the State of Israel and in the Adjudication of the (Civil) Courts and the Rabbinical Courts"] (Tel Aviv 1968).

Englard, I., *Religious Law in the Israeli Legal System* (Jerusalem 1975).

Friedmann, D., "The Effect of Foreign Law on the Law of Israel: Remnants of the Ottoman Period," *Israel Law Review* 10 (1975), 192–206.

Friedmann, Y., *Tolerance and Coercion in Islam. Interfaith Relations in the Muslim Tradition* (Cambridge 2003).

Hooker, M.B., *Legal Pluralism: An Introduction to Colonial and New-Colonial Laws* (Oxford 1975).

Karpat, H.K., "*Millet*s and Nationality: The Roots of the Incongruity of Nation and State," in B. Braude and B. Lewis (eds.), *Christians and Jews in the Ottoman Empire. The Functioning of a Plural Society*, vol. 1, *The Central Lands* (New York 1982), 141–69.

Kupferschmidt, U., *The Supreme Muslim Council. Islam under the British Mandate for Palestine* (Leiden 1987).

Lapidoth, Ruth, *Hoq-yesod: Yerushalayim birat yisra'el* ["The Basic Law: Jerusalem, Capital of Israel"] (Jerusalem 1999).

Layish, A., "Adaptation of a Jurists' Law to Modern Times in an Alien Environment: The *Shari'a* in Israel." *Die Welt des Islams* 46/2 (2006), 168–222.

Layish, A., "Reformist Matrimonial Legislation and the Collapse of the Muslim Patrilineal Family," *Awrāq* 21 (2000), 57–80.

Layish, A., *Marriage, Divorce and Succession in the Druze Family. A Study Based on Decisions of Druze Arbitrators and Religious Courts in Israel and the Golan Heights* (Leiden 1982).

Layish, A., "The Muslim *Waqf* in Israel." *Asian and African Studies* 2 (1966): 41–76.

Layish, A., "The Status of the *Sharīʿa* in a Non-Muslim State: The Case of Israel," *Asian and African Studies* 27 (1993), 171–87.

Layish, A., "The Transformation of the *Shari'a* from Jurists' Law to Statutory Law in the Contemporary Muslim World," *Die Welt des Islams* 44 (2004), 85–112.

Layish, A., *Women and Islamic Law in a Non-Muslim State. A Study Based on the Decisions of the Shari'a Courts in Israel* (New York 1975).

Lewis, B., *The Emergence of Modern Turkey* (London 1961).

Lewis, B., *The Jews of Islam* (Princeton, N.J. 1984).

Likhovski, A., "The Invention of 'Hebrew Law' in Mandatory Palestine." *The American Journal of Comparative Law* 46 (1998), 339–73.

Likhovski, A., *Law and Identity in Mandate Palestine* (Chapel Hill, N.C. 2006).

Peled, Alisa Rubin, *Debating Islam in the Jewish State. The Development of Policy Toward Islamic Institutions in Israel* (Albany, N.Y. 2001).

Peters, R., *Crime and Punishment in Islamic Law. Theory and Practice from the Sixteenth to the Twenty-first Century* (Cambridge 2005).

Porath, Y., *The Emergence of the Palestinian Arab National Movement, 1918–1929* (London 1974).

Reiter, Y., "Haʿarakhat ha-reforma be-mosad ha-heqdesh ha-muslemi be-yisra'el: Ha-waqf be-ʿAcco" ["An Assessment of the Reform in the Muslim *Waqf* in Israel: The *Waqf* in Acre"], *Hamizrah Hehadash* 32 (1989), 21–45.

Reiter, Y., *Islamic Endowments in Jerusalem under the British Mandate* (London 1996).

Reiter, Y., *Islamic Institutions in Jerusalem. Palestinian Muslim Organization under Jordanian and Israeli Rule* (The Hague 1997).

Schacht, J., *An Introduction to Islamic Law* (Oxford 1964).

Ursinus, M.O.H., "Millet," *The Encyclopaedia of Islam*, New ed. (1993), 7:61–4.

Vitta, E., *The Conflict of Laws in Matters of Personal Status in Palestine* (Tel Aviv 1947).

CHAPTER 20

# Adaptation of a Jurists' Law to Modern Times in an Alien Environment: The Case of the *Sharīʿa* in Israel

*In memoriam Dr. Immanuel Naveh*

## 1 Introduction[1]

The title of this essay may sound strange, if not disturbing, to a person for whom the conception of jurists' law constitutes a basic tenet of personal belief. The Qāḍī Aḥmad Nāṭūr, President of the Sharīʿa Court of Appeal, for instance, has expressed the opinion that the *sharīʿa* is not required to adapt itself to changes of time and place since it is, in his terms, appropriate for all times and places,[2] and his judgments conform to this view.[3] This opinion is also shared

---

1 I am grateful to his honor, the Qāḍī Aḥmad Nāṭūr, President of the Sharīʿa Court of Appeal, for the generous help extended to me during all stages of writing this article. I am especially indebted to him for detailed and penetrating comments on an earlier draft of this essay. While respecting his religious sensibilities to the topic under review, my approach here, remains that of a legal historian. I consider his comments a vital complementary source to the judicial practice of the Sharʿī Court of Appeal vis-à-vis the relations between the *sharʿī* judiciary and both the Knesset and the Supreme Court. I am also grateful to my colleagues, Professor Yaʿakov Meron, Professor Yohanan Friedmann, Professor Aron Zysow, Haim Kedar, B.A. Econ. M. Juris. and to my student Ido Shahar for their valuable remarks. Obviously, all remaining shortcomings in this article are my own responsibility. This essay is an expanded version of a lecture delivered at the Israel Academy of Sciences and Humanities in Jerusalem on March 16, 2004.

[Originally published in *Die Welt des Islams*, 46/2 (2006), pp. 168–225.]

2 Personal communication, 29.12.03. As a Muslim, Qāḍī Nāṭūr consequently objects to the use of terms such as "adaptation" of the *sharīʿa*, "a norm complementary to the *sharīʿa*", and "absorption [in the sense of Islamization]" of non- *sharʿī* rules and concepts into the *sharʿī* adjudication (Nāṭūr, *Comments*, Secs. 2–3). Cf. Englard, *Integration of Jewish Law*, 112. The Supreme Court Justice, the late Prof. M. Silberg, too, claimed that the Jewish law is universal to such an extent that it does not recognize boundaries of time nor of place. HCJ 301/63 Streit v. Chief Rabbi of Israel, *Piskei Din*, 17 (1), 598. I am indebted to Yaʿakov Meron for this reference.

3 Reiter, "Qāḍīs", 213, n. 17 (with references to judgments), 227.

 | DOI:10.1163/9789004680920_022

by Qāḍī Fārūq Zuʿbī, member of the Sharīʿa Court of Appeal, who states in one of his judgments: "The *sharīʿa* is complete, general, comprehensive, and valid at all times and places."[4]

Islamic law crystallized at a time when Islam had reached the peak of its territorial expansion and when the issue that preoccupied the rulers and exercised the legal minds of the *fuqahāʾ* – the *sharīʿa*'s exponents responsible for solving specific problems arising from time to time – was how to define the legal status of members of the revealed religions, Jews and Christians, and other faiths who came under the domination of Islam. The degree of tolerance or coercion exercised in their regard was essentially contingent on the relative strength or weakness of Islam at different times.[5]

By way of contrast, the status of Muslim communities under non-Muslim rule was adjudged irrelevant over the centuries although the issue preoccupied the *ʿulamāʾ* on a theoretical plane. Between the 2/8th and 11/17th centuries, legal discourse addressed the following issues: 1. Are Muslims allowed to live in non-Muslim territories (*dār al-ḥarb*)?; 2. The nature of relations desirable between Muslims living in *dār al-ḥarb* and those residing in *dār al-islām* territory under Muslim sovereignty; and 3. The obligations vis-à-vis the *sharīʿa* and a hosting non-Muslim sovereign; and the possibility of imposing a Muslim life-style entailing observance of the entire body of religious and cultic commandments in cases where the head of state is a non-Muslim sovereign.[6] In this respect, the *sharīʿa* is not properly equipped to be applied in an alien, non-Muslim territory.

It is interesting to note in this connection ʿAbd al-Qādir's view – an Algerian *ʿālim* and *ṣūfī* and one of the leaders who resisted the French occupation – of Muslims living under Christian rule: since it was impossible to prevent the occupation, there was no alternative, in his view, but to encourage the emigration of Muslims to countries under Muslim rule. His reasons in favour of emigration (*hijra*) are as follows: the personal example of the Prophet; the ability of *dār al-islām* to absorb all the immigrants; lack of *sharʿī* validity to cultic commandments performed in a non-Muslim territory; and the presumption that life under the protection (*dhimma*) of an infidel is tantamount to heresy.[7] The Muslim press in Tunisia characterized the acceptance of French citizenship as apostasy from Islam (*ridda*).[8]

4 Abou Ramadan, "Custody", 612 (cites App. File 127/97, 24.11.97).
5 For further details, see Friedmann.
6 Abou El Fadl, 141–143.
7 Shinar, "ʿAbd al-Qādir", 154–155.
8 Shinar, *Tunisia*, 94–95.

During the first Islamic centuries, legal discourse on these issues was somewhat vague; clearer legal approaches emerged only after the 6/12th century, again by way of a reaction to the changing political situation.[9] The issue began to draw concrete attention only after Muslim territories came under non-Muslim domination starting with the Tatar Khanate of Crimea and India at the end of the 18th century[10] down to North Africa and the Middle East in the 19th and 20th centuries.

The status of the Muslims[11] in Israel has a special character due to political circumstances: specifically, their recent transition from a sovereign status to that of citizens in a Jewish state, and the conflict between Israel, the Palestinians and the Arab and Muslim world in general. The situation in Israel reflects the polarization between the majority and the minority not only in national, but also in religious, social, and cultural terms.[12] It seems that the Muslims have not completely internalized the changes in their legal status. Characteristic in this context is the decision of the Sharīʿa Court of Appeal which was handed down incidentally to a debate on an issue of dissolution of a marriage contract on grounds of absence of the spouse relict abroad. The Court ruled: "The Muslim *sharīʿa* is a personal, rather than territorial, law in the sense that it [the personal law] is not restricted to a given territory, but bound on a Muslim qua Muslim regardless of his domicile" (*inna al-sharīʿa al-islāmiyya hiya qānūn shakhṣī wa-laysa arḍiyyan – bi-maʿnā annahu ghayr maḥdūd bi 'l-makān bal huwa mulzim lil-muslim ka-muslim aynamā kān*).[13]

9 For a detailed discussion on this issue, see Abou El Fadl, 143ff.

10 See Lewis, 37n. and Schacht, 94ff., respectively.

11 I do not use the term "religious community" because it is alien and loaded with respect to the Muslims. The term appears in Palestine Order-in-Council, 1922–47 with respect to Jews and Christians (but not Muslims); this is a heritage from the Ottoman *millet* system. Cf. Englard, *Religious Law*, 13, 30, 122.

12 Cf. Englard, *Religious Law*, 46.

13 Appeals, *Selection*, file 39/89, 26.7.89 (written by Qāḍī Aḥmad Nāṭūr, subsequently President of the Sharīʿa Court of Appeal). In one case, the Sharīʿa Court of Beer Sheva ruled that the wife living in Hebron should obey her husband in his conjugal dwelling in Abū Rabīʿa tribe in the Negev on grounds that Article 52 of Palestine Order-in-Council, 1922–47 is applicable to the entirety of Palestine, and that the *sharīʿa* is the same *sharīʿa* everywhere. The ruling, which ignores the fact that the *sharīʿa* has undergone codification in each of the two territories, was overruled by the *sharīʿa* Court of Appeal; the latter deciding that the Israeli *sharīʿa* court had no jurisdiction with respect to the Administered Territories. See Abū Ghūsh, *Appeals*, file 31/86, pp. 50–53. In yet another case, the Court of Appeal ruled that a court order preventing the father from leaving the country due to a debt of maintenance to a minor child, is a matter that should be regulated by *sharʿī*, rather than Israeli civil, procedure since under Ḥanafī doctrine a *qāḍī* may imprison a well-to-do father on account of his refusal to pay a debt of maintenance. However, the

Another characteristic in this context is that the *sharīʿa* court deals with conversion to Islam in much the same way that it used to during the Ottoman period,[14] although conversion is not a matter of personal status. Moreover, the *sharīʿa* court deals with cases of mixed marriages between Muslim men and Jewish or Christian women, including disputes between the spouses arising in such marriages, in the manner followed in a Muslim state. As is well known, Article 55 of Palestine Order-in-Council provides that where the two parties belong to different communities, the Chief Justice (in Israel this is the President of the Supreme Court) is to choose the court before which the matter is to be brought.[15]

With the collapse of the Ottoman Empire at the end of the First World War, and the occupation of Palestine by Britain, the country ceased to be part of a Muslim state with all the legal consequences involved. Thus, for instance, the *sharīʿa* courts' jurisdiction with respect to non-Muslims dating back to the Ottoman Empire or the incidental jurisdiction of the *sharīʿa* courts functioning in their capacity as state courts, was removed from their competence during the British Mandate. In the circumstances ensuing with the emergence of the state of Israel, the Muslim community became a religious minority in a Jewish state. From a *sharʿī* point of view, an anomalous situation emerged: the Muslims who had, for centuries, granted the Jews (and Christians) a protected status (*ahl al-dhimma*) in the Muslim state, have themselves been transformed into a tolerated minority in Israel. The Muslim Supreme Council, established by the British Mandate in 1921 to compensate the Muslim community for the lack of a Muslim sovereign (indeed, some defined the Council as "a state within a state,"[16]) ceased to exist, and with it collapsed the entire Muslim establishment – the *sharīʿa* courts, the *waqf* administration, the religious services, the educational system, etc. The religious elite – the *qāḍī*s in charge of the application of the *sharīʿa* in the *sharīʿa* courts, the *muftī*s whose historical

---

*qāḍī* added, "nowadays *al-mulāzama ghayr wārida* (imprisonment of the husband is impossible [since the sovereign is not a Muslim]); see *al-Kashshāf*, 1997, part 2, 43/97, 57; cf. Englard, *Integration of Jewish Law*, 111. Article 52 of Palestine Order-in-Council extends the *sharīʿa* courts' exclusive jurisdiction in matters of personal status to Muslim foreigners who, under the law of their nationality, are subject in such matters to the jurisdiction of Muslim *sharīʿa* courts. Such a jurisdiction is not granted to Rabbinical courts and the religious courts of the Christian communities; see Welchman, 41. On the Islamic concept of international law, see al-Ghuneimi.

14 See, e.g., Sharīʿa Court of Jaffa, *Sijill Qarārāt*, nos. 5–12, 15–17, 19–20.

15 See Englard, *Religious Law*, 89 fn. 5.

16 Porath, 197. Cf. Welchman, 43.

task was to reconcile religious law and social reality,[17] the functionaries of the mosques – all these left Israel during the events that preceded its emergence and left behind a flock without a shepherd.[18]

How do Muslims in Israel cope with circumstances entailed by the accommodation of their religious law to the changing conditions of modern times? This question of course preoccupies many Muslim countries in our regions. These countries, however, cope with this question under congenial domestic conditions, that is, in territories dominated by Muslim sovereigns. Israel in this context is an alien environment.[19] The government of Israel has so far declined to reinstate the Muslim communal autonomy of the British Mandate. Hence, the *sharʿī* judiciary has been integrated into the general judicial system:[20] The law applicable in the *sharīʿa* courts is an integral part of the Israeli judicial system; the *sharīʿa* courts are subject to the control of the High Court Justice (hereinafter: HCJ);[21] the *qāḍīs* are nominated by the President of the State and are bound by an oath of allegiance to the state (but not to its laws).[22]

From an Islamic dogmatic-legalistic standpoint, this is apparently an intolerable situation. Since under the *sharīʿa* a non-Muslim cannot testify against a Muslim,[23] the prevalent *sharʿī* opinion is that a non-Muslim cannot appoint a Muslim *qāḍī*.[24] Until recently, however, the *sharīʿa* courts wielded the widest substantive jurisdiction (exclusive jurisdiction in almost all matters of

---

17 After the emergence of the State of Israel no *muftī* of any stature remained in the country. Shaykh Ṭāhir al-Ṭabarī, the Muftī of Tiberias prior to the establishment of the state, tried in the early 1950s, before he was nominated as the Qāḍī of the Sharīʿa Court of Nazareth, to obtain recognition as the Supreme Muftī. It happened occasionally that *qāḍīs* of a recognized *shārʿī* authority, such as Shaykh Ṭāhir Ḥammād and Shaykh Tawfīq ʿAsaliyya, issued *fatwās* pertaining to actual matters, such as the removal of the sanctity from cemeteries (cf. the *fatwā* allowing the sale of the cemetery of Waqf Istiqāl in Haifa by the local *qāḍī* (Abū Ghūsh, *Appeals*, 3/76, 184–186).

18 For further details, see Layish, "*Qāḍīs* and *Sharīʿa*", 237–238; idem, *Women and Islamic Law*, 1–4.

19 See Abu-Gosh, "Pluralism", 45.

20 In 2002, the *sharʿī* judiciary was subject to the Ministry of Justice instead of the Ministry for Religious Affairs. *Sefer Haḥuqim* [official publication of Israeli laws] 1860, 30.7.02, p. 505, Article 6; Shetreet, 122–124. Cf. Abou Ramadan, "Custody", 618, 622 (cites from a judgment by Justice Barak, HCJ 1000/92).

21 See Englard, *Religious Law*, 148, 162–164.

22 The Sharīʿa Court of Appeal is fully aware of the *qāḍīs*' commitment towards the state. See Abū Ghūsh, *Appeals*, 22/74, 203–204. See Shetreet, 131–132, 209 (the words "and its laws" were omitted from Section 7 of the Qāḍīs law).

23 Friedmann, 35.

24 Ibn ʿĀbidīn cites a source to the effect that a non-Muslim is not prevented from appointing a Muslim *qāḍī*; see Abou Ramadan, "Custody", 641, notes 150–151; idem, "Judicial Activism", 292 (a Ḥanafī *fatwā* allows an infidel ruler to appoint a *qāḍī*). Qāḍī Nāṭūr has

personal status and *waqf*) compared to that of other religious courts, including the Rabbinical courts; this is a heritage from the late Ottoman period. Since 2001, the Family Court shares jurisdiction (not in marriage and divorce) with the *sharīʿa* courts.[25] Characteristic in this context is a dispute over jurisdiction between different religious courts in a case of a mixed marriage. In one case, a *sharīʿa* court ruled that the children of a couple be transferred to the custody (*ḥiḍāna*) of the Muslim father. The Christian mother refused to accept the jurisdiction of the *sharīʿa* court and resorted, instead, to the Family Court; the latter ruled that she was entitled to custody and maintenance. Qāḍī Nāṭūr ruled that the issue of jurisdiction had to be decided in accordance with the minor's, rather than his parents', religion: the minor son was to follow his father's religion, his mother's religion being irrelevant.[26]

## 2 The Law Applicable in the *sharīʿa* Court

The law applicable in the *sharīʿa* court comprises several historical strata, each of which made a vital contribution to the accommodation of the *sharīʿa* to the changing conditions of the time:

A. The Ottoman Family Rights Law, 1917 is the first official codification of matters of personal status performed with a view to adapting the family law to the conditions prevailing then, and especially to improve the status of women. The eclectic system (*takhayyur*), that is, the adoption of appropriate elements from various schools of law and early independent jurists, provided that their doctrines could be reconciled with the reformist norm, was the main method for the introduction of the reforms. Thus, for instance, the Ottoman legislator adopted the Ḥanbalī doctrine with respect to the validity of a condition inserted in the marriage contract which enables the wife to stipulate that her husband is prohibited from marrying another wife; and that if he violates the condition, either she or her co-wife is divorced. Similarly, the legislator adopted the Mālikī doctrine which makes it possible to dissolve the marriage contract through legal proceedings, on the wife's initiative, on the basis of legal grounds,

---

found no basis in the *sharīʿa* to support the prevalent opinion that a non-Muslim cannot appoint a Muslim *qāḍī*; Nāṭūr, *Comments*, Sec. 21.

25 Family Court Law (Amendment No. 5), 2001. *Sefer Haḥuqim*, 1810, 14.11.01; Shetreet, 123.

26 *Al-Kashshāf*, 1997, part 1, 135/96, 298–301, 303. The HCJ overruled the Sharīʿa Court of Appeal's decision ruling that the President of the Supreme Court had to be resorted to and that he alone would decide which court was to handle the dispute; see Abou Ramadan, "Judicial Activism", 267.

such as the husband's absence. The Ottoman family law heralded the advent of legal modernism in matters of personal status in the Arab countries. State codification by means of the eclectic expedient has become the main method for the introduction of reforms, though at a great cost, from the viewpoint of Orthodox Islam, of transforming the *sharīʿa* from jurists' law into statutory law.[27]

B. The *sharʿī* inheritance rules have not undergone a process of codification. Their applicability, however, was restricted in the late Ottoman period to immovable property of the *mulk* category (i.e., estates in full ownership); immovable property of the *mīrī* category, the bare ownership (*raqaba*) of which belongs to the Sultan while the individual is entitled only to the usufruct (*taṣarruf*) thereof, was regulated under the inheritance law, 1913 of German origin. The law abolished the discrimination, in respect to inheritance, between the sexes and between agnates (relatives through males) and cognates (relatives through females). This law reflects far-reaching innovations from the viewpoint of the *sharʿī* inheritance rules and was also applied in the *sharīʿa* courts.[28]

C. The Procedure Law of the Religious Muslim Courts, 1333H. (1917) defines the role and authority of the courts, the rules of procedure and appeals; generally speaking, the institution of appeals is not recognized in the classical *sharīʿa*.[29]

D. The *Mejelle*, the Ottoman civil law of 1876, is also based on the eclectic expedient though within the framework of the Ḥanafī doctrine alone. This is an attempt *par excellence* to adapt the *sharīʿa* to the economic conditions of the time, and it includes far-reaching innovations, such as the transformation of custom into a formal source of law, unlike its position in classical legal theory (*uṣūl al-fiqh*).[30] The *Mejelle* was intended to be applied in the civil (*niẓāmī*) courts established alongside the *sharīʿa* courts; in actual fact, however, it was also applied in the *sharīʿa* courts. In 1984, the *Mejelle* was abolished with the proviso that its validity remains intact in the *sharīʿa* courts.[31]

---

27 For further details, see Layish, "Jurists' Law"; cf. Englard, "Integration of Jewish Law", 115–116, 121.

28 Cf. Welchman, 44–45.

29 The provisions of the law pertaining to appeals were amended by the British military regulations of 10.10.1918 and 1.8.1919; Goitein and Ben Shemesh, 275–283.

30 Libson, "Custom", 154–155; idem, "ʿUrf", 888; cf. Meron, "Custom", 222ff.; Messick, 54–58; Welchman, 36–37.

31 See Englard, *Religious Law*, 55 and the references in fn. 11. The Abolition of the *Mejelle* Law, 1984; *Sefer Haḥuqim* 1119, 20.6.84, 156. Section 2 (preservation of laws) explicitly provides

The British legislator maintained the Ottoman heritage of legal pluralism,[32] gave effect to the recent Ottoman reforms and scrupulously preserved the *status quo* in the judicial system, of course, with the indispensable changes arising from the new political situation.[33] Thus, for instance, in 1919 he adopted the Ottoman Family Rights Law, but restricted its applicability to Muslims alone. Similarly, when introducing reforms in matters of marriage and divorce under the inspiration of Western norms, he did this by means of penal legislation that does not abrogate the validity of the religious law. This method was brought to bear, for instance, on registration of marriage and divorce (1919). Thus, "customary marriage" (*ʿaqd ʿurfī*), i.e., without registration, entails a criminal sanction but the marriage remains intact according to the religious law.[34] This applies also to the ban on marriage of minor girls and on polygamy; moreover, the legislator even provided a "good defense" against a charge of violating this ban to Muslims *qua* Muslims and exempted them from the criminal sanction.[35]

## 3 Accommodation of the *sharīʿa* within the Framework of the State

### 3.1 *The Knesset's Legislation*

Until recently the main effort to adjust the *sharīʿa* to changing circumstances came from outside. The Knesset's legislation was the most efficient means to adapt the legal norm in matters of personal status to the conditions of a modern society. It introduced many reforms in this domain, some of which are most daring. Thus, the Knesset recognized the mother as a natural guardian of her children along with their father (the *sharīʿa* recognizes only the father as a natural guardian, and after him the minor's male agnates in a specified order), introduced equality with respect to inheritance between the sexes and between agnates and cognates (according to the *sharʿī* rules of inheritance, males and the agnates respectively have priority), and equalized the resources between the spouses (the *sharīʿa* recognizes the complete separation between the spouses' properties). The keynote, on the declaratory level,

that the law shall not be interpreted as if it is meant to reduce the validity of any given law applicable in the *sharīʿa* courts, and the Explanatory Note to the law explicitly notes that the abolition of the *Mejelle* is by no means intended to uproot custom to the extent that it still exists as a source of law in Israel (Bills 1681, 14.5.84, 246); see Naveh, 379–380.

32 Cf. Botiveau, "Palestinian Law", 77–83; Shahar, "Palestinians", 45; Bälz, 231–233 (models of legal pluralism); Shetreet, 59.

33 Cf. Englard, *Religious Law*, 13; Shetreet, 65; Welchman, 39–40.

34 Cf. *al-Kashshāf*, 1995, 64/95, 246–247.

35 Layish, *Women and Islamic Law*, 3–4.

of these reforms is Section 1 of the Women's Equal Rights Law, 1951 which provides: "A man and a woman shall have equal status with regard to any legal act; any provision of law which discriminates, with regard to any legal act, against women as women, shall be of no effect." These reforms, initiated by the Israeli socio-political elite with a view to bringing about full equality between the sexes, were imposed from above on the Muslim society the majority of which was not ready to absorb them.[36]

For obvious reasons, the Knesset could not adopt the technique customary in Muslim countries for introducing reforms. This technique consisting of methods such as the eclectic expedient (*takhayyur*), i.e., absorption of convenient elements from the abundant Muslim legal heritage in statutory legislation, and the reinterpretation of the textual sources (the Qur'ān and the *ḥadīth*), was intended to confer on the reforms the character of internal refurbishing of the *sharīʿa*, though in actual fact this technique should be assessed as extra development of the *sharīʿa*. The absorption of religious-legal elements in legislation is common practice in the Knesset (the so-called "religious legislation"), with the difference that the declaratory source of inspiration of the Knesset is Jewish law and the Israeli heritage by virtue of the Law of Legal Foundations of 1980.[37]

However, out of regard for the legal systems of the various religious communities, the Knesset subjected its legislation in matters pertaining to personal status to two severe restrictions: 1. Abstention from interfering with any religious prohibition or permission to marriage and divorce, while instead adopting procedural provisions and penal sanctions as deterrents in preference to substantive provisions which would have invalidated the relevant religious law;[38] and 2. In matters for which provisions superseding religious law were enacted, the parties were usually given the option to litigate in accordance with religious law. In matters pertaining to inheritance, the realization of this option was contingent on the parties' consent to the jurisdiction of the religious court.

### 3.2 *The Judicial Practice of the Civil Court*

The Israeli civil courts, especially the HCJ, fulfill a vital role, alongside the Knesset, in the adaptation of the *sharīʿa* from outside, to modern conditions.

36 Cf. Abu-Gosh, "Pluralism", 46–50.

37 Elon (for definition, see p. 171); Englard, "Integration of Jewish Law", 115ff. (claims that the absorption of the religious law in Knesset legislation is liable to substantially prejudice the completeness of the Jewish law); cf. Naveh, 377. On the source of inspiration of the Knesset, see Meron, *Moslem Law*, 1–11.

38 See Englard, *Religious Law*, 155; Abu-Gosh, "Pluralism", 50.

Until recently, the civil courts had jurisdiction only in some matters of personal status pertaining to the Muslims (such as permission to the marriage of a minor girl below seventeen, though the dissolution of the marriage was performed in accordance with religious law, and jurisdiction in matters of inheritance in accordance with the Israeli Succession Law, 1965). Following the reform in the jurisdiction of the *sharīʿa* courts in 2001, the Family Court was granted jurisdiction in all matters of personal status (excluding marriage and divorce) alongside the *sharīʿa* court. Moreover, the civil court has incidental jurisdiction in matters of personal status while adjudicating matters pertaining to civil and penal law. The HCJ may intervene in decisions of religious courts not as a court of appeal, but rather in circumstances giving rise to violation of natural justice, disregard of binding statutory provisions, i.e., explicitly addressed to religious courts (excess of authority), and default in the composition of the court.[39]

The civil judicial practice in Israel in matters of personal status relating to Muslims is based on secular legislation totally unrelated to the *sharīʿa*. However, in criminal offenses pertaining to marriage and divorce, the establishment of the religious-legal validity of the marriage and divorce is a precondition to the existence of the criminal offense. The majority of the judges in the civil courts have no legal training in Islamic law. When a need to identify a *sharʿī* rule arises, the judges resort to secondary sources, reference books, mainly on Anglo-Muhammadan law.[40] Naturally, the civil judge is less attentive than the *qāḍī sharʿī* to the distress and sensitivities of the Muslim public. He deems himself committed first and foremost to the principles of Israeli law, to enforcement of constitutional norms such as those embodied in the Women's Equal Rights Law, 1951, or Basic Law: Human Dignity and Liberty, 1992, or issues that have no explicit expression in legislation. Thus, for instance, the woman's right to compensation by virtue of being divorced against her will on grounds of breach of statutory duty is a rule that has been established by the Supreme Court (on the basis of Article 63 of the Civil Wrongs Ordinance), rather than by the Knesset.[41]

In 1954, it was pleaded in the HCJ that the Knesset's ban on polygamy constituted an infringement of the Muslims' freedom of religion and that it conflicted with Section 5 of the Women's Equal Rights Law, which provides that "this Law shall not affect any religious-legal prohibition or permission relating

---

39 See Englard, *Religious Law*, 112, 154–155.

40 Naveh, 374, 389–392; Meron, *Moslem Law*, 57–59.

41 Layish, "Women in Court", 373; cf. Meron, 'Répudiation", 934–936; idem, Illegitimate Child, 414; idem, *Moslem Law*, 212–213, 226; Naveh, 374–375.

to marriage or divorce." The HCJ rejected the plea on grounds that freedom of religion is the freedom to do what religion commands, and not what it permits, and since Islam does not command, but merely permits polygamy, its prohibition does not infringe upon the freedom of religion.[42] In a letter to the President of the Supreme Court, Qāḍī Ṭāhir Ḥammād contended that the HCJ was expected to assess freedom of religion in terms of the five *sharʿī* legal-ethical qualifications (*al-aḥkām al-khamsa*) under which any aspect of Muslim behavior is categorized. These are: obligatory (*wājib*), recommended (*mandūb*), indifferent (*mubāḥ*), reprehensible (*makrūh*), and forbidden (*ḥarām*). According to these categories, freedom of religion means also the freedom to do what religion permits; moreover, in certain circumstances, as in the case where a husband tends to commit adultery, it is obligatory for him to marry another woman.[43]

Occasionally, the civil courts are used as recourse for Muslims seeking relief when this is not available in the *sharīʿa* court.[44] As a matter of fact, the Supreme Court does not hesitate to interfere in such circumstances by creating a civil legal norm complementary to the *sharīʿa*. In one case, an unmarried woman admitted in the *sharīʿa* court that she had agreed to cohabit with a married Muslim, the father of eight children, after he had promised to divorce his wife and marry her. She claimed that after she had given birth to a girl, the man had not kept his promise. The woman requested that the court oblige the defendant to undergo a DNA test in order to establish his paternity, and to issue a declarative judgment to the effect that the defendant is the father of her daughter. She also requested that the court oblige the defendant to pay her and her daughter maintenance. The defendant denied paternity and refused to undergo a DNA test. The *sharīʿa* court rejected the woman's plea ruling that under Islamic law, in the absence of a valid *sharʿī* marriage contract between the parties, there is no ground for claiming filiation (*ilḥāq nasab*); hence the claim for maintenance from the defendant was also rejected. The court further ruled that under Islamic procedural law it is impossible to oblige the defendant to undergo a DNA test in order to establish his paternity.[45] According to the Ḥanafī doctrine, a child born out of wedlock is deemed illegitimate, even if

---

42 HCJ 49/54 Milḥim v. the *sharʿī* judge of Acre and the District; *Pisqei Din* 8, 910, 913 (Justice M. Silberg's decision). For further details, see Naveh, 126–131. The court does not provide any *sharʿī* reference to the distinction between a commandment and permission; Naveh, 384; Abou Ramadan, "Custody", 618.

43 Layish, "*Qāḍīs* and *Sharīʿa*", 268; idem, *Women and Islamic Law*, 81ff.; Abu-Gosh, "Pluralism", 50–51; Meron, "Polygamy". Cf. Kremnitzer, 235ff.

44 Naveh, 387.

45 The Sharīʿa Court of Haifa, 34/87 (*ilḥāq nasab*), 3.5.87.

the biological father is ready to acknowledge (*iqrār*) paternity; he has no right to maintenance or inheritance from his biological father. An illegitimate child is nevertheless considered a *maḥram*, i.e., blood relative prohibited for marriage. The Shāfiʿī school (to which the majority of the Israeli Muslims belong) maintains that an illegitimate daughter is deemed totally alien to her biological father to the extent that he may marry her.[46] The Sharīʿa Court of Appeal, to which the woman resorted, reasserted that the *sharīʿa* court had no competence to obligate the claimant to undergo a test of DNA and that in any case, such a test in itself did not constitute a *sharʿī* paternity.[47]

In her distress, the woman sought relief in the District Court, but was rejected *in limine* on grounds of lack of competence since paternity and maintenance are matters of personal status and fell, at the time, within the sole jurisdiction of the *sharīʿa* court. Subsequently, the claimant and her daughter presented their case before the Israeli Supreme Court sitting as a Court of Appeal on civil matters. Having regard to the minor's civil rights, and on the basis of Basic Law: Human Dignity and Liberty, 1992, the Supreme Court ruled in 1995 that the minor, born out of wedlock and hence debarred from legal paternity under Islamic law, was entitled to benefit from "civil paternity" that is, biological, natural paternity. The Court further ruled that human dignity was a supreme right by virtue of which minors were entitled to know their filiation in order to ensure their property, family and human rights. The Court also ruled that this substantial right to dignity created a secondary right for legal relief in the civil (rather than religious) court whenever the right to dignity had been violated. Once civil paternity is established, the minor daughter will also be entitled to maintenance from her father and to her share in his estate. The Supreme Court's decision introduced a new civil constitutional legal norm alongside the *sharʿī* norm, totally separated from it, the civil norm entailing civil basic rights. The Supreme Court's decision is based on the Israeli legislation and courts' judicial practice, on the norms of the State of Israel as a Jewish democratic state,[48] on Jewish law and on American and English courts' judicial practice. The Supreme Court clarified the position of Islamic law on the relevant issues in terms of the Anglo-Muhammadan law.[49]

---

46 An expert (Aharon Layish)'s legal opinion submitted to the Attorney of the State, 17.1.95; based on Shalabī, 683–694; cf. Abū Zahra, 454; ʿAbd al-Ḥamīd, 470ff.

47 The Sharīʿa Court of Appeal, 41/87, 20.10.87.

48 Cf. Barak, *The Judge*, 80 ff.

49 Civil Appeal 3077/90, *Pisqei Din* 49, part 2, 1995, 578–629 (written by Justice M. Cheshin); cf. Naveh, 223ff.; Meron, "Illegitimate Child", 407–415; Abou Ramadan, "Custody", 610. Qāḍī Nāṭūr claims that the intervention of the Supreme Court in this case could be spared, "since the *sharīʿa* has its own legal solutions to any problem that may arise, including

## 4 Adaptation of the *sharīʿa* to Modern Conditions by the *qāḍīs*

### 4.1 *Conferences of* qāḍīs *in Matters of Religious Law*

Already in the early years of the State of Israel, *qāḍīs*, in the absence of *muftīs*, used their legal authority, beyond their judicial role, for adjusting the law of personal status to changes in family structure and the status of women. In conferences convened from time to time to discuss problems of religious law, an effort was made to interpret the *sharīʿa* liberally. There was no pretension to re-open the gate of *ijtihād*, that is, to give a new interpretation to the textual sources of the *Qurʾān* and the *ḥadīth*. The *qāḍīs* preferred to resort to the eclectic method, that is, to enlist convenient elements from schools of law other than the Ḥanafī school, with a view to supporting desired reforms. The *qāḍīs*' approach was pragmatic: they sought a method to reform family law by expanding the scope of interpretation of the religious law, provided this did not entail an explicit contradiction to the *sharīʿa*. Practically, however, this approach occasionally resulted in deviation from the established doctrine of the *sharīʿa*.

At the *qāḍīs*' conferences convened in 1963, 1966 and 1974, important reforms, inspired by reforms promulgated in Arab countries, were passed. These pertain to matters such as stipulation in the marriage contract, conditional divorce, family arbitration as a mechanism to transform unilateral divorce into dissolution by means of legal proceedings,[50] and alimony to divorced women. Since *qāḍīs*' conferences are not statutory bodies authorized to decide on matters pertaining to the material law applicable in the *sharīʿa* courts, the reforms are not legally binding. At most, the *qāḍīs*' decisions may be regarded as collective legal opinions; to the extent that the *qāḍīs* undertake to apply them in their own judicial decisions, they do so voluntarily. In the context of judicial practice, the *qāḍīs*' decisions may be regarded as interpretations of the *sharīʿa*, and the degree of acceptability of such interpretations by the litigants depends on the personal legal authority of the *qāḍī* before whom the hearing takes place. There were in fact cases when one of the parties appealed to the Sharīʿa Court of Appeal on the ground that the *qāḍī*'s interpretation was "an error on a point

[the provision of] maintenance for an [illegitimate] girl from the Treasury (*bayt al-māl*)". However he does not suggest any *sharʿī* solution to the filiation of the girl to her father through union other than contract of marriage, and to the mutual right of inheritance between the girl and her biological father (Nāṭūr, *Comments*, Sec. 19).

50 On an attempt to transform unilateral divorce into judicial dissolution, see Abū Ghūsh, *Appeals*, 18/74, 68; on this tendency in reformist legislation in Iraq and Iran, see Layish, "Ṭalāq", 155.

of Islamic law".[51] On rare occasions *qāḍīs* referred to a legal authority outside Israel on a point of *sharʿī* law, as in the case of the dissolution of the marriage of women whose husbands were absent, having left Israel as a result of the 1948 war.[52]

The extent of the *qāḍīs*' readiness to adapt the *sharīʿa* to the requirements of modern society, to the age of science and technology, in matters other than family law, may be gauged from their legal opinions on issues such as permission for women to be photographed and have their pictures affixed to their identity cards, birth control and family planning, autopsies, and transplants of organs of the human body.[53]

### 4.2 *The Legal Circular*

Another mechanism for introducing reforms in matters of personal status in the spirit of the reforms introduced in Arab countries and outside the framework of the Knesset's legislation, is the judicial regulation or legal circular (*marsūm qaḍāʾī*) introduced in the mid-1990s. It was initiated by the President of the Sharīʿa Court of Appeal, Aḥmad al-Nāṭūr under the inspiration of the Sudanese Legal Circular (*manshūr qaḍāʾī*). Britain introduced the legal circular in Sudan, after the failure of the Mahdī's rebellion in 1886, with a view to using it as an instrument for adapting the *sharīʿa* to the changing conditions of the time under the normative control of the British "Legal Officer". The Grand Qāḍī (*qāḍī al-quḍāt*), placed at the top of the *sharʿī* legal system, indeed fulfilled this expectation. The legal circulars issued by him from time to time dealt with a variety of subjects deviating occasionally from the authoritative view in the Ḥanafī school; this was done by means of the eclectic expedient (*takhayyur*). Until the country attained its independence in 1956, many of the Grand Qāḍīs in Sudan were recruited from among senior *ʿulamāʾ* in Egypt, graduates of al-Azhar with a reformist orientation. The legal circular also fulfilled a vital role in reinstating the *sharīʿa* in Sudan under Numayrī.[54]

However, contrary to the Sudanese legal circular, the Israeli *marsūm* is not anchored in law. Actually, the *marsūms* are regulations issued by the President of the Sharīʿa Court of Appeal. The members of this court, as well as the *qāḍīs* of the *sharīʿa* courts of first instance, voluntarily commit themselves to apply the *marsūm* in their decisions. It is argued that the *marsūm* is tantamount to

51 For further details, see Layish, "*Qāḍīs* and *Sharīʿa*", 240–248; idem, "Ṭalāq", 155–157.

52 For further details, see Layish, "*Qāḍīs and Sharīʿa*", 249–250.

53 For further details, see Layish, "*Qāḍīs and Sharīʿa*", 251–255; Meron, "Forensic Medicine", 248–249 (autopsies), 249–251 and 260 (transplants of organs); idem, "Medical Treatment", 392–395.

54 Layish & Warburg, 72–75, 98–101.

*siyāsa sharʿiyya*, "governance in accordance with the *sharīʿa*", that is, state regulation that takes into account practical considerations of the government and the public interest.[55] However, in the absence of a Muslim sovereign, the *qāḍīs* are in charge of dispensing social justice (*ʿadl*).[56] It is further argued that in the absence of a statutory basis, the *marsūms* are deemed interpretation of the *sharīʿa*. In other words, this is another attempt to enlist the legal authority of the *qāḍīs* and their public reputation for the cause of conducting legal reforms in the *sharīʿa* courts.

Between the years 1994–1996 three *marsūms* were issued. The first deals with *waqf*,[57] and concerns coping with the results of the reforms embodied in Absentees' Property (Amendment No. 3) (Release and Use of Endowment Property), 1965 which transferred to the Custodian on Absentees' Property, retroactively from 1950, not only the right of management of and the right of entitlement (*istiḥqāq*) to the proceeds of the *waqf*, but also the full ownership of the property. According to the dominant view in the Ḥanafī school, the right of ownership in the *waqf* is vested in Allāh (hence, *waqf* property cannot be absentee property).[58] The law enables the custodian to release the full ownership of family (*dhurrī, ahlī*) *waqf* to the beneficiaries, and the full ownership of *waqf* property for public welfare (*khayrī*) to boards of trustees established in various towns. The boards may use the proceeds from *waqf* property and the consideration received for property sold – to educational, social welfare, health, religious worship and like purposes without being bound by the *sharʿī* rules pertaining to *waqf*.[59]

The eagerness on the part of some of the boards to sell *waqf* property, or to alienate such property for long periods of time to factors outside the Muslim community,[60] urged Qāḍī Nāṭūr to issue the *marsūm*, since he was disturbed by the possible liquidation of the *waqf* institution as well as by desecration of the sanctity of cemeteries and mosques. The *marsūm* prohibits *qāḍīs* to issue *fatwās* permitting the use of *waqf* property for purposes other than the original ones for which the *waqf* has been founded, on the grounds that deviation from

55 See Vogel.

56 Cf. Abou Ramadan, "Judicial Activism", 286.

57 The *marsūm* was published on 21.6.1994 (*al-Kashshāf*, 1995, 5–8).

58 The Sharīʿa Court of Appeal endorsed a decision of the first instance which had repealed an arbitration decision relating to a family *waqf* on the grounds that arbitration is permissible only with respect to the rights of human beings (*ḥuqūq al-ʿibād*) which may be compromised, whereas the *waqf* pertains exclusively to the right (*ḥaqq*) of Allāh, with respect to which no compromise can be made, i.e., human beings may not share such a right. Abū Ghūsh, *Appeals*, 14/81, 189–191.

59 Layish, "Waqf in Israel", 61–67. Cf. Damper, chap. 3.

60 Abū Ghūsh, *Appeals*, 22/74, 203–205; cf. Reiter, "Waqf in Acre", 29–45.

the founder's stipulation causes prejudice to the welfare of the Muslim community (*maṣlaḥat al-umma*).[61] The *marsūm* ignores the legal significance of the Knesset's legislation pertaining to *waqf.* The HCJ reasserted that once a *waqf* property has been declared an absentee property under Absentees' Property (Amendment No. 3) Law, "the full ownership is vested in the Custodian while [the property] is free from any restriction, stipulation, or limitation whatsoever. Allegedly, the property ceases to be a *waqf*, and the Custodian ceases to be the trustee of the *waqf*; hence the *sharīʿa* court is not competent [anymore] to deal with claims against the Custodian or claims pertaining to rights deriving from the *waqf*."[62]

The second *marsūm* deals with the role of the *mukhbirūn*,[63] informants from the close vicinity of the disputed spouses who are assumed to have the required information for fixing the rate of maintenance (*nafaqa*) to the wife. In President Nāṭūr's view, the current procedure for fixing maintenance by the *mukhbirūn* causes prejudice to women. The transfer of this function to the *qāḍī*s is intended to facilitate the adaptation of the rate of maintenance to the real needs. This reform is allegedly based on the *maṣlaḥa* (public interest) doctrine, creative interpretation, and the eclectic expedient. For the purpose of fixing criteria for the rates of maintenance, President Nāṭūr distinguishes between two fundamental approaches in the legal literature of the schools: According to the first approach, the rate of maintenance should be fixed in accordance with the economic situation of the two spouses; according to the second approach in accordance with the husband's economic situation. The Egyptian law (No. 25) of 1929 adopted the second approach (Article 16), and it seems that President Nāṭūr also is inclined towards this approach.

The *marsūm* introduced an important innovation into the domain of evidential rules; this too was inspired by modern legislation in Arab countries. A *qāḍī* may fix maintenance on the basis of written evidence, that is, official written documents (*wathāʾiq*) – as part of the entire evidence – in cases where no witnesses could be enlisted to prove the husband's wealth. President Nāṭūr claims that it is possible to find support in the *sharīʿa* for this view – though irregular (*shādhdh*) – to the effect that official documents pertaining to salary payments, income tax, national insurance, employment service, etc. are deemed valid legal evidence.[64]

61 Abū Ghūsh, *Appeals*, 3/76, 184–189.

62 HCJ 6452/96 (written by Justice Dorit Beinich); cf. Abou Ramadan, "Judicial Activism", 269–270.

63 The *marsūm* was issued in 4.1.95; *al-Kashshāf*, 1995, 9–19.

64 See *al-Kashshāf*, 1995, 17–18.

On the basis of my attendance at sessions of the Sharīʿa Court in West Jerusalem during the period of Ziyād ʿAsaliyya's term of office as the Qāḍī, I was impressed that he was applying the *marsūm* pertaining to the *mukhbirūn* in both spirit and letter. He decided on matters of maintenance according to evidence brought before him rather than on *mukhbirūn*'s recommendations. The rate of maintenance granted was so high that women from East Jerusalem preferred to present their claims for maintenance before him rather than seeking relief in the Sharīʿa Court in East Jerusalem.[65] Qāḍī ʿAsaliyya used to resort quite often to the professional opinions of the social welfare services, and enjoyed the reputation of a protector of women's interests.[66]

The third *marsūm* adopts the device of "compulsory bequest" within the limits of one-third of the estate, in favour of an orphaned grandchild.[67] This is a far-reaching substantive reform. The orphaned grandson, that is, one whose father predeceased the praepositus (i.e., the grandfather), is totally deprived of the estate by his uncles, the praepositus' sons, by virtue of the rule of degree: among relatives of the same class (parentela),[68] the one nearer in degree to the praepositus excludes the more remote from the estate. The *sharīʿa* does not recognize the doctrine of representation (*tanzīl, tamthīl, niyāba*) in succession: the orphaned grandchild does not take the portion his father would have been entitled to had he died *after* the praepositus; neither does the *sharīʿa* recognize absolute freedom of testamentary disposition. The division of the estate in accordance with the *sharʿī* inheritance and testamentary rules have been settled once and for all in the textual sources (the *Qurʾān* and the *ḥadīth*), and the individual has almost no control over his estate after his death. By virtue of *ultra vires* rules in the Sunnī law, in the absence of the heirs' consent, a will in excess of one-third of the estate or in favour of a legal heir is not valid. The Shīʿī law admits a will in favour of a legal heir.[69]

This *marsūm* was inspired by the Egyptian Law of Testamentary Disposition of 1946, and the Jordanian and Syrian laws of personal status of 1976 and 1953, respectively. The *marsūm* deviates from the Jordanian and Syrian laws in that

---

65 Cf. Reiter, "Qāḍīs", 220; Shahar, "Modernizer", 206–207. On the Sharīʿa Court in East Jerusalem, see Welchman, 56–67; Reiter, *Islamic Institutions in Jerusalem*, 11–22.

66 Shahar, "Modernizer", 196–197.

67 The *marsūm* was issued on 4.2.96; *al-Kashshāf*, 1995, 20–30.

68 Parentela is a class (*ṭabaqa*) of male agnates who share the same parent, and their issue. The order of parentelas in Islamic rules of inheritance are: the praepositus' son and his issue; the praepositus' father and his issue (i.e., brothers); the praepositus' paternal grandfather and his issue (i.e., uncles); etc.; the "parents" in this order are the praepositus' son, father, paternal grandfather etc., respectively; see Coulson, *Succession*, 33.

69 Coulson, *Succession*, 213–214, 235.

cognate grandchildren too, though only within the first degree with regard to the testator (i.e., excluding great-grandchildren and their issue), benefit from the "compulsory bequest."[70] "Compulsory bequest" is a distinctly unsophisticated device. Since the orphaned grandchild is not a legal heir, there is no *sharʿī* prohibition on making a will in his favour within the aforementioned limitations. The legislator provides that a bequest in favour of a grandchild is legally compulsory and hence should be taken into account in the division of the estate as if it has been actually made. The main *sharʿī* justification for the "compulsory bequest" is "public interest" (*maṣlaḥa*). Also, there is an attempt to derive support from the Mālikī jurist Ibn Rushd (d. 595/1198), who defines a will as a gift (*hiba*) that becomes valid only after the testator's death, regardless of whether he used an explicit expression (*lafẓ*) or not. The Explanatory Note to the Syrian law of 1953 claims that the "compulsory bequest" is based on Ibn Ḥazm (d. 456/1065) who advocates making a testamentary disposition in favour of relatives other than legal heirs; this seems to refer to the Qurʾānic verse of bequests which ordains making generous provision for parents and relatives, something regarded as an obligation upon the pious (2:180). The reference is to *ẓāhirī* (i.e. literal) interpretation, of the verse of bequests which was later abrogated by the Qurʾānic rules of inheritance.[71] Another justification for the reform, which pertains exclusively to Muslims in Israel, is the nationalization of the *waqf* property that by definition is designed for charity and public welfare purposes as well as for the strengthening of social solidarity. What seems to be inferred here is an attempt to prevent – by means of the compulsory bequest – the devolution of absentees' rights in estates or heirless estates to the Custodian of Absentees' property and the General Custodian, respectively.[72] In Pakistan, the reform intended to prevent the orphaned grandchild from being deprived of his grandfather's estate was carried out by means of the adoption of the doctrine of representation in inheritance.

Circles closely related to the Sharīʿa Court of Appeal estimate that the *marsūms* have become an integral part of the binding law applicable in the *sharīʿa* courts.[73] So far, the legal validity of the *marsūms* has not been put to the test of the HCJ; thus, for instance, it is not clear what will be the ruling of the HCJ in the case that one of the legal heirs claims to have been deprived of his *sharʿī* share in the estate by a compulsory bequest.[74]

70 Coulson, *Succession*, 255–258; Layish, "Mīrāth", 112.

71 Powers, *Inheritance*, 143 ff.; Coulson, *Succession*, 213ff.

72 *al-Kashshāf*, 1995, 28–29; for further details, see Layish, *Bequests*, 313–314.

73 *al-Kashshāf*, 1995, 2.

74 HCJ 6452/96 deals with issue of the *sharīʿa* court's competence with respect to *waqf* property vested in the Custodian on Absentees' Property (see above), rather than the issue of

### 4.3 *The Judicial Practice of the* Sharīʿa *Court of Appeal*[75]

Most of the *qāḍīs* nominated in the first years after the emergence of the state were graduates of al-Azhar. In the present generation of the *qāḍīs* there are no graduates of al-Azhar. One *qāḍī* (Ziyād ʿAsaliyya) has recently obtained a M. A. degree at the Sharʿī University in Hebron. Most of the other *qāḍīs* have degrees (undergraduates and graduates) from faculties of humanities, social sciences and education. Two (Aḥmad Nāṭūr and Fāruq Zuʿbī) have degrees in law. In several instances, members of the same families from different generations (father, son, and even grandson) were appointed as *qāḍīs* though not at one and the same time (of course, each of them was nominated on the basis of his own merits).[76] The Qāḍīs Law (Amendment No. 10), 2002 provides that, to qualify for the position, a candidate should possess higher education in the *sharīʿa* and precepts of Islam, or, alternatively, be an experienced attorney.[77]

In theory, Islamic law does not recognize a hierarchy of judicial instances, an instance of appeal,[78] and collegial composition of a court. All these innovations have been introduced in the Muslim world under the influence of Western law. A *sharīʿa* court of appeal with a permanent composition was instituted in Israel only in 1994. Until then, the decisions of the Sharīʿa Court of Appeal did not have the effect of binding precedent in relation to the *sharīʿa* courts of first instance; nor was the Court of Appeal itself bound by its own decisions. Thus, for instance, in one case from the 1980s, the Sharīʿa Court of Appeal revoked its own decision ruling that the deferred dower should not be linked to the cost-of-living, on the grounds that the revocation constituted an act of justice. The Court further ruled that according to the *sharīʿa*, "withdrawal from a mistake is a virtue" (*al-rujūʿ min al-khaṭaʾ faḍīla*).[79] On July 23, 1996, the

---

the *marsūm*'s legal validity with respect to *waqf*. Abou Ramadan ("Judicial Activism", 287, n. 153) claims that the *marsūms*, being an act of legislation, violate the principle of the separation of powers. Cf. Dotan, 49ff. (the HCJ's intervention in considerations of Jewish law in Rabbinical courts).

75 This section of the essay is based on decisions of the Sharīʿa Court of Appeal collected from the following sources: Abū Ghūsh, *Appeals; al-Kashshāf*; and Appeals, *Selection* (see Bibliography). For the purpose of discussion, we distinguish in the following between three generations of *qāḍīs*: the first generation starts with the emergence of the state; the second generation from 1980s to mid 1990s (hereinafter: "interim generation"), and the *qāḍīs* of the permanent Sharīʿa Court of Appeal established in1994; cf. Reiter, "Qāḍīs", 209.

76 For further details, see Reiter, "Qāḍīs", 207–210, 226; Abou Ramadan, "Custody", 647, 649.

77 *Sefer Hahuqim*, 1860, 30.7.02, p. 505, art. 3. Cf. Shetreet, 133, 303–305.

78 In actual fact, however, in 14th-century North Africa, there is evidence of appeals within a hierarchy of judicial instances and within a *sharīʿa* court of first instance (a *qāḍī* may repeal a decision of his predecessor); see Powers, "Judicial Review".

79 Abū Ghūsh, *Appeals*, 30/86, 120–121; *ibid.*, 26/88, 122–124 (the linkage of the dower to the cost-of living was in order). Cf., in contrast, the legal opinion of a Libyan *qāḍī*, who

binding precedent was introduced in the *sharʿī* judiciary. In a decision pertaining to a dispute over maintenance, the Sharīʿa Court of Appeal ruled that, although the Court "is not bound by its decisions, the decisions are binding on the *sharīʿa* court of first instance with respect to the issue which is the object of the appeal but not otherwise, due to the difference in the substantial and personal circumstances of every case". This decision was made by Qāḍī Zuʿbī with Qāḍī ʿAsaliyya consenting. A year later, Qāḍī Nāṭūr reasserted the decision pertaining to the binding precedent. This innovation was justified by the need to strengthen legal stability and certainty with respect to the law applicable in the *sharīʿa* courts.[80]

The nomination of Qāḍī Nāṭūr as President of the Sharīʿa Court of Appeal signifies a new era in the judicial practice of this court. Circles close to the court estimate that Qāḍī Nāṭūr leads "a revolutionary reformist process" (*ʿamaliyyat iṣlāḥ thawriyya*).[81] To this end several methods were developed or refined. These methods were used to various extents in the judiciary practice of the *qāḍī*s of previous generations.

#### 4.3.1 Methods of Reformist Judicial Practice

##### 4.3.1.1 *Takhayyur*

Qāḍī Nāṭūr strives consciously to apply the eclectic method (*takhayyur*) in the judicial practice of the Sharīʿa Court of Appeal. He views the legal literature of the schools as one large reservoir out of which it is possible to derive elements in harmony with the conditions of modern times. The multiplicity of the schools in the *sharīʿa* and the variety of the *ʿulamā*'s *ijtihādāt* (to use his phrase) can provide an appropriate answer to any problem at any time and under any circumstances. The "*ʿulamā*'s *ijtihādāt*" seems to refer to the reservoir of the religious-legal thought based on *al-ijtihād fī 'l-madhhab*, creative interpretation within a given school which does not deviate from the *taqlīd*, the adherence to the school. In other words: the *sharīʿa* is the basis for judicial decisions (*qāʿida lil-ḥukm*).[82] The *Sharʿī* rules of personal status are

---

maintains that the linkage to a foreign currency is tantamount to usury; see Layish, *Sharīʿa and Custom*, Document 71.

80 *al-Kashshāf*, 1996, 41/96, 188; *ibid.*, 1997, part 1, 39/97, 135 (cites decision handed down in 41/96); Nāṭūr, *Comments*, Sec. 51; Abou Ramadan, "Judicial Activism", 274–275. On the effect of the binding precedent in religious courts on the judicial practice of secular courts, see Englard, *Religious Law*, 109ff.

81 *al-Kashshāf*, 1995, 4.

82 *al-Kashshāf*, 1995, 2. On another occasion Qāḍī Nāṭūr ruled that "the *sharīʿa* courts rely on the *sharīʿa* as a foundation for judicial decision (*taʿtamid al-sharīʿa asāsan lil-ḥukm*)" *al-Kashshāf*, 1997, part 1, 39/97, 135.

so abundant that there is no need to seek remedies from other sources. This seems to apply to the Knesset's legislation and to the judicial practice of the Supreme Court. The eclectic method was rejected by some *qāḍīs* of the first generation, graduates of al-Azhar, who strictly adhered to the Ḥanafī school to the point that they were not ready to respect provisions in the Ottoman Family Rights Law deviating from this school.[83]

Similarly, the Sharīʿa Court of Appeal consisting of *qāḍīs* from the interim generation rejected interpretation based on the Mālikī school. Thus, for instance, in one case, the regional *qāḍī* requested the husband who had raped his wife, to repudiate and compensate her. Since the husband declined to comply, the *qāḍī* dissolved the marriage, apparently on the Mālikī ground of prejudice caused to the wife. The Sharīʿa Court of Appeal overruled the decision, ruling that the *qāḍī* had to activate the mechanism of arbitration by virtue of Article 130 of the Ottoman Family Rights Law having regard to Article 14 of the *Mejelle*. This article provides that there is no reason for exercising *ijtihād* – here in the sense of interpretation – in the presence of statutory provision (*naṣṣ*), i.e., in the absence of a lacuna. The Court of Appeal repealed the dissolution on the ground of prejudice since this ground does not exist in the Ottoman Family Rights Law.[84]

The eclectic expedient is reflected in the judicial practice of the Sharīʿa Court of Appeal. The aforementioned Article 130 of the Ottoman Family Rights Law dealing with the dissolution of the marriage contract by means of legal proceedings on grounds of disputes between the spouses, is based on the Mālikī doctrine which – contrary to the Ḥanafī doctrine – enables the arbitrators to dissolve the marriage contract even without preliminary authorization of the spouses. Moreover, Qāḍī Zuʿbī maintains that in the event of uncertainty, literal interpretation of the provision is not sufficient; it is necessary to resort to the treatises of Mālik ibn Anas, the founder of the school, who is the historical source of the norm anchored in Article 130, in order to perceive the intention (*qaṣd*) of the legislator.[85] Mālik bases the pecuniary consequences resulting from the dissolution on prejudice (*ḍarar*) caused to the parties, relying in this matter on the divorce verses in the *Qurʾān*, and on the *ḥadīth*. The element of prejudice is not mentioned in Article 130; the pecuniary consequences in

83 Layish, *Women and Islamic Law*, 333.

84 Abū Ghūsh, *Appeals*, 12/80, 92–94 (presiding by Shaykh Ḥasan Amīn al-Ḥabash, with Shaykh Farīd Wajdī al-Ṭabarī consenting).

85 *al-Kashshāf*, 1997, part 2, 127/97, 146; on the competence of the arbitrators according to the Ḥanafī and Māikī doctrines, see *ibid.*, 143–144.

this article are based on the degree of responsibility of each of the parties to the dissolution.

#### 4.3.1.2 *Maṣlaḥa*

Public interest (*Maṣlaḥa*) is not an independent source of law in the classical theory of Islamic law. Nevertheless, *istiṣlāḥ*, taking account of public interest, is anchored in the mechanism of *qiyās*, analogical reasoning, as a source of law for deriving new rules from the textual sources. *Istiṣlāḥ* is recognized especially in the Mālikī school.[86] The modernists in Islam of Muḥammad ʿAbduh's school raised *maṣlaḥa* to an independent source of law.[87]

The doctrine of *maṣlaḥa* was applied by the Sharīʿa Court of Appeal long before the present generation of the *qāḍīs*. Thus, for instance, in one case, the regional court, having endorsed a divorce by mutual consent of the parties, ruled to disconnect the filiation (*qaṭʿ nasab*) of the minor to his father after the mother had admitted that the minor was born out of wedlock. The Court of Appeal ruled that the disconnection of filiation prejudiced the minor's interest and sought a way out of this predicament. The Court relied on the formal pretext that the process of *liʿān* had not taken place. This procedure consists of mutual imprecation by the spouses and denial (*nafy*) of paternity resulting in dissolution of the marriage, disconnection of the child from his father, and immunity of the Qurʾānic punishments imposed on adultery (*zinā*) and on false accusation of illicit intercourse (*qadhf*). The Court sought support in *Ḥāshiyat Radd al-muḥtār ʿalā Durr al-mukhtār sharḥ tanwīr al-abṣār*, compiled by the 19th-century Ḥanafī jurist of Damascus. This commentary provides that, if the procedure of *liʿān* has not taken place, or if paternity is established by explicit or implicit (*ḥukman*) acknowledgment, it is impossible to deny paternity at a later stage. And since the spouses shared the view that the minor was their common son ever since he was born until the dissolution of their marriage, and since "a human being is held responsible for his admission" (as phrased in Article 79 of the *Mejelle*), they may not deny their admission at this stage. Moreover, since the marriage was valid and has been consummated, it is required to follow the Prophetic *ḥadīth* which provides that "the child belongs to the bed of the marriage" (*al-walad lil-firāsh*), i.e., born in wedlock and hence legitimate.[88]

In one case, the Court of Appeal ruled that the woman was entitled to renounce her own portion of the estate, but not the portions of the minor

---

86 Schacht, 61, 109; Hallaq, *Legal Theories*, 112–113.

87 Layish, "Modernists", 266–267.

88 Abū Ghūsh, *Appeals*, 48/88, 198–199.

children in her guardianship since the renouncement was contrary to their interest (*maṣlaḥa*). In another case, the court rejected a request by one of the heirs to amend the order of succession claiming that the praepositus' widow had renounced her share in the estate in his favour; the court, by virtue of its position as the guardian of the public's interest, made a distinction (recognized in both the Ḥanafī and the Israeli law of succession), between withdrawal from the circle of the legal heirs (*takhāruj*) and renouncement of right in the estate in favour of a specified heir, and ruled that in the case under review the renouncement could be implemented only after an order of succession has been issued. It seems that the ruling was meant to grant the widow a space of discretion before she decided to renounce her share in the estate.[89]

The Court of Appeal presided over by Qāḍī Nāṭūr expanded the application of the doctrine of *maṣlaḥa*, taking into account, in the space of interpretation of prejudice (*ḍarar*), the political circumstances of the time. Thus, in one case, a woman refused to obey her husband in the conjugal dwelling her husband had prepared for her in Jenin (in the West Bank) on grounds that the dwelling did not meet the requirements of *maskan sharʿī*, legal conjugal dwelling. The specific reason for the wife's disobedience was that the transfer of the residence outside the municipal boundaries of Jerusalem caused her and her children "personal and civil" prejudice; moreover, it was stipulated in the marriage contract that the location of the conjugal dwelling would be in Jerusalem (though such a stipulation is not valid under Ḥanafī doctrine). Qāḍī Nāṭūr adopted the woman's view and ruled that the transfer of residence as mentioned above had caused a loss of rights and many other advantages, such as the National Insurance's allocations, and identity card – all these are tantamount to "prejudice that cannot be ignored in our time".[90]

#### 4.3.1.3 *Siyāsa sharʿiyya*

The mechanism of *siyāsa sharʿiyya*, state regulation that takes into account practical considerations, which was originally intended to be applied by the Muslim sovereign, apparently provides the *sharʿī* theoretical basis for introducing daring innovations by the *sharʿī* judiciary. We have already noted that this mechanism was meant to legitimize the *marsūm qaḍāʾī*, which is instrumental for introducing reforms in the substantive and procedural law applicable in

89 Abū Ghūsh, *Appeals*, 49/88, 173–174, and 42/90, 174–177, respectively.

90 *al-Kashshāf*, 1997, part 2, 155/97, 287–291. Cf. Shahar, "Palestinians", 71 n. 9, 111–112. On "blue marriages" with a view to obtaining a Jerusalem residential card by means of "customary" marriage (*zawāj ʿurfī*) entailing offer and acceptance [but not registration of the marriage], see *ibid.*, 122, 124.

the *sharīʿa* court. The status of binding precedent granted to decisions of the Sharīʿa Court of Appeal is also anchored in this mechanism.[91]

#### 4.3.1.4 *Judicial* ijtihād

In cases of lacunae in the Ottoman Family Rights Law, the Sharīʿa Court of Appeal resorts to the private code of personal status compiled by the Egyptian Muḥammad Qadrī Pāshā, *al-Aḥkām al-sharʿiyya fī 'l-aḥwāl al-shakhṣiyya*[92] based on the preferable view (*qawl rājiḥ*) in the Ḥanafī school although the code is not valid in Israel (nor in Egypt), and hence not binding on the *sharīʿa* courts.[93] The *qāḍīs* who graduated from al-Azhar apparently became acquainted with this code during their studies at al-Azhar. Quite often, the *qāḍīs* would resort to this code even in the presence of explicit provisions in the Ottoman Family Rights Law on the ground that these provisions deviate from the Ḥanafī doctrine.[94] The *qāḍīs* resort to classical treatises of all schools, to modern jurists such as Ibn ʿĀbidīn's *Ḥāshiyat Radd al-muḥtār*, as well as to legal literature based on concise versions of classical treatises by way of comparison between the schools of law. Out of convenience, the *qāḍīs* prefer to resort to the *Mejelle* due to its arrangement by chapters and provisions, rather than classical treatises.[95]

Quite often *qāḍīs* of the Sharīʿa Court of Appeal cite Qurʾānic verses and Prophetic *ḥadīth*s in matters pertaining to personal status[96] with a view to identifying the basic legal norm and providing support to their decisions. Qāḍī Nāṭūr maintains that judicial decisions should be based on the revealed sources (*bi-mā anzala Allāh*), which seems to imply both the *Qurʾān* and the *ḥadīth*; he does not refer to other sources of law required for *ijtihād* (*ijmāʿ*, the jurists' consensus, and *qiyās*, systematic analogy).[97]

In contrast, Qāḍī Zuʿbī recommends reopening the gate of *ijtihād* and enlists the support of Article 39 of the *Mejelle*, which provides: "It cannot be denied that changes of time entails changes in law" (*lā yunkar taghayyur al-aḥkām bi-taghayyur al-azmān*), which implies a recommendation to adjust the *sharīʿa*

91 See Nāṭūr, *Comments*, Sec. 51.

92 See Bibliography.

93 *al-Kashshāf*, 1997, part 2, 63/97, 15; Meron, *Moslem Law*, 59.

94 *al-Kashshāf*, 1995 ,92/95, 355; *ibid.*, 1997, part 1, 63/97, 15; cf. Abou Ramadan, "Custody", 599.

95 Appeals, *Selection*, 41/94 (Articles 1827, 1828); *al-Kashshāf*, 1997, part 2, 60/97, 47–48; 9/38, 61 (Articles 1816–1820); 87/97, 79 (the chapter on arbitration in the *Mejelle*, e.g., art. 1849); cf. Layish, "*Qāḍīs* and *Sharīʿa*", 249; Welchman, 36–37.

96 See, for instance, Qurʾān, 4:4 (dower); *al-Kashshāf*, 1997, part 2, 71/97, 34; *ibid.*, 1997, part 2, 60/97, 44. Qāḍī Nāṭūr requests that *qāḍīs* demonstrate their knowledge of the Qurʾān; see Abou Ramadan, "Judicial Activism", 275.

97 *al-Kashshāf*, 1995, 2.

to the changes of the times. Zuʿbī is inspired by Muḥammad ʿAbduh who prefers a *qāḍī* who is a creative *mujtahid* to application of statutory provisions. What we have here, however, is not a classical *ijtihād,* because the *qāḍī*, according to Zuʿbī, is expected to base his decision on the following legal sources in this order: the *Qurʾān*, the *ḥadīth*; the *ijtihād* of the first *khulafāʾ*, and that of the founders of the schools and other *mujtahid*s, i.e., the legal literature of all schools; the Ottoman laws derived from these sources; and in the event of lacuna – personal discretion (*raʾy*) which is close to the original significance of this term. Zuʿbī suggests interesting elements of legal methodology, but certainly not a systematic established methodology. He defines his legal methodology as "judicial legislation" (*tashrīʿ qaḍāʾī*) or "legislative adjudication" (*qaḍāʾ tashrīʿī*) and finds support for his methodology in the Common Law, and the principles of justice of the English law.[98]

I did not come across a single case of *ijtihād* in its classical sense in the judicial practice of the Sharīʿa Court of Appeal in the last decade. In one case, which occurred decades ago, one of the *qāḍī*s attempted, apparently in the wake of the modernists of Muḥammad ʿAbduh's school, to prohibit polygamy by alluding to the polygamous verses in the Qurʾān that make polygamy contingent on the obligation to treat co-wives justly and equitably.[99]

### 4.3.2 Absorption and Islamization of Israeli-inspired Legal Institutions

#### 4.3.2.1 *The Welfare of the Child*

One of the most daring innovations in the judicial practice of the present Sharīʿa Court of Appeal is the adoption of the principle of the welfare of the child. The *Sharīʿa* places the child's mother first among the women entitled to custody (*ḥiḍāna*). The mother's legally institutionalized right to custody exists as long as she qualifies for the position, and provided she is not disqualified on grounds of her marriage to a non-relative or to a relative within the prohibited degrees for marriage with respect to the child (*maḥram*). The mother is followed in order of priority to custody, by female relatives according to the rule of class (parentela, *ṭabaqa*) of heirs (to the exclusion of the first parentela of the immediate issue). Within each class of female relatives, entitlement to custody is assigned according to the degree of relationship with respect to the child; the nearer in degree excludes the more remote. Among females of the same degree, cognates exclude agnates: after the child's mother comes

---

98 *al-Kashshāf*, 1997, part 2, 60/97, 50–54; Schacht, Glossary, s.v. *raʾy*. On the application of the Common Law in the event of lacuna, see Englard, "Integration of Jewish Law", 127.

99 Layish, "*Qāḍīs* and *Sharīʿa*", 249. The judicial *ijtihād* in Sudan during the period of Numayrī seems to be extremely rare; see Layish & Warburg, 184–186.

the maternal grandmother in ascending line (the grandmother's mother, the great-grandmother's mother, etc.). After the extinction of the branch or in the event that the maternal grandmothers disqualify for custody, the paternal grandmother in ascending line is assigned to custody. After her, custody is transferred to the class of the sisters according to this order of priority: full sister (*shaqīqa*), maternal sister and paternal sister. After them, custody is assigned to the sisters' daughters according to the same order and so on and so forth, in accordance with the order of the parentelas. In other words, we are here dealing with an established, fixed order of entitlement to custody anchored in the *sharīʿa* with a clear preference of cognatic over agnatic relationship.[100] Although there is an attempt to justify the order of entitlement to custody with the principle of the child's welfare, it is obvious that his welfare is secondary to the entitlement of female relatives according to the rule of class. In fact, the child's welfare is not recognized in the *sharīʿa* as a general principle;[101] it is used as rationalization for the special position of the mother and female cognates, rather than as the source of their right which, as mentioned above, is anchored in law.

Qāḍī Nāṭūr, in contrast, strongly insists that the welfare of the child is an independent fundamental principle anchored in the *sharīʿa*. In his view, the two parents have an equal right to custody. The principle of welfare of the child should guide in each case, according to its special circumstances, which of the two parents (who reside separately) has priority to custody. To this end, it is required to consult social welfare officers, expert holders of a diploma, etc. Moreover, he maintains that the welfare of the child in the *sharīʿa* is in harmony with Article 25 of the Capacity and Guardianship Law which provides that when the minor's parents reside separately, and in the absence of an agreement between them, the religious court will decide in matters pertaining to custody according to its own discretion having regard to the minor's welfare.[102]

---

100 See Shalabī, 737–738; cf. Appeals, *Selection*, 151/2003, 15.10.2003, 4 (in Qāḍī Nāṭūr's wording: *fa'l-ḥiḍāna ḥaqq lil-ḥāḍin ayḍan bi-iʿtibār awlawiyyat al-qiyām bihā ḥasab al-tartīb alladhī waḍaʿahu al-shāriʿ*). Qāḍī Nāṭūr (*Comments*, Sec. 34): the order of females entitled to custody in the *sharīʿa* is based on practical experience accumulated over generations; the Sharīʿa Court of Appeal always rules according to this order unless it has been established that the welfare of the child requires ruling otherwise.

101 Cf. Motzki, 135. The welfare of the child is recognized as a principle only in extraordinary circumstances, such as the foundling (*laqīṭ*). It is required to transfer him to the richest man having regard to "the welfare of the foundling" (*mā huwa anfaʿ li-laqīṭ*); Ibn ʿĀbidīn, *Radd al-muḥtār*, Vol. 4, 273; see also *ibid.*, 271. I owe this reference to Yaʿakov Meron.

102 *al-Kashshāf*, 1995, 92/95, 358–359; cf. Abū Ghūsh, *Appeals*, 13/83, 140 (The court ruled that the welfare of the child is a principle shared by both the *sharīʿa* and the Capacity and Guardianship Law.); Abu-Gosh, "Pluralism", 47.

What we witness here seems to be an attempt to absorb and Islamize the principle of the welfare of the child as conceived in Israeli law.

The welfare of the child, as it emerges from the judicial practice of the Sharīʿa Court of Appeal, is based on the theory of presumptions (*farḍiyya*), e.g., children in tender age are presumed to be in the custody of their mother, unless it is established that there are good reasons to rule otherwise.[103] In one case, a *sharīʿa* court ruled that the presumption is that the father has the right to see his child and take him abroad on a long journey, unless the child's mother proves that the journey may cause harm to the child. The court, in its turn, has to choose between the degree of benefit (*nafʿ*) entailed in the child's journey, and the degree of harm (*ḍarar*) it may cause; "if harm exceeds benefit, its prevention is preferable to seeking benefit" (*fa-in kān al-ḍarar yafūq al-manfaʿa fa-darʾuhu muqaddam ʿalā jalb al-manfaʿa*).[104]

In one case, Qāḍī Nāṭūr ruled that, if the period of custody expired, the presumption was that the child was weaned from women's service and that his welfare (*maṣlaḥa*) required his transfer to the custody of his father and that thus the burden of proof rested with the mother who claimed the contrary of this presumption.[105] On various occasions, the Sharīʿa Court of Appeal opined that, since the Qurʾān and the *ḥadīth* do not indicate explicitly a specified age for termination of custody, and since the fixing of the age is a matter of *ijtihād fiqhī*, (i.e. *sharʿī* interpretation by the *fuqahāʾ*), it is permissible to deviate from the *sharʿī* norm provided the welfare of the minor requires this.[106]

In one case, a woman was deprived of her right to *ḥiḍāna* on the ground that she had married someone who was not *maḥram* in relation to her children. Qāḍī Nāṭūr ruled that the custody in the case under review had to be decided on the basis of the Prophetic *ḥadīth*: 'You are the worthiest [for *ḥiḍāna*] so long as you are not married" (*anti aḥaqqu bihi mā lam tunkaḥī*), and only if it was established, contrary to this presumption, that the minor had been neglected by a person who had replaced the minor's mother in custody, whereas the [mother's] husband treated the minor properly, was the child to remain in his mother's custody.[107]

Similarly, Qāḍī Zuʿbī ruled – contrary to an explicit view of the *sharīʿa* – that the marriage of a mother to a stranger (in relation to her children) did not

---

103 Cf. Shifman, 537.

104 *al-Kashshāf*, 1995, 92/95, 352–357, 359; the quote is from p. 355.

105 Appeals, *Selection*, 192/99, 27.4.2000, 4–7; cf. *al-Kashshāf*, 1997, part 1, 135/96, 296 (Qāḍī Nāṭūr: the mother is the worthiest for *ḥiḍāna*, but this presumption can be refuted by a proof to the contrary established by the minor's father).

106 Abū Ghūsh, *Appeals*, 39/90, 143–145; *ibid.*, 42/86, 157.

107 Appeals, *Selection*, 28/98, 26.5.98, 4–6.

automatically disqualify her for *ḥiḍāna*. In his view, the welfare of the child should be the supreme consideration regarding the *ḥiḍāna*. If someone alleges that the minor's journey abroad with his mother (in order to enable her to marry a stranger) disqualifies her for custody, he has to prove his allegation that the journey may cause harm, since the criterion for *maṣlaḥa* is the prevention of prejudice: *lā ḍarar wa-lā ḍirār* and similar phrases of *maṣlaḥa*.[108]

#### 4.3.2.2 *Natural Justice*

Usually, the Sharīʿa Court of Appeal uses the term "justice" within its Islamic meaning: "justice of God".[109] This concept of justice is anchored in Qurʾānic verses, the *ḥadīth* and exegesis.[110] *ʿAdl*, in the sense of God's justice, in connection with the requital of human acts, constitutes one of the five fundamental dogmas (*uṣūl*) in the Muʿtazilī doctrine. The *qāḍī* must adjudicate in the light of God's justice. The idea of material justice does not constitute a vital element in the theory of the *sharīʿa*.[111]

However, alongside the references to God's justice in the judicial practice of the Sharīʿa Court of Appeal, there is occasionally explicit or implicit reference to "natural justice" within the meaning used by the Supreme Court. [112] Thus, for instance, in one case the Court of Appeal ruled that the court of first instance should have been guided by the rules of natural justice (*aḥkām al-ʿadl al-ṭabīʿī*) regarding the right of standing of a third party in matters pertaining to interdiction (*ḥajr*). In one case the court ruled that the linkage of the dower to the cost of living is the closest act to making "justice by virtue of nature" (*al-ʿadl bi-ḥukm al-ṭabīʿa*). In yet another case, the regional court was instructed to make sure that detailed reasoning (*taʿlīl*) to the sentence was provided with a view to preserving the element of justice (*ʿadl, inṣāf*), which in turn would enable the parties to appeal to a higher instance, appeal (which, as already noted, is alien to Islamic law) being one of the "natural rights" (*ḥuqūq ṭabīʿiyya*) of the parties of the dispute. In another case, the Court of Appeal ruled that the refusal of the court of the first instance to delay the hearing of a dispute of maintenance "did not cause any hardship in the process of making justice (*sayr al-ʿadāla*) or break any of the principles of justice (*lam yatakharraq mabdaʾ*

---

108 Appeals, *Selection*, 187/99, 10.4.01, 1–3.

109 See, e.g., *al-Kashshāf*, 1997, part 2, 153/97, 219 (*iqāmat al-ʿadl wafqan li-mā anzala allāh*), 75/98, 198/98 (cited in Nāṭūr, *Comments*, Sec. 25).

110 For references on the use of the term *ʿadl* in these sources, see Nāṭūr, *Comments*, Sec. 22.

111 Tyan, 209i; Watt, 334ii; Gardet, "Allāh", 410i; Gardet, "ʿIlm al-Kalām", 1143ii.

112 On the principles of the Israeli natural justice, see Englard, *Religious Law*, 161 ff.

*min mabādi' al-ʿadl)*".[113] It seems that in all these cases the Court of Appeal was inspired by the concept of justice as perceived by the Supreme Court, rather than by God's justice. This may indicate readiness, within various degrees of awareness, to absorb legal-technical terms from an Israeli conceptual framework.[114] In all these cases the concept of natural justice was translated into terms pertaining to substantive and procedural law.

The detailed legal reasoning (*taʿlīl*) in the judicial sentences is indeed part of Qāḍī Nāṭūr's new concept of justice. He instructs the *qāḍī*s to strictly adhere to *taʿlīl* so that justice will be seen by all.[115] By virtue of the same rationale he allows the appearance of witnesses in the Sharīʿa Court of Appeal (instead of presenting the allegations in writing, as required by the regulations of the Court of Appeal) and releases the litigants from court fees due for the appearance. This concept of justice (*ʿadl*) has a social aspect *par excellence* that can be easily connected to the concept of "Islamic justice",[116] which in turn may legitimize the concept of natural justice. As noted earlier,[117] social justice also provides a theoretical basis for issuing legal circulars.

#### 4.3.2.3 *The Right of Standing*

According to the *sharīʿa*, a legal action requires a claimant. There is no public prosecutor whose function is to take action in criminal offenses. However, a *qāḍī* has competence to take action in matters of public welfare (homicide and bodily harm are within the domain of private law). In theory, the "Inspector of the Market" (*muḥtasib*) is the public representative in charge of the propagation of virtuous acts and prevention of vicious acts (*al-amr bi 'l-maʿrūf wa'l-nahy ʿan al-munkar*); his status is in fact that of a public prosecutor.[118] In civil claims between two parties, a third party has no right of standing.

In one case, a woman claimed the deferred dower on the plea that the marriage had been dissolved by the *sharīʿa* court on the grounds of the husband's absence (*ghayba*) and prejudice (*ḍarar*) caused to the wife. The husband's

113 *al-Kashshāf*, 1995, 15/95, 170, 172 (written by Qāḍī Nāṭūr); *ibid.*, 1995, 116/94, 157 (Qāḍī Nāṭūr); *ibid.*, 1995, 8/95, 88 (Qāḍī Nāṭūr); and *ibid.*, 1996, 41/96, 186 (Qāḍī Zuʿbī), respectively.

114 On the religious courts' duty to observe the principles of the natural justice, see Englard, *Religious Law*, 112.

115 See, e.g., Appeals, *Selection*, 41/94, 21.6.94, 2 (reasoning pertaining to principles of [natural?] justice, *uṣūl al-ʿadl; ibid.*, 32/94, 21.6.94, 2 (legal reasoning, *taʿlīl al-ḥukm*, is required for a request for addition to minor's maintenance); *al-Kashshāf*, 1994, 38/94, 116, 117 (the regional court and the family arbitrator are required to provide reasoning to their decisions). Cf. Barak, *Legal Discretion*, 46, 98, 242, 364; idem, *The Judge*, 38.

116 Cf. Abou Ramadan, "Judicial Activism", 282–283.

117 See p. 185, above.

118 Schacht, 189–190; cf. *Mejelle*, Sec. 1634; Black, 1222, s.v. "public prosecutor".

agnatic aunt submitted a counterclaim in which she alleged that the woman was anxious to remarry someone else although the dissolution of her first marriage had not been properly endorsed by court. The woman's attorney reacted by claiming that the aunt had no right of standing since she was not a party to the contract of marriage. It is worth mentioning that the law of procedure of the *sharīʿa* courts, 1917 has no reference to a third party's right of standing, though Article 46 of the law enables a third party to submit a rejection to a sentence of a *sharīʿa* court, but this option is based on the Ottoman civil procedure law. Qāḍī Nāṭūr, the future president of the Sharīʿa Court of Appeal, justified the aunt's intervention in the legal proceedings, as follows: "Since marriage and divorce touch upon the right (*ḥaqq*) of Allāh, be He exalted, because they entail [rules pertaining to] permission and prohibition (*yartabiṭ bihimā al-ḥall wa'l-ḥurma*); hence, every Muslim has the right to sue [i.e., right of standing] in this case, the more so a relative. This right [of standing] is valid according to the *sharīʿa*". It seems that we are here dealing with an attempt to stretch matters that are within private law (*ḥuqūq al-ʿibād*), with respect to which there is no right of standing for a third party, towards public law (*ḥuqūq allāh*), on the ground that the marriage of a woman to two husbands simultaneously, as alleged by the aunt, is tantamount to adultery, which is an offense against *ḥaqq allāh* entailing a Qurʾānic sanction. Moreover, Article 77 of the Ottoman Family Rights Law, 1917 requires the spouses of an invalid (*bāṭil*) or irregular (*fāsid*) marriage to dissolve the marriage contract; and if they fail to do so on their initiative, the *qāḍī* will separate between them. Qāḍī Nāṭūr strongly insists that the aunt's intervention in the legal proceedings is anchored in the right, even duty, of every Muslim to function as *muḥtasib* whenever there is a violation of the right of Allāh.[119] The *muḥtasib* controls public ethics; he is in charge of imposing Islamic norms of behavior and values on the Muslim community. Any individual in this community can step into the *muḥtasib*'s shoes and he has the right of standing (*khuṣūma*) as a private prosecutor.[120] Marriage and divorce are, however, within the domain of private, rather than public, law and the *sharīʿa* courts in Israel have no jurisdiction in matters pertaining to offenses entailing Qurʾānic punishments (a divorced woman whose marriage had been consummated, who committed adultery is liable to lapidation). Qāḍī Nāṭūr is anxious to apply the right of standing also to matters of personal status by

---

119 Abū Ghūsh, *Appeals*, 39/89, 125–131 Nāṭūr, *Comments*, Sec. 27.

120 Schacht, 52; Layish & Warburg, Glossary, s.v. *ḥisba, muḥtasib*. Cf. the right of standing (*khuṣūma*) granted to the inhabitants of Haifa in the case of the sale of Waqf Istiqlāl (Abū Ghūsh, *Appeals*, 3/76, 185). Another example of adoption of a principle from the general law: In a dispute pertaining to the attorney's wages in a case of maintenance, Qāḍī Fārūq Zuʿbī ruled: It is common knowledge in civil law that "a specific provision of law overrules a general provision" (*al-Kashshāf*, 1997, part 2, 113/97, 129–130).

stretching the principle to the level of Islamic public law; the legal justification for such a move is apparently obtained by bringing the right of standing within the orbit of the institution of the *muḥtasib*. As a jurist attuned to the general law, Qāḍī Nāṭūr was naturally fully aware of the HCJ's inclination to broaden the scope of the right of standing: This right is granted not only to individuals claiming that their personal interests have been prejudiced but also to pleaders claiming to present an issue of a constitutional or public nature which touches directly upon the rule of law.[121] It seems that the Sharīʿa Court of Appeal was inspired in this regard by the judicial practice of the Supreme Court and translated "an issue of public nature" into Islamic terms.

By the same token, Qāḍī Nāṭūr also regards custody (*ḥidāna*) as *ḥaqq allāh* on the grounds that it touches upon public interest (*maṣlaḥat al-ʿāmma*). He explains that custody is not a civil matter, such as the right to property (*māliyya*, or *ʿayn*); hence, it is impossible to renounce it even if the woman who has custody (*ḥāḍin*) of a child gives up her right or the renunciation is being made with the ward (*maḥḍūn*)'s consent.[122] Qāḍī Nāṭūr supports the concept of custody as *ḥaqq allāh* by views enlisted from legal treatises of *ʿulamāʾ* of various schools, modern legislation in Arab countries, books by sociologists and psychologists dealing with socialization of the child and the harm caused to him by the parents' divorce.[123] Moreover, Qāḍī Nāṭūr maintains that the minor's welfare is within the category of *farḍ kifāya*, a duty the fulfillment of which by a sufficient number of individuals excuses the other individuals from fulfilling it: a Muslim eyewitness to a minor's welfare being prejudiced by a sinner (*fāsiq*, *fājir*) custodian, must notify the *qāḍī* of this.[124] Here too, the attempt to connect the minor's welfare to the institution of the *muḥtasib* is inferred.

#### 4.3.2.4 *The Precedent*

As noted above,[125] the decisions of the Sharīʿa Court of Appeal are binding with respect to the regional courts of first instance. Judicial precedent is alien to Islamic law. It is very likely that its source of inspiration in the *sharʿī* judiciary is the Israeli Supreme Court, whose decisions are binding on all kinds of courts in Israel, secular and religious alike.[126] The introduction of the precedent is justified by the need to create legal certainty regarding the binding

121 Kremnitzer, 185; Dotan, 11–13; cf. Barak, *The Judge*, 69.

122 Appeals, *Selection*, 67/99, 31.5.99, 3–4 (Qāḍī Zuʿbī consents to the sentence).

123 Appeals, *Selection*, 92/98, 18.8.98, 9–16, 19; Nāṭūr, *Comments*, Sec. 47.

124 Appeals, *Selection*, 187/99, 10.4.01, 1–3; *ibid.*, 151/2003, 15.10.03, 5; cf. Schacht, 121.

125 See p. 191, above.

126 Barak, *Judicial Discretion*, 150–151; idem, *The Judge*, 67. Englard (*Religious Law*, 134), in contrast, is of the opinion that the decisions of the Supreme Court do not bind the religious courts.

legal norm in the *sharīʿa* courts; this certainty is expected to contribute to the stability of the *sharʿī* judiciary which is intensively exposed to the Knesset's legislation and to the judicial practice of the Supreme Court. Qāḍī Nāṭūr seeks to adopt the binding precedent by the mechanism of *siyāsa sharʿiyya*, which – as already noted – is traditionally reserved to the Muslim sovereign.[127] The terms "judicial legislation" (*tashrīʿ qaḍāʾī*) and "legislative adjudication" (*qaḍāʾ tashrīʿī*) in Zuʿbī's legal methodology also seem to be inspired by the Israeli Supreme Court.[128]

#### 4.3.2.5 *Civil Rules of Evidence and Procedure*

On the basis of my personal impression and that of others attained through attendance of sessions of the Sharīʿa Court in West Jerusalem presided by Qāḍī Ziyād ʿAsaliyya, it is safe to conclude that the following changes have been introduced into the judicial practice of this court (and apparently in the Sharīʿa Court of Haifa, where he is now presiding): the identification of the parties to the case and the witnesses on the basis of identity card or passport rather than the traditional *sharʿī* procedure (*taʿrīf*); legal documents are acceptable evidence (*bayyināt, adilla*);[129] application of civil rules of procedure; and the introduction of counter investigation of witnesses. According to the *sharīʿa*, the testimony of the claimant's witnesses is acceptable once they stand the test of credibility (*tazkiya*) without recourse to counter-investigation; the acceptance of circumstantial evidence (which is alien to traditional law),[130] as well as medical opinions and social welfare officials' opinions.[131] Shahar informs, on the basis of personal knowledge, that the "procedural revolution" (as he calls it) takes place not only in the *sharīʿa* courts presided by Qāḍī ʿAsaliyya, but also in the Sharīʿa Court of Beer Sheva presided over by Qāḍī Dūkān al-ʿAtāwna, in the Sharīʿa Court of West Jerusalem presided over by Qāḍī Muḥammad Rashīd Zabda, and in the Sharīʿa Court of Jaffa presided over by Qāḍī ʿAbd al-Ḥalīm Sammāra. Naturally, experts' opinions may have decisive weight in the court's decision.[132]

---

127 On the penetration of Western legal terminology into modern *uṣūlī* textbooks, see Cardinal, 246–253. Thus Shalabī considers the doctrine of precedent akin to *ijmāʿ*, and Abū Zahra classifies it as a form of inferential *qiyās*.

128 On judicial legislation, see Barak, *Judicial Discretion*, 147ff.; idem, *The Judge*, 25–26; cf. Englard, *Religious Law*, 115 (the religious court as a legislative organ).

129 Muḥammad ʿAbduh acknowledged written documents (*al-tawthīq bi'l-kitāba*) as legal evidence; ʿAbduh, 34; Layish, "*Shahādat naql*".

130 Excluding the Mālikī school in the event that there is a strong suspicion (*lawth*) connecting the suspect to the murder; Layish & Warburg, 152.

131 Shahar, "Palestinians", 49–50, 62; Reiter, "Qāḍīs", 213–214, 227.

132 Shahar's electronic letter to me, 27.5.04.

Other innovations pertain to the adjustment of the *sharīʿa* to changing social and economic conditions: the linkage of the rates of dower and maintenance to the cost-of-living,[133] acknowledgment of a flat in a condominium house as a legal conjugal dwelling (*maskan sharʿī*), although the dwelling does not meet all the required qualifications according to the classical definition.[134]

The absorption of legal institutions from foreign sources by means of their Islamization has also been observed in the judicial practice of the Supreme Court in Sudan under Numayrī where an attempt was made to reinstate the *sharīʿa*. Thus, for instance, the Supreme Court adopted the Western concept of compulsory insurance on vehicles which entails legal and financial accountability even with respect to a third party (pedestrians injured in road accidents), thus deviating from the *sharʿī* concept which acknowledges only contractual commitment between the parties to the contract. The adoption of compulsory insurance took place by allegedly relying on the doctrine of *maṣlaḥa*. Similarly, the Supreme Court legitimized the practice which permits retroactive application of provisions in the Penal Code, 1983, i.e., prior to its endorsement as a law, provided the new law is "more favorable for the accused" (*aṣlaḥ lil-muttaham*). This English-inspired principle is likewise anchored in the doctrine of *maṣlaḥa*.[135]

### 4.3.3 The *qāḏīs* and the Israeli Law

#### 4.3.3.1 *The Approach to Israeli Legislation*

The attitude of the *q̲āḏīs* of the first and interim generation to the Knesset's legislation was ambivalent. On the one hand, not all of them were fully aware of the reforms intended to improve the status of women or to use to this end the wide discretion granted them by the Knesset.[136] On the other hand, some of the *q̲āḏīs* ruled faithfully in accordance with the Knesset's legislation

133 *al-Kashshāf*, 1995, 116/94, 156–157 (Qāḏī Nāṭūr: the linkage of the dower to the cost-of-living in inflationary conditions is deemed just because in this way it is possible to preserve the real value of the money); *ibid.*, 1997, part 2, 60/97, 48–49, 55; Appeals, *Selection*, 41/94, 21.6.94, 1–3; *al-Kashshāf*, 1997, part 2, 65/97, 52 (dower of various kinds: the prompt dower with its appurtenance, *tawābiʿ*, and the deferred dower); Appeals, *Selection*, 32+35/2000, 14.5.00, 7; cf. Abū Ghūsh, *Appeals*, 23/85, 47–50 (maintenance); Reiter, "Qāḏīs", 223. Retroactive maintenance starting from the day of submission of the claim for maintenance (as required by the Ḥanafī school), rather than the day of handing down the court decision (in Egypt and Iraq – from the day that the husband ceased to pay maintenance); Layish & Shaham, 31.

134 Reiter, "Qāḏīs", 220–222. On bridging the gap between law and social reality with respect to community property, see Barak, *The Judge*, 62, 71.

135 For further details, see Layish & Warburg, 188–194.

136 Layish, *Women and Islamic Law*, 334–335.

even in cases where this legislation was not in harmony with the *sharīʿa*. Occasionally, the Sharīʿa Court of Appeal would draw the regional *qāḍī*'s attention to Article 1 of the Women's Equal Rights Law which provides that a man and a woman shall have equal status with regard to any legal act, or to the Capacity and Guardianship Law that provides that both parents are natural guardians of their children. In one case, the Court of Appeal ruled: "We cannot ignore the statutory laws (*lā yumkinuna ihmāl al-qawānīn al-waḍʿiyya*) which view any person below 18 as minor in accordance with Article 3 of the Capacity and Guardianship Law, and equalizes between the two parents for the matter of guardianship on minors in accordance with Article 14".[137] Qāḍī Nāṭūr, representing a new school of *qāḍīs* since the constitution of a permanent court of appeal in 1994, is of the opinion (which is indeed in harmony with the Knesset's intention) that the Israeli law is binding for the religious court only when it is explicitly addressed to it.[138] Otherwise, the *sharīʿa* court must apply the *sharīʿa* alone, since this is, in his view, the rationale of the judicial autonomy granted to the religious courts. He opposes the application of Property Relations between Spouses Law, 1973[139] and Basic Law: Human Dignity and Liberty, 1992, although he regards the latter as a "revolutionary law" (*qānūn thawrī*) of tremendous importance in social respects.[140] The Qāḍīs Nāṭūr and Mudlij are of the opinion that the Capacity and Guardianship Law is not addressed to religious courts although the HCJ ruled otherwise.[141] These attitudes reflect a retreat from the attitudes of the first and the interim generation of *qāḍīs* in the Sharīʿa Court of Appeal, who did not hesitate to apply the Women's Equal Rights Law and the Capacity and Guardianship Law, which place the welfare of the minor above any other consideration.[142]

The first and the interim generation of the *qāḍīs* also assisted in bringing to trial violators of criminal legislation pertaining to marriage and divorce. Thus, for instance, in one case, after it was established in the Sharīʿa Court of Appeal that the wife had objected to her divorce, this court instructed that the divorce,

---

137 Abū Ghūsh, *Appeals*, 42/86, 157; cf. Layish, *Women and Islamic Law*, 264.

138 Cf. Englard, *Religious law*, 153–154.

139 Reiter, "Qāḍīs", 215–217 (the *qāḍīs* tried to circumvent the law by guiding the marriage registrars to insert into the marriage contract a stipulation to the effect that the parties commit themselves not to apply the law). On property relations between the spouses in Islamic law, see Meron, "Property Relations", 279–298; idem, "Muslim Solution", 315–318.

140 Appeals, *Selection*, 237/98, 30.12.98, 8–10. In another case, Qāḍī Nāṭūr ruled that protection on human dignity and liberty should be based, in the judicial practice, on the *sharīʿa* rather than the Israeli law; Nāṭūr, *Comments*, Sec. 20 (reference to Appeals, 1944/99). Cf. Abou Ramadan, "Judicial Activism", 278–279.

141 *al-Kashshāf*, 1995, 92/95, 358–359; *ibid.*, 1997, part 1, 135/96, 297; Appeals, *Selection*, 237/98, 30.12.98, 8–10; *ibid.*, 93/99, 18.7.99, 6; cf. Shifman, 536.

142 Abū Ghūsh, *Appeals*, 33/85, 32–34.

which is deemed valid under the *sharīʿa*, be registered not only in order to enable the woman to remarry, but also in order to activate the criminal sanction anchored in law for divorcing one's wife against her will. The Sharīʿa Court of Appeal made it clear that the regional court should have clarified whether or not the wife consented to the divorce.[143] In another case, the *qāḍīs* Yūsuf Dasūqī and Ḥasan Asadī, sitting as members of the Sharīʿa Court of Appeal, ruled that the husband's contention to the effect that the wife was barren did not constitute a "dispute"(*nizāʿ wa-shiqāq*) within the meaning of Article 130 of the Ottoman Family Rights Law, and that as a matter of fact, the resort to this Article was used as a device to avoid the criminal sanction applicable to divorcing one's wife against her will.[144]

The *qāḍīs* of the first and interim generation deemed themselves bound by the Israeli legislation; moreover, they did not hesitate to invite the Knesset's intervention in issues where it was impossible to apply the *sharīʿa* without committing a criminal offense. Thus, for instance, since the wife's barrenness is not a ground for legal dissolution of the marriage under the Ottoman Family Rights Law, they requested that the Knesset promulgate that barrenness should be deemed a "good defense" against a charge of divorcing one's wife against her will, or a charge of taking a co-wife without the court's permission. The Court of Appeal requested "to find a solution that will ensure the Muslims' right to progeny (*ḥaqquhum fī 'l-dhurriyya*)," in the same manner that the issue was handled with respect to the Jewish population in Article 179 of the Criminal Law, 1977. This Article provides immunity against the sanction applicable to polygamy provided permission for marriage has been granted by a Rabbinical court and endorsed by the two Chief Rabbis. It was claimed that the absence of such permission with respect to Muslims consisted of discrimination against Muslims in relation to Jews.[145] In contrast, the Sharīʿa Court of Appeal presided by Qāḍī Nāṭūr deliberately refrains from initiating legislation by the Knesset as a means of solving distressing problems; rather, he seeks ways outside the framework of the state to this end.

#### 4.3.3.2 *The Attitude towards the Supreme Court*

From the early years of its establishment, the Sharīʿa Court of Appeal was sensitive to the intervention of the HCJ in matters pertaining to freedom of religion. Thus, for instance, the court presided by Shaykh Ḥasan Amīn al-Ḥabash

143 Abū Ghūsh, *Appeals*, 24/82, 19–20; cf. Abu-Gosh, "Pluralism", 48.

144 As well as to avoid payment of the divorced woman's rights. Abū Ghūsh, *Appeals*, 2/88, 77–81; Layish, *Women and Islamic Law*, 335; idem, "*Qāḍīs* and *Sharīʿa*", 266 ff.

145 Abū Ghūsh, *Appeals*, 23/88, 103–107 (the "common-law wife" is not a practical solution with respect to the Muslims); cf. *ibid.*, 25/76, 197; Layish, *Women and Islamic Law*, 86, n. 10.

expressed its concern at the possibility that the Supreme Court would ignore Qur'ānic verses which embody the superiority of men to women, such as the verse that provides that men are in control of women (*al-rijāl qawwāmūn ʿalā al-nisāʾ*) (34:4).[146] Qāḍī Nāṭūr formulated his concern in a harsher manner: the introduction of the norm "civil paternity" by the Supreme Court is assessed by him as "a religious disaster" and "biting interference" in the *sharʿī* rules pertaining to permission and prohibition.[147] At the same time, *qāḍīs* of the present Court of Appeal, especially those trained in Israeli law, are fully alert to the judicial practice of the Supreme Court, some of them even reveal a sense of empathy. Thus, for instance, Qāḍī Fārūq Zuʿbī supports the judicial activism initiated by the President of the Supreme Court, Aharon Barak, and cites in his sentences the President's book and judgments of the Supreme Court.[148] Qāḍī Nāṭūr frequently cites the HCJ's judgments and legal research literature in his sentences, while taking a critical stand towards various issues.[149]

*Qāḍīs* of the Sharīʿa Court of Appeal of all generations are attentive to the legislation and judicial practice in Arab countries, and quite often cite them in order to support their reformist attitudes in issues such as triple repudiation, family arbitration, maintenance and custody. Notwithstanding, they are aware that they are not bound by the legislation and the judicial practice in the Arab countries since they are an integral part of the Israeli legal system.[150]

## 5 Conclusion

The *qāḍīs* of the present generation in the Sharīʿa Court of Appeal strive to introduce reforms inspired by the legislation and judicial practice in the Arab countries. However, contrary to *qāḍīs* of previous generations, who consciously deemed themselves bound by and identified with the Knesset's legislation to the extent of being ready to invite statutory legislation as remedies to occasional problems, the *qāḍīs* of the present generation, though fully aware of the Knesset's legislation and the Supreme Court's judiciary's practice due to the

146 Abū Ghūsh, *Appeals*, 12/80, 92–98.

147 Nāṭūr, *Comments*, Sec. 19. See 180–182, below.

148 *al-Kashshāf*, 1997, part 2, 60/97, 49; cf. Abou Ramadan, "Judicial Activism", 275.

149 Appeals, *Selection*, 237/98, 30. 12. 98, 5, 8 *ibid.*, 93/99, 18.7.99, 4 *al-Kashshāf*, 1997, part 1, 135/96, 297, 298, 302.

150 Abū Ghūsh, *Appeals*, 33/85, 32–34; *ibid.*, 31/88, 81–85, 88; *al-Kashshāf*, 1997, part 2, 60/97, 41–43, 52; *ibid.*, 104/97, 90–94; Appeals, *Selection*, 28/98, 26.5.98, 4–6.

*sharʿī* judiciary integration into the general legal system, are anxious to preserve to the utmost the unique religious character of the *sharʿī* judiciary.[151]

It has recently been suggested to Qāḍī Nāṭūr to consider the replacement of the Ottoman Family Rights Law by a new law of personal status for the Muslims in Israel which will absorb the variety of reforms introduced in Middle Eastern and North African countries.[152] Since the Muslims in Israel do not have a *sharʿī* legislative body, it is impossible to introduce reforms outside the framework of the Knesset.[153] According to this suggestion, the Minister of Justice, in consultation with the president of the Sharīʿa Court of Appeal, will appoint a committee consisting of religious functionaries and experts on Islamic law of personal status, whose task is to prepare a bill of family law to be endorsed as a law by the Knesset *en bloc*, i.e., without interference in its substance. Qāḍī Nāṭūr turned down the suggestion on the spot, although he was fully aware of the advantages of a comprehensive integrative law of personal status that overnight will replace the Ottoman Family Rights Law of 1917 which is not in harmony with the present conditions. The reason for the rejection of the legislative initiative was Qāḍī Nāṭūr's reluctance to allow the Knesset's involvement in the process of preparing such a law. In his view, statutory codification is appropriate for independent Muslim countries; in the absence of a Muslim sovereignty or legislative authority in Israel, the only way left for introducing reforms is by means of the legal circular and the judicial practice of the Sharīʿa Court of Appeal.

Indeed, the legal reformism introduced by these means reflects first and foremost the desire to adjust the legal norm to the changing circumstances of the time, and especially to the transition from the multi-generational family to the nuclear family, and to the improvement of the status of women. Moreover, the members of the Court of Appeal, whose social and cultural identity has been shaped in Israel, bring with them to their judicial function a modern philosophy with a view to using the legal reform as an instrument for

151 On the attitude of the Rabbinical courts regarding the independence of the Jewish law, see Englard, *Religious Law*, 86.

152 A meeting with Qāḍī Nāṭūr on 29.12.03.

153 The Druze "Religious Council", within the meaning of the Religious Communities (Organization) Ordinance of 1926, in 1961 adopted the Lebanese Druze law of personal status, 1948 (Layish, *Druze*, 1, 10). Abou Ramadan suggests granting the Muslims autonomy similarly to that of the Christian and Druze communities in Israel. A body to be elected in general elections by the Muslim community, will be empowered to nominate *qāḍīs*, adopt a new family law, and promote high *sharʿī* education in Israel. Shaykh Rāʾid Ṣalāḥ, the head of the northern branch of the Islamic movement in Israel, suggests to constitute an independent *sharʿī* judiciary, separate from the state judiciary (Abou Ramadan, "Judiciary Activism", 292–296).

social change.[154] The *qāḍīs* are the bearers of the banner of reform, its legislators and in charge of its application. Indeed, legal reformism brought about a range of legal innovations in matters of personal status, succession and rules of evidence and procedure that in the long run will leave their imprint on Muslim society in Israel, and especially on the status of women.

The desire to preserve the Muslim religious character of the *sharʿī* judiciary is reflected in an incessant effort to present the traditional *sharīʿa* as a source of inspiration. A typical expression to this effort can be seen in Qāḍī Fārūq Zuʿbī's pronouncements in one of his judgments, the main substance of which is as follows: the fundamental element in legislation is the truth of Islamic law, which is an act of legislation by Allāh himself; the *sharīʿa* in its entirety was brought down to the Prophet Muḥammad, and consists of all matters pertaining to the relations between human beings and God and between human beings and themselves; the Prophet interpreted the *sharīʿa* in the *ḥadīth*, and this was followed, by means of *ijtihād*, by the Prophet's Companions, the righteous *khulafāʾ*, the founders of the schools of law (*madhāhib*) and other *fuqahāʾ*.[155] Similarly, Qāḍī Nāṭūr, too, opined that Muslims are requested to adjudicate in accordance with the Qurʾān not only in matters pertaining to substantive law, but also in matters of evidence and procedure.[156] These pronouncements are of special interest given the fact that these *qāḍīs* attained their legal education in Israeli universities and that they lack formal *sharʿī* education.

Similar to *qāḍīs* of previous generations, the attitude of the *qāḍīs* of the present generation to the Knesset and the Supreme Court is ambivalent: on the one hand, they still have inhibitions towards these authorities originating from the status of a Muslim-Arab minority in a state that defines itself as Jewish (in religious and national terms) and still is in perpetual conflict with the Palestinian people. Some contend that the initiative for issuing the legal circulars was inspired by the desire to strengthen the public authority of the *sharʿī* judiciary against the background of struggles for power with the Islamic movement and the movement for the liberation of women, the latter supporting the expansion of the jurisdiction of the Family Court at the expense of the *sharīʿa* court's jurisdiction.[157] In these circumstances it is no wonder that the efforts to introduce reforms are directed outside the parliament and the Supreme Court. On the other hand, the *qāḍīs*, and especially those who have a secular legal education and a rich practical experience as attorneys, are aware

---

154 Cf. Shahar, "Modernizer", 197, 209; cf. Barak, *The Judge*, 55ff.

155 *al-Kashshāf*, 1997, part 2, 60/97, 43–44; cf. Abu-Gosh, "Pluralism", 45.

156 Appeals, *Selection*, 237/98, 30.12.98, 4–5. Cf. Abou Ramadan, "Judicial Activism", 278 (the Sharīʿa Court of Appeal ruled that Israeli rules of evidence were not applicable in the *sharīʿa* court).

157 Abou Ramadan, "Judicial Activism", 283, 287.

of the fact that the *sharʿī* judiciary cannot operate independently from the general judiciary; on the contrary, the *sharʿī* judiciary is bound by the Knesset's legislation and the Supreme Court's judgments.

The tension between these two poles, segregation *vis-à-vis* openness, brought about the amazing experiment of absorption and Islamization of legal principles and institutions, such as the welfare of the child, natural justice, legal precedent and the right of standing, whose source of inspiration is Israeli law.[158] Some contend that absorption of legal institutions from Israeli law caused normative "depletion of the *sharīʿa*"[159] in the sense that the *sharīʿa* is being conquered on its soil. This contention cannot be accepted as a self-evident truth; rather, Islamization of legal institutions from foreign cultures was characteristic of the *sharīʿa* in its formative period in which it displayed an impressive assimilative power on reaching close contact with the conquered cultures in the west and east.[160] However, the process of Islamization was carried out by *fuqahāʾ* and *ʿulamāʾ*, the authoritative exponents and interpreters of the *sharīʿa*; hence the results of their efforts were binding and enduring.

In Israel, in contrast, in the absence of prominent *muftī*s and *fuqahāʾ*, the efforts to introduce reforms are carried by *qāḍī*s, whose historical contribution to the elaboration of the *sharīʿa* has been modest (excluding the period of the Umayyads prior to the crystallization of Islamic legal methodology).[161] The judicial practice of the *qāḍī*s in the *sharīʿa* courts had no impact on the formation of the classical doctrine of the *sharīʿa*. The *qāḍī*s in Israel have not created a new legal methodology capable of carrying on its shoulders the burden of reform. Although they make extensive use of the principle of *maṣlaḥa* that has become the principal instrument for reforms (utilitarianism) in the modernists' legal methodologies,[162] it is doubtful whether they managed to raise it, on the theoretical level, to the rank of an independent source of law. The use of other methods, such as *ẓāhirī* interpretation of Qurʾānic verses or reinterpretation of textual sources, *siyāsa shaʿriyya*, and especially *takhayyur*, which combines different legal doctrines for the sole sake of their adaptation to reformist norms which have been predetermined – the use of all these methods does not create a comprehensive, systematic integrative methodology.[163] Qāḍī Zuʿbī's legal methodology, though deriving inspiration from the classical methodology,

---

158 On Islamization of English principles of law in the Sudanese Supreme Court by means of anchoring them in the doctrine of *maṣlaḥa*, see Layish & Warburg, 190–191, 279.

159 Abou Ramadan, "Custody", 635.

160 Schacht, 15–22.

161 Schacht, 25–27, 75; Coulson, *History*, 28–35; Hallaq, *Authority*, 76–77.

162 Cf. Hallaq, *Legal Theories*, 214, 226.

163 Cf. Hallaq, *Legal Theories*, 211. Qāḍī Nāṭūr does not share this evaluation. In his view, the legal regulation (*marsūm qaḍāʾī*) and the binding precedent granted to the judgments of

strives at the same time to draw on the Ottoman legislation and English principles of law, yielding ultimately an unacceptable fusion from the point of view of orthodox Islam.[164] The judicial practice of the *qāḍīs* has no impact outside Israel; similarly, the legal reforms introduced by means of statutory legislation and state codification, and the Supreme Court's judicial practice in Arab countries are not binding outside the territorial boundaries of the relevant countries.

It seems that the phenomenon of Anglo-Muhammadan law will not repeat itself in Israel. In British India there were no *sharīʿa* courts ever since the late 18th century and the English courts, with the Privy Council in London at the top of the hierarchy, applied Islamic law in the light of the English principles of law (common law and equity). Nor will the phenomenon of *Droit Musulman Algérien* repeat itself, because in French Algeria the *sharīʿa* courts were amenable to a French supreme court of appeal, the *Chambre de révision musulmane*, located in Algiers, and this court applied Islamic law in the light of the French principles of law (fairness, justice and humanity).[165] In Israel, in contrast, the Muslims have a complete judiciary that until recently enjoyed exclusive jurisdiction in almost all matters of personal status. Moreover, in contrast to Algeria, the Supreme Court does not interfere in the judgments of the *sharīʿa* court as an appellate court. So far, the *sharīʿa* in Israel has not developed along the pattern of the colonial tradition, though in academic discourse this notion is not totally alien.[166]

The adaptation of Islamic law in Israel to the conditions of the time is regulated on two channels: the main channel has already been paved by the Ottoman legislator who codified the law of personal status using the eclectic device, thus blurring the boundaries between the various schools of law. The replacement of the Ottoman family law by a new family law for the Muslims in Israel, based on the reforms in matters of personal status introduced in Arab countries, provided such a law is endorsed by the Knesset, will not deviate from this channel. Statutory codification excludes the *sharīʿa* from the category of jurists' law with all the consequences involved: the destruction of the legal methodology of the classical *sharīʿa* and the schools of law, and the deprivation of the *ʿulamāʾ* of their monopoly on the elaboration of the *sharīʿa*.[167]

---

the Sharīʿa Court of Appeal, based in turn on the doctrine of *siyāsa*, are (to use his wording) a "solid methodology". Nāṭūr, *Comments*, Sec. 51.

164 Cf. Ḥasan al-Turābī's legal methodology in Layish & Warburg, 79–94.

165 Schacht, 94–99; Fyzee, *Outlines*, 47ff.; idem, *India and Pakistan* (Introduction, xviiff.); Charnay, 7–8.

166 Shahar, "Palestinians", 47 fn. 10; see also 41, 50, 84, 130.

167 On the repercussions of the "religious legislation" with respect to Jewish law, see Englard, "Integration of Jewish Law", 115–130.

The same phenomenon has been observed in the reformist legislation in Arab countries which is also based on the eclectic method.[168] In the Israeli context it has been contended that the application of the eclectic method in the judicial practice of the Sharīʿa Court of Appeal "causes legal anarchy or even a state of *non droit*".[169]

In the second channel, the *sharīʿa* courts have been extensively exposed to the impact of Israeli law. Beyond the Knesset's legislation which, as already noted, has interfered in many matters of personal status, occasionally in a daring manner, the impact of the Israeli law is discernible to some extent in the *sharīʿa* courts in so far as the reformist statutes have been explicitly addressed to religious courts. Concurrently, the Knesset's reforms are discernible in matters of personal status pertaining to Muslims only to the extent that these matters are adjudicated in the civil courts, first and foremost, the Supreme Court. It is too early to assess the restriction of the *sharīʿa* court's exclusive jurisdiction (to be shared, in matters of personal status other than marriage and divorce, by the Family Court) on the extent of Muslims' recourse to civil courts. It seems that religious, social, linguistic, cultural and national inhibitions still obstruct the way to civil courts whenever there arises an option to litigate in a *sharīʿa* court which naturally is the domestic, congenial, court for Muslims (especially women[170]) in Israel.[171] If the resort to the family courts increases significantly in future, it stands to reason that the *sharīʿa* will be exposed to the increasing influence of Israeli principles of law.

It is highly likely that legal interpretations resorted to in future in civil courts in issues pertaining to matters of personal status will be influenced by new norms shaped in the light of the principles of Basic Law: Human Dignity and Liberty and other basic laws promulgated in early 1990s.[172] The Supreme Court imposes on the *sharʿī* judiciary legal norms, which occasionally may not be in harmony with the *sharīʿa*, in matters of personal status pertaining to basic civil rights.[173] The late Immanuel Naveh, who wrote his dissertation on the application of the *sharīʿa* in civil courts in Egypt and Israel, estimated that the precedent set by the Supreme Court with respect to civil paternity might

168 Layish, *Jurists' Law*, 92–96.

169 Abou Ramadan, "Custody", 627.

170 Shahar, "Modernizer", 196 (it is estimated that 70% of the files in the Sharīʿa Court in West Jerusalem have been initiated by women), 208.

171 Cf. Reiter, "Qāḍīs", 208; Shahar, "Palestinians", 66, 73 (from the Palestinians' point of view, the resort to Israeli legal institutions bears a negative national symbolic weight), 74 (the court in West Jerusalem has also the advantage of being able to enforce and execute its judgments, unlike the court in East Jerusalem), 84 (many inhabitants of East Jerusalem prefer the *sharīʿa* court in the western part of the city because of this advantage).

172 Cf. Naveh, 378.

173 Naveh, 398.

have far-reaching repercussions on matters of personal status of Muslims in Israel. In his opinion, the possibility that basic rights in these matters will be reshaped once the civil court is requested to constitute for them a civil normative pattern, cannot be ruled out. In that event, it is possible to anticipate the development of a dual legal system in matters of personal status according to the division of the judiciary: the *sharīʿa* courts will apply the codified *sharīʿa*, subject to the changes introduced by the Knesset's legislation, and the civil courts will apply a pure civil law.[174] It is worth mentioning, in this context, the tendency of some of the *qāḍīs* to absorb inspiration from the Supreme Court. This tendency may be strengthened in the future when the number of *qāḍīs* with secular legal education and modern social philosophy increases.[175]

The Israeli judiciary is characterized by pluralism. However, this does not imply two independent legal systems, civil and religious, that coexist side by side; rather, we are facing autonomy exercised by the *sharīʿa* within the space reserved for it by Israeli law.[176] In any event, alongside the contribution of the Sharīʿa Court of Appeal, one may expect the increasing contribution of the Knesset, and especially the Supreme Court, to the adaptation of the *sharīʿa*, in its codified version, to the changing conditions of Muslim society.

## Bibliography

### *Primary Sources*

Abū Ghūsh, *Appeals. Qarārāt sharʿiyya min al-maḥkama al-istiʾnāfiyya*, ed. Ṣubḥī Abū Ghūsh. The Ministry for Religious Affairs. Jerusalem 1992.

Appeals, *Selection* A selection of judgments from the Sharīʿa Court of Appeal, 1998–2003 (unpublished).

al-Kashshāf, *al-Kashshāf ʿan qarārāt al-istiʾnāf al-ṣādira ʿan maḥkamat al-istiʾnāf al-sharʿiyya al-ʿulyā fī ʾl-quds al-sharīf, 1992–1997*. 7 Vols. Herzliya 1999.

174 Naveh, 223ff.

175 Cf. Abou Ramadan, "Judicial Activism", 292 (the lack of *qāḍīs* with *sharʿī* education supported by a class of *ʿulamāʾ* outside the establishment, exposes the *sharīʿa* to processes of secularization).

176 Some attribute the tendency of Islamization prevalent in the Sharīʿa Court of Appeal to the desire to prove that the *sharīʿa* is an independent legal system totally separated from the general legal system and as an expression of legal pluralism in the sense that every community has a measure of choice between a religious and a secular legal system. Shahar, "Palestinians", 67. Cf. Sezgin, 213–216; Abou Ramadan, "Custody", 618. On different kinds of relationship between two normative orders, see Englard, *Religious Law*, 37. On legal pluralism in the Arab world from a sociological and anthropological perspective, see Dupret, Berger and al-Zwaini.

### *Secondary Sources*

ʿAbd al-Ḥamīd, Muḥammad Muḥyī al-Dīn. *al-Aḥwāl al-shakhṣiyya fī 'l-sharīʿa al-islāmiyya maʿa al-ishāra ilā mā yuqābiluhā fī 'l-sharāʾiʿ al-ukhrā*. Cairo 1942.

ʿAbduh, Muḥammad. *Taqrīr fī iṣlāḥ al-maḥākim al-sharʿiyya*, ed. Muḥammad Rashīd Riḍā. Cairo 1317/1900.

Abou El Fadl, Khaled. "Islamic Law and Muslim Minorities: The Juristic Discourse on Muslim Minorities from the Second/Eighth to the Eleventh/Seventeenth Centuries" in: *Islamic Law and Society* 1 (1994), 141–187.

Abou Ramadan, Moussa. "Judicial Activism of the Shariʿah Appeals Court in Israel (1994–2001): Rise and Crisis" in: *Fordham International Journal* 27 (2003), 254–298.

Abou Ramadan, Moussa. "The Transition from Tradition to Reform: The Shariʿa Appeals Court Rulings on Child Custody (1992–2001)" in: *Fordham International Journal* 26 (2003), 594–655.

Abu-Ghosh, Subhi. "The Shariʿa Courts from the Perspective of Israeli Pluralism" in: K.O. Cohen and J.S. Gerber (eds.), *Perspectives on Israeli Pluralism: Proceedings of a Conference on Pluralism in Israel*. New York 1991, 45–52.

Abū Zahra, Muḥammad. *al-Aḥwāl al-shakhṣiyya*. Cairo n.d. [after 1957].

Bälz, K. "The Secular Reconstruction of Islamic Law: The Islamic Supreme Constitutional Court and the 'Battle over the Veil' in State-Run Schools" in: Dupret, B., M. Berger and Laila al-Zwaini (eds.), *Legal Pluralism in the Arab World*. The Hague, London, Boston 1999, 229–243.

Barak, A. *The Judge in a Democracy*. Haifa and Jerusalem 2004.

Barak, A. *Judicial Discretion*. Tel Aviv 1987.

Black, H.C., et al. *Black's Law Dictionary*. 6th ed. St. Paul, Minn. 1990.

Botiveau, B. *Loi islamique et droit dans les sociétés arabes*. Paris 1993.

Botiveau, B. "Palestinian Law: Social Segmentation Versus Centralization" in: Dupret, B., M. Berger and Laila al-Zwaini (eds.), *Legal Pluralism in the Arab World*. The Hague, London, Boston 1999, 73–87.

Cardinal, Monique C. "Islamic Legal Theory Curriculum: Are the Classics Taught Today?" in: *Islamic Law and Society* 12 (2005), 224–272.

Charnay, J.-P. *La vie musulmane en Algérie d'après la jurisprudence de la première moitié du xx^e siècle*. Paris 1965.

Coulson, N.J. *A History of Islamic Law*. Edinburgh 1964.

Coulson, N.J. *Succession in the Muslim Family*. Cambridge 1971.

Damper, M. *Islam and Israel. Muslim Religious Endowments and the Jewish State*. Washington, DC 1994.

Dotan, Y. "Activism shipuṭi be-vaga"tz" [Judicial Activism in the High Court of Justice] in: Ruth Gavison, M. Kremnitzer, and Y. Dotan. *Activism shipuṭi: beʿad ve-neged. meqomo shel BG"TS ba-ḥevra ha-yisreʾelit* [*Judicial Activism: For and Against. The Role of the High Court of Justice in Israeli Society*]. Jerusalem 2000, 5–68.

Dupret, B., M. Berger and Laila al-Zwaini (eds.), *Legal Pluralism in the Arab World.* The Hague, London, Boston 1999.

Elon, M. *Ḥaqiqa datit be-ḥuqei medinat Yisraʾel uba-shephiṭa shel batei mishpaṭ u-batei din rabaniyim* [Religious Legislation in the Laws of the State of Israel and in the Adjudication of the Civil Courts and the Rabbinical Courts]. Tel Aviv 1968.

Englard, I. *Religious Law in the Israeli Legal System.* Jerusalem 1975.

Englard, I. "Shiluv ha-din ha-yehudi be-maʿarekhet ha-mishpaṭ ha-yisreʾeli" [The Integration of Jewish Law in the Israeli Legal System] in: J. Bazak (ed.), *Ha-Mishpaṭ ha-ʿivri u-medinat Yisraʾel* [The Jewish Law and the State of Israel]. Jerusalem 1969, 110–134.

Friedmann, Y. *Tolerance and Coercion in Islam. Interfaith Relations in the Muslim Tradition.* Cambridge 2003.

Fyzee, Asaf A.A. *Cases in Muhammadan Law of India and Pakistan.* Oxford 1965.

Fyzee, Asaf A.A. *Outlines of Muhammadan Law.* 3rd ed. London 1964.

Gardet, L. "Allāh" in: *The Encyclopaedia of Islam.* New ed. I (1986), 406–417.

Gardet, L. "ʿIlm al-Kalām" in: *The Encyclopaedia of Islam.* New ed. III (1986), 1141–1150.

al-Ghuneimi, Mohammad Talaat. *The Muslim Conception of International Law and the Western Approach.* The Hague 1968.

Goitein, S.D. and Ben Shemesh, A. *ha-Mishpaṭ ha-muslemi bi-Yisraʾel* [Muslim Law in Israel]. Jerusalem 1957.

Hallaq, W.H. *Authority, Continuity, and Change in Islamic Law.* Cambridge 2001.

Hallaq, W.H. *A History of Islamic Legal Theories. An Introduction to Sunnī uṣūl al-fiqh.* Cambridge 1997.

Ibn ʿĀbidīn, Muḥammad Amīn. *Durr al-Mukhtār.* 8 Vols. Cairo 1966.

Kremnitzer, M. "BG"TS veha-tefisa ha-reḥava shel tafqido: ketav hagana" [High Court of Justice and the Broad Conception of its Role: Pleading in Defence] in: Ruth Gavison, M. Kremnitzer, and Y. Dotan. *Activism shipuṭi: beʿad ve-neged. meqomo shel BG"TS ba-ḥevra ha-yisreʾelit* [Judicial Activism: For and Against. The Role of the High Court of Justice in Israeli Society]. Jerusalem 2000, 185–252.

Layish, A. "Bequests as an Instrument for Accommodating Inheritance Rules: Israel as a Case Study" in: *Islamic Law and Society* 2 (1995), 282–319.

Layish, A. "The Contribution of the Modernists to the Secularization of Islamic Law" in: *Middle Eastern Studies* 14 (1978), 263–277.

Layish, A. "Maʿamad ha-ʾisha ha-muslemit be-veit ha-din ha-sharʿi be-Yisraʾel" [The Status of Women in the Sharīʿa Court in Israel] in: F. Raday, et al. (eds.), *Maʿamad ha-ʾisha ba-ḥevra uva-mishpaṭ* [Women's Status in Israeli Law and Society]. Tel Aviv 1995, 364–379.

Layish, A. *Marriage, Divorce and Succession in the Druze Family. A Study Based on Decisions of Druze Arbitrators and Religious Courts in Israel and the Golan Heights.* Leiden 1982.

Layish, A. "Mīrāth, 2. In Modern Islamic Countries" in: *The Encyclopaedia of Islam*. New ed. VII (1993), 111–113.

Layish, A. "The Muslim Waqf in Israel" in: *Asian and African Studies* 2 (1966), 41–76.

Layish, A. "*Qāḍīs* and *Sharīʿa* in Israel" in: *Asian and African Studies* 7 (1971), 237–272.

Layish, A. "*Shahādat naql* in the Judicial Practice in Modern Libya" in: M.Kh. Masud, R. Peters and D.S. Powers (eds.), *Dispensing Justice in Muslim Courts: Qadis, Procedures and Judgments*. Leiden 2006, 495–516.

Layish, A. *Sharīʿa and Custom in Libyan Tribal Society. An Annotated Translation of Decisions from the Sharīʿa Courts of Ajdābiya and Kufra*. Leiden 2005.

Layish, A. "Ṭalāq, II. Reforms in the Modern Middle East and North Africa" in: *The Encyclopaedia of Islam*. New ed., IX (1997), 155–157.

Layish, A. "The Transformation of the Sharīʿa from Jurists' Law to Statutory Law in the Contemporary Muslim World" in: *Die Welt des Islams* 44 (2004), 85–112.

Layish, A. "Waqf, 5: In the Modern Middle East and North Africa" in: *The Encyclopaedia of Islam*. New ed., XI (2000), 78–81.

Layish, A. *Women and Islamic Law in a Non-Muslim State. A Study Based on the Decisions of the Sharīʿa Courts in Israel*. New York and Jerusalem 1975.

Layish, A. & R. Shaham. "Nikāḥ, II. In the Modern Islamic World, 1. The Arab, Persian and Turkish Lands of the Middle East" in: *The Encyclopaedia of Islam*. New ed., VIII (1995), 29–32.

Layish, A. & G.R. Warburg. *The Reinstatement of Islamic Law in Sudan under Numayrī. An Evaluation of a Legal Experiment in the Light of Its Historical Context, Methodology, and Repercussions*. Leiden 2002.

Lewis, B. *The Emergence of Modern Turkey*. London 1961.

Libson, G. "On the Development of Custom as a Source of Law in Islamic Law: al-rujūʿu ilā al-ʿurfi aḥadu al-qawāʿidi al-khamsi allatī yatabannā ʿalayhā al-fiqhu" in: *Islamic Law and Society* 4 (1992), 131–155.

Libson, G. "ʿUrf, 1. The Status of Custom in Islamic Law" in: *The Encyclopaedia of Islam*. New ed., X (2000), 887–888.

*Mejelle* The *Mejelle*, the Ottoman Civil Code, 1869–76. trans. (into Hebrew) and annot. G. Frumkin. Jerusalem 1952.

Meron, Y. "L'Accomodation de la répudiation musulmane" in: *Revue Internationale de Droit Comparé* 47 (1995), 921–939.

Meron, Y. "Is Custom a Source of Law in Israel?" in: *Israel Law Review* 9 (1974), 221–233.

Meron, Y. "Din shtuqi ba-mishpaṭ ha-moslemi" [The Law of the Illegitimate Child in Islamic Law] in: *Ha-Praqliṭ* 43 (1997), 407–415.

Meron, Y. *ha-Din ha-moslemi be-re'iya ha-shva'atit* [Moslem Law in Comparative Perspective]. Jerusalem 2001.

Meron, Y. "Elements of Moslem Forensic Medicine" in: S.S. Kotteck and L. García-Ballester (eds.), *Medicine and Medical Ethics in Medieval and Early Modern Spain: An Intercultural Approach*. Jerusalem, 1966, 245–260.

Meron, Y. "Ribui nashim la-moslemim ve-ḥuqatiyut ʾisuro" [Muslim Polygamy and the Constitutionality of its Prohibition] in: *Mishpaṭim* 3 (1972), 515–539.

Meron, Y. "Tipul refuʾi be-ʿenei ha-mishpaṭ ha-moslemi" [Medical Treatment from a Muslim Point of View] in: *ʿIyunei Mishpaṭ* 2 (1972), 388–395.

Meron, Y. "Women's Equal Rights (A Muslim Solution)" in: *Israel Law Review* 7 (1972), 315–318.

Meron, Y. "Yeḥasei mamon bein benei zug moslemim" [Property Relations between Muslim Spouses] in: *ʿIyunei Mishpaṭ* 3 (1973), 279–301.

Messick, B. *The Calligraphic State. Textual Domination and History in a Muslim Society.* Berkeley and Los Angeles 1993.

Motzki, H. "Child Marriage in Seventeenth-Century Palestine" in: M.Kh. Masud, B. Messick and D.S. Powers (eds.), *Islamic Legal Interpretation. Muftis and their Fatwas.* Cambridge, M.A. 1966, 129–140.

Nāṭūr, Qāḍī Aḥmad's comments on an earlier draft of this essay, May 20, 2004, 9 pp.

Naveh, I. "Yesum ha-shariʿa be-ʿarkaʾot ezraḥiyot ba-meʾa ha-ʿesrim: meḥqar hashvaʾati lefi pesiqa be-ʿinyanei maʿamad ʿishi ve-waqf shel muslemim be-medina muslemit (mitzrayim) uve-medina lo-muslemit (Yisraʾel)" [Application of the *Sharīʿa* in Civil Courts in the Twentieth Century: A Comparative Study Based on Decisions of Civil Courts in Matters of Personal Status and Waqf of Muslims in a Muslim State (Egypt) and in a Non-Muslim State (Israel)]. Ph.D. thesis, submitted to the Hebrew University, Jerusalem, 1997.

Porath, Y. *The Emergence of the Palestinian Arab National Movement, 1918–1929.* London 1974.

Powers, D.S. "On Judicial Review in Islamic Law" in: *Law & Society Review* 26 (1992), 315–341.

Powers, D.S. *Studies in Qurʾan and Ḥadīth: The Formation of the Islamic Law of Inheritance.* Berkeley 1986.

Qadrī Pāshā, Muḥammad. *al-Aḥkām al-sharʿiyya fī ʾl-aḥwāl al-shakhṣiyya*, in: Rushdī al-Sarrāj. *Jāmiʿ kitāb majmūʿat al-qawānīn al-sharʿiyya.* Jaffa 1363/1944, 80–182.

Reiter, Y. "Haʿarakhat ha-reforma be-mosad ha-heqdesh ha-muslemi be-Yisraʾel: ha-waqf be-ʿAcco" [An Assessment of the Reform in the Muslim Waqf Institution in Israel – The *Waqf* in Israel] in: *Hamizraḥ Heḥadash* 32 (1989), 21–45.

Reiter, Y. *Islamic Institutions in Jerusalem. Palestinian Muslim Organization under Jordanian and Israeli Rule.* The Hague, London, Boston 1997.

Reiter, Y. "Qāḍīs and the Implementation of Islamic Law in Present Israel" in: R. Gleave and E. Kermeli (eds.), *Islamic Law: Theory and Practice.* London, New York 1997, 205–231.

Schacht, J. *An Introduction to Islamic Law.* Oxford 1964.

Sezgin, Y. "A Political Account for Legal Confrontation between State and Society: The Case of Israeli Legal Pluralism" in: *Studies in Law, Politics, and Society* 32 (2004), 199–235.

Shahar, I. "Palesṭinim be-veit din yisre'eli: tarbut, shliṭa ve-hitnagdut be-veit ha-din ha-shar'i be-ma'arav Yerushalayim" [Palestinians in an Israeli Court: Culture, Domination and Resistance in the Sharī'a Court in West Jerusalem]. M.A. Thesis, Faculty of Social Sciences, The Hebrew University, Jerusalem, 2000.

Shahar, I. "'Sokhen shinui' ve-'shomer ḥomot': beit ha-din ha-shar'i ha-yisre'eli bi-[ye]rushalayim u-ma'amad ha-'isha" ['Modernizer' and 'Guardian of Tradition': The Sharī'a Court and Women's Status] in: *Hamizraḥ Heḥadash* 44 (2004), 195–211.

Shalabī, Muḥammad Muṣṭafā. *Aḥkām al-usra fī 'l-islām. Dirāsa muqārana bayna fiqh al-madhāhib al-sunniyya wa'l-madhhab al-ja'farī wa'l-qānūn*. Beirut 1973.

Shetreet, Sh. *'Al ha-shefiṭa. Ma'arechet ha-tzedeq ba-mishpaṭ* [On Adjudication. Justice on Trial]. Tel-Aviv 2004.

Shifman, P. "Mishmoret u-mezonot yeladim" [Custody and Maintenance for Children] in: F. Raday, et al. (eds.), *Ma'amad ha-'isha ba-ḥevra uva-mishpaṭ* [Women's Status in Israeli Society and Law]. Tel Aviv 1995, 534–545.

Shinar, P. "'Abd al-Qādir and 'Abd al-Krīm. Religious Influences on their Thought and Action" in: *Asian and African Studies* 1 (1965), 139–174.

Shinar, P. "ha-Reformism ha-orthodoxi be-Tunisia (1882–1939)" [Orthodox Reformism in Tunisia (1882–1939)] in: Special issue on Renewal (*tajdīd*) and Reform (*iṣlāḥ*) in Islam. *Hamizrah Heḥadash* 31 (1986), 71–103.

Tyan, E. "'Adl" in: *The Encyclopaedia of Islam*. New ed., I (1986), 209–210.

Vogel, F.E. "Siyāsa, 3. In the sense of *siyāsa s̲h̲ar'iyya*" in: *The Encyclopaedia of Islam*. New ed., IX (1995), 694–696.

Watt, W. Montgomery. "'Aḳīda" in: *The Encyclopaedia of Islam*. New ed., I (1986), 333–336.

Welchman, Lynn. *Beyond the Code: Muslim Family Law and the Shari'a Judiciary in the Palestinian West Bank*. The Hague, London, Boston 2000.

# Index

Printed in the United States
by Baker & Taylor Publisher Services